D1809191

THE DAILY POCKET LECTIONARY AND MASS BOOK

Volume 1:
Sunday and Weekday Readings from Advent to Pentecost

This volume contains the Sunday and major feast day readings for all three years, and the readings for every day of the week, for the period Advent – Pentecost. A further volume will provide the readings from the Week after Pentecost to the Last Week of the Year.

The Sunday and major feast-day readings are complete for the three year cycle, and the weekday readings are complete for the two year cycle, from the Lectionary of the Roman Missal.

These readings give the Christian people, who take part in the celebration of Mass day by day, the opportunity of hearing the most important parts of the revealed word of God. For those who are not able to attend daily Mass, this book provides in convenient form the cycle of readings used by the Church in her public worship, and recommended to the people for their private devotion.

The Sundays are arranged according to a three year cycle. Three readings are given for each Sunday and solemnity:
i. a first reading from the Old Testament or from the Acts of the Apostles
ii. a second reading from an apostle
iii. a third reading from a Gospel.

The Weekdays are arranged according to a two year cycle. Two readings are given for each Day of the Week:
i. a first reading from the Old Testament or the Apostles
ii. a second reading from a Gospel.

The songs between the readings: after each first reading a psalm is given, to which the people respond by singing or saying the Response. Before the Gospel, a brief Alleluia verse (or Acclamation, during Lent) is given, so that the people may express their welcome of the Word in the Gospel.

Sunday and Weekday Cycles are independent of each other, and taken together provide the faithful with a comprehensive and semi-continuous reading of the scriptures.

At each particular season of the year (Advent, Christmastide, Lent, Easter, Pentecost), the readings follow the theme of the season.

During the days which fall outside particular seasons, semi-continuous readings from a particular Gospel are given, so that the people may become familiar with the entire Gospel; the Old Testament readings are chosen for the light they throw on the Gospel readings, and the readings from the letters of the Apostles are also semi-continuous.

The Daily Pocket Lectionary and Mass Book

Volume 1

Sunday and Weekday Readings
from Advent to Pentecost

Three year cycle of Sunday Readings
Two year cycle of Weekday Readings

Complete in this volume

Together with the Order of Mass

Jerusalem Bible texts with Grail Psalms

GEOFFREY CHAPMAN
LONDON   DUBLIN   1971

Geoffrey Chapman
18 High Street, Wimbledon, London SW19

Geoffrey Chapman (Ireland)
5–7 Main Street, Blackrock, Co Dublin

© compilation, 1971, Geoffrey Chapman Publishers

ISBN 0 225 65845 3
First published 1971

ACKNOWLEDGEMENTS

The scripture texts are taken from the Jerusalem Bible Version of the Scriptures, copyrighted © in 1966, 1967 and 1968 by Darton, Longman and Todd Ltd and Doubleday and Company Inc., and used by permission.

The version of the Psalms is that translated from the Hebrew by the Grail, © The Grail (England) 1963, and published by Collins in Fontana Books, London, 1963. Used by permission. Canticles from the Old and New Testament are translated from Hebrew and Greek, © The Grail (England) 1963.

New English translation of the Order of Mass (with the exceptions noted below) copyright © 1969 and 1971, International Committee on English in the Liturgy, Inc. All rights reserved.

The texts of the Gloria, Sanctus, Creed, Our Father, Dialogue before the Preface are those agreed by the Hierarchies of England, Wales, Scotland and Ireland in 1966.

This volume follows the *editio typica* of the Lectionary, approved for use in England, Wales, Scotland, Ireland and South Africa.

Concordat cum originali: John Humphreys JCD
  Secretary to the National Liturgical Commission of England and Wales
Imprimatur: ✠Victor Guazzelli, VG,
Westminster 24.5.71

Made and printed in Great Britain by
C. Nicholls & Company Ltd,
The Philips Park Press, Manchester M11 4AU

CONTENTS

Calendar of Moveable feasts and Sundays

Year	Sunday Cycle	Week-day Cycle	Feast of the Baptism of the Lord	No. of Weeks of the Year	No. of Sundays after Epiphany	Date of 1st Sunday of Lent	Date of Easter	Date of Pentecost	Week after Pentecost corresponds to Week of the Year	Date of Solemnity of the Holy Trinity	Sunday after Trinity Sunday corresponds to Sunday of the Year	Date of 1st Sunday of Advent*
1971	3 (C)	I	January 10	33	7	February 28	April 11	May 30	9	June 6	11	November 28
1972	1 (A)	II	January 9	34	6	February 20	April 2	May 21	7	May 28	9	December 3
1973	2 (B)	II	January 7	34	9	March 11	April 22	June 10	10	June 17	13	December 2
1974	3 (C)	I	January 13	33	7	March 3	April 14	June 2	9	June 9	11	December 1
1975	1 (A)	I	January 12	33	5	February 16	March 30	May 18	7	May 25	9	November 30
1976	2 (B)	II	January 11	33	8	March 7	April 18	June 6	10	June 13	12	November 28
1977	3 (C)	I	January 9	33	7	February 27	April 10	May 29	9	June 5	11	November 27
1978	1 (A)	II	January 8	34	5	February 12	March 26	May 14	6	May 21	8	December 3
1979	2 (B)	I	January 7	34	8	March 4	April 15	June 3	9	June 10	11	December 2
1980	3 (C)	II	January 13	33	6	February 24	April 6	May 25	8	June 1	10	November 30

*NB. The Sunday Cycle changes to that of the following calendar year on the First Sunday of Advent.

THE SEASON OF ADVENT

1st SUNDAY OF ADVENT

Year 1 (Year A)

First Reading (2:1–5)

A reading from the prophet Isaiah
*The Lord gathers all nations together into the eternal peace
of God's kingdom*

The vision of Isaiah son of Amoz, concerning Judah and
Jerusalem.

In the days to come
the mountain of the Temple of the Lord
shall tower above the mountains
and be lifted higher than the hills.
All the nations will stream to it,
peoples without number will come to it;
and they will say:
'Come, let us go up to the mountain of the Lord,
to the Temple of the God of Jacob
that he may teach us his ways
so that we may walk in his paths;
since the Law will go out from Zion,
and the oracle of the Lord from Jerusalem.''

He will wield authority over the nations
and adjudicate between many peoples;
these will hammer their swords into ploughshares,
their spears into sickles.

Nation will not lift sword against nation,
there will be no more training for war.

O House of Jacob, come,
let us walk in the light of the Lord.

This is the word of the Lord.

Responsorial Psalm   (Ps 121:1–4. 8–9 *R*. v. 1)

Response
I rejoiced when I heard them say:
"Let us go to God's house."

1. I rejoiced when I heard them say:
"Let us go to God's house."
And now our feet are standing
within your gates, O Jerusalem. (*R*.)

2. Jerusalem is built as a city
strongly compact.
It is there that the tribes go up,
the tribes of the Lord. (*R*.)

3. For love of my brethren and friends
I say: "Peace upon you!"
For love of the house of the Lord
I will ask for your good. (*R*.)

Second Reading   (13:11–14)

A reading from the letter of St Paul to the Romans
Our salvation is near.

You know "the time" has come: you must wake up now:
our salvation is even nearer than it was when we were con-

verted. The night is almost over, it will be daylight soon—let us give up all the things we prefer to do under cover of the dark; let us arm ourselves and appear in the light. Let us live decently as people do in the daytime: no drunken orgies, no promiscuity or licentiousness, and no wrangling or jealousy. Let your armour be the Lord Jesus Christ; forget about satisfying your bodies with all their cravings.

This is the word of the Lord.

Alleluia (Ps 84:8)

Alleluia, alleluia!
Let us see, O Lord, your mercy
and give us your saving help.
Alleluia!

Gospel (24:37–44)

A reading from the holy Gospel according to Matthew
Stay awake so that you may be ready.

Jesus said to his disciples: "As it was in Noah's day, so will it be when the Son of Man comes. For in those days before the Flood people were eating, drinking, taking wives, taking husbands, right up to the day Noah went into the ark, and they suspected nothing till the Flood came and swept all away. It will be like this when the Son of Man comes. Then of two men in the fields one is taken, one left; of two women at the millstone grinding, one is taken, one left. So stay awake, because you do not know the day when your master is coming. You may be quite sure of this that if the householder had known at what time of the night the burglar would come, he would have stayed awake and would not have allowed anyone to break through the wall of his house. Therefore, you too must stand ready because the Son of Man is coming at an hour you do not expect."

This is the Gospel of the Lord.

1st SUNDAY OF ADVENT
Year 2 (Year B)

First Reading   (63:16–17; 64:1.3–8)

A reading from the prophet Isaiah
Oh, that you would tear the heavens open and come down.

You, Lord, yourself are our Father,
Our Redeemer is your ancient name.
Why, Lord, leave us to stray from your ways
and harden our hearts against fearing you?
Return, for the sake of your servants,
the tribes of your inheritance.
Oh, that you would tear the heavens open and come down
– at your Presence the mountains would melt.
No ear has heard,
no eye has seen
any god but you act like this
for those who trust him.
You guide those who act with integrity
and keep your ways in mind.
You were angry when we were sinners;
we had long been rebels against you.
We were all like men unclean,
all that integrity of ours like filthy clothing.
We have all withered like leaves
and our sins blew us away like the wind.
No one invoked your name
or roused himself to catch hold of you.
For you hid your face from us
and gave us up to the power of our sins.
And yet, Lord you are our Father;
we the clay, you the potter,
we are all the work of your hand.

This is the word of the Lord.

Responsorial Psalm   (Ps 79:2–3. 15–16. 18–19. *R*. v. 4)

Response
God of hosts, bring us back;
let your face shine on us and we shall be saved.

1. O shepherd of Israel, hear us,
shine forth from your cherubim throne.
O Lord, rouse up your might,
O Lord, come to our help. (*R*.)

2. God of hosts, turn again, we implore,
look down from heaven and see.
Visit this vine and protect it,
the vine your right hand has planted. (*R*.)

3. May your hand be on the man you have chosen,
the man you have given your strength.
And we shall never forsake you again:
give us life that we may call upon your name. (*R*.)

Second Reading   (1:3–9)

A reading from the first letter of St Paul to the Corinthians
We are waiting for our Lord Jesus Christ to be revealed.

May God our Father and the Lord Jesus Christ send you
grace and peace.

I never stop thanking God for all the graces you have
received through Jesus Christ. I thank him that you have
been enriched in so many ways, especially in your teachers
and preachers; the witness to Christ has indeed been strong
among you so that you will not be without any of the gifts
of the Spirit while you are waiting for our Lord Jesus
Christ to be revealed; and he will keep you steady and without blame until the last day, the day of our Lord Jesus

Christ, because God by calling you has joined you to his Son, Jesus Christ; and God is faithful.

This is the word of the Lord.

Alleluia (Ps 84:8)

Alleluia, alleluia!
Let us see, O Lord, your mercy
and give us your saving help.
Alleluia!

Gospel (13:33–37)

A reading from the holy Gospel according to Mark
Stay awake, because you do not know when the master of the house is coming.

Jesus said to his disciples: "Be on your guard, stay awake, because you never know when the time will come. It is like a man travelling abroad: he has gone from home, and left his servants in charge, each with his own task; and he has told the doorkeeper to stay awake. So stay awake, because you do not know when the master of the house is coming, evening, midnight, cockcrow, dawn; if he comes unexpectedly, he must not find you asleep. And what I say to you I say to all: Stay awake!"

This is the Gospel of the Lord.

1st SUNDAY OF ADVENT
Year 3 (Year C)

First Reading (33:14–16)

A reading from the prophet Jeremiah
I will make a virtuous Branch grow for David.

See, the days are coming – it is the Lord who speaks – when I am going to fulfil the promise I made to the House of Israel and the House of Judah:

"In those days and at that time,
I will make a virtuous Branch grow for David,
who shall practise honesty and integrity in the land.
In those days Judah shall be saved
and Israel shall dwell in confidence.
And this is the name the city will be called:
The Lord-our-integrity."

This is the word of the Lord.

Responsorial Psalm   (Ps 24:4–5. 8–9. 10. 14. *R*. v.1)

Response
To you, O Lord, I lift up my soul.

1. Lord, make me know your ways.
Lord, teach me your paths.
Make me walk in your truth, and teach me:
for you are God my saviour. (*R*.)

2. The Lord is good and upright.
He shows the path to those who stray,
he guides the humble in the right path;
he teaches his way to the poor. (*R*.)

3. His ways are faithfulness and love
for those who keep his covenant and will.
The Lord's friendship is for those who revere him;
to them he reveals his covenant. (*R*.)

Second Reading   (3:12–4:2)

A reading from the first letter of St Paul to the Thessalonians
May the Lord confirm your hearts in holiness when Christ comes.

May the Lord be generous in increasing your love and make you love one another and the whole human race as much as we love you. And may he so confirm your hearts in holiness that you may be blameless in the sight of our God and Father when our Lord Jesus Christ comes with all his saints.

Finally, brothers, we urge you and appeal to you in the Lord Jesus to make more and more progress in the kind of life that you are meant to live: the life that God wants, as you learnt from us, and as you are already living it. You have not forgotten the instructions we gave you on the authority of the Lord Jesus.

This is the word of the Lord.

Alleluia   (Ps 84:8)

Alleluia, alleluia!
Let us see, O Lord, your mercy
and give us your saving help.
Alleluia!

Gospel   (21:25–28. 34–36)

A reading from the holy Gospel according to Luke
Your liberation is near at hand.

Jesus said to his disciples: "There will be signs in the sun and moon and stars; on earth nations in agony, bewildered by the clamour of the ocean and its waves; men dying of fear as they await what menaces the world, for the powers of heaven will be shaken. And then they will see the Son of Man coming in a cloud with power and great glory. When these things begin to take place, stand erect, hold your heads high, because your liberation is near at hand."

"Watch yourselves, or your hearts will be coarsened with debauchery and drunkenness and the cares of life, and that day will be sprung on you suddenly, like a trap. For it will come down on every living man on the face of the earth. Stay awake, praying at all times for the strength to survive all that is going to happen, and to stand with confidence before the Son of Man.''

This is the Gospel of the Lord.

MONDAY

First Reading   (2:1–5)

A reading from the prophet Isaiah
The Lord draws all nations together into the eternal peace of God's kingdom.

The vision of Isaiah son of Amoz, concerning Judah and Jerusalem.

In the days to come
the mountain of the Temple of the Lord
shall tower above the mountains
and be lifted higher than the hills.
All the nations will stream to it,
peoples without number will come to it; and they will say:
"Come, let us go up to the mountain of the Lord,
to the Temple of the God of Jacob
that he may teach us his ways
so that we may walk in his paths;
since the Law will go out from Zion,
and the oracle of the Lord from Jerusalem."

He will wield authority over the nations
and adjudicate between many peoples;
these will hammer their swords into ploughshares,
their spears into sickles.
Nation will not lift sword against nation,
there will be no more training for war.

O House of Jacob, come,
let us walk in the light of the Lord.

This is the word of the Lord.

Alternative Reading   (Year 1 only)

A reading from the prophet Isaiah   (4:2–6)
*The fruit of the earth shall be the pride and adornment of
Israel's survivors.*

That day, the branch of the Lord
shall be beauty and glory,
and the fruit of the earth
shall be the pride and adornment
of Israel's survivors.
Those who are left of Zion
and remain of Jerusalem
shall be called holy
and those left in Jerusalem, noted down for survival.
When the Lord has washed away
the filth of the daughters of Zion
and cleansed Jerusalem of the blood shed in her
with the blast of judgement and the blast of destruction,
the Lord will come and rest
on the whole stretch of Mount Zion
and on those who are gathered there,
a cloud by day, and smoke,
and by night the brightness of a flaring fire.
For, over all, the glory of the Lord
will be a canopy and a tent
to give shade by day from the heat,
refuge and shelter from the storm and the rain.

This is the word of the Lord.

Responsorial Psalm   (Ps 121:1–4. 8. 9. *R.* v. 1)

Response
I rejoiced when I heard them say:
"Let us go to God's house."

1. I rejoiced when I heard them say:
"Let us go to God's house."
And now our feet are standing
within your gates, O Jerusalem. (*R.*)

2. Jerusalem is built as a city
strongly compact.
It is there that the tribes go up,
the tribes of the Lord. (*R.*)

3. For love of my brethren and friends
I say: "Peace upon you!"
For love of the house of the Lord
I will ask for your good. (*R.*)

Alleluia   (Ps 79:4)

Alleluia, alleluia!
God of hosts, bring us back;
let your face shine on us and we shall be saved.
Alleluia!

Alternative Alleluias p. 837.

Gospel   (8:5–11)

A reading from the holy Gospel according to Matthew
*Many will come from east and west to take their places in the
kingdom of heaven.*

When Jesus went into Capernaum a centurion came up and
pleaded with him. "Sir," he said "my servant is lying at

home paralysed, and in great pain." "I will come myself and cure him" said Jesus. The centurion replied, "Sir, I am not worthy to have you under my roof; just give the word and my servant will be cured. For I am under authority myself, and have soldiers under me; and I say to one man: Go, and he goes; to another: Come here, and he comes; to my servant: Do this, and he does it." When Jesus heard this he was astonished and said to those following him, "I tell you solemnly, nowhere in Israel have I found faith like this. And I tell you that many will come from east and west to take their places with Abraham and Isaac and Jacob at the feast in the kingdom of heaven."

This is the Gospel of the Lord.

TUESDAY

First Reading (11:1–10)

A reading from the prophet Isaiah
On him the spirit of the Lord rests.

A shoot springs from the stock of Jesse,
a scion thrusts from his roots:
on him the spirit of the Lord rests,
a spirit of wisdom and insight,
a spirit of counsel and power,
a spirit of knowledge and of the fear of the Lord.
(The fear of the Lord is his breath.)
He does not judge by appearances,
he gives no verdict on hearsay,
but judges the wretched with integrity,
and with equity gives a verdict for the poor of the land.
His word is a rod that strikes the ruthless,
his sentences bring death to the wicked.
Integrity is the loincloth round his waist,
faithfulness the belt about his hips.

The wolf lives with the lamb,
the panther lies down with the kid,
calf and lion cub feed together
with a little boy to lead them.
The cow and the bear make friends,
their young lie down together.
The lion eats straw like the ox.
The infant plays over the cobra's hole;
into the viper's lair
the young child puts his hand.
They do no hurt, no harm,
on all my holy mountain,
for the country is filled with the knowledge of the Lord
as the waters swell the sea.

That day, the root of Jesse
shall stand as a signal to the peoples.
It will be sought out by the nations
and its home will be glorious.

This is the word of the Lord.

Responsorial Psalm   (Ps 71:1–2. 7–8. 12–13. 17. *R*. v. 7)

Response
In his days justice shall flourish
and peace till the moon fails.

1. O God, give your judgement to the king,
to a king's son your justice,
that he may judge your people in justice
and your poor in right judgement. (*R*.)

2. In his days justice shall flourish
and peace till the moon fails.
He shall rule from sea to sea,
from the Great River to earth's bounds. (*R*.)

3. For he shall save the poor when they cry
and the needy who are helpless.
He will have pity on the weak
and save the lives of the poor. (*R*.)

4. May his name be blessed for ever
and endure like the sun.
Every tribe shall be blessed in him,
all nations bless his name. (*R*.)

Alleluia   (Ps 84:8)

Alleluia, alleluia!
Let us see, O Lord, your mercy
and give us your saving help.
Alleluia!

Alternative Alleluias p. 837.

Gospel   (10:21–24)

A reading from the holy Gospel according to Luke
Jesus is filled with joy by the Holy Spirit.

It was then that, filled with joy by the Holy Spirit, Jesus said, "I bless you, Father, Lord of heaven and of earth, for hiding these things from the learned and the clever and revealing them to mere children. Yes, Father, for that is what it pleased you to do. Everything has been entrusted to me by my Father; and no one knows who the Son is except the Father, and who the Father is except the Son and those to whom the Son chooses to reveal him."

Then turning to his disciples he spoke to them in private. "Happy the eyes that see what you see, for I tell you that many prophets and kings wanted to see what you see, and never saw it; to hear what you hear, and never heard it."

This is the Gospel of the Lord.

WEDNESDAY

First Reading   (25:6–10)

A reading from the prophet Isaiah
*The Lord invites us to his banquet and wipes away the tears
from every cheek.*

On this mountain,
the Lord of hosts will prepare for all peoples
a banquet of rich food, a banquet of fine wines,
of food rich and juicy, of fine strained wines.
On this mountain he will remove
the mourning veil covering all peoples,
and the shroud enwrapping all nations,
he will destroy Death for ever.
The Lord will wipe away
the tears from every cheek;
he will take away his people's shame
everywhere on earth,
for the Lord has said so.
That day, it will be said: See, this is our God
in whom we hoped for salvation;
the Lord is the one in whom we hoped.
We exult and we rejoice
that he has saved us;
for the hand of the Lord
rests on this mountain.

    This is the word of the Lord.

Responsorial Psalm   (Ps 22:1–3. 5–6. *R.* v. 6)

Response
In the Lord's own house shall I dwell
for ever and ever.

1. The Lord is my shepherd;
there is nothing I shall want.
Fresh and green are the pastures
where he gives me repose. (*R*.)

2. Near restful waters he leads me,
to revive my drooping spirit.
He guides me along the right path;
he is true to his name. (*R*.)

3. You have prepared a banquet for me
in the sight of my foes.
My head you have anointed with oil;
my cup is overflowing. (*R*.)

4. Surely goodness and kindness shall follow me
all the days of my life.
In the Lord's own house shall I dwell
for ever and ever. (*R*.)

Alleluia   (Is 33:22)

Alleluia, alleluia!
The Lord is our judge, the Lord our lawgiver,
the Lord our king and our saviour.
Alleluia!

Alternative Alleluias p. 837.

Gospel   (15:29–37)

A reading from the holy Gospel according to Matthew
Jesus cures many and multiplies the loaves.

Jesus went on from there and reached the shores of the Sea
of Galilee, and he went up into the hills. He sat there, and

large crowds came to him bringing the lame, the crippled, the blind, the dumb and many others; these they put down at his feet, and he cured them. The crowds were astonished to see the dumb speaking, the cripples whole again, the lame walking and the blind with their sight, and they praised the God of Israel.

But Jesus called his disciples to him and said, "I feel sorry for all these people; they have been with me for three days now and have nothing to eat. I do not want to send them off hungry, they might collapse on the way." The disciples said to him, "Where could we get enough bread in this deserted place to feed such a crowd?" Jesus said to them, "How many loaves have you?" "Seven" they said "and a few small fish." Then he instructed the crowd to sit down on the ground, and he took the seven loaves and the fish, and he gave thanks and broke them and handed them to the disciples who gave them to the crowds. They all ate as much as they wanted, and they collected what was left of the scraps, seven baskets full.

This is the Gospel of the Lord.

THURSDAY

First Reading   (26:1–6)

A reading from the prophet Isaiah

Let the upright nation come in, she, the faithful one.

That day, this song will be sung in the land of Judah:
We have a strong city;
to guard us he has set
wall and rampart about us.
Open the gates! Let the upright nation come in,
she, the faithful one

whose mind is steadfast, who keeps the peace,
because she trusts in you.
Trust in the Lord for ever,
for the Lord is the everlasting Rock;
he has brought low those who lived high up
in the steep citadel;
he brings it down, brings it down to the ground,
flings it down in the dust:
the feet of the lowly, the footsteps of the poor
trample on it.

This is the word of the Lord.

Responsorial Psalm (Ps 117:1. 8–9. 19–21. 25–27. *R.* v. 26)
Response
Blessed in the name of the Lord
is he who comes.

Alternative Response
Alleluia!

1. Give thanks to the Lord for he is good,
for his love has no end.
It is better to take refuge in the Lord
than to trust in men;
it is better to take refuge in the Lord
than to trust in princes. (*R.*)

2. Open to me the gates of holiness:
I will enter and give thanks.
This is the Lord's own gate
where the just may enter.
I will thank you for you have given answer
and you are my saviour. (*R.*)

3. O Lord, grant us salvation;
O Lord, grant success.
Blessed in the name of the Lord
is he who comes.
We bless you from the house of the Lord;
the Lord God is our light. (*R*.)

Alleluia   (Is 40:9–10)

Alleluia, alleluia!
Shout with a loud voice, joyful messenger to Jerusalem.
Here is the Lord God coming with power.
Alleluia!

Alternative Alleluias p. 837.

Gospel   (7:21. 24–27)

A reading from the holy Gospel according to Matthew
The person who does the will of my Father will enter the kingdom of heaven.

Jesus said to his disciples: "It is not those who say to me, 'Lord, Lord', who will enter the kingdom of heaven, but the person who does the will of my Father in heaven.

"Therefore, everyone who listens to these words of mine and acts on them will be like a sensible man who built his house on rock. Rain came down, floods rose, gales blew and hurled themselves against that house, and it did not fall: it was founded on rock. But everyone who listens to these words of mine and does not act on them will be like a stupid man who built his house on sand. Rain came down, floods rose, gales blew and struck that house, and it fell; and what a fall it had!"

This is the Gospel of the Lord.

FRIDAY

First Reading   (29:17–24)

A reading from the prophet Isaiah
That day the eyes of the blind will see.

The Lord says this:
In a short time, a very short time,
shall not Lebanon become fertile land
and fertile land turn into forest?
The deaf, that day,
will hear the words of a book
and, after shadow and darkness,
the eyes of the blind will see.

But the lowly will rejoice in the Lord even more
and the poorest exult in the Holy One of Israel;
for tyrants shall be no more, and scoffers vanish,
and all be destroyed who are disposed to do evil:

those who gossip to incriminate others,
those who try at the gate to trip the arbitrator
and get the upright man's case dismissed for groundless
    reasons.

Therefore the Lord speaks, the God of the House of Jacob,
Abraham's redeemer:
No longer shall Jacob be ashamed,
no more shall his face grow pale,
for he shall see what my hands have done in his midst,
he shall hold my name holy.
They will hallow the Holy One of Jacob,
stand in awe of the God of Israel.
Erring spirits will learn wisdom
and murmurers accept instruction.

This is the word of the Lord.

Responsorial Psalm   (Ps 26:1. 4. 13–14. *R*. v. 1)

Response
The Lord is my light and my help.

1. The Lord is my light and my help;
whom shall I fear?
The Lord is the stronghold of my life;
before whom shall I shrink? (*R*.)

2. There is one thing I ask of the Lord,
for this I long,
to live in the house of the Lord,
all the days of my life,
to savour the sweetness of the Lord,
to behold his temple. (*R*.)

3. I am sure I shall see the Lord's goodness
in the land of the living.
Hope in him, hold firm and take heart.
Hope in the Lord! (*R*.)

Alleluia   (Is 45:8)

Alleluia, alleluia!
Send victory like a dew, you heavens,
and let the clouds rain it down.
Let the earth open
and bring forth the saviour.
Alleluia!

Alternative Alleluias p. 837.

Gospel   (9:27–31)

A reading from the holy Gospel according to Matthew
Two blind men who believe in Jesus are cured.

As Jesus went on his way two blind men followed him shouting, "Take pity on us, Son of David." And when Jesus reached the house the blind men came up with him and he said to them. "Do you believe I can do this," They said, "Sir, we do." Then he touched their eyes saying, "Your faith deserves it, so let this be done for you." And their sight returned. Then Jesus sternly warned them. "Take care that no one learns about this." But when they had gone, they talked about him all over the countryside.

This is the Gospel of the Lord.

SATURDAY

First Reading (30:19–21. 23–26)

A reading from the prophet Isaiah
He will be gracious to you when he hears your cry.

Thus says the Lord God, the Holy One of Israel:
People of Zion, you will live in Jerusalem and weep no more. He will be gracious to you when he hears your cry; when he hears he will answer. When the Lord has given you the bread of suffering and the water of distress, he who is your teacher will hide no longer, and you will see your teacher with your own eyes. Whether you turn to right or left, your ears will hear these words behind you, "This is the way, follow it." He will send rain for the seed you sow in the ground, and the bread that the ground provides will be rich and nourishing. Your cattle will graze, that day, in wide pastures. Oxen and donkeys that till the ground will eat a salted fodder, winnowed with shovel and fork. On every lofty mountain, on every high hill there will be streams and watercourses, on the day of the great slaughter when the strongholds fall. Then moonlight will be bright as sunlight and sunlight itself be seven times brighter – like the light of seven days in one – on the day the Lord dresses the

wound of his people and heals the bruises his blows have left.

This is the word of the Lord.

Responsorial Psalm   (Ps 146:1–6. *R.* Is 30:18)

Response

Happy are all who hope in him.

Alternative Response

Alleluia!

1. Praise the Lord for he is good;
sing to our God for he is loving:
to him our praise is due.
The Lord builds up Jerusalem
and brings back Israel's exiles. (*R.*)

2. He heals the broken-hearted,
he binds up all their wounds.
He fixes the number of the stars;
he calls each one by its name. (*R.*)

3. Our Lord is great and almighty;
his wisdom can never be measured.
The Lord raises the lowly;
he humbles the wicked in the dust. (*R.*)

Alleluia   (Is 55:6)

Alleluia, alleluia!
Seek the Lord while he is still to be found,
call to him while he is still near.
Alleluia!

Alternative Alleluias p. 837.

Gospel   (9:35–10:1.6–8)

A reading from the holy Gospel according to Matthew
When he saw the crowds he felt sorry for them.

Jesus made a tour through all the towns and villages, teaching in their synagogues, proclaiming the Good News of the kingdom and curing all kinds of diseases and sickness.

And when he saw the crowds he felt sorry for them because they were harassed and dejected, like sheep without a shepherd. Then he said to his disciples, "The harvest is rich but the labourers are few, so ask the Lord of the harvest to send labourers, to his harvest.'

He summoned his twelve disciples, and gave them authority over unclean spirits with power to cast them out and to cure all kinds of diseases and sickness. These twelve Jesus sent out, instructing them as follows: "Go rather to the lost sheep of the House of Israel. And as you go, proclaim that the kingdom of heaven is close at hand. Cure the sick, raise the dead, cleanse the lepers, cast out devils. You received without charge, give without charge.'

This is the Gospel of the Lord.

2nd SUNDAY OF ADVENT
Year 1 (Year A)

First Reading   (11:1–10)

A reading from the prophet Isaiah
He judges the wretched with integrity.

A shoot springs from the stock of Jesse,
a scion thrusts from his roots :
on him the spirit of the Lord rests,
a spirit of wisdom and insight,
a spirit of counsel and power,

a spirit of knowledge and of the fear of the Lord.
(The fear of the Lord is his breath.)
He does not judge by appearances,
he gives no verdict on hearsay,
but judges the wretched with integrity,
and with equity gives a verdict for the poor of the land.
His word is a rod that strikes the ruthless,
his sentences bring death to the wicked.
Integrity is the loincloth round his waist,
faithfulness the belt about his hips.

The wolf lives with the lamb,
the panther lies down with the kid,
calf and lion cub feed together
with a little boy to lead them.
The cow and the bear make friends,
their young lie down together.
The lion eats straw like the ox.
The infant plays over the cobra's hole;
into the viper's lair
the young child puts his hand.
They do no hurt, no harm,
on all my holy mountain,
for the country is filled with the knowledge of the Lord
as the waters swell the sea.

That day, the root of Jesse
shall stand as a signal to the peoples.
It will be sought out by the nations
and its home will be glorious.

This is the word of the Lord.

Responsorial Psalm   (Ps 71:1–2. 7–8. 12–13. 17. *R*. v. 7)
Response
In his days justice shall flourish
and peace till the moon fails.

1. O God, give your judgement to the king,
to a king's son your justice,
that he may judge your people in justice
and your poor in right judgement. (R.)

2. In his days justice shall flourish
and peace till the moon fails.
He shall rule from sea to sea,
from the Great River to earth's bounds. (R.)

3. For he shall save the poor when they cry
and the needy who are helpless.
He will have pity on the weak
and save the lives of the poor. (R.)

4. May his name be blessed for ever
and endure like the sun.
Every tribe shall be blessed in him,
all nations bless his name. (R.)

Second Reading (15:4–9)

A reading from the letter of St Paul to the Romans
Christ is the saviour of all men.

Everything that was written long ago in the scriptures was meant to teach us something about hope from the examples scripture gives of how people who did not give up were helped by God. And may he who helps us when we refuse to give up, help you all to be tolerant with each other, following the example of Christ Jesus, so that united in mind and voice you may give glory to the God and Father of our Lord Jesus Christ.

It can only be to God's glory, then, for you to treat each other in the same friendly way as Christ treated you. The reason Christ became the servant of circumcised Jews was not only so that God could faithfully carry out the promises made to the patriarchs, it was also to get the pagans to give glory to God for his mercy, as scripture says in one place: For this I shall praise you among the pagans and sing to your name.

This is the word of the Lord.

Alleluia (Lk 3:4.6)

Alleluia, alleluia!
Prepare a way for the Lord,
make his paths straight.
And all mankind shall see the salvation of God.
Alleluia!

Gospel (3:1–12)

A reading from the holy Gospel according to Matthew
Repent, for the kingdom of heaven is close at hand.

In due course John the Baptist appeared; he preached in the wilderness of Judaea and this was his message: "Repent, for the kingdom of heaven is close at hand." This was the man the prophet Isaiah spoke of when he said:

A voice cries in the wilderness:
Prepare a way for the Lord,
make his paths straight.

This man John wore a garment made of camel-hair with a leather belt round his waist, and his food was locusts and wild honey. Then Jerusalem and all Judaea and the whole Jordan district made their way to him, and as they were baptised by him in the river Jordan they confessed their sins. But when he saw a number of Pharisees and Sadducees coming for baptism he said to them, "Brood of vipers, who warned you to fly from the retribution that is coming? But if you are repentant, produce the appropriate fruit, and do not presume to tell yourselves, 'We have Abraham for our father,' because, I tell you, God can raise children for Abraham from these stones. Even now the axe is laid to the roots of the trees, so that any tree which fails to produce good fruit will be cut down and thrown on the fire. I baptise you in water for repentance, but the one who follows me is more powerful than I am, and I am not fit to carry his sandals; he will baptise you with the Holy Spirit and fire. His winnowing-fan is in his hand; he will clear his threshing-floor and gather his wheat into the barn; but the chaff he will burn in a fire that will never go out."

This is the Gospel of the Lord.

2nd SUNDAY OF ADVENT
Year 2 (Year B)

First Reading (40:1–5. 9–11)

A reading from the prophet Isaiah
Prepare a way for the Lord

"Console my people, console them"
says your God.
"Speak to the heart of Jerusalem
and call to her
that her time of service is ended,
that her sin is atoned for,
that she has received from the hand of the Lord
double punishment for all her crimes."
A voice cries, "Prepare in the wilderness
a way for the Lord.
Make a straight highway for our God
across the desert.

Let every valley be filled in,
every mountain and hill be laid low,
let every cliff become a plain,
and the ridges a valley;
then the glory of the Lord shall be revealed
and all mankind shall see it;
for the mouth of the Lord has spoken."

Go up on a high mountain,
joyful messenger to Zion.
Shout with a loud voice,
joyful messenger to Jerusalem.
Shout without fear,
say to the towns of Judah,
"Here is your God."
Here is the Lord coming with power,
his arm subduing all things to him.
The prize of his victory is with him,
his trophies all go before him.
He is like a shepherd feeding his flock,
gathering lambs in his arms,
holding them against his breast
and leading to their rest the mother ewes.

This is the word of the Lord.

Responsorial Psalm (Ps 84:9–14. *R*. v. 8)

Response
Let us see, O Lord, your mercy
and give us your saving help.

1. I will hear what the Lord God has to say,
a voice that speaks of peace,
peace for his people.
His help is near for those who fear him
and his glory will dwell in our land. (*R*.)

2. Mercy and faithfulness have met;
justice and peace have embraced.
Faithfulness shall spring from the earth
and justice look down from heaven. (*R.*)

3. The Lord will make us prosper
and our earth shall yield its fruit.
Justice shall march before him
and peace shall follow his steps. (*R.*)

Second Reading (3:8–14)

A reading from the second letter of St Peter
We are waiting for the new heavens and new earth.

There is one thing, my friends, that you must never forget: that with the Lord, "a day" can mean a thousand years, and a thousand years is like a day. The Lord is not being slow to carry out his promises, as anybody else might be called slow; but he is being patient with you all, wanting nobody to be lost and everybody to be brought to change his ways. The Day of the Lord will come like a thief, and then with a roar the sky will vanish, the elements will catch fire and fall apart, the earth and all that it contains will be burnt up.

Since everything is coming to an end like this, you should be living holy and saintly lives while you wait and long for the Day of God to come, when the sky will dissolve in flames and the elements melt in the heat. What we are waiting for is what he promised: the new heavens and new earth, the place where righteousness will be at home. So then, my friends, while you are waiting, do your best to live lives without spot or stain so that he will find you at peace.

This is the word of the Lord.

Alleluia (Lk 3:4.6)

Alleluia, alleluia!

Prepare a way for the Lord,
make his paths straight.
And all mankind shall see the salvation of God.
Alleluia!

Gospel   (1:1–8)

The beginning of the holy Gospel according to Mark
Make his paths straight.

The beginning of the Good News about Jesus Christ, the
Son of God. It is written in the book of the prophet Isaiah:

Look, I am going to send my messenger before you;
he will prepare your way.
A voice cries in the wilderness:
Prepare a way for the Lord,
make his paths straight,

and so it was that John the Baptist appeared in the wilderness, proclaiming a baptism of repentance for the forgiveness of sins. All Judaea and all the people of Jerusalem
made their way to him, and as they were baptised by him
in the river Jordan they confessed their sins. John wore a
garment of camel-skin, and he lived on locusts and wild
honey. In the course of his preaching he said, "Someone is
following me, someone who is more powerful than I am,
and I am not fit to kneel down and undo the strap of his
sandals. I have baptised you with water, but he will baptise
you with the Holy Spirit."

This is the Gospel of the Lord.

2nd SUNDAY OF ADVENT
Year 3 (Year C)

First Reading   (5:1–9)

A reading from the prophet Baruch
God means to show your splendour to every nation.

Jerusalem, take off your dress of sorrow and distress,
put on the beauty of the glory of God for ever,
wrap the cloak of the integrity of God around you,
put the diadem of the glory of the Eternal on your head:
since God means to show your splendour to every nation
     under heaven,
since the name God gives you for ever will be,
"Peace through integrity, and honour through devotedness."
Arise, Jerusalem, stand on the heights
and turn your eyes to the east:
see your sons reassembled from west and east
at the command of the Holy One, jubilant that God has
     remembered them.
Though they left you on foot,
with enemies for an escort,
now God brings them back to you
like royal princes carried back in glory.
For God has decreed the flattening
of each high mountain, of the everlasting hills,
the filling of the valleys to make the ground level
so that Israel can walk in safety under the glory of God.
And the forests and every fragrant tree will provide shade
for Israel at the command of God;
for God will guide Israel in joy by the light of his glory
with his mercy and integrity for escort.

    This is the word of the Lord.

Responsorial Psalm   (Ps 125. *R*. v. 3)
Response
What marvels the Lord worked for us!
Indeed we were glad.

1. When the Lord delivered Zion from bondage,
It seemed like a dream.

Then was our mouth filled with laughter,
on our lips there were songs. (*R.*)

2. The heathens themselves said: "What marvels
the Lord worked for them!"
What marvels the Lord worked for us!
Indeed we were glad. (*R.*)

3. Deliver us, O Lord, from our bondage
as streams in dry land.
Those who are sowing in tears
will sing when they reap. (*R.*)

4. They go out, they go out, full of tears,
carrying seed for the sowing:
they come back, they come back, full of song,
will sing when they reap. (*R.*)

Second Reading   (1:3–6. 8–11)

A reading from the letter of St Paul to the Philippians
Be pure and blameless for the day of Christ.

Every time I pray for all of you, I pray with joy, remembering how you have helped to spread the Good News from the
day you first heard it right up to the present. I am quite
certain that the One who began this good work in you will
see that it is finished when the Day of Christ Jesus comes.
God knows how much I miss you all, loving you as Christ
Jesus loves you. My prayer is that your love for each other
may increase more and more and never stop improving
your knowledge and deepening your perception so that you
can always recognise what is best. This will help you to
become pure and blameless, and prepare you for the Day of
Christ, when you will reach the perfect goodness which
Jesus Christ produces in us for the glory and praise of God.

This is the word of the Lord.

Alleluia (Lk 3:4. 6)

Alleluia, alleluia!
Prepare a way for the Lord,
make his paths straight.
And all mankind shall see the salvation of God.
Alleluia!

Gospel (3:1–6)

A reading from the holy Gospel according to Luke
All mankind shall see the salvation of God.

In the fifteenth year of Tiberius Caesar's reign, when Pontius Pilate was governor of Judaea, Herod tetrarch of Galilee, his brother Philip tetrarch of the lands of Ituraea and Trachonitis, Lysanias tetrarch of Abilene, during the pontificate of Annas and Caiaphas, the word of God came to John son of Zechariah, in the wilderness. He went through the whole Jordan district proclaiming a baptism of repentance for the forgiveness of sins, as it is written in the book of the sayings of the prophet Isaiah:

A voice cries in the wilderness:
Prepare a way for the Lord,
make his paths straight.
Every valley will be filled in,
every mountain and hill be laid low,
winding ways will be straightened
and rough roads made smooth.
And all mankind shall see the salvation of God.

This is the Gospel of the Lord.

MONDAY

First Reading   (35:1–10)

A reading from the prophet Isaiah
God himself is coming to save you.

Let the wilderness and the dry-lands exult,
let the wasteland rejoice and bloom,
let it bring forth flowers like the jonquil,
let it rejoice and sing for joy.

The glory of Lebanon is bestowed on it,
the splendour of Carmel and Sharon;
they shall see the glory of the Lord,
the splendour of our God.

Strengthen all weary hands,
steady all trembling knees
and say to all faint hearts,
"Courage! Do not be afraid.

"Look, your God is coming,
vengeance is coming,
the retribution of God;
he is coming to save you."

Then the eyes of the blind shall be opened,
the ears of the deaf unsealed,
then the lame shall leap like a deer
and the tongues of the dumb sing for joy;

for water gushes in the desert,
streams in the wasteland,
the scorched earth becomes a lake,
the parched land springs of water.
The lairs where the jackals used to live
become thickets of reed and papyrus.

And through it will run a highway undefiled
which shall be called the Sacred Way;
the unclean may not travel by it,
nor fools stray along it.

No lion will be there
nor any fierce beast roam about it,
but the redeemed will walk there,
for those the Lord has ransomed shall return.

They will come to Zion shouting for joy,
everlasting joy on their faces;
joy and gladness will go with them
and sorrow and lament be ended.

This is the word of the Lord.

Responsorial Psalm   (Ps 84:9–14. *R.* Is 35:4)

Response
Look, our God is coming to save us.

1. I will hear what the Lord God has to say,
a voice that speaks of peace,
peace for his people.
His help is near for those who fear him
and his glory will dwell in our land. (*R.*)

2. Mercy and faithfulness have met;
justice and peace have embraced.
Faithfulness shall spring from the earth
and justice look down from heaven. (*R.*)

3. The Lord will make us prosper
and our earth shall yield its fruit.

Justice shall march before him
and peace shall follow his steps. (*R.*)

Alleluia   (Lk 3:4. 6)

Alleluia, alleluia!
Prepare a way for the Lord,
make his paths straight.
And all mankind shall see the salvation of God.
Alleluia!

Alternative Alleluias p. 837.

Gospel   (5:17–26)

A reading from the holy Gospel according to Luke
We have seen strange things today.

Now Jesus was teaching one day, and among the audience
there were Pharisees and doctors of the Law who had come
from every village in Galilee, from Judaea and from Jerusalem. And the Power of the Lord was behind his works of
healing. Then some men appeared, carrying on a bed a
paralysed man whom they were trying to bring in and lay
down in front of him. But as the crowd made it impossible
to find a way of getting him in, they went up on to the flat
roof and lowered him and his stretcher down through the
tiles into the middle of the gathering, in front of Jesus. Seeing their faith he said, "My friend, your sins are forgiven
you." The scribes and the Pharisees began to think this
over. "Who is this man talking blasphemy? Who can forgive sins but God alone?" But Jesus, aware of their
thoughts, made them this reply, "What are these thoughts
you have in your hearts? Which of these is easier: to say,
'Your sins are forgiven you' or to say, 'Get up and walk'?
But to prove to you that the son of Man has authority on
earth to forgive sins", – he said to the paralysed man – "I
order you: get up, and pick up your stretcher and go home."

And immediately before their very eyes he got up, picked up what he had been lying on and went home praising God.

They were all astounded and praised God, and were filled with awe, saying, "We have seen strange things today."

This is the Gospel of the Lord.

TUESDAY

First Reading (40:1–11)

A reading from the prophet Isaiah
God consoles his people.

"Console my people, console them"
says your God.
"Speak to the heart of Jerusalem
and call to her
that her time of service is ended,
that her sin is atoned for,
that she has received from the hand of the Lord
double punishment for all her crimes."

A voice cries, "Prepare in the wilderness
a way for the Lord.
Make a straight highway for our God
across the desert.
Let every valley be filled in,
every mountain and hill be laid low,
let every cliff become a plain,
and the ridges a valley;
then the glory of the Lord shall be revealed
and all mankind shall see it;
for the mouth of the Lord has spoken.
A voice commands: "Cry!"
and I answered, "What shall I cry?"
– "All flesh is grass
and its beauty like the wild flower's.

The grass withers, the flower fades
when the breath of the Lord blows on them.
(The grass is without doubt the people.)
The grass withers, the flower fades,
but the word of our God remains for ever."
Go up on a high mountain,
joyful messenger to Zion.
Shout with a loud voice,
joyful messenger to Jerusalem.
Shout without fear,
say to the towns of Judah,
"Here is your God."

Here is the Lord coming with power,
his arm subduing all things to him.
The prize of his victory is with him,
his trophies all go before him.
He is like a shepherd feeding his flock,
gathering lambs in his arms,
holding them against his breast
and leading to their rest the mother ewes.

This is the word of the Lord.

Responsorial Psalm   (Ps 95:1–3. 10–13. R. Is 40:9–10)

Response
Here is our God coming with power.

1. O sing a new song to the Lord,
sing to the Lord all the earth.
O sing to the Lord, bless his name.
Proclaim his help day by day. (*R.*)

2. Tell among the nations his glory
and his wonders among all the peoples.
Proclaim to the nations: "God is king."
he will judge the peoples in fairness. (*R.*)

3. Let the heavens rejoice and earth be glad,
let the sea and all within it thunder praise,
let the land and all it bears rejoice,
all the trees of the wood shout for joy
at the presence of the Lord for he comes,
he comes to rule the earth. (*R.*)

4. With justice he will rule the world,
he will judge the peoples with his truth. (R.)

Alleluia

Alleluia, alleluia!
Come Lord! Do not delay.
Forgive the sins of your people.
Alleluia!

Alternative Alleluias p. 837.

Gospel   (18:12–14)

A reading from the holy Gospel according to Matthew
God does not wish the little ones to be lost.

Jesus said to his disciples: "Tell me. Suppose a man has a
hundred sheep and one of them strays; will he not leave
the ninety-nine on the hillside and go in search of the stray?
I tell you solemnly, if he finds it, it gives him more joy than
do the ninety-nine that did not stray at all. Similarly, it is
never the will of your Father in heaven that one of these
little ones should be lost."

This is the Gospel of the Lord.

WEDNESDAY

First Reading   (40:25–31)

A reading from the prophet Isaiah
The Lord almighty gives strength to the wearied.

"To whom could you liken me
and who could be my equal?" says the Holy One.
Lift your eyes and look.
Who made these stars
if not he who drills them like an army,
calling each one by name?
So mighty is his power, so great his strength,
that not one fails to answer.

How can you say, Jacob,
how can you insist, Israel,
"My destiny is hidden from the Lord,
my rights are ignored by my God"?
Did you not know?
Had you not heard?

The Lord is an everlasting God,
he created the boundaries of the earth.
He does not grow tired or weary,
his understanding is beyond fathoming.
He gives strength to the wearied,
he strengthens the powerless.
Young men may grow tired and weary,
youths may stumble,
but those who hope in the Lord renew their strength,
they put out wings like eagles.
They run and do not grow weary,
walk and never tire.

This is the word of the Lord.

Responsorial Psalm (Ps 102:1–4. 8.10. *R*. v. 1)

Response

My soul, give thanks to the Lord.

1. My soul, give thanks to the Lord,
all my being, bless his holy name.
My soul, give thanks to the Lord
and never forget all his blessings. (*R*.)

2. It is he who forgives all your guilt,
who heals every one of your ills,
who redeems your life from the grave,
who crowns you with love and compassion. (*R*.)

3. The Lord is compassion and love,
slow to anger and rich in mercy.
He does not treat us according to our sins
nor repay us according to our faults. (*R*.)

Alleluia

Alleluia, alleluia!
Behold, our Lord will come with power
and will enlighten the eyes of his servants.
Alleluia!

Alternative Alleluias p. 837.

Gospel (11:28–30)

A reading from the holy Gospel according to Matthew
Come to me, all you who labour.

At that time Jesus exclaimed, "Come to me, all you who labour and are overburdened, and I will give you rest. Shoulder my yoke and learn from me, for I am gentle and humble in heart, and you will find rest for your souls. Yes, my yoke is easy and my burden light."

This is the Gospel of the Lord.

THURSDAY

First Reading   (41:13–20)

A reading from the prophet Isaiah
I, the Holy One of Israel, am your redeemer.

For I, the Lord, your God,
I am holding you by the right hand;
I tell you, "Do not be afraid,
I will help you."

Do not be afraid, Jacob, poor worm,
Israel, puny mite.
I will help you – it is the Lord who speaks –
the Holy One of Israel is your redeemer.

See, I turn you into a threshing-sled,
new, with doubled teeth;
you shall thresh and crush the mountains,
and turn the hills to chaff.

You shall winnow them and the wind will blow them away,
the gale will scatter them.
But you yourself will rejoice in the Lord,
and glory in the Holy One of Israel.

The poor and needy ask for water, and there is none,
their tongue is parched with thirst.
I, the Lord, will answer them,
I, the God of Israel, will not abandon them.

I will make rivers well up on barren heights,
and fountains in the midst of valleys;
turn the wilderness into a lake,
and dry ground into waterspring.

In the wilderness I will put cedar trees,
acacias, myrtles, olives.

In the desert I will plant juniper,
plane tree and cypress side by side;

so that men may see and know,
may all observe and understand
that the hand of the Lord has done this,
that the Holy One of Israel has created it.

This is the word of the Lord.

Responsorial Psalm (Ps 144:1. 9–13. *R*. v. 8)

Response
The Lord is kind and full of compassion,
slow to anger, abounding in love.

1. I will give you glory,
O God my King,
I will bless your name for ever.
How good is the Lord to all,
compassionate to all his creatures. (*R*.)

2. All your creatures shall thank you, O Lord,
and your friends shall repeat their blessing.
They shall speak of the glory of your reign
and declare your might, O God,
to make known to men your mighty deeds
and the glorious splendour of your reign. (*R*.)

3. Yours is an everlasting kingdom;
your rule lasts from age to age. (*R*.)

Alleluia

Alleluia, alleluia!
Come to us, Lord, with your peace
that we may rejoice in your presence with sincerity of heart.
Alleluia!
Alternative Alleluias p. 837.

Gospel   (11:11–15)

A reading from the holy Gospel according to Matthew
A greater than John the Baptist has never been seen.

Jesus spoke to the crowds: "I tell you solemnly, of all the
children born of women, a greater than John the Baptist
has never been seen; yet the least in the kingdom of heaven
is greater than he is. Since John the Baptist came, up to this
present time, the kingdom of heaven has been subjected to
violence and the violent are taking it by storm. Because it
was towards John that all the prophecies of the prophets
and of the Law were leading; and he, if you will believe me,
is the Elijah who was to return. If anyone has ears to hear,
let him listen!"

This is the Gospel of the Lord.

FRIDAY

First Reading   (48:17–19)

A reading from the prophet Isaiah
If only you had been alert to my commandments.

Thus says the Lord, your redeemer, the Holy One of Israel:
I, the Lord, your God, teach you what is good for you,
I lead you in the way that you must go.
If only you had been alert to my commandments,
your happiness would have been like a river,
your integrity like the waves of the sea.
Your children would have been numbered like the sand,
your descendants as many as its grains.
Never would your name have been cut off or blotted out
    before me.

This is the word of the Lord.

Responsorial Psalm (Ps 1:1–4. 6. *R*. Jn 8:12)

Response
Anyone who follows you, Lord, will have the light of life.

1. Happy indeed is the man
who follows not the counsel of the wicked;
nor lingers in the way of sinners
nor sits in the company of scorners,
but whose delight is the law of the Lord
and who ponders his law day and night. (*R*.)

2. He is like a tree that is planted
beside the flowing waters,
that yields its fruit in due season
and whose leaves shall never fade;
and all that he does shall prosper. (*R*.)

3. Not so are the wicked, not so!
For they like winnowed chaff
shall be driven away by the wind.
For the Lord guards the way of the just
but the way of the wicked leads to doom. (*R*.)

Alleluia

Alleluia, alleluia!
See, the king, the Lord of the world, will come.
He will free us from the yoke of our bondage.
Alleluia!

Alternative Alleluias p. 837.

Gospel (11:16–19)

A reading from the holy Gospel according to Matthew
They heed neither John nor the Son of Man.

Jesus spoke to the crowds: "What description can I find

for this generation? It is like children shouting to each other
as they sit in the market place:

'We played the pipes for you,
and you wouldn't dance;
we sang dirges,
and you wouldn't be mourners.'

"For John came, neither eating nor drinking, and they say,
'He is possessed.' The Son of Man came, eating and drinking, and they say, 'Look, a glutton and a drunkard, a friend
of tax collectors and sinners.' Yet wisdom has been proved
right by her actions."

This is the Gospel of the Lord.

SATURDAY

First Reading   (48:1–4. 9–11)

A reading from the book of Ecclesiasticus
Elijah will come again.

Then the prophet Elijah arose like a fire,
his word flaring like a torch.
It was he who brought famine on them,
and who decimated them in his zeal.
By the word of the Lord, he shut up the heavens,
he also, three times, brought down fire.
How glorious you were in your miracles, Elijah!
Has anyone reason to boast as you have? –
taken up in the whirlwind of fire,
in a chariot with fiery horses;
designated in the prophecies of doom
to allay God's wrath before the fury breaks,
to turn the hearts of fathers towards their children,
and to restore the tribes of Jacob.

Happy shall they be who see you,
and those who have fallen asleep in love.

This is the word of the Lord.

Responsorial Psalm   (Ps 79:2–3. 15–16. 18–19. *R.* v. 4)

Response
God of hosts, bring us back;
let your face shine on us and we shall be saved.

1. O shepherd of Israel, hear us,
shine forth from your cherubim throne.
O Lord, rouse up your might,
O Lord, come to our help. (*R.*)

2. God of hosts, turn again, we implore,
look down from heaven and see.
Visit this vine and protect it,
the vine your right hand has planted. (*R.*)

3. May your hand be on the man you have chosen,
the man you have given your strength.
And we shall never forsake you again:
give us life that we may call upon your name. (*R.*)

Alleluia

Alleluia, alleluia!
The day of the Lord is near;
Look, he comes to save us.
Alleluia!

Alternative Alleluias p. 837.

Gospel   (17:10–13)

A reading from the holy Gospel according to Matthew
Elijah has come already and they did not recognise him.

As they came down from the mountain the disciples put this question to Jesus, "Why do the scribes say then that Elijah has to come first?" "True," he replied "Elijah is to come to see that everything is once more as it should be; however, I tell you that Elijah has come already and they did not recognise him but treated him as they pleased; and the Son of Man will suffer similarly at their hands." The disciples understood then that he had been speaking of John the Baptist.

This is the Gospel of the Lord.

3rd SUNDAY OF ADVENT
Year 1 (Year A)

First Reading   (35:1–6. 10)

A reading from the prophet Isaiah
God himself is coming to save you.

Let the wilderness and the dry-lands exult,
let the wasteland rejoice and bloom,
let it bring forth flowers like the jonquil,
let it rejoice and sing for joy.

The glory of Lebanon is bestowed on it,
the splendour of Carmel and Sharon;
they shall see the glory of the Lord,
the splendour of our God.

Strengthen all weary hands, steady all trembling knees
and say to all faint hearts,
"Courage! Do not be afraid.

"Look, your God is coming,
vengeance is coming,
the retribution of God;
he is coming to save you."

Then the eyes of the blind shall be opened,
the ears of the deaf unsealed,
then the lame shall leap like a deer
and the tongues of the dumb sing for joy;
for those the Lord has ransomed shall return.

They will come to Zion shouting for joy,
everlasting joy on their faces;
joy and gladness will go with them
and sorrow and lament be ended.

This is the word of the Lord.

Responsorial Psalm (Ps 145:6–10. *R*. Is 35:4)

Response
Come, Lord, and save us.

Alternative Response
Alleluia!

1. It is he who keeps faith for ever,
who is just to those who are oppressed.
It is he who gives bread to the hungry,
the Lord, who sets prisoners free. (*R*.)

2. The Lord who gives sight to the blind,
who raises up those who are bowed down,
the Lord, who protects the stranger
and upholds the widow and orphan. (*R*.)

3. It is the Lord who loves the just
but thwarts the path of the wicked.
The Lord will reign for ever,
Zion's God, from age to age. (*R*.)

Second Reading   (5:7–10)

A reading from the letter of St James
Do not lose heart for the Lord's coming will be soon.

Be patient, brothers, until the Lord's coming. Think of a
farmer: how patiently he waits for the precious fruit of the
ground until it has had the autumn rains and the spring
rains! You too have to be patient; do not lose heart, because the Lord's coming will be soon. Do not make complaints against one another, brothers, so as not to be brought
to judgement yourselves; the Judge is already to be seen
waiting at the gates. For your example, brothers, in submitting with patience, take the prophets who spoke in the name
of the Lord.

This is the word of the Lord.

Alleluia   (Lk 4:18)

Alleluia, alleluia!
The spirit of the Lord has been given to me.
He has sent me to bring good news to the poor.
Alleluia!

Gospel   (11:2–11)

A reading from the holy Gospel according to Matthew
*Are you the one who is to come, or have we got to wait for
someone else?*

John in his prison had heard what Christ was doing and he
sent his disciples to ask him, "Are you the one who is to
come, or have we got to wait for someone else?" Jesus
answered, "Go back and tell John what you hear and see;
the blind see again, and the lame walk, lepers are cleansed,
and the deaf hear, and the dead are raised to life and the
Good News is proclaimed to the poor; and happy is the
man who does not lose faith in me."

As the messengers were leaving, Jesus began to talk to the people about John: "What did you go out into the wilderness to see? A reed swaying in the breeze? No? Then what did you go out to see? A man wearing fine clothes? Oh no, those who wear fine clothes are to be found in palaces. Then what did you go out for? To see a prophet? Yes, I tell you, and much more than a prophet: he is the one of whom scripture says: Look, I am going to send my messenger before you; he will prepare your way before you. I tell you solemnly, of all the children born of women, a greater than John the Baptist has never been seen; yet the least in the kingdom of heaven is greater than he is."

This is the Gospel of the Lord.

3rd SUNDAY OF ADVENT
Year 2 (Year B)

First Reading   (61:1–2. 10–11)

A reading from the prophet Isaiah
I exult for joy in the Lord.

The spirit of the Lord has been given to me,
for the Lord has anointed me.
He has sent me to bring good news to the poor,
to bind up hearts that are broken;

to proclaim liberty to captives,
freedom to those in prison;
to proclaim a year of favour from the Lord.

"I exult for joy in the Lord,
my soul rejoices in my God,
for he has clothed me in the garments of salvation,
he has wrapped me in the cloak of integrity,
like a bridegroom wearing his wreath,
like a bride adorned in her jewels.

"For as the earth makes fresh things grow,
as a garden makes seeds spring up,
so will the Lord make both integrity and praise
spring up in the sight of the nations."

This is the word of the Lord.

Responsorial Psalm   (Lk 1:46–50. 53–54. *R.* Is 61:10)
Response
My soul rejoices in my God.

1. My soul glorifies the Lord,
my spirit rejoices in God, my Saviour.
He looks on his servant in her nothingness;
henceforth all ages will call me blessed. (*R.*)

2. The Almighty works marvels for me.
Holy his name!
His mercy is from age to age,
on those who fear him. (*R.*)

3. He fills the starving with good things,
sends the rich away empty.
He protects Israel, his servant,
remembering his mercy. (*R.*)

Second Reading   (5:16–24)

A reading from the first letter of St Paul to the Thessalonians
*May you all be kept safe, spirit, soul and body, for the coming
of the Lord.*

Be happy at all times; pray constantly; and for all things
give thanks to God, because this is what God expects you to
do in Christ Jesus.

Never try to suppress the Spirit or treat the gift of prophecy with contempt; think before you do anything – hold on to what is good and avoid every form of evil.

May the God of peace make you perfect and holy; and may you all be kept safe and blameless, spirit, soul and body, for the coming of our Lord Jesus Christ. God has called you and he will not fail you.

This is the word of the Lord.

Alleluia (Lk 4:18)

Alleluia, alleluia!
The spirit of the Lord has been given to me.
He has sent me to bring good news to the poor.
Alleluia!

Gospel (1:6–8. 19–28)

A reading from the holy Gospel according to John
There stands among you – unknown to you – the one who is coming after me.

A man came, sent by God.
His name was John.
He came as a witness,
as a witness to speak for the light,
so that everyone might believe through him.
He was not the light,
only a witness to speak for the light.

This is how John appeared as a witness. When the Jews sent priests and Levites from Jerusalem to ask him, "Who are you?" he not only declared, but he declared quite openly, "I am not the Christ." "Well then," they asked "are you Elijah?" "I am not" he said. "Are you the Prophet?"

He answered, "No." So they said to him, "Who are you? We must take back an answer to those who sent us. What have you to say about yourself?" So John said, "I am, as Isaiah prophesied:

a voice that cries in the wilderness:
Make a straight way for the Lord."

Now these men had been sent by the Pharisees, and they put this further question to him, "Why are you baptising if you are not the Christ, and not Elijah, and not the prophet?" John replied, "I baptise with water; but there stands among you – unknown to you – the one who is coming after me; and I am not fit to undo his sandal-strap." This happened at Bethany, on the far side of the Jordan, where John was baptising.

This is the Gospel of the Lord.

3rd SUNDAY OF ADVENT
Year 3 (Year C)

First Reading   (3:14–18)

A reading from the prophet Zephaniah
The Lord will dance with shouts of joy for you as on a day of festival.

Shout for joy, daughter of Zion,
Israel, shout aloud!
Rejoice, exult with all your heart,
daughter of Jerusalem!
The Lord has repealed your sentence;
he has driven your enemies away.
The Lord, the king of Israel, is in your midst;
you have no more evil to fear.

When that day comes, word will come to Jerusalem:
Zion, have no fear,
do not let your hands fall limp.
The Lord your God is in your midst,
a victorious warrior.
He will exult with joy over you,
he will renew you by his love;
he will dance with shouts of joy for you
as on a day of festival.

This is the word of the Lord.

Responsorial Psalm (Is 12:2–6. R. v. 6)

Response
Sing and shout for joy
for great in your midst is the Holy One of Israel.

1. Truly, God is my salvation,
I trust, I shall not fear.
For the Lord is my strength, my song,
he became my saviour.
With joy you will draw water
from the wells of salvation. (R.)

2. Give thanks to the Lord, give praise to his name!
make his mighty deeds known to the peoples!
Declare the greatness of his name. (R.)

3. Sing a psalm to the Lord
for he has done glorious deeds,
make them known to all the earth!
People of Zion, sing and shout for joy
for great in your midst is the Holy One of Israel. (R.)

Second Reading   (4:4–7)

A reading from the letter of St Paul to the Philippians
The Lord is very near.

I want you to be happy, always happy in the Lord; I repeat, what I want is your happiness. Let your tolerance be evident to everyone: the Lord is very near. There is no need to worry; but if there is anything you need, pray for it, asking God for it with prayer and thanksgiving, and that peace of God, which is so much greater than we can understand, will guard your hearts and your thoughts, in Christ Jesus.

This is the word of the Lord.

Alleluia   (Lk 4:18)

Alleluia, alleluia!
The spirit of the Lord has been given to me.
He has sent me to bring good news to the poor.
Alleluia!

Gospel   (3:10–18)

A reading from the holy Gospel according to Luke
What must we do?

When all the people asked John, "What must we do, then?" he answered, "If anyone has two tunics he must share with the man who has none, and the one with something to eat must do the same." There were tax collectors too who came for baptism, and these said to him, "Master, what must we do?" He said to them, "Exact no more than your rate." Some soldiers asked him in their turn, "What about us? What must we do?" He said to them, "No intimidation! No extortion! Be content with your pay!"

A feeling of expectancy had grown among the people, who were beginning to think that John might be the Christ, so John declared before them all, "I baptise you with water, but someone is coming, someone who is more powerful than I am, and I am not fit to undo the strap of his sandals; he will baptise you with the Holy Spirit and fire. His winnowing-fan is in his hand to clear his threshing-floor and to gather the wheat into his barn; but the chaff he will burn in a fire that will never go out." As well as this, there were many other things he said to exhort the people and to announce the Good News to them.

This is the Gospel of the Lord.

MONDAY

Special readings and chants are given for ferias from 17–24 December. See pp. 85 ff.

First Reading   (24:2–7. 15–17)

A reading from the book of Numbers
A star from Jacob takes the leadership.

Raising his eyes Balaam saw Israel, encamped by tribes; the spirit of God came on him and he declaimed his poem. He said:

"The oracle of Balaam son of Beor,
the oracle of the man with far-seeing eyes,
the oracle of the one who hears the word of God.
He sees what Shaddai makes him see,
receives the divine answer, and his eyes are opened.
How fair are your tents, O Jacob!
How fair your dwellings, Israel!
Like valleys that stretch afar,
like gardens by the banks of a river,
like aloes planted by the Lord,
like cedars beside the waters!
A hero arises from their stock,
he reigns over countless peoples.

His king is greater than Agag,
his majesty is exalted."

Then Balaam declaimed his poem. He said:

"The oracle of Balaam son of Beor,
the oracle of the man with far-seeing eyes,
the oracle of one who hears the word of God,
of one who knows the knowledge of the Most High.
He sees what Shaddai makes him see,
receives the divine answer, and his eyes are opened.
I see him – but not in the present,
I behold him – but not close at hand:
a star from Jacob takes the leadership,
a sceptre arises from Israel."

    This is the word of the Lord.

Responsorial Psalm   (Ps 24:4–9. *R*. v. 4)

Response
Lord, make me know your ways.

1. Lord, make me know your ways.
Lord, teach me your paths.
Make me walk in your truth, and teach me:
for you are God my saviour. (*R*.)

2. Remember your mercy, Lord,
and the love you have shown from of old.
In your love remember me,
because of your goodness, O Lord. (*R*.)

3. The Lord is good and upright.
He shows the path to those who stray,
he guides the humble in the right path;
he teaches his way to the poor. (*R*.)

Alleluia

Alleluia, alleluia!
The Lord will come, go out to meet him.
Great is his beginning and his reign will have no end.
Alleluia!

Alternative Alleluias p. 838.

Gospel   (21:23–27)

A reading from the holy Gospel according to Matthew
John's baptism: where did it come from?

Jesus had gone into the Temple and was teaching, when the chief priests and the elders of the people came to him and said, "What authority have you for acting like this? And who gave you this authority?" "And I" replied Jesus "will ask you a question, only one; if you tell me the answer to it, I will then tell you my authority for acting like this. John's baptism: where did it come from: heaven or man?" And they argued it out this way among themselves, "If we say from heaven, he will retort, 'Then why did you refuse to believe him?'; but if we say from man, we have the people to fear, for they all hold that John was a prophet." So their reply to Jesus was, "We do not know." And he retorted, "Nor will I tell you my authority for acting like this."

This is the Gospel of the Lord.

TUESDAY

Special readings and chants are given for ferias from 17–24 December. See pp. 85 ff.

First Reading   (3:1–2. 9–13)

A reading from the prophet Zephaniah
Messianic salvation is promised to all the poor in spirit.

Trouble is coming to the rebellious, the defiled,
the tyrannical city!
She would never listen to the call,
would never learn the lesson;
she has never trusted in the Lord,
never drawn near to her God.
Yes, I will then give the peoples
lips that are clean,
so that all may invoke the name of the Lord
and serve him under the same yoke.
From beyond the banks of the rivers of Ethiopia my sup-
    pliants
will bring me offerings.
When that day comes
you need feel no shame for all the misdeeds
you have committed against me,
for I will remove your proud boasters
from your midst;
and you will cease to strut
on my holy mountain.
In your midst I will leave
a humble and lowly people,
and those who are left in Israel will seek refuge in the name
    of the Lord.
They will do no wrong,
will tell no lies;
and the perjured tongue will no longer
be found in their mouths.
But they will be able to graze and rest
with no one to disturb them.

    This is the word of the Lord.

Responsorial Psalm (Ps 33:2–3. 6–7. 16. 18–19. 23. *R*. v. 7)
Response
This poor man called; the Lord heard him.

1. I will bless the Lord at all times,
his praise always on my lips;
in the Lord my soul shall make its boast.
The humble shall hear and be glad. (*R.*)

2. Look towards him and be radiant;
let your faces not be abashed.
This poor man called; the Lord heard him
and rescued him from all his distress. (*R.*)

3. The Lord turns his face against the wicked
to destroy their remembrance from the earth.
The just call and the Lord hears
and rescues them in all their distress. (*R.*)

4. The Lord is close to the broken-hearted;
those whose spirit is crushed he will save.
The Lord ransoms the souls of his servants.
Those who hide in him shall not be condemned. (*R.*)

Alleluia

Alleluia, alleluia!
Look, the Lord will come to save his people.
Blessed those who are ready to meet him.
Alleluia!

Alternative Alleluias p. 837.

Gospel   (21:28–32)

A reading from the holy Gospel according to Matthew
John came, but it was the sinners who believed in him.

Jesus said to the chief priests and the elders of the people,
"What is your opinion? A man had two sons. He went and
said to the first, 'My boy, you go and work in the vineyard
today.' He answered, 'I will not go,' but afterwards thought
better of it and went. The man then went and said the same

thing to the second who answered, 'Certainly, sir,' but did not go. Which of the two did the father's will?" "The first" they said. Jesus said to them, "I tell you solemnly, tax collectors and prostitutes are making their way into the kingdom of God before you. For John came to you, a pattern of true righteousness, but you did not believe him, and yet the tax collectors and prostitutes did. Even after seeing that, you refused to think better of it and believe in him."

This is the Gospel of the Lord.

WEDNESDAY

Special readings and chants are given for ferias from 17–24 December. See pp. 85 ff.

First Reading   (45:6–8. 18. 21–26)

A reading from the prophet Isaiah
Send victory like a dew, you heavens!

Apart from me, all is nothing.
I am the Lord, unrivalled,
I form the light and create the dark.
I make good fortune and create calamity,
it is I, the Lord, who do all this.

Send victory like a dew, you heavens,
and let the clouds rain it down.
Let the earth open
for salvation to spring up.
Let deliverance, too, bud forth
which I, the Lord, shall create.
Yes, thus says the Lord,
creator of the heavens,
who is God,
who formed the earth and made it,
who set it firm,
created it no chaos,
but a place to be lived in:

"I am the Lord, unrivalled.
There is no other god besides me,
a God of integrity and a saviour;
there is none apart from me.
Turn to me and be saved,
all the ends of the earth,
for I am God unrivalled.

"By my own self I swear it;
what comes from my mouth is truth,
a word irrevocable:
before me every knee shall bend,
by me every tongue shall swear,
saying, 'From the Lord alone
come victory and strength.'
To him shall come, ashamed,
all who raged against him.
Victorious and glorious through the Lord shall be
all the descendants of Israel."

This is the word of the Lord.

Responsorial Psalm   (Ps 84:9–14. *R*. Is 45:8)

Response
Send victory like a dew, you heavens,
and let the clouds rain it down.

1. I will hear what the Lord God has to say,
a voice that speaks of peace,
peace for his people.
His help is near for those who fear him
and his glory will dwell in our land. (*R*.)

2. Mercy and faithfulness have met;
justice and peace have embraced.

Faithfulness shall spring from the earth
and justice look down from heaven. (*R.*)

3. The Lord will make us prosper
and our earth shall yield its fruit.
Justice shall march before him
and peace shall follow his steps. (*R.*)

Alleluia   (Is 55:6)

Alleluia, alleluia!
Seek the Lord while he is still to be found,
call to him while he is still near.
Alleluia!

Alternative Alleluias p. 837.

Gospel   (7:19–23)

A reading from the holy Gospel according to Luke
Go back and tell John what you have seen and heard.

John, summoning two of his disciples, sent them to the
Lord to ask, "Are you the one who is to come, or must we
wait for someone else?" When the men reached Jesus they
said, "John the Baptist has sent us to you, to ask, 'Are you
the one who is to come or have we to wait for someone
else?'" It was just then that he cured many people of diseases and afflictions and of evil spirits, and gave the gift of
sight to many who were blind. Then he gave the messengers
their answer, "Go back and tell John what you have seen
and heard: the blind see again, the lame walk, lepers are
cleansed, and the deaf hear, the dead are raised to life, the
Good News is proclaimed to the poor and happy is the
man who does not lose faith in me."
    This is the Gospel of the Lord.

THURSDAY

Special readings and chants are given for ferias from 17–24 December.
See pp. 85 ff.

First Reading (54:1–10)

A reading from the prophet Isaiah
Like a forsaken wife, the Lord calls you back.

Shout for joy, you barren women who bore no children!
Break into cries of joy and gladness, you who were never
  in labour!
For the sons of the forsaken one are more in number
than the sons of the wedded wife, says the Lord.

Widen the space of your tent,
stretch out your hangings freely,
lengthen your ropes, make your pegs firm;
for you will burst out to right and to left.
Your race will take possession of the nations,
and people the abandoned cities.
Do not be afraid, you will not be put to shame,
do not be dismayed, you will not be disgraced;
for you will forget the shame of your youth
and no longer remember the curse of your widowhood.
For now your creator will be your husband,
his name, the Lord of hosts;
your redeemer will be the Holy One of Israel,
he is called the God of the whole earth.
Yes, like a forsaken wife, distressed in spirit,
the Lord calls you back.
Does a man cast off the wife of his youth?
says your God.

I did forsake you for a brief moment,
but with great love will I take you back.
In excess of anger, for a moment
I hid my face from you.

But with everlasting love I have taken pity on you,
says the Lord, your redeemer.

I am now as I was in the days of Noah
when I swore that Noah's waters
should never flood the world again.
So now I swear concerning my anger with you
and the threats I made against you;

for the mountains may depart,
the hills be shaken,
but my love for you will never leave you
and my covenant of peace with you will never be shaken,
says the Lord who takes pity on you.

This is the word of the Lord.

Responsorial Psalm   (Ps 29:2. 4–6. 11–13. *R*. v. 2)

Response
I will praise you, Lord, you have rescued me.

1. I will praise you, Lord, you have rescued me
and have not let my enemies rejoice over me.
O Lord, you have raised my soul from the dead,
restored me to life from those who sink into the grave. (*R*.)

2. Sing psalms to the Lord, you who love him,
give thanks to his holy name.
His anger lasts but a moment; his favour through life.
At night there are tears, but joy comes with dawn. (*R*.)

3. The Lord listened and had pity.
The Lord came to my help.
For me you have changed my mourning into dancing,
O Lord my God, I will thank you for ever. (*R*.)

Alleluia

Alleluia, alleluia!
The day of the Lord is near.
Look, he comes to save us.
Alleluia!

Alternative Alleluias p. 837.

Gospel (7:24–30

A reading from the holy Gospel according to Luke
John is the messenger who prepares the way of the Lord.

When John's messengers had gone Jesus began to talk to the people about John, "What did you go out into the wilderness to see? A reed swaying in the breeze? No? Then what did you go out to see? A man dressed in fine clothes? Oh no, those who go in for fine clothes and live luxuriously are to be found at court! Then what did you go out to see? A prophet? Yes, I tell you, and much more than a prophet: he is the one of whom scripture says: See, I am going to send my messenger before you; he will prepare the way before you. I tell you, of all the children born of women, there is no one greater than John; yet the least in the kingdom of God is greater than he is. All the people who heard him, and the tax collectors too, acknowledged God's plan by accepting baptism from John; but by refusing baptism from him the Pharisees and the lawyers had thwarted what God had in mind for them."

This is the Gospel of the Lord.

FRIDAY

Special readings and chants are given for ferias from 17–24 December. See pp. 85ff.

First Reading (56:1–3. 6–8)

A reading from the prophet Isaiah
My house will be called a house of prayer for all the peoples.

Thus says the Lord: Have a care for justice, act with integrity, for soon my salvation will come and my integrity be manifest.

Blessed is the man who does this and the son of man who clings to it: observing the sabbath, not profaning it, and keeping his hand from every evil deed.

Let no foreigner who has attached himself to the Lord say, "The Lord will surely exclude me from his people."

Foreigners who have attached themselves to the Lord to serve him and to love his name and be his servants – all who observe the sabbath, not profaning it, and cling to my covenant – these I will bring to my holy mountain. I will make them joyful in my house of prayer. Their holocausts and their sacrifices will be accepted on my altar, for my house will be called a house of prayer for all the peoples.

It is the Lord God who speaks, who gathers the outcasts of Israel: there are others I will gather besides those already gathered.

This is the word of the Lord.

Responsorial Psalm   (Ps 66:2–3.5. 7–8. *R*. v. 4)

Response
Let the peoples praise you, O God;
let all the peoples praise you.

1. O God, be gracious and bless us
and let your face shed its light upon us.
So will your ways be known upon earth
and all nations learn your saving help. (*R*.)

2. Let the nations be glad and exult
for you rule the world with justice.
With fairness you rule the peoples,
you guide the nations on earth. (*R*.)

3. The earth has yielded its fruit
for God, our God, has blessed us.
May God still give us his blessing
till the ends of the earth revere him. (*R.*)

Alleluia (Ps 84:8)

Alleluia, alleluia!
Let us see, O Lord, your mercy
and give us your saving help.
Alleluia!

Alternative Alleluias p. 837.

Gospel (5:33–36)

A reading from the holy Gospel according to John
John was a lamp alight and shining.

Jesus said to the Jews:
You sent messengers to John,
and he gave his testimony to the truth:
not that I depend on human testimony;
no, it is for your salvation that I speak of this.
John was a lamp alight and shining
and for a time you were content to enjoy the light that he
    gave.
But my testimony is greater than John's:
the works my Father has given me to carry out,
these same works of mine
testify that the Father has sent me.

This is the Gospel of the Lord.

4th SUNDAY OF ADVENT

Year 1 (Year A)

First Reading   (7:10–14)

A reading from the prophet Isaiah
The maiden is with child.

Once again the Lord spoke to Ahaz and said, "Ask the
Lord your God for a sign for yourself coming either from
the depths of Sheol or from the heights above." "No," Ahaz
answered "I will not put the Lord to the test."

Then he said:

"Listen now, House of David:
are you not satisfied with trying the patience of men without
trying the patience of my God, too?
The Lord himself, therefore,
will give you a sign.
It is this: the maiden is with child
and will soon give birth to a son
whom she will call Immanuel,

a name which means 'God-is-with-us'."

This is the word of the Lord.

Responsorial Psalm   (Ps 23:1–6. *R.* v. 7. 10)

Response
Let the Lord enter! He is the king of glory.

1. The Lord's is the earth and its fullness,
the world and all its peoples.
It is he who set it on the seas;
on the waters he made it firm. (*R.*)

2. Who shall climb the mountain of the Lord?
Who shall stand in his holy place?
The man with clean hands and pure heart,
who desires not worthless things. (*R.*)

3. He shall receive blessings from the Lord
and reward from the God who saves him.
Such are the men who seek him,
seek the face of the God of Jacob. (*R.*)

Second Reading   (1:1–7)

A reading from the letter of St Paul to the Romans
Jesus Christ, descendant of David, Son of God.

From Paul, a servant of Christ Jesus who has been called to
be an apostle, and specially chosen to preach the Good
News that God promised long ago through his prophets in
the scriptures.

This news is about the Son of God who, according to the
human nature he took, was a descendant of David: it is
about Jesus Christ our Lord who, in the order of the spirit,
the spirit of holiness that was in him, was proclaimed Son
of God in all his power through his resurrection from the
dead. Through him we received grace and our apostolic
mission to preach the obedience of faith to all pagan nations
in honour of his name. You are one of these nations, and by
his call belong to Jesus Christ. To you all, then, who are
God's beloved in Rome, called to be saints, may God our
Father and the Lord Jesus Christ send grace and peace.

This is the word of the Lord.

Alleluia   (Mt 1:23)

Alleluia, alleluia!

The virgin will conceive and give birth to a son
and they will call him Emmanuel,
a name which means "God-is-with-us".
Alleluia!

Gospel (1:18–25)

A reading from the holy Gospel according to Matthew
*Jesus is born of Mary who was betrothed to Joseph, son of
David.*

This is how Jesus Christ came to be born. His mother Mary
was betrothed to Joseph; but before they came to live together she was found to be with child through the Holy
Spirit. Her husband Joseph, being a man of honour and
wanting to spare her publicity, decided to divorce her informally. He had made up his mind to do this when the
angel of the Lord appeared to him in a dream and said,
"Joseph son of David, do not be afraid to take Mary home
as your wife, because she has conceived what is in her by the
Holy Spirit. She will give birth to a son and you must name
him Jesus, because he is the one who is to save his people
from their sins." Now all this took place to fulfil the words
spoken by the Lord through the prophet:

The virgin will conceive and give birth to a son
and they will call him Emmanuel,

a name which means "God-is-with-us". When Joseph woke
up he did what the angel of the Lord had told him to do:
he took his wife to his home.

    This is the Gospel of the Lord.

4th SUNDAY OF ADVENT

Year 2 (Year B)

First Reading   (7:1–5. 8–11. 16)

A reading from the second book of Samuel
The kingdom of David will always stand secure before the Lord.

Once David had settled into his house and the Lord had given him rest from all the enemies surrounding him, the king said to the prophet Nathan, "Look, I am living in a house of cedar while the ark of God dwells in a tent." Nathan said to the king, "Go and do all that is in your mind, for the Lord is with you."

But that very night the word of the Lord came to Nathan:

"Go and tell my servant David, 'Thus the Lord speaks: Are you the man to build me a house to dwell in? I took you from the pasture, from following the sheep, to be leader of my people Israel; I have been with you on all your expeditions; I have cut off all your enemies before you. I will give you fame as great as the fame of the greatest on earth. I will provide a place for my people Israel; I will plant them there and they shall dwell in that place and never be disturbed again; nor shall the wicked continue to oppress them as they did, in the days when I appointed judges over my people Israel; I will give them rest from all their enemies. The Lord will make you great; the Lord will make you a House. Your House and your sovereignty will always stand secure before me and your throne be established for ever.' "

This is the word of the Lord.

Responsorial Psalm   (Ps 88:2–5. 27. 29. *R*. v. 2)

Response
I will sing for ever of your love, O Lord.

1. I will sing for ever of your love, O Lord;
through all ages my mouth will proclaim your truth.

Of this I am sure, that your love lasts for ever,
that your truth is firmly established as the heavens. (*R.*)

2. "I have made a covenant with my chosen one;
I have sworn to David my servant:
I will establish your dynasty for ever
and set up your throne through all ages." (*R.*)

3. He will say to me: "You are my father,
my God, the rock who saves me."
I will keep my love for him always;
for him my covenant shall endure. (*R.*)

Second Reading   (16:25–27)

A reading from the letter of St Paul to the Romans
The mystery, which was kept secret for endless ages, is now made clear.

Glory to him who is able to give you the strength to live according to the Good News I preach, and in which I proclaim Jesus Christ, the revelation of a mystery kept secret for endless ages, but now so clear that it must be broadcast to pagans everywhere to bring them to the obedience of faith. This is only what scripture has predicted, and it is all part of the way the eternal God wants things to be. He alone is wisdom; give glory therefore to him through Jesus Christ for ever and ever. Amen.

This is the word of the Lord.

Alleluia   (Lk 1:38)

Alleluia, alleluia!
I am the handmaid of the Lord:
let what you have said be done to me.
Alleluia!

Gospel (1:26–38)

A reading from the holy Gospel according to Luke
Listen! You are to conceive and bear a son.

In the sixth month the angel Gabriel was sent by God to a town in Galilee called Nazareth, to a virgin betrothed to a man named Joseph, of the House of David; and the virgin's name was Mary. He went in and said to her, "Rejoice, so highly favoured! The Lord is with you." She was deeply disturbed by these words and asked herself what this greeting could mean, but the angel said to her, "Mary, do not be afraid; you have won God's favour. Listen! You are to conceive and bear a son, and you must name him Jesus. He will be great and will be called Son of the Most High. The Lord God will give him the throne of his ancestor David; he will rule over the House of Jacob for ever and his reign will have no end." Mary said to the angel, "But how can this come about, since I am a virgin?" "The Holy Spirit will come upon you" the angel answered "and the power of the Most High will cover you with its shadow. And so the child will be holy and will be called Son of God. Know this too: your kinswoman Elizabeth has, in her old age, herself conceived a son, and she whom people called barren is now in her sixth month, for nothing is impossible to God." "I am the handmaid of the Lord," said Mary "let what you have said be done to me." And the angel left her.

This is the Gospel of the Lord.

4th SUNDAY OF ADVENT

Year 3 (Year C)

First Reading (5:1–4)

A reading from the prophet Micah
Out of you will be born the one who is to rule over Israel.

The Lord says this:

You, (Bethlehem) Ephrathah,
the least of the clans of Judah,
out of you will be born for me
the one who is to rule over Israel;
his origin goes back to the distant past,
to the days of old.
The Lord is therefore going to abandon them
till the time when she who is to give birth gives birth.
Then the remnant of his brothers will come back
to the sons of Israel.
He will stand and feed his flock
with the power of the Lord,
with the majesty of the name of his God.
They will live secure, for from then on he will extend his
    power
to the ends of the land.
He himself will be peace.

This is the word of the Lord.

Responsorial Psalm   (Ps 79:2–3. 15–16. 18–19. *R*. v. 4)
Response
God of hosts, bring us back;
let your face shine on us and we shall be saved.

1. O shepherd of Israel, hear us,
shine forth from your cherubim throne.
O Lord, rouse up your might,
O Lord, come to our help. (*R*.)

2. God of hosts, turn again, we implore,
look down from heaven and see.
Visit this vine and protect it,
the vine your right hand has planted. (*R*.)

3. May your hand be on the man you have chosen,
the man you have given your strength.
And we shall never forsake you again:
give us life that we may call upon your name. (*R.*)

Second Reading   (10:5–10)

A reading from the letter to the Hebrews
Here I am! I am coming to obey your will.

This is what Christ said, on coming into the world:

You who wanted no sacrifice or oblation,
prepared a body for me.
You took no pleasure in holocausts or sacrifices for sin;
then I said,
just as I was commanded in the scroll of the book,
"God, here I am! I am coming to obey your will."

Notice that he says first: You did not want what the Law
lays down as the things to be offered, that is: the sacrifices,
the oblations, the holocausts and the sacrifices for sin, and
you took no pleasure in them; and then he says: Here I
am! I am coming to obey your will. He is abolishing the
first sort to replace it with the second. And this will was for
us to be made holy by the offering of his body made once
and for all by Jesus Christ.

This is the word of the Lord.

Alleluia   (Lk 1:38)

Alleluia, alleluia!
I am the handmaid of the Lord:
let what you have said be done to me.
Alleluia!

Gospel   (1:39–44)

A reading from the holy Gospel according to Luke
*Why should I be honoured with a visit from the mother of my
Lord?*

Mary set out at that time and went as quickly as she could
to a town in the hill country of Judah. She went into Zechariah's house and greeted Elizabeth. Now as soon as Elizabeth heard Mary's greeting, the child leapt in her womb and
Elizabeth was filled with the Holy Spirit. She gave a loud
cry and said, "Of all women you are the most blessed, and
blessed is the fruit of your womb. Why should I be honoured with a visit from the mother of my Lord? For the
moment your greeting reached my ears, the child in my
womb leapt for joy. Yes, blessed is she who believed that
the promise made her by the Lord would be fulfilled."

This is the Gospel of the Lord.

The following readings are used from 17–24 December. The readings
of the day on which Sunday falls are omitted, but they may be
anticipated or used later on another day, especially in place of those
readings which occur on the Sunday of the current year.

DECEMBER 17

First Reading   (49:2. 8–10)

A reading from the book of Genesis
The sceptre shall not pass from Judah.

Jacob called his sons and said,
"Gather round, sons of Jacob, and listen;
listen to Israel your father.
Judah, your brothers shall praise you:
you grip your enemies by the neck,
your father's sons shall do you homage,

Judah is a lion cub,
you climb back, my son, from your kill;
like a lion he crouches and lies down,
or a lioness: who dare rouse him?
The sceptre shall not pass from Judah,
nor the mace from between his feet,
until he come to whom it belongs,
to whom the peoples shall render obedience."

This is the word of the Lord.

Responsorial Psalm   (Ps 71:1–4. 7–8. 17. *R*. v. 7)

Response
In his days justice shall flourish
and peace till the moon fails.

1. O God, give your judgement to the king,
to a king's son your justice,
that he may judge your people in justice
and your poor in right judgement. (*R*.)

2. May the mountains bring forth peace for the people
and the hills, justice.
May he defend the poor of the people
and save the children of the needy. (*R*.)

3. In his days justice shall flourish
and peace till the moon fails.
He shall rule from sea to sea,
from the Great River to earth's bounds. (*R*.)

4. May his name be blessed for ever
and endure like the sun.
Every tribe shall be blessed in him,
all nations bless his name. (*R*.)

Gospel   (1:1–17)

The beginning of the holy Gospel according to Matthew
Genealogy of Jesus Christ, son of David.

A genealogy of Jesus Christ, son of David, son of Abraham:

Abraham was the father of Isaac,
Isaac the father of Jacob,
Jacob the father of Judah and his brothers,
Judah was the father of Perez and Zerah, Tamar being
    their mother,
Perez was the father of Hezron,
Hezron the father of Ram,
Ram was the father of Amminadab,
Amminadab the father of Nahshon,
Nahshon the father of Salmon,
Salmon was the father of Boaz, Rahab being his mother,
Boaz was the father of Obed, Ruth being his mother,
Obed was the father of Jesse;
and Jesse was the father of King David.

David was the father of Solomon, whose mother had been
    Uriah's wife,
Solomon was the father of Rehoboam,
Rehoboam the father of Abijah,
Abijah the father of Asa,
Asa was the father of Jehoshaphat,
Jehoshaphat the father of Joram,
Joram the father of Azariah,
Azariah was the father of Jotham,
Jotham the father of Ahaz,
Ahaz the father of Hezekiah,
Hezekiah was the father of Manasseh,
Manasseh the father of Amon,

Amon the father of Josiah;
and Josiah was the father of Jechoniah and his brothers.
Then the deportation to Babylon took place.
After the deportation to Babylon:
Jechoniah was the father of Shealtiel,
Shealtiel the father of Zerubbabel,
Zerubbabel was the father of Abiud,
Abiud the father of Eliakim,
Eliakim the father of Azor,

Azor was the father of Zadok,
Zadok the father of Achim,
Achim the father of Eliud,
Eliud was the father of Eleazer,
Eleazer the father of Matthan,
Matthan the father of Jacob;
and Jacob was the father of Joseph the husband of Mary;
of her was born Jesus who is called Christ.

The sum of generations is therefore: fourteen from Abraham to David; fourteen from David to the Babylonian deportation; and fourteen from the Babylonian deportation to Christ.

This is the Gospel of the Lord.

DECEMBER 18

First Reading   (23:5–8)

A reading from the prophet Jeremiah
I will raise a virtuous Branch for David.

"See, the days are coming – it is the Lord who speaks –
when I will raise a virtuous Branch for David,
who will reign as true king and be wise,
practising honesty and integrity in the land.

In his days Judah will be saved
and Israel dwell in confidence.
And this is the name he will be called:
The Lord-our-integrity.

"So, then, the days are coming – it is the Lord who speaks
– when people will no longer say, 'As the Lord lives who
brought the sons of Israel out of the land of Egypt!' but,
'As the Lord lives who led back and brought home the descendants of the House of Israel out of the land of the North
and from all the countries to which he had dispersed them,
to live on their own soil.' "

This is the word of the Lord.

Responsorial Psalm   (Ps 71:1–2. 12–13. 18–19. R. v. 7)

Response
In his days justice shall flourish
and peace till the moon fails.

1. O God, give your judgement to the king,
to a king's son your justice,
that he may judge your people in justice
and your poor in right judgement. (R.)

2. For he shall save the poor when they cry
and the needy who are helpless.
He will have pity on the weak
and save the lives of the poor. (R.)

3. Blessed be the Lord, God of Israel,
who alone works wonders,
ever blessed his glorious name.
Let his glory fill the earth.
Amen! Amen! (R.)

Alleluia

Alleluia, alleluia!
Wisdom of the Most High,
ordering all things with strength and gentleness,
come and teach us the way of truth.
Alleluia!

Alternative Alleluias p. 839.

Gospel (1:18–24)

A reading from the holy Gospel according to Matthew
Jesus is born of Mary who was betrothed to Joseph, son of David.

This is how Jesus Christ came to be born. His mother Mary was betrothed to Joseph, but before they came to live together she was found to be with child through the Holy Spirit. Her husband Joseph, being a man of honour and wanting to spare her publicity, decided to divorce her informally. He had made up his mind to do this when the angel of the Lord appeared to him in a dream and said, "Joseph son of David, do not be afraid to take Mary home as your wife, because she has conceived what is in her by the Holy Spirit. She will give birth to a son and you must name him Jesus, because he is the one who is to save his people from their sins." Now all this took place to fulfil the words spoken by the Lord through the prophet:

> The virgin will conceive and give birth to a son
> and they will call him Emmanuel,

a name which means "God-is-with-us". When Joseph woke up he did what the angel of the Lord had told him to do: he took his wife to his home.

This is the Gospel of the Lord.

DECEMBER 19

First Reading   (13:2–7. 24–25)

A reading from the book of Judges
The birth of Samson is announced by an angel.

There was a man of Zorah of the tribe of Dan, called Man-
oah. His wife was barren, she had borne no children. The
angel of the Lord appeared to this woman and said to her,
"You are barren and have had no child. But from now on
take great care. Take no wine or strong drink, and eat nothing unclean. For you will conceive and bear a son. No razor
is to touch his head, for the boy shall be God's nazirite from
his mother's womb. It is he who will begin to rescue Israel
from the power of the Philistines." Then the woman went
and told her husband, "A man of God has just come to me;
his presence was like the presence of the angel of God, he
was so majestic. I did not ask him where he came from, and
he did not reveal his name to me. But he said to me, 'You
will conceive and bear a son. From now on, take no wine
or strong drink, and eat nothing unclean. For the boy shall
be God's nazirite from his mother's womb to his dying
day.' "

The woman gave birth to a son and called him Samson.
The child grew, and the Lord blessed him; and the spirit of
the Lord began to move him.

This is the word of the Lord.

Responsorial Psalm   (Ps 70:3–6. 16–17. *R.* v. 8)

Response
My lips are filled with your praise,
with your glory all the day long.

1. Be a rock where I can take refuge,
a mighty stronghold to save me;

for you are my rock, my stronghold.
Free me from the hand of the wicked. (*R.*)

2. It is you, O Lord, who are my hope,
my trust, O Lord, since my youth.
On you I have leaned from my birth,
from my mother's womb you have been my help. (*R.*)

3. I will declare the Lord's mighty deeds
proclaiming your justice, yours alone.
O God, you have taught me from my youth
and I proclaim your wonders still. (*R.*)

Alleluia

Alleluia, alleluia!
Ruler of the House of Israel,
Who gave the law to Moses on Sinai,
come and save us with outstretched arm.
Alleluia!

Alternative Alleluias p. 839.

Gospel   (1:5–25)

A reading from the holy Gospel according to Luke
The birth of John the Baptist is announced by Gabriel.

In the days of King Herod of Judaea there lived a priest
called Zechariah who belonged to the Abijah section of the
priesthood, and he had a wife, Elizabeth by name, who was
a descendant of Aaron. Both were worthy in the sight of
God, and scrupulously observed all the commandments and
observances of the Lord. But they were childless: Elizabeth
was barren and they were both getting on in years.

Now it was the turn of Zechariah's section to serve, and
he was exercising his priestly office before God when it fell

to him by lot, as the ritual custom was, to enter the Lord's sanctuary and burn incense there. And at the hour of incense the whole congregation was outside, praying.

Then there appeared to him the angel of the Lord, standing on the right of the altar of incense. The sight disturbed Zechariah and he was overcome with fear. But the angel said to him, "Zechariah, do not be afraid, your prayer has been heard. Your wife Elizabeth is to bear you a son and you must name him John. He will be your joy and delight and many will rejoice at his birth, for he will be great in the sight of the Lord; he must drink no wine, no strong drink. Even from his mother's womb he will be filled with the Holy Spirit, and he will bring back many of the sons of Israel to the Lord their God. With the spirit and power of Elijah, he will go before him to turn the hearts of fathers towards their children and the disobedient back to the wisdom that the virtuous have, preparing for the Lord a people fit for him." Zechariah said to the angel, "How can I be sure of this? I am an old man and my wife is getting on in years." The angel replied, "I am Gabriel who stand in God's presence, and I have been sent to speak to you and bring you this good news. Listen! Since you have not believed my words, which will come true at their appointed time, you will be silenced and have no power of speech until this has happened." Meanwhile the people were waiting for Zechariah and were surprised that he stayed in the sanctuary so long. When he came out he could not speak to them, and they realised that he had received a vision in the sanctuary. But he could only make signs to them, and remained dumb.

When his time of service came to an end he returned home. Some time later his wife Elizabeth conceived, and for five months she kept to herself. "The Lord has done this for me" she said "now that it has pleased him to take away the humiliation I suffered among men."

This is the Gospel of the Lord.

DECEMBER 20

First Reading (7:10–14)

A reading from the prophet Isaiah
The maiden is with child.

Once again the Lord spoke to Ahaz and said, "Ask the
Lord your God for a sign for yourself coming either from
the depths of Sheol or from the heights above." "No," Ahez
answered "I will not put the Lord to the test."

Then he said:
"Listen now, House of David:
are you not satisfied with trying the patience of men without
trying the patience of my God, too?
The Lord himself, therefore,
will give you a sign.
It is this: the maiden is with child
and will soon give birth to a son
whom she will call Immanuel,
a name which means 'God-is-with-us'."

This is the word of the Lord.

Responsorial Psalm (Ps 23:1–6. *R.* vv. 7. 10)

Response
Let the Lord enter! He is the king of glory.

1. The Lord's is the earth and its fullness,
the world and all its peoples.
It is he who set it on the seas;
on the waters he made it firm. (*R.*)

2. Who shall climb the mountain of the Lord?
Who shall stand in his holy place?
The man with clean hands and pure heart,
who desires not worthless things. (*R.*)

3. He shall receive blessings from the Lord
and reward from the God who saves him.
Such are the men who seek him,
seek the face of the God of Jacob. (*R*.)

Alleluia

Alleluia, alleluia!
Root of Jesse, set up as a sign to the peoples,
come to save us and delay no more.
Alleluia!

Alternative Alleluias p. 839.

Gospel   (1:26–38)

A reading from the holy Gospel according to Luke
Listen! You are to conceive and bear a son.

In the sixth month the angel Gabriel was sent by God to a
town in Galilee called Nazareth, to a virgin betrothed to a
man named Joseph, of the House of David; and the virgin's
name was Mary. He went in and said to her, "Rejoice, so
highly favoured! The Lord is with you." She was deeply
disturbed by these words and asked herself what this greeting could mean, but the angel said to her, "Mary, do not be
afraid; you have won God's favour. Listen! You are to
conceive and bear a son, and you must name him Jesus. He
will be great and will be called Son of the Most High. The
Lord God will give him the throne of his ancestor David;
he will rule over the House of Jacob for ever and his reign
will have no end." Mary said to the angel, "But how can
this come about, since I am a virgin?" "The Holy Spirit will
come upon you" the angel answered "and the power of the
Most High will cover you with its shadow. And so the child
will be holy and will be called Son of God. Know this too:
your kinswoman Elizabeth has, in her old age, herself conceived a son, and she whom people called barren is now in

her sixth month, for nothing is impossible to God." "I am
the handmaid of the Lord," said Mary "let what you have
said to be done to me." And the angel left her.

This is the Gospel of the Lord.

DECEMBER 21

First Reading   (2:8–14)

A reading from the Song of Songs
See how my beloved comes leaping over the mountains.

I hear my Beloved.
See how he comes
leaping on the mountains,
bounding over the hills.
My Beloved is like a gazelle,
like a young stag.

See where he stands
behind our wall.
He looks in at the window,
he peers through the lattice.

My Beloved lifts up his voice,
he says to me,
"Come then, my love,
my lovely one, come.
For see, winter is past
the rains are over and gone.
The flowers appear on the earth.
The season of glad songs has come,
the cooing of the turtledove is heard
in our land.
The fig tree is forming its first figs
and the blossoming vines give out their fragrance.

Come then, my love,
my lovely one, come.
My dove, hiding in the clefts of the rock,
in the coverts of the cliff,
show me your face,
let me hear your voice;
for your voice is sweet
and your face is beautiful."

This is the word of the Lord.

Alternative Reading   (3:14–18)

A reading from the prophet Zephaniah
The Lord, the king of Israel, is in your midst.

Shout for joy, daughter of Zion,
Israel, shout aloud!
Rejoice, exult with all your heart,
daughter of Jerusalem!
The Lord has repealed your sentence;
he has driven your enemies away.
The Lord, the king of Israel, is in your midst;
you have no more evil to fear.

When that day comes, word will come to Jerusalem:
Zion, have no fear,
do not let your hands fall limp.
The lord your God is in your midst,
a victorious warrior.
He will exult with joy over you,
he will renew you by his love;
he will dance with shouts of joy for you
as on a day of festival.

This is the word of the Lord.

Responsorial Psalm   (Ps 32:2–3. 11–12. 20–21. *R*. vv. 1. 3)
Response
Ring out your joy to the Lord, O you just;
O sing him a song that is new.

1. Give thanks to the Lord upon the harp,
with a ten-stringed lute sing him songs.
O sing him a song that is new,
play loudly, with all your skill. (*R*.)

2. His own designs shall stand for ever,
the plans of his heart from age to age.
They are happy, whose God is the Lord,
the people he has chosen as his own. (*R*.)

3. Our soul is waiting for the Lord.
The Lord is our help and our shield.
In him do our hearts find joy.
We trust in his holy name. (*R*.)

Alleluia

Alleluia, alleluia!
Key of David, who open the gates of the eternal kingdom,
come to liberate from prison
the captive who lives in darkness.
Alleluia!
Alternative Alleluias p. 839.

Gospel   (1:39–45)
A reading from the holy Gospel according to Luke
*Why should I be honoured with a visit from the mother of my
Lord?*

Mary set out at that time and went as quickly as she could
to a town in the hill country of Judah. She went into Zecha-

riah's house and greeted Elizabeth. Now as soon as Elizabeth heard Mary's greeting, the child leapt in her womb and Elizabeth was filled with the Holy Spirit. She gave a loud cry and said, "Of all women you are the most blessed, and blessed is the fruit of your womb. Why should I be honoured with a visit from the mother of my Lord? For the moment your greeting reached my ears, the child in my womb leapt for joy. Yes, blessed is she who believed that the promise made her by the Lord would be fulfilled."

This is the Gospel of the Lord.

DECEMBER 22

First Reading   (1:24–28)

A reading from the first book of Samuel
Hannah gives thanks for Samuel's birth.

When Hannah had weaned Samuel, she took him up with her together with a three-year old bull, an ephah of flour and a skin of wine, and she brought him to the temple of the Lord at Shiloh; and the child was with them. They slaughtered the bull and the child's mother came to Eli. She said, "If you please, my lord. As you live, my lord, I am the woman who stood here beside you, praying to the Lord. This is the child I prayed for, and the Lord granted me what I asked him. Now I make him over to the Lord for the whole of his life. He is made over to the Lord."

There she left him, for the Lord.

This is the word of the Lord.

Responsorial Psalm   (1 Sam 2:1. 4–8. *R*. v. 1)

Response
My heart exults in the Lord my saviour.

1. My heart exults in the Lord,
I find my strength in my God;
my mouth laughs at my enemies
as I rejoice in your saving help. (*R*.)

2. The bows of the mighty are broken,
but the weak are clothed with strength.
Those with plenty must labour for bread,
but the hungry need work no more.
The childless wife has children now
but the fruitful wife bears no more. (*R*.)

3. It is the Lord who gives life and death,
he brings men to the grave and back;
it is the Lord who gives poverty and riches.
He brings men low and raises them on high. (*R*.)

4. He lifts up the lowly from the dust,
from the dungheap he raises the poor
to set him in the company of princes,
to give him a glorious throne.
For the pillars of the earth are the Lord's,
on them he has set the world. (*R*.)

Alleluia

Alleluia, alleluia!
Morning star, radiance of eternal light,
sun of justice,
come and enlighted those who live in darkness
and in the shadow of death.
Alleluia!

Alternative Alleluias p. 839.

Gospel   (1:46–56)

A reading from the holy Gospel according to Luke
The Almighty has done great things for me.

Mary said:
"My soul proclaims the greatness of the Lord
and my spirit exults in God my saviour;
because he has looked upon his lowly handmaid.
Yes, from this day forward all generations will call me
    blessed,
for the Almighty has done great things for me.
Holy is his name,
and his mercy reaches from age to age for those who fear
    him.

He has shown the power of his arm,
he has routed the proud of heart.
He has pulled down princes from their thrones and exalted
    the lowly.
The hungry he has filled with good things, the rich sent
    empty away.
He has come to the help of Israel his servant, mindful of
    his mercy
– according to the promise he made to our ancestors –
of his mercy to Abraham and to his descendants for ever."

Mary stayed with Elizabeth about three months and then
went back home.
    This is the Gospel of the Lord.

DECEMBER 23

First Reading   (3:1–4. 23–24)

A reading from the prophet Malachi
I am going to send you Elijah the prophet before the day of the Lord comes.

The Lord God says this: Look, I am going to send my messenger to prepare a way before me. And the Lord you are seeking will suddenly enter his Temple; and the angel of the covenant whom you are longing for, yes, he is coming, says the Lord of hosts. Who will be able to resist the day of his coming? Who will remain standing when he appears? For he is like the refiner's fire and the fullers' alkali. He will take his seat as refiner and purifier; he will purify the sons of Levi and refine them like gold and silver, and then they will make the offering to the Lord as it should be made. The offering of Judah and Jerusalem will then be welcomed by the Lord as in former days, as in the years of old.

Know that I am going to send you Elijah the prophet before my day comes, that great and terrible day. He shall turn the hearts of fathers towards their children and the hearts of children towards their fathers, lest I come and strike the land with a curse.

This is the word of the Lord.

Responsorial Psalm   (Ps 24:4–5. 8–10. 14. *R.* Lk 21:28)

Response
Stand erect, hold your heads high,
because your liberation is near at hand.

1. Lord, make me know your ways.
Lord, teach me your paths.
Make me walk in your truth, and teach me:
for you are God my saviour. (*R.*)

2. The Lord is good and upright.
He shows the path to those who stray.
He guides the humble in the right path;
he teaches his way to the poor. (*R.*)

3. His ways are faithfulness and love
for those who keep his covenant and will.
The Lord's friendship is for those who revere him;
to them he reveals his covenant. (*R.*)

Alleluia

Alleluia, alleluia!
King of the peoples and corner-stone of the Church,
come and save man whom you made from the dust of the
    earth.
Alleluia!

Alternative Alleluias p. 839.

Gospel   (1:57–66)

A reading from the holy Gospel according to Luke
The birth of John the Baptist.

The time came for Elizabeth to have her child, and she gave
birth to a son; and when her neighbours and relations heard
that the Lord had shown her so great a kindness, they
shared her joy.

Now on the eighth day they came to circumcise the child;
they were going to call him Zechariah after his father, but
his mother spoke up. "No," she said "he is to be called
John." They said to her, "But no one in your family has that
name", and made signs to his father to find out what he
wanted him called. The father asked for a writing-tablet
and wrote, "His name is John". And they were all astonished. At that instant his power of speech returned and he
spoke and praised God. All their neighbours were filled

with awe and the whole affair was talked about throughout the hill country of Judaea. All those who heard of it treasured it in their hearts. "What will this child turn out to be?" they wondered. And indeed the hand of the Lord was with him.

This is the Gospel of the Lord.

DECEMBER 24 (Morning Mass)

First Reading (7:1–5. 8–11. 16)

A reading from the second book of Samuel
The kingdom of David will always stand secure before the Lord.

Once David had settled into his house and the Lord had given him rest from all the enemies surrounding him, the king said to the prophet Nathan, "Look, I am living in a house of cedar while the ark of God dwells in a tent". Nathan said to the kind, "Go and do all that is in your mind, for the Lord is with you".

But that very night the word of the Lord came to Nathan:

"Go and tell my servant David, 'Thus the Lord speaks: Are you the man to build me a house to dwell in? I took you from the pasture, from following the sheep, to be a leader of my people Israel; I have been with you on all your expeditions; I have cut off all your enemies before you. I will give you fame as great as the fame of the greatest on earth. I will provide a place for my people Israel; I will plant them there and they shall dwell in that place and never be disturbed again; nor shall the wicked continue to oppress them as they did, in the days when I appointed judges over my people Israel; I will give them rest from all their enemies. The Lord will make you great; the Lord will make you a House. Your House and your sovereignty will always

stand secure before me and your throne be established for
ever.' "

This is the word of the Lord.

Responsorial Psalm   (Ps 88:2–5. 27. 29. *R*. v. 2)
Response
I will sing for ever of your love, O Lord.

1. I will sing for ever of your love, O Lord;
through all ages my mouth will proclaim your truth.
Of this I am sure, that your love lasts for ever.
that your truth is firmly established as the heavens. (*R*.)

2. "I have made a covenant with my chosen one;
I have sworn to David my servant;
I will establish your dynasty for ever
and set up your throne through all ages." (*R*.)

3. He will say to me: "You are my father,
my God, the rock who saves me."
I will keep my love for him always;
for him my covenant shall endure. (*R*.)

Alleluia

Emmanuel, our king and lawgiver,
come and save us, Lord our God.
Alleluia!

Alternative Alleluias p. 839.

Gospel   (1:67–79)

A reading from the holy Gospel according to Luke
Our God from on high will bring the rising Sun to visit us.

John's father Zechariah was filled with the Holy Spirit and
spoke this prophecy:

"Blessed be the Lord, the God of Israel,
for he has visited his people, he has come to their rescue
and he has raised up for us a power for salvation
in the House of his servant David,
even as he proclaimed,
by the mouth of his holy prophets from ancient times,
that he would save us from our enemies
and from the hands of all who hate us.
Thus he shows mercy to our ancestors,
thus he remembers his holy covenant,
the oath he swore
to our father Abraham
that he would grant us, free from fear,
to be delivered from the hands of our enemies,
to serve him in holiness and virtue
in his presence, all our days.
And you, little child,
you shall be called Prophet of the Most High,
for you will go before the Lord
to prepare the way for him.
To give his people knowledge of salvation
through the forgiveness of their sins;
this by the tender mercy of our God
who from on high will bring the rising Sun to visit us,
to give light to those who live
in darkness and the shadow of death,
and to guide our feet
into the way of peace."

This is the Gospel of the Lord.

THE SEASON OF CHRISTMAS

DECEMBER 24

Evening Mass

These readings are to be used at the Afternoon Mass on 24 December, either before or after first Vespers of Christmas. They may also be used on Christmas Day, with a choice of readings from one of the Christmas Masses, as the pastoral needs of the congregation suggest.

First Reading (62:1-5)

A reading from the prophet Isaiah
The Lord takes delight in you.

About Zion I will not be silent,
about Jerusalem I will not grow weary,
until her integrity shines out like the dawn
and her salvation flames like a torch.
The nation then will see your integrity,
all the kings your glory,
and you will be called by a new name,
one which the mouth of the Lord will confer.
You are to be a crown of splendour in the hand of the Lord,
a princely diadem in the hand of your God;
no longer are you to be named "Forsaken",
nor your land "Abandoned",
but you shall be called "My Delight"
and your land "The Wedded";
for the Lord takes delight in you
and your land will have its wedding.

Like a young man marrying a virgin,
so will the one who built you wed you,
and as the bridegroom rejoices in his bride,
so will your God rejoice in you.

This is the word of the Lord.

Responsorial Psalm   (Ps 88:4–5. 16–17. 27. 29. *R*. v. 2)

Response

I will sing for ever of your love, O Lord.

1. "I have made a covenant with my chosen one;
I have sworn to David my servant:
I will establish your dynasty for ever
and set up your throne through all ages." (*R*.)

2. Happy the people who acclaim such a king,
who walk, O Lord, in the light of your face,
who find their joy every day in your name,
who make your justice the source of their bliss. (*R*.)

3. "He will say to me: 'You are my father,
my God, the rock who saves me.'
I will keep my love for him always;
for him my covenant shall endure." (*R*.)

Second Reading   (13:16–17. 22–25)

A reading from the Acts of the Apostles
Paul's witness to Christ, the son of David.

When Paul reached Antioch in Pisidia, he stood up in the
synagogue, held up a hand for silence and began to speak:

"Men of Israel, and fearers of God, listen! The God of
our nation Israel chose our ancestors, and made our people
great when they were living as foreigners in Egypt; then by
divine power he led them out.

"Then he made David their king, of whom he approved
in these words, 'I have selected David son of Jesse, a man
after my own heart, who will carry out my whole purpose'.
To keep his promise, God has raised up for Israel one of
David's descendants, Jesus, as Saviour, whose coming was

heralded by John when he proclaimed a baptism of repentance for the whole people of Israel. Before John ended his career he said, 'I am not the one you imagine me to be; that one is coming after me and I am not fit to undo his sandal'."

This is the word of the Lord.

Alleluia

Alleluia, alleluia!
Tomorrow there will be an end to the sin of the world
and the saviour of the world will be our king.
Alleluia!

Gospel   (1:1–25)

The beginning of the holy Gospel according to Matthew
The ancestry of Jesus Christ, the son of David.

A genealogy of Jesus Christ, son of David, son of Abraham:

Abraham was the father of Isaac,
Isaac the father of Jacob,
Jacob was the father of Judah and his brothers,
Judah was the father of Perez and Zerah, Tamar being their
    mother,
Perez was the father of Hezron,
Hezron the father of Ram,
Ram was the father of Amminadab,
Amminadab the father of Nahshon,
Nahshon the father of Salmon,
Salmon was the father of Boaz, Rahab being his mother,
Boaz was the father of Obed, Ruth being his mother,
Obed was the father of Jesse;
and Jesse was the father of King David.

David was the father of Solomon, whose mother had been
Uriah's wife,
Solomon was the father of Rehoboam,
Rehoboam the father of Abijah,
Abijah the father of Asa,
Asa was the father of Jehoshaphat,
Jehoshaphat the father of Joram,
Joram the father of Azariah,
Azariah was the father of Jotham,
Jotham the father of Ahaz,
Ahaz the father of Hezekiah,
Hezekiah was the father of Manasseh,
Manasseh the father of Amon,
Amon the father of Josiah;
and Josiah was the father of Jechoniah and his brothers.
Then the deportation to Babylon took place.

After the deportation to Babylon:
Jechoniah was the father of Shealtiel,
Shealtiel the father of Zerubbabel,
Zerubbabel was the father of Abiud,
Abiud the father of Eliakim,
Eliakim the father of Azor,
Azor was the father of Zadok,
Zadok the father of Achim,
Achim the father of Eliud,
Eliud was the father of Eleazar,
Eleazar the father of Matthan,
Matthan the father of Jacob;
and Jacob was the father of Joseph the husband of Mary;
of her was born Jesus who is called Christ.

The sum of generations is therefore: fourteen from Abraham to David; fourteen from David to the Babylonian
deportation; and fourteen from the Babylonian deportation to Christ.

*This is how Jesus Christ came to be born. His mother Mary was betrothed to Joseph; but before they came to live together she was found to be with child through the Holy Spirit. Her husband Joseph, being a man of honour and wanting to spare her publicity, decided to divorce her informally. He had made up his mind to do this when the angel of the Lord appeared to him in a dream and said, "Joseph son of David, do not be afraid to take Mary home as your wife, because she has conceived what is in her by the Holy Spirit. She will give birth to a son and you must name him Jesus, because he is the one who is to save his people from their sins." Now all this took place to fulfil the words spoken by the Lord through the prophet:

> The Virgin will conceive and give birth to a son
> and they will call him Emmanuel,

a name which means "God-is-with-us". When Joseph woke up he did what the angel of the Lord told him to do: he took his wife to his home and, though he had not had intercourse with her, she gave birth to a son; and he named him Jesus.

This is the Gospel of the Lord.*

* Shorter form, read between*

December 25

THE NATIVITY OF OUR LORD

Midnight Mass

First Reading   (9:1–7)

A reading from the prophet Isaiah
A Son is given to us.

The people that walked in darkness
has seen a great light;
on those who live in a land of deep shadow
a light has shone.

You have made their gladness greater,
you have made their joy increase;
they rejoice in your presence
as men rejoice at harvest time,
as men are happy when they are dividing the spoils.

For the yoke that was weighing on him,
the bar across his shoulders,
the rod of his oppressor,
these you break as on the day of Midian.

For all the footgear of battle,
every cloak rolled in blood,
is burnt
and consumed by fire.

For there is a child born for us,
a son given to us
and dominion is laid on his shoulders;
and this is the name they give him:
Wonder-Counsellor, Mighty-God,
Eternal-Father, Prince-of-Peace.
Wide is his dominion
in a peace that has no end,
for the throne of David
and for his royal power,
which he establishes and makes secure
in justice and integrity.
From this time onwards and for ever,
the jealous love of the Lord of hosts will do this.

This is the word of the Lord.

Responsorial Psalm   (Ps 95:1–3. 11–13. *R*. Lk 2:11)

Response
Today a saviour has been born to us;
he is Christ the Lord.

1. O sing a new song to the Lord,
sing to the Lord all the earth.
O sing to the Lord, bless his name. (*R.*)

2. Proclaim his help day by day,
tell among the nations his glory
and his wonders among all the peoples. (*R.*)

3. Let the heavens rejoice and earth be glad,
let the sea and all within it thunder praise,
let the land and all it bears rejoice,
all the trees of the wood shout for joy
at the presence of the Lord for he comes,
he comes to rule the earth. (*R.*)

4. With justice he will rule the world,
he will judge the peoples with his truth. (*R.*)

Second Reading   (2:11–14)
A reading from the letter of St Paul to Titus
God's grace has been revealed to the whole human race.

God's grace has been revealed, and it has made salvation
possible for the whole human race and taught us that what
we have to do is to give up everything that does not lead to
God, and all our worldly ambitions; we must be self-
restrained and live good and religious lives here in this
present world, while we are waiting in hope for the blessing
which will come with the Appearing of the glory of our
great God and saviour Christ Jesus. He sacrificed himself
for us in order to set us free from all wickedness and to
purify a people so that it could be his very own and would
have no ambition except to do good.

This is the word of the Lord.

Alleluia (Lk 2:10–11)

Alleluia, alleluia!
I bring you news of great joy:
today a saviour has been born to us, Christ the Lord.
Alleluia!

Gospel (2:1–14)

A reading from the holy Gospel according to Luke
Today a saviour has been born to you.

Now at this time Caesar Augustus issued a decree for a census of the whole world to be taken. This census – the first – took place while Quirinius was governor of Syria, and everyone went to his own town to be registered. So Joseph set out from the town of Nazareth in Galilee and travelled up to Judaea, to the town of David called Bethlehem, since he was of David's House and line, in order to be registered together with Mary, his betrothed, who was with child. While they were there the time came for her to have her child, and she gave birth to a son, her first-born. She wrapped him in swaddling clothes, and laid him in a manger because there was no room for them at the inn. In the countryside close by there were shepherds who lived in the fields and took it in turns to watch their flocks during the night. The angel of the Lord appeared to them and the glory of the Lord shone round them. They were terrified, but the angel said, "Do not be afraid. Listen, I bring you news of great joy, a joy to be shared by the whole people. Today in the town of David a saviour has been born to you; he is Christ the Lord. And here is a sign for you: you will find a baby wrapped in swaddling clothes and lying in a manger." And suddenly with the angel there was a great throng of the heavenly host, praising God and singing:

> "Glory to God in the highest heaven,
> and peace to men who enjoy his favour".

This is the Gospel of the Lord.

THE NATIVITY OF OUR LORD

Dawn Mass

First Reading   (62:11–12)

A reading from the prophet Isaiah
Look, your saviour comes.

This the Lord proclaims
to the ends of the earth:

Say to the daughter of Zion, "Look,
your saviour comes,
the prize of his victory with him,
his trophies before him".

They shall be called "The Holy People",
"The Lord's Redeemed".
And you shall be called "The-sought-after",
"City-not-forsaken".
    This is the word of the Lord.

Responsorial Psalm   (Ps 96:1. 6. 11–12)

Response
This day new light will shine upon the earth:
the Lord is born for us.

1. The Lord is king, let earth rejoice,
the many coastlands be glad.
The skies proclaim his justice;
all peoples see his glory. (*R.*)

2. Light shines forth for the just
and joy for the upright of heart.
Rejoice, you just, in the Lord:
give glory to his holy name. (*R.*)

Second Reading   (3:4–7)

A reading from the letter of St Paul to Titus
It was for no reason except his own compassion that he saved us.

When the kindness and love of God our saviour for mankind were revealed, it was not because he was concerned with any righteous actions we might have done ourselves; it was for no reason except his own compassion that he saved us, by means of the cleansing water of rebirth and by renewing us with the Holy Spirit which he has so generously poured over us through Jesus Christ our saviour. He did this so that we should be justified by his grace, to become heirs looking forward to inheriting eternal life.

This is the word of the Lord.

Alleluia   (Lk 2:14)

Alleluia, alleluia!
Glory to God in the highest heaven,
and peace to men who enjoy his favour.
Alleluia!

Gospel   (2:15–20)

A reading from the holy Gospel according to Luke
The shepherds found Mary and Joseph and the baby.

Now when the angels had gone from them into heaven, the shepherds said to one another, "Let us go to Bethlehem and see this thing that has happened which the Lord has made known to us." So they hurried away and found Mary and Joseph, and the baby lying in the manger. When they saw the child they repeated what they had been told about him, and everyone who heard it was astonished at what the shepherds had to say. As for Mary, she treasured all these things and pondered them in her heart. And the shepherds went

back glorifying and praising God for all they had heard
and seen; it was exactly as they had been told.

   This is the Gospel of the Lord.

THE NATIVITY OF OUR LORD

Christmas Day Mass

First Reading (52:7–10)

A reading from the prophet Isaiah
All the ends of the earth shall see the salvation of our God.

How beautiful on the mountains,
are the feet of one who brings good news,
who heralds peace, brings happiness,
proclaims salvation,
and tells Zion,
"Your God is king!"
Listen! Your watchmen raise their voices,
they shout for joy together,
for they see the Lord face to face,
as he returns to Zion.

Break into shouts of joy together,
you ruins of Jerusalem;
for the Lord is consoling his people,
redeeming Jerusalem.
The Lord bares his holy arm
in the sight of all the nations,
and all the ends of the earth shall see
the salvation of our God.

   This is the word of the Lord.

Responsorial Psalm (97:1–6. *R*. v. 3)

Response
All the ends of the earth have seen
the salvation of our God.

1. Sing a new song to the Lord
for he has worked wonders.
His right hand and his holy arm
have brought salvation. (*R.*)

2. The Lord has made known his salvation;
has shown his justice to the nations.
He has remembered his truth and love
for the house of Israel. (*R.*)

3. All the ends of the earth have seen
the salvation of our God.
Shout to the Lord all the earth,
ring out your joy. (*R.*)

4. Sing psalms to the Lord with the harp,
with the sound of music.
With trumpets and the sound of the horn
acclaim the King, the Lord. (*R.*)

Second Reading (1:1–6)

A reading from the letter to the Hebrews
God has spoken to us through his Son.

At various times in the past and in various different ways,
God spoke to our ancestors through the prophets; but in
our own time, the last days, he has spoken to us through
his Son, the Son that he has appointed to inherit everything
and through whom he made everything there is. He is the
radiant light of God's glory and the perfect copy of his
nature, sustaining the universe by his powerful command;
and now that he has destroyed the defilement of sin, he has
gone to take his place in heaven at the right hand of divine
Majesty. So he is now as far above the angels as the title
which he has inherited is higher than their own name.

God has never said to any angel: You are my Son, today
I have become your father, or: I will be a father to him and
he a son to me. Again, when he brings the First-born into
the world, he says: Let all the angels of God worship him.

This is the word of the Lord.

Alleluia

Alleluia, alleluia!
A hallowed day has dawned upon us.
Come, you nations, worship the Lord,
for today a great light has shone down upon the earth.
Alleluia!

Gospel   (1:1–18)

The beginning of the holy Gospel according to John
The Word was made flesh, and lived among us.

*In the beginning was the Word:
the Word was with God
and the Word was God.
He was with God in the beginning.
Through him all things came to be,
not one thing had its being but through him.
All that came to be had life in him
and that life was the light of men,
a light that shines in the dark,
a light that darkness could not overpower.*

A man came, sent by God.
His name was John.
He came as a witness,
as a witness to speak for the light,
so that everyone might believe through him.
He was not the light,
only a witness to speak for the light.

*The Word was the true light
that enlightens all men;
and he was coming into the world.
He was in the world
that had its being through him,
and the world did not know him.
He came to his own domain
and his own people did not accept him.
But to all who did accept him
he gave power to become children of God,
to all who believe in the name of him
who was born not out of human stock
or urge of the flesh
or will of man
but of God himself.
The Word was made flesh,
he lived among us,
and we saw his glory,
the glory that is his as the only Son of the Father,
full of grace and truth.*

John appears as his witness. He proclaims:
"This is the one of whom I said:
He who comes after me
ranks before me
because he existed before me."

Indeed, from his fulness we have, all of us, received –
yes, grace in return for grace,
since, though the Law was given through Moses,
grace and truth have come through Jesus Christ.
No one has ever seen God;
it is the only Son, who is nearest to the Father's heart,
who has made him known.

This is the Gospel of the Lord.

*Shorter Form, verses 1–5, 9–14. Read between *.

Sunday in the Octave of Christmas

FEAST OF THE HOLY FAMILY

First Reading   (3:2–6. 12–14)

A reading from the book of Ecclesiasticus
He who fears the Lord respects his parents.

The Lord honours the father in his children,
and upholds the rights of a mother over her sons.
Whoever respects his father is atoning for his sins,
he who honours his mother is like someone amassing a
    fortune.
Whoever respects his father will be happy with children of
    his own,
he shall be heard on the day when he prays.
Long life comes to him who honours his father,
he who sets his mother at ease is showing obedience to the
    Lord.
My son, support your father in his old age,
do not grieve him during his life.
Even if his mind should fail, show him sympathy,
do not despise him in your health and strength;
for kindness to a father shall not be forgotten
but will serve as reparation for your sins.

This is the word of the Lord.

Responsorial Psalm   (Ps. 127:1–5. *R.* v. 1)

Response
O blessed are those who fear the Lord
and walk in his ways!

1. O blessed are those who fear the Lord
and walk in his ways!
By the labour of your hands you shall eat.
You will be happy and prosper. (*R.*)

2. Your wife like a fruitful vine
in the heart of your house;
your children like shoots of the olive,
around your table. (*R.*)

3. Indeed thus shall be blessed
the man who fears the Lord.
May the Lord bless you from Zion
all the days of your life! (*R.*)

Second Reading   (3:12–21)
A reading from the letter of St Paul to the Colossians
Family life in the Lord.

You are God's chosen race, his saints; he loves you and
you should be clothed in sincere compassion, in kindness
and humility, gentleness and patience. Bear with one another; forgive each other as soon as a quarrel begins. The
Lord has forgiven you; now you must do the same. Over
all these clothes, to keep them together and complete them,
put on love. And may the peace of Christ reign in your
hearts, because it is for this that you were called together
as parts of one body. Always be thankful.

Let the message of Christ, in all its richness, find a home
with you. Teach each other, and advise each other, in all
wisdom. With gratitude in your hearts sing psalms and
hymns and inspired songs to God; and never say or do
anything except in the name of the Lord Jesus, giving thanks
to God the Father through him.

Wives, give way to your husbands, as you should in the
Lord. Husbands, love your wives and treat them with
gentleness. Children, be obedient to your parents always,
because that is what will please the Lord. Parents, never
drive your children to resentment or you will make them
feel frustrated.

This is the word of the Lord.

Alleluia   (Col. 3:15. 16)

Alleluia, alleluia!
May the peace of Christ reign in your hearts;
let the message of Christ find a home with you.
Alleluia!

Year 1 (Year A)

Gospel   (2:13–15. 19–23)

A reading from the holy Gospel according to Matthew
Take the child and his mother and escape into Egypt.

After the wise men had left, the angel of the Lord appeared
to Joseph in a dream and said, "Get up, take the child and
his mother with you, and escape into Egypt, and stay there
until I tell you, because Herod intends to search for the
child and do away with him". So Joseph got up and, taking
the child and his mother with him, left that night for Egypt,
where he stayed until Herod was dead. This was to fulfil
what the Lord had spoken through the prophet:

I called my son out of Egypt.

After Herod's death, the angel of the Lord appeared in a
dream to Joseph in Egypt and said, "Get up, take the child
and his mother with you and go back to the land of Israel,
for those who wanted to kill the child are dead". So Joseph
got up and, taking the child and his mother with him, went
back to the land of Israel. But when he learnt that Arche-
laus had succeeded his father Herod as ruler of Judaea he
was afraid to go there, and being warned in a dream he
left for the region of Galilee. There he settled in a town
called Nazareth. In this way the words spoken through the
prophets were to be fulfilled:

He will be called a Nazarene.

This is the Gospel of the Lord.

Year 2 (Year B)

Gospel   (2:22–40)

A reading from the holy Gospel according to Luke
The child grew, filled with wisdom.

*When the day came for them to be purified as laid down by
the Law of Moses, they took him up to Jerusalem to present
him to the Lord* – observing what stands written in the
Law of the Lord: Every first-born male must be consecrated to the Lord – and also to offer in sacrifice, in accordance with what is said in the Law of the Lord, a pair of
turtledoves or two young pigeons. Now in Jerusalem there
was a man named Simeon. He was an upright and devout
man; he looked forward to Israel's comforting and the Holy
Spirit rested on him. It had been revealed to him by the
Holy Spirit that he would not see death until he had set eyes
on the Christ of the Lord. Prompted by the Spirit he came to
the Temple; and when the parents brought in the child Jesus
to do for him what the Law required, he took him into his
arms and blessed God; and he said:

"Now, Master, you can let your servant go in peace,
just as you promised;
because my eyes have seen the salvation
which you have prepared for all the nations to see,
a light to enlighten the pagans
and the glory of your people Israel."

As the child's father and mother stood there wondering
at the things that were being said about him, Simeon blessed
them and said to Mary his mother, "You see this child: he
is destined for the fall and for the rising of many in Israel,
destined to be a sign that is rejected – and a sword will pierce
your own soul too – so that the secret thoughts of many
may be laid bare."

There was a prophetess also, Anna the daughter of Phanuel, of the tribe of Asher. She was well on in years. Her days of girlhood over, she had been married for seven years before becoming a widow. She was now eighty-four years old and never left the Temple, serving God night and day with fasting and prayer. She came by just at that moment and began to praise God; and she spoke of the child to all who looked forward to the deliverance of Jerusalem.

*When they had done everything the Law of the Lord required, they went back to Galilee, to their own town of Nazareth. Meanwhile the child grew to maturity, and he was filled with wisdom; and God's favour was with him.

This is the Gospel of the Lord.*

* Shorter Form, verses 22. 39–40. Read between *.

Year 3 (Year C)

Gospel   (2:41–52)

A reading from the holy Gospel according to Luke
Jesus is found by his parents sitting among the doctors.

Every year the parents of Jesus used to go to Jerusalem for the feast of the Passover. When he was twelve years old, they went up for the feast as usual. When they were on their way home after the feast, the boy Jesus stayed behind in Jerusalem without his parents knowing it. They assumed he was with the caravan, and it was only after a day's journey that they went to look for him among their relations and acquaintances. When they failed to find him they went back to Jerusalem looking for him everywhere.

Three days later, they found him in the Temple, sitting among the doctors, listening to them, and asking them questions; and all those who heard him were astounded at his intelligence and his replies. They were overcome when they saw him, and his mother said to him, "My child, why have you done this to us? See how worried your father and I have been, looking for you." "Why were you looking for me?" he replied. "Did you not know that I must be busy with my Father's affairs?" But they did not understand what he meant.

He then went down with them and came to Nazareth and lived under their authority. His mother stored up all these things in her heart. And Jesus increased in wisdom, in stature, and in favour with God and men.

This is the Gospel of the Lord.

DECEMBER 29

First Reading   (2:3–11)

A reading from the first letter of St John
Anyone who loves his brother is living in the light.

We can be sure that we know God
only by keeping his commandments.
Anyone who says, "I know him",
and does not keep his commandments,
is a liar,
refusing to admit the truth.
But when anyone does obey what he has said,
God's love comes to perfection in him.
We can be sure
that we are in God
only when the one who claims to be living in him
is living the same kind of life as Christ lived.
My dear people,
this is not a new commandment that I am writing to tell
    you,
but an old commandment
that you were given from the beginning,
the original commandment which was the message brought
    to you.
Yet in another way, what I am writing to you,
and what is being carried out in your lives as it was in his,
is a new commandment;

because the night is over
and the real light is already shining.
Anyone who claims to be in the light
but hates his brother
is still in the dark.
But anyone who loves his brother is living in the light
and need not be afraid of stumbling;
unlike the man who hates his brother and is in the darkness,
not knowing where he is going,
because it is too dark to see.

This is the word of the Lord.

Responsorial Psalm   (Ps 95:1–3. 5–6. *R*. v. 11)
Response
Let the heavens rejoice and earth be glad.

1. O sing a new song to the Lord,
sing to the Lord all the earth.
O sing to the Lord, bless his name. (*R*.)

2. Proclaim his help day by day,
tell among the nations his glory
and his wonders among all the peoples. (*R*.)

3. It was the Lord who made the heavens,
his are majesty and state and power
and splendour in his holy place. (*R*.)

Alleluia   (Jn 1:14. 12)
Alleluia, alleluia!
The Word became flesh, and dwelt among us.
To all who received him he gave power to become children
of God.
Alleluia!
Alternative Alleluias p. 840.

Gospel   (2:22–35)

A reading from the holy Gospel according to Luke
A light to enlighten the pagans.

When the day came for them to be purified as laid down by
the Law of Moses, the parents of Jesus took him up to
Jerusalem to present him to the Lord – observing what
stands written in the Law of the Lord: Every first-born
male must be consecrated to the Lord – and also to offer in
sacrifice, in accordance with what is said in the Law of the
Lord, a pair of turtledoves or two young pigeons. Now in
Jerusalem there was a man called Simeon. He was an
upright and devout man; he looked forward to Israel's
comforting and the Holy Spirit rested on him. It had been
revealed to him by the Holy Spirit that he would not see
death until he had set eyes on the Christ of the Lord. Prompted by the Spirit he came to the Temple: and when the parents brought in the child Jesus to do for him what the Law
required, he took him into his arms and blessed God; and
he said:

"Now, Master, you can let your servant go in peace,
just as you promised;
because my eyes have seen the salvation
which you have prepared for all the nations to see,
a light to enlighten the pagans
and the glory of your people Israel."

As the child's father and mother stood there wondering at
the things that were being said about him, Simeon blessed
them and said to Mary his mother, "You see this child: he
is destined for the fall and for the rising of many in Israel,
destined to be a sign that is rejected – and a sword will
pierce your own soul too – so that the secret thoughts of
many may be laid bare."
    This is the Gospel of the Lord.

DECEMBER 30

First Reading   (2:12–17)

A reading from the first letter of St John
Anyone who does the will of God remains for ever.

I am writing to you, my own children,
whose sins have already been forgiven through his name;
I am writing to you, fathers,
who have come to know the one
who has existed since the beginning;
I am writing to you, young men,
who have already overcome the Evil One;
I have written to you, children,
because you already know the Father;
I have written to you, fathers,
because you have come to know the one
who has existed since the beginning;
I have written to you, young men,
because you are strong and God's word has made its home
    in you,
and you have overcome the Evil One.
You must not love this passing world
or anything that is in the world.
The love of the Father cannot be
in any man who loves the world,
because nothing the world has to offer
– the sensual body,
the lustful eye,
pride in possessions –
could ever come from the Father
but only from the world;
and the world, with all it craves for,
is coming to an end;
but anyone who does the will of God
remains for ever.

This is the word of the Lord.

Responsorial Psalm (Ps 95:7–10. *R.* v. 11)

Response
Let the heavens rejoice and earth be glad.

1. Give the Lord, you families of peoples,
give the Lord glory and power,
give the Lord the glory of his name. (*R.*)

2. Bring an offering and enter his courts,
worship the Lord in his temple.
O earth, tremble before him. (*R.*)

3. Proclaim to the nations: "God is king".
The world he made firm in its place;
he will judge the peoples in fairness. (*R.*)

Alleluia (Heb 1:1–2)

Alleluia, alleluia!
At various times in the past
and in various different ways,
God spoke to our ancestors through the prophets;
but in our own time, the last days,
he has spoken to us through his Son.
Alleluia!

Alternative Alleluias p. 840.

Gospel (2:36–40)

A reading from the holy Gospel according to Luke
She spoke of the child to all who looked forward to the
deliverance of Jerusalem.

There was a prophetess, Anna the daughter of Phanuel, of
the tribe of Asher. She was well on in years. Her days of
girlhood over, she had been married for seven years before

becoming a widow. She was now eighty-four years old and
never left the Temple, serving God night and day with fasting and prayer. She came by just at that moment and began
to praise God; and she spoke of the child to all who looked
forward to the deliverance of Jerusalem. When they had
done everything the Law of the Lord required, they went
back to Galilee, to their own town of Nazareth. Meanwhile
the child grew to maturity, and he was filled with wisdom;
and God's favour was with him.

This is the Gospel of the Lord.

DECEMBER 31

First Reading   (2:18–21)

A reading from the first letter of St John
You have been anointed by the Holy One and have all received
the knowledge.

Children, these are the last days;
you were told that an Antichrist must come,
and now several antichrists have already appeared;
we know from this that these are the last days.
Those rivals of Christ came out of your own number,
   but they had never really belonged;
if they had belonged, they would have stayed with us;
but they left us, to prove that not one of them
ever belonged to us.
But you have been anointed by the Holy One,
and have all received the knowledge.
It is not because you do not know the truth that I am writing
   to you
but rather because you know it already
and know that no lie can come from the truth.

This is the word of the Lord.

Responsorial Psalm   (Ps 95:1–2. 11–13. *R*. v. 11)

Response

Let the heavens rejoice and earth be glad.

1. O sing a new song to the Lord,
sing to the Lord all the earth.
O sing to the Lord, bless his name.
Proclaim his help day by day. (*R*.)

2. Let the heavens rejoice and earth be glad,
let the sea and all within it thunder praise,
let the land and all it bears rejoice,
all the trees of the wood shout for joy
at the presence of the Lord for he comes,
he comes to rule the earth. (*R*.)

3. With justice he will rule the world,
he will judge the peoples with his truth. (*R*.)

Alleluia

Alleluia, alleluia!
A hallowed day has dawned upon us.
Come, you nations, worship the Lord,
for today a great light has shone down upon the earth.
Alleluia!

Alternative Alleluias p. 840.

Gospel   (1:1–18)

The beginning of the holy Gospel according to John
The Word was made flesh.

In the beginning was the Word:
the Word was with God
and the Word was God.

He was with God in the beginning.
Through him all things came to be,
not one thing had its being but through him.
All that came to be had life in him
and that life was the light of men,
a light that shines in the dark,
a light that darkness could not overpower.

A man came, sent by God.
His name was John.
He came as a witness,
as a witness to speak for the light,
so that everyone might believe through him.
He was not the light,
only a witness to speak for the light.

The Word was the true light
that enlightens all men;
and he was coming into the world.
He was in the world
that had its being through him,
and the world did not know him.
He came to his own domain
and his own people did not accept him.
But to all who did accept him
he gave power to become children of God,
to all who believe in the name of him
who was born not out of human stock
or urge of the flesh
or will of man
but of God himself.
The Word was made flesh,
he lived among us,
and we saw his glory,
the glory that is his as the only Son of the Father,
full of grace and truth.

John appears as his witness. He proclaims:
"This is the one of whom I said:
He who comes after me
ranks before me
because he existed before me."

Indeed, from his fulness we have, all of us, received –
yes, grace in return for grace,
since, though the Law was given through Moses,
grace and truth have come through Jesus Christ.
No one has ever seen God;
it is the only Son, who is nearest to the Father's heart,
who has made him known.

This is the Gospel of the Lord.

January 1

OCTAVE OF CHRISTMAS

and Solemnity of Mary Mother of God

First Reading   (6:22–27)

A reading from the book of Numbers
They are to call down my name on the sons of Israel, and I will bless them.

The Lord spoke to Moses and said, "Say this to Aaron and his sons: 'This is how you are to bless the sons of Israel. You shall say to them:

May the Lord bless you and keep you.
May the Lord let his face shine on you and be gracious to you.
May the Lord uncover his face to you and bring you peace.'

This is how they are to call down my name on the sons of Israel, and I will bless them."
This is the word of the Lord.

Responsorial Psalm   (Ps 66:2–3. 5. 6. 8. *R*. v. 2)

Response
O God, be gracious and bless us.

1. God, be gracious and bless us
and let your face shed its light upon us.
So will your ways be known upon earth
and all nations learn your saving help. (*R*.)

2. Let the nations be glad and exult
for you rule the world with justice.
With fairness you rule the peoples,
you guide the nations on earth. (*R*.)

3. Let the peoples praise you, O God;
let all the peoples praise you.
May God still give us his blessing
till the ends of the earth revere him. (*R*.)

Second Reading   (4:4–7)

A reading from the letter of St Paul to the Galatians
God sent his Son, born of a woman.

When the appointed time came, God sent his Son, born of
a woman, born a subject of the Law, to redeem the subjects
of the Law and to enable us to be adopted as sons. The
proof that you are sons is that God has sent the Spirit of his
Son into our hearts: the Spirit that cries, "Abba, Father",
and it is this that makes you a son, you are not a slave any
more; and if God has made you son, then he has made you
heir.

This is the word of the Lord.

Alleluia   (Heb 1:1–2)

Alleluia, Alleluia!
At various times in the past
and in various different ways,
God spoke to our ancestors through the prophets;
but in our own time, the last days,
he has spoken to us through his Son.
Alleluia!

Gospel   (2:16–21)

A reading from the holy Gospel according to Luke
They found Mary and Joseph and the baby . . . When the
eighth day came, they gave him the name Jesus.

The shepherds hurried away to Bethlehem and found Mary
and Joseph, and the baby lying in the manger. When they
saw the child they repeated what they had been told about
him, and everyone who heard it was astonished at what
the shepherds had to say. As for Mary, she treasured all
these things and pondered them in her heart. And the shepherds went back glorifying and praising God for all they
had heard and seen; it was exactly as they had been told.

When the eighth day came and the child was to be circumcised, they gave him the name Jesus, the name the angel had
given him before his conception.

This is the Gospel of the Lord.

2nd SUNDAY AFTER CHRISTMAS

First Reading   (24:1–2. 8–12)

A reading from the book of Ecclesiasticus
The wisdom of God has pitched her tent among the chosen
people.

Wisdom speaks her own praises,
in the midst of her people she glories in herself.

She opens her mouth in the assembly of the Most High,
she glories in herself in the presence of the Mighty One;
Then the creator of all things instructed me,
and he who created me fixed a place for my tent.
He said, "Pitch your tent in Jacob,
make Israel your inheritance."
From eternity, in the beginning, he created me,
and for eternity I shall remain.
I ministered before him in the holy tabernacle,
and thus was I established on Zion.
In the beloved city he has given me rest,
and in Jerusalem I wield my authority.
I have taken root in a privileged people,
in the Lord's property, in his inheritance.

This is the word of the Lord.

Responsorial Psalm   (Ps 147:12–15. 19–20. *R.* Jn 1:14)

Response
The Word was made flesh,
and lived among us.

Alternative Response
Alleluia!

1. O praise the Lord, Jerusalem!
Zion, praise your God!
He has strengthened the bars of your gates,
he has blessed the children within you. (*R.*)

2. He established peace on your borders,
he feeds you with finest wheat.
He sends out his word to the earth
and swiftly runs his command. (*R.*)

3. He makes his word known to Jacob,
to Israel his laws and decrees.
He has not dealt thus with other nations;
he has not taught them his decrees.
Alleluia! (*R.*)

Second Reading   (1:3–6. 15–18)

A reading from the letter of St Paul to the Ephesians
He determined that we should become his adopted sons through Jesus.

Blessed be God the Father of our Lord Jesus Christ, who
has blessed us with all the spiritual blessings of heaven in
Christ. Before the world was made, he chose us, chose us in
Christ, to be holy and spotless, and to live through love in
his presence, determining that we should become his adopted sons, through Jesus Christ, for his own kind purposes,
to make us praise the glory of his grace, his free gift to us in
the Beloved.

That will explain why I, having once heard about your
faith in the Lord Jesus, and the love that you show towards
all the saints, have never failed to remember you in my
prayers and to thank God for you. May the God of our
Lord Jesus Christ, the Father of glory, give you a spirit of
wisdom and perception of what is revealed, to bring you to
full knowledge of him. May he enlighten the eyes of your
mind so that you can see what hope his call holds for you,
what rich glories he has promised the saints will inherit.

This is the word of the Lord.

Alleluia   (cf.1 Tim 3:16)

Alleluia, alleluia!
Glory be to you, O Christ, proclaimed to the pagans;
Glory be to you, O Christ, believed in by the world.
Alleluia!

Gospel   (1:1–18)

The beginning of the holy Gospel according to John
The Word was made flesh, and lived among us.

*In the beginning was the Word:
the Word was with God
and the Word was God.
He was with God in the beginning.
Through him all things came to be,
not one thing had its being but through him.
All that came to be had life in him
and that life was the light of men,
a light that shines in the dark,
a light that darkness could not overpower.*

A man came, sent by God.
His name was John.
He came as a witness,
as a witness to speak for the light,
so that everyone might believe through him.
He was not the light,
only a witness to speak for the light.

*The Word was the true light
that enlightens all men;
and he was coming into the world.
He was in the world
that had its being through him,
and the world did not know him.
He came to his own domain
and his own people did not accept him.
But to all who did accept him
he gave power to become children of God,
to all who believe in the name of him
who was born not out of human stock

or urge of the flesh
or will of man
but of God himself.
The Word was made flesh,
he lived among us,
and we saw his glory,
the glory that is his as the only Son of the Father,
full of grace and truth.*

John appears as his witness. He proclaims:
"This is the one of whom I said:
He who comes after me
ranks before me
because he existed before me."

Indeed, from his fulness we have, all of us, received –
yes, grace in return for grace,
since, though the Law was given through Moses,
grace and truth have come through Jesus Christ.
No one has ever seen God;
it is the only Son, who is nearest to the Father's heart,
who has made him known.

   This is the Gospel of the Lord.

*Shorter Form, verses 1–5. 9–14. Read between *.

JANUARY 2

First Reading   (2:22–28)

A reading from the first letter of St John
Keep alive in yourselves what you were taught in the be-
ginning.

The man who denies that Jesus is the Christ –
he is the liar,
he is Antichrist;

and he is denying the Father as well as the Son,

because no one who has the Father can deny the Son,

and to acknowledge the Son is to have the Father as well.

Keep alive in yourselves what you were taught in the beginning:

as long as what you were taught in the beginning is alive
in you,

you will live in the Son

and in the Father;

and what is promised to you by his own promise

is eternal life.

This is all that I am writing to you about the people who
are trying to lead you astray.

But you have not lost the anointing that he gave you,

and you do not need anyone to teach you;

the anointing he gave teaches you everything;

you are anointed with truth, not with a lie,

and as it has taught you, so you must stay in him.

Live in Christ, then, my children,

so that if he appears, we may have full confidence,

and not turn from him in shame

at his coming.

This is the word of the Lord.

Responsorial Psalm   (Ps 97:1–4. *R*. v. 3)

Response

All the ends of the earth have seen
the salvation of our God.

1. Sing a new song to the Lord
for he has worked wonders.
His right hand and his holy arm
have brought salvation. (*R*.)

2. The Lord has made known his salvation;
has shown his justice to the nations.
He has remembered his truth and love
for the house of Israel. (*R*.)

3. All the ends of the earth have seen
the salvation of our God.
Shout to the Lord all the earth,
ring out your joy. (*R*.)

Alleluia (Jn 1:14. 12)

Alleluia, alleluia!
The Word became flesh, and dwelt among us.
To all who received him he gave power to become children
of God.
Alleluia!

Alternative Alleluias p. 840.

Gospel (1:19–28)

A reading from the holy Gospel according to John
One is coming after me who existed before me.

This is how John appeared as a witness. When the Jews
sent priests and Levites from Jerusalem to ask him, "Who
are you?" he not only declared, but he declared quite openly, "I am not the Christ". "Well then," they asked "are
you Elijah?" "I am not" he said. "Are you the Prophet?"
He answered, "No." So they said to him, "Who are you?
We must take back an answer to those who sent us. What
have you to say about yourself?" So John said, "I am, as
Isaiah prophesied:

> a voice that cries in the wilderness:
> Make a straight way for the Lord."

Now these men had been sent by the Pharisees, and they put this further question to him, "Why are you baptising if you are not the Christ, and not Elijah, and not the prophet?" John replied, "I baptise with water; but there stands among you – unknown to you – the one who is coming after me; and I am not fit to undo his sandal-strap." This happened at Bethany, on the far side of the Jordan, where John was baptising.

This is the Gospel of the Lord.

JANUARY 3

First Reading   (2:29–3:6)

A reading from the first letter of St John
Anyone who lives in God does not sin.

You know that God is righteous –
then you must recognise that everyone whose life is righteous has been begotten by him.

Think of the love that the Father has lavished on us,
by letting us be called God's children;
and that is what we are.
Because the world refused to acknowledge him,
therefore it does not acknowledge us.
My dear people, we are already the children of God
but what we are to be in the future has not yet been revealed;
all we know is, that when it is revealed
we shall be like him
because we shall see him as he really is.
Surely everyone who entertains this hope
must purify himself, must try to be as pure as Christ.
Anyone who sins at all
breaks the law,
because to sin is to break the law.

Now you know that he appeared in order to abolish sin,
and that in him there is no sin;
anyone who lives in God does not sin,
and anyone who sins
has never seen him or known him.

This is the word of the Lord.

Responsorial Psalm   (Ps 97:1. 3–6. *R*. v. 3)

Response
All the ends of the earth have seen
the salvation of our God.

1. Sing a new song to the Lord
for he has worked wonders.
His right hand and his holy arm
have brought salvation. (*R*.)

2. All the ends of the earth have seen
the salvation of our God.
Shout to the Lord all the earth,
ring out your joy. (*R*.)

3. Sing psalms to the Lord with the harp
with the sound of music.
With trumpets and the sound of the horn
acclaim the King, the Lord. (*R*.)

Alleluia
Alleluia, alleluia!
A hallowed day has dawned upon us.
Come you nations, worship the Lord,
for today a great light has shone down upon the earth.

Alternative Alleluias p. 840.

Gospel   (1:29–34)

A reading from the holy Gospel according to John
Look, there is the lamb of God.

The next day, seeing Jesus coming towards him, John said, "Look, there is the lamb of God that takes away the sin of the world. This is the one I spoke of when I said: A man is coming after me who ranks before me because he existed before me. I did not know him myself, and yet it was to reveal him to Israel that I came baptising with water." John also declared, "I saw the Spirit coming down on him from heaven like a dove and resting on him. I did not know him myself, but he who sent me to baptise with water had said to me, 'The man on whom you see the Spirit come down and rest is the one who is going to baptise with the Holy Spirit'. Yes, I have seen and I am the witness that he is the Chosen One of God."

This is the Gospel of the Lord.

JANUARY 4

First Reading   (3:7–10)

A reading from the first letter of St John
He cannot sin when he has been begotten by God.

My children, do not let anyone lead you astray:
to live a holy life
is to be holy just as God is holy;
to lead a sinful life is to belong to the devil,
since the devil was a sinner from the beginning.
It was to undo all that the devil has done
that the Son of God appeared.
No one who has been begotten by God sins;
because God's seed remains inside him,
he cannot sin when he has been begotten by God.

In this way we distinguish the children of God
from the children of the devil:
anybody not living a holy life
and not loving his brother
is no child of God's.

This is the word of the Lord.

Responsorial Psalm (Ps 97:1. 7–9. *R*. v. 3)

Response
All the ends of the earth have seen
the salvation of our God.

1. Sing a new song to the Lord
for he has worked wonders.
His right hand and his holy arm
have brought salvation. (*R*.)

2. Let the sea and all within it, thunder;
the world, and all its peoples.
Let the rivers clap their hands
and the hills ring out their joy
at the presence of the Lord: for he comes,
he comes to rule the earth. (*R*.)

3. He will rule the world with justice
and the peoples with fairness. (*R*.)

Alleluia (Jn 1:14. 12)

Alleluia, alleluia!
The word became flesh, and dwelt among us.
To all who received him he gave power to become children
of God.
Alleluia!

Alternative Alleluias p. 840.

Gospel   (1:35–42)

A reading from the holy Gospel according to John
We have found the Messiah.

As John stood there with two of his disciples, Jesus passed,
and John stared hard at him and said, "Look, there is the
lamb of God." Hearing this, the two disciples followed Jesus. Jesus turned round, saw them following and said,
"What do you want?" They answered, "Rabbi," – which
means Teacher – "where do you live?" "Come and see" he
replied; so they went and saw where he lived, and stayed
with him the rest of that day. It was about the tenth hour.

One of these two who became followers of Jesus after
hearing what John had said was Andrew, the brother of
Simon Peter. Early next morning, Andrew met his brother
and said to him, "We have found the Messiah" – which
means the Christ – and he took Simon to Jesus. Jesus looked
hard at him and said, "You are Simon son of John; you are
to be called Cephas" – meaning Rock.

This is the Gospel of the Lord.

JANUARY 5

First Reading   (3:11–12)

A reading from the first letter of St John
*We have passed out of death and into life because we love our
brothers.*

This is the message
as you heard it from the beginning:
that we are to love one another;
not to be like Cain, who belonged to the Evil One
and cut his brother's throat;
cut his brother's throat simply for this reason,
that his own life was evil and his brother lived a good life.

You must not be surprised, brothers, when the world hates
  you;
we have passed out of death and into life,
and of this we can be sure
because we love our brothers.
If you refuse to love, you must remain dead;
to hate your brother is to be a murderer,
and murderers, as you know, do not have eternal life in
  them.
This has taught us love –
that he gave up his life for us;
and we, too, ought to give up our lives for our brothers.
If a man who was rich enough in this world's goods
saw that one of his brothers was in need,
but closed his heart to him,
how could the love of God be living in him?
My children,
our love is not to be just words or mere talk,
but something real and active;
only by this can we be certain
that we are children of the truth
and be able to quieten our conscience in his presence,
whatever accusations it may raise against us,
because God is greater than our conscience and he knows
  everything.
My dear people,
if we cannot be condemned by our own conscience,
we need not be afraid in God's presence.

This is the word of the Lord.

Responsorial Psalm (Ps 99. *R*. v. 1)

Response
Cry out with joy to the Lord, all the earth.

1. Cry out with joy to the Lord, all the earth.
Serve the Lord with gladness.
Come before him, singing for joy. (*R.*)

2. Know that he, the Lord, is God.
He made us, we belong to him,
we are his people, the sheep of his flock. (*R.*)

3. Go within his gates, giving thanks.
Enter his courts with songs of praise.
Give thanks to him and bless his name. (*R.*)

4. Indeed, how good is the Lord,
eternal his merciful love.
He is faithful from age to age. (*R.*)

Alleluia   (Heb 1:1–2)

Alleluia, alleluia!
At various times in the past
and in various different ways,
God spoke to our ancestors through the prophets;
but in our own time, the last days,
he has spoken to us through his Son.
Alleluia!

Alternative Alleluias p. 840.

Gospel   (1:43–51)

A reading from the holy Gospel according to John
You are the Son of God, you are the King of Israel.

After Jesus had decided to leave for Galilee, he met Philip
and said, "Follow me." Philip came from the same town,
Bethsaida, as Andrew and Peter. Philip found Nathanael
and said to him, "We have found the one Moses wrote about
in the Law, the one about whom the Prophets wrote: he is

Jesus son of Joseph, from Nazareth." "From Nazareth?" said Nathanael "Can anything good come from that place?" "Come and see" replied Philip. When Jesus saw Nathanael coming he said of him, "There is an Israelite who deserves the name, incapable of deceit." "How do you know me?" said Nathanael. "Before Philip came to call you," said Jesus "I saw you under the fig tree." Nathanael answered, "Rabbi, you are the Son of God, you are the King of Israel." Jesus replied, "You believe that just because I said: I saw you under the fig tree. You will see greater things than that." And then he added, "I tell you most solemnly, you will see heaven laid open and, above the Son of Man, the angels of God ascending and descending."

This is the Gospel of the Lord.

January 6
EPIPHANY

First Reading   (60:1–6)

A reading from the prophet Isaiah
Above you the glory of the Lord appears.

Arise, shine out, for your light has come,
the glory of the Lord is rising on you,
though night still covers the earth
and darkness the peoples.

Above you the Lord now rises
and above you his glory appears.
The nations come to your light
and kings to your dawning brightness.

Lift up your eyes and look round:
all are assembling and coming towards you,
your sons from far away
and your daughters being tenderly carried.

At this sight you will grow radiant,
your heart throbbing and full;
since the riches of the sea will flow to you,
the wealth of the nations come to you;

camels in throngs will cover you,
and dromedaries of Midian and Ephah;
everyone in Sheba will come,
bringing gold and incense
and singing the praise of the Lord.

This is the word of the Lord.

Responsorial Psalm   (Ps 71:1–2. 7–8. 10–13. *R*. v. 11)
Response
All nations shall fall prostrate before you, O Lord.

1. O God, give your judgement to the king,
to a king's son your justice,
that he may judge your people in justice
and your poor in right judgement. (*R*.)

2. In his days justice shall flourish
and peace till the moon fails.
He shall rule from sea to sea,
from the Great River to earth's bounds. (*R*.)

3. The kings of Tarshish and the sea coasts
shall pay him tribute.
The kings of Sheba and Seba
shall bring him gifts.
Before him all kings shall fall prostrate,
all nations shall serve him.(*R*.)

4. For he shall save the poor when they cry
and the needy who are helpless.

He will have pity on the weak
and save the lives of the poor. (*R*.)

Second Reading   (3:2–3. 5–6)

A reading from the letter of St Paul to the Ephesians
*It has now been revealed that pagans share the same
inheritance.*

You have probably heard how I have been entrusted by
God with the grace he meant for you, and that it was by a
revelation that I was given the knowledge of the mystery.
This mystery that has now been revealed through the Spirit
to his holy apostles and prophets was unknown to any men
in past generations; it means that pagans now share the
same inheritance, that they are parts of the same body, and
that the same promise has been made to them, in Christ
Jesus, through the gospel.

 This is the word of the Lord.

Alleluia   (Mt 2:2)

Alleluia, alleluia!
We saw his star as it rose
and have come to do the Lord homage.
Alleluia!

Gospel   (2:1–12)

A reading from the holy Gospel according to Matthew
We saw his star and have come to do the king homage.

After Jesus had been born at Bethlehem in Judaea during
the reign of King Herod, some wise men came to Jerusalem
from the east. "Where is the infant king of the Jews?" they
asked. "We saw his star as it rose and have come to do him
homage." When King Herod heard this he was perturbed,
and so was the whole of Jerusalem. He called together all

the chief priests and the scribes of the people, and enquired of them where the Christ was to be born. "At Bethlehem in Judaea," they told him "for this is what the prophet wrote:

And you, Bethlehem, in the land of Judah
you are by no means least among the leaders of Judah,
for out of you will come a leader
who will shepherd my people Israel."

Then Herod summoned the wise men to see him privately. He asked them the exact date on which the star had appeared, and sent them on to Bethlehem. "Go and find out all about the child," he said "and when you have found him, let me know, so that I too may go and do him homage." Having listened to what the king had to say, they set out. And there in front of them was the star they had seen rising; it went forward and halted over the place where the child was. The sight of the star filled them with delight, and going into the house they saw the child with his mother Mary, and falling to their knees they did him homage. Then, opening their treasures, they offered him gifts of gold and frankincense and myrrh. But they were warned in a dream not to go back to Herod, and returned to their own country by a different way.

This is the Gospel of the Lord.

The readings given for 7–12 January are used only on the days between the Epiphany and the following Sunday.

JANUARY 7

First Reading   (3:22–4:6)

A reading from the first letter of St John
Test the spirits, to see if they come from God.

Whatever we ask God,
we shall receive,
because we keep his commandments

and live the kind of life that he wants.
His commandments are these:
that we believe in the name of his Son Jesus Christ
and that we love one another
as he told us to.
Whoever keeps his commandments
lives in God and God lives in him.
We know that he lives in us
by the Spirit that he has given us.

It is not every spirit, my dear people, that you can trust;
test them, to see if they come from God,
there are many false prophets, now, in the world.
You can tell the spirits that come from God by this:
every spirit which acknowledges that Jesus the Christ has
    come in the flesh
is from God;
but any spirit which will not say this of Jesus
is not from God,
but is the spirit of Antichrist,
whose coming you were warned about.
Well, now he is here, in the world.
Children,
you have already overcome these false prophets,
because you are from God and you have in you
one who is greater than anyone in this world;
as for them, they are of the world,
and so they speak the language of the world
and the world listens to them.
But we are children of God,
and those who know God listen to us;
those who are not of God refuse to listen to us.
This is how we can tell
the spirit of truth from the spirit of falsehood.

    This is the word of the Lord.

Responsorial Psalm   (Ps 2:7–8. 10–11. *R.* v. 8)
Response
I will give you the nations for your heritage.

1. The Lord said to me: "You are my Son.
It is I who have begotten you this day.
Ask and I shall bequeath you the nations,
put the ends of the earth in your possession." (*R.*)

2. Now, O kings, understand,
take warning, rulers of the earth;
serve the Lord with awe
and trembling, pay him your homage. (*R.*)

Alleluia   (Mt 4:16)
Alleluia, alleluia!
The people that lived in darkness
has seen a great light;
on those who dwell in the land and shadow of death
a light has dawned.
Alleluia!

Alternative Alleluias p. 841.

Gospel   (4:12–17. 23–25)
A reading from the holy Gospel according to Matthew
The kingdom of heaven is close at hand.

Hearing that John had been arrested, Jesus went back to
Galilee, and leaving Nazareth he went and settled in Capernaum, a lakeside town on the borders of Zebulun and
Naphtali. In this way the prophecy of Isaiah was to be
fulfilled:

Land of Zebulun! Land of Naphtali!
Way of the sea on the far side of Jordan,
Galilee of the nations!

The people that lived in darkness
has seen a great light;
on those who dwell in the land and shadow of death
a light has dawned.

From that moment Jesus began his preaching with the message, "Repent, for the kingdom of heaven is close at hand."

He went round the whole of Galilee teaching in their synagogues, proclaiming the Good News of the kingdom and curing all kinds of diseases and sickness among the people. His fame spread throughout Syria, and those who were suffering from diseases and painful complaints of one kind or another, the possessed, epileptics, the paralysed, were all brought to him, and he cured them. Large crowds followed him, coming from Galilee, the Decapolis, Jerusalem, Judaea and Transjordania.

This is the Gospel of the Lord.

JANUARY 8

First Reading (4:7–10)

A reading from the first letter of St John
God is love.

My dear people,
let us love one another
since love comes from God
and everyone who loves is begotten by God and knows
    God.
Anyone who fails to love can never have known God,
because God is love.
God's love for us was revealed
when God sent into the world his only Son
so that we could have life through him;
this is the love I mean:

not our love for God,
but God's love for us when he sent his Son
to be the sacrifice that takes our sins away.

This is the word of the Lord.

Responsorial Psalm   (Ps 71:1–4. 7–8. *R.* v. 11)
Response
All nations shall fall prostrate before you, O Lord.

1. O God, give your judgement to the king,
to a king's son your justice,
that he may judge your people in justice
and your poor in right judgement. (*R.*)

2. May the mountains bring forth peace for the people
and the hills, justice.
May he defend the poor of the people
and save the children of the needy. (*R.*)

3. In his days justice shall flourish
and peace till the moon fails.
He shall rule from sea to sea,
from the Great River to earth's bounds. (*R.*)

Alleluia   (Mt 4:23)
Alleluia, alleluia!
Jesus proclaimed the Good News of the kingdom
and cured all kinds of diseases among the people.
Alleluia!
Alternative Alleluias p. 841.

Gospel   (6:34–44)

A reading from the holy Gospel according to Mark
By multiplying the loaves Jesus shows that he is a prophet.

As Jesus stepped ashore he saw a large crowd; and he took
pity on them because they were like sheep without a shepherd, and he set himself to teach them at some length. By
now it was getting very late, and his disciples came up to
him and said, "This is a lonely place and it is getting very
late, so send them away, and they can go to the farms and
villages round about, to buy themselves something to eat."
He replied, "Give them something to eat yourselves." They
answered, "Are we to go and spend two hundred denarii on
bread for them to eat?" "How many loaves have you?" he
asked. "Go and see." And when they had found out they
said, "Five, and two fish." Then he ordered them to get all
the people together in groups on the green grass, and they
sat down on the ground in squares of hundreds and fifties.
Then he took the five loaves and the two fish, raised his eyes
to heaven and said the blessing; then he broke the loaves
and handed them to his disciples to distribute among the
people. He also shared out the two fish among them all.
They all ate as much as they wanted. They collected twelve
basketfuls of scraps of bread and pieces of fish. Those who
had eaten the loaves numbered five thousand men.

This is the Gospel of the Lord.

JANUARY 9

First Reading   (4:11–18)

A reading from the first letter of St John
As long as we love one another God will live in us.

My dear people,
since God has loved us so much,
we too should love one another.

No one has ever seen God;
but as long as we love one another
God will live in us
and his love will be complete in us.
We can know that we are living in him
and he is living in us
because he lets us share his Spirit.
We ourselves saw and we testify
that the Father sent his Son
as saviour of the world.
If anyone acknowledges that Jesus is the Son of God,
God lives in him, and he in God.

We ourselves have known and put our faith in
God's love towards ourselves.
God is love
and anyone who lives in love lives in God,
and God lives in him.
Love will come to its perfection in us
when we can face the day of Judgement without fear;
because even in this world
we have become as he is.
In love there can be no fear,
but fear is driven out by perfect love:
because to fear is to expect punishment,
and anyone who is afraid is still imperfect in love.

This is the word of the Lord.

Responsorial Psalm   (Ps 71:1–2. 10. 12–13. R. v. 11)

Response

All nations shall fall prostrate before you, O Lord.

1. O God, give your judgement to the king,
to a king's son your justice,
that he may judge your people in justice
and your poor in right judgement.

2. The kings of Tarshish and the sea coasts
shall pay him tribute.
The kings of Sheba and Seba
shall bring him gifts. (*R.*)

3. For he shall save the poor when they cry
and the needy who are helpless.
He will have pity on the weak
and save the lives of the poor. (*R.*)

Alleluia (Lk 4:18–19)

Alleluia, alleluia!
The Lord has sent me to bring the Good News to the poor,
to proclaim liberty to the captives.
Alleluia!

Alternative Alleluias p. 841.

Gospel (6:45–52)

A reading from the holy Gospel according to Mark

They saw him walking on the lake.

After the five thousand had eaten and were filled, Jesu
made his disciples get into the boat and go on ahead t
Bethsaida, while he himself sent the crowd away. After say
ing good-bye to them he went off into the hills to pray
When evening came, the boat was far out on the lake, an
he was alone on the land. He could see they were worn ou
with rowing, for the wind was against them; and about th
fourth watch of the night he came towards them, walking c
the lake. He was going to pass them by, but when they sa
him walking on the lake they thought it was a ghost an
cried out, for they had all seen him and were terrified. B
he at once spoke to them, and said, "Courage! It is I! D
not be afraid." Then he got into the boat with them, an
the wind dropped. They were utterly and completely dum

founded, because they had not seen what the miracle of the
loaves meant; their minds were closed.

This is the Gospel of the Lord.

JANUARY 10

First Reading   (4:19–5:4)

A reading from the first letter of St John
Anyone who loves God must also love his brother.

We are to love, then,
because God loved us first.
Anyone who says, "I love God",
and hates his brother,
is a liar,
since a man who does not love the brother that he can see
cannot love God, whom he has never seen.
So this is the commandment that he has given us,
that anyone who loves God must also love his brother.

Whoever believes that Jesus is the Christ
has been begotten by God;
and whoever loves the Father that begot him
loves the child whom he begets.
We can be sure that we love God's children
if we love God himself and do what he has commanded
    us;
this is what loving God is –
keeping his commandments;
and his commandments are not difficult,
because anyone who has been begotten by God
has already overcome the world;
this is the victory over the world –
our faith.

This is the word of the Lord.

Responsorial Psalm   (Ps 71:1–2. 14–15. 17. *R*. v. 11)
Response
All nations shall fall prostrate before you, O Lord.

1. O God, give your judgement to the king,
to a king's son your justice,
that he may judge your people in justice
and your poor in right judgement. (*R*.)

2. From oppression he will rescue their lives,
to him their blood is dear.
They shall pray for him without ceasing
and bless him all the day. (*R*.)

3. May his name be blessed for ever
and endure like the sun.
Every tribe shall be blessed in him,
all nations bless his name. (*R*.)

Alleluia   (Lk 7:16)

Alleluia, alleluia!
A great prophet has appeared among us;
God has visited his people.
Alleluia!

Alternative Alleluias p. 841.

Gospel   (4:14–22)

A reading from the holy Gospel according to Luke
This text is being fulfilled today.

Jesus, with the power of the Spirit in him, returned to Gali-
lee; and his reputation spread throughout the countryside.
He taught in their synagogues and everyone praised him.
  He came to Nazara, where he had been brought up, and

went into the synagogue on the sabbath day as he usually did. He stood up to read, and they handed him the scroll of the prophet Isaiah. Unrolling the scroll he found the place where it is written:

The spirit of the Lord has been given to me,
for he has anointed me.
He has sent me to bring the good news to the poor,
to proclaim liberty to captives
and to the blind new sight,
to set the downtrodden free,
to proclaim the Lord's year of favour.

He then rolled up the scroll, gave it back to the assistant and sat down. And all eyes in the synagogue were fixed on him. Then he began to speak to them, "This text is being fulfilled today even as you listen." And he won the approval of all, and they were astonished by the gracious words that came from his lips.

This is the Gospel of the Lord.

JANUARY 11

First Reading   (5:5–13)

A reading from the first letter of St John
The Spirit, the water and the blood.

Who can overcome the world?
Only the man who believes that Jesus is the Son of God:
Jesus Christ who came by water and blood,
not with water only,
but with water and blood,
with the Spirit as another witness –
since the Spirit is the truth –
so that there are three witnesses,
the Spirit, the water and the blood,
and all three of them agree.

We accept the testimony of human witnesses,
but God's testimony is much greater,
and this is God's testimony,
given as evidence for his Son.
Everybody who believes in the Son of God
has this testimony inside him;
and anyone who will not believe God
is making God out to be a liar,
because he has not trusted
the testimony God has given about his Son.
This is the testimony:
God has given us eternal life
and this life is in his Son;
anyone who has the Son has life,
anyone who does not have the Son does not have life.
I have written all this to you
so that you who believe in the name of the Son of God
may be sure that you have eternal life.

This is the word of the Lord.

Responsorial Psalm (Ps 147:12–15. 19–20. *R.* v. 12)
Response
O praise the Lord, Jerusalem!

Alternative Response
Alleluia!

1. O praise the Lord, Jerusalem!
Zion, praise your God!
He has strengthened the bars of your gates,
he has blessed the children within you. (*R.*)

2. He established peace on your borders,
he feeds you with finest wheat.

He sends out his word to the earth
and swiftly runs his command. (*R.*)

3. He makes his word known to Jacob,
to Israel his laws and decrees.
He has not dealt thus with other nations;
he has not taught them his decrees. (*R.*)

Alleluia　　　　　　　　　　　　　　　　　　(cf. 1 Tim 3:16)

Alleluia, alleluia!
Glory be to you, O Christ, proclaimed to the pagans;
glory be to you, O Christ, believed in by the world.
Alleluia!

Alternative Alleluias p. 841.

Gospel　　　　　　　　　　　　　　　　　　　　(5:12–16)

A reading from the holy Gospel according to Luke
And the leprosy left him at once.

Jesus was in one of the towns when a man appeared, covered with leprosy. Seeing Jesus he fell on his face and implored him. "Sir," he said, "if you want to, you can cure me." Jesus stretched out his hand, touched him and said, "Of course I want to! Be cured!" And the leprosy left him at once. He ordered him to tell no one, "But go and show yourself to the priest and make the offering for your healing as Moses prescribed it, as evidence for them."

His reputation continued to grow, and large crowds would gather to hear him and to have their sickness cured, but he would always go off to some place where he could be alone and pray.

This is the Gospel of the Lord.

JANUARY 12

First Reading (5:14–21)

A reading from the first letter of St John
Whatever we may ask, he hears us.

We are quite confident that if we ask the Son of God for
    anything.
and it is in accordance with his will,
he will hear us;
and, knowing that whatever we may ask, he hears us,
we know that we have been granted what we asked of him.
If anybody sees his brother commit a sin
that is not a deadly sin,
he has only to pray, and God will give life to the sinner
– not those who commit a deadly sin;
for there is a sin that is death,
and I will not say that you must pray about that.
Every kind of wrong-doing is sin,
but not all sin is deadly.
We know that anyone who has been begotten by God
does not sin,
because the begotten Son of God protects him,
and the Evil One does not touch him.
We know that we belong to God,
but the whole world lies in the power of the Evil One.
We know, too, that the Son of God has come,
and has given us the power
to know the true God.
We are in the true God,
as we are in his Son, Jesus Christ.
This is the true God,
this is eternal life.
Children, be on your guard against false gods.

This is the word of the Lord.

Responsorial Psalm   (Ps 149:1–6. 9. *R*. v. 4)

Response
The Lord takes delight in his people.

Alternative Response
Alleluia!

1. Sing a new song to the Lord,
his praise in the assembly of the faithful.
Let Israel rejoice in its Maker,
let Zion's sons exult in their king. (*R*.)

2. Let them praise his name with dancing
and make music with timbrel and harp.
For the Lord takes delight in his people.
He crowns the poor with salvation. (*R*.)

3. Let the faithful rejoice in their glory,
shout for joy and take their rest.
Let the praise of God be on their lips;
this honour is for all his faithful.
Alleluia! (*R*.)

Alleluia   (Lk 7:16)

Alleluia, alleluia!
A great prophet has appeared among us;
God has visited his people.
Alleluia!

Alternative Alleluias p. 841.

Gospel (3:22–30)

A reading from the holy Gospel according to John
The bridegroom's friend is glad when he hears the bridegroom's voice.

Jesus went with his disciples into the Judaean countryside and stayed with them there and baptised. At the same time John was baptising at Aenon near Salim, where there was plenty of water, and people were going there to be baptised. This was before John had been put in prison.

Now some of John's disciples had opened a discussion with a Jew about purification, so they went to John and said, "Rabbi, the man who was with you on the far side of the Jordan, the man to whom you bore witness, is baptising now; and everyone is going to him." John replied:

"A man can lay claim
only to what is given him from heaven.

"You yourselves can bear me out: I said: I myself am not the Christ; I am the one who has been sent in front of him.

"The bride is only for the bridegroom;
and yet the bridegroom's friend,
who stands there and listens,
is glad when he hears the bridegroom's voice.
This same joy I feel, and now it is complete.
He must grow greater,
I must grow smaller."

This is the Gospel of the Lord.

Sunday after Epiphany

FEAST OF THE BAPTISM OF THE LORD

(1st Sunday of the Year)

First Reading   (42:1–4. 6–7)

A reading from the prophet Isaiah
Here is my servant in whom my soul delights.

Thus says the Lord:
Here is my servant whom I uphold,
my chosen one in whom my soul delights.
I have endowed him with my spirit
that he may bring true justice to the nations.

He does not cry out or shout aloud,
or make his voice heard in the streets.
He does not break the crushed reed,
nor quench the wavering flame.

Faithfully he brings true justice;
he will neither waver, nor be crushed
until true justice is established on earth,
for the islands are awaiting his law.

I, the Lord, have called you to serve the cause of right;
I have taken you by the hand and formed you;
I have appointed you as covenant of the people and light
   of the nations,

to open the eyes of the blind,
to free captives from prison,
and those who live in darkness from the dungeon.

This is the word of the Lord.

Responsorial Psalm   (Ps 28:1–4. 9–10. *R.* v. 11)

Response
The Lord will bless his people with peace.

1. O give the Lord you sons of God,
give the Lord glory and power;
give the Lord the glory of his name.
Adore the Lord in his holy court. (*R.*)

2. The Lord's voice resounding on the waters,
the Lord on the immensity of waters;
the voice of the Lord, full of power,
the voice of the Lord, full of splendour. (*R.*)

3. The God of glory thunders.
In his temple they all cry: "Glory!"
The Lord sat enthroned over the flood;
the Lord sits as king for ever. (*R.*)

Second Reading   (10:34–38)

A reading from the Acts of the Apostles
God anointed him with the Holy Spirit.

Peter addressed Cornelius and his household: "The truth
I have now come to realise" he said "is that God does not
have favourites, but that anybody of any nationality who
fears God and does what is right is acceptable to him.

"It is true, God sent his word to the people of Israel, and
it was to them that the good news of peace was brought by
Jesus Christ – but Jesus Christ is Lord of all men. You
must have heard about the recent happenings in Judaea;
about Jesus of Nazareth and how he began in Galilee, after
John had been preaching baptism. God had anointed him
with the Holy Spirit and with power, and because God was

with him, Jesus went about doing good and curing all who had fallen into the power of the devil."

This is the word of the Lord.

Alleluia   (Mk 9:8)

Alleluia, alleluia!
The heavens opened and the Father's voice resounded:
"This is my Son, the Beloved. Listen to him."
Alleluia!

Year 1 (Year A)

Gospel   (3:13–17)

A reading from the holy Gospel according to Matthew
As soon as Jesus was baptised he saw the Spirit of God coming down on him.

Jesus came from Galilee to the Jordan to be baptised by John. John tried to dissuade him. "It is I who need baptism from you," he said "and yet you come to me!" But Jesus replied, "Leave it like this for the time being; it is fitting that we should, in this way, do all that righteousness demands." At this, John gave in to him.

As soon as Jesus was baptised he came up from the water, and suddenly the heavens opened and he saw the Spirit of God descending like a dove and coming down on him. And a voice spoke from heaven, "This is my Son, the Beloved; my favour rests on him."

This is the Gospel of the Lord.

Year 2 (Year B)

Gospel   (1:7–11)

A reading from the holy Gospel according to Mark
You are my Son, the Beloved; my favour rests on you.

In the course of his preaching John the Baptist said, "Someone is following me, someone who is more powerful than
I am, and I am not fit to kneel down and undo the strap of
his sandals. I have baptised you with water, but he will baptise you with the Holy Spirit."

It was at this time that Jesus came from Nazareth in Galilee and was baptised in the Jordan by John. No sooner had
he come up out of the water than he saw the heavens torn
apart and the Spirit, like a dove, descending on him. And a
voice came from heaven, "You are my Son, the Beloved;
my favour rests on you."

This is the Gospel of the Lord.

Year 3 (Year C)

Gospel   (3:15–16. 21–22)

A reading from the holy Gospel according to Luke
*While Jesus after his own baptism was at prayer, heaven
opened.*

A feeling of expectancy had grown among the people, who
were beginning to think that John might be the Christ, so
John declared before them all, "I baptise you with water,
but someone is coming, someone who is more powerful
than I am, and I am not fit to undo the strap of his sandals;
he will baptise you with the Holy Spirit and fire."

Now when all the people had been baptised and while
Jesus after his own baptism was at prayer, heaven opened
and the Holy Spirit descended on him in bodily shape, like
a dove. And a voice came from heaven, "You are my Son,
the Beloved; my favour rests on you."

This is the Gospel of the Lord.

THE WEEKS OF THE YEAR

The first Sunday of the Year is the feast of the Baptism of the Lord (p. 169). The number of the Weeks of the Year that may fall between the Baptism of the Lord and Ash Wednesday is variable: see the Table of Moveable Feasts on p. 879. Those Weeks of the Year which may fall between the Baptism and Ash Wednesday are given here.

MONDAY

Year I

First Reading (1:1–6)

A reading from the letter to the Hebrews
God has spoken to us through his Son.

At various times in the past and in various different ways, God spoke to our ancestors through the prophets; but in our own time, the last days, he has spoken to us through his Son, the Son that he has appointed to inherit everything and through whom he made everything there is. He is the radiant light of God's glory and the perfect copy of his nature, sustaining the universe by his powerful command; and now that he has destroyed the defilement of sin, he has gone to take his place in heaven at the right hand of divine Majesty. So he is now as far above the angels as the title he has inherited is higher than their own name.

God has never said to any angel: You are my Son, today I have become your father; or: I will be a father to him and he a son to me. Again, when he brings the First-born into the world, he says: Let all the angels of God worship him.

This is the word of the Lord.

Responsorial Psalm (Ps 96:1–2. 6–7. 9. *R.* v. 7)

Response
All you spirits, worship him.

1. The Lord is king, let earth rejoice,
the many coastlands be glad.
Cloud and darkness are his raiment;
his throne, justice and right. (*R.*)

2. The skies proclaim his justice;
all peoples see his glory.
All you spirits, worship him. (*R.*)

3. For you indeed are the Lord
most high above all the earth
exalted far above all spirits. (R.)

ALLELUIA and GOSPEL. As for Year II, see p. 175.

Year II

First Reading   (1:1–8)

A reading from the first book of Samuel
Hannah's rival would taunt her because the Lord had made her barren.

There was a man of Ramathaim, a Zuphite from the highlands of Ephraim whose name was Elkanah son of Jeroham, son of Elihu, son of Tohu, son of Zuph, an Ephraimite. He had two wives, one called Hannah, the other Peninnah; Peninnah had children but Hannah had none. Every year this man used to go up from his town to worship and to sacrifice to the Lord of hosts in Shiloh. The two sons of Eli, Hophni and Phinehas, were there as priests of the Lord.

One day Elkanah offered sacrifice. He used to give portions to Peninnah and to all her sons and daughters; to Hannah, however, he would give only one portion, although he loved her more, since the Lord had made her barren. Her rival would taunt her to annoy her, because the Lord had made her barren. And this went on year after year; every time they went up to the temple of the Lord she used to taunt her. And so Hannah wept and would not eat. Then Elkanah her husband said to her, "Hannah, why are you

crying and why are you not eating? Why so sad? Am I not
more to you than ten sons?"

This is the word of the Lord.

Responsorial Psalm   (Ps 115:12–19. R. v. 17)

Response

A thanksgiving sacrifice I make to you, O Lord.

Alternative Response
Alleluia!

1. How can I repay the Lord
for his goodness to me?
The cup of salvation I will raise;
I will call on the Lord's name. (R.)

2. My vows to the Lord I will fulfil
before all his people.
O precious in the eyes of the Lord
is the death of his faithful. (R.)

3. Your servant, Lord, your servant am I;
you have loosened my bonds.
A thanksgiving sacrifice I make:
I will call on the Lord's name. (R.)

4. My vows to the Lord I will fulfil
before all his people,
in the courts of the house of the Lord,
in your midst, O Jerusalem. (R.)

                    Years I and II

Alleluia   (Acts 16:14)

Alleluia, alleluia!
Open our heart, O Lord,
to accept the words of your Son.
Alleluia!

Alternative Alleluias p. 847.

Gospel (1:14–20)

A reading from the holy Gospel according to Mark
Repent and believe the Good News.

After John had been arrested, Jesus went into Galilee. There he proclaimed the Good News from God. "The time has come" he said "and the kingdom of God is close at hand. Repent, and believe the Good News."

As he was walking along by the Sea of Galilee he saw Simon and his brother Andrew casting a net in the lake – for they were fishermen. And Jesus said to them, "Follow me and I will make you into fishers of men." And at once they left their nets and followed him.

Going on a little further, he saw James son of Zebedee and his brother John; they too were in their boat, mending their nets. He called them at once and, leaving their father Zebedee in the boat with the men he employed, they went after him.

This is the Gospel of the Lord.

TUESDAY

Year I

First Reading (2:5–12)

A reading from the letter to the Hebrews
It was appropriate that God should make perfect through suffering the leader who would take them to their salvation.

God did not appoint angels to be rulers of the world to come, and that world is what we are talking about. Somewhere there is a passage that shows us this. It runs: What is man that you should spare a thought for him, the son of man that you should care for him? For a short while you made him lower than the angels; you crowned him with glory and splendour. You have put him in command of everything. Well then, if he has put him in command of everything, he has left nothing which is not under his command. At present, it is true, we are not able to see that everything has been put under his command, but we do see in Jesus one who was for a short while made lower than the angels and is now crowned with glory and splendour because he submitted to death; by God's grace he had to experience death for all mankind.

As it was his purpose to bring a great many of his sons into glory, it was appropriate that God, for whom everything exists and through whom everything exists, should make perfect, through suffering, the leader who would take them to their salvation. For the one who sanctifies, and the ones who are sanctified, are of the same stock; that is why he openly calls them brothers in the text: I shall announce your name to my brothers, praise you in full assembly.

This is the word of the Lord.

Responsorial Psalm   (Ps 8:2. 5–9. *R*. v. 7)

Response

Your Son you gave power
over the works of your hand.

1. How great is your name, O Lord our God,
through all the earth!
what is man that you should keep him in mind,
mortal man that you care for him? (*R*.)

2. Yet you have made him little less than a god;
with glory and honour you crowned him,
gave him power over the works of your hand.
put all things under his feet. (*R*.)

3. All of them, sheep and cattle,
yes, even the savage beasts,
birds of the air, and fish
that make their way through the waters. (*R*.)

ALLELUIA and GOSPEL. As for Year II, see p. 180.

Year II

First Reading   (1:9–20)

A reading from the first book of Samuel
The Lord was mindful of Hannah and she gave birth to Samuel.

After they had eaten in the hall, Hannah rose and took her stand before the Lord, while Eli the priest was sitting on his seat by the doorpost of the temple of the Lord. In the bitterness of her soul she prayed to the Lord with many tears and made a vow, saying, "Lord of hosts! If you will take notice of the distress of your servant, and bear me in mind and not forget your servant and give her a man-child, I will give him to the Lord for the whole of his life and no razor shall ever touch his head."

While she prayed before the Lord which she did for some time, Eli was watching her mouth, for she was speaking under her breath; her lips were moving but her voice could not be heard. He therefore supposed that she was drunk and said to her, "How long are you going to be in this drunken state? Rid yourself of your wine." "No, my lord," Hannah replied "I am a woman in great trouble; I have taken neither wine nor strong drink – I was pouring out my soul before the Lord. Do not take your maidservant for a worthless woman; all this time I have been speaking from the depth of my grief and my resentment." Then Eli answered her: "Go in peace," he said "and may the God of Israel grant what you have asked of him." And she said, "May your maidservant find favour in your sight"; and with that the woman went away; she returned to the hall and ate and was dejected no longer.

They rose early in the morning and worshipped before the Lord and then set out and returned to their home in Ramah. Elkanah had intercourse with Hannah his wife and the Lord was mindful of her. She conceived and gave birth to a son, and called him Samuel "since" she said "I asked the Lord for him."

This is the word of the Lord.

Responsorial Psalm   (1 Sam 2:1. 4–8. *R*. v. 1)

Response
My heart exults in the Lord.

1. My heart exults in the Lord.
I find my strength in my God;
my mouth laughs at my enemies
as I rejoice in your saving help. (*R*.)

2. The bows of the mighty are broken,
but the weak are clothed with strength.
Those with plenty must labour for bread,
but the hungry need work no more.
The childless wife has children now
but the fruitful wife bears no more. (*R*.)

3. It is the Lord who gives life and death,
he brings men to the grave and back;
it is the Lord who gives poverty and riches.
He brings men low and raises them on high. (*R*.)

4. He lifts up the lowly from the dust,
from the dungheap he raises the poor
to set him in the company of princes,
to give him a glorious throne. (*R*.)

Years I and II

Alleluia   (James 1:21)

Alleluia, alleluia!
Accept and submit to the word
which has been planted in you
and can save your souls.
Alleluia!

Alternative Alleluias p. 847.

Gospel   (1:21–28)

A reading from the Holy Gospel according to Mark
He taught them with authority.

Jesus and his disciples went as far as Capernaum, and as soon as the sabbath came he went to the synagogue and began to teach. And his teaching made a deep impression on them because, unlike the scribes, he taught them with authority.

In their synagogue just then there was a man possessed by an unclean spirit, and it shouted, "What do you want with us, Jesus of Nazareth? Have you come to destroy us? I know who you are: the Holy One of God." But Jesus said sharply, "Be quiet! Come out of him!" And the unclean spirit threw the man into convulsions and with a loud cry went out of him. The people were so astonished that they started asking each other what it all meant. "Here is a teaching that is new" they said "and with authority behind it: he gives orders even to unclean spirits and they obey him." And his reputation rapidly spread everywhere, through all the surrounding Galilean countryside.

This is the Gospel of the Lord.

WEDNESDAY
Year I

First Reading   (2:14–18)

A reading from the letter to the Hebrews
*It was essential that he should in this way become completely
like his brothers so that he could be compassionate.*

Since all the children share the same blood and flesh, Jesus
too shared equally in it, so that by his death he could take
away all the power of the devil, who had power over death,
and set free all those who had been held in slavery all their
lives by the fear of death. For it was not the angels that he
took to himself; he took to himself descent from Abraham.
It was essential that he should in this way become completely like his brothers so that he could be a compassionate
and trustworthy high priest of God's religion, able to atone
for human sins. That is, because he has himself been through
temptation he is able to help others who are tempted.

This is the word of the Lord.

Responsorial Psalm   (Ps 104:1–4. 6–9. *R*. v. 8)

Response
The Lord remembers his covenant for ever.

Alternative Response
Alleluia!

1. Alleluia!
Give thanks to the Lord, tell his name,
make known his deeds among the peoples.
O sing to him, sing his praise;
tell all his wonderful works! (*R*.)

2. Be proud of his holy name,
let the hearts that seek the Lord rejoice.

Consider the Lord and his strength;
constantly seek his face. (*R.*)

3. O children of Abraham, his servant,
O sons of the Jacob he chose.
He, the Lord, is our God:
·his judgements prevail in all the earth. (*R.*)

4. He remembers his covenant for ever,
his promise for a thousand generations,
the covenant he made with Abraham,
the oath he swore to Isaac. (*R.*)

ALLELUIA and GOSPEL. As for Year II, see p. 184.

Year II

First Reading   (3:1–10. 19–20)

A reading from the first book of Samuel
Speak, Lord, your servant is listening.

The boy Samuel was ministering to the Lord in the presence
of Eli; it was rare for the Lord to speak in those days; visions were uncommon. One day, it happened that Eli was
lying down in his room. His eyes were beginning to grow
dim; he could no longer see. The lamp of God had not yet
gone out, and Samuel was lying in the sanctuary of the Lord
where the ark of God was, when the Lord called, "Samuel!
Samuel!" He answered, "Here I am." Then he ran to Eli
and said, "Here I am, since you called me." Eli said, "I did
not call. Go back and lie down." So he went and lay down.
Once again the Lord called, "Samuel! Samuel!" Samuel
got up and went to Eli and said, "Here I am, since you
called me." He replied, "I did not call you, my son; go back
and lie down." Samuel had as yet no knowledge of the Lord
and the word of the Lord had not yet been revealed to him.
Once again the Lord called, the third time. He got up and

went to Eli and said, "Here I am, since you called me." Eli
then understood that it was the Lord who was calling the
boy, and he said to Samuel, "Go and lie down, and if someone calls say, 'Speak, Lord, your servant is listening.'" So
Samuel went and lay down in his place.

The Lord then came and stood by, calling as he had done
before, "Samuel! Samuel!" Samuel answered, "Speak,
Lord, your servant is listening."

Samuel grew up and the Lord was with him and let no
word of his fall to the ground. All Israel from Dan to Beersheba came to know that Samuel was accredited as a prophet of the Lord.

This is the word of the Lord.

Responsorial Psalm   (Ps 39:2. 5. 7–10. *R.* vv. 8. 9)

Response
Behold, Lord, I come to do your will.

1. I waited, I waited for the Lord
and he stooped down to me;
he heard me cry.
Happy the man who has placed
his trust in the Lord
and has not gone over to the rebels
who follows false gods. (*R.*)

2. You do not ask for sacrifice and offerings,
but an open ear.
You do not ask for holocaust and victim.
Instead, here am I. (*R.*)

3. In the scroll of the book it stands written
that I should do your will.
My God, I delight in your law
in the depth of my heart. (*R.*)

4. Your justice I have proclaimed
in the great assembly.
My lips I have not sealed;
you know it, O Lord. (*R.*)

Years I and II

Alleluia   (Col 3:16. 17)

Alleluia, alleluia!
Let the message of Christ, in all its richness,
find a home with you;
through him give thanks to God the Father.
Alleluia!

Alternative Alleluias p. 847.

Gospel   (1:29–39)

A reading from the holy Gospel according to Mark
*He cured many who were suffering from diseases of one kind
or another.*

On leaving the synagogue, Jesus went with James and John
straight to the house of Simon and Andrew. Now Simon's
mother-in-law had gone to bed with fever, and they told him
about her straightaway. He went to her, took her by the
hand and helped her up. And the fever left her and she began
to wait on them.

That evening, after sunset, they brought to him all who
were sick and those who were possessed by devils. The
whole town came crowding round the door, and he cured
many who were suffering from diseases of one kind or another; he also cast out many devils, but he would not allow
them to speak, because they knew who he was.

In the morning, long before dawn, he got up and left the
house, and went off to a lonely place and prayed there.
Simon and his companions set out in search of him, and
when they found him they said, "Everybody is looking for

you." He answered, "Let us go elsewhere, to the neighbouring country towns, so that I can preach there too, because that is why I came." And he went all through Galilee, preaching in their synagogues and casting out devils.

This is the Gospel of the Lord.

THURSDAY

Year I

First Reading   (3:7–14)

A reading from the letter to the Hebrews
As long as this "today" lasts, keep encouraging one another.

The Holy Spirit says: If only you would listen to him to-day; do not harden your hearts, as happened in the Rebellion, on the Day of Temptation in the wilderness, when your ancestors challenged me and tested me, though they had seen what I could do for forty years. That was why I was angry with that generation and said: How unreliable these people who refuse to grasp my ways! And so, in anger, I swore that not one would reach the place of rest I had for them. Take care, brothers, that there is not in any one of your community a wicked mind, so unbelieving as to turn away from the living God. Every day, as long as this "today" lasts, keep encouraging one another so that none of you is hardened by the lure of sin, because we shall remain co-heirs with Christ only if we keep a grasp on our first confidence right to the end.

This is the word of the Lord.

Responsorial Psalm   (Ps 94:6–11. *R*. v. 8)

Response
O that today you would listen to his voice!
"Harden not your hearts."

1. Come in; let us bow and bend low;
let us kneel before the God who made us
for he is our God and we
the people who belong to his pasture,
the flock that is led by his hand. (*R.*)

2. O that today you would listen to his voice!
"Harden not your hearts as at Meribah,
as on that day at Massah in the desert
when your fathers put me to the test;
when they tried me, though they saw my work. (*R.*)

3. For forty years I was wearied of these people
and I said: 'Their hearts are astray,
these people do not know my ways.'
Then I took an oath in my anger:
'Never shall they enter my rest.' " (*R.*)

ALLELUIA and GOSPEL. As for Year II, see p. 188.

Year II

First Reading   (4:1–11)

A reading from the first book of Samuel
Israel was defeated and the ark of God was captured.

It happened that the Philistines mustered to fight Israel and
Israel went out to meet them in battle, encamping near Eb-
enezer while the Philistines were encamped at Aphek. The
Philistines drew up their battle line against Israel, the battle
was hotly engaged, and Israel was defeated by the Philistines and about four thousand of their army were killed on
the field. The troops returned to the camp and the elders of
Israel said, "Why has the Lord allowed us to be defeated
today by the Philistines? Let us fetch the ark of our God
from Shiloh so that it may come among us and rescue us
from the power of our enemies." So the troops sent to Shiloh

and brought away the ark of the Lord of hosts, he who is
seated on the cherubs; the two sons of Eli, Hophni and
Phinehas, came with the ark. When the ark of the Lord arrived in the camp, all Israel gave a great shout so that the
earth resounded. When the Philistines heard the noise of
the shouting, they said, "What can this great shouting in
the Hebrew camp mean?" And they realised that the ark of
the Lord had come into the camp. At this the Philistines
were afraid; and they said, "God has come to the camp."
"Alas!" they cried "This has never happened before. Alas!
Who will save us from the power of this mighty God? It
was he who struck down Egypt with every kind of plague!
But take courage and be men, Philistines, or you will become slaves to the Hebrews as they have been slaves to you.
Be men and fight." So the Philistines joined battle and Israel
was defeated, each man fleeing to his tent. The slaughter
was great indeed, and there fell of the Israelites thirty thousand foot soldiers. The ark of God was captured too, and
the two sons of Eli died, Hophni and Phinehas.

This is the word of the Lord.

Responsorial Psalm   (Ps 43:10–11. 14–15. 24–25. *R.* v. 27)
Response
Redeem us, O Lord,
because of your love.

1. Yet now you have rejected us, disgraced us:
you no longer go forth with our armies.
You make us retreat from the foe
and our enemies plunder us at will. (*R.*)

2. You make us the taunt of our neighbours,
the mockery and scorn of all who are near.
Among the nations, you make us a byword,
among the peoples a thing of derision. (*R.*)

3. Awake, O Lord, why do you sleep?
Arise, do not reject us for ever!
Why do you hide your face
and forget our oppression and misery. (*R.*)

Years I and II

Alleluia (Ps 118:88)

Alleluia, alleluia!
Because of your love give me life,
and I will do your will.
Alleluia!

Alternative Alleluias p. 847.

Gospel (1:40–45)

A reading from the holy Gospel according to Mark
The leprosy left him and he was cured.

A leper came to Jesus and pleaded on his knees: "If you want to" he said "you can cure me." Feeling sorry for him, Jesus stretched out his hand and touched him. "Of course I want to!" he said. "Be cured!" And the leprosy left him at once and he was cured. Jesus immediately sent him away and sternly ordered him, "Mind you say nothing to anyone, but go and show yourself to the priest, and make offering for your healing prescribed by Moses as evidence of your recovery." The man went away, but then started talking about it freely and telling the story everywhere, so that Jesus could no longer go openly into any town, but had to stay outside in places where nobody lived. Even so, people from all around would come to him.

This is the Gospel of the Lord.

FRIDAY
Year I

First Reading   (4:1–5. 11)

A reading from the letter to the Hebrews
We must therefore do everything we can to reach this place of rest.

Be careful: the promise of reaching the place of rest God
had for the Israelites still holds good, and none of you must
think that he has come too late for it. We received the Good
News exactly as they did; but hearing the message did them
no good because they did not share the faith of those who
listened. We, however, who have faith, shall reach a place
of rest, as in the text: And so, in anger, I swore that not
one would reach the place of rest I had for them. God's
work was undoubtedly all finished at the beginning of the
world; as one text says, referring to the seventh day: After
all his work God rested on the seventh day. The text we
are considering says: They shall not reach the place of rest
I had for them.

We must therefore do everything we can to reach this
place of rest, or some of you might copy this example of
disobedience and be lost.

This is the word of the Lord.

Responsorial Psalm   (Ps 77:3–4. 6–8. *R*. v. 7)

Response
Never forget God's deeds.

. The things we have heard and understood,
the things our fathers have told us
we will not hide from their children
but will tell them to the next generation:
the glories of the Lord and his might
and the marvellous deeds he has done. (*R*.)

2. They too should arise and tell their sons
that they too should set their hope in God
and never forget God's deeds
but keep every one of his commands. (*R.*)

3. So that they might not be like their fathers,
a defiant and rebellious race,
a race whose heart was fickle,
whose spirit was unfaithful to God. (*R.*)

ALLELUIA and GOSPEL. As for Year II, see p. 191.

Year II

First Reading   (8:4–7. 10–22)

A reading from the first book of Samuel
*You will cry out on account of the king you have chosen for
yourselves, but God will not answer you.*

All the elders of Israel gathered together and came to Samuel at Ramah. "Look," they said to him "you are old, and your sons do not follow your ways. So give us a king to rule over us, like the other nations." It displeased Samuel that they should say, "Let us have a king to rule us," so he prayed to the Lord. But the Lord said to Samuel, "Obey the voice of the people in all that they say to you, for it is not you they have rejected; they have rejected me from ruling over them."

All that the Lord had said Samuel repeated to the people who were asking him for a king. He said, "These will be the rights of the king who is to reign over you. He will take your sons and assign them to his chariotry and cavalry, and they will run in front of his chariot. He will use them as leaders of a thousand and leaders of fifty; he will make them plough his ploughland and harvest his harvest and make his weapons of war and the gear for his chariots. He will also take your daughters as perfumers, cooks and bakers. He will take the best of your fields, of your vine-

yards and olive groves and give them to his officials. He
will tithe your crops and vineyards to provide for his eun-
uchs and his officials. He will take the best of your man-
servants and maidservants, of your cattle and your donkeys,
and make them work for him. He will tithe your flocks, and
you yourselves will become his slaves. When that day
comes, you will cry out on account of the king you have
chosen for yourselves, but on that day God will not answer
you."

The people refused to listen to the words of Samuel. They
said, "No! We want a king, so that we in our turn can be
like the other nations; our king shall rule us and be our
leader and fight our battles." Samuel listened to all that the
people had to say and repeated it in the ears of the Lord.
The Lord then said to Samuel, "Obey their voice and give
them a king."

This is the word of the Lord.

Responsorial Psalm (Ps 88:16–19. *R*. v. 2)

Response
I will sing for ever of your love, O Lord.

1. Happy the people who acclaim such a king,
who walk, O Lord, in the light of your face,
who find their joy every day in your name,
who make your justice the source of their bliss. (*R*.)

2. For it is you, O Lord, who are the glory of their strength;
it is by your favour that our might is exalted:
for our ruler is in the keeping of the Lord;
our king in the keeping of the Holy One of Israel. (*R*.)

Years I and II

Alleluia (Eph 1:17. 18)

Alleluia, alleluia!
May the Father of our Lord Jesus Christ
enlighten the eyes of our mind,

so that we can see what hope his call holds for us.
Alleluia!

Alternative Alleluias p. 847.

Gospel (2:1–12)

A reading from the holy Gospel according to Mark
The Son of Man has authority on earth to forgive sins.

When Jesus returned to Capernaum, word went round that he was back; and so many people collected there that there was no room left, even in front of the door. He was preaching the word to them when some people came bringing him a paralytic carried by four men, but as the crowd made it impossible to get the man to him, they stripped the roof over the place where Jesus was; and when they had made an opening, they lowered the stretcher on which the paralytic lay. Seeing their faith, Jesus said to the paralytic, "My child, your sins are forgiven." Now some scribes were sitting there, and they thought to themselves, "How can this man talk like that? He is blaspheming. Who can forgive sins but God?" Jesus, inwardly aware that this was what they were thinking, said to them, "Why do you have these thoughts in your hearts? Which of these is easier: to say to the paralytic, 'Your sins are forgiven' or to say, 'Get up, pick up your stretcher and walk'? But to prove to you that the Son of Man has authority on earth to forgive sins," – he said to the paralytic – "I order you: get up, pick up your stretcher, and go off home." And the man got up, picked up his stretcher at once and walked out in front of everyone so that they were all astounded and praised God saying "We have never seen anything like this."

This is the Gospel of the Lord.

SATURDAY
Year I

First Reading   (4:12–16)

A reading from the letter to the Hebrews
Let us be confident in approaching the throne of grace.

The word of God is something alive and active: it cuts like
any double-edged sword but more finely: it can slip through
the place where the soul is divided from the spirit, or joints
from the marrow; it can judge the secret emotions and
thoughts. No created thing can hide from him; everything
is uncovered and open to the eyes of the one to whom we
must give account of ourselves.

Since in Jesus, the Son of God, we have the supreme high
priest who has gone through to the highest heaven, we must
never let go of the faith that we have professed. For it is not
as if we had a high priest who was incapable of feeling our
weaknesses with us; but we have one who has been tempted
in every way that we are, though he is without sin. Let us
be confident, then, in approaching the throne of grace, that
we shall have mercy from him and find grace when we are
in need of help.

This is the word of the Lord.

Responsorial Psalm   (18:8–10. 15. *R*. Jn 6:63)

Response
Your words, Lord, are spirit,
and they are life.

1. The law of the Lord is perfect,
it revives the soul.
The rule of the Lord is to be trusted,
it gives wisdom to the simple. (*R*.)

2. The precepts of the Lord are right,
they gladden the heart.

The command of the Lord is clear,
it gives light to the eyes. (*R.*)

3. The fear of the Lord is holy,
abiding for ever.
The decrees of the Lord are truth
and all of them just. (*R.*)

4. May the spoken words of my mouth,
the thoughts of my heart,
win favour in your sight, O Lord,
my rescuer, my rock! (*R.*)

ALLELUIA and GOSPEL. As for Year II, see p. 195.

Year II

First Reading (9:1–4. 17–19. 10:1)

A reading from the first book of Samuel
The Lord told Samuel, "That is the man of whom I told you;
Saul shall rule my people."

Among the men of Benjamin there was a man named Kish
son of Abiel, son of Zeror, son of Becorath, son of Aphiah;
a Benjaminite and a man of rank. He had a son named
Saul, a handsome man in the prime of life. Of all the Israelites there was no one more handsome than he; he stood
head and shoulders taller than the rest of the people. Now
some of the she-donkeys of Saul's father Kish had strayed,
so Kish said to Saul, "My son, take one of the servants with
you and be off; go and look for the she-donkeys." They
passed through the highlands of Ephraim and passed
through the land of Shalishah, but did not find them; they
passed through the land of Shaalim, they were not there;
they passed through the land of Benjamin, but did not find
them.

When Samuel saw Saul, the Lord told him, "That is the

man of whom I told you; he shall rule my people." Saul accosted Samuel in the gateway and said, "Tell me, please, where the seer's house is?" Samuel replied to Saul, "I am the seer. Go up ahead of me to the high place. You are to eat with me today. In the morning I shall take leave of you and tell you all that is in your heart."

Samuel took a phial of oil and poured it on Saul's head; then he kissed him, saying, "Has not the Lord anointed you prince over his people Israel? You are the man who must rule the Lord's people, and who must save them from the power of the enemies surrounding them."

This is the word of the Lord.

Responsorial Psalm (Ps 20:2–7. *R.* v. 2)

Response
O Lord, your strength gives joy to the king.

1. O Lord, your strength gives joy to the king;
how your saving help makes him glad!
You have granted him his heart's desire;
you have not refused the prayer of his lips. (*R.*)

2. You came to meet him with the blessing of success,
you have set on his head a crown of pure gold.
He asked you for life and this you have given,
days that will last from age to age. (*R.*)

3. Your saving help has given him glory.
You have laid upon him majesty and splendour,
you have granted your blessings to him for ever.
You have made him rejoice with the joy of your presence. (*R.*)

Years I and II

Alleluia (Ps 118:29. 35)

Alleluia, alleluia!
Bend my heart to your will, O Lord,

and teach me your law.
Alleluia!

Alternative Alleluias p. 847.

Gospel (2:13–17)

A reading from the holy Gospel according to Mark
I did not come to call the virtuous, but sinners.

Jesus went out to the shore of the lake; and all the people
came to him, and he taught them. As he was walking on he
saw Levi the son of Alphaeus, sitting by the customs house,
and he said to him, "Follow me." And he got up and fol-
owed him.

When Jesus was at dinner in his house, a number of tax
collectors and sinners were also sitting at the table with
Jesus and his disciples; for there were many of them among
his followers. When the scribes of the Pharisee party saw
him eating with sinners and tax collectors, they said to his
disciples, "Why does he eat with tax collectors and sinners?" When Jesus heard this he said to them, "It is not
the healthy who need the doctor, but the sick. I did not come
to call the virtuous, but sinners."

This is the Gospel of the Lord.

2nd SUNDAY OF THE YEAR
Year I (Year A)

First Reading (49:3. 5–6)

A reading from the prophet Isaiah
*I will make you the light of the nations so that my salvation
may reach to the ends of the earth.*

The Lord said to me, "You are my servant (Israel)
in whom I shall be glorified";
I was honoured in the eyes of the Lord,
my God was my strength.

And now the Lord has spoken,
he who formed me in the womb to be his servant,
to bring Jacob back to him,
to gather Israel to him:

"It is not enough for you to be my servant,
to restore the tribes of Jacob and bring back the survivors
    of Israel;
I will make you the light of the nations
so that my salvation may reach to the ends of the earth."

    This is the word of the Lord.

Responsorial Psalm   (Ps 39:2. 4. 7–10. R. vv. 8. 9)

Response
Here I am Lord!
I come to do your will.

1. I waited, I waited for the Lord
and he stooped down to me;
he heard my cry.
He put a new song into my mouth,
praise of our God. (*R.*)

2. You do not ask for sacrifice and offerings,
but an open ear.
You do not ask for holocaust and victim.
Instead, here am I. (*R.*)

3. In the scroll of the book it stands written
that I should do your will.
My God, I delight in your law
in the depth of my heart. (*R.*)

4. Your justice I have proclaimed
in the great assembly.
My lips I have not sealed;
you know it, O Lord. (*R.*)

Second Reading   (1:1–3)

A reading from the first letter of St Paul to the Corinthians
May God our Father and the Lord Jesus Christ send you grace and peace.

I, Paul, appointed by God to be an apostle, together with brother Sosthenes, send greetings to the church of God in Corinth, to the holy people of Jesus Christ, who are called to take their place among all the saints everywhere who pray to our Lord Jesus Christ; for he is their Lord no less than ours. May God our Father and the Lord Jesus Christ send you grace and peace.

This is the word of the Lord.

Alleluia   (Lk 19:38)

Alleluia, alleluia!
Blessings on the King who comes,
in the name of the Lord!
Peace in heaven
and glory in the highest heavens!
Alleluia!

Alternative Alleluias p. 854.

Gospel   (1:29–34)

A reading from the holy Gospel according to John
Look, there is the lamb of God that takes away the sin of the world.

Seeing Jesus coming towards him, John said, "Look, there is the lamb of God that takes away the sin of the world. This is the one I spoke of when I said: A man is coming after me who ranks before me because he existed before me. I did not know him myself, and yet it was to reveal him to Israel that I came baptising with water." John also declared, "I saw the Spirit coming down on him from heaven like a dove and resting on him. I did not know him myself, but he who sent me to baptise with water had said to me, 'The man on whom you see the Spirit come down and rest is the one who is going to baptise with the Holy Spirit.' Yes, I have seen and I am the witness that he is the Chosen One of God."

This is the Gospel of the Lord.

2nd SUNDAY OF THE YEAR

Year 2 (Year B)

First Reading   (3:3–10. 19)

A reading from the first book of Samuel
Speak, Lord, your servant is listening.

Samuel was lying in the sanctuary of the Lord where the ark of God was, when the Lord called, "Samuel! Samuel!" He answered, "Here I am." Then he ran to Eli and said, "Here I am, since you called me." Eli said, "I did not call. Go back and lie down." So he went and lay down. Once again the Lord called, "Samuel! Samuel!" Samuel got up and went to Eli and said, "Here I am, since you called me." He replied, "I did not call you, my son; go back and lie down." Samuel had as yet no knowledge of the Lord and the word of the Lord had not yet been revealed to him. Once again the Lord called, the third time. He got up and went to Eli and said, "Here I am, since you called me." Eli then understood that it was the Lord who was calling the boy, and he said to Samuel. "Go and lie down, and if someone calls say, 'Speak, Lord, your servant is listening.'" So Samuel went and lay down in his place.

The Lord then came and stood by, calling as he had done before, "Samuel! Samuel!" Samuel answered, "Speak, Lord, your servant is listening."

Samuel grew up and the Lord was with him and let no word of his fall to the ground.

This is the word of the Lord.

RESPONSORIAL PSALM, as for Year 1 (Year A), p. 197.

Second Reading   (6:13–15. 17–20)

A reading from the first letter of St Paul to the Corinthians
Your bodies are members making up the body of Christ.

The body is not meant for fornication; it is for the Lord,
and the Lord for the body. God who raised the Lord from
the dead, will by his power raise us up too.

You know, surely, that your bodies are members making
up the body of Christ; anyone who is joined to the Lord is
one spirit with him.

Keep away from fornication. All the other sins are committed outside the body; but to fornicate is to sin against
your own body. Your body, you know, is the temple of the
Holy Spirit, who is in you since you received him from God.
You are not your own property; you have been bought and
paid for. That is why you should use your body for the
glory of God.

This is the word of the Lord.

Alleluia   (1 Sam 3:9; Jn 6:68)

Alleluia, alleluia!
Speak, Lord, your servant is listening:
you have the message of eternal life.
Alleluia!

Alternative Alleluias p. 854.

Gospel   (1:35–42)

A reading from the holy Gospel according to John
They saw where he lived, and stayed with him.

As John stood with two of his disciples, Jesus passed, and
John stared hard at him and said, "Look, there is the lamb
of God." Hearing this, the two disciples followed Jesus.
Jesus turned round, saw them following and said, "What
do you want?" They answered, "Rabbi," – which means

Teacher – "where do you live?" "Come and see" he replied; so they went and saw where he lived, and stayed with him the rest of that day. It was about the tenth hour.

One of these two who became followers of Jesus after hearing what John had said was Andrew, the brother of Simon Peter. Early next morning, Andrew met his brother and said to him, "We have found the Messiah" – which means the Christ – and he took Simon to Jesus. Jesus looked hard at him and said, "You are Simon son of John; you are to be called Cephas" – meaning Rock.

This is the Gospel of the Lord.

2nd SUNDAY OF THE YEAR
Year 3 (Year C)

First Reading   (62:1–5)

A reading from the prophet Isaiah
The bridegroom rejoices in his bride.

About Zion I will not be silent,
about Jerusalem I will not grow weary,
until her integrity shines out like the dawn
and her salvation flames like a torch.

The nations then will see your integrity,
all the kings your glory,
and you will be called by a new name,
one which the mouth of the Lord will confer.
You are to be a crown of splendour in the hand of the Lord,
a princely diadem in the hand of your God;
no longer are you to be named "Forsaken",
nor your land "Abandoned",
but you shall be called "My Delight"
and your land "The Wedded";
for the Lord takes delight in you
and your land will have its wedding.

Like a young man marrying a virgin,
so will the one who built you wed you,
and as the bridegroom rejoices in his bride,
so will your God rejoice in you.

This is the word of the Lord.

Responsorial Psalm   (Ps 95:1–3. 7–10. *R.* v. 3)
Response
Proclaim the wonders of the Lord
among all the peoples.

1. O sing a new song to the Lord,
sing to the Lord all the earth.
O sing to the Lord, bless his name. (*R.*)

2. Proclaim his help day by day,
tell among the nations his glory
and his wonders among all the peoples. (*R.*)

3. Give the Lord, you families of peoples,
give the Lord glory and power,
give the Lord the glory of his name. (*R.*)

4. Worship the Lord in his temple.
O earth, tremble before him.
Proclaim to the nations: "God is king."
He will judge the peoples in fairness. (*R.*)

Second Reading   (12:4–11)
A reading from the first letter of St Paul to the Corinthians
*One and the same Spirit, who distributes gifts to different
people just as he chooses.*

There is a variety of gifts but always the same Spirit; there
are all sorts of service to be done, but always to the same
Lord; working in all sorts of different ways in different

people, it is the same God who is working in all of them. The particular way in which the Spirit is given to each person is for a good purpose. One may have the gift of preaching with wisdom given him by the Spirit; another may have the gift of preaching instruction given him by the same Spirit; and another the gift of faith given by the same Spirit; another again the gift of healing, through this one Spirit; one, the power of miracles; another, prophecy; another the gift of recognising spirits; another the gift of tongues and another the ability to interpret them. All these are the work of one and the same Spirit, who distributes different gifts to different people just as he chooses.

This is the word of the Lord.

Alleluia   (Jn 6:63. 68)

Alleluia, alleluia!
Your words are spirit, Lord,
and they are life:
you have the message of eternal life.
Alleluia!

Alternative Alleluias p. 854.

Gospel   (2:1–12)

A reading from the holy Gospel according to John
*This was the first of the signs given by Jesus: it was given at
Cana in Galilee.*

There was a wedding at Cana in Galilee. The mother of Jesus was there, and Jesus and his disciples had also been invited. When they ran out of wine, since the wine provided for the wedding was all finished, the mother of Jesus said to him, "They have no wine." Jesus said, "Woman, why turn to me? My hour has not come yet." His mother said to the servants, "Do whatever he tells you." There were six stone water jars standing there, meant for the ablutions that are customary among the Jews: each could hold twenty or thirty gallons. Jesus said to the servants, "Fill the jars with water," and they filled them to the brim. "Draw some out now" he told them "and take it to the steward." They did this; the steward tasted the water, and it had turned into wine. Having no idea where it came from – only the servants who had drawn the water knew – the steward called the bridegroom and said, "People generally serve the best wine first, and keep the cheaper sort till the guests have had plenty to drink; but you have kept the best wine till now."

This was the first of the signs given by Jesus: it was given at Cana in Galilee. He let his glory be seen, and his disciples believed in him. After this he went down to Capernaum with his mother and the brothers, but they stayed there only a few days.

This is the Gospel of the Lord.

MONDAY
Year I

First Reading   (5:1–10)

A reading from the letter to the Hebrews
Although he was Son, he learnt to obey through suffering.

Every high priest has been taken out of mankind and is appointed to act for men in their relations with God, to offer gifts and sacrifices for sins; and so he can sympathise with those who are ignorant or uncertain because he too lives in the limitations of weakness. That is why he has to make sin offerings for himself as well as for the people. No one takes this honour on himself, but each one is called by God, as Aaron was. Nor did Christ give himself the glory of becoming high priest, but he had it from the one who said to him: You are my son, today I have become your father, and in another text: You are a priest of the order of Melchizedek, and for ever. During his life on earth, he offered up prayer and entreaty, aloud and in silent tears, to the one who had the power to save him out of death, and he submitted so humbly that his prayer was heard. Although he was Son, he learnt to obey through suffering; but having been made perfect, he became for all who obey him the source of eternal salvation and was acclaimed by God with the title of high priest of the order of Melchizedek.

This is the word of the Lord.

Responsorial Psalm   (Ps 109:1–4. *R*. v. 4)

Response
You are a priest for ever,
a priest like Melchizedek of old.

1. The Lord's revelation to my Master:
"Sit on my right:
I will put your foes beneath your feet." (*R*.)

2.The Lord will send from Zion
your sceptre of power:
rule in the midst of all your foes. (*R*.)

3. A prince from the day of your birth
on the holy mountains;
from the womb before the daybreak I begot you. (*R*.)

4. The Lord has sworn an oath he will not change.
"You are a priest for ever,
a priest like Melchizedek of old." (*R*.)

ALLELUIA and GOSPEL. As for Year II, see p. 207.

Year II

First Reading   (15:16–23)

A reading from the first book of Samuel
Obedience is better than sacrifice. The Lord has rejected you as king.

Samuel said to Saul, "Stop! Let me tell you what the Lord said to me last night." Saul said, "Tell me." Samuel continued, "Small as you may be in your own eyes, are you not head of the tribes of Israel? The Lord has anointed you king over Israel. The Lord sent you on a mission and said to you, 'Go, put these sinners, the Amalekites, under the ban and make war on them until they are exterminated.' Why then did you not obey the voice of the Lord? Why did you fall on the booty and do what is displeasing to the Lord?" Saul replied to Samuel, "But I did obey the voice of the Lord. I went on the mission which the Lord gave me; I brought back Agag king of the Amalekites; I put the Amalekites under the ban. From the booty the people took the best sheep and oxen of what was under the ban to sacrifice them to the Lord your God in Gilgal." But Samuel replied:

"Is the pleasure of the Lord in holocausts and sacrifices
or in obedience to the voice of the Lord?
Yes, obedience is better than sacrifice,
submissiveness better than the fat of rams.
Rebellion is a sin of sorcery,
presumption a crime of teraphim.

"Since you have rejected the word of the Lord, he has rejected you as king."
This is the word of the Lord.

Responsorial Psalm   (Ps 49:8–9. 16–17. 21. 23. R. v. 23)
Response
I will show God's salvation to the upright.

1. "I find no fault with your sacrifices,
your offerings are always before me.
I do not ask more bullocks from your farms,
nor goats from among your herds. (R.)

2. "But how can you recite my commandments
and take my covenant on your lips,

you who despise my law
and throw my words to the winds. (*R.*)

3. "You do this, and should I keep silence?
Do you think that I am like you?
a sacrifice of thanksgiving honours me
and I will show God's salvation to the upright." (*R.*)

Years I and II

Alleluia   (1 Thess 2:13)

Alleluia, alleluia!
Accept God's message for what it really is:
God's message, and not some human thinking.
Alleluia!

Alternative Alleluias p. 847.

Gospel   (2:18–22)

A reading from the holy Gospel according to Mark
The bridegroom is with them.

One day when John's disciples and the Pharisees were fasting, some people came and said to Jesus, "Why is it that
John's disciples and the disciples of the Pharisees fast, but
your disciples do not?" Jesus replied, "Surely the bridegroom's attendants would never think of fasting while the
bridegroom is still with them? As long as they have the
bridegroom with them, they could not think of fasting. But
the time will come for the bridegroom to be taken away
from them, and then, on that day, they will fast. No one
sews a piece of unshrunken cloth on an old cloak; if he
does, the patch pulls away from it, the new from the old, and
the tear gets worse. And nobody puts new wine into old
wineskins; if he does, the wine will burst the skins, and the

wine is lost and the skins too. No! New wine, fresh skins!"

This is the Gospel of the Lord.

TUESDAY
Year I

First Reading   (6:10–20)

A reading from the letter to the Hebrews

In the hope that is held out to us we have an anchor for our
soul, as sure as it is firm.

God would not be so unjust as to forget all you have done,
the love that you have for his name or the services you have
done, and are still doing, for the saints. Our one desire is
that every one of you should go on showing the same earnestness to the end, to the perfect fulfilment of our hopes,
never growing careless, but imitating those who have the
faith and the perseverance to inherit the promises.

When God made the promise to Abraham, he swore by
his own self, since it was impossible for him to swear by
anyone greater: I will shower blessings on you and give
you many descendants. Because of that, Abraham perse-
vered and saw the promise fulfilled. Men, of course, swear
an oath by something greater than themselves, and between
men, confirmation by an oath puts an end to all dispute. In
the same way, when God wanted to make the heirs to the
promise thoroughly realise that his purpose was unalterable, he conveyed this by an oath; so that there would be
two unalterable things in which it was impossible for God
to be lying, and so that we, now we have found safety,
should have a strong encouragement to take a firm grip on
the hope that is held out to us. Here we have an anchor for
our soul, as sure as it is firm, and reaching right through
beyond the veil where Jesus has entered before us and on
our behalf, to become a high priest of the order of Melchizedek, and for ever.

This is the word of the Lord.

Responsorial Psalm　　　(Ps 110:1–2. 4–5. 9. 10. *R*. v. 5)

Response

The Lord keeps his covenant ever in mind.

Or: Alleluia!

1. Alleluia!
I will thank the Lord with all my heart
in the meeting of the just and their assembly.
Great are the works of the Lord;
to be pondered by all who love them. (*R*.)

2 He makes us remember his wonders.
The Lord is compassion and love.
He gives food to those who fear him;
keeps his covenant ever in mind. (*R*.)

3. He has sent deliverance to his people
and established his covenant for ever.
Holy his name, to be feared.
His praise shall last for ever! (*R*.)

ALLELUIA and GOSPEL. As for Year II, see p. 211.

Year II

First Reading　　　　　　　(16:1–13)

A reading from the first book of Samuel
*Samuel anointed David where he stood with his brothers; and
the Spirit of the Lord seized on David.*

The Lord said to Samuel, "How long will you go on mourning over Saul when I have rejected him as king of Israel?
Fill your horn with oil and go. I am sending you to Jesse
of Bethlehem, for I have chosen myself a king among his
sons." Samuel replied, "How can I go? When Saul hears of
it he will kill me." Then the Lord said, "Take a heifer with
you and say, 'I have come to sacrifice to the Lord.' Invite

Jesse to the sacrifice, and then I myself will tell you what you must do; you must anoint me the one I point out to you."

Samuel did what the Lord ordered and went to Bethlehem. The elders of the town came trembling to meet him and asked, "Seer, have you come with good intentions towards us?" "Yes," he replied "I have come to sacrifice to the Lord. Purify yourselves and come with me to the sacrifice." He purified Jesse and his sons and invited them to the sacrifice.

When they arrived, he caught sight of Eliab and thought, "Surely the Lord's anointed one stands there before him," but the Lord said to Samuel, "Take no notice of his appearance or his height for I have rejected him; God does not see as man sees; man looks at appearances but the Lord looks at the heart." Jesse then called Abinadab and presented him to Samuel, who said, "The Lord has not chosen this one either." Jesse then presented Shammah, but Samuel said, "The Lord has not chosen this one either." Jesse presented his seven sons to Samuel, but Samuel said to Jesse, "The Lord has not chosen these." He then asked Jesse, "Are these all the sons you have?" He answered, "There is still one left, the youngest; he is out looking after the sheep." Then Samuel said to Jesse, "Send for him; we will not sit down to eat until he comes." Jesse had him sent for, a boy of fresh complexion, with fine eyes and pleasant bearing. The Lord said, "Come, anoint him, for this is the one." At this, Samuel took the horn of oil and anointed him where he stood with his brothers; and the spirit of the Lord seized on David and stayed with him from that day on. As for Samuel, he rose and went to Ramah.

This is the word of the Lord.

Responsorial Psalm   (Ps 88:20–22. 27–28. R. v. 21)

Response
I have found David my servant.

1. Of old you spoke in a vision.
To your friends the prophets you said:
"I have set the crown on a warrior,
I have exalted one chosen from the people. (R.)

2. "I have found David my servant
and with my holy oil anointed him.
My hand shall always be with him
and my arm shall make him strong. (R.)

3. "He will say to me: 'You are my father,
my God, the rock who saves me.'
And I will make him my first-born,
the highest of the kings of the earth." (R.)

Years I and II

Alleluia   (Ps 118:18)

Alleluia, alleluia!
Open my eyes, O Lord, that I may consider
the wonders of your law.
Alleluia!

Alternative Alleluias p. 847.

Gospel   (2:23–28)

A reading from the holy Gospel according to Mark
The sabbath was made for man, not man for the sabbath.

One sabbath day Jesus happened to be taking a walk
through the cornfields, and his disciples began to pick ears
of corn as they went along. And the Pharisees said to him,
"Look, why are they doing something on the sabbath day
that is forbidden?" And he replied, "Did you never read
what David did in his time of need when he and his followers were hungry – how he went into the house of God when
Abiathar was high priest, and ate the loaves of offering

which only the priests are allowed to eat, and how he also gave some to the men with him?"

And he said to them. "The sabbath was made for man, not man for the sabbath; so the Son of Man is master even of the sabbath."

This is the Gospel of the Lord.

WEDNESDAY
Year I

First Reading   (7:1–3. 15–17)

A reading from the letter to the Hebrews
You are a priest of the order of Melchizedek, and for ever.

You remember that Melchizedek, king of Salem, a priest of God Most High, went to meet Abraham who was on his way back after defeating the kings, and blessed him; and also that it was to him that Abraham gave a tenth of all that he had. By the interpretation of his name, he is, first, "king of righteousness" and also king of Salem, that is, "king of peace"; he has no father, mother or ancestry, and his life has no beginning or ending; he is like the Son of God. He remains a priest for ever.

This becomes even more clearly evident when there appears a second Melchizedek, who is a priest not by virtue of a law about physical descent, but by the power of an indestructible life. For it was about him that the prophecy was made: You are a priest of the order of Melchizedek, and for ever.

This is the word of the Lord.

Responsorial Psalm   (Ps 109:1–4. *R.* v. 4)

Response
You are a priest for ever,
a priest like Melchizedek of old.

1. The Lord's revelation to my Master:
"Sit on my right:
I will put your foes beneath your feet." (*R.*)

2. The Lord will send from Zion
your sceptre of power;
rule in the midst of all your foes. (*R.*)

3. A prince from the day of your birth
on the holy mountains;
from the womb before the daybreak I begot you. (*R.*)

4. The Lord has sworn an oath he will not change.
"You are a priest for ever,
a priest like Melchizedek of old." (*R.*)

ALLELUIA and GOSPEL. As for Year II, see p. 215.

Year II

First Reading   (17:32–33. 37. 40–51)

A reading from the first book of Samuel
David triumphed over the Philistine with a sling and a stone.

David said to Saul, "Let no one lose heart on his account;
your servant will go and fight this Philistine." But Saul
answered David, "You cannot go and fight the Philistine;
you are only a boy and he has been a warrior from his
youth." "The Lord who rescued me from the claws of lion
and bear" David said "will rescue me from the power of
this Philistine." Then Saul said to David, "Go, and the Lord
be with you!"

He took his staff in his hand, picked five smooth stones
from the river bed, put them in his shepherd's bag, in his
pouch, and with his sling in his hand he went to meet the
Philistine. The Philistine, his shield-bearer in front of him,
came nearer and nearer to David; and the Philistine looked
at David, and what he saw filled him with scorn, because
David was only a youth, a boy of fresh complexion and
pleasant bearing. The Philistine said to him, "Am I a dog

for you to come against me with sticks?" And the Philistine cursed David by his gods. The Philistine said to David, "Come over here and I will give your flesh to the birds of the air and the beasts of the field." But David answered the Philistine, "You come against me with sword and spear and javelin, but I come against you in the name of the Lord of hosts, the God of the armies of Israel that you have dared to insult. Today the Lord will deliver you into my hand and I shall kill you; I will cut off your head, and this very day I will give your dead body and the bodies of the Philistine army to the birds of the air and the wild beasts of the earth, so that all the earth may know that there is a God in Israel, and that all this assembly may know that it is not by sword or by spear that the Lord gives the victory, for he is lord of the battle and he will deliver you into our power."

No sooner had the Philistine started forward to confront David than David left the line of battle and ran to meet the Philistine. Putting his hand in his bag, he took out a stone and slung it and struck the Philistine on the forehead; the stone penetrated his forehead and he fell on his face to the ground. Thus David triumphed over the Philistine with a sling and a stone and struck the Philistine down and killed him. David had no sword in his hand. Then David ran and, standing over the Philistine, seized his sword and drew it from the scabbard, and with this he killed him, cutting off his head. The Philistines saw that their champion was dead and took to flight.

This is the word of the Lord.

Responsorial Psalm   (Ps 143:1–2. 9–10. *R*. v. 1)

Response
Blessed be the Lord, my rock.

1. Blessed be the Lord, my rock
who trains my arms for battle,
who prepares my hands for war. (*R*.)

2. He is my love, my fortress;
he is my stronghold, my saviour,
my shield, my place of refuge.
He brings peoples under my rule. (R.)

3. To you, O God, will I sing a new song;
I will play on the ten-stringed lute
to you who give kings their victory,
who set David your servant free. (R.)

Years I and II

Alleluia (Heb 4:12)

Alleluia, alleluia!
The word of God is something alive and active;
it can judge secret emotions and thoughts.
Alleluia!

Alternative Alleluias p. 847.

Gospel (3:1–6)

A reading from the holy Gospel according to Mark
Is it against the law on the sabbath day to save life?

Jesus went into a synagogue, and there was a man there
who had a withered hand. And they were watching him to
see if he would cure him on the sabbath day, hoping for
something to use against him. He said to the man with the
withered hand, "Stand up out in the middle!" Then he said
to them, "Is it against the law on the sabbath day to do
good, or to do evil; to save life, or to kill?" But they said
nothing. Then, grieved to find them so obstinate, he looked
angrily round at them, and said to the man, "Stretch out
your hand." He stretched it out and his hand was better.
The Pharisees went out and at once began to plot with the
Herodians against him, discussing how to destroy him.

This is the Gospel of the Lord.

THURSDAY
Year I

First Reading (7:25–8:6)

A reading from the letter to the Hebrews
He offered sacrifices by offering himself once and for all.

The power of Jesus to save is utterly certain, since he is living for ever to intercede for all who come to God through him.

To suit us, the ideal high priest would have to be holy, innocent and uncontaminated, beyond the influence of sinners, and raised up above the heavens; one who would not need to offer sacrifices every day, as the other high priests do for their own sins and then for those of the people, because he has done this once and for all by offering himself. The Law appoints high priests who are men subject to weakness; but the promise on oath, which came after the Law, appointed the Son who is made perfect for ever.

The great point of all that we have said is that we have a high priest of exactly this kind. He has his place at the right of the throne of divine Majesty in the heavens, and he is the minister of the sanctuary and of the true Tent of Meeting which the Lord, and not any man, set up. It is the duty of every high priest to offer gifts and sacrifices, and so this one too must have something to offer. In fact, if he were on earth, he would not be a priest at all, since there are others who make offerings laid down by the Law and these only maintain the service of a model or a reflection of the heavenly realities. For Moses, when he had the Tent to build, was warned by God who said: See that you make everything according to the pattern shown you on the mountain.

We have seen that he has been given a ministry of a far higher order, and to the same degree it is a better covenant of which he is the mediator, founded on better promises.

This is the word of the Lord.

Responsorial Psalm   (Ps 39:7–10. 17. *R.* vv. 8. 9)

Response
Behold, Lord, I come to do your will.

1. You do not ask for sacrifice and offerings,
but an open ear.
You do not ask for holocaust and victim.
Instead, here am I. (*R.*)

2. In the scroll of the book it stands written
that I should do your will.
My God, I delight in your law
in the depth of my heart. (*R.*)

3. Your justice I have proclaimed
in the great assembly.
My lips I have not sealed;
you know it, O Lord. (*R.*)

4. O let there be rejoicing and gladness
for all who seek you.
Let them ever say: "The Lord is great".
who love your saving help. (*R.*)

ALLELUIA and GOSPEL. As for Year II, see p. 219.

Year II

First Reading   (18:6–9; 19:1–7)

A reading from the first book of Samuel
My father Saul is looking for a way to kill you.

On their way back, as David was returning after killing the
Philistine, the women came out to meet King Saul from all
the towns of Israel, singing and dancing to the sound of
tambourine and lyre and cries of joy; and as they danced
the women sang:

"Saul has killed his thousands,
and David his tens of thousands."

Saul was very angry; the incident was not to his liking.
"They have given David the tens of thousands," he said
"but me only the thousands; he has all but the kingship
now." And Saul turned a jealous eye on David from that
day forward.

Saul told Jonathan his son and all his servants of his
intention to kill David. Now Jonathan, Saul's son, held
David in great affection; and so Jonathan warned David;
"My father Saul is looking for a way to kill you," he said,
"so be on your guard tomorrow morning; hide away in
some secret place. Then I will go out and keep my father
company in the fields where you are hiding, and will talk to
my father about you; I will find out what the situation is
and let you know."

So Jonathan spoke well of David to Saul his father; he
said, "Let not the king sin against his servant David, for he
has not sinned against you, and what he has done has been
greatly to your advantage. He took his life in his hands
when he killed the Philistine, and the Lord brought about a
great victory for all Israel. You saw it yourself and rejoiced;
why then sin against innocent blood in killing David without cause?" Saul was impressed by Jonathan's words and
took an oath, "As the Lord lives, I will not kill him," Jonathan called David and told him all these things. Then Jonathan brought him to Saul, and David attended on him as
before.

This is the word of the Lord.

Responsorial Psalm   (Ps 55:2–3. 9–14. R̸. v. 5)

Response
In God I trust, I shall not fear.

1. Have mercy on me, God, men crush me;
they fight me all day long and oppress me.

My foes crush me all the day long,
for many fight proudly against me. (*R.*)

2. You have kept an account of my wanderings;
you have kept a record of my tears;
(are they not written in your book?)
Then my foes will be put to flight
on the day that I call to you. (*R.*)

3. This I know, that God is on my side.
In God, whose word I praise,
in the Lord, whose word I praise,
in God I trust; I shall not fear:
what can mortal man do to me? (*R.*)

4. I am bound by the vows I have made you.
O God, I will offer you praise
for you rescued my soul from death,
you kept my feet from stumbling
that I may walk in the presence of God
in the light of the living. (*R.*)

Years I and II

Alleluia   (Jn 6:63. 68)

Alleluia, alleluia!
Your words are spirit, Lord,
and they are life:
you have the message of eternal life.
Alleluia!

Alternative Alleluias p. 847.

Gospel   (3:7–12)

A reading from the holy Gospel according to Mark
The unclean spirits would shout, 'You are the Son of God!'
But he warned them strongly not to make him known.

Jesus withdrew with his disciples to the lakeside, and great crowds from Galilee followed him. From Judaea, Jerusalem, Idumaea, Transjordania and the region of Tyre and Sidon, great numbers who had heard of all he was doing came to him. And he asked his disciples to have a boat ready for him because of the crowd, to keep him from being crushed. For he had cured so many that all who were afflicted in any way were crowding forward to touch him. And the unclean spirits, whenever they saw him, would fall down before him and shout, "You are the Son of God!" But he warned them strongly not to make him known.

This is the Gospel of the Lord.

FRIDAY

Year I

First Reading (8:6–13)

A reading from the letter to the Hebrews
It is a better covenant of which he is the mediator.

We have seen that Jesus has been given a ministry of a far higher order, and to the same degree it is a better covenant of which he is the mediator, founded on better promises. If that first covenant had been without a fault, there would have been no need for a second one to replace it. And in fact God does find fault with them; he says:

See, the days are coming – it is the Lord who speaks –
when I will establish a new covenant
with the House of Israel and the House of Judah,
but not a covenant like the one I made with their ancestors
on the day I took them by the hand
to bring them out of the land of Egypt.
They abandoned that covenant of mine,
and so I on my side deserted them. It is the Lord who
    speaks.

No, this is the covenant I will make
with the House of Israel
when those days arrive – it is the Lord who speaks.
I will put my laws into their minds
and write them on their hearts.
Then I will be their God
and they shall be my people.
There will be no further need for neighbour to try to teach
    neighbour,
or brother to say to brother,
"Learn to know the Lord."
No, they will all know me,
the least no less than the greatest,
since I will forgive their iniquities
and never call their sins to mind.

By speaking of a new covenant, he implies that the first one
is already old. Now anything old only gets more antiquated
until in the end it disappears.

　　This is the word of the Lord.

Responsorial Psalm   (Ps 84:8. 10–14. *R*. v. 11)
Response

Mercy and faithfulness have met.

1. Let us see, O Lord, your mercy
and give us your saving help.
His help is near for those who fear him
and his glory will dwell in our land. (*R*.)

2. Mercy and faithfulness have met;
justice and peace have embraced.
Faithfulness shall spring from the earth
and justice look down from heaven. (*R*.)

3. The Lord will make us prosper
and our earth shall yield its fruit.
Justice shall march before him
and peace shall follow his steps. (*R*.)

ALLELUIA and GOSPEL. As for Year 11, see p. 224.

Year II

First Reading (24:3–21)

A reading from the first book of Samuel

I will not raise my hand against him, for he is the anointed of the Lord.

Saul took three thousand men chosen from the whole of Israel and went in search of David and his men east of the Rocks of the Wild Goats. He came to the sheep-folds along the route where there was a cave, and went in to cover his feet. Now David and his men were sitting in the recesses of the cave; David's men said to him, "Today is the day of which the Lord said to you, 'I will deliver your enemy into your power, do what you like with him.'" David stood up and, unobserved, cut off the border of Saul's cloak. Afterwards David reproached himself for having cut off the border of Saul's cloak. He said to his men, "The Lord preserve me from doing such a thing to my lord and raising my hand against him, for he is the anointed of the Lord." David gave his men strict instructions, forbidding them to attack Saul.

Saul then left the cave and went on his way. After this David too left the cave and called after Saul, "My lord king!" Saul looked behind him and David bowed to the ground and did homage. Then David said to Saul, "Why do you listen to the men who say to you, 'David means to harm you'? Why, your own eyes have seen today how the Lord put you in my power in the cave and how I refused to kill you, but spared you. 'I will not raise my hand against my lord,' I said 'for he is the anointed of the Lord.' O my

father, see, look at the border of your cloak in my hand.
Since I cut off the border of your cloak, yet did not kill you,
you must acknowledge frankly that there is neither malice
nor treason in my mind. I have not offended against you,
yet you hunt me down to take my life. May the Lord be
judge between me and you, and may the Lord avenge me
on you; but my hand shall not be laid on you. (As the old
proverb says: Wickedness goes out from the wicked, and
my hand will not be laid on you.) On whose trail has the
king of Israel set out? On whose trail are you in hot pur-
suit? On the trail of a dead dog! On the trail of a single
flea! May the Lord be the judge and decide between me and
you; may he take up my cause and defend it and give judgement for me, freeing me from your power."

When David had finished saying these words to Saul,
Saul said, "Is that your voice, my son David?" And Saul
wept aloud. "You are a more upright man than I," he said
to David "for you have repaid me with good while I have
repaid you with evil. Today you have crowned your goodness toward me since the Lord had put me in your power
yet you did not kill me. When a man comes on his enemy,
does he let him go unmolested? May the Lord reward you
for the goodness you have shown me today. Now I know
you will indeed reign and that the sovereignty in Israel will
be secure in your hands."

This is the word of the Lord.

Responsorial Psalm   (Ps 56:2–4. 6. 11. *R*. v. 2)
Response

Have mercy on me, God, have mercy.

1. Have mercy on me, God, have mercy
for in you my soul has taken refuge.
In the shadow of your wings I take refuge
till the storms of destruction pass by. (*R*.)

2. I call to God the Most High,
to God who has always been my help.
May he send from heaven and save me
and shame those who assail me.
May God send his truth and his love. (*R.*)

3. O God, arise above the heavens;
may your glory shine on earth!
for your love reaches to the heavens
and your truth to the skies. (*R.*)

Years I and II

Alleluia   (2 Thess 2:14)

Alleluia, alleluia!
Through the Good News God called us
to share the glory of our Lord Jesus Christ.
Alleluia!

Alternative Alleluias p. 847.

Gospel   (3:13–19)

A reading from the holy Gospel according to Mark
He summoned those he wanted to be his companions.

Jesus went up into the hills and summoned those he wanted. So they came to him and he appointed twelve; they were to be his companions and to be sent out to preach, with power to cast out devils. And so he appointed the Twelve: Simon to whom he gave the name Peter, James the son of Zebedee and John the brother of James, to whom he gave the name Boanerges or "Sons of Thunder"; then Andrew, Philip, Bartholomew, Matthew, Thomas, James the son of Alphaeus, Thaddaeus, Simon the Zealot and Judas Iscariot, the man who was to betray him.

This is the Gospel of the Lord.

SATURDAY

Year I

First Reading (9:2–3. 11–14)

A reading from the letter to the Hebrews

He has entered the sanctuary once and for all through his own blood.

There was a tent which comprised two compartments: the first, in which the lamp-stand, the table and the presentation loaves were kept, was called the Holy Place; then beyond the second veil, an innermost part which was called the Holy of Holies.

But now Christ has come, as the high priest of all the blessings which were to come. He has passed through the greater, the more perfect tent, which is better than the one made by men's hands because it is not of this created order; and he has entered the sanctuary once and for all, taking with him not the blood of goats and bull calves, but his own blood, having won an eternal redemption for us. The blood of goats and bulls and the ashes of a heifer are sprinkled on those who have incurred defilement and they restore the holiness of their outward lives; how much more effectively the blood of Christ, who offered himself as the perfect sacrifice to God through the eternal Spirit, can purify our inner self from dead actions so that we do our service to the living God.

This is the word of the Lord.

Responsorial Psalm (Ps 46:2–3. 6–9. *R.* v. 6)

Response
God goes up with shouts of joy;
the Lord goes up with trumpet blast.

1. All peoples, clap your hands,
cry to God with shouts of joy!

For the Lord, the Most High, we must fear,
great king over all the earth. (R.)

2. God goes up with shouts of joy;
the Lord goes up with trumpet blast.
Sing praise for God, sing praise,
sing praise to our king, sing praise. (R.)

3. God is king of all the earth.
Sing praise with all your skill.
God is king over the nations;
God reigns on his holy throne. (R.)

ALLELUIA and GOSPEL. As for Year II, see p. 228.

Year II

First Reading   (1:1–4. 11–12. 17. 19. 23–27)

A reading from the second book of Samuel
How did the heroes fall in the thick of the battle.

After the death of Saul, David returned from his rout of the Amalekites and spent two days in Ziklag. On the third day a man came from the camp where Saul had been, his garments torn and earth on his head. When he came to David, he fell to the ground and did homage. "Where do you come from?" David asked him. "I have escaped from the Israelite camp," he said. David said to him, "What happened? Tell me." He replied, "The people have fled from the battlefield and many of them have fallen. Saul and his son Jonathan are dead too."

Then David took hold of his garments and tore them, and all the men did the same. They mourned and wept and fasted until the evening for Saul and his son Jonathan, for the people of the Lord and for the House of Israel, because they had fallen by the sword.

Then David made this lament over Saul and his son Jonathan:

Alas, the glory of Israel has been slain on your heights!
How did the heroes fall?

Saul and Jonathan, loved and lovely,
neither in life, nor in death, were divided.

Swifter than eagles were they,
stronger were they than lions.

O daughters of Israel, weep for Saul
who clothed you in scarlet and fine linen,
who set brooches of gold
on your garments.

How did the heroes fall
in the thick of the battle?

O Jonathan, in your death I am stricken,
I am desolate for you, Jonathan my brother.
Very dear to me you were,
your love to me more wonderful
than the love of a woman.

How did the heroes fall
and the battle armour fail?

This is the word of the Lord.

Responsorial Psalm   (Ps 79:2–3. 5–7. R. v. 4)
Response
Let your face shine on us, O Lord,
and we shall be saved.

1. O shepherd of Israel, hear us,
you who lead Joseph's flock,
shine forth from your cherubim throne
upon Ephraim, Benjamin, Manasseh.
O Lord, rouse up your might,
O Lord, come to our help. (R.)

2. Lord God of hosts, how long
will you frown on your people's plea?
You have fed them with tears for their bread,
an abundance of tears for their drink.
You have made us the taunt of our neighbours,
our enemies laugh us to scorn.(R.)

Years I and II

Alleluia (2 Cor 5:19)

Alleluia, alleluia!
God in Christ was reconciling the world to himself,
and he has entrusted to us the news that they are reconciled.
Alleluia!

Alternative Alleluias p. 847.

Gospel (3:20–21)

A reading from the holy Gospel according to Mark
His relatives said he was out of his mind.

Jesus went home, and such a crowd collected that they could
not even have a meal. When his relatives heard of this, they
set out to take charge of him, convinced he was out of his
mind.
    This is the Gospel of the Lord.

3rd SUNDAY OF THE YEAR
Year 1 (Year A)

First Reading   (8:23–9:3)

A reading from the prophet Isaiah
In Galilee of the nations the people has seen a great light.

In days past the Lord humbled the land of Zebulun and the
land of Naphtali, but in days to come he will confer glory
on the Way of the Sea on the far side of Jordan, province
of the nations.

The people that walked in darkness
has seen a great light;
on those who live in a land of deep shadow
a light has shone.
You have made their gladness greater,
you have made their joy increase;
they rejoice in your presence
as men rejoice at harvest time,
as men are happy when they are dividing the spoils.

For the yoke that was weighing on him,
the bar across his shoulders,
the rod of his oppressor,
these you break as on the day of Midian.

This is the word of the Lord.

Responsorial Psalm   (Ps 26:1. 4. 13–14. *R*. v. 1)

Response
The Lord is my light and my help.

1. The Lord is my light and my help;
whom shall I fear?
The Lord is the stronghold of my life;
before whom shall I shrink? (*R*.)

2. There is one thing I ask of the Lord,
for this I long,
to live in the house of the Lord,
all the days of my life,
to savour the sweetness of the Lord,
to behold his temple. (*R.*)

3. I am sure I shall see the Lord's goodness
in the land of the living.
Hope in him, hold firm and take heart.
Hope in the Lord! (*R.*)

Second Reading   (1:10–13. 17)

A reading from the first letter of St Paul to the Corinthians
*Make up the differences between you instead of disagreeing
among yourselves.*

I do appeal to you, brothers, for the sake of our Lord Jesus
Christ, to make up the differences between you, and instead
of disagreeing among yourselves, to be united again in your
belief and practice. From what Chloe's people have been
telling me, my dear brothers, it is clear that there are serious
differences among you. What I mean are all these slogans
that you have, like: "I am for Paul", "I am for Apollos",
"I am for Cephas", "I am for Christ". Has Christ been
parcelled out? Was it Paul that was crucified for you? Were
you baptised in the name of Paul?

   For Christ did not send me to baptise, but to preach the
Good News, and not to preach that in the terms of philosophy in which the crucifixion of Christ cannot be expressed.

   This is the word of the Lord.

Alleluia   (Mt 4:23)

Alleluia, alleluia!
Jesus proclaimed the Good News of the kingdom,

and cured all kinds of sickness among the people.
Alleluia!

Gospel   (4:12–23)

A reading from the holy Gospel according to Matthew
He went and settled in Capernaum: in this way the prophecy
of Isaiah was to be fulfilled.

*Hearing that John had been arrested Jesus went back to
Galilee, and leaving Nazareth he went and settled in Capernaum, a lakeside town on the borders of Zebulun and Naphtali. In this way the prophecy of Isaiah was to be fulfilled:

Land of Zebulun! Land of Naphtali!
Way of the sea on the far side of Jordan,
Galilee of the nations!
The people that lived in darkness
has seen a great light;
on those who dwell in the land and shadow of death
a light has dawned.

From that moment Jesus began his preaching with the
message, "Repent, for the kingdom of heaven is close at
hand."*

As he was walking by the Sea of Galilee he saw two brothers, Simon, who was called Peter, and his brother Andrew;
they were making a cast in the lake with their net, for they
were fishermen. And he said to them, "Follow me and I will
make you fishers of men." And they left their nets at once
and followed him.

Going on from there he saw another pair of brothers,
James son of Zebedee and his brother John; they were in
their boat with their father Zebedee, mending their nets,
and he called them. At once, leaving the boat and their
father, they followed him.

He went round the whole of Galilee teaching in their

synagogues, proclaiming the Good News of the kingdom and curing all kinds of diseases and sickness among the people.

| *This is the Gospel of the Lord.*

Shorter form, verses 12–17. Read between.

3rd SUNDAY OF THE YEAR

Year 2 (Year B)

First Reading   (3:1–5. 10)

A reading from the prophet Jonah
The people of Nineveh renounce their evil behaviour.

The word of the Lord was addressed a second time to Jonah: "Up!" he said "Go to Nineveh, the great city, and preach to them as I told you to." Jonah set out and went to Nineveh in obedience to the word of the Lord. Now Nineveh was a city great beyond compare: it took three days to cross it. Jonah went on into the city, making a day's journey. He preached in these words, "Only forty days more and Nineveh is going to be destroyed." And the people of Nineveh believed in God; they proclaimed a fast and put on sackcloth, from the greatest to the least.

God saw their efforts to renounce their evil behaviour. And God relented: he did not inflict on them the disaster which he had threatened.

This is the word of the Lord.

Responsorial Psalm   (Ps 24:4–9. *R.* v. 4)

Response
Lord, make me know your ways.

1. Lord, make me know your ways.
Lord, teach me your paths.
Make me walk in your truth, and teach me:
for you are God my saviour. (*R.*)

2. Remember your mercy, Lord,
and the love you have shown from of old.
In your love remember me,
because of your goodness, O Lord. (*R.*)

3. The Lord is good and upright.
He shows the path to those who stray,
He guides the humble in the right path;
he teaches his way to the poor. (*R.*)

Second Reading   (7:29–31)

A reading from the first letter of St Paul to the Corinthians
The world as we know it is passing away.

Brothers, this is what I mean: our time is growing short.
Those who have wives should live as though they had none,
and those who mourn should live as though they had nothing to mourn for; those who are enjoying life should live as
though there were nothing to laugh about; those whose life
is buying things should live as though they had nothing of
their own; and those who have to deal with the world should
not become engrossed in it. I say this because the world as
we know it is passing away.

   This is the word of the Lord.

Alleluia   (Mk 1:15)

Alleluia, alleluia!
The kingdom of God is close at hand;
believe the Good News.
Alleluia!

Gospel   (1:14–20)

A reading from the holy Gospel according to Mark
Repent, and believe the Good News.

After John had been arrested, Jesus went into Galilee. There he proclaimed the Good News from God. "The time has come" he said "and the kingdom of God is close at hand. Repent, and believe the Good News."

As he was walking along by the Sea of Galilee he saw Simon and his brother Andrew casting a net in the lake – for they were fishermen. And Jesus said to them, "Follow me and I will make you into fishers of men." And at once they left their nets and followed him.

Going on a little further, he saw James son of Zebedee and his brother John; they too were in their boat, mending their nets. He called them at once and, leaving their father Zebedee in the boat with the men he employed, they went after him.

This is the Gospel of the Lord.

3rd SUNDAY OF THE YEAR

Year 3 (Year C)

First Reading   (8:2–6. 8–10)

A reading from the book of Nehemiah
Ezra read from the law of God and the people understood what was read.

Ezra the priest brought the Law before the assembly, consisting of men, women, and children old enough to understand. This was the first day of the seventh month. On the square before the Water Gate, in the presence of the men and women, and children old enough to understand, he read from the book from early morning till noon; all the people listened attentively to the Book of the Law.

Ezra the scribe stood on a wooden dais erected for the purpose. In full view of all the people – since he stood higher than all the people – Ezra opened the book; and when he opened it all the people stood up. Then Ezra blessed the Lord, the great God, and all the people raised their hands and answered, "Amen! Amen!"; then they bowed down and, face to the ground, prostrated themselves before the Lord. And Ezra read from the Law of God, translating and giving the sense, so that the people understood what was read.

Then (Nehemiah – His Excellency – and) Ezra, priest and scribe (and the Levites who were instructing the people) said to all the people, "This day is sacred to the Lord your God. Do not be mournful, do not weep." For the people were all in tears as they listened to the words of the Law.

He then said, "Go, eat the fat, drink the sweet wine, and send a portion to the man who has nothing prepared ready. For this day is sacred to our Lord. Do not be sad: the joy of the Lord is your stronghold."

This is the word of the Lord.

Responsorial Psalm (Ps 18:8–10. 15. R. Jn 6:63)

Response
Your words are spirit, Lord,
and they are life.

1. The law of the Lord is perfect,
it revives the soul.
The rule of the Lord is to be trusted,
it gives wisdom to the simple. (R.)

2. The precepts of the Lord are right,
they gladden the heart.
The command of the Lord is clear,
it gives light to the eyes. (R.)

3. The fear of the Lord is holy,
abiding for ever.
The decrees of the Lord are truth
my rescuer, my rock! (R.)

4. May the spoken words of my mouth,
the thoughts of my heart,
win favour in your sight, O Lord,
my rescuer, my rock! (*R*.)

Second Reading   (12:12–30)

A reading from the first letter of St Paul to the Corinthians
You together are Christ's body; but each of you is a different part of it.

*Just as a human body, though it is made up of many parts, is a single unit because all these parts, though many, make one body, so it is with Christ. In the one Spirit we were all baptised, Jews as well as Greeks, slaves as well as citizens, and one Spirit was given to us all to drink.

Nor is the body to be identified with any one of its many parts.* If the foot were to say, "I am not a hand and so I do not belong to the body", would that mean that it stopped being part of the body? If the ear were to say, "I am not an eye, and so I do not belong to the body," would that mean that it was not a part of the body? If your whole body was just one eye, how would you hear anything? If it was just one ear, how would you smell anything?

Instead of that, God put all the separate parts into the body on purpose. If all the parts were the same, how could it be a body? As it is, the parts are many but the body is one. The eye cannot say to the hand, "I do not need you," nor can the head say to the feet, "I do not need you."

What is more, it is precisely the parts of the body that seem to be the weakest which are the indispensable ones; and it is the least honourable parts of the body that we clothe with the greatest care. So our more improper parts get decorated in a way that our more proper parts do not need. God has arranged the body so that more dignity is given to the parts which are without it, and so that there

may not be disagreements inside the body, but that each
part may be equally concerned for all the others. If one part
is hurt, all parts are hurt with it. If one part is given special
honour, all parts enjoy it.

*Now you together are Christ's body; but each of you
is a different part of it.* In the Church, God has given the
first place to apostles, the second to prophets, the third to
teachers; after them, miracles, and after them the gift of
healing; helpers, good leaders, those with many languages.
Are all of them apostles, or all of them prophets, or all of
them teachers? Do they all have the gift of miracles, or all
have the gift of healing? Do all speak strange languages,
and all interpret them?

This is the word of the Lord.

Shorter form, verses 12–14. 17. Read between.

Alleluia   (Lk 4:18–19)

Alleluia, alleluia!
The Lord has sent me
to bring the Good News to the poor,
to proclaim liberty to the captives.
Alleluia!

Gospel   (1:1–4; 4:14–21)

A reading from the holy Gospel according to Luke
This text is being fulfilled today.

Seeing that many others have undertaken to draw up accounts of the events that have taken place among us, exactly
as these were handed down to us by those who from the
outset were eyewitnesses and ministers of the word, I in my
turn, after carefully going over the whole story from the
beginning, have decided to write an ordered account for
you, Theophilus, so that your Excellency may learn how
well founded the teaching is that you have received.

Jesus, with the power of the Spirit in him, returned to Galilee; and his reputation spread throughout the countryside. He taught in their synagogues and everyone praised him.

He came to Nazara, where he had been brought up, and went into the synagogue on the sabbath day as he usually did. He stood up to read, and they handed him the scroll of the prophet Isaiah. Unrolling the scroll he found the place where it is written:

The spirit of the Lord has been given to me,
for he has anointed me.
He has sent me to bring the good news to the poor,
to proclaim liberty to captives
and to the blind new sight,
to set the downtrodden free,
to proclaim the Lord's year of favour.

He then rolled up the scroll, gave it back to the assistant and sat down. And all eyes in the synagogue were fixed on him. Then he began to speak to them, "This text is being fulfilled today even as you listen."

This is the Gospel of the Lord.

MONDAY
Year I

First Reading (9:15. 24–28)

A reading from the letter to the Hebrews
He sacrificed himself once and for all to do away with sin; when he appears a second time it will be to those who are waiting for him.

Christ brings a new covenant, as the mediator, only so that the people who were called to an eternal inheritance may actually receive what was promised: his death took place to cancel the sins that infringed the earlier covenant. It is not as though Christ had entered a man-made sanctuary which was only modelled on the real one; but it was heaven itself, so that he could appear in the actual presence of God on our behalf. And he does not have to offer himself again and again, like the high priest going into the sanctuary year after year with the blood that is not his own, or else he would have had to suffer over and over again since the world began. Instead of that, he has made his appearance once and for all, now at the end of the last age, to do away with sin by sacrificing himself. Since men only die once, and after that comes judgement, so Christ, too, offers himself only once to take the faults of many on himself, and when he appears a second time, it will not be to deal with sin but to reward with salvation those who are waiting for him.

This is the word of the Lord.

Responsorial Psalm   (Ps 97:1–6. *R*. v. 1)

Response

Sing a new song to the Lord
for he has worked wonders.

1. Sing a new song to the Lord
for he has worked wonders.
His right hand and his holy arm
have brought salvation. (*R*.)

2. The Lord has made known his salvation;
has shown his justice to the nations.
He has remembered his truth and love
for the house of Israel (*R*.)

3. All the ends of the earth have seen
the salvation of our God.

Shout to the Lord all the earth,
ring out your joy. (*R.*)

4. Sing psalms to the Lord with the harp
with the sound of music.
With trumpets and the sound of the horn
acclaim the King, the Lord. (*R.*)

ALLELUIA and GOSPEL. As for Year II, see p. 241.

Year II

First Reading   (5:1–7. 10)

A reading from the second book of Samuel
You shall be shepherd of my people Israel.

All the tribes of Israel came to David at Hebron. "Look" they said "we are your own flesh and blood. In days past when Saul was our king, it was you who led Israel in all their exploits; and the Lord said to you, 'You are the man who shall be shepherd of my people Israel, you shall be the leader of Israel.'" So all the elders of Israel came to the king at Hebron, and King David made a pact with them at Hebron in the presence of the Lord, and they anointed David king of Israel.

David was thirty years old when he became king, and he reigned for forty years. He reigned in Hebron over Judah for seven years and six months; then he reigned in Jerusalem over all Israel and Judah for thirty-three years.

David and his men marched on Jerusalem against the Jebusites living there. These said to David, "You will not get in here. The blind and the lame will hold you off." (That is to say: David will never get in here.) But David captured the fortress of Zion, that is, the Citadel of David.

He grew greater and greater, and the Lord, the God of hosts, was with him.

This is the word of the Lord.

Responsorial Psalm   (Ps 88:20–22. 25–26. *R*. v. 25)

Response
My truth and my love shall be with him.

1. Of old you spoke in a vision.
To your friends the prophets you said:
"I have set the crown on a warrior,
I have exalted one chosen from the people. (*R*.)

2. I have found David my servant
and with my holy oil anointed him.
My hand shall always be with him
and my arm shall make him strong. (*R*.)

3. My truth and my love shall be with him;
by my name his might shall be exalted.
I will stretch out his hand to the Sea
and his right hand as far as the River." (*R*.)

Years I and II

Alleluia   (Ps 24:4. 5)

Alleluia, alleluia!
Teach me your paths, my God,
make me walk in your truth.
Alleluia!

Alternative Alleluias p. 847.

Gospel   (3:22–30)

A reading from the holy Gospel according to Mark
It is the end of Satan.

The scribes who had come down from Jerusalem were saying: "Beelzebul is in him" and, "It is through the prince of
devils that he casts devils out." So Jesus called them to him

and spoke to them in parables, "How can Satan cast out Satan? If a kingdom is divided against itself, that kingdom cannot last. And if a household is divided against itself, that household can never stand. Now if Satan has rebelled against himself and is divided, he cannot stand either – it is the end of him. But no one can make his way into a strong man's house and burgle his property unless he has tied up the strong man first. Only then can he burgle his house.

"I tell you solemnly, all men's sins will be forgiven, and all their blasphemies; but let anyone blaspheme against the Holy Spirit and he will never have forgiveness: he is guilty of an eternal sin." This was because they were saying, "An unclean spirit is in him."

This is the Gospel of the Lord.

TUESDAY
Year I

First Reading   (10:1–10)

A reading from the letter to the Hebrews
God, here I am! I am coming to obey your will.

Since the Law has no more than a reflection of these realities, and no finished picture of them, it is quite incapable of bringing the worshippers to perfection, with the same sacrifices repeatedly offered year after year. Otherwise, the offering of them would have stopped, because the worshippers, when they had been purified once, would have no awareness of sins. Instead of that, the sins are recalled year after year in the sacrifices. Bulls' blood and goats' blood are useless for taking away sins, and this is what he said, on coming into the world:

You who wanted no sacrifice or oblation,
prepared a body for me.

You took no pleasure in holocausts or sacrifices for sin;
then I said,
just as I was commanded in the scroll of the book,
"God, here I am! I am coming to obey your will."

Notice that he says first: You did not want what the Law
lays down as the things to be offered, that is: the sacrifices,
the oblations, the holocausts and the sacrifices for sin, and
you took no pleasure in them; and then he says: Here I am!
I am coming to obey your will. He is abolishing the first sort
to replace it with the second. And this will was for us to be
made holy by the offering of his body made once and for all
by Jesus Christ.

This is the word of the Lord.

Responsorial Psalm   (Ps 39: 2. 4. 7–8. 10. 11. *R*. vv. 8. 9)
Response
Behold, I come to do your will,
O my God.

1. I waited, I waited for the Lord
and he stooped down to me.
He put a new song into my mouth,
praise of our God. (*R*.)

2. You do not ask for sacrifice and offerings,
but an open ear.
You do not ask for holocaust and victim.
Instead, here am I. (*R*.)

3. Your justice I have proclaimed
in the great assembly.
My lips I have not sealed;
you know it, O Lord. (*R*.)

4. I have not hidden your justice in my heart
but declared your faithful help.
I have not hidden your love and your truth
from the great assembly. (*R.*)

ALLELUIA and GOSPEL. As for Year II see p. 245.

Year II

First Reading (6:12–15. 17–19)

A reading from the second book of Samuel
*David and all the house of Israel brought up the ark of the
Lord with acclaim.*

David went and brought the ark of God up from Obed-
edom's house to the Citadel of David with great rejoicing.
When the bearers of the ark of the Lord had gone six paces,
he sacrificed an ox and a fat sheep. And David danced
whirling round before the Lord with all his might, wearing
a linen loincloth round him. Thus David and all the House
of Israel brought up the ark of the Lord with acclaim and
the sound of the horn. They brought the ark of the Lord
and put it in position inside the tent that David had pitched
for it; and David offered holocausts before the Lord, and
communion sacrifices. And when David had finished offering holocausts and communion sacrifices, he blessed the
people in the name of the Lord of hosts. He then distributed
among all the people, among the whole multitude of Israelites, men and women, a roll of bread to each, a portion of
dates, and a raisin cake. Then they all went away, each to
his own house.

    This is the word of the Lord.

Responsorial Psalm (Ps 23:7–10. *R.* v. 8)

Response
Who is the king of glory?
He, the Lord, he is the king of glory.

1. O gates, lift high your heads;
grow higher, ancient doors.
Let him enter, the king of glory! (R.)

2. Who is the king of glory?
The Lord, the mighty, the valiant,
the Lord, the valiant in war. (R.)

3. O gates, lift high your heads;
grow higher, ancient doors.
Let him enter, the king of glory! (R.)

4. Who is he, the king of glory?
He, the Lord of armies,
he is the king of glory. (R.)

Years I and II

Alleluia (Ps 118:135)

Alleluia, alleluia!
Let your face shine on your servant,
and teach me your decrees.
Alleluia!

Alternative Alleluias p. 847.

Gospel (3:31–35)

A reading from the holy Gospel according to Mark
*Anyone who does the will of God, that person is my brother and
sister and mother.*

The mother and brothers of Jesus arrived and, standing
outside, sent in a message asking for him. A crowd was
sitting round him at the time the message was passed to him,
'Your mother and brothers and sisters are outside asking
for you." He replied, "Who are my mother and my brothers?" And looking round at those sitting in a circle about

him, he said, "Here are my mother and my brothers. Anyone who does the will of God, that person is my brother and
sister and mother."

This is the Gospel of the Lord.

WEDNESDAY

Year I

First Reading   (10:11–18)

A reading from the letter to the Hebrews
He achieved the eternal perfection of all whom he is sanctifying.

All the priests stand at their duties every day, offering over
and over again the same sacrifices which are quite incapable
of taking sins away. Jesus, on the other hand, has offered
one single sacrifice for sins, and then taken his place for
ever, at the right hand of God, where he is now waiting until
his enemies are made into a footstool for him. By virtue of
that one single offering, he has achieved the eternal perfection of all whom he is sanctifying. The Holy Spirit assures
us of this; for he says, first:

This is the covenant I will make with them
when those days arrive;

and the Lord then goes on to say:

I will put my laws into their hearts
and write them on their minds.
I will never call their sins to mind,
or their offences.

When all sins have been forgiven, there can be no more sin
offerings.

This is the word of the Lord.

Responsorial Psalm   (Ps 109:1–4. *R.* v. 4)

Response
You are a priest for ever,
a priest like Melchizedek of old.

1. The Lord's revelation to my Master:
"Sit on my right:
I will put your foes beneath your feet." (*R.*)

2. The Lord will send from Zion
your sceptre of power:
rule in the midst of all your foes. (*R.*)

3. A prince from the day of your birth
on the holy mountains;
from the womb before the daybreak I begot you. (*R.*)

4. The Lord has sworn an oath he will not change.
"You are a priest for ever,
a priest like Melchizedek of old." (*R.*)

ALLELUIA and GOSPEL. As for Year II, see p. 249.

Year II

First Reading   (7:4–17)

A reading from the second book of Samuel
Your House and your sovereignty will always stand secure
before me.

The word of the Lord came to Nathan:
"Go and tell my servant David, 'Thus the Lord speaks:
Are you the man to build me a house to dwell in? I have
never stayed in a house from the day I brought the Israelites out of Egypt until today, but have always led a wanderer's life in a tent. In all my journeying with the whole
people of Israel, did I say to any one of the judges of Israel,
whom I had appointed as shepherds of Israel my people:

Why have you not built me a house of cedar?' This is what you must say to my servant David, 'The Lord of hosts says this: I took you from the pasture, from following the sheep, to be leader of my people Israel; I have been with you on all your expeditions; I have cut off all your enemies before you. I will give you fame as great as the fame of the greatest on earth. I will provide a place for my people Israel; I will plant them there and they shall dwell in that place and never be disturbed again; nor shall the wicked continue to oppress them as they did, in the days when I appointed judges over my people Israel; I will give them rest from all their enemies. The Lord will make you great; the Lord will make you a House. And when your days are ended and you are laid to rest with your ancestors, I will preserve the offspring of your body after you and make his sovereignty secure. (It is he who shall build a house for my name, and I will make his royal throne secure for ever.) I will be a father to him and he a son to me; if he does evil, I will punish him with the rod such as men use, with strokes such as mankind gives. Yet I will not withdraw my favour from him, as I withdrew it from your predecessor. Your House and your sovereignty will always stand secure before me and your throne be established for ever.' "

Nathan related all these words to David and this whole revelation.

This is the word of the Lord.

Responsorial Psalm   (Ps 88:4–5. 27–30. R. v. 29)

Response
I will keep my love for him always.

1. I have made a covenant with my chosen one;
I have sworn to David my servant:
I will establish your dynasty for ever
and set up your throne through all ages. (R.)

2. He will say to me: "You are my father,
my God, the rock who saves me."
And I will make him my first-born,
the highest of the kings of the earth. (*R*.)

3. I will keep my love for him always;
for him my covenant shall endure.
I will establish his dynasty for ever,
make his throne as lasting as the heavens. (*R*.)

Years I and II

Alleluia   (1 Sam 3:9; Jn 6:68)

Alleluia, alleluia!
Speak, Lord, your servant is listening:
you have the message of eternal life.
Alleluia!

Alternative Alleluias p. 847.

Gospel   (4:1–20)

A reading from the holy Gospel according to Mark
Imagine a sower going out to sow.

Jesus began to teach by the lakeside, but such a huge crowd
gathered round him that he got into a boat on the lake and
sat there. The people were all along the shore, at the water's
edge. He taught them many things in parables, and in the
course of his teaching he said to them, "Listen! Imagine a
sower going out to sow. Now it happened that, as he sowed,
some of the seed fell on the edge of the path, and the birds
came and ate it up. Some seeds fell on rocky ground where
it found little soil and sprang up straightaway, because
there was no depth of earth; and when the sun came up it
was scorched and, not having any roots, it withered away.
Some seed fell into thorns, and the thorns grew up and
choked it, and it produced no crop. And some seed fell into

rich soil and, growing tall and strong, produced crop; and yielded thirty, sixty, even a hundredfold." And he said, "Listen, anyone who has ears to hear!"

When he was alone, the Twelve, together with the others who formed his company, asked what the parables meant. He told them, "The secret of the kingdom of God is given to you, but to those who are outside everything comes in parables, so that they may see and see again, but not perceive; may hear and hear again, but not understand; otherwise they might be converted and be forgiven."

He said to them, "Do you not understand this parable? Then how will you understand any of the parables? What the sower is sowing is the word. Those on the edge of the path where the word is sown are people who have no sooner heard it than Satan comes and carries away the word that was sown in them. Similarly, those who receive the seed on patches of rock are people who, when first they hear the word, welcome it at once with joy. But they have no root in them, they do not last; should some trial come, or some persecution on account of the word, they fall away at once. Then there are others who receive the seed in thorns. These have heard the word, but the worries of this world, the lure of riches and all the other passions come in to choke the word, and so it produces nothing. And there are those who have received the seed in rich soil: they hear the word and accept it and yield a harvest, thirty and sixty and a hundredfold."

This is the Gospel of the Lord.

THURSDAY

Year I

First Reading (10:19–25

A reading from the letter to the Hebrews

Let us keep firm in the hope we profess and be concerned for each other, to stir a response in love.

Through the blood of Jesus we have the right to enter the
sanctuary, by a new way which he has opened for us, a living opening through the curtain, that is to say, his body.
And we have the supreme high priest over all the house of
God. So as we go in, let us be sincere in heart and filled with
faith, our minds sprinkled and free from any trace of bad
conscience and our bodies washed with pure water. Let us
keep firm in the hope we profess, because the one who made
the promise is faithful. Let us be concerned for each other,
to stir a response in love and good works. Do not stay away
from the meetings of the community, as some do, but en-
courage each other to go; the more so as you see the Day
drawing near.

   This is the word of the Lord.

Responsorial Psalm   (Ps 23:1–6. *R*. v. 6)

Response

Such are the men who seek your face, O Lord.

1. The Lord's is the earth and its fullness,
 he world and all its peoples.
 t is he who set it on the seas;
 on the waters he made it firm. (*R*.)

. Who shall climb the mountain of the Lord?
Who shall stand in his holy place?
 he man with clean hands and pure heart,
 ho desires not worthless things. (*R*.)

 He shall receive blessings from the Lord
 nd reward from the God who saves him.
 uch are the men who seek him,
 ek the face of the God of Jacob. (*R*.)

LLELUIA and GOSPEL. As for Year II, see p. 253

Year II
First Reading (7:18–19. 24–29)

A reading from the second book of Samuel
Who am I, Lord, and what is my House?

King David went in and, seated before the Lord, said:

"Who am I, Lord, and what is my House, that you have led me as far as this? Yet in your sight, Lord, this is still not far enough, and you make your promises extend to the House of your servant for a far-distant future. You have constituted your people Israel to be your own people for ever; and you, Lord, have become their God. Now, Lord, always keep the promise you have made your servant and his House, and do as you have said. Your name will be exalted for ever and men will say, 'The Lord of hosts is God over Israel.' The House of your servant David will be made secure in your presence, since you yourself, Lord of hosts, God of Israel, have made this revelation to your servant, 'I will build you a House'; hence your servant has ventured to offer this prayer to you. Yes, Lord, you are God indeed, your words are true and you have made this fair promise to your servant. Be pleased, then, to bless the House of your servant, that it may continue for ever in your presence; for you, Lord, have spoken; and with your blessing the House of your servant will be for ever blessed."

This is the word of the Lord.

Responsorial Psalm (Ps 131:1–5. 11–14. *R.* Lk 1:32)
Response
The Lord God will give to him
the throne of his father David.

1. O Lord, remember David
and all the hardships he endured,
the oath he swore to the Lord,
his vow to the Strong One of Jacob. (*R.*)

2. "I will not enter the house where I live
nor go to the bed where I rest.
I will give no sleep to my eyes
to my eyelids will give no slumber
till I find a place for the Lord,
a dwelling for the Strong One of Jacob." (*R.*)

3. The Lord swore an oath to David;
he will not go back on his word:
"A son, the fruit of your body,
will I set upon your throne. (*R.*)

4. If they keep my covenant in truth
and my laws that I have taught them,
their sons also shall rule
on your throne from age to age." (*R.*)

5. For the Lord has chosen Zion;
he has desired it for his dwelling:
"This is my resting-place for ever,
here have I chosen to live." (*R.*)

Years I and II

Alleluia   (Phil 2:15–16)
Alleluia, alleluia!
You will shine in the world like bright stars
because you are offering it the word of life.
Alleluia!

Alternative Alleluias p. 847.

Gospel   (4:21–25)
A reading from the holy Gospel according to Mark
*A lamp is to be put on a lamp-stand. The amount you measure
out is the amount you will be given.*

Jesus said to his disciples: "Would you bring in a lamp to put it under a tub or under the bed? Surely you will put it on the lamp-stand? For there is nothing hidden but it must be disclosed, nothing kept secret except to be brought to light. If anyone has ears to hear, let him listen to this."

He also said to them, "Take notice of what you are hearing. The amount you measure out is the amount you will be given – and more besides; for the man who has will be given more; from the man who has not, even what he has will be taken away."

This is the Gospel of the Lord.

FRIDAY

Year I

First Reading   (10:32–39)

A reading from the letter to the Hebrews
Remember all the sufferings you had to meet. Be as confident now.

Remember all the sufferings that you had to meet after you received the light, in earlier days; sometimes by being yourselves publicly exposed to insults and violence, and sometimes as associates of others who were treated in the same way. For you not only shared in the sufferings of those who were in prison, but you happily accepted being stripped of your belongings, knowing that you owned something that was better and lasting. Be as confident now, then, since the reward is so great. You will need endurance to do God's will and gain what he has promised.

Only a little while now, a very little while,
and the one that is coming will have come; he will not delay.
The righteous man will live by faith,
but if he draws back, my soul will take no pleasure in him.

You and I are not the sort of people who draw back, and

are lost by it; we are the sort who keep faithful until our
souls are saved.

This is the word of the Lord.

Responsorial Psalm   (Ps 36:3–6. 23–24. 39–40. *R*. v. 39)
Response
The salvation of the just comes from the Lord.

1. If you trust in the Lord and do good,
then you will live in the land and be secure.
If you find your delight in the Lord,
he will grant your heart's desire.

2. Commit your life to the Lord,
trust in him and he will act,
so that your justice breaks forth like the light,
your cause like the noon-day sun. (*R*.)

3. The Lord guides the steps of a man
and makes safe the path of one he loves.
Though he stumble he shall never fall
for the Lord holds him by the hand. (*R*.)

4. The salvation of the just comes from the Lord,
their stronghold in time of distress.
The Lord helps them and delivers them
and saves them: for their refuge is in him. (*R*.)

ALLELUIA and GOSPEL. As for Year II, see p. 257.

Year II

First Reading   (11:1–10. 13–17)
A reading from the second book of Samuel
*You have shown contempt for me and taken the wife of Uriah
to be your wife.*

At the turn of the year, the time when kings go campaigning, David sent Joab and with him his own guards and the whole of Israel. They massacred the Ammonites and laid siege to Rabbah. David however remained in Jerusalem.

It happened towards evening when David had risen from his couch and was strolling on the palace roof, that he saw from the roof a woman bathing; the woman was very beautiful. David made inquiries about this woman and was told, "Why, that is Bathsheba, Eliam's daughter, the wife of Uriah the Hittite". Then David sent messengers and had her brought. She came to him, and he slept with her; now she had just purified herself from her courses. She then went home again. The woman conceived and sent word to David, "I am with child".

Then David sent Joab a message, "Send me Uriah the Hittite," whereupon Joab sent Uriah to David. When Uriah came into his presence, David asked after Joab and the army and how the war was going. David then said to Uriah, "Go down to your house and enjoy yourself." Uriah left the palace, and was followed by a present from the king's table. Uriah however slept by the palace door with his master's bodyguard and did not go down to his house.

This was reported to David; "Uriah" they said "did not go down to his house." The next day David invited him to eat and drink in his presence and made him drunk. In the evening Uriah went out and lay on his couch with his master's bodyguard, but he did not go down to his house.

Next morning David wrote a letter to Joab and sent it by Uriah. In the letter he wrote, "Station Uriah in the thick of the fight and then fall back behind him so that he may be struck down and die." Joab, then besieging the town, posted Uriah in a place where he knew there were fierce fighters. The men of the town sallied out and engaged Joab; the army suffered casualties, including some of David's bodyguard; and Uriah the Hittite was killed too.

This is the word of the Lord.

Responsorial Psalm   (Ps 50:3–7. 10–11. *R*. v. 3)

Response
Have mercy on us, Lord, for we have sinned.

1. Have mercy on me, God, in your kindness.
In your compassion blot out my offence.
O wash me more and more from my guilt
and cleanse me from my sin. (*R*.)

2. My offences truly I know them;
my sin is always before me.
Against you, you alone, have I sinned;
what is evil in your sight I have done. (*R*.)

3. That you may be justified when you give sentence
and be without reproach when you judge,
O see, in guilt I was born,
a sinner was I conceived. (*R*.)

4. Make me hear rejoicing and gladness,
that the bones you have crushed may thrill.
From my sins turn away your face
and blot out all my guilt. (*R*.)

Years I and II

Alleluia   (Ps 118:27)

Alleluia, alleluia!
Make me grasp the way of your precepts,
and I will muse on your wonders.
Alleluia!

Alternative Alleluias, p. 847.

Gospel   (4:26–34)

A reading from the holy Gospel according to Mark
A man throws seed on the land. While he sleeps the seed is
growing; how, he does not know.

Jesus said to his disciples: "This is what the kingdom of God is like. A man throws seed on the land. Night and day, while he sleeps, when he is awake, the seed is sprouting and growing; how, he does not know. Of its own accord the land produces first the shoot, then the ear, then the full grain in the ear. And when the crop is ready, he loses no time: he starts to reap because the harvest has come."

He also said, "What can we say the kingdom of God is like? What parable can we find for it? It is like a mustard seed which at the time of its sowing in the soil is the smallest of all the seeds on earth; yet once it is sown it grows into the biggest shrub of them all and puts out big branches so that the birds of the air can shelter in its shade."

Using many parables like these, he spoke the word to them, so far as they were capable of understanding it. He would not speak to them except in parables, but he explained everything to his disciples when they were alone.

This is the Gospel of the Lord.

SATURDAY
Year I

First Reading   (11:1–2. 8–19)

A reading from the letter to the Hebrews
He looked forward to a city founded, designed and built by God.

Only faith can guarantee the blessings that we hope for, or prove the existence of the realities that at present remain unseen. It was for faith that our ancestors were commended.

It was by faith that Abraham obeyed the call to set out for a country that was the inheritance given to him and his descendants, and that he set out without knowing where he was going. By faith he arrived, as a foreigner, in the Promised Land, and lived there as if in a strange country, with Isaac and Jacob, who were heirs with him of the same promise.

They lived there in tents while he looked forward to a city founded, designed and built by God.

It was equally by faith that Sarah, in spite of being past the age, was made able to conceive, because she believed that he who had made the promise would be faithful to it. Because of this, there came from one man, and one who was already as good as dead himself, more descendants than could be counted, as many as the stars of heaven or the grains of sand on the sea-shore.

All these died in faith, before receiving any of the things that had been promised, but they saw them in the far distance and welcomed them, recognising that they were only strangers and nomads on earth. People who use such terms about themselves make it quite plain that they are in search of their real homeland. They can hardly have meant the country they came from, since they had the opportunity to go back to it; but in fact they were longing for a better homeland, their heavenly homeland. That is why God is not ashamed to be called their God, since he has founded the city for them.

It was by faith that Abraham, when put to the test, offered up Isaac. He offered to sacrifice his only son even though the promises had been made to him and he had been told: It is through Isaac that your name will be carried on. He was confident that God had the power even to raise the dead; and so, figuratively speaking, he was given back Isaac from the dead.

This is the word of the Lord.

Responsorial Psalm   (Lk 1:69–75. *R*. v. 68)

Response
Blessed be the Lord, the God of Israel!
He has visited his people and redeemed them.

1. He has raised up for us a mighty saviour
in the house of David his servant,

as he promised by the lips of holy men,
those who were his prophets from of old. (*R.*)

2. A saviour who would free us from our foes,
from the hands of all who hate us.
So his love for our fathers is fulfilled
and his holy covenant remembered. (*R.*)

3. He swore to Abraham our father
to grant us, that free from fear,
and saved from the hands of our foes,
we might serve him in holiness and justice
all the days of our life in his presence. (*R.*)

ALLELUIA and GOSPEL. As for Year II, see p. 262.

Year II

First Reading   (12:1–7. 10–17)

A reading from the second book of Samuel
I have sinned against the Lord.

The Lord sent Nathan the prophet to David. He came to
him and said.
"In the same town were two men,
one rich, the other poor.
The rich man had flocks and herds
in great abundance;
the poor man had nothing but a ewe lamb,
one only, a small one he had bought.
This he fed, and it grew up with him and his children,
eating his bread, drinking from his cup,
sleeping on his breast; it was like a daughter to him.
When there came a traveller to stay the rich man
refused to take one of his own flock or herd
to provide for the wayfarer who had come to him.
Instead he took the poor man's lamb
and prepared it for his guest."

David's anger flared up against the man. "As the Lord lives," he said to Nathan "the man who did this deserves to die! He must make fourfold restitution for the lamb, for doing such a thing and showing no compassion."

Then Nathan said to David, "You are the man. So now the sword will never be far from your House, since you have shown contempt for me and taken the wife of Uriah the Hittite to be your wife."

"Thus the Lord speaks, 'I will stir up evil for you out of your own House. Before your very eyes I will take your wives and give them to your neighbour, and he shall lie with your wives in the sight of this sun. You worked in secret, I will work this in the face of all Israel and in the face of the sun.'"

David said to Nathan, "I have sinned against the Lord." Then Nathan said to David, "The Lord, for his part, forgives your sin; you are not to die. Yet because you have outraged the Lord by doing this, the child that is born to you is to die." Then Nathan went home.

The Lord struck the child that Uriah's wife had borne to David and it fell gravely ill. David pleaded with the Lord for the child; he kept a strict fast and went home and spent the night on the bare ground, covered with sacking. The officials of his household came and stood round him to get him to rise from the ground, but he refused, nor would he take food with them.

This is the word of the Lord.

Responsorial Psalm   (Ps 50:12–17. *R*. v. 12)

Response
A pure heart create for me, O God.

1. A pure heart create for me, O God,
put a steadfast spirit within me.
Do not cast me away from your presence,
nor deprive me of your holy spirit. (*R*.)

2. Give me again the joy of your help;
with a spirit of fervour sustain me,
that I may teach transgressors your ways
and sinners may return to you. (*R.*)

3. O rescue me, God, my helper,
and my tongue shall ring out your goodness.
O Lord, open my lips
and my mouth shall declare your praise. (*R.*)

Years I and II

Alleluia (Ps 26:11)

Alleluia, alleluia!
Instruct me, Lord, in your way;
on an even path lead me.
Alleluia!

Alternative Alleluias p. 847.

Gospel (4:35–41)

A reading from the holy Gospel according to Mark
Who can this be? Even the wind and the sea obey him.

With the coming of evening, Jesus said to his disciples, "Let
us cross over to the other side." And leaving the crowd
behind they took him, just as he was, in the boat; and there
were other boats with him. Then it began to blow a gale and
the waves were breaking into the boat so that it was almost
swamped. But he was in the stern, his head on the cushion,
asleep. They woke him and said to him, "Master, do you
not care? We are going down!" And he woke up and rebuked the wind and said to the sea, "Quiet now! Be calm!"
And the wind dropped, and all was calm again. Then he
said to them, "Why are you so frightened? How is it that
you have no faith?" They were filled with awe and said to

one another, "Who can this be? Even the wind and the sea obey him."

This is the Gospel of the Lord.

4th SUNDAY OF THE YEAR
Year 1 (Year A)

First Reading   (2:3;3:12–13)

A reading from the prophet Zephaniah
In your midst I will leave a humble and lowly people.

Seek the Lord
all you, the humble of the earth,
who obey his commands.
Seek integrity,
seek humility:
you may perhaps find shelter
on the day of the anger of the Lord.
In your midst I will leave
a humble and lowly people,
and those who are left in Israel will seek refuge in the name
    of the Lord.
They will do no wrong,
will tell no lies;
and the perjured tongue will no longer
be found in their mouths.
But they will be able to graze and rest
with no one to disturb them.

This is the word of the Lord.

Responsorial Psalm   (Ps 145:7–10. *R*. Mt 5:3)

Response
How happy are the poor in spirit;
theirs is the kingdom of heaven.
Or: Alleluia!

1. It is he who keeps faith for ever,
who is just to those who are oppressed.
It is he who gives bread to the hungry,
the lord, who sets prisoners free. (*R.*)

2. It is the Lord who gives sight to the blind,
who raises up those who are bowed down,
the Lord, who protects the stranger
and upholds the widow and orphan. (*R.*)

3. It is the Lord who loves the just
but thwarts the path of the wicked.
The Lord will reign for ever,
Zion's God, from age to age. (*R.*)

Second Reading (1:26–31)

A reading from the first letter of St Paul to the Corinthians
God chose what is foolish by human reckoning.

Take yourselves for instance, brothers, at the time when you
were called: how many of you were wise in the ordinary
sense of the word, how many were influential people, or
came from noble families? No, it was to shame the wise
that God chose what is foolish by human reckoning, and
to shame what is strong that he chose what is weak by human reckoning; those whom the world thinks common and
contemptible are the ones that God has chosen – those who
are nothing at all to show up those who are everything. The
human race has nothing to boast about to God, but you,
God has made members of Christ Jesus and by God's doing
he has become our wisdom, and our virtue, and our holiness, and our freedom. As scripture says: if anyone wants
to boast, let him boast about the Lord.

This is the word of the Lord.

Alleluia   (Mt 11:25)

Alleluia, alleluia!
Blessed are you, Father,
Lord of heaven and earth,
for revealing the mysteries of the kingdom
to mere children.
Alleluia!

Gospel   (5:1–12)

A reading from the holy Gospel according to Matthew
How happy are the poor in spirit.

Seeing the crowds, Jesus went up the hill. There he sat down
and was joined by his disciples. Then he began to speak.
This is what he taught them:

"How happy are the poor in spirit;
theirs is the kingdom of heaven.
Happy the gentle:
they shall have the earth for their heritage.
Happy those who mourn:
they shall be comforted.
Happy those who hunger and thirst for what is right:
they shall be satisfied.
Happy the merciful:
they shall have mercy shown them.
Happy the pure in heart:
they shall see God.
Happy the peacemakers:
they shall be called sons of God.
Happy those who are persecuted in the cause of right:
theirs is the kingdom of heaven.

"Happy are you when people abuse you and persecute you
and speak all kinds of calumny against you on my account.

Rejoice and be glad, for your reward will be great in heaven."

This is the Gospel of the Lord.

4th SUNDAY OF THE YEAR
Year 2 (Year B)

First Reading (18:15–20)

A reading from the book of Deuteronomy
I will raise up a prophet and I will put my words into his mouth.

Moses said to the people: "Your God will raise up for you a prophet like myself, from among yourselves, from your own brothers; to him you must listen. This is what you yourselves asked of the Lord your God at Horeb on the day of the Assembly. 'Do not let me hear again' you said 'the voice of the Lord my God, nor look any longer on this great fire, or I shall die'; and the Lord said to me, 'All they have spoken is well said. I will raise up a prophet like yourself for them from their own brothers; I will put my words into his mouth and he shall tell them all I command him. The man who does not listen to my words that he speaks in my name, shall be held answerable to me for it. But the prophet who presumes to say in my name a thing I have not commanded him to say, or who speaks in the name of other gods, that prophet shall die.'"

This is the word of the Lord.

Responsorial Psalm (Ps 94:1–2. 6–9. *R.* v. 8)

Response
O that today you would listen to his voice!
Harden not your hearts.

1. Come, ring out our joy to the Lord;
hail the rock who saves us.
Let us come before him, giving thanks,
with songs let us hail the Lord. (*R.*)

2. Come in; let us kneel and bend low;
let us kneel before the God who made us
for he is our God and we
the people who belong to his pasture,
the flock that is led by his hand. (*R*.)

3. O that today you would listen to his voice!
"Harden not your hearts as at Meribah,
as on that day at Massah in the desert
when your fathers put me to the test;
when they tried me, though they saw my work." (*R*.)

Second Reading   (7:32–35)

A reading from the first letter of St Paul to the Corinthians
*An unmarried woman can devote herself to the Lord's affairs;
all she need worry about is being holy.*

I would like to see you free from all worry. An unmarried
man can devote himself to the Lord's affairs, all he need
worry about is pleasing the Lord; but a married man has to
bother about the world's affairs and devote himself to pleasing his wife: he is torn two ways. In the same way an unmarried woman, like a young girl, can devote herself to the
Lord's affairs; all she need worry about is being holy in
body and spirit. The married woman, on the other hand,
has to worry about the world's affairs and devote herself to
pleasing her husband. I say this only to help you, not to put
a halter round your necks, but simply to make sure that
everything is as it should be, and that you give your un-
divided attention to the Lord.

This is the word of the Lord.

ALLELUIA. As for year 1(A), p. 265.

Gospel   (1:21–28)

A reading from the holy Gospel according to Mark
He taught them with authority.

They went as far as Capernaum, and as soon as the sabbath came Jesus went to the synagogue and began to teach. And his teaching made a deep impression on them because, unlike the scribes, he taught them with authority.

In their synagogue just then there was a man possessed by an unclean spirit, and it shouted, "What do you want with us, Jesus of Nazareth? Have you come to destroy us? I know who you are: the Holy One of God." But Jesus said sharply, "Be quiet! Come out of him!" And the unclean spirit threw the man into convulsions and with a loud cry went out of him. The people were so astonished that they started asking each other what it all meant. "Here is a teaching that is new" they said "and with authority behind it: he gives orders even to unclean spirits and they obey him." And his reputation rapidly spread everywhere, through all the surrounding Galilean countryside.

This is the Gospel of the Lord.

4th SUNDAY OF THE YEAR

Year 3 (Year C)

First Reading   (1:4–5. 17–19)

A reading from the prophet Jeremiah
I have appointed you as prophet to the nations.

The word of the Lord was addressed to me, saying,
"Before I formed you in the womb I knew you;
before you came to birth I consecrated you;
I have appointed you as prophet to the nations.
So now brace yourself for action.
Stand up and tell them
all I command you.
Do not be dismayed at their presence,
or in their presence I will make you dismayed.
I, for my part, today will make you

into a fortified city,
a pillar of iron,
and a wall of bronze
to confront all this land:
the kings of Judah, its princes,
its priests and the country people.
They will fight against you
but shall not overcome you,
for I am with you to deliver you –
it is the Lord who speaks."

This is the word of the Lord.

Responsorial Psalm   (Ps 70:1–6. 15. 17. *R*. v. 15)

Response
My lips will tell of your help.

1. In you, O Lord, I take refuge;
let me never be put to shame.
In your justice rescue me, free me:
pay heed to me and save me. (*R*.)

2. Be a rock where I can take refuge,
a mighty stronghold to save me;
for you are my rock, my stronghold.
Free me from the hand of the wicked. (*R*.)

3. It is you, O Lord, who are my hope,
my trust, O Lord, since my youth.
On you I have leaned from my birth,
from my mother's womb you have been my help. (*R*.)

4. My lips will tell of your justice
and day by day of your help.

O God, you have taught me from my youth
and I proclaim your wonders still. (*R.*)

Second Reading   (12:31–13:13)

A reading from the first letter of St Paul to the Corinthians
There are three things that last: faith, hope and love; and the
greatest of these is love.

Be ambitious for the higher gifts. And I am going to show
you a way that is better than any of them.

If I have all the eloquence of men or of angels, but speak
without love, I am simply a gong booming or a cymbal
clashing. If I have the gift of prophecy, understanding all
the mysteries there are, and knowing everything, and if I
have faith in all its fulness, to move mountains, but without
love, then I am nothing at all. If I give away all that I possess, piece by piece, and if I even let them take my body to
burn it, but am without love, it will do me good whatever.

*Love is always patient and kind; it is never jealous; love
is never boastful or conceited; it is never rude or selfish; it
does not take offence, and is not resentful. Love takes no
pleasure in other people's sins but delights in the truth; it is
always ready to excuse, to trust, to hope, and to endure
whatever comes.

Love does not come to an end. But if there are gifts of
prophecy, the time will come when they must fail; or the
gift of languages, it will not continue for ever; and knowledge – for this, too, the time will come when it must fail.
For our knowledge is imperfect and our prophesying is
imperfect; but once perfection comes, all imperfect things
will disappear. When I was a child, I used to talk like a
child, and think like a child, and argue like a child, but now
I am a man, all childish ways are put behind me. Now we
are seeing a dim reflection in a mirror; but then we shall be
seeing face to face. The knowledge that I have now is imperfect; but then I shall know as fully as I am known.

In short, there are three things that last: faith, hope and love; and the greatest of these is love.

This is the word of the Lord.*

* Shorter form, verses 4–13, read between*

Alleluia   (Jn 14:15)

'Alleluia, alleluia!
I am the Way, the Truth and the Life, says the Lord;
no one can come to the Father except through me.
Alleluia!

Alternative Alleluias, p. 854.

Gospel   (4:21–30)

A reading from the holy Gospel according to Luke
Like Elijah and Elisha, Jesus is not sent to the Jews only.

Jesus began to speak to them in the synagogue, "This text is being fulfilled today even as you listen." And he won the approval of all, and they were astonished by the gracious words that came from his lips.

They said, "This is Joseph's son, surely?" But he replied, "No doubt you will quote me the saying, 'Physician, heal yourself' and tell me, 'We have heard all that happened in Capernaum, do the same here in your own countryside.' " And he went on, "I tell you solemnly, no prophet is ever accepted in his own country.

"There were many widows in Israel, I can assure you, in Elijah's day, when heaven remained shut for three years and six months and a great famine raged throughout the land, but Elijah was not sent to any one of these: he was sent to a widow at Zarephath, a Sidonian town. And in the prophet Elisha's time there were many lepers in Israel, but none of these was cured, except the Syrian, Naaman."

When they heard this everyone in the synagogue was enraged. They sprang to their feet and hustled him out of the town; and they took him up to the brow of the hill their town was built on, intending to throw him down the cliff, but he slipped through the crowd and walked away.

This is the Gospel of the Lord.

MONDAY
Year I

First Reading   (11:32–40)

A reading from the letter to the Hebrews
Through faith they conquered kingdoms. God will make provision for us to have something better.

Is there any need to say more? There is not time for me to give an account of Gideon, Barak, Samson, Jephthah, or of David, Samuel and the prophets. These were men who through faith conquered kingdoms, did what is right and earned the promises. They could keep a lion's mouth shut, put out blazing fires and emerge unscathed from battle. They were weak people who were given strength, to be brave in war and drive back foreign invaders. Some came back to their wives from the dead, by resurrection; and others submitted to torture, refusing release so that they would rise again to a better life. Some had to bear being pilloried and flogged, or even chained up in prison. They were stoned, or sawn in half, or beheaded; they were homeless, and dressed in the skins of sheep and goats; they were penniless and were given nothing but ill-treatment. They were too good for the world and they went out to live in deserts and mountains and in caves and ravines. These are all heroes of faith, but they did not receive what was promised, since God had made provision for us to have something better, and they were not to reach perfection except with us.

This is the word of the Lord.

Responsorial Psalm   (Ps 30:20–24. R. v. 25)

Response
Let your heart take courage,
all who hope in the Lord.

1. How great is the goodness, Lord,
that you keep for those who fear you,
that you show to those who trust you
in the sight of men. (R.)

2. You hide them in the shelter of your presence
from the plotting of men:
you keep them safe within your tent
from disputing tongues. (R.)

3. Blessed be the Lord who has shown me
the wonders of his love
in a fortified city. (R.)

4. "I am far removed from your sight"
I said in my alarm.
Yet you heard the voice of my plea
when I cried for help. (R.)

5. Love the Lord, all you saints.
He guards his faithful
but the Lord will repay to the full
those who act with pride. (R.)

ALLELUIA and GOSPEL. As for Year II, p. 275.

Year II

First Reading   (15:13–14. 30;16:5–13)

A reading from the second book of Samuel
Let us fly, or we shall never escape Absalom.

A messenger came to tell David, "The hearts of the men of
Israel are now with Absalom." So David said to all his

officers who were with him in Jerusalem, "Let us be off, let us fly, or we shall never escape from Absalom. Leave as quickly as you can in case he mounts a surprise attack and worsts us and puts the city to the sword."

David then made his way up the Mount of Olives, weeping as he went, his head covered and his feet bare. And all the people with him had their heads covered and made their way up, weeping as they went.

As David was reaching Bahurim, out came a man of the same clan as Saul's family. His name was Shimei son of Gera, and as he came he uttered curse after curse and threw stones at David and at all King David's officers, though the whole army and all the champions flanked the king right and left. The words of his curse were these, "Be off, be off, man of blood, scoundrel! The Lord has brought on you all the blood of the House of Saul whose sovereignty you have usurped; and the Lord has transferred that same sovereignty to Absalom your son. Now your doom has overtaken you, man of blood that you are." Abishai son of Zeruiah said to the king, "Is this dead dog to curse my lord the king? Let me go over and cut his head off." But the king replied, "What business is it of mine and yours, son of Zeruiah? Let him curse. If the Lord said to him, 'Curse David,' what right has anyone to say, 'Why have you done this?'" David said to Abishai and all his officers, "Why, my own son, sprung from my body, is now seeking my life; so now how much the more this Benjaminite? Let him curse on if the Lord has told him to. Perhaps the Lord will look on my misery and repay me with good for his curse today." So David and his men went on their way.

This is the word of the Lord.

Responsorial Psalm (Ps 3:2–8. *R.* v. 8)
Response
Arise, Lord; save me, my God.

1. How many are my foes, O Lord!
How many are rising up against me!
How many are saying about me:
"There is no help for him in God." (R.)

2. But you, Lord, are a shield about me,
my glory, who lift up my head.
I cry aloud to the Lord.
He answers from his holy mountain. (R.)

3. I lie down to rest and I sleep.
I wake, for the Lord upholds me.
I will not fear even thousands of people
who are ranged on every side against me.
Arise, Lord; save me, my God. (R.)

Years I and II

Alleluia   (Jn 17:17)

Alleluia, alleluia!
Your word is truth, O Lord,
consecrate us in the truth.
Alleluia!

Alternative Alleluias, p. 847.

Gospel   (5:1-20)

A reading from the holy Gospel according to Mark
Come out of that man, unclean spirit.

Jesus and his disciples reached the country of the Geras-
enes on the other side of the lake, and no sooner had he left
the boat than a man with an unclean spirit came out from
the tombs towards him. The man lived in the tombs and no
one could secure him any more, even with a chain, because
he had often been secured with fetters and chains but had
snapped the chains and broken the fetters, and no one had

the strength to control him. All night and all day, among the tombs and in the mountains, he would howl and gash himself with stones. Catching sight of Jesus from a distance, he ran up and fell at his feet and shouted at the top of his voice, "What do you want with me, Jesus, son of the Most High God? Swear by God you will not torture me!" – For Jesus had been saying to him, "Come out of the man, unclean spirit." "What is your name?" Jesus asked. "My name is legion," he answered "for there are many of us." And he begged him earnestly not to send them out of the district. Now there was there on the mountainside a great herd of pigs feeding, and the unclean spirits begged him, "Send us to the pigs, let us go into them." So he gave them leave. With that, the unclean spirits came out and went into the pigs, and the herd of about two thousand pigs charged down the cliff into the lake, and there they were drowned. The swineherds ran off and told their story in the town and in the country round about; and the people came to see what had really happened. They came to Jesus and saw the demoniac sitting there, clothed and in his full senses – the very man who had had the legion in him before – and they were afraid. And those who had witnessed it reported what had happened to the demoniac and what had become of the pigs. Then they began to implore Jesus to leave the neighbourhood. As he was getting into the boat, the man who had been possessed begged to be allowed to stay with him. Jesus would not let him but said to him, "Go home to your people and tell them all that the Lord in his mercy has done for you." So the man went off and proceeded to spread throughout the Decapolis all that Jesus had done for him. And everyone was amazed.

This is the Gospel of the Lord.

TUESDAY

Year I

First Reading   (12:1–4)

A reading from the letter to the Hebrews
We should keep running steadily in the race we have started.

With so many witnesses in a great cloud on every side of
us, we too, then, should throw off everything that hinders
us, especially the sin that clings so easily, and keep running
steadily in the race we have started. Let us not lose sight of
Jesus, who leads us in our faith and brings it to perfection:
for the sake of the joy which was still in the future, he endured the cross, disregarding the shamefulness of it, and
from now on has taken his place at the right of God's
throne. Think of the way he stood such opposition from
sinners and then you will not give up for want of courage.
In the fight against sin, you have not yet had to keep fighting
to the point of death.

This is the word of the Lord.

Responsorial Psalm   (Ps 21:26–28.30–32. R. v. 27)

Response
They shall praise you, Lord,
those who seek you.

1. My vows I will pay before those who fear him.
The poor shall eat and shall have their fill.
They shall praise the Lord, those who seek him.
May their hearts live for ever and ever! (R.)

2. All the earth shall remember and return to the Lord,
all families of the nations worship before him.
They shall worship him, all the mighty of the earth;
before him shall bow all who go down to the dust. (R.)

3. And my soul shall live for him, my children serve him.
They shall tell of the Lord to generations yet to come,
declare his faithfulness to peoples yet unborn:
"These things the Lord has done." (R.)

ALLELUIA and GOSPEL. As for year II, p. 279.

Year II

First Reading   (18:9–10. 14. 24–25. 30–19:3)

A reading from the second book of Samuel
My son Absalom! Would I had died in your place.

Absalom happened to run into some of David's followers.
Absalom was riding a mule and the mule passed under the
thick branches of a great oak. Absalom's head caught fast in
the oak and he was left hanging between heaven and earth,
while the mule he was riding went on. Someone saw this
and told Joab. "I have just seen Absalom" he said "hanging from an oak." And Joab took three lances in his hand
and thrust them into Absalom's heart while he was still alive
there in the oak tree.

David was sitting between the two gates. The look-out
had gone up to the roof of the gate, on the ramparts; he
looked up and saw a man running all by himself. The watch
called out to the king and told him. The king said, "Move
aside and stand there." He moved aside and stood waiting.

Then the Cushite arrived. "Good news for my lord the
king!" cried the Cushite. "The Lord has vindicated your
cause today by ridding you of all who rebelled against you."
"Is all well with young Absalom?" the king asked the Cushite. "May the enemies of my lord the king" the Cushite
answered "and all who rebelled against you to your hurt,
share the lot of that young man."

The king shuddered. He went up to the room over the
gate and burst into tears, and weeping said, "My son Absalom! My son! My son Absalom! Would I had died in

your place! Absalom, my son, my son!" Word was brought to Joab. "The king is now weeping and mourning for Absalom." And the day's victory was turned to mourning for all the troops, because they learned that the king was grieving for his son. And the troops returned stealthily that day to the town, as troops creep back ashamed when routed in battle.

This is the word of the Lord.

Responsorial Psalm   (Ps 85:1–6. *R*. v. 1)

Response

Turn your ear, O Lord, and give answer.

1. Turn your ear, O Lord, and give answer
for I am poor and needy.
Preserve my life, for I am faithful:
save the servant who trusts in you. (*R*.)

2. You are my God, have mercy on me, Lord,
for I cry to you all the day long.
Give joy to your servant, O Lord,
for to you I lift up my soul. (*R*.)

3. O Lord, you are good and forgiving,
full of love to all who call.
Give heed, O Lord, to my prayer
and attend to the sound of my voice. (*R*.)

Years I and II

Alleluia   (Jn 14:5)

Alleluia, alleluia!
I am the Way, the Truth and the Life, says the Lord;
no one can come to the Father except through me.
Alleluia!

Alternative Alleluias, p. 847.

Gospel   (5:21–43)

A reading from the holy Gospel according to Mark
Little girl, I tell you get up.

When Jesus had crossed in the boat to the other side, a
large crowd gathered round him and he stayed by the lakeside. Then one of the synagogue officials came up, Jairus
by name, and seeing him, fell at his feet and pleaded with
him earnestly, saying, "My little daughter is desperately
sick. Do come and lay your hands on her to make her better
and save her life." Jesus went with him and a large crowd
followed him; they were pressing all round him.

Now there was a woman who had suffered from a
haemorrhage for twelve years; after long and painful treat-
ment under various doctors, she had spent all she had without being any the better for it, in fact, she was getting worse.
She had heard about Jesus, and she came up behind him
through the crowd and touched his cloak. "If I can touch
even his clothes," she had told herself "I shall be well again."
And the source of the bleeding dried up instantly, and she
felt in herself that she was cured of her complaint. Immediately aware that power had gone out from him, Jesus turned
round in the crowd and said, "Who touched my clothes?"
His disciples said to him, "You see how the crowd is pressing round you and yet you say, 'Who touched me?' " But he
continued to look all round to see who had done it. Then
the woman came forward, frightened and trembling because
she knew what had happened to her, and she fell at his feet
and told him the whole truth. "My daughter," he said "your
faith has restored you to health; go in peace and be free
from your complaint."

While he was still speaking some people arrived from the
house of the synagogue official to say, "Your daughter is
dead: why put the Master to any further trouble?" But
Jesus had overheard this remark of theirs and he said to the

official, "Do not be afraid; only have faith." And he allowed no one to go with him except Peter and James and John the brother of James. So they came to the official's house and Jesus noticed all the commotion, with people weeping and wailing unrestrainedly. He went in and said to them, "Why all this commotion and crying? The child is not dead, but asleep." But they laughed at him. So he turned them all out and, taking with him the child's father and mother and his own companions, he went into the place where the child lay. And taking the child by the hand he said to her, "Talitha, kum!" which means, "Little girl, I tell you to get up." The little girl got up at once and began to walk about, for she was twelve years old. At this they were overcome with astonishment, and he ordered them strictly not to let anyone know about it, and told them to give her something to eat.

This is the Gospel of the Lord.

WEDNESDAY

Year I

First Reading (12:4–7. 11–15)

A reading from the letter to the Hebrews
The Lord trains the ones that he loves.

In the fight against sin, you have not yet had to keep fighting to the point of death.

Have you forgotten that encouraging text in which you are addressed as sons? My son, when the Lord corrects you, do not treat it lightly; but do not get discouraged when he reprimands you. For the Lord trains the ones that he loves and he punishes all those that he acknowledges as his sons. Suffering is part of your training; God is treating you as his sons. Has there ever been any son whose father did not train him?

Of course, any punishment is most painful at the time, and far from pleasant; but later, in those on whom it has been used, it bears fruit in peace and goodness. So hold up your limp arms and steady your trembling knees and smooth out the path you tread; then the injured limb will not be wrenched, it will grow strong again.

Always be wanting peace with all people, and the holiness without which no one can ever see the Lord. Be careful that no one is deprived of the grace of God and that no root of bitterness should begin to grow and make trouble; this can poison a whole community.

This is the word of the Lord.

Responsorial Psalm   (Ps 102:1–2. 13–14. 17–18. R. 17)

Response
The love of the Lord is everlasting
upon those who hold him in fear.

1. My soul, give thanks to the Lord,
all my being, bless his holy name.
My soul, give thanks to the Lord
and never forget all his blessings. (*R.*)

2. As a father has compassion on his sons,
the Lord has pity on those who fear him;
for he knows of what we are made,
he remembers that we are dust. (*R.*)

3. But the love of the Lord is everlasting
upon those who hold him in fear;
his justice reaches out to children's children
when they keep his covenant in truth. (*R.*)

ALLELUIA and GOSPEL. As for year II, see p. 285.

Year II

First Reading   (24:2. 9–17)

A reading from the second book of Samuel

*It was I who sinned, taking a census of the people. But these,
this flock, what have they done?*

King David said to Joab and to the senior army officers
who were with him, "Now go throughout the tribes of Israel
from Dan to Beersheba and take a census of the people;
I wish to know the size of the population."

Joab gave the king the figures for the census of the people;
Israel numbered eight hundred thousand armed men capable of drawing sword, and Judah five hundred thousand
men.

But afterwards David's heart misgave him for having
taken a census of the people. "I have committed a grave sin"
David said to the Lord "But now, Lord, I beg you to forgive your servant for this fault. I have been very foolish."
But when David got up the next morning, the following
message had come from the Lord to the prophet Gad, David's seer, "Go and say to David, 'The Lord says this: I
offer you three things; choose one of them for me to do to
you.'"

So Gad went to David and told him. "Are three years of
famine to come on you in your country" he said "or will you
flee for the three months before your pursuing enemy, or
would you rather have three days' pestilence in your country? Now think, and decide how I am to answer him who
sends me." David said to Gad, "This is a hard choice. But
let us rather fall into the power of the Lord, since his mercy
is great, and not into the power of men." So David chose
pestilence.

It was the time of the wheat harvest. The Lord sent a
pestilence on Israel from the morning till the time appointed
and plague ravaged the people, and from Dan to Beersheba

seventy thousand men of them died. The angel stretched out his hand towards Jerusalem to destroy it, but the Lord thought better of this evil, and he said to the angel who was destroying the people, "Enough! now withdraw your hand." The angel of the Lord was beside the threshing-floor of Araunah the Jebusite. When David saw the angel who was ravaging the people, he spoke to the Lord. "It was I who sinned;" he said "I who did this wicked thing. But these, this flock, what have they done? Let your hand lie heavy on me then, and on my family."

This is the word of the Lord.

Responsorial Psalm   (Ps 31:1–2. 5–7. *R*. v. 5)

Response
Forgive, Lord, the guilt of my sin.

1. Happy the man whose offence is forgiven,
whose sin is remitted.
O happy the man to whom the Lord
imputes no guilt,
in whose spirit is no guile. (*R*.)

2. But now I have acknowledged my sins;
my guilt I did not hide.
I said: "I will confess
my offence to the Lord."
And you, Lord, have forgiven
the guilt of my sin. (*R*.)

3. So let every good man pray to you
in the time of need.
The floods of water may reach high
but him they shall not reach.
You are my hiding place, O Lord;
you save me from distress.
You surround me with cries of deliverance. (*R*.)

Years I and II

Alleluia   (Mt 4:4)

Alleluia, alleluia!
Man does not live on bread alone,
but on every word that comes from the mouth of God.
Alleluia!

Alternative Alleluias p. 847.

Gospel   (6:1–6)

A reading from the holy Gospel according to Mark

A prophet is only despised in his own country.

Jesus went to his home town and his disciples accompanied
him. With the coming of the sabbath he began teaching in
the synagogue and most of them were astonished when they
heard him. They said, "Where did the man get all this?
What is this wisdom that has been granted him, and these
miracles that are worked through him? This is the carpen-
ter, surely, the son of Mary, the brother of James and Joset
and Jude and Simon? His sisters, too, are they not here with
us?" And they would not accept him. And Jesus said to
them, "A prophet is only despised in his own country, among his own relations and in his own house"; and he could
work no miracle there, though he cured a few sick people by
laying his hands on them. He was amazed at their lack of
faith.

This is the Gospel of the Lord.

THURSDAY
Year I

First Reading   (12:18–19. 21–24)

A reading from the letter to the Hebrews

*What you have come to is Mount Zion and the city of the
living God.*

What you have come to is nothing known to the senses:
not a blazing fire, or a gloom turning to total darkness, or a

storm; or trumpeting thunder or the great voice speaking which made everyone that heard it beg that no more should be said to them. The whole scene was so terrible that Moses said: I am afraid, and was trembling with fright. But what you have come to is Mount Zion and the city of the living God, the heavenly Jerusalem where the millions of angels have gathered for the festival, with the whole Church in which everyone is a "first-born son" and a citizen of heaven. You have come to God himself, the supreme Judge, and been placed with spirits of the saints who have been made perfect; and to Jesus, the mediator who brings a new covenant and a blood for purification which pleads more insistently than Abel's.

This is the word of the Lord.

Responsorial Psalm   (Ps 47:2–4. 9–11. *R*. v. 10)

Response
O God, we ponder your love
within your temple.

1. The Lord is great and worthy to be praised
in the city of our God.
His holy mountain rises in beauty,
the joy of all the earth. (*R*.)

2. Mount Zion, true pole of the earth,
the Great King's city!
God, in the midst of its citadels,
has shown himself its stronghold. (*R*.)

3. As we have heard, so we have seen
in the city of our God,
in the city of the Lord of hosts
which God upholds for ever. (*R*.)

4. O God, we ponder your love
within your temple.

Your praise, O God, like your name
reaches to the ends of the earth.
With justice your right hand is filled. (*R.*)

ALLELUIA and GOSPEL. As for Year II, see p. 288.

Year II

First Reading   (2:1–4. 10–12)

A reading from the first book of the Kings

*I am going the way of all the earth. Be strong, Solomon, and
show yourself a man.*

As David's life drew to its close he laid this charge on his
son Solomon, "I am going the way of all the earth. Be strong
and show yourself a man. Observe the injunctions of the
Lord your God, following his ways and keeping his laws,
his commandments, his customs and his decrees, as it
stands written in the Law of Moses, that so you may be
successful in all you do and undertake, so that the Lord may
fulfil the promise he made me, 'If your sons are careful how
they behave, and walk loyally before me with all their heart
and soul, you shall never lack for a man on the throne of
Israel.' "

So David slept with his ancestors and was buried in the
Citadel of David. David's reign over Israel lasted forty
years: he reigned in Hebron for seven years, and in Jerusalem for thirty-three.

Solomon was seated upon the throne of David, and his
sovereignty was securely established.

This is the word of the Lord.

Responsorial Psalm   (1 Chron 29:10–12.*R*.v.12)

Response
You, Lord, are the ruler of all.

1. Blessed are you, O Lord,
the God of Israel, our father,
for ever, for ages unending. (*R.*)

2. Yours, Lord, are greatness and power,
and splendour, triumph and glory.
All is yours, in heaven and on earth. (*R.*)

3. Yours, O Lord, is the kingdom,
you are supreme over all.
Both honour and riches come from you. (*R.*)

4. You are the ruler of all,
from your hand come strength and power,
from your hand come greatness and might. (*R.*)

Years I and II

Alleluia   (Jn 15:15)

Alleluia, alleluia!
I call you friends, says the Lord,
because I have made known to you
everything I have learnt from my Father.
Alleluia!

Alternative Alleluias p. 847.

Gospel   (6:7–13

A reading from the holy Gospel according to Mark
He began to send them out.

Jesus made a tour round the villages, teaching. Then h
summoned the Twelve and began to send them out in pai
giving them authority over the unclean spirits. And he i
structed them to take nothing for the journey except a sta
– no bread, no haversack, no coppers for their purses. The
were to wear sandals but, he added, "Do not take a spa
tunic." And he said to them, "If you enter a house anywher
stay there until you leave the district. And if any place do
not welcome you and people refuse to listen to you, as yo
walk away shake off the dust from under your feet as a si

to them." So they set off to preach repentance; and they cast out many devils, and anointed many sick people with oil and cured them.

This is the Gospel of the Lord.

FRIDAY
Year I

First Reading   (13:1–8)

A reading from the letter to the Hebrews
Jesus Christ is the same today as he was yesterday and as he will be for ever.

Continue to love each other like brothers, and remember always to welcome strangers, for by doing this, some people have entertained angels without knowing it. Keep in mind those who are in prison, as though you were in prison with them; and those who are being badly treated, since you too are in the one body. Marriage is to be honoured by all, and marriages are to be kept undefiled, because fornicators and adulterers will come under God's judgement. Put greed out of your lives and be content with whatever you have; God himself has said: I will not fail you or desert you, and so we can say with confidence: With the Lord to help me, I fear nothing: what can man do to me?

Remember your leaders, who preached the word of God to you, and as you reflect on the outcome of their lives, imitate their faith. Jesus Christ is the same today as he was yesterday and as he will be for ever.

This is the word of the Lord.

Responsorial Psalm   (Ps 26:1. 3. 5. 8–9. *R̊*. v. 1)

Response
The Lord is my light and my help.

1. The Lord is my light and my help;
whom shall I fear?

The Lord is the stronghold of my life;
before whom shall I shrink? (*R.*)

2. Though an army encamp against me
my heart would not fear.
Though war break out against me
even then would I trust. (*R.*)

3. For there he keeps me safe in his tent
in the day of evil.
He hides me in the shelter of his tent,
on a rock he sets me safe. (*R.*)

4. It is your face, O Lord, that I seek;
hide not your face.
Dismiss not your servant in anger;
you have been my help. (*R.*)

ALLELUIA and GOSPEL. As for Year II, see p. 292.

Year II

First Reading   (47:2–11)

A reading from the book of Ecclesiasticus
David put all his heart into his songs out of love for his Maker.

As the fat is set apart from the communion sacrifice,
so David was chosen out of all the sons of Israel.
He played with lions as though with kids,
and with bears as though with lambs of the flock.
While still a boy, did he not slay the giant,
and relieve the people of their shame,
by putting out a hand to sling a stone
which brought down the arrogance of Goliath?
For he called on the Lord Most High,
who gave strength to his right arm
to put a mighty warrior to death,
and lift up the horn of his people.

Hence they gave him credit for ten thousand,
and praised him while they blessed the Lord,
by offering him a crown of glory;
for he massacred enemies on every side,
he annihilated his foes the Philistines,
and crushed their horn to this very day.
In all his activities he gave thanks
to the Holy One, the Most High, in words of glory;
he put all his heart into his songs
out of love for his Maker.
He placed harps before the altar
to make the singing sweeter with their music;
he gave the feasts their splendour,
the festivals their solemn pomp,
causing the Lord's holy name to be praised
and the sanctuary to resound from dawn.
The Lord took away his sins,
and exalted his horn for ever;
he gave him a royal covenant,
and a glorious throne in Israel.

This is the word of the Lord.

Responsorial Psalm   (Ps 17:31. 47. 50–51. R. v. 47)

Response
Praised be the God who saves me.

1. As for God, his ways are perfect;
the word of the Lord, purest gold.
He indeed is the shield
of all who make him their refuge. (R.)

2. Long life to the Lord, my rock!
Praised be the God who saves me.
I will praise you, Lord, among the nations:
I will sing a psalm to your name. (R.)

3. He has given great victories to his king
and shown his love for his anointed,
for David and his sons for ever. (*R.*)

Years I and II

Alleluia (Lk 8:15)

Alleluia, alleluia!
Blessed are those who,
with a noble and generous heart,
take the word of God to themselves
and yield a harvest through their perseverence.
Alleluia!

Alternative Alleluias p. 847.

Gospel (6:14–29)

A reading from the holy Gospel according to Mark
It is John whose head I cut off; he has risen from the dead.

Meanwhile King Herod had heard about Jesus, since by
now his name was well-known. Some were saying, "John
the Baptist has risen from the dead, and that is why miracu-
lous powers are at work in him." Others said, "He is Elijah"; others again, "He is a prophet, like the prophets we
used to have." But when Herod heard this he said, "It is
John whose head I cut off; he has risen from the dead."

Now it was this same Herod who had sent to have John
arrested, and had him chained up in prison because of Herodias, his brother Philip's wife whom he had married. For
John had told Herod, "It is against the law for you to have
your brother's wife." As for Herodias, she was furious with
him and wanted to kill him; but she was not able to, because
Herod was afraid of John, knowing him to be a good and
holy man, and gave him his protection. When he had heard
him speak he was greatly perplexed, and yet he liked to
listen to him.

An opportunity came on Herod's birthday when he gave
a banquet for the nobles of his court, for his army officers
and for the leading figures in Galilee. When the daughter
of this same Herodias came in and danced, she delighted
Herod and his guests; so the king said to the girl, "Ask me
anything you like and I will give it you." And he swore her
an oath, "I will give you anything you ask, even half my
kingdom." She went out and said to her mother, "What
shall I ask for?" She replied, "The head of John the Baptist." The girl hurried straight back to the king and made
her request, "I want you to give me John the Baptist's head,
here and now, on a dish." The king was deeply distressed
but, thinking of the oaths he had sworn and of his guests,
he was reluctant to break his word to her. So the king at
once sent one of the bodyguard with orders to bring John's
head. The man went off and beheaded him in prison; then
he brought the head on a dish and gave it to the girl, and the
girl gave it to her mother. When John's disciples heard
about this, they came and took his body and laid it in a
tomb.

This is the Gospel of the Lord.

SATURDAY
Year I

First Reading   (13:15–17. 20–21)

A reading from the letter to the Hebrews
*May the God of peace, who brought back from the dead the
great Shepherd, make you ready to do his will in any kind of
good action.*

Through Jesus, let us offer God an unending sacrifice of
praise, a verbal sacrifice that is offered every time we acknowledge his name. Keep doing good works and sharing
your resources, for these are sacrifices that please God.

Obey your leaders and do as they tell you, because they
must give an account of the way they look after your souls;

make this a joy for them to do, and not a grief – you yourselves would be the losers.

I pray that the God of peace, who brought our Lord
Jesus back from the dead to become the great Shepherd of
the sheep by the blood that sealed an eternal covenant, may
make you ready to do his will in any kind of good action;
and turn us all into whatever is acceptable to himself
through Jesus Christ, to whom be glory for ever and ever,
Amen.

This is the word of the Lord.

Responsorial Psalm   (Ps 22. *R.* v. 1)

Response
The Lord is my shepherd;
there is nothing I shall want.

1. The Lord is my shepherd;
there is nothing I shall want.
Fresh and green are the pastures
where he gives me repose.
Near restful waters he leads me,
to revive my drooping spirit. (*R.*)

2. He guides me along the right path;
he is true to his name.
If I should walk in the valley of darkness
no evil would I fear.
You are there with your crook and your staff;
with these you give me comfort. (*R.*)

3. You have prepared a banquet for me
in the sight of my foes.
My head you have anointed with oil;
my cup is overflowing. (*R.*)

4. Surely goodness and kindness shall follow me
all the days of my life.

In the Lord's own house shall I dwell
for ever and ever. (R.)

ALLELUIA and GOSPEL. As for Year II, see p. 296.

Year II

First Reading   (3:4–13)

A reading from the first book of the Kings

Give your servant a heart to understand how to discern between good and evil.

The king went to Gibeon to sacrifice there, since that was the greatest of the high places – Solomon offered a thousand holocausts on that altar. At Gibeon the Lord appeared in a dream to Solomon during the night. God said, "Ask what you would like me to give you." Solomon replied, "You showed great kindness to your servant David, my father, when he lived his life before you in faithfulness and justice and integrity of heart; you have continued this great kindness to him by allowing a son of his to sit on his throne to-day. Now, Lord my God, you have made your servant king in succession to David my father. But I am a very young man, unskilled in leadership. Your servant finds himself in the midst of this people of yours that you have chosen, a people so many its number cannot be counted or reckoned. Give your servant a heart to understand how to discern between good and evil, for who could govern this people of yours that is so great?" It pleased the Lord that Solomon should have asked for this. "Since you have asked for this" the Lord said "and not asked for long life for yourself or riches or the lives of your enemies, but have asked for a discerning judgement for yourself, here and now I do what you ask. I give you a heart wise and shrewd as none before you has had and none will have after you. What you have not asked I shall give you too : such riches and glory as no other king ever had."

This is the word of the Lord.

Responsorial Psalm   (Ps 118:9–14. *R*. v. 12)

Response
Lord, teach me your statutes.

1. How shall the young remain sinless?
By obeying your word.
I have sought you with all my heart:
let me not stray from your commands. (*R*.)

2. I treasure your promise in my heart
lest I sin against you.
Blessed are you, O Lord;
teach me your statutes. (*R*.)

3. With my tongue I have recounted
the decrees of your lips.
I rejoiced to do your will
as though all riches were mine. (*R*.)

Years I and II

Alleluia   (Jn 10:27)

Alleluia, alleluia!
The sheep that belong to me listen to my voice,
says the Lord,
I know them and they follow me.
Alleluia!

Alternative Alleluias p. 847.

Gospel   (6:30–34)

A reading from the holy Gospel according to Mark
They were like sheep without a shepherd.

The apostles rejoined Jesus and told him all they had done
and taught. Then he said to them, "You must come away to
some lonely place all by yourselves and rest for a while";

for there were so many coming and going that the apostles had no time even to eat. So they went off in a boat to a lonely place where they could be by themselves. But people saw them going, and many could guess where; and from every town they all hurried to the place on foot and reached it before them. So as he stepped ashore he saw a large crowd; and he took pity on them because they were like sheep without a shepherd, and he set himself to teach them at some length.

This is the Gospel of the Lord.

5th SUNDAY OF THE YEAR

Year 1 (Year A)

First Reading   (58:7–10)

A reading from the prophet Isaiah
Then will your light shine like the dawn.

Thus says the Lord:
Share your bread with the hungry,
and shelter the homeless poor,

clothe the man you see to be naked
and turn not from your own kin.
Then will your light shine like the dawn
and your wound be quickly healed over.

Your integrity will go before you
and the glory of the Lord behind you.
Cry, and the Lord will answer;
call, and he will say, "I am here."

If you do away with the yoke,
the clenched fist, the wicked word,
if you give your bread to the hungry,
and relief to the oppressed,

your light will rise in the darkness,
and your shadows become like noon.

This is the word of the Lord.

Responsorial Psalm (Ps 111 : 4–9. *R.* v. 4)

Response
The good man is a light in the darkness for the upright.

Or: Alleluia!

1. He is a light in the darkness for the upright :
he is generous, merciful and just.
The good man takes pity and lends,
he conducts his affairs with honour. (*R.*)

2. The just man will never waver :
he will be remembered for ever.
He has no fear of evil news ;
with a firm heart he trusts in the Lord. (*R.*)

3. With a steadfast heart he will not fear ;
Open-handed, he gives to the poor ;
his justice stands firm for ever.
His head will be raised in glory. (*R.*)

Second Reading (2 : 1–5)

A reading from the first letter of St Paul to the Corinthians
*During my stay with you, the only knowledge I claimed to have
was about Jesus as the crucified Christ.*

As for me, brothers, when I came to you, it was not with
any show of oratory or philosophy, but simply to tell you
what God had guaranteed. During my stay with you, the
only knowledge I claimed to have was about Jesus, and
only about him as the crucified Christ. Far from relying on

any power of my own, I came among you in great "fear and trembling" and in my speeches and the sermons that I gave, there were none of the arguments that belong to philosophy; only a demonstration of the power of the Spirit. And I did this so that your faith should not depend on human philosophy but on the power of God.

This is the word of the Lord.

Alleluia   (Jn 8:12)

Alleluia, alleluia!
I am the light of the world, says the Lord,
anyone who follows me
will have the light of life.
Alleluia!

Alternative Alleluias p. 854.

Gospel   (5:13–16)

A reading from the holy Gospel according to Matthew
You are the light of the world.

Jesus said to his disciples: "You are the salt of the earth. But if salt becomes tasteless, what can make it salty again? It is good for nothing, and can only be thrown out to be trampled underfoot by men.

"You are the light of the world. A city built on a hill-top cannot be hidden. No one lights a lamp to put it under a tub; they put it on the lamp-stand where it shines for everyone in the house. In the same way your light must shine in the sight of men, so that, seeing your good works, they may give the praise to your Father in heaven."

This is the Gospel of the Lord.

5th SUNDAY OF THE YEAR
Year 2 (Year B)

First Reading   (7:1–4. 6–7)

A reading from the book of Job
Restlessly I fret till twilight falls.

Job began to speak:
Is not man's life on earth nothing more than pressed service,
his time no better than hired drudgery?
Like the slave, sighing for the shade,
or the workman with no thought but his wages,
months of delusion I have assigned to me,
nothing for my own but nights of grief.
Lying in bed I wonder, "When will it be day?"
Risen I think, "How slowly evening comes!"
Restlessly I fret till twilight falls.
Swifter than a weaver's shuttle my days have passed,
and vanished, leaving no hope behind.
Remember that my life is but a breath,
and that my eyes will never again see joy.

This is the word of the Lord.

Responsorial Psalm   (Ps 146:1–6. *R*. v. 3)

Response
Praise the Lord who heals the broken-hearted.

Or: Alleluia!

1. Alleluia!
Praise the Lord for he is good;
sing to our God for he is loving:
to him our praise is due. (*R*.)

2. The Lord builds up Jerusalem
and brings back Israel's exiles,

he heals the broken-hearted,
he binds up all their wounds.
He fixes the number of the stars;
he calls each one by its name. (R.)

3. Our Lord is great and almighty;
his wisdom can never be measured.
The Lord raises the lowly;
he humbles the wicked to the dust. (R.)

Second Reading   (9:16–19. 22–23)

A reading from the first letter of St Paul to the Corinthians
I should be punished if I did not preach the Gospel.

I do not boast of preaching the gospel, since it is a duty
which has been laid on me; I should be punished if I did not
preach it! If I had chosen this work myself, I might have
been paid for it, but as I have not, it is a responsibility which
has been put into my hands. Do you know what my reward
is? It is this: in my preaching, to be able to offer the Good
News free, and not insist on the rights which the gospel
gives me.

So though I am not a slave of any man I have made myself the slave of everyone so as to win as many as I could.
For the weak I made myself weak. I made myself all things
to all men in order to save some at any cost; and I still do
this, for the sake of the gospel, to have a share in its blessings.

This is the word of the Lord.

ALLELUIA. As for Year I (A) see p. 299.

Gospel   (1:29–39)

A reading from the holy Gospel according to Mark
*He cured many who were suffering from diseases of one kind
or another.*

On leaving the synagogue, Jesus went with James and John straight to the house of Simon and Andrew. Now Simon's mother-in-law had gone to bed with fever, and they told him about her straightaway. He went to her, took her by the hand and helped her up. And the fever left her and she began to wait on them.

That evening, after sunset, they brought to him all who were sick and those who were possessed by devils. The whole town came crowding round the door, and he cured many who were suffering from diseases of one kind or another; he also cast out many devils, but he would not allow them to speak, because they knew who he was.

In the morning, long before dawn, he got up and left the house, and went off to a lonely place and prayed there. Simon and his companions set out in search of him, and when they found him they said, "Everybody is looking for you." He answered, "Let us go elsewhere, to the neighbouring country towns, so that I can preach there too, because that is why I came." And he went all through Galilee, preaching in their synagogues and casting out devils.

This is the Gospel of the Lord.

5th SUNDAY OF THE YEAR

Year 3 (Year C)

First Reading   (6:1–8)

A reading from the prophet Isaiah
Here I am, send me.

In the year of King Uzziah's death I saw the Lord seated on a high throne; his train filled the sanctuary; above him stood seraphs, each one with six wings.

And they cried out one to another in this way,
"Holy, holy, holy is the Lord of hosts.
His glory fills the whole earth."

The foundations of the threshold shook with the voice of the one who cried out, and the Temple was filled with smoke. I said:

"What a wretched state I am in! I am lost,
for I am a man of unclean lips
and I live among a people of unclean lips,
and my eyes have looked at the King, the Lord of hosts."

Then one of the seraphs flew to me, holding in his hand a live coal which he had taken from the altar with a pair of tongs. With this he touched my mouth and said:

"See now, this has touched your lips,
your sin is taken away,
your iniquity is purged."

Then I heard the voice of the Lord saying:

"Whom shall I send? Who will be our messenger?"

I answered, "Here I am, send me."

This is the word of the Lord.

Responsorial Psalm   (Ps 137:1–5. 7–8. R. v. 1)

Response

Before the angels I will bless you, O Lord.

1. I thank you, Lord, with all my heart,
you have heard the words of my mouth.
Before the angels I will bless you.
I will adore before your holy temple. (R.)

2. I thank you for your faithfulness and love
which excel all we ever knew of you.

On the day I called, you answered;
you increased the strength of my soul. (*R.*)

3. All earth's kings shall thank you
when they hear the words of your mouth.
They shall sing of the Lord's ways:
"How great is the glory of the Lord!" (*R.*)

4. You stretch out your hand and save me,
your hand will do all things for me.
Your love, O Lord, is eternal,
discard not the work of your hands. (*R.*)

Second Reading (15:1–11)

A reading from the first letter of St Paul to the Corinthians
I preach what they preach, and this is what you all believed.

Brothers, I want to remind you of the gospel I preached to you, the gospel that you received and in which you are firmly established; because the gospel will save you only if you keep believing exactly what I preached to you – believing anything else will not lead to anything.

Well then *in the first place, I taught you what I had been taught myself, namely that Christ died for our sins, in accordance with the scriptures; that he was buried; and that he was raised to life on the third day, in accordance with the scriptures; that he appeared first to Cephas and secondly to the Twelve. Next he appeared to more than five hundred of the brothers at the same time, most of whom are still alive, though some have died; then he appeared to James, and then to all the apostles; and last of all he appeared to me too; it was as though I was born when no one expected it.

I am the least of the apostles; in fact, since I persecuted the Church of God, I hardly deserve the name apostle; but by God's grace that is what I am, and the grace that he gave me has not been fruitless. On the contrary, I, or rather the grace of God that is with me, have worked harder than any of the others; but what matters is that I preach what they preach, and this is what you all believed.*

This is the word of the Lord.

*Shorter form, verses 3–8. 11, read between *.

Alleluia   (Jn 15:15)

Alleluia, alleluia!
I call you friends, says the Lord,
because I have made known to you
everything I have learnt from my Father.
Alleluia!

Alternative Alleluias p. 854.

Gospel   (5:1–11)

A reading from the holy Gospel according to Luke
They left everything and followed him.

Jesus was standing one day by the Lake of Gennesaret, with the crowd pressing round him listening to the word of God, when he caught sight of two boats close to the bank. The fishermen had gone out of them and were washing their nets. He got into one of the boats – it was Simon's – and asked him to put out a little from the shore. Then he sat down and taught the crowds from the boat.

When he had finished speaking he said to Simon, "Put out into deep water and pay out your nets for a catch." "Master," Simon replied "we worked hard all night long and caught nothing, but if you say so, I will pay out the nets." And when they had done this they netted such a huge number of fish that their nets began to tear, so they signalled to their companions in the other boat to come and help them; when these came, they filled the two boats to sinking point.

When Simon Peter saw this he fell at the knees of Jesus saying, "Leave me, Lord; I am a sinful man." For he and all his companions were completely overcome by the catch they had made; so also were James and John, sons of Zebedee, who were Simon's partners. But Jesus said to Simon, "Do not be afraid; from now on it is men you will catch." Then, bringing their boats back to land, they left everything and followed him.

This is the Gospel of the Lord.

MONDAY
Year I

First Reading   (1:1–19)

A reading from the book of Genesis
God said, and so it was.

In the beginning God created the heavens and the earth. Now the earth was a formless void, there was darkness over the deep, and God's spirit hovered over the water.

God said, "Let there be light," and there was light. God saw that light was good, and God divided light from darkness. God called light "day," and darkness he called "night". Evening came and morning came: the first day.

God said, "Let there be a vault in the waters to divide the waters in two." And so it was. God made the vault, and it divided the waters above the vault from the waters under the vault. God called the vault "heaven". Evening came and morning came: the second day.

God said, "Let the waters under heaven come together into a single mass, and let dry land appear." And so it was. God called the dry land "earth" and the mass of waters "seas", and God saw that it was good.

God said, "Let the earth produce vegetation: seed-bearing plants, and fruit trees bearing fruit with their seed inside, on the earth." And so it was. The earth produced vegetation: plants bearing seed in their several kinds, and trees bearing fruit with their seed inside in their several kinds. God saw that it was good. Evening came and morning came: the third day.

God said, "Let there be lights in the vault of heaven to divide day from night, and let them indicate festivals, days and years. Let them be lights in the vault of heaven to shine on the earth." And so it was. God made the two great lights: the greater light to govern the day, the smaller light to govern the night, and the stars. God set them in the vault of heaven to shine on the earth, to govern the day and the night and to divide light from darkness. God saw that it was good. Evening came and morning came: the fourth day.

This is the word of the Lord.

Responsorial Psalm (Ps 103:1–2. 5–6. 10. 12. 24. 35. *R.* v. 31)

Response
May the Lord rejoice in his works!

1. Bless the Lord, my soul!
Lord God, how great you are,
clothed in majesty and glory,
wrapped in light as in a robe! (*R.*)

2. You founded the earth on its base,
to stand firm from age to age.
You wrapped it with the ocean like a cloak:
the waters stood higher than the mountains. (*R.*)

3. You make springs gush forth in the valleys:
they flow in between the hills.
On their banks dwell the birds of heaven;
from the branches they sing their song. (*R.*)

4. How many are your works, O Lord!
In wisdom you have made them all.
The earth is full of your riches.
Bless the Lord, my soul! (*R.*)

ALLELUIA and GOSPEL. As for Year II, see p. 309.

Year II

First Reading (8:1–7. 9–13)

A reading from the first book of the Kings
They brought the ark of the covenant into the Holy of Holies,
and the cloud filled the Temple of the Lord.

Solomon called the elders of Israel together in Jerusalem
to bring the ark of the covenant of the Lord up from the
Citadel of David, which is Zion. All the men of Israel assembled round King Solomon in the month of Ethanim,
at the time of the feast (that is, the seventh month), and the
priests took up the ark and the Tent of Meeting with all the
sacred vessels that were in it. In the presence of the ark,
King Solomon and all Israel sacrificed sheep and oxen,
countless, innumerable. The priests brought the ark of the
covenant of the Lord to its place, in the Debir of the Temple,
that is, in the Holy of Holies, under the cherubs' wings. For
there where the ark was placed the cherubs spread out their
wings and sheltered the ark and its shafts. There was nothing in the ark except the two stone tablets Moses had placed
in it at Horeb, the tablets of the covenant which the Lord
had made with the Israelites when they came out of the land
of Egypt; they are still there today.

Now when the priests came out of the sanctuary, the cloud
filled the Temple of the Lord, and because of the cloud the
priests could no longer perform their duties: the glory of
the Lord filled the Lord's Temple.

Then Solomon said:

"The Lord has chosen to dwell in the thick cloud.
Yes, I have built you a dwelling,
a place for you to live in for ever."

This is the word of the Lord.

Responsorial Psalm   (Ps 131:6–10. *R*. v .8)
Response
Go up, Lord, to the place of your rest!

1. At Ephrata we heard of the ark;
we found it in the plains of Yearim.
"Let us go to the place of his dwelling;
let us go to kneel at his footstool." (*R*.)

2. Go up, Lord, to the place of your rest,
you and the ark of your strength.
Your priests shall be clothed with holiness:
your faithful shall ring out their joy.
For the sake of David your servant
do not reject your anointed. (*R*.)

Years I and II
Alleluia   (Jn 8:12)

Alleluia, alleluia!
I am the light of the world, says the Lord,
anyone who follows me
will have the light of life.
Alleluia!

Alternative Alleluias p. 847.

Gospel   (6:53–56)
A reading from the holy Gospel according to Mark
All those who touched him were cured.

Having made the crossing, Jesus and his disciples came to
and at Genessaret and tied up. No sooner had they stepped

out of the boat than people recognised him, and started hurrying all through the countryside and brought the sick on stretchers to wherever they heard he was. And wherever he went, to village, or town, or farm, they laid down the sick in the open spaces, begging him to let them touch even the fringe of his cloak. And all those who touched him were cured.

This is the Gospel of the Lord.

TUESDAY
Year I

First Reading (1:20–2:4)

A reading from the book of Genesis
Let us make man in our own image, in the likeness of ourselves.

God said, "Let the waters teem with living creatures, and let birds fly above the earth within the vault of heaven." And so it was. God created great sea-serpents and every kind of living creature with which the waters teem, and every kind of winged creature. God saw that it was good. God blessed them, saying, "Be fruitful, multiply, and fill the waters of the seas; and let the birds multiply upon the earth." Evening came and morning came: the fifth day.

God said, "Let the earth produce every kind of living creature: cattle, reptiles, and every kind of wild beast." And so it was. God made every kind of wild beast, every kind of cattle, and every kind of land reptile. God saw that it was good.

God said, "Let us make man in our own image, in the likeness of ourselves, and let them be masters of the fish of the sea, the birds of heaven, the cattle, all the wild beasts and all the reptiles that crawl upon the earth."

God created man in the image of himself,
in the image of God he created him,
male and female he created them.

God blessed them, saying to them, "Be fruitful, multiply, fill the earth and conquer it. Be masters of the fish of the sea, the birds of heaven and all living animals on the earth." God said, "See, I give you all the seed-bearing plants that are upon the whole earth, and all the trees with seed-bearing fruit; this shall be your food. To all wild beasts, all birds of heaven and all living reptiles on the earth I give all the foliage of plants for food." And so it was. God saw all he had made, and indeed it was very good. Evening came and morning came: the sixth day.

Thus heaven and earth were completed with all their array. On the seventh day God completed the work he had been doing. He rested on the seventh day after all the work he had been doing. God blessed the seventh day and made it holy, because on that day he had rested after all his work of creating.

Such were the origins of heaven and earth when they were created.

This is the word of the Lord.

Responsorial Psalm   (Ps 8:4–9. *R*. v. 2)

Response
How great is your name,
O Lord our God,
through all the earth!

1. When I see the heavens, the work of your hands,
the moon and the stars which you arranged,
what is man that you should keep him in mind,
mortal man that you care for him? (*R*.)

2. Yet you have made him little less than a god;
with glory and honour you crowned him,
gave him power over the works of your hand,
put all things under his feet. (*R*.)

3. All of them, sheep and cattle,
yes, even the savage beasts,
birds of the air, and fish
that make their way through the waters. (*R.*)

ALLELUIA and GOSPEL. As for Year II, see p. 313.

Year II

First Reading   (8:22–23. 27–30)

A reading from the first book of the Kings

You have said, "My name shall be there." Hear the entreaty of your people Israel.

In the presence of the whole assembly of Israel, Solomon stood before the altar of the Lord and, stretching out his hands towards heaven, said, "Lord God of Israel, not in heaven above nor on earth beneath is there such a God as you, true to your covenant and your kindness towards your servants when they walk wholeheartedly in your way. Yet will God really live with men on the earth? Why, the heavens and their own heavens cannot contain you. How much less this house that I have built! Listen to the prayer and entreaty of your servant, Lord my God; listen to the cry and to the prayer your servant makes to you today. Day and night let your eyes watch over this house, over this place of which you have said, 'My name shall be there.' Listen to the prayer that your servant will offer in this place.

"Hear the entreaty of your servant and of Israel your people as they pray in this place. From heaven where your dwelling is, hear; and, as you hear, forgive."

This is the word of the Lord.

Responsorial Psalm   (Ps 83:3–5. 10–11. *R.* v. 2)

Response

How lovely is your dwelling place,
Lord, God of hosts.

1. My soul is longing and yearning,
is yearning for the courts of the Lord.
My heart and my soul ring out their joy
to God, the living God. (*R*)

2. The sparrow herself finds a home
and the swallow a nest for her brood;
she lays her young by your altars,
Lord of hosts, my king and my God. (*R.*)

3. They are happy, who dwell in your house,
for ever singing your praise.
Turn your eyes, O God, our shield,
look on the face of your anointed. (*R.*)

4. One day within your courts
is better than a thousand elsewhere.
The threshold of the house of God
I prefer to the dwellings of the wicked. (*R.*)

Years I and II

Alleluia   (Ps 118:34)

Alleluia, alleluia!
Train me, Lord, to observe your law,
to keep it with my heart.
Alleluia!

Alternative Alleluias p. 847.

Gospel   (7:1–13)

A reading from the holy Gospel according to Mark
*You put aside the commandment of God to cling to human
traditions.*

The Pharisees and some of the scribes who had come from
Jerusalem gathered round Jesus, and they noticed that some

of his disciples were eating with unclean hands, that is, without washing them. For the Pharisees, and the Jews in general, follow the tradition of the elders and never eat without washing their arms as far as the elbow; and on returning from the market place they never eat without first sprinkling themselves. There are also many other observances which have been handed down to them concerning the washing of cups and pots and bronze dishes. So these Pharisees and scribes asked him, "Why do your disciples not respect the tradition of the elders but eat their food with unclean hands?" He answered, "It was of you hypocrites that Isaiah so rightly prophesied in this passage of scripture:

This people honours me only with lip-service,
while their hearts are far from me.
The worship they offer me is worthless,
the doctrines they teach are only human regulations.

You put aside the commandment of God to cling to human traditions." And he said to them. "How ingeniously you get round the commandment of God in order to preserve your own tradition! For Moses said: Do your duty to your father and your mother, and, Anyone who curses father or mother must be put to death. But you say, 'If a man says to his father or mother: Anything I have that I might have used to help you is Corban (that is, dedicated to God), then he is forbidden from that moment to do anything for his father or mother.' In this way you make God's word null and void for the sake of your tradition which you have handed down. And you do many other things like this."
    This is the Gospel of the Lord.

WEDNESDAY
Year I

First Reading   (2:4–9. 15–17)

A reading from the book of Genesis

The Lord God took the man and settled him in the garden of Eden.

At the time when the Lord God made earth and heaven there was as yet no wild bush on the earth nor had any wild plant yet sprung up, for the Lord God had not sent rain on the earth, nor was there any man to till the soil. However, a flood was rising from the earth and watering all the surface of the soil. The Lord God fashioned man of dust from the soil. Then he breathed into his nostrils a breath of life, and thus man became a living being.

The Lord God planted a garden in Eden which is in the east, and there he put the man he had fashioned. The Lord God caused to spring up from the soil every kind of tree, enticing to look at and good to eat, with the tree of life and the tree of the knowledge of good and evil in the middle of the garden. The Lord God took the man and settled him in the garden of Eden to cultivate and take care of it. Then the Lord God gave the man this admonition, "You may eat indeed of all the trees in the garden. Nevertheless of the tree of the knowledge of good and evil you are not to eat, for on the day you eat of it you shall most surely die."

This is the word of the Lord.

Responsorial Psalm   (Ps 103:1–2. 27–30. R. v .1)

Response
Bless the Lord, my soul!

. Bless the Lord my soul!
Lord God, how great you are,
clothed in majesty and glory,
wrapped in light as in a robe. (*R.*)

2. All of these look to you
to give them their food in due season.
You give it, they gather it up:
you open your hand, they have their fill. (R.)

3. You take back your spirit, they die,
returning from the dust from which they came.
You send forth your spirit, they are created;
and you renew the face of the earth. (R.)

ALLELUIA and GOSPEL. As for Year II, see p. 317.

Year II

First Reading   (10:1–10)

A reading from the first book of the Kings
The queen of Sheba saw all the wisdom of Solomon.

The fame of Solomon having reached the queen of Sheba
she came to test him with difficult questions. She brough
immense riches to Jerusalem with her, camels laden witl
spices, great quantities of gold, and precious stones. O
coming to Solomon, she opened her mind freely to him
and Solomon had an answer for all her questions, not on
of them was too obscure for the king to expound. When th
queen of Sheba saw all the wisdom of Solomon, the palac
he had built, the food at his table, the accommodation fo
his officials, the organisation of his staff and the way the
were dressed, his cup-bearers, and the holocausts he of
ered in the Temple of the Lord, it left her breathless, and sh
said to the king, "What I heard in my own country abou
you and your wisdom was true, then! Until I came an
saw it with my own eyes I could not believe what they tol
me, but clearly they told me less than half: for wisdom an
prosperity you surpass the report I heard. How happy yo
wives are! How happy are these servants of yours who wa
on you always and hear your wisdom! Blessed be the Lo

your God who has granted you his favour, setting you on
the throne of Israel! Because of the Lord's everlasting love
for Israel, he has made you king to deal out law and justice."
And she presented the king with a hundred and twenty talents of gold and great quantities of spices and precious
stones; no such wealth of spices ever came again as those
given to King Solomon by the queen of Sheba.
This is the word of the Lord.

Responsorial Psalm   (Ps 36:5–6. 30–31. 39–40. *R*. v. 30)
Response
The just man's mouth utters wisdom.

1. Commit your life to the Lord,
trust in him and he will act,
so that your justice breaks forth like the light,
your cause like the noon-day sun. (*R*.)

2. The just man's mouth utters wisdom
and his lips speak what is right;
the law of his God is in his heart,
his steps shall be saved from stumbling. (*R*.)

3. The salvation of the just comes from the Lord,
their stronghold in time of distress.
The Lord helps them and delivers them
and saves them: for their refuge is in him. (*R*.)

Years I and II

Alleluia   (2 Tim 1:10)
Alleluia, alleluia!
Our Saviour Christ Jesus abolished death,
and he has proclaimed life through the Good News.
Alleluia!

Alternative Alleluias p. 847.

Gospel   (7:14–23)

A reading from the holy Gospel according to Mark
It is what comes out of a man that makes him unclean.

Jesus called the people to him and said, "Listen to me, all of you, and understand. Nothing that goes into a man from outside can make him unclean; it is the things that come out of a man that make him unclean. If anyone has ears to hear, let him listen to this."

When he had gone back into the house, away from the crowd, his disciples questioned him about the parable. He said to them, "Do you not understand either? Can you not see that whatever goes into a man from outside cannot make him unclean, because it does not go into his heart but through his stomach and passes out into the sewer?" (Thus he pronounced all foods clean.) And he went on, "It is what comes out of a man that makes him unclean. For it is from within, from men's hearts, that evil intentions emerge: fornication, theft, murder, adultery, avarice, malice, deceit, indecency, envy, slander, pride, folly. All these evil things come from within and make a man unclean."

This is the Gospel of the Lord.

THURSDAY

Year I

First Reading   (2:18–25)

A reading from the book of Genesis
He brought her to the man. They became one body.

The Lord God said, "It is not good that the man should be alone. I will make him a helpmate." So from the soil the Lord God fashioned all the wild beasts and all the birds of heaven. These he brought to the man to see what he would call them; each one was to bear the name the man would give it. The man gave names to all the cattle, all the birds of heaven, and all the wild beasts. But no helpmate suitable for man was found for him. So the Lord God made the man fall into a deep sleep. And while he slept, he took one of his ribs and enclosed it in flesh. The Lord God built the rib he had taken from the man into a woman, and brought her to the man. The man exclaimed:

"This at last is bone from my bones,
and flesh from my flesh!
This is to be called woman,
for this was taken from man."

This is why a man leaves his father and mother and joins himself to his wife, and they become one body.

Now both of them were naked, the man and his wife, but they felt no shame in front of each other.

This is the word of the Lord.

Responsorial Psalm   (Ps 127:1–5. *R*. v. 1)

Response
O blessed are those who fear the Lord.

1. O blessed are those who fear the Lord
and walk in his ways! (*R*.)

2. By the labour of your hands you shall eat.
You will be happy and prosper;
your wife like a fruitful vine
in the heart of your house;
your children like shoots of the olive,
round your table. (*R*.)

3. Indeed thus shall be blessed
the man who fears the Lord.

May the Lord bless you from Zion
all the days of your life! (*R.*)

ALLELUIA and GOSPEL. As for Year II, see p. 321.

Year II

First Reading   (11:4–13)

A reading from the first book of the Kings

*Since you do not keep my covenant I will tear the kingdom
away from you. For the sake of my servant David, I will leave
your son one tribe.*

When Solomon grew old his wives swayed his heart to other
gods; and his heart was not wholly with the Lord his God
as his father David's had been. Solomon became a follower
of Astarte, the goddess of the Sidonians, and of Milcom
the Ammonite abomination. He did what was displeasing to
the Lord, and was not a wholehearted follower of the Lord
as his father David had been. Then it was that Solomon
built a high place for Chemosh the god of Moab on the
mountain to the east of Jerusalem, and to Milcom the god
of the Ammonites. He did the same for all his foreign wives
who offered incense and sacrifice to their gods.

The Lord was angry with Solomon because his heart had
turned from the Lord the God of Israel who had twice appeared to him and who had then forbidden him to follow
other gods; but he did not carry out the Lord's order. The
Lord therefore said to Solomon, "Since you behave like
this and do not keep my covenant or the laws I laid down
for you, I will most surely tear the kingdom away from you
and give it to one of your servants. For your father David's
sake, however, I will not do this during your lifetime, but
will tear it out of your son's hands. Even so, I will not tear
the whole kingdom from him. For the sake of my servant
David, and for the sake of Jerusalem which I have chosen,
I will leave your son one tribe."

This is the word of the Lord.

Responsorial Psalm (Ps 105:3–4. 35–37. 40. *R.* v. 4)

Response
O Lord, remember me
out of the love you have for your people.

1. They are happy who do what is right,
who at all times do what is just.
O Lord, remember me
out of the love you have for your people. (*R.*)

2. But instead they mingled with the nations
and learned to act like them.
They worshipped the idols of the nations
and these became a snare to entrap them. (*R.*)

3. They even offered their own sons
and their daughters in sacrifice to demons,
till his anger blazed against his people:
he was filled with horror at his chosen ones. (*R.*)

Years I and II

Alleluia (Ps 144:13)

Alleluia, alleluia!
The Lord is faithful in all his words
and loving in all his deeds.
Alleluia!

Alternative Alleluias p. 847.

Gospel (7:24–30)

A reading from the holy Gospel according to Mark
The house-dogs under the table can eat the children's scraps.

Jesus left Gennesaret and set out for the territory of Tyre.
There he went into a house and did not want anyone to
know he was there, but he could not pass unrecognised. A
woman whose little daughter had an unclean spirit heard
about him straightaway and came and fell at his feet. Now

the woman was a pagan, by birth a Syrophoenician, and she begged him to cast the devil out of her daughter. And he said to her, "The children should be fed first, because it is not fair to take the children's food and throw it to the house-dogs." But she spoke up: "Ah yes, sir," she replied "but the house-dogs under the table can eat the children's scraps." And he said to her, "For saying this, you may go home happy: the devil has gone out of your daughter." So she went off to her home and found the child lying on the bed and the devil gone.

This is the Gospel of the Lord.

FRIDAY
Year I

First Reading   (3:1–8)

A reading from the book of Genesis
You will be like gods, knowing good and evil.

The serpent was the most subtle of all the wild beasts that the Lord God had made. It asked the woman, "Did God really say you were not to eat from any of the trees in the garden?" The woman answered the serpent, "We may eat the fruit of the trees in the garden. But of the fruit of the tree in the middle of the garden God said, 'You must not eat it, nor touch it, under pain of death.'" Then the serpent said to the woman, "No! You will not die! God knows in fact that on the day you eat it your eyes will be opened and you will be like gods, knowing good and evil." The woman saw that the tree was good to eat and pleasing to the eye, and that it was desirable for the knowledge that it could give. So she took some of its fruit and ate it. She gave some also to her husband who was with her, and he ate it. Then the eyes of both of them were opened and they realised that they were naked. So they sewed fig-leaves together to make themselves loin-cloths.

The man and his wife heard the sound of the Lord God

walking in the garden in the cool of the day, and they hid
from the Lord God among the trees of the garden.

This is the word of the Lord.

Responsorial Psalm   (Ps 31:1–2. 5–7. R. v. 1)

Response
Happy the man whose offence is forgiven.

1. Happy the man whose offence is forgiven,
whose sin is remitted.
O happy the man to whom the Lord
imputes no guilt,
in whose spirit is no guile (R.)

2. But now I have acknowledged my sins;
my guilt I did not hide.
I said: "I will confess
my offence to the Lord."
And you, Lord, have forgiven
the guilt of my sin. (R.)

3. So let every good man pray to you
in the time of need.
The floods of water may reach high
but him they shall not reach.
You are my hiding place, O Lord;
you save me from distress.
You surround me with cries of deliverance. (R.)

ALLELUIA and GOSPEL. As for Year II, see p. 324.

Year II

First Reading   (11:29–32;12:19)

A reading from the first book of the Kings
Israel has been separated from the House of David.

One day when Jeroboam had gone out of Jerusalem, the
prophet Ahijah of Shiloh accosted him on the road. Ahijah

was wearing a new cloak; the two of them were in the open country by themselves. Ahijah took the new cloak he was wearing and tore it into twelve strips, saying to Jeroboam, "Take ten strips for yourself, for thus the Lord God speaks, the God of Israel, 'I am going to tear the kingdom from Solomon's hand and give ten tribes to you. He shall keep one tribe for the sake of my servant David and for the sake of Jerusalem, the city I have chosen out of all the tribes of Israel.' " And Israel has been separated from the House of David until the present day.

This is the word of the Lord.

Responsorial Psalm   (Ps 80:10–15. *R.* vv. 11. 9)
Response
I am the Lord your God,
listen to my warning.

1. Let there be no foreign god among you,
no worship of an alien god.
I am the Lord your God,
who brought you from the land of Egypt. (*R.*)

2. But my people did not heed my voice
and Israel would not obey,
so I left them in their stubbornness of heart
to follow their own designs. (*R.*)

3. O that my people would heed me,
that Israel would walk in my ways!
At once I would subdue their foes,
turn my hand against their enemies. (*R.*)

Years I and II

Alleluia   (Jn 6:63. 68)
Alleluia, alleluia!
Your words are spirit, Lord,
and they are life:

you have the message of eternal life.
Alleluia!

Alternative Alleluias p. 847.

Gospel   (7:31–37)

A reading from the holy Gospel according to Mark
He makes the deaf hear and the dumb speak.

Returning from the district of Tyre, Jesus went by way of
Sidon towards the Sea of Galilee, right through the Decapolis region. And they brought him a deaf man who had an
impediment in his speech; and they asked him to lay his
hand on him. He took him aside in private, away from the
crowd, put his fingers into the man's ears and touched his
tongue with spittle. Then looking up to heaven he sighed;
and he said to him, "Ephphatha," that is, "Be opened." And
his ears were opened, and the ligament of his tongue was
loosened and he spoke clearly. And Jesus ordered them to
tell no one about it, but the more he insisted, the more widely
they published it. Their admiration was unbounded. "He
has done all things well," they said "he makes the deaf hear
and the dumb speak."

This is the Gospel of the Lord.

SATURDAY
Year I

First Reading   (3:9–24)

A reading from the book of Genesis
*The Lord God expelled him from the garden of Eden, to till the
soil.*

The Lord God called to the man. "Where are you?" he
asked. "I heard the sound of you in the garden," he replied
"I was afraid because I was naked, so I hid." "Who told
you that you were naked?" he asked. "Have you been eating

of the tree I forbade you to eat?" The man replied, "It was the woman you put with me; she gave me the fruit, and I ate it." Then the Lord God asked the woman, "What is this you have done?" The woman replied, "The serpent tempted me and I ate."

Then the Lord God said to the serpent, "Because you have done this,

"Be accursed beyond all cattle,
all wild beasts.
You shall crawl on your belly and eat dust
every day of your life.
I will make you enemies of each other:
you and the woman,
your offspring and her offspring.
It will crush your head
and you will strike its heel."

To the woman he said:

"I will multiply your pains in childbearing,
you shall give birth to your children in pain.
Your yearning shall be for your husband,
yet he will lord it over you."

To the man he said, "Because you listened to the voice of your wife and ate from the tree of which I had forbidden you to eat,

"Accursed be the soil because of you.
With suffering shall you get your food from it
every day of your life.
It shall yield you brambles and thistles,
and you shall eat wild plants.
With sweat on your brow
shall you eat your bread,
until you return to the soil,

as you were taken from it.
For dust you are
and to dust you shall return."

The man named his wife "Eve" because she was the
mother of all those who live. The Lord God made clothes
out of skins for the man and his wife, and they put them on.
Then the Lord God said, "See, the man has become like one
of us, with his knowledge of good and evil. He must not be
allowed to stretch his hand out next and pick from the tree
of life also, and eat some and live for ever." So the Lord
God expelled him from the garden of Eden, to till the soil
from which he had been taken. He banished the man, and in
front of the garden of Eden he posted the cherubs, and the
flame of a flashing sword, to guard the way to the tree of
life.

This is the word of the Lord.

Responsorial Psalm   (Ps 89:2–6. 12–13. *R*. v .1)

Response
O Lord, you have been our refuge
from one generation to the next.

1. Before the mountains were born
or the earth or the world brought forth,
You are God, without beginning or end. (*R*.)

2. You turn men back into dust
and say: "Go back, sons of men."
To your eyes a thousand years
are like yesterday, come and gone,
no more than a watch in the night. (*R*.)

3. You sweep men away like a dream,
like grass which springs up in the morning.
In the morning it springs up and flowers:
by evening it withers and fades. (*R*.)

4. Make us know the shortness of our life
that we may gain wisdom of heart.
Lord, relent! Is your anger for ever?
Show pity on your servants. (*R.*)

ALLELUIA and GOSPEL. As for Year II, see p. 329.

Year II

First Reading   (12:26–32;13:33–34)

A reading from the first book of the Kings
Jeroboam made two golden calves.

Jeroboam thought to himself, "As things are, the kingdom
will revert to the House of David. If this people continues
to go up to the Temple of the Lord in Jerusalem to offer
sacrifices, the people's heart will turn back again to their
lord, Rehoboam king of Judah, and they will put me to
death." So the king thought this over and then made two
golden calves; he said to the people, "You have been going
up to Jerusalem long enough. Here are your gods, Israel;
these brought you up out of the land of Egypt!" He set up
one in Bethel and the people went in procession all the way
to Dan in front of the other. He set up the temple of the high
places and appointed priests from ordinary families, who
were not of the sons of Levi. Jeroboam also instituted a
feast in the eighth month, on the fifteenth of the month, like
the feast that was kept in Judah, and he went up to the altar.
That was how he behaved in Bethel, sacrificing to the calves
he had made; and at Bethel he put the priests of the high
places he had established.

Jeroboam did not give up his wicked ways after this incident, but went on appointing priests for the high places
from the common people. He consecrated as priests of the
high places any who wished to be. Such conduct made the
House of Jeroboam a sinful House, and caused its ruin and
extinction from the face of the earth.

This is the word of the Lord.

Responsorial Psalm (Ps 118:1–2. 4–5. 17–18. 33–34. *R*. v. 1)

Response
They are happy who follow God's law!

1. They are happy whose life is blameless,
who follow God's law!
They are happy those who do his will,
seeking him with all their hearts. (*R*.)

2. You have laid down your precepts
to be obeyed with care.
May my footsteps be firm
to obey your statutes. (*R*.)

3. Bless your servant and I shall live
and obey your word.
Open my eyes that I may consider
the wonders of your law. (*R*.)

4. Teach me the demands of your statutes
and I will keep them to the end.
Train me to observe your law,
to keep it with my heart. (*R*.)

Second Reading   (2:6–10)

A reading from the first letter of St Paul to the Corinthians
*God predestined wisdom to be for our glory before the ages
began.*

We have a wisdom to offer those who have reached maturity: not a philosophy of our age, it is true, still less of the
masters of our age, which are coming to their end. The
hidden wisdom of God which we teach in our mysteries is
the wisdom that God predestined to be for our glory before
the ages began. It is a wisdom that none of the masters of
this age have ever known, or they would not have crucified

the Lord of Glory; we teach what scripture calls: the things that no eye has seen and no ear has heard, things beyond the mind of man, all that God has prepared for those who love him.

These are the very things that God has revealed to us through the Spirit, for the Spirit reaches the depths of everything, even the depths of God.

This is the word of the Lord.

Alleluia   (1 Sam 3:9; Jn 6:68)

Alleluia, alleluia!
Speak, Lord, your servant is listening:
you have the message of eternal life.
Alleluia!

Alternative Alleluias p. 854.

Gospel   (5:17–37)

A reading from the holy Gospel according to Matthew
You have learnt how it was said to our ancestors; but I say this to you.

Jesus said to his disciples: "Do not imagine that I have come to abolish the Law or the Prophets. I have come not to abolish them but to complete them. I tell you solemnly, till heaven and earth disappear, not one dot, one little stroke, shall disappear from the Law until its purpose is achieved. Therefore, the man who infringes even one of the least of these commandments and teaches others to do the same will be considered the least in the kingdom of heaven; but the man who keeps them and teaches them will be considered great in the kingdom of heaven.

*"For I tell you, if your virtue goes no deeper than that of the scribes and Pharisees, you will never get into the kingdom of heaven.

"You have learnt how it was said to our ancestors: You must not kill; and if anyone does kill he must answer for it before the court. But I say this to you: anyone who is angry with his brother will answer for it before the court;* if a man calls his brother 'Fool' he will answer for it before the Sanhedrin; and if a man calls him 'Renegade' he will answer for it in hell fire. So then, if you are bringing your offering to the altar and there remember that your brother has something against you, leave your offering there before the altar, go and be reconciled with your brother first, and then come back and present your offering. Come to terms with your opponent in good time while you are still on the way to the court with him, or he may hand you over to the judge and the judge to the officer, and you will be thrown into prison. I tell you solemnly, you will not get out till you have paid the last penny.

"You have learnt how it was said: You must not commit adultery. But I say this to you: if a man looks at a woman lustfully, he has already committed adultery with her in his heart. If your right eye should cause you to sin, tear it out and throw it away; for it will do you less harm to lose one part of you than to have your whole body thrown into hell. And if your right hand should cause you to sin, cut it off and throw it away; for it will do you less harm to lose one part of you than to have your whole body go to hell.

"It has also been said: Anyone who divorces his wife must give her a writ of dismissal. But I say this to you: everyone who divorces his wife, except for the case of fornication, makes her an adulteress; and anyone who marries a divorced woman commits adultery.

"Again, you have learnt how it was said to our ancestors: You must not break your oath, but must fulfil your oaths to the Lord. But I say this to you: do not swear at all, either by heaven, since that is God's throne; or by the earth, since that is his footstool; or by Jerusalem, since that is the city of the great king. Do not swear by your own head either, since you cannot turn a single hair white or black.

*All you need say is 'Yes' if you mean yes, 'No' if you mean no; anything more than this comes from the evil one."

   This is the Gospel of the Lord.*

* Shorter Form, verses 20–22, 27–28. 33–34. 37. Read between*.

6th SUNDAY OF THE YEAR
Year 2 (Year B)

First Reading   (13:1–2. 45–46)

A reading from the book of Leviticus
The leper must live apart: he must live outside the camp.

The Lord said to Moses and Aaron, "If a swelling or scab or shiny spot appears on a man's skin, a case of leprosy of the skin is to be suspected. The man must be taken to Aaron, the priest, or to one of the priests who are his sons.

   "A man infected with leprosy must wear his clothing torn and his hair disordered; he must shield his upper lip and cry, 'Unclean, unclean'. As long as the disease lasts he must be unclean; and therefore he must live apart: he must live outside the camp."

   This is the word of the Lord.

Responsorial Psalm   (Ps 31:1–2. 5. 11. *R*. v. 7)

Response
You are my hiding place, O Lord;
you surround me with cries of deliverance.

1. Happy the man whose offence is forgiven,
whose sin is remitted.
O happy the man to whom the Lord
imputes no guilt,
in whose spirit is no guile. (*R*.)

2. But now I have acknowledged my sins;
my guilt I did not hide.
I said: "I will confess
my offence to the Lord."

And you, Lord, have forgiven
the guilt of my sin. (*R.*)

3. Rejoice, rejoice in the Lord,
exult, you just!
O come, ring out your joy,
all you upright of heart. (*R.*)

Second Reading   (10:31–11:1)

A reading from the first letter of St Paul to the Corinthians
Take me for your model, as I take Christ.

Whatever you eat, whatever you drink, whatever you do at
all, do it for the glory of God. Never do anything offensive
to anyone – to Jews or Greeks or to the Church of God; just
as I try to be helpful to everyone at all times, not anxious
for my own advantage but for the advantage of everybody
else, so that they may be saved.

   Take me for your model, as I take Christ.
   This is the word of the Lord.

Alleluia   (Eph 1:17. 18)

Alleluia, alleluia!
May the Father of our Lord Jesus Christ
enlighten the eyes of our mind,
so that we can see what hope his call holds for us.
Alleluia!

Alternative Alleluias p. 854.

Gospel   (1:40–45)

A reading from the holy Gospel according to Mark
The leprosy left him at once and he was cured.

A leper came to Jesus and pleaded on his knees: "If you
want to" he said "you can cure me." Feeling sorry for him,

Jesus stretched out his hand and touched him. "Of course I want to!" he said. "Be cured!" And the leprosy left him at once and he was cured. Jesus immediately sent him away and sternly ordered him, "Mind you say nothing to anyone, but go and show yourself to the priest, and make the offering for your healing prescribed by Moses as evidence of your recovery." The man went away, but then started talking about it freely and telling the story everywhere, so that Jesus could no longer go openly into any town, but had to stay outside in places where nobody lived. Even so, people from all around would come to him.

This is the Gospel of the Lord.

6th SUNDAY OF THE YEAR

Year 3 (Year C)

First Reading   (17:5–8)

A reading from the prophet Jeremiah
A curse on the man who puts his trust in man, a blessing on the man who puts his trust in the Lord.

The Lord says this:

"A curse on the man who puts his trust in man,
who relies on things of flesh,
whose heart turns from the Lord.
He is like dry scrub in the wastelands:
if good comes, he has no eyes for it,
he settles in the parched places of the wilderness,
a salt land, uninhabited.
A blessing on the man who puts his trust in the Lord,
with the Lord for his hope.
He is like a tree by the waterside
that thrusts its roots to the stream:
when the heat comes it feels no alarm,
its foliage stays green;

it has no worries in a year of drought,
and never ceases to bear fruit."

This is the word of the Lord.

Responsorial Psalm   (Ps 1:1–4. 6. *R.* Ps 39:5)
Response
Happy the man who has placed
his trust in the Lord.

1. Happy indeed is the man
who follows not the counsel of the wicked;
nor lingers in the way of sinners
nor sits in the company of scorners,
but whose delight is the law of the Lord
and who ponders his law day and night. (*R.*)

2. He is like a tree that is planted
beside the flowing waters,
that yields its fruit in due season
and whose leaves shall never fade;
and all that he does shall prosper. (*R.*)

3. Not so are the wicked, not so!
For they like winnowed chaff
shall be driven away by the wind.
For the Lord guards the way of the just
but the way of the wicked leads to doom. (*R.*)

Second Reading   (15:12. 16–20)
A reading from the first letter of St Paul to the Corinthians
If Christ has not been raised, your believing is useless.

If Christ raised from the dead is what has been preached,
how can some of you be saying that there is no resurrection

of the dead? For if the dead are not raised, Christ has not been raised, and if Christ has not been raised, you are still in your sins. And what is more serious, all who have died in Christ have perished. If our hope in Christ has been for this life only, we are the most unfortunate of all people.

But Christ has in fact been raised from the dead, the first-fruits of all who have fallen asleep.

This is the word of the Lord.

Alleluia   (Mt 11:25)

Alleluia, alleluia!
Blessed are you, Father,
Lord of heaven and earth,
for revealing the mysteries of the kingdom
to mere children.
Alleluia!

Alternative Alleluias p. 854.

Gospel   (6:17. 20–26)

A reading from the holy Gospel according to Luke
How happy are you who are poor. Alas for you who are rich.

Jesus came down with the Twelve and stopped at a piece of level ground where there was a large gathering of his disciples with a great crowd of people from all parts of Judaea and from Jerusalem and from the coastal region of Tyre and Sidon who had come to hear him and to be cured of their diseases.

Then fixing his eyes on his disciples he said:

"How happy are you who are poor: your is the kingdom of God.
Happy you who are hungry now: you shall be satisfied.
Happy you who weep now: you shall laugh.

"Happy are you when people hate you, drive you out, ab-

use you, denounce your name as criminal, on account of the
Son of Man. Rejoice when that day comes and dance for
joy, for then your reward will be great in heaven. This was
the way their ancestors treated the prophets.

"But alas for you who are rich: you are having your con-
    solation now.
Alas for you who have your fill now: you shall go hungry.
Alas for you who laugh now: you shall mourn and weep.

"Alas for you when the world speaks well of you! This
was the way their ancestors treated the false prophets."
    This is the Gospel of the Lord.

MONDAY
Year I

First Reading   (4:1–15. 25)

A reading from the book of Genesis
Cain set on his brother Abel and killed him.

The man had intercourse with his wife Eve, and she conceived and gave birth to Cain. "I have acquired a man with
the help of the Lord" she said. She gave birth to a second
child, Abel, the brother of Cain. Now Abel became a shepherd and kept flocks, while Cain tilled the soil. Time passed
and Cain brought some of the produce of the soil as an
offering for the Lord, while Abel for his part brought the
first-born of his flock and some of their fat as well. The
Lord looked with favour on Abel and his offering. But he
did not look with favour on Cain and his offering, and Cain
was very angry and downcast. The Lord asked Cain, "Why
are you angry and downcast? If you are well disposed,
ought you not to lift up your head? But if you are ill disposed, is not sin at the door like a crouching beast hunger-
ing for you, which you must master?" Cain said to his bro-

ther Abel, "Let us go out"; and while they were in the open country, Cain set on his brother Abel and killed him.

The Lord asked Cain, "Where is your brother Abel?" "I do not know" he replied. "Am I my brother's guardian?" "What have you done?" the Lord asked. "Listen to the sound of your brother's blood, crying out to me from the ground. Now be accursed and driven from the ground that has opened its mouth to receive your brother's blood at your hands. When you till the ground it shall no longer yield you any of its produce. You shall be a fugitive and a wanderer over the earth." Then Cain said to the Lord, "My punishment is greater than I can bear. See! Today you drive me from this ground. I must hide from you, and be a fugitive and a wanderer over the earth. Why, whoever comes across me will kill me!" "Very well, then," the Lord replied "if anyone kills Cain, sevenfold vengeance shall be taken for him." So the Lord put a mark on Cain, to prevent whoever might come across him from striking him down.

Adam had intercourse with his wife, and she gave birth to a son whom she named Seth, "because God has granted me other offspring" she said "in place of Abel, since Cain has killed him."

This is the word of the Lord.

Responsorial Psalm   (Ps 49:1. 8. 16–17. 20–21. *R*. v. 14)
Response
Pay your sacrifice of thanksgiving to God.

1. The God of gods, the Lord,
has spoken and summoned the earth,
from the rising of the sun to its setting.
"I find no fault with your sacrifices,
your offerings are always before me." (*R*.)

2. "But how can you recite my commandments
and take my covenant on your lips,

you who despise my law
and throw my words to the winds. (*R.*)

3. "You who sit and malign your brother
and slander your own mother's son.
You do this, and should I keep silence?
Do you think that I am like you?" (*R.*)

ALLELUIA and GOSPEL. As for Year II, see p. 342.

Year II

First Reading   (1:1–11)

A reading from the letter of St James

*Your faith is only put to the test to make you patient so that
you will become fully-developed, complete.*

From James, servant of God and of the Lord Jesus Christ.
Greetings to the twelve tribes of the Dispersion.

My brothers, you will always have your trials but, when
they come, try to treat them as a happy privilege; you understand that your faith is only put to the test to make you
patient, but patience too is to have its practical results so
that you will become fully-developed, complete, with nothing missing.

If there is any one of you who needs wisdom, he must ask
God, who gives to all freely and ungrudgingly; it will be
given to him. But he must ask with faith, and no trace of
doubt, because a person who has doubts is like the waves
thrown up in the sea when the wind drives. That sort of
person, in two minds, wavering between going different
ways, must not expect that the Lord will give him anything.

It is right for the poor brother to be proud of his high
rank, and the rich one to be thankful that he has been humbled, because riches last no longer than the flowers in the
grass; the scorching sun comes up, and the grass withers,
the flower falls; what looked so beautiful now disappears.

It is the same with the rich man: his business goes on; he himself perishes.

This is the word of the Lord.

Responsorial Psalm (Ps 118:67–68. 71–72. 75–76. *R*. v. 77)
Response
Let your love come to me and I shall live.

1. Before I was afflicted I went astray
but now I keep your word.
You are good and your deeds are good;
teach me your statutes. (*R*.)

2. It was good for me to be afflicted,
to learn your statutes.
The law from your mouth means more to me
than silver and gold. (*R*.)

3. Lord, I know that your decrees are right,
that you afflicted me justly.
Let your love be ready to console me
by your promise to your servant. (*R*.)

Years I and II
Alleluia   (Ps 94:8)
Alleluia, alleluia!
Harden not your hearts today,
but listen to the voice of the Lord.
Alleluia!
Alternative Alleluias p. 847.

Gospel   (8:11–13)
A reading from the holy Gospel according to Mark
Why does this generation demand a sign?

The Pharisees came up and started a discussion with Jesus;
they demanded of him a sign from heaven, to test him. And

with a sigh that came straight from the heart he said, "Why does this generation demand a sign? I tell you solemnly, no sign shall be given to this generation." And leaving them again and re-embarking he went away to the opposite shore.

This is the Gospel of the Lord.

TUESDAY
Year I

First Reading   (6:5–8;7:1–5. 10)

A reading from the book of Genesis
I will rid the earth's face of man, my own creation.

The Lord saw that the wickedness of man was great on the earth, and that the thoughts in his heart fashioned nothing but wickedness all day long. The Lord regretted having made man on the earth, and his heart grieved. "I will rid the earth's face of man, my own creation," the Lord said "and of animals also, reptiles too, and the birds of heaven; for I regret having made them." But Noah had found favour with the Lord.

The Lord said to Noah, "Go aboard the ark, you and all your household, for you alone among this generation do I see as a good man in my judgement. Of all the clean animals you must take seven of each kind, both male and female; of the unclean animals you must take two, a male and its female (and of the birds of heaven also, seven of each kind, both male and female), to propagate their kind over the whole earth. For in seven days' time I mean to make it rain on the earth for forty days and nights, and I will rid the earth of every living thing that I made." Noah did all that the Lord ordered.

Seven days later the waters of the flood appeared on the earth.

This is the word of the Lord.

Responsorial Psalm   (Ps 28:1–4. 9–10. *R*. v. 11)

Response
The Lord will bless his people with peace.

1. O give the Lord you sons of God,
give the Lord glory and power;
give the Lord the glory of his name.
Adore the Lord in his holy court. (*R*.)

2. The Lord's voice resounding on the waters,
the Lord on the immensity of waters;
the voice of the Lord, full of power,
the voice of the Lord, full of splendour. (*R*.)

3. The God of glory thunders.
In his temple they all cry: "Glory!"
The Lord sat enthroned over the flood;
the Lord sits as king for ever. (*R*.)

ALLELUIA and GOSPEL. As for Year II, see p. 345.

Year II

First Reading   (1:12–18)

A reading from the letter of St James
God does not tempt anybody.

Happy the man who stands firm when trials come. He has
proved himself, and will win the prize of life, the crown that
the Lord has promised to those who love him.

  Never, when you have been tempted, say, "God sent the
temptation"; God cannot be tempted to do anything wrong,
and he does not tempt anybody. Everyone who is tempted
is attracted and seduced by his own wrong desire. Then the
desire conceives and gives birth to sin, and when sin is fully
grown, it too has a child, and the child is death.

Make no mistake about this, my dear brothers: it is all that is good, everything that is perfect, which is given us from above; it comes down from the Father of all light; with him there is no such thing as alteration, no shadow of a change. By his own choice he made us his children by the message of the truth so that we should be a sort of first-fruits of all that he had created.

This is the word of the Lord.

Responsorial Psalm   (Ps 93:12–15. 18–19. *R*. v. 12)
Response
Happy the man whom you teach, O Lord.

1. Happy the man whom you teach, O Lord,
whom you train by means of your law:
to him you give peace in evil days. (*R*.)

2. The Lord will not abandon his people
nor forsake those who are his own:
for judgement shall again be just
and all true hearts shall uphold it. (*R*.)

3. When I think: "I have lost my foothold";
your mercy, Lord, holds me up.
When cares increase in my heart
your consolation calms my soul. (*R*.)

                        Years I and II
Alleluia   (Acts 16:14)
Alleluia, alleluia!
Open our heart, O Lord,
  to accept the words of your Son.
Alleluia!

Alternative Alleluias p. 847.

Gospel   (8:14–21)

A reading from the holy Gospel according to Mark
Be on your guard against the yeast of the Pharisees.

The disciples had forgotten to take any food and they had
only one loaf with them in the boat. Then Jesus gave them
this warning, "Keep your eyes open; be on your guard
against the yeast of the Pharisees and the yeast of Herod."
And they said to one another, "It is because we have no
bread." And Jesus knew it, and he said to them, "Why are
you talking about having no bread? Do you not yet understand? Have you no perception? Are your minds closed?
Have you eyes that do not see, ears that do not hear? Or
do you not remember? When I broke the five loaves among
the five thousand, how many baskets full of scraps did you
collect?" They answered, "Twelve." "And when I broke the
seven loaves for the four thousand, how many baskets full
of scraps did you collect?" And they answered, "Seven".
Then he said to them, "Are you still without perception?"

This is the Gospel of the Lord.

WEDNESDAY
Year I

First Reading   (8:6–13. 20–22)

A reading from the book of Genesis
He looked out; the surface of the ground was dry.

At the end of forty days Noah opened the porthole he had
made in the ark and he sent out the raven. This went off
and flew back and forth until the waters dried up from the
earth. Then he sent out the dove, to see whether the waters
were receding from the surface of the earth. The dove, finding nowhere to perch, returned to him in the ark, for there
was water over the whole surface of the earth; putting out

his hand he took hold of it and brought it back into the ark
with him. After waiting seven more days, again he sent out
the dove from the ark. In the evening, the dove came back
to him and there it was with a new olive-branch in its beak.
So Noah realised that the waters were receding from the
earth. After waiting seven more days he sent out the dove,
and now it returned to him no more.

It was in the six hundred and first year of Noah's life, in
the first month and on the first of the month, that the water
dried up from the earth. Noah lifted back the hatch of the
ark and looked out. The surface of the ground was dry!

Noah built an altar for the Lord, and choosing from all
the clean animals and all the clean birds he offered burnt
offerings on the altar. The Lord smelt the appeasing fragrance and said to himself, "Never again will I curse the
earth because of man, because his heart contrives evil from
his infancy. Never again will I strike down every living thing
as I have done.

'As long as earth lasts,
sowing and reaping,
cold and heat,
summer and winter,
day and night
shall cease no more."

This is the word of the Lord.

Responsorial Psalm   (Ps 115:12–15. 18–19. R. v. 17)

Response
A thanksgiving sacrifice I make to you, O Lord.

Alternative Response
Alleluia!

1. How can I repay the Lord
for his goodness to me?
The cup of salvation I will raise;
I will call on the Lord's name. (*R*.)

2. My vows to the Lord I will fulfil
before all his people.
O precious in the eyes of the Lord
is the death of his faithful (*R*.)

3. My vows to the Lord I will fulfil
before all his people,
in the courts of the house of the Lord,
in your midst, O Jerusalem. (*R*.)

ALLELUIA and GOSPEL. As for Year II, see p. 349.

Year II

First Reading   (1:19–27)

A reading from the letter of St James
You must do what the word tells you, and not just listen to it.

Remember this, my dear brothers: be quick to listen but
slow to speak and slow to rouse your temper; God's right
eousness is never served by man's anger; so do away with
all the impurities and bad habits that are still left in you
accept and submit to the word which has been planted i
you and can save your souls. But you must do what th
word tells you, and not just listen to it and deceive your
selves. To listen to the word and not obey is like lookin
at your own features in a mirror and then, after a quic
look, going off and immediately forgetting what you looke
like. But the man who looks steadily at the perfect law
freedom and makes that his habit – not listening and the
forgetting, but actively putting it into practice – will b
happy in all that he does.

Nobody must imagine that he is religious while he still goes on deceiving himself and not keeping control over his tongue; anyone who does this has the wrong idea of religion. Pure, unspoilt religion, in the eyes of God our Father is this: coming to the help of orphans and widows when they need it, and keeping oneself uncontaminated by the world.

This is the word of the Lord.

Responsorial Psalm   (Ps 14:2–5. *R.* v. 1)
Response
The just shall dwell on your holy mountain, Lord.

1. Lord, who shall dwell on your holy mountain?
He who walks without fault;
he who acts with justice
and speaks the truth from his heart;
he who does not slander with his tongue. (*R.*)

2. He who does no wrong to his brother,
who casts no slur on his neighbour,
who holds the godless in disdain,
but honours those who fear the Lord. (*R.*)

3. He who keeps his pledge, come what may;
who takes no interest on a loan
and accepts no bribes against the innocent.
Such a man will stand firm for ever. (*R.*)

Years I and II

Alleluia   (Ps 118:105)
Alleluia, alleluia!
Your word is a lamp for my steps
and a light for my path.
Alleluia!

Alternative Alleluias, p. 847.

Gospel   (8:22–26)

A reading from the holy Gospel according to Mark
He was cured and he could see everything plainly and distinctly.

Jesus and his disciples came to Bethsaida, and some people brought to him a blind man whom they begged him to touch. He took the blind man by the hand and led him outside the village. Then putting spittle on his eyes and laying his hands on him, he asked, "Can you see anything?" The man, who was beginning to see, replied, "I can see people; they look like trees to me, but they are walking about." Then he laid his hands on the man's eyes again and he saw clearly; he was cured, and he could see everything plainly and distinctly. And Jesus sent him home, saying, "Do not even go into the village."

This is the Gospel of the Lord.

THURSDAY
Year I

First Reading   (9:1–13)

A reading from the book of Genesis
I set my bow in the clouds and it shall be a sign of the Covenant between me and the earth.

God blessed Noah and his sons, saying to them, "Be fruitful multiply and fill the earth. Be the terror and the dread of al the wild beasts and all the birds of heaven, of everything that crawls on the ground and all the fish of the sea; the are handed over to you. Every living and crawling thing shall provide food for you, no less than the foliage of plants I give you everything, with this exception: you must no eat flesh with life, that is to say blood, in it. I will deman an account of your life-blood. I will demand an accoun from every beast and from man. I will demand an accoun of every man's life from his fellow men.

"He who sheds man's blood,
shall have his blood shed by man,
for in the image of God
man was made.

"As for you, be fruitful, multiply, teem over the earth
and be lord of it."

God spoke to Noah and his sons, "See, I establish my
Covenant with you, and with your descendants after you;
also with every living creature to be found with you, birds,
cattle and every wild beast with you: everything that came
out of the ark, everything that lives in the earth. I establish
my Covenant with you: no thing of flesh shall be swept
away again by the waters of the flood. There shall be no
flood to destroy the earth again."

God said, "Here is the sign of the Covenant I make between myself and you and every living creature with you for
all generations: I set my bow in the clouds and it shall be a
sign of the Covenant between me and the earth."

This is the word of the Lord.

Responsorial Psalm   (Ps 101:16–21. 29. 22–23. *R.* v. 20)
Response
The Lord looked down from heaven to the earth.

1. The nations shall fear the name of the Lord
and all the earth's kings your glory,
when the Lord shall build up Zion again
and appear in all his glory.
Then he will turn to the prayers of the helpless;
he will not despise their prayers. (*R.*)

2. Let this be written for ages to come
that a people yet unborn may praise the Lord;
for the Lord leaned down from his sanctuary on high.

He looked down from heaven to the earth
that he might hear the groans of the prisoners
and free those condemned to die. (*R.*)

3. The sons of your servants shall dwell untroubled
and their race shall endure before you
that the name of the Lord may be proclaimed in Zion
and his praise in the heart of Jerusalem,
when peoples and kingdoms are gathered together
to pay their homage to the Lord. (*R.*)

ALLELUIA and GOSPEL. As for Year II, see p. 353.

Year II

First Reading (2:1–9)

A reading from the letter of St James
*Did not God choose those who are poor? But you have no
respect for anybody who is poor.*

My brothers, do not try to combine faith in Jesus Christ,
our glorified Lord, with the making of distinctions between
classes of people. Now suppose a man comes into your
synagogue, beautifully dressed and with a gold ring on, and
at the same time a poor man comes in, in shabby clothes,
and you take notice of the well-dressed man, and say,
"Come this way to the best seats"; then you tell the poor
man, "Stand over there" or "You can sit on the floor by
my foot-rest." Can't you see that you have used two different standards in your mind, and turned yourselves into
judges, and corrupt judges at that?

Listen, my dear brothers: it was those who are poor according to the world that God chose, to be rich in faith and
to be the heirs to the kingdom which he promised to those
who love him. In spite of this, you have no respect for anybody who is poor. Isn't it always the rich who are against
you? Isn't it always their doing when you are dragged b

fore the court? Aren't they the ones who insult the honourable name to which you have been dedicated? Well, the
right thing to do is to keep the supreme law of scripture:
you must love your neighbour as yourself; but as soon as
you make distinctions between classes of people, you are
committing sin, and under condemnation for breaking the
Law.

This is the word of the Lord.

Responsorial Psalm   (Ps 33:2–7. *R*. v. 7)
Response
This poor man called;
the Lord heard him.

1. I will bless the Lord at all times,
his praise always on my lips;
in the Lord my soul shall make its boast.
The humble shall hear and be glad. (*R*.)

2. Glorify the Lord with me.
Together let us praise his name.
I sought the Lord and he answered me;
from all my terrors he set me free. (*R*.)

3. Look towards him and be radiant;
let your faces not be abashed.
This poor man called; the Lord heard him
and rescued him from all his distress. (*R*.)

Years I and II
Alleluia   (James 1:18)
Alleluia, alleluia!
By his own choice the Father made us his children
by the message of the truth,

so that we should be a sort of first-fruits
of all that he created.
Alleluia!

Alternative Alleluias p. 847.

Gospel (8:27–33)

A reading from the holy Gospel according to Mark
*You are the Christ. The Son of Man is destined to suffer
grievously.*

Jesus and his disciples left for the villages round Caesarea
Philippi. On the way he put this question to his disciples,
"Who do people say I am?" And they told him. "John the
Baptist," they said, "others Elijah; others again, one of the
prophets." "But you," he asked, "who do you say I am?"
Peter spoke up and said to him, "You are the Christ." And
he gave them strict orders not to tell anyone about him.

And he began to teach them that the Son of Man was
destined to suffer grievously, to be rejected by the elders and
the chief priests and the scribes, and to be put to death, and
after three days to rise again; and he said all this quite
openly. Then, taking him aside, Peter started to remon-
strate with him. But, turning and seeing his disciples, he rebuked Peter and said to him, "Get behind me, Satan! Because the way you think is not God's way but man's."

This is the Gospel of the Lord.

FRIDAY
Year I

First Reading (11:1–9)

A reading from the book of Genesis
Let us go down and confuse their language.

Throughout the earth men spoke the same language, with
the same vocabulary. Now as they moved eastwards they

found a plain in the land of Shinar where they settled. They said to one another, "Come, let us make bricks and bake them in the fire." – For stone they used bricks, and for mortar they used bitumen. – "Come," they said, "let us build ourselves a town and a tower with its top reaching heaven. Let us make a name for ourselves, so that we may not be scattered about the whole earth."

Now the Lord came down to see the town and the tower that the sons of man had built. "So they are all a single people with a single language!" said the Lord. "This is but the start of their undertakings! There will be nothing too hard for them to do. Come, let us go down and confuse their language on the spot so that they can no longer understand one another." The Lord scattered them hence over the whole face of the earth, and they stopped building the town. It was named Babel therefore, because there the Lord confused the language of the whole earth. It was from there that the Lord scattered them over the whole face of the earth.

This is the word of the Lord.

Responsorial Psalm   (Ps 32:10–15. *R*. v. 12)

Response
Happy are the people
whom the Lord has chosen as his own.

1. He frustrates the designs of the nations,
he defeats the plans of the peoples.
His own designs shall stand for ever,
the plans of his heart from age to age. (*R.*)

2. They are happy, whose God is the Lord,
the people he has chosen as his own.
From the heavens the Lord looks forth,
he sees all the children of men. (*R.*)

3. From the place where he dwells he gazes
on all the dwellers on the earth,
he who shapes the hearts of them all
and considers all their deeds. (*R.*)

ALLELUIA and GOSPEL. As for Year II, see p. 357.

Year II

First Reading   (2:14–24. 26)

A reading from the letter of St James

*A body dies when it is separated from the spirit, and in the
same way faith is dead if it is separated from good deeds.*

Take the case, my brothers, of someone who has never done
a single good act but claims that he has faith. Will that
faith save him? If one of the brothers or one of the sisters is
in need of clothes and has not enough food to live on, and
one of you says to them, "I wish you well; keep yourself
warm and eat plenty", without giving them these bare neces-
sities of life, then what good is that? Faith is like that: if
good works do not go with it, it is quite dead.

This is the way to talk to people of that kind: "You say
you have faith and I have good deeds; I will prove to you
that I have faith by showing you my good deeds – now you
prove to me that you have faith without any good deeds to
show. You believe in the one God – that is creditable
enough, but the demons have the same belief, and they
tremble with fear. Do realise, you senseless man, that faith
without good deeds is useless. You surely know that
Abraham our father was justified by his deed, because he
offered his son Isaac on the altar? There you see it: faith
and deeds were working together; his faith became perfect
by what he did. This is what scripture really means when it
says: Abraham put his faith in God, and this was counted
as making him justified; and that is why he was called "the
friend of God."

You see now that it is by doing something good, and not only by believing that a man is justified. A body dies when it is separated from the spirit, and in the same way faith is dead if it is separated from good deeds.

This is the word of the Lord.

Responsorial Psalm   (Ps 111:1–6. *R*. v. 1)

Response
Happy the man who takes delight
in the commands of the Lord.

1. Alleluia!
Happy the man who fears the Lord,
who takes delight in his commands.
His sons will be powerful on earth;
the children of the upright are blessed. (*R*.)

2. Riches and wealth are in his house;
his justice stands firm for ever.
He is a light in the darkness for the upright:
he is generous, merciful and just. (*R*.)

3. The good man takes pity and lends,
he conducts his affairs with honour.
The just man will never waver:
he will be remembered for ever. (*R*.)

Years I and II

Alleluia   (1 Jn 2:5)

Alleluia, alleluia!
When anyone obeys what Christ has said,
God's love comes to perfection in him.
Alleluia!

Alternative Alleluias p. 847.

Gospel   (8:34–39:1)

A reading from the holy Gospel according to Mark
Anyone who loses his life for my sake, and for the sake of the gospel, will save it.

Jesus called the people and his disciples to him and said, "If anyone wants to be a follower of mine, let him renounce himself and take up his cross and follow me. For anyone who wants to save his life will lose it; but anyone who loses his life for my sake, and for the sake of the gospel, will save it. What gain, then, is it for a man to win the whole world and ruin his life? And indeed what can man offer in exchange for his life? For if anyone in this adulterous and sinful generation is ashamed of me and of my words, the Son of Man will also be ashamed of him when he comes in the glory of his Father with the holy angels."

And he said to them, "I tell you solemnly, there are some standing here who will not taste death before they see the kingdom of God come with power."

This is the Gospel of the Lord.

SATURDAY
Year I

First Reading   (11:1–7)

A reading from the letter to the Hebrews
It is by faith that we understand that the world was created by one word from God.

Only faith can guarantee the blessings that we hope for, or prove the existence of the realities that at present remain unseen. It was for faith that our ancestors were commended.

It is by faith that we understand that the world was created by one word from God, so that no apparent cause can account for the things we can see.

It was because of his faith that Abel offered God a better

sacrifice than Cain, and for that he was declared to be righteous when God made acknowledgement of his offerings.
Though he is dead, he still speaks by faith.

It was because of his faith that Enoch was taken up and
did not have to experience death: he was not to be found
because God had taken him. This was because before his
assumption it is attested that he had pleased God. Now it is
impossible to please God without faith, since anyone who
comes to him must believe that he exists and rewards those
who try to find him.

It was through his faith that Noah, when he had been
warned by God of something that had never been seen before, felt a holy fear and built an ark to save his family. By
his faith the world was convicted, and he was able to claim
the righteousness which is the reward of faith.

This is the word of the Lord.

Responsorial Psalm   (Ps 144:2–5. 10–11. R. v. 1)

Response
I will bless your name, O Lord, for ever.

1. I will bless you day after day
and praise your name for ever.
The Lord is great, highly to be praised
his greatness cannot be measured. (R.)

2. Age to age shall proclaim your works,
shall declare your mighty deeds,
shall speak of your splendour and glory,
tell the tale of your wonderful works. (R.)

3. All your creatures shall thank you, O Lord,
and your friends shall repeat their blessing.
They shall speak of the glory of your reign
and declare your might, O God. (R.)

ALLELUIA and GOSPEL. As for year II, see p. 359.

Year II

First Reading   (3:1–10)

A reading from the letter to St James
Nobody can tame the tongue.

Only a few of you, my brothers, should be teachers, bearing in mind that those of us who teach can expect a stricter judgement.

After all, every one of us does something wrong, over and over again; the only man who could reach perfection would be someone who never said anything wrong – he would be able to control every part of himself. Once we put a bit into the horse's mouth, to make it do what we want, we have the whole animal under our control. Or think of ships: no matter how big they are, even if a gale is driving them, the man at the helm can steer them anywhere he likes by controlling a tiny rudder. So is the tongue only a tiny part of the body, but it can proudly claim that it does great things. Think how small a flame can set fire to a huge forest; the tongue is a flame like that. Among all the parts of the body, the tongue is a whole wicked world in itself: it infects the whole body; catching fire itself from hell, it sets fire to the whole wheel of creation. Wild animals and birds, reptiles and fish can all be tamed by man, and often are; but nobody can tame the tongue – it is a pest that will not keep still, full of deadly poison. We use it to bless the Lord and Father, but we also use it to curse men who are made in God's image: the blessing and the curse come out of the same mouth. My brothers, this must be wrong.

This is the word of the Lord.

Responsorial Psalm   (Ps 11:2–5. 7–8. *R.* v. 8)

Response
It is you, O Lord,
who will take us in your care.

1. Help, O Lord, for good men have vanished:
truth has gone from the sons of men.
Falsehood they speak one to another,
with lying lips, with a false heart. (R.)

2. May the Lord destroy all lying lips,
the tongue speaking high-sounding words,
those who say: "Our tongue is our strength;
our lips are our own, who is our master?" (R.)

3. The words of the Lord are words without alloy,
silver from the furnace, seven times refined.
It is you, O Lord, who will take us in your care
and protect us for ever from this generation. (R.)

Years I and II

Alleluia   (Ps 147:12. 15)

Alleluia, alleluia!
O praise the Lord, Jerusalem!
He sends out his word to the earth.
Alleluia!

Alternative Alleluias p. 847.

Gospel   (9:2–13)

A reading from the holy Gospel according to Mark
In their presence he was transfigured.

Jesus took with him Peter and James and John and led
them up a high mountain where they could be alone by
themselves. There in their presence he was transfigured:
his clothes became dazzlingly white, whiter than any earthly
bleacher could make them. Elijah appeared to them with
Moses; and they were talking with Jesus. Then Peter spoke
to Jesus: "Rabbi," he said, "it is wonderful for us to be
here; so let us make three tents, one for you, one for Moses

and one for Elijah." He did not know what to say; they were so frightened. And a cloud came, covering them in shadow; and there came a voice from the cloud, "This is my Son, the Beloved. Listen to him." Then suddenly, when they looked round, they saw no one with them any more but only Jesus.

As they came down from the mountain he warned them to tell no one what they had seen, until after the Son of Man had risen from the dead. They observed the warning faithfully, though among themselves they discussed what "rising from the dead" could mean. And they put this question to him, "Why do the scribes say that Elijah has to come first?" "True," he said, "Elijah is to come first and to see that everything is as it should be; yet how is it that the scriptures say about the Son of Man that he is to suffer grievously and be treated with contempt? However, I tell you that Elijah has come and they have treated him as they pleased, just as the scriptures say about him."

This is the Gospel of the Lord.

7th SUNDAY OF THE YEAR
Year 1 (Year A)

First Reading   (19:1–2. 17–18)

A reading from the book of Leviticus
You must love your neighbour as yourself.

The Lord spoke to Moses; he said: "Speak to the whole community of the sons of Israel and say to them: 'Be holy, for I, the Lord your God, am holy.'"

You must not bear hatred for your brother in your heart. You must openly tell him, your neighbour, of this offence; this way you will not take a sin upon yourself. You must not exact vengeance, nor must you bear a grudge against the children of your people. You must love your neighbour as yourself. I am the Lord.

This is the word of the Lord.

Responsorial Psalm   (Ps 102:1–4. 8. 10. 12–13. *R*. v. 8)

Response
The Lord is compassion and love.

1. My soul, give thanks to the Lord,
all my being, bless his holy name.
My soul, give thanks to the Lord
and never forget all his blessings (*R*.)

2. It is he who forgives all your guilt,
who heals every one of your ills,
who redeems your life from the grave,
who crowns you with love and compassion. (*R*.)

3. The Lord is compassion and love,
slow to anger and rich in mercy.
He does not treat us according to our sins
nor repay us according to our faults. (*R*.)

4. As far as the east is from the west
so far does he remove our sins.
As a father has compassion on his sons,
the Lord has pity on those who fear him. (*R*.)

Second Reading   (3:16–23)

A reading from the first letter of St Paul to the Corinthians
*All are your servants, but you belong to Christ and Christ
belongs to God.*

Didn't you realise that you were God's temple and that the
Spirit of God was living among you? If anybody should
destroy the temple of God, God will destroy him, because
the temple of God is sacred; and you are that temple.

Make no mistake about it: if any one of you thinks of
himself as wise, in the ordinary sense of the word, then he
must learn to be a fool before he really can be wise. Why?

Because the wisdom of this world is foolishness to God. As scripture says: The Lord knows wise men's thoughts: he knows how useless they are or again: God is not convinced by the arguments of the wise. So there is nothing to boast about in anything human: Paul, Apollos, Cephas, the world, life and death, the present and the future, are all your servants; but you belong to Christ and Christ belongs to God.

This is the word of the Lord.

Alleluia (Jn 14:23)

Alleluia, alleluia!
If anyone loves me he will keep my word,
and my Father will love him,
and we shall come to him.
Alleluia!

Alternative Alleluias p. 854.

Gospel (5:38–48)

A reading from the holy Gospel according to Matthew
Love your enemies.

Jesus said to his disciples: "You have learnt how it was said: Eye for eye and tooth for tooth. But I say this to you: offer the wicked man no resistance. On the contrary, if anyone hits you on the right cheek, offer him the other as well; if a man takes you to law and would have your tunic, let him have your cloak as well. And if anyone orders you to go one mile, go two miles with him. Give to anyone who asks, and if anyone wants to borrow, do not turn away.

"You have learnt how it was said: You must love your neighbour and hate your enemy. But I say this to you: love your enemies and pray for those who persecute you; in this Way you will be sons of your Father in heaven, for he causes his sun to rise on bad men as well as good, and his rain to fall on honest and dishonest men alike. For if you love those who love you, what right have you to claim any credit? Even the tax collectors do as much, do they not? And if you save your greetings for your brothers, are you doing anything exceptional? Even the pagans do as much, do they not? You must therefore be perfect just as your heavenly Father is perfect."

This is the Gospel of the Lord.

7th SUNDAY OF THE YEAR
Year 2 (Year B)

First Reading   (43:18–19. 21–22. 24–25)

A reading from the prophet Isaiah
I it is who must blot out everything.

Thus says the Lord:
No need to recall the past,
no need to think about what was done before.
See, I am doing a new deed,
even now it comes to light; can you not see it?
Yes, I am making a road in the wilderness,
paths in the wilds.
The people I have formed for myself
will sing my praises.

Jacob, you have not invoked me,
you have not troubled yourself, Israel, on my behalf.
Instead you have burdened me with your sins,
troubled me with your iniquities.
I it is, I it is, who must blot out everything
and not remember your sins.

This is the word of the Lord.

Responsorial Psalm   (Ps 40:2–5. 13–14. R. v. 5)

Response
Heal my soul for I have sinned against you.

1. Happy the man who considers the poor and the weak.
The Lord will save him in the day of evil,
will guard him, give him life, make him happy in the land
and will not give him up to the will of his foes. (*R*.)

2. The Lord will help him on his bed of pain,
he will bring him back from sickness to health.
As for me, I said: "Lord, have mercy on me,
heal my soul for I have sinned against you." (*R*.)

3. If you uphold me I shall be unharmed
and set in your presence for evermore.
Blessed be the Lord, the God of Israel
from age to age. Amen. Amen. (*R*.)

Second Reading (1:18–22)

A reading from the second letter of St Paul to the
Corinthians
Jesus was never Yes and No: with him it was always Yes.

I swear by God's truth, there is no Yes and No about what
we say to you. The Son of God, the Christ Jesus that we
proclaimed among you – I mean Silvanus and Timothy
and I – was never Yes and No: with him it was always
Yes, and however many the promises God made, the Yes
to them all is in him. That is why it is "through him" that
we answer Amen to the praise of God. Remember it is God
himself who assures us all, and you, of our standing in
Christ, and has anointed us, marking us with his seal and
giving us the pledge, the Spirit, that we carry in our hearts.
    This is the word of the Lord.

Alleluia (Jn 1:12. 14)
Alleluia, alleluia!
The Word was made flesh and lived among us;
to all who did accept him

he gave power to become children of God.
Alleluia!

Alternative Alleluias p. 854.

Gospel   (2:1–12)

A reading from the holy Gospel according to Mark
The Son of Man has authority on earth to forgive sins.

When Jesus returned to Capernaum, word went round that
he was back; and so many people collected that there was
no room left, even in front of the door. He was preaching
the word to them when some people came bringing him a
paralytic carried by four men, but as the crowd made it impossible to get the man to him, they stripped the roof over
the place where Jesus was; and when they had made an
opening, they lowered the stretcher on which the paralytic
lay. Seeing their faith, Jesus said to the paralytic, "My child,
your sins are forgiven." Now some scribes were sitting there,
and they thought to themselves, "How can this man talk
like that? He is blaspheming. Who can forgive sins but
God?" Jesus, inwardly aware that this was what they were
thinking, said to them, "Why do you have these thoughts in
your hearts? Which of these is easier: to say to the paralytic, 'Your sins are forgiven' or to say, 'Get up, pick up
your stretcher and walk'? But to prove to you that the Son
of Man has authority on earth to forgive sins," – he said to
the paralytic – "I order you: get up, pick up your stretcher,
and go off home." And the man got up, picked up his
stretcher at once and walked out in front of everyone, so
that they were all astounded and praised God saying, "We
have never seen anything like this."

This is the Gospel of the Lord.

7th SUNDAY OF THE YEAR

Year 3 (Year C)

First Reading   (26:2. 7–9. 12–13. 22–23)

A reading from the first book of Samuel
The Lord put you in my power, but I would not raise my hand.

Saul set off and went down to the wilderness of Ziph, accompanied by three thousand men chosen from Israel to search for David in the wilderness of Ziph.

So in the dark David and Abishai made their way towards the force, where they found Saul asleep inside the camp, his spear stuck in the ground beside his head, with Abner and the troops lying round him.

Then Abishai said to David, "Today God has put your enemy in your power; so now let me pin him to the ground with his own spear. Just one stroke! I will not need to strike him twice." David answered Abishai, "Do not kill him, for who can lift his hand against the Lord's anointed and be without guilt?" David took the spear and the pitcher of water from beside Saul's head, and they made off. No one saw, no one knew, no one woke up; they were all asleep, for a deep sleep from the Lord had fallen on them.

David crossed to the other side and halted on the top of the mountain a long way off; there was a wide space between them. David then called out, "Here is the king's spear. Let one of the soldiers come across and take it. The Lord repays everyone for his uprightness and loyalty. Today the Lord put you in my power, but I would not raise my hand against the Lord's anointed."

This is the word of the Lord.

Responsorial Psalm   (Ps 102:1–4. 8. 10. 12–13. *R*. v. 8)
Response
The Lord is compassion and love.

1. My soul, give thanks to the Lord,
all my being, bless his holy name.
My soul, give thanks to the Lord
and never forget all his blessings. (*R.*)

2. It is he who forgives all your guilt,
who heals every one of your ills,
who redeems your life from the grave,
who crowns you with love and compassion. (*R.*)

3. The Lord is compassion and love,
slow to anger and rich in mercy.
He does not treat us according to our sins
nor repay us according to our faults. (*R.*)

4. As far as the east is from the west
so far does he remove our sins.
As a father has compassion on his sons,
the Lord has pity on those who fear him. (*R.*)

Second Reading   (15:45–49)

A reading from the first letter of St Paul to the Corinthians
*We who have been modelled on the earthly man will be modelled
on the heavenly man.*

The first man, Adam, as scripture says, became a living
soul; but the last Adam has become a life-giving spirit. That
is, first the one with the soul, not the spirit, and after that,
the one with the spirit. The first man, being from the earth,
is earthly by nature; the second man is from heaven. As this
earthly man was, so are we on earth; and as the heavenly
man is, so are we in heaven. And we, who have been modelled on the earthly man, will be modelled on the heavenly
man.

This is the word of the Lord.

Alleluia   (Acts 16:14)

Alleluia, alleluia!
Open our heart, O Lord,
to accept the words of your Son.
Alleluia!

Alternative Alleluias p. 854.

Gospel   (6:27–38)

A reading from the holy Gospel according to Luke
Be compassionate as your Father is compassionate.

Jesus said to his disciples: "But I say this to you who are
listening: Love your enemies, do good to those who hate
you, bless those who curse you, pray for those who treat
you badly. To the man who slaps you on one cheek, present the other cheek too; to the man who takes your cloak
from you, do not refuse your tunic. Give to everyone who
asks you, and do not ask for your property back from the
man who robs you. Treat others as you would like them to
treat you. If you love those who love you, what thanks can
you expect? Even sinners love those who love them. And if
you do good to those who do good to you, what thanks can
you expect? For even sinners do that much. And if you
lend to those from whom you hope to receive, what thanks
can you expect? Even sinners lend to sinners to get back the
same amount. Instead, love your enemies and do good, and
lend without any hope of return. You will have a great reward, and you will be sons of the Most High, for he himself
is kind to the ungrateful and the wicked.

"Be compassionate as your Father is compassionate. Do
not judge, and you will not be judged yourselves; do not
condemn, and you will not be condemned yourselves; grant
pardon, and you will be pardoned. Give, and there will be
gifts for you: a full measure, pressed down, shaken together, and running over, will be poured into your lap; be-

cause the amount you measure out is the amount you will
be given back."

This is the Gospel of the Lord.

MONDAY
Year I

First Reading   (1:1–10)

A reading from the book of Ecclesiasticus
Before all other things wisdom was created.

All wisdom is from the Lord,
and it is his own for ever.
The sand of the sea and the raindrops,
and the days of eternity, who can assess them?
The height of the sky and the breadth of the earth,
and the depth of the abyss, who can probe them?
Before all other things wisdom was created,
shrewd understanding is everlasting.
For whom has the root of wisdom ever been uncovered?
Her resourceful ways, who knows them?
One only is wise, terrible indeed,
seated on his throne, the Lord.
He himself has created her, looked on her and assessed her,
and poured her out on all his works
to be with all mankind as his gift,
and he conveyed her to those who love him.

This is the word of the Lord.

Responsorial Psalm   (Ps 92:1-2. 5. *R*. v. 1)
Response
The Lord is king, with majesty enrobed.

1. The Lord is king, with majesty enrobed;
the Lord has robed himself with might,
he has girded himself with power. (*R*.)

2. The world you made firm, not to be moved;
your throne has stood firm from of old.
From all eternity, O Lord, you are. (*R.*)

3. Truly your decrees are to be trusted.
Holiness is fitting to your house,
O Lord, until the end of time. (*R.*)

ALLELUIA and GOSPEL. As for Year II, see p. 373.

Year II

First Reading   (3:13–18)

A reading from the letter of St James

*If at heart you have a self-seeking ambition, never make any
claims for yourself.*

If there are any wise or learned men among you, let them
show it by their good lives, with humility and wisdom in
their actions. But if at heart you have the bitterness of jealousy, or a self-seeking ambition, never make any claims for
yourself or cover up the truth with lies – principles of this
kind are not the wisdom that comes down from above:
they are only earthly, animal and devilish. Wherever you
find jealousy and ambition, you find disharmony, and
wicked things of every kind being done; whereas the wisdom that comes down from above is essentially something
pure; it also makes for peace, and is kindly and consider-
ate; it is full of compassion and shows itself by doing good;
nor is there any trace of partiality or hypocrisy in it. Peacemakers, when they work for peace, sow the seeds which
will bear fruit in holiness.

This is the word of the Lord.

Responsorial Psalm   (Ps 18:8–11. *R.* v. 9)

Response
The precepts of the Lord
gladden the heart.

1. The law of the Lord is perfect,
it revives the soul.
The rule of the Lord is to be trusted,
it gives wisdom to the simple. (*R.*)

2. The precepts of the Lord are right,
they gladden the heart.
The command of the Lord is clear,
it gives light to the eyes. (*R.*)

3. The fear of the Lord is holy,
abiding for ever.
The decrees of the Lord are truth
and all of them just. (*R.*)

4. May the spoken words of my mouth,
the thoughts of my heart,
win favour in your sight, O Lord,
my rescuer, my rock. (*R.*)

Years I and II

Alleluia   (1 Peter 1:25)

Alleluia, alleluia!
The word of the Lord remains for ever:
What is this word?
It is the Good News that has been brought to you.
Alleluia!

Alternative Alleluias p. 847.

Gospel   (9:14–29)

A reading from the holy Gospel according to Mark
I do have faith. Help the little faith I have.

When Jesus, with Peter, James and John rejoined the disciples they saw a large crowd round them and some scribes
arguing with them. The moment they saw him the whole

crowd were struck with amazement and ran to greet him. "What are you arguing about with them?" he asked. A man answered him from the crowd, "Master, I have brought my son to you; there is a spirit of dumbness in him, and when it takes hold of him it throws him to the ground, and he foams at the mouth and grinds his teeth and goes rigid. And I asked your disciples to cast it out and they were unable to." "You faithless generation," he said to them in reply. "How much longer must I be with you? How much longer must I put up with you? Bring him to me." They brought the boy to him, and as soon as the spirit saw Jesus it threw the boy into convulsions, and he fell to the ground and lay writhing there, foaming at the mouth. Jesus asked the father, "How long has this been happening to him?" "From childhood," he replied and it has often thrown him into the fire and into the water, in order to destroy him. But if you can do anything, have pity on us and help us." "If you can?" retorted Jesus. "Everything is possible for anyone who has faith." Immediately the father of the boy cried out, "I do have faith. Help the little faith I have!" And when Jesus saw how many people were pressing round him, he rebuked the unclean spirit. "Deaf and dumb spirit," he said, "I command you: come out of him and never enter him again." Then throwing the boy into violent convulsions it came out shouting, and the boy lay there so like a corpse that most of them said, "He is dead." But Jesus took him by the hand and helped him up, and he was able to stand. When he had gone indoors his disciples asked him privately, "Why were we unable to cast it out?" "This is the kind," he answered "that can only be driven out by prayer."

This is the Gospel of the Lord.

TUESDAY
Year I

First Reading   (2:1–11)

A reading from the book of Ecclesiasticus
Prepare yourself for an ordeal.

My son, if you aspire to serve the Lord,
prepare yourself for an ordeal.
Be sincere of heart, be steadfast,
and do not be alarmed when disaster comes.
Cling to him and do not leave him,
so that you may be honoured at the end of your days.
Whatever happens to you, accept it,
and in the uncertainties of your humble state, be patient,
since gold is tested in the fire,
and chosen men in the furnace of humiliation.
Trust him and he will uphold you,
follow a straight path and hope in him.
You who fear the Lord, wait for his mercy;
do not turn aside in case you fall.
You who fear the Lord, trust him,
and you will not be baulked of your reward.
You who fear the Lord hope for good things,
for everlasting happiness and mercy.
Look at the generations of old and see:
who ever trusted in the Lord and was put to shame?
Or who ever feared him steadfastly and was left forsaken?
Or who ever called out to him, and was ignored?
For the Lord is compassionate and merciful,
he forgives sins, and saves in days of distress.

This is the word of the Lord.

Responsorial Psalm (Ps 36:3–4. 18–19. 27–28. 39–40. R. v. 5)
Response
Commit your life to the Lord,
trust him and he will act.

1. If you trust in the Lord and do good,
then you will live in the land and be secure.
If you find your delight in the Lord,
he will grant your heart's desire. (*R.*)

2. He protects the lives of the upright,
their heritage will last for ever.
They shall not be put to shame in evil days,
in time of famine their food shall not fail. (*R.*)

3. Then turn away from evil and do good
and you shall have a home for ever;
for the Lord loves justice
and will never forsake his friends. (*R.*)

4. The salvation of the just comes from the Lord,
their stronghold in time of distress.
The Lord helps them and delivers them
and saves them: for their refuge is in him. (*R.*)

ALLELUIA and GOSPEL. As for Year II, see p. 378.

Year II

First Reading   (4:1–10)

A reading from the letter of St James
When you do pray and don't get it, it is because you have not prayed properly.

Where do these wars and battles between yourselves first start? Isn't it precisely in the desires fighting inside your own selves? You want something and you haven't got it; so you are prepared to kill. You have an ambition that you cannot satisfy; so you fight to get your way by force. Why you don't have what you want is because you don't pray for it; when you do pray and don't get it, it is because you have not prayed properly, you have prayed for something to indulge your own desires.

You are as unfaithful as adulterous wives; don't you realise that making the world your friend is making God your enemy? Anyone who chooses the world for his friend turns himself into God's enemy. Surely you don't think scripture is wrong when it says: the spirit which he sent to live in us wants us for himself alone? But he has been even more generous to us, as scripture says: God opposes the proud but he gives generously to the humble. Give in to God, then; resist the devil, and he will run away from you. The nearer you go to God, the nearer he will come to you. Clean your hands, you sinners, and clear your minds, you waverers. Look at your wretched condition, and weep for it in misery; be miserable instead of laughing, gloomy instead of happy. Humble yourselves before the Lord and he will lift you up.

This is the word of the Lord.

Responsorial Psalm   (Ps 54:7–11. 23. *R*. v. 23)

Response
Entrust your cares to the Lord
and he will support you.

1. O that I had wings like a dove
to fly away and be at rest.
So I would escape far away
and take refuge in the desert. (*R*.)

2. I would hasten to find a shelter
from the raging wind,
from the destructive storm, O Lord,
and from their plotting tongues. (*R*.)

3. For I can see nothing but violence
and strife in the city.
Night and day they patrol
high on the city walls. (*R*.)

4. Entrust your cares to the Lord
and he will support you.
He will never allow
the just man to stumble. (*R*.)

Years I and II

Alleluia (Jn 14:23)

Alleluia, alleluia!
If anyone loves me he will keep my word,
and my Father will love him,
and we shall come to him.
Alleluia!
Alternative Alleluias p. 847.

Gospel (9:30–37)

A reading from the holy Gospel according to Mark
*The Son of Man will be delivered into the hands of men. If
anyone wants to be first, he must make himself the last of all.*

Jesus and his disciples made their way through Galilee; and
he did not want anyone to know, because he was instructing
his disciples; he was telling them, "The Son of Man will be
delivered into the hands of men; they will put him to death;
and three days after he has been put to death he will rise
again." But they did not understand what he said and were
afraid to ask him.

They came to Capernaum, and when he was in the house
he asked them, "What were you arguing about on the
road?" They said nothing because they had been arguing
which of them was the greatest. So he sat down, called the
Twelve to him and said, "If anyone wants to be first, he
must make himself last of all and servant of all." He then
took a little child, set him in front of them, put his arms
round him, and said to them, "Anyone who welcomes one
of these little children in my name, welcomes me; and anyone who welcomes me welcomes not me but the one who
sent me."

This is the Gospel of the Lord.

WEDNESDAY

Year I

First Reading (4:11–19)

A reading from the book of Ecclesiasticus

The Lord loves those who love wisdom.

Wisdom brings up her own sons,
and cares for those who seek her.
Whoever loves her loves life,
those who wait on her early will be filled with happiness.
Whoever holds her close will inherit honour,
and wherever he walks the Lord will bless him.
Those who serve her minister to the Holy One,
and the Lord loves those who love her.
Whoever obeys her judges aright,
and whoever pays attention to her dwells secure.
If he trusts himself to her he will inherit her,
and his descendants will remain in possession of her;
for though she takes him at first through winding ways,
bringing fear and faintness on him,
plaguing him with her discipline until she can trust him,
and testing him with her ordeals,
in the end she will lead him back to the straight road,
and reveal her secrets to him.
If he wanders away she will abandon him,
and hand him over to his fate.

    This is the word of the Lord.

Responsorial Psalm (Ps 118:165. 168. 171–2. 174–5. *R.* v. 165)

Response
The lovers of your law
have great peace, O Lord.

The lovers of your law have great peace;
they never stumble.

I obey your precepts and your will;
all that I do is before you. (*R.*)

2. Let my lips proclaim your praise
because you teach me your statutes.
Let my tongue sing your promise
for your commands are just. (*R.*)

3. Give life to my soul that I may praise you.
Let your decrees give me help.
Lord, I long for your saving help
and your law is my delight. (*R.*)

ALLELUIA and GOSPEL. As for Year II, see p. 381.

Year II

First Reading   (4:13–17)

A reading from the letter of St James
*You never know what will happen tomorrow. The most you
should ever say is: 'If it is the Lord's will.'*

Here is the answer for those of you who talk like this: "Today or tomorrow, we are off to this or that town; we are
going to spend a year there, trading, and make some
money." You never know what will happen tomorrow: you
are no more than a mist that is here for a little while and
then disappears. The most you should ever say is: "If it is
the Lord's will, we shall still be alive to do this or that."
But how proud and sure of yourselves you are now! Pride
of this kind is always wicked. Everyone who knows what
is the right thing to do and doesn't do it commits a sin.

   This is the word of the Lord.

Responsorial Psalm   (Ps 48:2–3. 6–11. *R.* Mt 5:3

Response
How happy are the poor in spirit;
theirs is the kingdom of heaven.

1. Hear this, all you peoples,
give heed, all who dwell in the world,
men both low and high,
rich and poor alike! (*R.*)

2. Why should I fear in evil days
the malice of the foes who surround me,
men who trust in their wealth,
and boast of the vastness of their riches? (*R.*)

3. For no man can buy his own ransom,
or pay a price to God for his life.
The ransom of his soul is beyond him.
He cannot buy life without end,
nor avoid coming to the grave. (*R.*)

4. He knows that wise men and fools must both perish
and leave their wealth to others. (*R.*)

Years I and II

Alleluia   (Jn 14:5)

Alleluia, alleluia!
I am the Way, the Truth and the Life, says the Lord;
no one can come to the Father except through me.
Alleluia!

Alternative Alleluias p. 847.

Gospel   (9:38–40)

A reading from the holy Gospel according to Mark
Anyone who is not against us is for us.

John said to Jesus, "Master, we saw a man who is not one
of us casting out devils in your name; and because he was
not one of us we tried to stop him." But Jesus said, "You
must not stop him: no one who works a miracle in my
name is likely to speak evil of me. Anyone who is not against
us is for us."

This is the Gospel of the Lord.

THURSDAY
Year I

First Reading (5:1–8)

A reading from the book of Ecclesiasticus
Do not delay your return to the Lord.

Do not give your heart to your money,
or say, "With this I am self-sufficient."
Do not be led by your appetites and energy
to follow the passions of your heart.
And do not say, "Who has authority over me?"
for the Lord will certainly be avenged on you.
Do not say, "I sinned, and what happened to me?"
for the Lord's forbearance is long.
Do not be so sure of forgiveness
that you add sin to sin.
And do not say, "His compassion is great,
he will forgive me my many sins";
for with him are both mercy and wrath,
and his rage bears heavy on sinners.
Do not delay your return to the Lord,
do not put it off day after day;
for suddenly the Lord's wrath will blaze out,
and at the time of vengeance you will be utterly destroyed.
Do not set your heart on ill-gotten gains,
they will be of no use to you on the day of disaster.

This is the word of the Lord.

Responsorial Psalm (Ps 1:1–4. 6. R. Ps 39:5

Response
Happy the man who has placed
his trust in the Lord.

1. Happy indeed is the man
who follows not the counsel of the wicked;

nor lingers in the way of sinners
nor sits in the company of scorners,
but whose delight is the law of the Lord
and who ponders his law day and night. (*R.*)

2. He is like a tree that is planted
beside the flowering waters,
that yields its fruit in due season
and whose leaves shall never fade;
and all that he does shall prosper. (*R.*)

3. Not so are the wicked, not so!
For they like winnowed chaff
shall be driven away by the wind.
For the Lord guards the way of the just
but the way of the wicked leads to doom. (*R.*)

ALLELUIA and GOSPEL. As for Year II, see p. 384.

Year II

First Reading   (5:1–6)

A reading from the letter of St James
*The cries of the reapers you cheated have reached the ears of
the Lord.*

The answer for the rich: start crying, weep for the mis-
eries that are coming to you. Your wealth is all rotting,
your clothes are all eaten up by moths. All your gold and
your silver are corroding away, and the same corrosion will
be your own sentence, and eat into your body. It was a burning fire that you stored up as your treasure for the last days.
Labourers mowed your fields, and you cheated them – listen
to the wages that you kept back, calling out; realise that the
cries of the reapers have reached the ears of the Lord of
hosts. On earth you have had a life of comfort and luxury;
in the time of slaughter you went on eating to your heart's

content. It was you who condemned the innocent and killed them; they offered you no resistance.

This is the word of the Lord.

Responsorial Psalm   (Ps 48:14–20. *R*. Mt 5:3)

Response
How happy are the poor in spirit;
theirs is the kingdom of heaven.

1. This is the lot of the self-confident,
who have others at their beck and call.
Like sheep they are driven to the grave,
where death shall be their shepherd
and the just shall become their rulers. (*R*.)

2. With the morning their outward show vanishes
and the grave becomes their home.
But God will ransom me from death
and take my soul to himself. (*R*.)

3. Then do not fear when a man grows rich,
when the glory of his house increases.
He takes nothing with him when he dies,
his glory does not follow him below. (*R*.)

4. Though he flattered himself while he lived:
"Men will praise me for doing well for myself,"
yet he will go to join his fathers,
who will never see the light any more. (*R*.)

Years I and II

Alleluia   (Lk 8:15

Alleluia, alleluia!
Blessed are those who,
with a noble and generous heart,
take the word of God to themselves
and yield a harvest through their perseverance.
Alleluia!

Alternative Alleluias p. 847.

Gospel   (9:41–50)

A reading from the holy Gospel according to Mark
*It is better for you to enter into life crippled, than to have two
hands and go to hell.*

Jesus said to his disciples: "If anyone gives you a cup of
water to drink just because you belong to Christ, then I tell
you solemnly, he will most certainly not lose his reward.

"But anyone who is an obstacle to bring down one of
these little ones who have faith, would be better thrown
into the sea with a great millstone round his neck. And if
your hand should cause you to sin, cut it off; it is better for
you to enter into life crippled, than to have two hands and
go to hell, into the fire that cannot be put out. And if your
foot should cause you to sin, cut it off; it is better for you
to enter into life lame, than to have two feet and be thrown
into hell. And if your eye should cause you to sin, tear it
out; it is better for you to enter into the kingdom of God
with one eye, than to have two eyes and be thrown into hell
where their worm does not die nor their fire go out. For
everyone will be salted with fire. Salt is a good thing, but if
salt has become insipid, how can you season it again? Have
salt in yourselves and be at peace with one another."

This is the Gospel of the Lord.

FRIDAY

Year I

First Reading   (6:5–17)

A reading from the book of Ecclesiasticus
A faithful friend is something beyond price.

A kindly turn of speech multiplies a man's friends,
and a courteous way of speaking invites many a friendly
reply.

Let your acquaintances be many,
but your advisers one in a thousand.
If you want to make a friend, take him on trial,
and be in no hurry to trust him;
for one kind of friend is only so when it suits him
but will not stand by you in your day of trouble.
Another kind of friend will fall out with you
and to your dismay make your quarrel public,
and a third kind of friend will share your table,
but not stand by you in your day of trouble:
when you are doing well he will be your second self,
ordering your servants about;
but if ever you are brought low he will turn against you
and will hide himself from you.
Keep well clear of your enemies,
and be wary of your friends.
A faithful friend is a sure shelter,
whoever finds one has found a rare treasure.
A faithful friend is something beyond price,
there is no measuring his worth.
A faithful friend is the elixir of life,
and those who fear the Lord will find one.
Whoever fears the Lord makes true friends,
for as a man is, so is his friend.

This is the word of the Lord.

Responsorial Psalm (Ps 118:12. 16. 18. 27. 34–35. *R.* v. 35)
Response
Guide me, Lord, in the path of your commands.

1. Blessed are you, O Lord;
teach me your statutes.
I take delight in your statutes;
I will not forget your word. (*R.*)

2. Open my eyes that I may consider
the wonders of your law.
Make me grasp the way of your precepts
and I will muse on your wonders. (R.)

3. Train me to observe your law,
to keep it with my heart.
Guide me in the path of your commands;
for there is my delight. (R.)

ALLELUIA and GOSPEL. As for Year II, see p. 388.

Year II

First Reading   (5:9–12)

A reading from the letter of St James
The Judge is already to be seen waiting at the gates.

Do not make complaints against one another, brothers, so
as not to be brought to judgement yourselves; the Judge
is already to be seen waiting at the gates. For your example, brothers, in submitting with patience, take the
prophets who spoke in the name of the Lord; remember it is
those who had endurance that we say are the blessed ones.
You have heard of the patience of Job, and understood
the Lord's purpose, realising that the Lord is kind and
compassionate.

    Above all, my brothers, do not swear by heaven or by
the earth, or use any oaths at all. If you mean "yes", you
must say "yes"; if you mean "no", say "no". Otherwise you
make yourselves liable to judgement.

    This is the word of the Lord.

Responsorial Psalm   (Ps 102:1–4. 8–9. 11–12. R. v. 8)
Response
The Lord is compassion and love.

1. My soul, give thanks to the Lord,
all my being, bless his holy name.

My soul, give thanks to the Lord
and never forget all his blessings. (*R.*)

2. It is he who forgives all your guilt,
who heals every one of your ills,
who redeems your life from the grave,
who crowns you with love and compassion. (*R.*)

3. The Lord is compassion and love,
slow to anger and rich in mercy.
His wrath will come to an end;
he will not be angry for ever. (*R.*)

4. For as the heavens are high above the earth
so strong is his love for those who fear him.
As far as the east is from the west
so far does he remove our sins. (*R.*)

Years I and II

Alleluia (Ps 110:7:8)

Alleluia, alleluia!
Your precepts, O Lord, are all of them sure;
they stand firm for ever and ever,
Alleluia!

Alternative Alleluias p. 847.

Gospel (10:1–12)

A reading from the holy Gospel according to Mark
What God has united, man must not divide.

Jesus came to the district of Judaea and the far side of the
Jordan. And again crowds gathered round him, and again
he taught them, as his custom was. Some Pharisees approached him and asked, "Is it against the law for a man
to divorce his wife?" They were testing him. He answered
them, "What did Moses command you?" "Moses allowed

us" they said "to draw up a writ of dismissal and so to divorce." Then Jesus said to them, "It was because you were so unteachable that he wrote this commandment for you. But from the beginning of creation God made them male and female. This is why a man must leave father and mother, and the two become one body. They are no longer two, therefore, but one body. So then, what God has united, man must not divide." Back in the house the disciples questioned him again about this, and he said to them, "The man who divorces his wife and marries another is guilty of adultery against her. And if a woman divorces her husband and marries another she is guilty of adultery too."

This is the Gospel of the Lord.

SATURDAY
Year I

First Reading   (17:1–15)

A reading from the book of Ecclesiasticus
The Lord God made man in his own image.

The Lord fashioned man from the earth,
to consign him back to it.
He gave them so many days' determined time,
he gave them authority over everything on earth.
He clothed them with strength like his own,
and made them in his own image.
He filled all living things with dread of man,
making him master over beasts and birds.
He shaped for them a mouth and tongue, eyes and ears,
and gave them a heart to think with.
He filled them with knowledge and understanding,
and revealed to them good and evil.
He put his own light in their hearts
to show them the magnificence of his works.
They will praise his holy name,
as they tell of his magnificent works.

He set knowledge before them,
he endowed them with the law of life.
He established an eternal covenant with them,
and revealed his judgements to them.
Their eyes saw his glorious majesty,
and their ears heard the glory of his voice.
He said to them, "Beware of all wrong-doing";
he gave each a commandment concerning his neighbour.
Their ways are always under his eye,
they cannot be hidden from his sight.

This is the word of the Lord.

Responsorial Psalm   (Ps 102:13–18. *R*. v. 17)

Response
The love of the Lord is everlasting
upon those who hold him in fear.

1. As a father has compassion on his sons,
the Lord has pity on those who fear him;
for he knows of what we are made,
he remembers that we are dust. (*R*.)

2. As for man, his days are like grass;
he flowers like the flower of the field;
the wind blows and he is gone
and his place never sees him again. (*R*.)

3. But the love of the Lord is everlasting
upon those who hold him in fear;
his justice reaches out to children's children
when they keep his covenant in truth,
when they keep his will in their mind. (*R*.)

ALLELUIA and GOSPEL. As for Year II, see p. 392.

Year II

First Reading   (5:13–20)

A reading from the letter of St James
The heartfelt prayer of a good man works very powerfully.

If any one of you is in trouble, he should pray; if anyone is
feeling happy, he should sing a psalm. If one of you is ill,
he should send for the elders of the church, and they must
anoint him with oil in the name of the Lord and pray over
him. The prayer of faith will save the sick man and the
Lord will raise him up again; and if he has committed any
sins, he will be forgiven. So confess your sins to one another, and pray for one another, and this will cure you;
the heartfelt prayer of a good man works very powerfully.
Elijah was a human being like ourselves – he prayed hard
for it not to rain, and no rain fell for three-and-a-half years;
then he prayed again and the sky gave rain and the earth
gave crops.

My brothers, if one of you strays away from the truth,
and another brings him back to it, he may be sure that anyone who can bring back a sinner from the wrong way that
he has taken will be saving a soul from death and covering
up a great number of sins.

This is the word of the Lord.

Responsorial Psalm   (Ps 140: 1–3. 8. *R*. v. 2)

Response
Let my prayer come before you like incense.

1. I have called to you, Lord; hasten to help me!
Hear my voice when I cry to you.
Let my prayer come before you like incense,
the raising of my hands like an evening oblation. (*R*.)

2. Lord, set a guard over my mouth;
keep watch at the door of my lips!

To you, Lord God, my eyes are turned:
in you I take refuge; spare my soul! (*R.*)

Years I and II

Alleluia   (Mt 11:25)

Alleluia, alleluia!
Blessed are you, Father,
Lord of heaven and earth,
for revealing the mysteries of the kingdom
to mere children.
Alleluia!

Alternative Alleluias p. 847.

Gospel   (10:13–16)

A reading from the holy Gospel according to Mark
*Anyone who does not welcome the kingdom of God like a little
child will never enter it.*

People were bringing little children to Jesus, for him to
touch them. The disciples turned them away, but when
Jesus saw this he was indignant and said to them, "Let the
little children come to me; do not stop them; for it is to
such as these that the kingdom of God belongs. I tell you
solemnly, anyone who does not welcome the kingdom of
God like a little child will never enter it." Then he put his
arms round them, laid his hands on them and gave them his
blessing.

This is the Gospel of the Lord.

8th SUNDAY OF THE YEAR
Year 1 (Year A)

First Reading   (49:14–15)

A reading from the prophet Isaiah
I will never forget you.

Zion was saying, "The Lord has abandoned me,
the Lord has forgotten me."

Does a woman forget her baby at the breast,
or fail to cherish the son of her womb?
Yet even if these forget,
I will never forget you.

This is the word of the Lord.

Responsorial Psalm   (Ps 61:2–3. 6–9. *R.* v. 6)

Response
In God alone is my soul at rest.

1. In God alone is my soul at rest;
my help comes from him.
He alone is my rock, my stronghold,
my fortress: I stand firm. (*R.*)

2. In God alone be at rest, my soul;
for my hope comes from him.
He alone is my rock, my stronghold
my fortress: I stand firm. (*R.*)

3. In God is my safety and glory,
the rock of my strength.
Take refuge in God all you people.
Trust him at all times.
Pour out your hearts before him. (*R.*)

Second Reading   (4:1–5)

A reading from the first letter of St Paul to the Corinthians
The Lord will reveal the secret intentions of men's hearts.

People must think of us as Christ's servants, stewards entrusted with the mysteries of God. What is expected of
stewards is that each one should be found worthy of his
trust. Not that it makes the slightest difference to me
whether you, or indeed any human tribunal, find me worthy

or not. I will not even pass judgement on myself. True, my conscience does not reproach me at all, but that does not prove that I am acquitted: the Lord alone is my judge. There must be no passing of premature judgement. Leave that until the Lord comes: he will light up all that is hidden in the dark and reveal the secret intentions of men's hearts. Then will be the time for each one to have whatever praise he deserves, from God.

This is the word of the Lord.

Alleluia (Jn 17:17)

Alleluia, alleluia!
Your word is truth, O Lord,
consecrate us in the truth.
Alleluia!

Alternative Alleluias p. 854.

Gospel (6:24–34)

A reading from the holy Gospel according to Matthew
Do not worry about tomorrow.

Jesus said to his disciples: "No one can be the slave of two masters: he will either hate the first and love the second, or treat the first with respect and the second with scorn. You cannot be the slave both of God and money.

"That is why I am telling you not to worry about your life and what you are to eat, nor about your body and how you are to clothe it. Surely life means more than food, and the body more than clothing! Look at the birds in the sky. They do not sow or reap or gather into barns; yet your heavenly Father feeds them. Are you not worth much more than they are? Can any of you, for all his worrying, add one single cubit to his span of life? And why worry about clothing? Think of the flowers growing in the fields; they never have to work or spin; yet I assure you that not even Solomon in all his regalia was robed like one of these. Now if that is how God clothes the grass in the field which is there today and thrown into the furnace tomorrow, will he not much more look after you, you men of little faith? So do not worry; do not say, 'What are we to eat? What are we to drink? How are we to be clothed?' It is the pagans who set their hearts on all these things. Your heavenly Father knows you need them all. Set your hearts on his kingdom first, and on his righteousness, and all these other things will be given you as well. So do not worry about to-morrow: tomorrow will take care of itself. Each day has enough trouble of its own."

This is the Gospel of the Lord.

8th SUNDAY OF THE YEAR

Year 2 (Year B)

First Reading   (2:16–17. 21–22)

A reading from the prophet Hosea
I will betroth you to myself for ever.

Thus says the Lord:

I am going to lure her
and lead her out into the wilderness
and speak to her heart.
There she will rsepond to me as she did when she was
    young,
as she did when she came out of the land of Egypt.
I will betroth you to myself for ever,
betroth you with integrity and justice,
with tenderness and love;
I will betroth you to myself with faithfulness,
and you will come to know the Lord.

This is the word of the Lord.

Responsorial Psalm   (Ps 102:1–4. 8. 10. 12–13. *R*. v. 8)
Response
The Lord is compassion and love.

1. My soul, give thanks to the Lord,
all my being, bless his holy name.
My soul, give thanks to the Lord
and never forget all his blessings. (*R*.)

2. It is he who forgives all your guilt,
who heals every one of your ills,
who redeems your life from the grave,
who crowns you with love and compassion. (*R*.)

3. The Lord is compassion and love,
slow to anger and rich in mercy.
He does not treat us according to our sins
nor repay us according to our faults. (*R*.)

4. As far as the east is from the west
so far does he remove our sins.
As a father has compassion on his sons,
The Lord has pity on those who fear him. (*R*.)

Second Reading   (3:1–6)

A reading from the second letter of St Paul to the
Corinthians
You are a letter from Christ drawn up by us.

Unlike other people, we need no letters of recommendation
either to you or from you, because you are yourselves our
letter, written in our hearts, that anybody can see and read,
and it is plain that you are a letter from Christ, drawn up
by us, and written not with ink but with the Spirit of the
living God, not on stone tablets but on the tablets of your
living hearts.

Before God, we are confident of this through Christ: not that we are qualified in ourselves to claim anything as our own work: all our qualifications come from God. He is the one who has given us the qualifications to be the administrators of this new covenant, which is not a covenant of written letters but of the Spirit: the written letters bring death, but the Spirit gives life.

This is the word of the Lord.

Alleluia   (Jn 10:27)

Alleluia, alleluia!
The sheep that belong to me listen to my voice,
says the Lord,
I know them and they follow me.
Alleluia!
Alternative Alleluias p. 854.

Gospel   (2:18–22)
A reading from the holy Gospel according to Mark
The bridegroom is with them.

One day when John's disciples and the Pharisees were fasting, some people came and said to Jesus, "Why is it that John's disciples and the disciples of the Pharisees fast, but your disciples do not?" Jesus replied, "Surely the bridegroom's attendants would never think of fasting while the bridegroom is still with them? As long as they have the bridegroom with them, they could not think of fasting. But the time will come for the bridegroom to be taken away from them, and then, on that day, they will fast. No one sews a piece of unshrunken cloth on an old cloak; if he does, the patch pulls away from it, the new from the old, and the tear gets worse. And nobody puts new wine into old wineskins; if he does, the wine will burst the skins, and the wine is lost and the skins too. No! New wine, fresh skins!"

This is the Gospel of the Lord.

8th SUNDAY OF THE YEAR

Year 3 (Year C)

First Reading   (27:4–7)

A reading from the book of Ecclesiasticus
Do not praise a man before he has spoken.

In a shaken sieve the rubbish is left behind,
so too the defects of a man appear in his talk.
The kiln tests the work of the potter,
the test of a man is in his conversation.
The orchard where the tree grows is judged on the quality
     of its fruit,
similarly a man's words betray what he feels.
Do not praise a man before he has spoken,
since this is the test of men.

   This is the word of the Lord.

Responsorial Psalm   (Ps 91:2–3. 13–16. *R*. v. 2)

Response
It is good to give you thanks, O Lord.

1. It is good to give thanks to the Lord
to make music to your name, O Most High,
to proclaim your love in the morning
and your truth in the watches of the night. (*R*.)

2. The just will flourish like the palm-tree
and grow like a Lebanon cedar. (*R*.)

3. Planted in the house of the Lord
they will flourish in the courts of our God,
still bearing fruit when they are old,
still full of sap, still green,
In him, my rock, there is no wrong. (*R*.)

Second Reading   (15:54–58)

A reading from the first letter of St Paul to the Corinthians
He has given us the victory through our Lord Jesus Christ.

When this perishable nature has put on imperishability,
and when this mortal nature has put on immortality, then
the words of scripture will come true: Death is swallowed
up in victory. Death, where is your victory? Death, where
is your sting? Now the sting of death is sin, and sin gets its
power from the Law. So let us thank God for giving us the
victory through our Lord Jesus Christ.

   Never give in then, my dear brothers, never admit defeat;
keep on working at the Lord's work always, knowing that,
in the Lord, you cannot be labouring in vain.

   This is the word of the Lord.

Alleluia   (Acts 16:14)

Alleluia, alleluia!
Open our heart, O Lord,
to accept the words of your Son.
Alleluia!

Alternative Alleluias p. 854.

Gospel   (6:39–45)

A reading from the holy Gospel according to Luke
A man's words flow out of what fills his heart.

Jesus told a parable to them, "Can one blind man guide another? Surely both will fall into a pit? The disciple is not
superior to his teacher; the fully trained disciple will always be like his teacher. Why do you observe the splinter
in your brother's eye and never notice the plank in your
own? How can you say to your brother, 'Brother, let me
take out the splinter that is in your eye,' when you cannot
see the plank in your own? Hypocrite! Take the plank

out of your own eye first, and then you will see clearly enough to take out the splinter that is in your brother's eye.

"There is no sound tree that produces rotten fruit, nor again a rotten tree that produces sound fruit. For every tree can be told by its own fruit: people do not pick figs from thorns, nor gather grapes from brambles. A good man draws what is good from the store of goodness in his heart; a bad man draws what is bad from the store of badness. For a man's words flow out of what fills his heart."

This is the Gospel of the Lord.

MONDAY
Year I

First Reading   (17:24–29)

A reading from the book of Ecclesiasticus
Return to the Lord and leave sin behind.

To those who repent God permits return,
and he encourages those who were losing hope.
Return to the Lord and leave sin behind,
plead before his face and lessen your offence.
Come back to the Most High and turn away from iniquity,
and hold in abhorrence all that is foul.
Who will praise the Most High in Sheol,
if the living do not do so by giving glory to him?
To the dead, as to those who do not exist, praise is unknown,
only those with life and health can praise the Lord.
How great is the mercy of the Lord,
his pardon on all those who turn towards him!

This is the word of the Lord.

Responsorial Psalm   (Ps 31:1–2. 5–7. R. v. 11)

Response
Rejoice, rejoice in the Lord,
exult, you just!

1. Happy the man whose offence is forgiven,
whose sin is remitted.
O happy the man to whom the Lord
imputes no guilt,
in whose spirit is no guile. (*R.*)

2. But now I have acknowledged my sins;
my guilt I did not hide.
I said: "I will confess
my offence to the Lord."
And you, Lord, have forgiven
the guilt of my sin. (*R.*)

3. So let every good man pray to you
in time of need.
The floods of water may reach high
but him they shall not reach.
You are my hiding place, O Lord;
you save me from distress.
You surround me with cries of deliverance. (*R.*)

ALLELUIA and GOSPEL. As for Year II, see p. 403.

Year II

First Reading   (1:3–9)

A reading from the first letter of St Peter
You did not see Christ, yet you love him; and you are already
filled with joy that cannot be described, because you believe.

Blessed be God the Father of our Lord Jesus Christ, who
in his great mercy has given us a new birth as his sons, by
raising Jesus Christ from the dead, so that we have a sure
hope and the promise of an inheritance that can never be
spoilt or soiled and never fade away, because it is being
kept for you in the heavens. Through your faith, God's
power will guard you until the salvation which has been
prepared is revealed at the end of time. This is a cause of
great joy for you, even though you may for a short time

have to bear being plagued by all sorts of trials; so that, when Jesus Christ is revealed, your faith will have been tested and proved like gold – only it is more precious than gold, which is corruptible even though it bears testing by fire – and then you will have praise and glory and honour. You did not see him, yet you love him; and still without seeing him, you are already filled with a joy so glorious that it cannot be described, because you believe; and you are sure of the end to which your faith looks forward, that is, the salvation of your souls.

This is the word of the Lord.

Responsorial Psalm   (Ps 110:1–2. 5–6. 9–10. *R.* v. 5)

Response
He keeps his covenant ever in mind.

Alternative Response
Alleluia!

1. Alleluia!
I will thank the Lord with all my heart
in the meeting of the just and their assembly.
Great are the works of the Lord;
to be pondered by all who love them. (*R.*)

2. He gives food to those who fear him;
keeps his covenant ever in mind.
He has shown his might to his people
by giving them the lands of the nations. (*R.*)

3. He has sent deliverance to his people
and established his covenant for ever.
Holy his name, to be feared. (*R.*)

4. To fear the Lord is the beginning of wisdom;
all who do so prove themselves wise.
His praise shall last for ever! (*R.*)

Years I and II

Alleluia   (1 Thess 2:13)

Alleluia, alleluia!
Accept God's message for what it really is:
God's message, and not some human thinking.
Alleluia!

Alternative Alleluias p. 847.

Gospel   (10:17–27)

A reading from the holy Gospel according to Mark
Sell everything you own and follow me.

Jesus was setting out on a journey when a man ran up, knelt before him and put this question to him, "Good master, what must I do to inherit eternal life?" Jesus said to him, "Why do you call me good? No one is good but God alone. You know the commandments: You must not kill; You must not commit adultery; You must not steal; You must not bring false witness; You must not defraud; Honour your father and mother." And he said to him, "Master, I have kept all these from my earliest days." Jesus looked steadily at him and loved him, and he said, "There is one thing you lack. Go and sell everything you own and give the money to the poor, and you will have treasure in heaven; then come, follow me." But his face fell at these words and he went away sad, for he was a man of great wealth.

Jesus looked round and said to his disciples, "How hard it is for those who have riches to enter the kingdom of God!" The disciples were astounded by these words, but Jesus insisted, "My children," he said to them "how hard it is to enter the kingdom of God! It is easier for a camel to pass through the eye of a needle than for a rich man to enter the kingdom of God. They were more astonished than ever. "In that case" they said to one another "who can be saved?" Jesus gazed at them. "For men" he said "it is impossible, but not for God: because everything is possible for God."

This is the Gospel of the Lord.

TUESDAY
Year I

First Reading   (35:1–12)

A reading from the book of Ecclesiasticus

A man offers communion sacrifices by following the commandments.

A man multiplies offerings by keeping the Law;
he offers communion sacrifices by following the commandments.
By showing gratitude he makes an offering of fine flour,
by giving alms he offers a sacrifice of praise.
Withdraw from wickedness and the Lord will be pleased,
withdraw from injustice and you make atonement.
Do not appear empty-handed in the Lord's presence;
for all these things are due under the commandment.
A virtuous man's offering graces the altar,
and its savour rises before the Most High.
A virtuous man's sacrifice is acceptable,
its memorial will not be forgotten.
Honour the Lord with generosity,
do not stint the first-fruits you bring.
Add a smiling face to all your gifts,
and be cheerful as you dedicate your tithes.
Give to the Most High as he has given to you,
generously as your means can afford;
for the Lord is a good rewarder,
he will reward you seven times over.
Offer him no bribe, he will not accept it,
do not put your faith in an unvirtuous sacrifice;

since the Lord is a judge
who is no respecter of personages.

   This is the word of the Lord.

Responsorial Psalm   (Ps 49:5–8. 14. 23. *R*. v. 23)
Response
I will show God's salvation to the upright.

1. "Summon before me my people
who made covenant with me by sacrifice."
The heavens proclaim his justice,
for he, God, is the judge. (*R*.)

2. "Listen, my people, I will speak;
Israel, I will testify against you,
for I am God your God.
I find no fault with your sacrifices,
your offerings are always before me. (*R*.)

3. "Pay your sacrifice of thanksgiving to God
and render him your votive offerings.
A sacrifice of thanksgiving honours me
and I will show God's salvation to the upright." (*R*.)

ALLELUIA and GOSPEL. As for Year II, see p. 406.

Year II

First Reading   (1:10–16)
A reading from the first letter of St Peter
Their prophecies were about the grace which was to come to
you. Free your minds then of encumbrances.

It was this salvation that the prophets were looking and
searching so hard for; their prophecies were about the grace
which was to come to you. The Spirit of Christ which was
in them foretold the sufferings of Christ and the glories that
would come after them, and they tried to find out at what
time and in what circumstances all this was to be expected.

It was revealed to them that the news they brought of all the things which have now been announced to you, by those who preached to you the Good News through the Holy Spirit sent from heaven, was for you and not for themselves. Even the angels long to catch a glimpse of these things.

Free your minds, then, of encumbrances; control them, and put your trust in nothing but the grace that will be given you when Jesus Christ is revealed. Do not behave in the way that you liked to before you learnt the truth; make a habit of obedience: be holy in all you do, since it is the Holy One who has called you, and scripture says: Be holy, for I am holy.

This is the word of the Lord.

Responsorial Psalm   (97:1-4. *R*. v. 2)
Response
The Lord has made known his salvation.

1. Sing a new song to the Lord
for he has worked wonders.
His right hand and his holy arm
have brought salvation. (*R*.)

2. The Lord has made known his salvation;
has shown his justice to the nations.
He has remembered his truth and love
for the house of Israel. (*R*)

3. All the ends of the earth have seen
the salvation of our God.
Shout to the Lord all the earth,
ring out your joy. (*R*.)

Years I and II

Alleluia   (Phil 2:15-16)
Alleluia, alleluia!
You will shine in the world like bright stars

because you are offering it the word of life.
Alleluia!

Alternative Alleluias p. 847.

Gospel   (10:28–31)

A reading from the holy Gospel according to Mark
You will be repaid a hundred times over, not without per-secutions, now in this present time and, in the world to come, eternal life.

"What about us?" Peter asked Jesus. "We have left every-thing and followed you." Jesus said, "I tell you solemnly, there is no one who has left house, brothers, sisters, father, children or land for my sake and for the sake of the gospel who will not be repaid a hundred times over, houses, brothers, sisters, mothers, children and land – not without persecutions – now in this present time and, in the world to come, eternal life.
    "Many who are first will be last, and the last first."
    This is the Gospel of the Lord.

WEDNESDAY
Year I

First Reading   (36:1. 4–5. 10–17)

A reading from the book of Ecclesiasticus
Let the nations know that there is no God but you, Lord.

Have mercy on us, Master, Lord of all, and look on us,
cast the fear of yourself over every nation.
Let them acknowledge you, just as we have acknowledged
that there is no God but you, Lord.
Send new portents, do fresh wonders,
win glory for your hand and your right arm.
Gather together all the tribes of Jacob,
restore them their inheritance as in the beginning.

Have mercy, Lord, on the people who have invoked your
    name,
on Israel whom you have treated as a first-born.
Show compassion on your holy city,
on Jerusalem the place of your rest.
Fill Zion with songs of your praise,
and your sanctuary with your glory.
Bear witness to those you created in the beginning,
and bring about what has been prophesied in your name.
Give those who wait for you their reward,
and let your prophets be proved worthy of belief.
Grant, Lord, the prayer of your servants,
in accordance with Aaron's blessing on your people,
so that all the earth's inhabitants may acknowledge
that you are the Lord, the everlasting God.

    This is the word of the Lord.

Responsorial Psalm   (Ps 78:8–9. 11. 13. *R*. Ecclus 36:1)
Response
Have mercy on us, Lord,
and look on us.

1. Do not hold the guilt of our fathers against us.
Let your compassion hasten to meet us
for we are in the depths of distress. (*R*.)

2. O God our saviour, come to our help,
come for the sake of the glory of your name.
O Lord our God, forgive us our sins;
rescue us for the sake of your name. (*R*.)

3. Let the groans of the prisoners come before you;
let your strong arm reprieve those condemned to die.
But we, your people, the flock of your pasture,
will give you thanks for ever and ever.
We will tell your praise from age to age. (*R*.)
ALLELUIA and GOSPEL. As for Year II, see p. 410.

Year II

First Reading   (1:18–25)

A reading from the first letter to St Peter
You were ransomed in the precious blood of a lamb without
spot or stain, namely Christ.

Remember, the ransom that was paid to free you from the
useless way of life your ancestors handed down was not
paid in anything corruptible, neither in silver nor gold,
but in the precious blood of a lamb without spot or stain,
namely Christ; who, though known since before the world
was made, has been revealed only in our time, the end of
the ages, for your sake. Through him you now have faith in
God, who raised him from the dead and gave him glory for
that very reason – so that you would have faith and hope in
God.

You have been obedient to the truth and purified your
souls until you can love like brothers, in sincerity; let your
love for each other be real and from the heart – your new
birth was not from any mortal seed but from the everlasting
word of the living and eternal God. All flesh is grass and its
glory like the wild flower's. The grass withers, the flower
falls, but the word of the Lord remains for ever. What is
this word? It is the Good News that has been brought to
you.

This is the word of the Lord.

Responsorial Psalm   (Ps 147:12–15. 19–20. *R.* v. 12)

Response
O praise the Lord, Jerusalem!

Or: Alleluia!

1. O praise the Lord, Jerusalem!
Zion, praise your God!

He has strengthened the bars of your gates,
he has blessed the children within you. (*R.*)

2. He established peace on your borders,
he feeds you with finest wheat.
He sends out his word to the earth
and swiftly runs his command. (*R.*)

3. He makes his word known to Jacob,
to Israel his laws and decrees.
He has not dealt thus with other nations.
he has not taught them his decrees.
Alleluia! (*R.*)

Years I and II

Alleluia (1 Jn 2:5)
Alleluia, alleluia!
When anyone obeys what Christ has said,
God's love comes to perfection in him.
Alleluia!
Alternative Alleluias p. 847.

Gospel (10:32–45)
A reading from the holy Gospel according to Mark
*Now we are going up to Jerusalem and the Son of Man is about
to be handed over.*

They were on the road, going up to Jerusalem; Jesus was
walking on ahead of them; they were in a daze, and those
who followed were apprehensive. Once more taking the
Twelve aside he began to tell them what was going to happen
to him: "Now we are going up to Jerusalem, and the
Son of Man is about to be handed over to the chief priests
and the scribes. They will condemn him to death and will
hand him over to the pagans, who will mock him and spit
at him and scourge him and put him to death; and after
three days he will rise again."

James and John, the sons of Zebedee, approached him.

"Master," they said to him "we want you to do us a favour." He said to them, "What is it you want me to do for you?" They said to him, "Allow us to sit one at your right hand and the other at your left in your glory." "You do not know what you are asking" Jesus said to them. "Can you drink the cup that I must drink, or be baptised with the baptism with which I must be baptised?" They replied, "We can." Jesus said to them, "The cup that I must drink you shall drink, and with the baptism with which I must be baptised you shall be baptised, but as for seats at my right hand or my left, these are not mine to grant; they belong to those to whom they have been allotted."

When the other ten heard this they began to feel indignant with James and John, so Jesus called them to him and said to them, "You know that among the pagans their so-called rulers lord it over them, and their great men make their authority felt. This is not to happen among you. No; anyone who wants to become great among you must be your servant, and anyone who wants to be first among you must be slave to all. For the Son of Man himself did not come to be served but to serve, and to give his life as a ransom for many."

This is the Gospel of the Lord.

THURSDAY
Year I

First Reading   (42:15–25)

A reading from the book of Ecclesiasticus
The work of the Lord is full of his glory.

Next, I will remind you of the works of the Lord,
and tell of what I have seen.
By the words of the Lord his works come into being
and all creation obeys his will.
As the sun in shining looks on all things,
so the work of the Lord is full of his glory.

The Lord has not granted to the holy ones
to tell of all his marvels
which the Almighty Lord has solidly constructed
for the universe to stand firm in his glory.
He has fathomed the deep and the heart,
and seen into their devious ways:
for the Most High knows all the knowledge there is,
and has observed the signs of the times.
He declares what is past and what will be,
and uncovers the traces of hidden things.
Not a thought escapes him,
not a single word is hidden from him.
He has imposed an order on the magnificent works of his
wisdom,
he is from everlasting to everlasting,
nothing can be added to him, nothing taken away,
he needs no one's advice.
How desirable are all his works,
how dazzling to the eye!
They all live and last for ever,
whatever the circumstances all obey him.
All things go in pairs, by opposites,
and he has made nothing defective;
the one consolidates the excellence of the other,
who could ever be sated with gazing at his glory?

This is the word of the Lord.

Responsorial Psalm   (Ps 32:2–9. *R*. v. 6)

Response
By the word of the Lord the heavens were made.

1. Give thanks to the Lord upon the harp,
with a ten-stringed lute sing him songs.
O sing him a song that is new,
play loudly, with all your skill. (*R*.)

2. For the word of the Lord is faithful
and all his works to be trusted.
The Lord loves justice and right
and fills the earth with his love. (R.)

3. By his word the heavens were made,
by the breath of his mouth all the stars.
He collects the waves of the ocean;
he stores up the depths of the sea. (R.)

4. Let all the earth fear the Lord,
all who live in the world revere him.
He spoke; and it came to be.
He commanded; it sprang into being. (R.)

ALLELUIA and GOSPEL. As for Year II, see p. 414.

Year II

First Reading   (2:2–5. 9–12)

A reading from the first letter of St Peter

*You are a royal priesthood, a people set apart to sing the
praises of him who called you.*

You are new born, and, like babies, you should be hungry
for nothing but milk – the spiritual honesty which will help
you to grow up to Salvation – now that you have tasted the
goodness of the Lord.

He is the living stone, rejected by men but chosen by God
and precious to him; set yourselves close to him so that
you too, the holy priesthood that offers the spiritual sacrifices which Jesus Christ has made acceptable to God, may
be living stones making a spiritual house.

But you are a chosen race, a royal priesthood, a consecrated nation, a people set apart to sing the praises of God
who called you out of the darkness into his wonderful light.
Once you were not a people at all and now you are the
People of God; once you were outside the mercy and now
you have been given mercy.

I urge you, my dear people, while you are visitors and pilgrims to keep yourselves free from the selfish passions that attack the soul. Always behave honourably among pagans so that they can see your good works for themselves and, when the day of reckoning comes, give thanks to God for the things which now make them denounce you as criminals.

This is the word of the Lord.

Responsorial Psalm (Ps 99:2–5. *R*. v. 2)

Response
Come before the Lord,
singing for joy.

1. Serve the Lord with gladness.
Come before him, singing for joy. (*R*.)

2. Know that he, the Lord, is God.
He made us, we belong to him,
we are his people, the sheep of his flock. (*R*.)

3. Go within his gates, giving thanks.
Enter his courts with songs of praise.
Give thanks to him and bless his name. (*R*.)

4. Indeed, how good is the Lord,
eternal his merciful love.
He is faithful from age to age. (*R*.)

Years I and II

Alleluia (Ps 129:5)

Alleluia, alleluia!
My soul is waiting for the Lord,
I count on his word.
Alleluia!

Alternative Alleluias p. 847.

Gospel   (10:46–52)

A reading from the holy Gospel according to Mark
Master, let me see again.

They reached Jericho; and as Jesus left Jericho with his
disciples and a large crowd, Bartimaeus (that is, the son of
Timaeus), a blind beggar, was sitting at the side of the road.
When he heard that it was Jesus of Nazareth, he began to
shout and to say, "Son of David, Jesus, have pity on me."
And many of them scolded him and told him to keep quiet,
but he only shouted all the louder, "Son of David, have pity
on me." Jesus stopped and said, "Call him here." So they
called the blind man. "Courage," they said "get up; he is
calling you." So throwing off his cloak, he jumped up and
went to Jesus. Then Jesus spoke, "What do you want me
to do for you?' "Rabbuni," the blind man said to him
"Master, let me see again." Jesus said to him, "Go; your
faith has saved you." And immediately his sight returned
and he followed him along the road.

This is the Gospel of the Lord.

FRIDAY
Year I

First Reading   (44:1. 9–13)

A reading from the book of Ecclesiasticus
*Our ancestors were generous men, and their name lives on for
all generations.*

Next let us praise illustrious men,
our ancestors in their successive generations.
While others have left no memory,
and disappeared as though they had not existed,
they are now as though they had never been,
and so too, their children after them.

But here is a list of generous men
whose good works have not been forgotten.
In their descendants there remains
a rich inheritance born of them.
Their descendants stand by the covenants
and, thanks to them, so do their children's children.
Their offspring will last for ever,
their glory will not fade.

This is the word of the Lord.

Responsorial Psalm (Ps 149:1–6. 9. *R*. v. 4)

Response
The Lord takes delight in his people.

Alternative Response
Alleluia!

1. Sing a new song to the Lord,
his praise in the assembly of the faithful.
Let Israel rejoice in its Maker,
let Zion's sons exult in their king. (*R*.)

2. Let them praise his name with dancing
and make music with timbrel and harp.
For the Lord takes delight in his people.
He crowns the poor with salvation. (*R*.)

3. Let the faithful rejoice in their glory,
shout for joy and take their rest.
Let the praise of God be on their lips;
this honour is for all his faithful.
Alleluia! (*R*.)

ALLELUIA and GOSPEL. As for year II, p. 418.

Year II

First Reading   (4:7–13)

A reading from the first letter of St Peter
Like good stewards responsible for all these different graces of God, put yourselves at the service of others.

Everything will soon come to an end, so, to pray better, keep a calm and sober mind. Above all, never let your love for each other grow insincere, since love covers over many a sin. Welcome each other into your houses without grumbling. Each one of you has received a special grace, so, like good stewards responsible for all these different graces of God, put yourselves at the service of others. If you are a speaker, speak in words which seem to come from God; if you are a helper, help as though every action was done at God's orders; so that in everything God may receive the glory, through Jesus Christ, since to him alone belong all glory and power for ever and ever. Amen.

My dear people, you must not think it unaccountable that you should be tested by fire. There is nothing extraordinary in what has happened to you. If you can have some share in the sufferings of Christ, be glad, because you will enjoy a much greater gladness when his glory is revealed.

This is the word of the Lord.

Responsorial Psalm   (Ps 95:10–13. R. v. 13)

Response
The Lord comes to rule the earth.

1. Proclaim to the nations: "God is king."
The world he made firm in its place;
he will judge the peoples in fairness. (R.)

2. Let the heavens rejoice and earth be glad.
Let the sea and all within it thunder praise,

let the land and all it bears rejoice,
all the trees of the wood shout for joy
at the presence of the Lord for he comes,
he comes to rule the earth. (*R.*)

3. With justice he will rule the world,
he will judge the peoples with his truth. (*R.*)

Years I and II

Alleluia (Ps 118:29. 35)

Alleluia, alleluia!
Bend my heart to your will, O Lord,
and teach me your law.
Alleluia!

Alternative Alleluias p. 847.

Gospel (11:11–26)

A reading from the holy Gospel according to Mark
*My house will be called a house of prayer for all the peoples.
Have faith in God.*

Jesus entered Jerusalem and went into the Temple. He
looked all round him, but as it was now late, he went out to
Bethany with the Twelve.

Next day as they were leaving Bethany, he felt hungry.
Seeing a fig tree in leaf some distance away, he went to see if
he could find any fruit on it, but when he came up to it he
found nothing but leaves; for it was not the season for figs.
And he addressed the fig tree. "May no one ever eat fruit
from you again" he said. And his disciples heard him say
this.

So they reached Jerusalem and he went into the Temple
and began driving out those who were selling and buying
there; he upset the tables of the money changers and the
chairs of those who were selling pigeons. Nor would he
allow anyone to carry anything through the Temple. And

he taught them and said, "Does not scripture say: My house will be called a house of prayer for all the peoples? But you have turned it into a robber's den." This came to the ears of the chief priests and the scribes, and they tried to find some way of doing away with him; they were afraid of him because the people were carried away by his teaching. And when evening came he went out of the city.

Next morning, as they passed by, they saw the fig tree withered to the roots. Peter remembered. "Look, Rabbi," he said to Jesus "the fig tree you cursed has withered away." Jesus answered, "Have faith in God. I tell you solemnly, if anyone says to this mountain, 'Get up and throw yourself into the sea,' with no hesitation in his heart but believing that what he says will happen, it will be done for him. I tell you therefore: everything you ask and pray for, believe that you have it already, and it will be yours. And when you stand in prayer, forgive whatever you have against anybody, so that your Father in heaven may forgive your failings too. But if you do not forgive, your Father in heaven will not forgive your failings either."

This is the Gospel of the Lord.

SATURDAY
Year I

First Reading   (51:12–20)

A reading from the book of Ecclesiasticus
Glory be to him who has given me wisdom.

Therefore I will thank you and praise you,
and bless the name of the Lord.
When I was still a youth, before I went travelling,
in my prayers I asked outright for wisdom.
Outside the sanctuary I would pray for her,
and to the last I will continue to seek her.
From her blossoming to the ripening of her grape
my heart has taken its delight in her.
My foot has pursued a straight path,

I have been following her steps ever since my youth.
By bowing my ear a little I have received her,
and have found much instruction.
Thanks to her I have advanced;
the glory be to him who has given me wisdom!
For I am determined to put her into practice,
I have earnestly pursued what is good, I will not be put to
    shame.
My soul has fought to possess her,
I have been scrupulous in keeping the Law;
I have stretched out my hands to heaven
and bewailed my ignorance of her;
I have directed my soul towards her,
and in purity have found her.

This is the word of the Lord.

Responsorial Psalm   (Ps 18:8–11. *R*. v. 9)

Response
The precepts of the Lord gladden the heart.

1. The law of the Lord is perfect,
it revives the soul.
The rule of the Lord is to be trusted,
it gives wisdom to the simple. (*R*.)

2. The precepts of the Lord are right,
they gladden the heart.
The command of the Lord is clear,
it gives light to the eyes. (*R*.)

3. The fear of the Lord is holy,
abiding for ever.
The decrees of the Lord are truth
and all of them just. (*R*.)

4. They are more to be desired than gold,
than the purest of gold
and sweeter are they than honey,
than honey from the comb. (*R.*)

ALLELUIA and GOSPEL. As for Year II, see p. 422.

Year II

First Reading   (17. 20–25)

A reading from the letter of St Jude
God can keep you from falling and bring you safe to his glorious presence, innocent and happy.

Remember, my dear friends, what the apostles of our Lord Jesus Christ told you to expect. You must use your holy faith as your foundation and build on that, praying in the Holy Spirit; keep yourselves within the love of God and wait for the mercy of our Lord Jesus Christ to give you eternal life. When there are some who have doubts, reassure them; when there are some to be saved from the fire, pull them out; but there are others to whom you must be kind with great caution, keeping your distance even from outside clothing which is contaminated by vice.

Glory be to him who can keep you from falling and bring you safe to his glorious presence, innocent and happy. To God, the only God, who saves us through Jesus Christ our Lord, be the glory, majesty, authority and power, which he had before time began, now and for ever. Amen.

This is the word of the Lord.

Responsorial Psalm   (Ps 62:2–6. *R.* v. 2)

Response
For you my soul is thirsting,
Lord, my God.

1. O God, you are my God, for you I long;
for you my soul is thirsting.

My body pines for you
like a dry, weary land without water. (*R.*)

2. So I gaze on you in the sanctuary
to see your strength and your glory.
For your love is better than life,
my lips will speak your praise. (*R.*)

3. So I will bless you all my life,
in your name I will lift up my hands.
My soul shall be filled as with a banquet,
my mouth shall praise you with joy. (*R.*)

Years I and II

Alleluia   (1 Peter 1:25)

Alleluia, alleluia!
The word of the Lord remains for ever:
What is this word?
It is the Good News that has been brought to you.
Alleluia!

Alternative Alleluias p. 847.

Gospel   (11:27–33)

A reading from the holy Gospel according to Mark
What authority have you for acting like this?

Jesus and his disciples came to Jerusalem, and as Jesus was
walking in the Temple, the chief priests and the scribes and
the elders came to him, and they said to him, "What authority have you for acting like this? Or who gave you authority
to do these things?" Jesus said to them, "I will ask you a
question, only one; answer me and I will tell you my
authority for acting like this. John's baptism: did it come
from heaven, or from man? Answer me that." And they
argued it out this way among themselves: "If we say from
heaven, he will say, 'Then why did you refuse to believe

him?' But dare we say from man?" – they had the people to fear, for everyone held that John was a real prophet. So their reply to Jesus was, "We do not know." And Jesus said to them, "Nor will I tell you my authority for acting like this."

This is the Gospel of the Lord.

9th SUNDAY OF THE YEAR
Year 1 (Year A)

First Reading   (11:18. 26–28)

A reading from the book of Deuteronomy
See, I set before you today a blessing and a curse.

Moses said to the people: "Let these words of mine remain in your heart and in your soul; fasten them on your hand as a sign and on your forehead as a circlet.

"See, I set before you today a blessing and a curse: a blessing, if you obey the commandments of the Lord our God that I enjoin on you today; a curse, if you disobey the commandments of the Lord your God and leave the way I have marked out for you today, by going after other gods you have not known."

This is the word of the Lord.

Responsorial Psalm   (Ps 30:2–4. 17. 25. *R*. v. 3)

Response
Be a rock of refuge for me, O Lord.

1. In you, O Lord, I take refuge.
Let me never be put to shame.
In your justice, set me free,
hear me and speedily rescue me. (*R*.)

2. Be a rock of refuge for me,
a mighty stronghold to save me,
for you are my rock, my stronghold.
For your name's sake, lead me and guide me. (*R*.)

3. Let your face shine on your servant.
Save me in your love.
Be strong, let your heart take courage,
all who hope in the Lord. (*R.*)

Second Reading   (3:21–25. 28)

A reading from the letter of St Paul to the Romans
*A man is justified by faith and not by doing something the Law
tells him to do.*

God's justice that was made known through the Law and
the Prophets has now been revealed outside the Law, since
it is the same justice of God that comes through faith to
everyone, Jew and pagan alike, who believes in Jesus
Christ. Both Jew and pagan sinned and forfeited God's
glory, and both are justified through the free gift of his
grace by being redeemed in Christ Jesus who was appointed
by God to sacrifice his life so as to win reconciliation
through faith since, as we see it, a man is justified by faith
and not by doing something the Law tells him to do.

This is the word of the Lord.

Alleluia   (Jn 14:23)

Alleluia, alleluia!
If anyone loves me he will keep my word,
and my Father will love him,
and we shall come to him.
Alleluia!
Alternative Alleluias p. 854.

Gospel   (7:21–27)

A reading from the holy Gospel according to Matthew
The house built on rock and the house built on sand.

Jesus said to his disciples: "It is not those who say to me,
'Lord, Lord', who will enter the kingdom of heaven, but the
person who does the will of my Father in heaven. When the

day comes many will say to me, 'Lord, Lord, did we not prophesy in your name, cast out demons in your name, work many miracles in your name?' Then I shall tell them to their faces: I have never known you; away from me, you evil men!'"

"Therefore, everyone who listens to these words of mine and acts on them will be like a sensible man who built his house on rock. Rain came down, floods rose, gales blew and hurled themselves against that house, and it did not fall: it was founded on rock. But everyone who listens to these words of mine and does not act on them will be like a stupid man who built his house on sand. Rain came down, floods rose, gales blew and struck that house, and it fell; and what a fall it had!'"

This is the Gospel of the Lord.

9th SUNDAY OF THE YEAR
Year 2 (Year B)

First Reading   (5:12–15)

A reading from the book of Deuteronomy
Remember that you were a servant in the land of Egypt.

The Lord says this: "Observe the sabbath day and keep it holy, as the Lord your God has commanded you. For six days you shall labour and do all your work, but the seventh day is a sabbath for the Lord your God. You shall do no work that day, neither you nor your son nor your daughter nor your servants, men or women, nor your ox nor your donkey nor any of your animals, nor the stranger who lives with you. Thus your servant, man or woman, shall rest as you do. Remember that you were a servant in the land of Egypt, and that the Lord your God brought you out from there with mighty hand and outstretched arm; because of this, the Lord your God has commanded you to keep the sabbath day."

This is the word of the Lord.

Responsorial Psalm   (Ps 80:3–8. 10–11. *R*. v. 2)

Response

Ring out your joy to God our strength.

1. Raise a song and sound the timbrel,
The sweet-sounding harp and the lute,
blow the trumpet at the new moon,
when the moon is full, on our feast. (*R*.)

2. For this is Israel's law,
a command of the God of Jacob.
He imposed it as a rule on Joseph,
when he went out against the land of Egypt. (*R*.)

3. A voice I did not know said to me:
"I freed your shoulder from the burden;
your hands were freed from the load.
You called in distress and I saved you. (*R*.)

4. "Let there be no foreign god among you,
no worship of an alien god.
I am the Lord your God,
who brought you from the land of Egypt." (*R*.)

Second Reading   (4:6–11)

A reading from the second letter of St Paul to the
Corinthians

In our mortal flesh the life of Jesus is openly shown.

It is the same God that said, "Let there be light shining out
of darkness," who has shone in our minds to radiate the
light of the knowledge of God's glory, the glory on the face
of Christ.

   We are only the earthenware jars that hold this treasure,
to make it clear that such an overwhelming power comes
from God and not from us. We are in difficulties on all
sides, but never cornered; we see no answer to our prob-

lems, but never despair; we have been persecuted, but never deserted; knocked down, but never killed; always, wherever we may be, we carry with us in our body the death of Jesus, so that the life of Jesus, too, may always be seen in our body. Indeed, while we are still alive, we are consigned to our death every day, for the sake of Jesus, so that in our mortal flesh the life of Jesus, too, may be openly shown.

This is the word of the Lord.

Alleluia   (Jn 6:63. 68)

Alleluia, alleluia!
Your words are spirit, Lord,
and they are life:
you have the message of eternal life.
Alleluia!

Alternative Alleluias p. 854.

Gospel   (2:23–3:6)

A reading from the holy Gospel according to Mark
The Son of Man is master even of the Sabbath.

*One sabbath day Jesus happened to be taking a walk through the cornfields, and his disciples began to pick ears of corn as they went along. And the Pharisees said to him, "Look, why are they doing something on the sabbath day that is forbidden?" And he replied, "Did you ever read what David did in his time of need when he and his followers were hungry – how he went into the house of God when Abiathar was high priest, and ate the loaves of offering which only the priests are allowed to eat, and how he also gave some to the men with him?"

And he said to them, "The sabbath was made for man, not man for the sabbath; so the Son of Man is master even of the sabbath."*

He went again into a synagogue, and there was a man there who had a withered hand. And they were watching him to see if he could cure him on the sabbath day, hoping for something to use against him. He said to the man with the withered hand, "Stand up out in the middle!" Then he said to them, "Is it against the law on the sabbath day to do good, or to do evil; to save life, or to kill?" But they said nothing. Then, grieved to find them so obstinate, he looked angrily round at them, and said to the man, "Stretch out your hand." He stretched it out and his hand was better. The Pharisees went out and at once began to plot with the Herodians against him, discussing how to destroy him.

This is the Gospel of the Lord.

*Shorter Form, verses 23–28, read between *.

9th SUNDAY OF THE YEAR
Year 3 (Year C)

First Reading   (8:41–43)

A reading from the first book of the Kings
If a foreigner comes, grant all he asks.

Solomon stood before the altar of the Lord and, stretching out his hands towards heaven, said:

"And the foreigner too, not belonging to your people Israel, if he comes from a distant country for the sake of your name – for men will hear of your name, of your mighty hand and outstretched arm – if he comes and prays in this Temple, hear from heaven where your home is, and grant all the foreigner asks, so that all the peoples of the earth may come to know your name and, like your people Israel, revere you, and know that your name is given to the Temple I have built."

This is the word of the Lord.

Responsorial Psalm   (Ps 116:1–2. R. Mk 16:15)

Response
Go out to the whole world
and proclaim the Good News.

Alternative Response
Alleluia!

1. Alleluia!
O praise the Lord, all you nations,
acclaim him all you peoples!
Strong is his love for us;
he is faithful for ever. (*R.*)

Second Reading   (1:1–2. 6–10)

A reading from the letter of St Paul to the Galatians
If I still wanted men's approval, I should not be a servant of Christ.

From Paul to the churches of Galatia, and from all the brothers who are here with me, an apostle who does not owe his authority to men or his appointment to any human being but who has been appointed by Jesus Christ and by God the Father who raised Jesus from the dead.

I am astonished at the promptness with which you have turned away from the one who called you and have decided to follow a different version of the Good News. Not that there can be more than one Good News; it is merely that some troublemakers among you want to change the Good News of Christ; and let me warn you that if anyone preaches a version of the Good News different from the one we have already preached to you, whether it be ourselves or an angel from heaven, he is to be condemned. I am only repeating what we told you before: if anyone preaches a version of the Good News different from the one you have already heard, he is to be condemned. So now whom am I trying to please – man, or God? Would you say it is men's approval I am looking for? If I still wanted that, I should not be what I am – a servant of Christ.

This is the word of God.

Alleluia   (Jn1:12. 14)

Alleluia, alleluia!
The Word was made flesh and lived among us;
to all who did accept him
he gave power to become children of God.
Alleluia!

Alternative Alleluias p. 854.

Gospel   (7:1–10)

A reading from the holy Gospel according to Luke
Not even in Israel have I found faith like this.

When Jesus had come to the end of all he wanted the people
to hear, he went into Capernaum. A centurion there had a
servant, a favourite of his, who was sick and near death.
Having heard about Jesus he sent some Jewish elders to
him to ask him to come and heal his servant. When they
came to Jesus they pleaded earnestly with him. "He deserves this of you," they said "because he is friendly towards our people; in fact, he is the one who built the
synagogue." So Jesus went with them, and was not very
far from the house when the centurion sent word to him
by some friends: "Sir," he said "do not put yourself to
trouble; because I am not worthy to have you under my
roof; and for this same reason I did not presume to come
to you myself; but give the word and let my servant be cured.
For I am under authority myself, and have soldiers under
me; and I say to one man: Go, and he goes: to another:
Come here, and he comes; to my servant: Do this, and he
does it." When Jesus heard these words he was astonished
at him and, turning round, said to the crowd following him,
"I tell you, not even in Israel have I found faith like this."
And when the messengers got back to the house they found
the servant in perfect health.

    This is the Gospel of the Lord.

MONDAY

Year I

First Reading   (1:1; 2:1–8)

A reading from the book of Tobit.
Tobit feared God more than he feared the king.

The tale of Tobit son of Tobiel, of the lineage of Asiel and tribe of Naphtali. In the days of Shalmaneser, king of Assyria, he was exiled from Thisbe, which is south of Kedesh-Naphtali in Upper Galilee, above Hazor, some distance to the west, north of Shephat.

At our feast of Pentecost (the feast of Weeks) there was a good dinner. I took my place for the meal; the table was brought to me and various dishes were brought. Then I said to my son Tobias, "Go, my child, and seek out some poor, loyal-hearted man among our brothers exiled in Nineveh, and bring him to share my meal. I will wait until you come back, my child." So Tobias went out to look for some poor man among our brothers, but he came back again and said, "Father!" I answered, "What is it, my child?" He went on, "Father, one of our nation has just been murdered; he has been strangled and then thrown down in the market place; he is there still." I sprang up at once, left my meal untouched, took the man from the market place and laid him in one of my rooms, waiting until sunset to bury him. I came in again and washed myself and ate my bread in sorrow, remembering the words of the prophet Amos concerning Bethel:

Your feasts will be turned to mourning,

and all your songs to lamentation.

And I wept. When the sun was down, I went and dug a grave and buried him. My neighbours laughed and said, "See! He is not afraid any more." (You must remember that a price had been set on my head earlier for this very thing.) "The time before this he had to flee, yet here he is, beginning to bury the dead again."

This is the word of the Lord.

Responsorial Psalm (Ps 111:1–6. *R.* v. 1)

Response
Happy the man who fears the Lord.
Or: Alleluia!

1. Alleluia!
Happy the man who fears the Lord,
who takes delight in his commands.
His sons will be powerful on earth;
the children of the upright are blessed. (*R.*)

2. Riches and wealth are in his house;
his justice stands firm for ever.
He is a light in the darkness for the upright:
he is generous, merciful and just. (*R.*)

3. The good man takes pity and lends,
he conducts his affairs with honour.
The just man will never waver:
he will be remembered for ever. (*R.*)

ALLELUIA and GOSPEL. As for Year II, see p. 433.

Year II

First Reading (1:2–7)

A reading from the second letter of St Peter
He has given us the guarantee of something very great: to be able to share the divine nature.

May you have more and more grace and peace as you come to know our Lord more and more.

By his divine power, he has given us all the things that we need for life and for true devotion, bringing us to know

God himself, who has called us by his own glory and goodness. In making these gifts, he has given us the guarantee of something very great and wonderful to come: through them you will be able to share the divine nature and to escape corruption in a world that is sunk in vice. But to attain this, you will have to do your utmost yourselves, adding goodness to the faith that you have, understanding to your goodness, self-control to your understanding, patience to your self-control, true devotion to your patience, kindness towards your fellow men to your devotion, and, to this kindness, love.

This is the word of the Lord.

Responsorial Psalm   (Ps 90:1–2. 14–16. *R*. v. 2)

Response
My God, in you I trust.

1. He who dwells in the shelter of the Most High
and abides in the shade of the Almighty
says to the Lord: "My refuge,
my stronghold, my God in whom I trust!" (R.)

2. His love he set on me, so I will rescue him;
protect him for he knows my name.
When he calls I shall answer: "I am with you." (*R*.)

3. I will save him in distress and give him glory.
With length of life I will content him;
I shall let him see my saving power. (*R*.)

Years I and II

Alleluia   (Col 3:16. 17)

Alleluia, alleluia!
Let the message of Christ, in all its richness,
find a home with you;
through him give thanks to God the Father.
Alleluia!
Alternative Alleluias p. 847.

Gospel   (12:1–12)

A reading from the holy Gospel according to Mark
*They seized the beloved son and killed him and threw him out
of the vineyard.*

Jesus spoke to the Pharisees in parables, "A man planted
a vineyard; he fenced it round, dug out a trough for the
winepress and built a tower; then he leased it to tenants and
went abroad. When the time came, he sent a servant to the
tenants to collect from them his share of the produce from
the vineyard. But they seized the man, thrashed him and sent
him away empty-handed. Next he sent another servant to
them; him they beat about the head and treated shamefully.
And he sent another and him they killed; then a number
of others, and they thrashed some and killed the rest. He
had still someone left: his beloved son. He sent him to them
last of all. 'They will respect my son' he said. But those
tenants said to each other, 'This is the heir. Come on, let us
kill him, and the inheritance will be ours.' So they seized
him and killed him and threw him out of the vineyard. Now
what will the owner of the vineyard do? He will come and
make an end of the tenants and give the vineyard to others
Have you not read this text of scripture:

It was the stone rejected by the builders
that became the keystone.
This was the Lord's doing
and it is wonderful to see?"

And they would have liked to arrest him, because the
realised that the parable was aimed at them, but they were
afraid of the crowds. So they left him alone and went away.
    This is the Gospel of the Lord.

TUESDAY
Year I

First Reading   (2:9–14)

A reading from the book of Tobit
Tobit did not complain against God at being struck blind.

I, Tobit, took a bath; then I went into the courtyard and
lay down by the courtyard wall. Since it was hot I left my
face uncovered. I did not know that there were sparrows in
the wall above my head; their hot droppings fell into my
eyes. White spots then formed, which I was obliged to
have treated by the doctors. But the more ointments they
tried me with, the more the spots blinded me, and in the end
I became blind altogether. I remained without sight four
years; all my brothers were distressed; and Ahikar provided
for my upkeep for two years, till he left for Elymais.

My wife Anna then undertook woman's work; she would
spin wool and take cloth to weave; she used to deliver
whatever had been ordered from her and then receive payment. Now on March the seventh she finished a piece of
work and delivered it to her customers. They paid her all
that was due, and into the bargain presented her with a kid
for a meal. When the kid came into my house, it began to
bleat. I called to my wife and said, "Where does this creature come from? Suppose it has been stolen! Quick, let the
owners have it back; we have no right to eat stolen goods."
She said, "No, it was a present given me over and above my
wages." I did not believe her, and told her to give it back
to the owners (I blushed at this in her presence). Then she
answered, "What about your own alms? What about your
own good works? Everyone knows what return you have
had for them."

This is the word of the Lord.

Responsorial Psalm   (Ps 111:1–2. 7–9. R. v. 7)
Response
With a firm heart he trusts in the Lord.

Alternative Response
Alleluia!

1. Alleluia!
Happy the man who fears the Lord,
who takes delight in his commands.
His sons will be powerful on earth;
the children of the upright are blessed. (*R.*)

2. He has no fear of evil news;
with a firm heart he trusts in the Lord.
With a steadfast heart he will not fear;
he will see the downfall of his foes. (*R.*)

3. Open-handed, he gives to the poor;
his justice stands firm for ever.
His head will be raised in glory. (*R.*)

ALLELUIA and GOSPEL. As for Year II, p. 437.

Year II

First Reading   (3:11–15. 17–18)

A reading from the second letter of St Peter
We are waiting for the new heavens and new earth.

You should be living holy and saintly lives while you wait
and long for the Day of God to come, when the sky will
dissolve in flames and the elements melt in the heat. What
we are waiting for is what he promised: the new heavens
and new earth, the place where righteousness will be a
home. So then, my friends, while you are waiting, do your
best to live lives without spot or stain so that he will find
you at peace. Think of our Lord's patience as your opportunity to be saved. You have been warned about this, my
friends; be careful not to get carried away by the errors of
unprincipled people, from the firm ground that you are
standing on. Instead, go on growing in the grace and in the

knowledge of our Lord and saviour Jesus Christ. To him be glory, in time and in eternity. Amen.

This is the word of the Lord.

Responsorial Psalm   (Ps 89:2–4. 10. 14. 16. *R*. v. 1)
Response
O Lord, you have been our refuge
from one generation to the next.

1. Before the mountains were born
or the earth or the world brought forth,
you are God, without beginning or end. (*R*.)

2. You turn men back into dust
and say: "Go back, sons of men."
To your eyes a thousand years
are like yesterday, come and gone,
no more than a watch in the night. (*R*.)

3. Our span is seventy years
or eighty for those who are strong.
And most of these are emptiness and pain.
They pass swiftly and we are gone. (R.)

4. In the morning, fill us with your love;
we shall exult and rejoice all our days.
Show forth your work to your servants;
let your glory shine on their children. (*R*.)

Years I and II

Alleluia   (Heb 4:12)
Alleluia, alleluia!
The word of God is something alive and active;
Alleluia!
It can judge secret emotions and thoughts.
Alternative Alleluias, p. 847.

Gospel   (12:13–17)

A reading from the holy Gospel according to Mark
Give back to Caesar what belongs to Caesar – and to God what belongs to God.

They sent to Jesus some Pharisees and some Herodians to catch him out in what he said. These came and said to him, "Master, we know you are an honest man, that you are not afraid of anyone, because a man's rank means nothing to you, and that you teach the way of God in all honesty. Is it permissible to pay taxes to Caesar or not? Should we pay, yes or no?" Seeing through their hypocrisy he said to them, 'Why do you set this trap for me? Hand me a denarius and let me see it." They handed him one and he said "Whose head is this? Whose name?" "Caesar's" they told him. Jesus said to them, "Give back to Caesar what belongs to Caesar – and to God what belongs to God." This reply took them completely by surprise.

This is the Gospel of the Lord.

Ash Wednesday follows.

SEASON OF LENT

ASH WEDNESDAY

When the blessing and distribution of ashes is done without Mass these readings may be used for a liturgy of the word before the blessing of ashes.

First Reading (2:12–18)

A reading from the prophet Joel
Let your hearts be broken, not your garments torn.

"But now, now – it is the Lord who speaks –
come back to me with all your heart,
fasting, weeping, mourning."
Let your hearts be broken, not your garments torn,
turn to the Lord your God again,
for he is all tenderness and compassion,
slow to anger, rich in graciousness,
and ready to relent.
Who knows if he will not turn again, will not relent,
will not leave a blessing as he passes,
oblation and libation
for the Lord your God?

Sound the trumpet in Zion!
Order a fast,
proclaim a solemn assembly,
call the people together,
summon the community,
assemble the elders,
gather the children,
even the infants at the breast.
Let the bridegroom leave his bedroom
and the bride her alcove.

Between vestibule and altar let the priests,
the ministers of the Lord, lament.
Let them say,
"Spare your people, Lord!
Do not make your heritage a thing of shame,
a byword for the nations.
Why should it be said among the nations,
'Where is their God?' "
Then the Lord, jealous on behalf of his land,
took pity on his people.

This is the word of the Lord.

Responsorial Psalm   (Ps 50:3–6. 12–14. 17. *R.* v. 3)
Response
Have mercy on us, O Lord, for we have sinned.

1. Have mercy on me, God, in your kindness.
In your compassion blot out my offence.
O wash me more and more from my guilt
and cleanse me from my sin. (*R.*)

2. My offences truly I know them;
my sin is always before me.
Against you, you alone, have I sinned:
what is evil in your sight I have done. (*R.*)

3. A pure heart create for me, O God,
put a steadfast spirit within me.
Do not cast me away from your presence,
nor deprive me of your holy spirit. (*R.*)

4. Give me again the joy of your help;
with a spirit of fervour sustain me,
O Lord, open my lips
and my mouth shall declare your praise. (*R.*)

Second Reading   (5:20–6:2)

A reading from the second letter of St Paul to the
Corinthians
Be reconciled to God . . . now is the favourable time.

We are ambassadors for Christ; it is as though God were
appealing through us, and the appeal that we make in
Christ's name is: be reconciled to God. For our sake God
made the sinless one into sin, so that in him we might become the goodness of God. As his fellow workers, we beg
you once again not to neglect the grace of God that you
have received. For he says: At the favourable time, I have
listened to you; on the day of salvation I came to your help.
Well, now is the favourable time; this is the day of salvation.

   This is the word of the Lord.

During Lent, both before and after the Acclamation, one or other
of the following phrases, or a similar phrase, may be used:

1. Praise to you, O Christ, king of eternal glory:
2. Praise and honour to you, Lord Jesus:
3. Glory and praise to you, O Christ:
4. Glory to you, O Christ, you are the Word of God.

Acclamation   (Ps 50:12. 14)

A pure heart create for me, O God,
and give me again the joy of your help.

Alternative Acclamations p. 842.

Gospel   (6:1–6. 16–18)

A reading from the holy Gospel according to Matthew
Your Father who sees all that is done in secret will reward you.

Jesus said to his disciples:

   "Be careful not to parade your good deeds before men
to attract their notice; by doing this you will lose all reward
from your Father in heaven. So when you give alms, do not
have it trumpeted before you; this is what the hypocrites do

in the synagogues and in the streets to win men's admiration. I tell you solemnly, they have had their reward. But when you give alms, your left hand must not know what your right is doing; your almsgiving must be secret, and your Father who sees all that is done in secret will reward you.

"And when you pray, do not imitate the hypocrites: they love to say their prayers standing up in the synagogues and at the street corners for people to see them. I tell you solemnly, they have had their reward. But when you pray, go to your private room and, when you have shut your door, pray to your Father who is in that secret place, and your Father who sees all that is done in secret will reward you.

"When you fast do not put on a gloomy look as the hypocrites do: they pull long faces to let men know they are fasting. I tell you solemnly, they have had their reward. But when you fast, put oil on your head and wash your face, so that no one will know you are fasting except your Father who sees all that is done in secret; and your Father who sees all that is done in secret will reward you."

This is the Gospel of the Lord.

THURSDAY AFTER ASH WEDNESDAY

First Reading   (30:15–20)

A reading from the book of Deuteronomy
See, I set before you today a blessing and a curse.

Moses said to the people: "See, today I set before you life and prosperity, death and disaster. If you obey the commandments of the Lord your God that I enjoin on you today, if you love the Lord your God and follow his ways, if you keep his commandments, his laws, his customs, you will live and increase, and the Lord your God will bless you in the land which you are entering to make your own. But if your heart strays, if you refuse to listen, if you let yourself be drawn into worshipping other gods and serving them, I tell you today, you will most certainly perish; you will not live long in the land you are crossing the Jordan to enter and possess. I call heaven and earth to witness against you today: I set before you life or death, blessing or curse. Choose life, then, so that you and your descendants may live, in the love of the Lord your God, obeying his voice, clinging to him; for in this your life consists, and on this depends your long stay in the land which the Lord swore to your fathers Abraham, Isaac and Jacob he would give them."

This is the word of the Lord.

Responsorial Psalm   (Ps 1:1–4. 6. *R.* Ps 39:5)

Response
Happy the man who has placed
his trust in the Lord.

1. Happy indeed is the man
who follows not the counsel of the wicked;
nor lingers in the way of sinners
nor sits in the company of scorners,
but whose delight is the law of the Lord
and who ponders his law day and night. (*R.*)

2. He is like a tree that is planted
beside the flowing waters,
that yields its fruit in due season
and whose leaves shall never fade;
and all that he does shall prosper. (*R.*)

3. Not so are the wicked, not so!
For they like winnowed chaff
shall be driven away by the wind;
for the Lord guards the way of the just
but the way of the wicked leads to doom. (*R.*)

Acclamation (Ps 50:12, 14)

A pure heart create for me, O God,
and give me again the joy of your help.

Alternative Acclamations p. 842.

Gospel (9:22–25)

A reading from the holy Gospel according to Luke
Anyone who loses his life for my sake, that man will save it.

Jesus said to his disciples: "The Son of Man is destined
to suffer grievously, to be rejected by the elders and chief
priests and scribes and to be put to death, and to be raised
up on the third day."

Then to all he said, "If anyone wants to be a follower
of mine, let him renounce himself and take up his cross
every day and follow me. For anyone who wants to save
his life will lose it; but anyone who loses his life for my
sake, that man will save it. What gain, then, is it for a man
to have won the whole world and to have lost or ruined his
very self?"

This is the Gospel of the Lord.

FRIDAY AFTER ASH WEDNESDAY

First Reading (58:1–9)

A reading from the prophet Isaiah
Is not this the sort of fast that pleases me?

Thus says the Lord:

Shout for all you are worth,
raise your voice like a trumpet.
Proclaim their faults to my people,
their sins to the House of Jacob.

They seek me day after day,
they long to know my ways,
like a nation that wants to act with integrity
and not ignore the law of its God.

They ask me for laws that are just,
they long for God to draw near:
"Why should we fast if you never see it,
why do penance if you never notice?"

Look, you do business on your fastdays,
you oppress all your workmen;
look, you quarrel and squabble when you fast
and strike the poor man with your fist.

Fasting like yours today
will never make your voice heard on high.
Is that the sort of fast that pleases me,
a truly penitential day for men?

Hanging your head like a reed,
lying down on sackcloth and ashes?
Is that what you call fasting,
a day acceptable to the Lord?

Is not this the sort of fast that pleases me
- it is the Lord who speaks –
to break unjust fetters
and undo the thongs of the yoke,

to let the oppressed go free,
and break every yoke,
to share your bread with the hungry,
and shelter the homeless poor,

to clothe the man you see to be naked
and not turn from your own kin?

Then will your light shine like the dawn
and your wound be quickly healed over.

Your integrity will go before you
and the glory of the Lord behind you.
Cry, and the Lord will answer;
call, and he will say, "I am here."

This is the word of the Lord.

Responsorial Psalm (Ps 50:3–6. 18–19. R. v. 19)
Response
A humbled, contrite heart, O God, you will not spurn.

1. Have mercy on me, God, in your kindness.
In your compassion blot out my offence.
O wash me more and more from my guilt
and cleanse me from my sin. (R.)

2. My offences truly I know them;
my sin is always before me.
Against you, you alone, have I sinned;
what is evil in your sight I have done. (R.)

3. For in sacrifice you take no delight,
burnt offering from me you would refuse,
my sacrifice, a contrite spirit.
A humbled, contrite heart you will not spurn. (R.)

Acclamation (Ps 129:5, 7)
My soul is waiting for the Lord,
I count on his word,
because with the Lord there is mercy
and fullness of redemption.

Alternative Acclamations p. 842.

Gospel   (9:14–15)

A reading from the holy Gospel according to Matthew
When the bridegroom is taken away from them, then they will
fast.

Then John's disciples came to Jesus and said, "Why is it
that we and the Pharisees fast, but your disciples do not?"
Jesus replied, "Surely the bridegroom's attendants would
never think of mourning as long as the bridegroom is still
with them? But the time will come for the bridegroom to be
taken away from them, and then they will fast."
    This is the Gospel of the Lord.

SATURDAY AFTER ASH WEDNESDAY

First Reading   (58:9–14)

A reading from the prophet Isaiah
Your light will rise in the darkness.

The Lord says this:

If you do away with the yoke,
the clenched fist, the wicked word,
if you give your bread to the hungry,
and relief to the oppressed,

your light will rise in the darkness,
and your shadows become like noon.
The Lord will always guide you,
giving you relief in desert places.

He will give strength to your bones
and you shall be like a watered garden,
like a spring of water
whose waters never run dry.

You will rebuild the ancient ruins,
build up on the old foundations.
You will be called "Breach-mender",
"Restorer of ruined houses".
If you refrain from trampling the sabbath,
and doing business on the holy day,
if you call the sabbath "Delightful",
and the day sacred to the Lord "Honourable",
if you honour it by abstaining from travel,
from doing business and from gossip,
then you shall find happiness in the Lord
and I will lead you triumphant over the heights of the land.
I will feed you on the heritage of Jacob your father.
For the mouth of the Lord has spoken.

This is the word of the Lord.

Responsorial Psalm (Ps 85:1–6. *R*. v. 11)

Response
Show me, Lord, your way
so that I may walk in your truth.

1. Turn your ear, O Lord, and give answer.
for I am poor and needy.
Preserve my life, for I am faithful:
save the servant who trusts in you. (*R*.)

2. You are my God, have mercy on me, Lord,
for I cry to you all the day long.
Give joy to your servant, O Lord,
for to you I lift up my soul. (*R*.)

3. O Lord, you are good and forgiving,
full of love to all who call.
Give heed, O Lord, to my prayer
and attend to the sound of my voice. (*R*.)

Acclamation   (Ps 94:8)

Harden not your hearts today,
but listen to the voice of the Lord.

Alternative Acclamations p. 842.

Gospel   (5:27–32)

A reading from the holy Gospel according to Luke
I have not come to call the virtuous, but sinners to repentance.

Jesus noticed a tax collector, Levi by name, sitting by the
customs house, and said to him, "Follow me." And leaving
everything he got up and followed him.

In his honour Levi held a great reception in his house,
and with them at table was a large gathering of tax collectors and others. The Pharisees and their scribes complained
to his disciples and said, "Why do you eat and drink with
tax collectors and sinners?" Jesus said to them in reply,
"It is not those who are well who need the doctor, but the
sick. I have not come to call the virtuous, but sinners to
repentance."

This is the Gospel of the Lord.

1st SUNDAY OF LENT

Year 1 (Year A)

First Reading   (2:7–9; 3:1–7)

A reading from the book of Genesis
The creation and sin of our first parents.

The Lord God fashioned man of dust from the soil. Then
he breathed into his nostrils a breath of life, and thus man
became a living being.

The Lord God planted a garden in Eden which is in the
east, and there he put the man he had fashioned. The Lord
God caused to spring up from the soil every kind of tree,

enticing to look at and good to eat, with the tree of life and the tree of the knowledge of good and evil in the middle of the garden.

The serpent was the most subtle of all the wild beasts that the Lord God had made. It asked the woman, "Did God really say you were not to eat from any of the trees in the garden?" The woman answered the serpent, "We may eat the fruit of the trees in the garden. But of the fruit of the tree in the middle of the garden God said, 'You must not eat it, nor touch it, under pain of death'." Then the serpent said to the woman, "No! You will not die! God knows in fact that on the day you eat it your eyes will be opened and you will be like gods, knowing good and evil." The woman saw that the tree was good to eat and pleasing to the eye, and that it was desirable for the knowledge that it could give. So she took some of its fruit and ate it. She gave some also to her husband who was with her, and he ate it. Then the eyes of both of them were opened and they realised that they were naked. So they sewed fig-leaves together to make themselves loin-cloths.

This is the word of the Lord.

Responsorial Psalm   (Ps 50:3–6. 12–14. 17. *R*. v. 3)
Response
Have mercy on us, O Lord, for we have sinned.

1. Have mercy on me, God, in your kindness.
In your compassion blot out my offence.
O wash me more and more from my guilt
and cleanse me from my sin. (*R*.)

2. My offences truly I know them;
my sin is always before me.
Against you, you alone, have I sinned;
what is evil in your sight I have done. (*R*.)

3. A pure heart create for me, O God,
put a steadfast spirit within me.
Do not cast me away from your presence,
nor deprive me of your holy spirit. (R.)

4. Give me again the joy of your help;
with a spirit of fervour sustain me.
O Lord, open my lips
and my mouth shall declare your praise. (R.)

Second Reading   (5:12–19)

A reading from the letter of St Paul to the Romans
However great the number of sins committed, grace was even greater.

Sin entered the world through one man, and through sin death, and thus death has spread through the whole human race because everyone has sinned. Sin existed in the world long before the Law was given. There was no law and so no one could be accused of the sin of "law-breaking", yet death reigned over all from Adam to Moses, even though their sin, unlike that of Adam, was not a matter of breaking a law.

Adam prefigured the One to come, but the gift itself considerably outweighed the fall. If it is certain that through one man's fall so many died, it is even more certain that divine grace, coming through the one man, Jesus Christ, came to so many as an abundant free gift. The results of the gift also outweigh the results of one man's sin: for after one single fall came judgement with a verdict of condemnation, now after many falls comes grace with its verdict of acquittal. *If it is certain that death reigned over everyone as the consequence of one man's fall, it is even more certain that one man, Jesus Christ, will cause everyone to reign in life who receives the free gift that he does not deserve, of being made righteous. Again, as one man's fall brought condemnation on everyone, so the good act of one man brings everyone life and makes them justified. As by one man's disobedience many were made sinners, so by one man's obedience many will be made righteous.

This is the word of the Lord.*

*Shorter Form, verses 12. 17–19, read between *.

Acclamation   (Mt 4:4)

Man does not live on bread alone
but on every word that comes from the mouth of God.

Gospel   (4:1–11)

A reading from the holy Gospel according to Matthew
Jesus fasts for forty days and is tempted.

Then Jesus was led by the Spirit out into the wilderness to be tempted by the devil. He fasted for forty days and forty nights, after which he was very hungry, and the tempter came and said to him, "If you are the Son of God, tell these stones to turn into loaves." But he replied, "Scripture says:

Man does not live on bread alone
but on every word that comes from the mouth of God."

The devil then took him to the holy city and made him stand on the parapet of the Temple. "If you are the Son of God" he said "throw yourself down; for scripture says:

He will put you in his angels' charge,
and they will support you on their hands
in case you hurt your foot against a stone."

Jesus said to him, "Scripture also says:
You must not put the Lord your God to the test."

Next, taking him to a very high mountain, the devil showed him all the kingdoms of the world and their splendour. "I will give you all these" he said, "if you fall at my feet and worship me." Then Jesus replied, "Be off, Satan! For scripture says:

You must worship the Lord your God,
and serve him alone."

Then the devil left him, and angels appeared and looked after him.

This is the Gospel of the Lord.

1st SUNDAY OF LENT

Year 2 (Year B)

First Reading   (9:8–15)

A reading from the book of Genesis
God's covenant with Noah after he had saved him from the waters of the flood.

God spoke to Noah and his sons, "See, I establish my Covenant with you, and with your descendants after you; also with every living creature to be found with you, birds, cattle and every wild beast with you: everything that came out of the ark, everything that lives on the earth. I establish my Covenant with you: no thing of flesh shall be swept away again by the waters of the flood. There shall be no flood to destroy the earth again."

God said, "Here is the sign of the Covenant I make between myself and you and every living creature with you for all generations: I set my bow in the clouds and it shall be a sign of the Covenant between me and the earth. When I gather the clouds over the earth and the bow appears in the clouds, I will recall the Covenant between myself and you and every living creature of every kind. And so the waters shall never again become a flood to destroy all things of flesh."

This is the word of the Lord.

Responsorial Psalm   (Ps 24:4–9. *R*. v. 10)
Response
Your ways, Lord, are faithfulness and love
for those who keep your covenant.

1. Lord, make me know your ways.
Lord, teach me your paths.
Make me walk in your truth, and teach me:
for you are God my saviour. (*R*.)

2. Remember your mercy, Lord,
and the love you have shown from of old.
In your love remember me,
because of your goodness, O Lord. (*R*.)

3. The Lord is good and upright.
He shows the path to those who stray,
he guides the humble in the right path;
he teaches his way to the poor. (*R*.)

Second Reading   (3:18–22)
A reading from the first letter of St Peter
That water is a type of the baptism which saves you now.

Christ himself, innocent though he was, died once for sins, died for the guilty, to lead us to God. In the body he was put to death, in the spirit he was raised to life, and, in the spirit, he went to preach to the spirits in prison. Now it was long ago, when Noah was still building that ark which saved only a small group of eight people "by water", and when God was still waiting patiently, that these spirits refused to believe. That water is a type of the baptism which saves you now, and which is not the washing off of physical dirt but a pledge made to God from a good conscience, through the resurrection of Jesus Christ, who has entered heaven and is at God's right hand, now that he has made the angels and Dominations and Powers his subjects.

This is the word of the Lord.

Acclamation   (Mt 4:4)

Man does not live on bread alone,
but on every word that comes from the mouth of God.

Gospel   (1:12–15)

A reading from the holy Gospel according to Mark
Jesus was tempted by Satan, and the angels looked after him.

The Spirit drove Jesus out into the wilderness and he remained there for forty days, and was tempted by Satan. He was with the wild beasts, and the angels looked after him.

After John had been arrested, Jesus went into Galilee. There he proclaimed the Good News from God. "The time has come" he said "and the kingdom of God is close at hand. Repent, and believe the Good News."

This is the Gospel of the Lord.

1st SUNDAY OF LENT
Year 3 (Year C)

First Reading   (26:4–10)

A reading from the book of Deuteronomy
The creed of the chosen people.

Moses said to the people: "The priest shall take the pannier from your hand and lay it before the altar of the Lord your God. Then, in the sight of the Lord your God, you must make this pronouncement:

'My father was a wandering Aramaean. He went down into Egypt to find refuge there, few in numbers; but there he became a nation, great, mighty, and strong. The Egyptians ill-treated us, they gave us no peace and inflicted harsh slavery on us. But we called on the Lord, the God of our fathers. The Lord heard our voice and saw our misery, our toil and our oppression; and the Lord brought us out of Egypt with mighty hand and outstretched arm, with great terror, and with signs and wonders. He brought us here and gave us this land, a land where milk and honey flow. Here then I bring the first-fruits of the produce of the soil that you, Lord, have given me.' You must then lay them before the Lord your God, and bow down in the sight of the Lord your God."

This is the word of the Lord.

Responsorial Psalm   (Ps 90:1–2. 10–15. R. v. 15)

Response
Be with me, O Lord, in my distress.

1. He who dwells in the shelter of the Most High
and abides in the shade of the Almighty
says to the Lord: "My refuge,
my stronghold, my God in whom I trust!" (R.)

2. Upon you no evil shall fall,
no plague approach where you dwell.
For you has he commanded his angels,
to keep you in all your ways. (R.)

3. They shall bear you upon their hands
lest you strike your foot against a stone.
On the lion and the viper you will tread
and trample the young lion and the dragon. (R.)

4. His love he set on me, so I will rescue him;
protect him for he knows my name.
When he calls I shall answer: "I am with you."
I will save him in distress and give him glory. (*R.*)

Second Reading   (10:8–13)

A reading from the letter of St Paul to the Romans
The creed of the Christian.

Scripture says: The word, that is the faith we proclaim, is
very near to you, it is on your lips and in your heart. If your
lips confess that Jesus is Lord and if you believe in your
heart that God raised him from the dead, then you will be
saved. By believing from the heart you are made righteous;
by confessing with your lips you are saved. When scripture
says: those who believe in him will have no cause for
shame, it makes no distinction between Jew and Greek: all
belong to the same Lord who is rich enough, however many
ask for his help, for everyone who calls on the name of the
Lord will be saved.

This is the word of the Lord.

Acclamation   (Mt 4:4)

Man does not live on bread alone,
but on every word that comes from the mouth of God.

Gospel   (4:1–13)

A reading from the holy Gospel according to Luke
*Jesus was led by the Spirit through the wilderness and was
tempted there.*

Filled with the Holy Spirit, Jesus left the Jordan and was
led by the Spirit through the wilderness, being tempted
there by the devil for forty days. During that time he ate

nothing and at the end he was hungry. Then the devil said to him, "If you are the Son of God, tell this stone to turn into a loaf." But Jesus replied, "Scripture says: Man does not live on bread alone."

Then leading him to a height, the devil showed him in a moment of time all the kingdoms of the world and said to him, "I will give you all this power and the glory of these kingdoms, for it has been committed to me and I give it to anyone I choose. Worship me, then, and it shall all be yours." But Jesus answered him, "Scripture says:

You must worship the Lord your God,
and serve him alone."

Then he led him to Jerusalem and made him stand on the parapet of the Temple. "If you are the Son of God," he said to him "throw yourself down from here, for scripture says:

He will put his angels in charge of you
to guard you,

and again:

They will hold you up on their hands
in case you hurt your foot against a stone."

But Jesus answered him, "It has been said:

You must not put the Lord your God to the test."

Having exhausted all these ways of tempting him, the devil left him, to return at the appointed time.

This is the Gospel of the Lord.

MONDAY

First Reading   (19:1–2. 11–18)

A reading from the book of Leviticus
You must pass judgement on your neighbour according to justice.

The Lord spoke to Moses; he said: "Speak to the whole community of the sons of Israel and say to them: 'Be holy, for I, the Lord your God, am holy.

'You must not steal nor deal deceitfully or fraudulently with your neighbour. You must not swear falsely by my name, profaning the name of your God. I am the Lord. You must not exploit or rob your neighbour. You must not keep back the labourer's wage until next morning. You must not curse the dumb, nor put an obstacle in the blind man's way, but you must fear your God. I am the Lord.

'You must not be guilty of unjust verdicts. You must neither be partial to the little man nor overawed by the great; you must pass judgement on your neighbour according to justice. You must not slander your own people, and you must not jeopardise your neighbour's life. I am the Lord. You must not bear hatred for your brother in your heart. You must openly tell him, your neighbour, of his offence; this way you will not take a sin upon yourself. You must not exact vengeance, nor must you bear a grudge against the children of your people. You must love your neighbour as yourself. I am the Lord.' "

This is the word of the Lord.

Responsorial Psalm   (Ps 18:8–10. 15. *R*. Jn 6:64)

Response
Your words are spirit, Lord,
and they are life.

1. The law of the Lord is perfect,
it revives the soul.

The rule of the Lord is to be trusted,
it gives wisdom to the simple. (*R.*)

2. The precepts of the Lord are right,
they gladden the heart.
The command of the Lord is clear,
it gives light to the eyes. (*R.*)

3. The fear of the Lord is holy,
abiding for ever.
The decrees of the Lord are truth
and all of them just. (*R.*)

4. May the spoken words of my mouth,
the thoughts of my heart,
win favour in your sight, O Lord,
my rescuer, my rock! (*R.*)

Acclamation (Ez 18:31)

Shake off all your sins – it is the Lord who speaks –
and make yourselves a new heart and a new spirit.

Alternative Acclamations p. 842.

Gospel (25:31–46)

A reading from the holy Gospel according to Matthew
In so far as you did this to one of the least of these brothers of
mine you did it to me.

Jesus said to his disciples: "When the Son of Man comes
in his glory, escorted by all the angels, then he will take
his seat on his throne of glory. All the nations will be assembled before him and he will separate men one from
another as the shepherd separates sheep from goats. He
will place the sheep on his right hand and the goats on his
left. Then the King will say to those on his right hand,

'Come, you whom my Father has blessed, take for your heritage the kingdom prepared for you since the foundation of the world. For I was hungry and you gave me food; I was thirsty and you gave me drink; I was a stranger and you made me welcome; naked and you clothed me, sick and you visited me, in prison and you came to see me.' Then the virtuous will say to him in reply, 'Lord, when did we see you hungry and feed you; or thirsty and give you drink? When did we see you a stranger and make you welcome; naked and clothe you; sick or in prison and go to see you?' And the King will answer, 'I tell you solemnly, in so far as you did this to one of the least of these brothers of mine, you did it to me'. Next he will say to those on his left hand, 'Go away from me, with your curse upon you, to the eternal fire prepared for the devil and his angels. For I was hungry and you never gave me food; I was thirsty and you never gave me anything to drink; I was a stranger and you never made me welcome, naked and you never clothed me, sick and in prison and you never visited me.' Then it will be their turn to ask, 'Lord, when did we see you hungry or thirsty, a stranger or naked, sick or in prison, and did not come to your help?' Then he will answer, 'I tell you solemnly, in so far as you neglected to do this to one of the least of these, you neglected to do it to me.' And they will go away to eternal punishment, and the virtuous to eternal life."

This is the Gospel of the Lord.

TUESDAY

First Reading   (55:10–11)

A reading from the prophet Isaiah
My word shall succeed in what it was sent to do.

Thus says the Lord:
    Yes, as the rain and the snow come down from the

heavens and do not return without watering the earth, making it yield and giving growth to provide seed for the sower and bread for the eating, so the word that goes from my mouth does not return to me empty, without carrying out my will and succeeding in what it was sent to do.

This is the word of the Lord.

Responsorial Psalm (Ps 33:4–7. 16–19. *R.* v. 18)
Response
The Lord rescues the just in all their distress.

1. Glorify the Lord with me.
Together let us praise his name.
I sought the Lord and he answered me;
from all my terrors he set me free. (*R.*)

2. Look towards him and be radiant;
let your faces not be abashed.
This poor man called; the Lord heard him
and rescued him from all his distress. (*R.*)

3. The Lord turns his face against the wicked
to destroy their remembrance from the earth.
The Lord turns his eyes to the just
and his ears to their appeal. (*R.*)

4. They call and the Lord hears
and rescues them in all their distress.
The Lord is close to the broken-hearted;
those whose spirit is crushed he will save. (*R.*)

Acclamation (Mt 4:4)
Man does not live on bread alone, but on every word that comes from the mouth of God.

Alternative Acclamations p. 842.

Gospel   (6:7–15)

A reading from the holy Gospel according to Matthew
You should pray like this.

Jesus said to his disciples: "In your prayers do not babble
as the pagans do, for they think that by using many words
they will make themselves heard. Do not be like them; your
Father knows what you need before you ask him. So you
should pray like this:

"Our Father in heaven,
may your name be held holy,
your kingdom come,
your will be done,
on earth as in heaven.
Give us today our daily bread.
And forgive us our debts,
as we have forgiven those who are in debt to us.
And do not put us to the test,
but save us from the evil one.

Yes, if you forgive others their failings, your heavenly
Father will forgive you yours; but if you do not forgive
others, your Father will not forgive your failings either."

This is the Gospel of the Lord.

WEDNESDAY

First Reading   (3:1–10)

A reading from the prophet Jonah
The people of Nineveh renounced their evil behaviour.

The word of the Lord was addressed a second time to
Jonah: "Up!" he said. "Go to Nineveh, the great city,
and preach to them as I told you to." Jonah set out and
went to Nineveh in obedience to the word of the Lord.

Now Nineveh was a city great beyond compare: it took three days to cross it. Jonah went on into the city, making a day's journey. He preached in these words, "Only forty days more and Nineveh is going to be destroyed." And the people of Nineveh believed in God; they proclaimed a fast and put on sackcloth, from the greatest to the least. The news reached the king of Nineveh, who rose from his throne, took off his robe, put on sackcloth and sat down in ashes. A proclamation was then promulgated throughout Nineveh, by decree of the king and his ministers, as follows: "Men and beasts, herds and flocks, are to taste nothing; they must not eat, they must not drink water. All are to put on sackcloth and call on God with all their might; and let everyone renounce his evil behaviour and the wicked things he has done. Who knows if God will not change his mind and relent, if he will not renounce his burning wrath, so that we do not perish?" God saw their efforts to renounce their evil behaviour. And God relented: he did not inflict on them the disaster which he had threatened.

This is the word of the Lord.

Responsorial Psalm   (Ps 50:3–4. 12–13. 18–19. R. v. 19)

Response
A humbled, contrite heart, O God, you will not spurn.

1. Have mercy on me, God, in your kindness.
In your compassion blot out my offence.
O wash me more and more from my guilt
and cleanse me from my sin. (R.)

2. A pure heart create for me, O God,
put a steadfast spirit within me.
Do not cast me away from your presence,
nor deprive me of your holy spirit. (R.)

3. For in sacrifice you take no delight,
burnt offering from me you would refuse,
my sacrifice a contrite spirit.
A humbled, contrite heart you will not spurn. (*R.*)

Acclamation   (Ez 33:11)

I take pleasure, not in the death of a wicked man – it is the
Lord who speaks – but in the turning back of a wicked man
who changes his ways to win life.

Alternative Acclamations p. 842.

Gospel   (11:29–32)

A reading from the holy Gospel according to Luke
The only sign given to this generation is the sign of Jonah.

The crowds got even bigger and Jesus addressed them.
"This is a wicked generation; it is asking for a sign. The
only sign it will be given is the sign of Jonah. For just as
Jonah became a sign to the Ninevites, so will the Son of
Man be to this generation. On Judgement day the Queen of
the South will rise up with the men of this generation and
condemn them, because she came from the ends of the earth
to hear the wisdom of Solomon; and there is something
greater than Solomon here. On Judgement day the men of
Nineveh will stand up with this generation and condemn it,
because when Jonah preached they repented; and there is
something greater than Jonah here."

This is the Gospel of the Lord.

THURSDAY

First Reading   (4:17)
A reading from the book of Esther
I have no helper but you.

Queen Esther took refuge with the Lord in the mortal peril
which had overtaken her. She besought the Lord God of
Israel in these words:

"My Lord, our King, the only one,
come to my help, for I am alone
and have no helper but you
and am about to take my life in my hands.

"I have been taught from my earliest years, in the bosom of
    my family, that you, Lord, chose
Israel out of all the nations
and our ancestors out of all the people of old times
to be your heritage for ever;
and that you have treated them as you promised.
Remember, Lord; reveal yourself
in the time of our distress.

"As for me, give me courage,
King of gods and master of all power.
Put persuasive words into my mouth
when I face the lion;
change his feeling into hatred for our enemy,
that the latter and all like him may be brought to their end.

"As for ourselves, save us by your hand,
and come to my help, for I am alone
and have no one but you, Lord."

   This is the word of the Lord.

Responsorial Psalm   (Ps 137:1–3. 7–8. *R*. v. 3)

Response

On the day I called, you answered me, O Lord.

1. I thank you, Lord, with all my heart,
you have heard the words of my mouth.
Before the angels I will bless you.
I will adore before your holy temple. (*R*.)

2. I thank you for your faithfulness and love
which excel all we ever knew of you.
On the day I called, you answered;
you increased the strength of my soul. (*R*.)

3. You stretch out your hand and save me,
your hand will do all things for me.
Your love, O Lord, is eternal,
discard not the work of your hands. (*R*.)

Acclamation   (Joel 2:12–13)

Now, now – it is the Lord who speaks –
come back to me with all your heart,
for I am all tenderness and compassion.

Alternative Acclamations p. 842.

Gospel   (7:7–12)

A reading from the holy Gospel according to Matthew
The one who asks always receives.

Jesus said to his disciples: "Ask, and it will be given to
you; search, and you will find; knock, and the door will be
opened to you. For the one who asks always receives; the
one who searches always finds; the one who knocks will
always have the door opened to him. Is there a man among

you who would hand his son a stone when he asked for bread? Or would hand him a snake when he asked for a fish? If you, then, who are evil, know how to give your children what is good, how much more will your Father in heaven give good things to those who ask him!

"So always treat others as you would like them to treat you; that is the meaning of the Law and the Prophets."

This is the Gospel of the Lord.

FRIDAY

First Reading (18:21–28)

A reading from the prophet Ezekiel
Am I likely to take pleasure in the death of a wicked man and not prefer to see him renounce his wickedness and live?

Thus says the Lord:

"But if the wicked man renounces all the sins he has committed, respects my laws and is law-abiding and honest, he will certainly live; he will not die. All the sins he committed will be forgotten from then on; he shall live because of the integrity he has practised. What! Am I likely to take pleasure in the death of a wicked man – it is the Lord who speaks – and not prefer to see him renounce his wickedness and live?

"But if the upright man renounces his integrity, commits sin, copies the wicked man and practises every kind of filth, is he to live? All the integrity he has practised shall be forgotten from then on; but this is because he himself has broken faith and committed sin, and for this he shall die. But you object, 'What the Lord does is unjust.' Listen, you House of Israel: is what I do unjust? Is it not what you do that is unjust? When the upright man renounces his integrity to commit sin and dies because of this, he dies because of the evil that he himself has committed. When the sinner renounces sin to become law-abiding and honest, he deserves to live. He has chosen to renounce all his previous sins, he shall certainly live; he shall not die."

This is the word of the Lord.

Responsorial Psalm   (Ps 129. *R*. v. 3)

Response
If you, O Lord, should mark our guilt,
Lord, who would survive?

1. Out of the depths I cry to you, O Lord,
Lord, hear my voice!
O let your ears be attentive
to the voice of my pleading. (*R*.)

2. If you, O Lord, should mark our guilt,
Lord, who would survive?
But with you is found forgiveness:
for this we revere you. (*R*.)

3. My soul is waiting for the Lord,
I count on his word.
My soul is longing for the Lord
more than watchman for daybreak.
Let the watchman count on daybreak
and Israel on the Lord. (*R*.)

4. Because with the Lord there is mercy
and fullness of redemption,
Israel indeed he will redeem
from all its iniquity. (*R*.)

Acclamation   (Amos 5:14)

Seek good and not evil so that you may live, and that the Lord God of hosts may really be with you.

Alternative Acclamations p. 842.

Gospel   (5:20–26)

A reading from the holy Gospel according to Matthew
Go and be reconciled with your brother first.

Jesus said to his disciples: "For I tell you, if your virtue
goes no deeper than that of the scribes and Pharisees, you
will never get into the kingdom of heaven.

"You have learnt how it was said to our ancestors: You
must not kill, and if anyone does kill he must answer for it
before the court. But I say this to you: anyone who is angry
with his brother will answer for it before the court; if a man
calls his brother 'Fool' he will answer for it before the Sanhedrin, and if a man calls him 'Renegade' he will answer for
it in hell fire. So then, if you are bringing your offering to
the altar and there remember that your brother has something against you, leave your offering there before the altar,
go and be reconciled with your brother first, and then come
back and present your offering. Come to terms with your
opponent in good time while you are still on the way to the
court with him, or he may hand you over to the judge and
the judge to the officer, and you will be thrown into prison.
I tell you solemnly, you will not get out till you have paid
the last penny."

This is the Gospel of the Lord.

SATURDAY

First Reading   (26:16–19)

A reading from the book of Deuteronomy
You will be a people consecrated to the Lord.

Moses said to the people: "The Lord your God today
commands you to observe these laws and customs; you
must keep and observe them with all your heart and with
all your soul.

"You have today made this declaration about the Lord;

that he will be your God, but only if you follow his ways, keep his statutes, his commandments, his ordinances, and listen to his voice. And the Lord has today made this declaration about you: that you will be his very own people as he promised you, but only if you keep all his commandments; then for praise and renown and honour he will set you high above all the nations he has made, and you will be a people consecrated to the Lord, as he promised."

This is the word of the Lord.

Responsorial Psalm   (Ps 118:1–2. 4–5. 7–8. *R.* v. 1)

Response
They are happy who follow God's law!

1. They are happy whose life is blameless,
who follow God's law!
They are happy those who do his will,
seeking him with all their hearts. (*R.*)

2. You have laid down your precepts
to be obeyed with care.
May my footsteps be firm
to obey your statutes. (*R.*)

3. I will thank you with an upright heart
as I learn your decrees.
I will obey your statutes;
do not forsake me. (*R.*)

Acclamation   (Lk 8:15)
Blessed are those who, with a noble and generous heart, take the word of God to themselves and yield a harvest through their perseverance.

Alternative Acclamations p. 842.

Gospel (5:43–48)

A reading from the holy Gospel according to Matthew
Be perfect just as your heavenly Father is perfect.

Jesus said to his disciples: "You have learnt how it was said: You must love your neighbour and hate your enemy. But I say this to you: love your enemies and pray for those who persecute you; in this way you will be sons of your Father in heaven, for he causes the sun to rise on bad men as well as good, and his rain to fall on honest and dishonest men alike. For if you love those who love you, what right have you to claim any credit? Even the tax collectors do as much, do they not? And if you save your greetings for your brothers, are you doing anything exceptional? Even the pagans do as much, do they not? You must therefore be perfect just as your heavenly Father is perfect."

This is the Gospel of the Lord.

2nd SUNDAY OF LENT
Year 1 (Year A)

First Reading (12:1–4)

A reading from the book of Genesis
The call of Abraham, father of the People of God.

The Lord said to Abram, "Leave your country, your family and your father's house, for the land I will show you. I will make you a great nation; I will bless you and make your name so famous that it will be used as a blessing.

"I will bless those who bless you:
I will curse those who slight you.
All the tribes of the earth
shall bless themselves by you."

So Abram went as the Lord told him.
    This is the word of the Lord.

Responsorial Psalm   (Ps 32:4–5. 18–20. 22. *R.* v. 22)

Response

May your love be upon us, O Lord,
as we place all our hope in you.

1. For the word of the Lord is faithful
and all his works to be trusted.
The Lord loves justice and right
and fills the earth with his love. (*R.*)

2. The Lord looks on those who revere him,
on those who hope in his love,
to rescue their souls from death,
to keep them alive in famine. (*R.*)

3. Our soul is waiting for the Lord.
The Lord is our help and our shield.
May your love be upon us, O Lord,
as we place all our hope in you. (*R.*)

Second Reading   (1:8–10)

A reading from the second letter of St Paul to Timothy

God calls and enlightens us.

With me, bear the hardships for the sake of the Good News,
relying on the power of God who has saved us and called
us to be holy – not because of anything we ourselves have
done but for his own purpose and by his own grace. This
grace had already been granted to us, in Christ Jesus, before the beginning of time, but it has only been revealed by
the Appearing of our saviour Christ Jesus. He abolished
death, and he has proclaimed life and immortality through
the Good News.

    This is the word of the Lord.

Acclamation (Mt 17:5)

From the bright cloud the Father's voice was heard:
"This is my Son, the Beloved. Listen to him."

Gospel (17:1–9)

A reading from the holy Gospel according to Matthew
His face shone like the sun.

Six days later, Jesus took with him Peter and James and
his brother John and led them up a high mountain where
they could be alone. There in their presence he was transfigured; his face shone like the sun and his clothes became
as white as the light. Suddenly Moses and Elijah appeared
to them; they were talking with him. Then Peter spoke to
Jesus. "Lord," he said "it is wonderful for us to be here;
if you wish, I will make three tents here, one for you, one
for Moses and one for Elijah." He was still speaking when
suddenly a bright cloud covered them with shadow, and
from the cloud there came a voice which said, "This is my
Son, the Beloved; he enjoys my favour. Listen to him."
When they heard this, the disciples fell on their faces, overcome with fear. But Jesus came up and touched them.
"Stand up," he said "do not be afraid." And when they
raised their eyes they saw no one but only Jesus.

As they came down from the mountain Jesus gave them
this order. "Tell no one about the vision until the Son of
Man has risen from the dead."

This is the Gospel of the Lord.

2nd SUNDAY OF LENT
Year 2 (Year B)

First Reading (22:1–2. 9–13. 15–18)

A reading from the book of Genesis
The sacrifice of Abraham, our father in faith.

God put Abraham to the test. "Abraham, Abraham" he called. "Here I am" he replied. "Take your son," God said "your only child Isaac, whom you love, and go to the land of Moriah. There you shall offer him as a burnt offering, on a mountain I will point out to you."

When they arrived at the place God had pointed out to him, Abraham stretched out his hand and seized the knife to kill his son.

But the angel of the Lord called to him from heaven. "Abraham, Abraham" he said. "I am here" he replied. "Do not raise your hand against the boy" the angel said. "Do not harm him, for now I know you fear God. You have not refused me your son, your only son." Then looking up, Abraham saw a ram caught by its horns in a bush. Abraham took the ram and offered it as a burnt-offering in place of his son.

The angel of the Lord called Abraham a second time from heaven. "I swear by my own self – it is the Lord who speaks – because you have done this, because you have not refused me your son, your only son, I will shower blessings on you, I will make your descendants as many as the stars of heaven and the grains of sand on the seashore. Your descendants shall gain possession of the gates of their enemies. All the nations of the earth shall bless themselves by your descendants, as a reward for your obedience."

This is the word of the Lord.

Responsorial Psalm   (Ps 115:10. 15–19. *R*. Ps 114:9)

Response
I will walk in the presence of the Lord
in the land of the living.

1. I trusted, even when I said:
"I am sorely afflicted."
O precious in the eyes of the Lord
is the death of his faithful. (*R*.)

2. Your servant, Lord, your servant am I;
you have loosened my bonds.
A thanksgiving sacrifice I make:
I will call on the Lord's name. (*R.*)

3. My vows to the Lord I will fulfil
before all his people,
in the courts of the house of the Lord,
in your midst, O Jerusalem. (*R.*)

Second Reading   (8:31–34)

A reading from the letter of St Paul to the Romans
God did not spare his own Son.

With God on our side who can be against us? Since God
did not spare his own Son, but gave him up to benefit us
all, we may be certain, after such a gift, that he will not refuse anything he can give. Could anyone accuse those that
God has chosen? When God acquits, could anyone condemn? Could Christ Jesus? No! He not only died for us –
he rose from the dead, and there at God's right hand he
stands and pleads for us.

This is the word of the Lord.

Acclamation   (Mt 17:5)

From the bright cloud the Father's voice was heard:
"This is my Son, the Beloved. Listen to him."

Gospel   (9:2–10)

A reading from the holy Gospel according to Mark
This is my Son, the Beloved.

Six days later, Jesus took with him Peter and James and
John and led them up a high mountain where they could

be alone by themselves. There in their presence he was transfigured: his clothes became dazzlingly white, whiter than any earthly bleacher could make them. Elijah appeared to them with Moses; and they were talking with Jesus. Then Peter spoke to Jesus. "Rabbi", he said "it is wonderful for us to be here; so let us make three tents, one for you, one for Moses and one for Elijah." He did not know what to say; they were so frightened. And a cloud came, covering them in shadow; and there came a voice from the cloud, "This is my Son, the Beloved. Listen to him." Then suddenly, when they looked round, they saw no one with them any more but only Jesus.

As they came down the mountain he warned them to tell no one what they had seen, until after the Son of Man had risen from the dead. They observed the warning faithfully, though among themselves they discussed what "rising from the dead" could mean.

This is the Gospel of the Lord.

2nd SUNDAY OF LENT
Year 3 (Year C)

First Reading   (15:5–12. 17–18)

A reading from the book of Genesis
God enters into a Covenant with Abraham, the man of faith.

Taking Abram outside the Lord said, "Look up to heaven and count the stars if you can. Such will be your descendants" he told him. Abram put his faith in the Lord, who counted this as making him justified.

"I am the Lord" he said to him "who brought you out of Ur of the Chaldaeans to make you heir to this land." "My Lord, the Lord" Abram replied "how am I to know that I shall inherit it?" He said to him, "Get me a three-year-old heifer, a three-year-old goat, a three-year-old ram, a turtledove and a young pigeon". He brought him all these, cut them in half and put half on one side and half facing it on the other; but the birds he did not cut in half. Birds of prey came down on the carcases but Abram drove them off.

Now as the sun was setting Abram fell into a deep sleep, and terror seized him. When the sun had set and darkness had fallen, there appeared a smoking furnace and a fire-brand that went between the halves. That day the Lord made a Covenant with Abram in these terms:

"To your descendants I give this land,
from the wadi of Egypt to the Great River."

This is the word of the Lord.

Responsorial Psalm   (Ps 26:1. 7–9. 13–14. *R.* v. 1)
Response
The Lord is my light and my help.

1. The Lord is my light and my help;
whom shall I fear?
The Lord is the stronghold of my life;
before whom shall I shrink? (*R.*)

2. O Lord, hear my voice when I call;
have mercy and answer.
Of you my heart has spoken:
"Seek his face." (*R.*)

3. It is your face, O Lord, that I seek;
hide not your face.
Dismiss not your servant in anger;
you have been my help. (*R.*)

4. I am sure I shall see the Lord's goodness
in the land of the living.
Hope in him, hold firm and take heart.
Hope in the Lord! (R.)

Second Reading   (3:17–4:1)

A reading from the letter of St Paul to the Philippians
Christ will transfigure our bodies into copies of his glorious
body.

My brothers, be united in following my rule of life. Take as
your models everybody who is already doing this and
study them as you used to study us. I have told you often,
and I repeat it today with tears, there are many who are
behaving as the enemies of the cross of Christ. They are
destined to be lost. They make foods into their god and
they are proudest of something they ought to think shameful; the things they think important are earthly things.

*For us, our homeland is in heaven, and from heaven
comes the saviour we are waiting for, the Lord Jesus Christ,
and he will transfigure these wretched bodies of ours into
copies of his glorious body. He will do that by the same
power with which he can subdue the whole universe.

So then, my brothers and dear friends, do not give way
but remain faithful in the Lord. I miss you very much, dear
friends; you are my joy and my crown.

This is the word of the Lord.*

*Shorter Form, 3:20–4:1. Read between *.

Acclamation   (Mt 17:5)

From the bright cloud the Father's voice was heard:
"This is my Son, the Beloved. Listen to him."

Gospel   (9:28–36)

A reading from the holy Gospel according to Luke
As Jesus prayed, the aspect of his face was changed.

Jesus took with him Peter and John and James and went up the mountain to pray. As he prayed, the aspect of his face was changed and his clothing became brilliant as lightning. Suddenly there were two men there talking to him; they were Moses and Elijah appearing in glory, and they were speaking of his passing which he was to accomplish in Jerusalem. Peter and his companions were heavy with sleep, but they kept awake and saw his glory and the two men standing with him. As these were leaving him, Peter said to Jesus, "Master, it is wonderful for us to be here; so let us make three tents, one for you, one for Moses and one for Elijah." – He did not know what he was saying. As he spoke, a cloud came and covered them with shadow; and when they went into the cloud the disciples were afraid. And a voice came from the cloud saying, "This is my Son, the Chosen One. Listen to him." And after the voice had spoken, Jesus was found alone. The disciples kept silence and, at that time, told no one what they had seen.

This is the Gospel of the Lord.

MONDAY

First Reading   (9:4–10)

A reading from the prophet Daniel
We have sinned, we have done wrong.

"O Lord, God great and to be feared, you keep the covenant and have kindness for those who love you and keep your commandments: we have sinned, we have done wrong, we have acted wickedly, we have betrayed your commandments and your ordinances and turned away from

them. We have not listened to your servants the prophets,
who spoke in your name to our kings, our princes, our
ancestors, and to all the people of the land. Integrity, Lord,
is yours; ours the look of shame we wear today, we, the
people of Judah, the citizens of Jerusalem, the whole of
Israel, near and far away, in every country to which you
have dispersed us because of the treason we have committed against you. To us, Lord, the look of shame belongs, to
our kings, our princes, our ancestors, because we have sinned against you. To the Lord our God mercy and pardon
belong, because we have betrayed him, and have not listened
to the voice of the Lord our God nor followed the laws he
has given us through his servants the prophets."

   This is the word of the Lord.

Responsorial Psalm   (Ps 78:8–9. 11. 13. *R.* Ps 102:10)

Response
Do not treat us according to our sins, O Lord.

1. Do not hold the guilt of our fathers against us.
Let your compassion hasten to meet us
for we are in the depths of distress. (*R.*)

2. O God our saviour, come to our help,
come for the sake of the glory of your name.
O Lord our God, forgive us our sins;
rescue us for the sake of your name. (*R.*)

3. Let the groans of the prisoners come before you;
let your strong arm reprieve those condemned to die.
But we, your people, the flock of your pasture,
will give you thanks for ever and ever.
We will tell your praise from age to age. (*R.*)

Acclamation

The seed is the word of God, Christ the sower; whoever finds this seed will remain for ever.

Alternative Acclamations p. 842.

Gospel (6:36–38)

A reading from the holy Gospel according to Luke
Grant pardon, and you will be pardoned.

Jesus said to his disciples: "Be compassionate as your Father is compassionate. Do not judge, and you will not be judged yourselves; do not condemn, and you will not be condemned yourselves; grant pardon, and you will be pardoned. Give, and there will be gifts for you: a full measure, pressed down, shaken together, and running over, will be poured into your lap; because the amount you measure out is the amount you will be given back."

This is the Gospel of the Lord.

TUESDAY

First Reading (1:10. 16–20)

A reading from the prophet Isaiah
Learn to do good, search for justice.

Hear the word of the Lord,
you rulers of Sodom;
listen to the command of our God,
you people of Gomorrah.

"Wash, make yourselves clean.
Take your wrong-doing out of my sight.

"Cease to do evil.
Learn to do good,
search for justice,
help the oppressed,

be just to the orphan,
plead for the widow.

"Come now, let us talk this over,
says the Lord.
Though your sins are like scarlet,
they shall be as white as snow;
though they are red as crimson,
they shall be like wool.

"If you are willing to obey,
you shall eat the good things of the earth.
But if you persist in rebellion,
the sword shall eat you instead."
The mouth of the Lord has spoken.

    This is the word of the Lord.

Responsorial Psalm   (Ps 49:8–9. 16–17. 21. 23. *R*. v. 23)
Response
I will show God's salvation to the upright.

1. "I find no fault with your sacrifices,
your offerings are always before me.
I do not ask more bullocks from your farms,
nor goats from among your herds. (*R*.)

2. "But how can you recite my commandments
and take my covenant on your lips,
you who despise my law
and throw my words to the winds. (*R*.)

3. "You do this, and should I keep silence?
Do you think that I am like you?
A sacrifice of thanksgiving honours me
and I will show God's salvation to the upright." (*R*.)

Acclamation   (Mt 4:17)

Repent, says the Lord, for the kingdom of heaven is close at hand.

Alternative Acclamations p. 842.

Gospel   (23:1–12)

A reading from the holy Gospel according to Matthew
They do not practise what they preach.

Addressing the people and his disciples Jesus said, "The scribes and the Pharisees occupy the chair of Moses. You must therefore do what they tell you and listen to what they say; but do not be guided by what they do, since they do not practise what they preach. They tie up heavy burdens and lay them on men's shoulders, but will they lift a finger to move them? Not they! Everything they do is done to attract attention, like wearing broader phylacteries and longer tassels, like wanting to take the place of honour at banquets and the front seats in the synagogues, being greeted obsequiously in the market squares and having people calling them Rabbi.

"You, however, must not allow yourselves to be called Rabbi, since you have only one Master, and you are all brothers. You must call no one on earth your father, since you have only one Father, and he is in heaven. Nor must you allow yourselves to be called teachers, for you have only one Teacher, the Christ. The greatest among you must be your servant. Anyone who exalts himself will be humbled, and anyone who humbles himself will be exalted."

This is the Gospel of the Lord.

WEDNESDAY

First Reading   (18:18–20)

A reading from the prophet Jeremiah
Come on, let us hit at him.

"Come on," they said "let us concoct a plot against Jeremiah; the priest will not run short of instruction without him, nor the sage of advice, nor the prophet of the word. Come on, let us hit at him with his own tongue; let us listen carefully to every word he says."

Listen to me, Lord,
hear what my adversaries are saying.
Should evil be returned for good?
For they are digging a pit for me.
Remember how I stood in your presence
to plead on their behalf,
to turn your wrath away from them.

This is the word of the Lord.

Responsorial Psalm   (Ps 30:5–6. 14–16. *R.* v. 17)
Response
Save me in your love, O Lord.

1. Release me from the snares they have hidden
for you are my refuge, Lord.
Into your hands I commend my spirit.
It is you who will redeem me, Lord. (*R.*)

2. I have heard the slander of the crowd,
fear is all around me,
as they plot together against me,
as they plan to take my life. (*R.*)

3. But as for me, I trust in you, Lord,
I say: "You are my God.
My life is in your hands, deliver me
from the hands of those who hate me." (*R.*)

Acclamation   (Jn 6:64. 69)

Your words are spirit, Lord, and they are life; you have
the message of eternal life.

Alternative Acclamations p. 842.

Gospel   (20:17–28)

A reading from the holy Gospel according to Matthew

They will condemn him to death.

Jesus was going up to Jerusalem, and on the way he took
the Twelve to one side and said to them, "Now we are going up to Jerusalem, and the Son of Man is about to be
handed over to the chief priests and scribes. They will condemn him to death and will hand him over to the pagans to
be mocked and scourged and crucified; and on the third
day he will rise again."

Then the mother of Zebedee's sons came with her sons
to make a request of him, and bowed low; and he said to
her, "What is it you want?" She said to him, "Promise
that these two sons of mine may sit one at your right hand
and the other at your left in your kingdom." "You do not
know what you are asking" Jesus answered. "Can you drink
the cup that I am going to drink?" They replied, "We can."
"Very well," he said "you shall drink my cup, but as for
seats at my right hand and my left, these are not mine to
grant; they belong to those to whom they have been allotted
by my Father."

When the other ten heard this they were indignant with
the two brothers. But Jesus called them to him and said,
"You know that among the pagans the rulers lord it over
them, and their great men make their authority felt. This is
not to happen among you. No; anyone who wants to be
great among you must be your servant, and anyone who
wants to be first among you must be your slave, just as the
Son of Man came not to be served but to serve, and to give
his life as a ransom for many."

This is the Gospel of the Lord.

THURSDAY

First Reading (17:5–10)

A reading from the prophet Jeremiah

A curse on the man who puts his trust in man,
a blessing on the man who puts his trust in the Lord.

The Lord says this:

"A curse on the man who puts his trust in man,
who relies on things of flesh,
whose heart turns from the Lord.
He is like dry scrub in the wastelands:
if good comes, he has no eyes for it,
he settles in the parched places of the wilderness,
a salt land, uninhabited.

"A blessing on the man who puts his trust in the Lord,
with the Lord for his hope.
He is like a tree by the waterside
that thrusts its roots to the stream:
when the heat comes it feels no alarm,
its foliage stays green;
it has no worries in a year of drought,
and never ceases to bear fruit.

"The heart is more devious than any other thing,
perverse too: who can pierce its secrets?
I, the Lord, search to the heart,
I probe the loins
to give each man what his conduct
and his actions deserve."

This is the word of the Lord.

Responsorial Psalm   (Ps 1:1–4. 6. *R.* Ps. 39:5)

Response

Happy the man who has placed his trust in the Lord.

1. Happy indeed is the man
who follows not the counsel of the wicked;
nor lingers in the way of sinners
nor sits in the company of scorners,
but whose delight is the law of the Lord
and who ponders his law day and night. (*R.*)

2. He is like a tree that is planted
beside the flowing waters,
that yields its fruit in due season
and whose leaves shall never fade;
and all that he does shall prosper. (*R.*)

3. Not so are the wicked, not so!
For they like winnowed chaff
shall be driven away by the wind.
For the Lord guards the way of the just
but the way of the wicked leads to doom. (R.)

Acclamation   (Lk 15:18)

I will leave this place and go to my father and say:
"Father, I have sinned against heaven and against you."

Alternative Acclamations p. 842.

Gospel   (16:19–31)

A reading from the holy Gospel according to Luke

*Good things came your way, just as bad things came the way of
Lazarus. Now he is being comforted here while you are in
agony.*

Jesus said to the Pharisees: "There was a rich man who
used to dress in purple and fine linen and feast magnifi-

cently every day. And at his gate there lay a poor man called Lazarus, covered with sores, who longed to fill himself with the scraps that fell from the rich man's table. Dogs even came and licked his sores. Now the poor man died and was carried away by the angels to the bosom of Abraham. The rich man also died and was buried.

"In his torment in Hades he looked up and saw Abraham a long way off with Lazarus in his bosom. So he cried out, 'Father Abraham, pity me and send Lazarus to dip the tip of his finger in water and cool my tongue, for I am in agony in these flames.' 'My son', Abraham replied 'remember that during your life good things came your way, just as bad things came the way of Lazarus. Now he is being comforted here while you are in agony. But that is not all: between us and you a great gulf has been fixed, to stop anyone, if he wanted to, crossing from our side to yours, and to stop any crossing from your side to ours.'

"The rich man replied, 'Father, I beg you then to send Lazarus to my father's house, since I have five brothers, to give them warning so that they do not come to this place of torment too.' 'They have Moses and the prophets,' said Abraham 'let them listen to them.' 'Ah no, father Abraham,' said the rich man 'but if someone comes to them from the dead, they will repent.' Then Abraham said to him, 'If they will not listen either to Moses or to the prophets, they will not be convinced even if someone should rise from the dead.' "

This is the Gospel of the Lord.

FRIDAY

First Reading   (37:3–4. 12–13. 17–28)
A reading from the book of Genesis
Here comes the man of dreams. Come on, let us kill him.

Israel loved Joseph more than all his other sons, for he was the son of his old age, and he had a coat with long sleeves made for him. But his brothers, seeing how his father loved him more than all his other sons, came to hate him so much that they could not say a civil word to him.

His brothers went to pasture their father's flock at Shechem. Then Israel said to Joseph, "Are not your brothers with the flock at Shechem? Come, I am going to send you to them." So Joseph went after his brothers and found them at Dothan.

They saw him in the distance, and before he reached them they made a plot among themselves to put him to death. "Here comes the man of dreams" they said to one another. "Come on, let us kill him and throw him into some well; we can say that a wild beast devoured him. Then we shall see what becomes of his dreams."

But Reuben heard, and he saved him from their violence. "We must not take his life" he said. "Shed no blood," said Reuben to them "throw him into this well in the wilderness, but do not lay violent hands on him" – intending to save him from them and to restore him to his father. So, when Joseph reached his brothers, they pulled off his coat, the coat with long sleeves that he was wearing, and catching hold of him they threw him into the well, an empty well with no water in it. They then sat down to eat.

Looking up they saw a group of Ishmaelites who were coming from Gilead, their camels laden with gum, tragacanth, balsam and resin, which they were taking down into Egypt. Then Judah said to his brothers, "What do we gain by killing our brother and covering up his blood? Come, let us sell him to the Ishmaelites, but let us not do any harm to him. After all, he is our brother, and our own flesh." His brothers agreed.

Now some Midianite merchants were passing, and they drew Joseph up out of the well. They sold Joseph to the Ishmaelites for twenty silver pieces, and these men took Joseph to Egypt.

This is the word of the Lord.

Responsorial Psalm   (Ps 104:16–21. R. v. 5)

Response
Remember the wonders the Lord has done.

1. God called down a famine on the land;
he broke the staff that supported them.
He had sent a man before them,
Joseph, sold as a slave. (*R.*)

2. His feet were put in chains,
his neck was bound with iron,
until what he said came to pass
and the Lord's word proved him true. (*R.*)

3. Then the king sent and released him;
the ruler of the peoples set him free,
making him master of his house
and ruler of all he possessed. (*R.*)

Acclamation   (Jn 3:16)

God loved the world so much that he gave his only Son;
everyone who believes in him has eternal life.

Alternative Acclamations p. 842.

Gospel   (21:33–43. 45–46)
A reading from the holy Gospel according to Matthew
This is the heir. Come on, let us kill him.

Jesus said to the chief priests and the elders of the people:
"Listen to another parable. There was a man, a landowner,
who planted a vineyard; he fenced it round, dug a winepress
in it and built a tower; then he leased it to tenants and went
abroad. When vintage time drew near he sent his servants to
the tenants to collect his produce. But the tenants seized
his servants, thrashed one, killed another and stoned a
third. Next he sent some more servants, this time a large

number, and they dealt with them in the same way. Finally he sent his son to them. 'They will respect my son,' he said. But when the tenants saw the son, they said to each other. 'This is the heir. Come on, let us kill him and take over his inheritance.' So they seized him and threw him out of the vineyard and killed him. Now when the owner of the vineyard comes, what will he do to those tenants?" They answered, "He will bring those wretches to a wretched end and lease the vineyard to other tenants who will deliver the produce to him when the season arrives." Jesus said to them, "Have you never read in the scriptures:

It was the stone rejected by the builders
that became the keystone.
This was the Lord's doing
and it is wonderful to see?

I tell you, then, that the kingdom of God will be taken from you and given to a people who will produce its fruit."

When they heard his parables, the chief priests and the scribes realised he was speaking about them but though they would have liked to arrest him they were afraid of the crowds, who looked on him as a prophet.

This is the Gospel of the Lord.

SATURDAY

First Reading (7:14-15. 18-20)
A reading from the prophet Micah
Tread down our faults to the bottom of the sea.

With shepherd's crook lead your people to pasture,
the flock that is your heritage,
living confined in a forest
with meadow land all around.
Let them pasture in Bashan and Gilead
as in the days of old.

As in the days when you came out of Egypt
grant us to see wonders.
What god can compare with you : taking fault away,
pardoning crime,
not cherishing anger for ever
but delighting in showing mercy?
Once more have pity on us,
tread down our faults,
to the bottom of the sea
throw all our sins.
Grant Jacob your faithfulness,
and Abraham your mercy,
as you swore to our fathers
from the days of long ago.

This is the word of the Lord.

Responsorial Psalm   (Ps 102:1–4. 9–12. *R*. v. 8)
Response
The Lord is compassion and love.

1. My soul, give thanks to the Lord
all my being, bless his holy name.
My soul, give thanks to the Lord
and never forget all his blessings. (*R*.)

2. It is he who forgives all your guilt,
who heals every one of your ills,
who redeems your life from the grave,
who crowns you with love and compassion. (*R*.)

3. His wrath will come to an end;
he will not be angry for ever.
He does not treat us according to our sins
nor repay us according to our faults. (*R*.)

4. For as the heavens are high above the earth
so strong is his love for those who fear him.
As far as the east is from the west
so far does he remove our sins. (*R.*)

Acclamation   (Lk 15:18)

I will leave this place and go to my father and say:
"Father, I have sinned against heaven and against you."

Alternative Acclamations p. 842.

Gospel   (15:1–3. 11–32)

A reading from the holy Gospel according to Luke
Your brother here was dead and has come to life.

The tax collectors and the sinners were all seeking the company of Jesus to hear what he had to say, and the Pharisees and the scribes complained. "This man" they said "welcomes sinners and eats with them." So he spoke this parable to them:

"A man had two sons. The younger said to his father, 'Father, let me have the share of the estate that would come to me.' So the father divided the property between them. A few days later, the younger son got together everything he had and left for a distant country where he squandered his money on a life of debauchery.

"When he had spent it all, that country experienced a severe famine, and now he began to feel the pinch, so he hired himself out to one of the local inhabitants who put him on his farm to feed the pigs. And he would willingly have filled his belly with the husks the pigs were eating but no one offered him anything. Then he came to his senses and said, 'How many of my father's paid servants have more food than they want, and here am I dying of hunger! I will leave this place and go to my father and say: Father, I have sinned against heaven and against you; I no longer deserve to be called your son; treat me as one of your paid servants.' So he left the place and went back to his father.

"While he was still a long way off, his father saw him and was moved with pity. He ran to the boy, clasped him in his arms and kissed him tenderly. Then his son said, 'Father, I have sinned against heaven and against you. I no longer deserve to be called your son.' But the father said to his servants, 'Quick! Bring out the best robe and put it on him; put a ring on his finger and sandals on his feet. Bring the calf we have been fattening, and kill it; we are going to have a feast, a celebration, because this son of mine was dead and has come back to life; he was lost and is found.' And they began to celebrate.

"Now the elder son was out in the fields, and on his way back, as he drew near the house, he could hear music and dancing. Calling one of the servants he asked what it was all about. 'Your brother has come' replied the servant 'and your father has killed the calf we had fattened because he has got him back safe and sound.' He was angry then and refused to go in, and his father came out to plead with him; but he answered his father, 'Look, all these years I have slaved for you and never once disobeyed your orders, yet you never offered me so much as a kid for me to celebrate with my friends. But, for this son of yours, when he comes back after swallowing up your property – he and his women – you kill the calf we had been fattening.'

"The father said, 'My son, you are with me always and all I have is yours. But it was only right we should celebrate and rejoice, because your brother here was dead and has come to life; he was lost and is found.' "

This is the Gospel of the Lord.

3rd SUNDAY OF LENT

Year 1 (Year A)

First Reading   (17:3–7)

A reading from the book of Exodus
Give us water to drink.

Tormented by thirst, the people complained against Moses.
"Why did you bring us out of Egypt?" they said. "Was it
so that I should die of thirst, my children too, and my
cattle?" Moses appealed to the Lord. "How am I to deal
with this people?" he said. "A little more and they will
stone me!" The Lord said to Moses, "Take with you some
of the elders of Israel and move on to the forefront of the
people; take in your hand the staff with which you struck
the river, and go. I shall be standing before you there on
the rock, at Horeb. You must strike the rock, and water
will flow from it for the people to drink." This is what
Moses did, in the sight of the elders of Israel. The place was
named Massah and Meribah because of the grumbling of
the sons of Israel and because they put the Lord to the test
by saying, "Is the Lord with us, or not?"

This is the word of the Lord.

Responsorial Psalm   (Ps 94:1–2. 6–9. *R.* v. 8)

Response
O that today you would listen to his voice!
Harden not your hearts.

1. Come, ring out our joy to the Lord;
hail the rock who saves us.
Let us come before him, giving thanks,
with songs let us hail the Lord. (*R.*)

2. Come in; let us bow and bend low;
let us kneel before the God who made us
for he is our God and we
the people who belong to his pasture,
the flock that is led by his hand. (*R.*)

3. O that today you would listen to his voice!
"Harden not your hearts as at Meribah,
as on that day at Massah in the desert
when your fathers put me to the test;
when they tried me, though they saw my work." (*R.*)

Second Reading   (5:1–2. 5–8)
A reading from the letter of St Paul to the Romans
The love of God has been poured into our hearts by the Holy
Spirit which has been given us.

So far then we have seen that, through our Lord Jesus
Christ, by faith we are judged righteous and at peace with
God, since it is by faith and through Jesus that we have
entered this state of grace in which we can boast about
looking forward to God's glory. This hope is not deceptive,
because the love of God has been poured into our hearts
by the Holy Spirit which has been given us. We were still
helpless when at his appointed moment Christ died for
sinful men. It is not easy to die even for a good man –
though of course for someone really worthy, a man might
be prepared to die – but what proves that God loves us is
that Christ died for us while we were still sinners.

　　This is the word of the Lord.

Acclamation   (Jn 4:42. 15)
Lord, you are really the saviour of the world;
give me the living water, so that I may never get thirsty.

Gospel   (4:5–42)

A reading from the holy Gospel according to John

A spring of water welling up to eternal life.

*Jesus came to the Samaritan town called Sychar, near the land that Jacob gave to his son Joseph. Jacob's well is there and Jesus, tired by the journey, sat straight down by the well. It was about the sixth hour. When a Samaritan woman came to draw water, Jesus said to her, "Give me a drink." His disciples had gone into the town to buy food. The Samaritan woman said to him. "What? You are a Jew and you ask me, a Samaritan, for a drink?" – Jews, in fact, do not associate with Samaritans. Jesus replied:

"If you only knew what God is offering
and who it is that is saying to you:
Give me a drink,
you would have been the one to ask,
and he would have given you living water."

"You have no bucket, sir," she answered "and the well is deep: how could you get this living water? Are you a greater man than our father Jacob who gave us this well and drank from it himself with his sons and his cattle?" Jesus replied:

"Whoever drinks this water
will get thirsty again;
but anyone who drinks the water that I shall
   give
will never be thirsty again:
the water that I shall give
will turn into a spring inside him, welling up
   to eternal life."

"Sir," said the woman "give me some of that water, so that I may never get thirsty and never have to come here again to draw water."* "Go and call your husband" said Jesus to her "and come back here." The woman answered, "I have no husband." He said to her, "You are right to say, 'I have no husband'; for although you have had five, the one you have now is not your husband. You spoke the truth there." *"I see you are a prophet, sir" said the woman. "Our fathers worshipped on this mountain, while you say that Jerusalem is the place where one ought to worship." Jesus said:

"Believe me, woman, the hour is coming
when you will worship the Father
neither on this mountain nor in Jerusalem.
You worship what you do not know;
we worship what we do know;
for salvation comes from the Jews.
But the hour will come – in fact it is here already –
when true worshippers will worship the Father in
   spirit and truth:
that is the kind of worshipper
the Father wants.
God is spirit,
and those who worship
must worship in spirit and truth."

The woman said to him. "I know that Messiah – that is, Christ – is coming; and when he comes, he will tell us everything." "I who am speaking to you," said Jesus "I am he."*
At this point his disciples returned, and were surprised to find him speaking to a woman, though none of them asked, "What do you want from her?" or, "Why are you talking to her?" The woman put down her water jar and hurried back to the town to tell the people, "Come and see a man who has told me everything I ever did; I wonder if he is the Christ?" This brought people out of the town and they started walking towards him.

Meanwhile, the disciples were urging him, "Rabbi, do have something to eat"; but he said, "I have food to eat that you do not know about." So the disciples asked one another, "Has someone been bringing him food?" But Jesus said:

"My food
is to do the will of the one who sent me,
and to complete his work.
Have you not got a saying:
Four months and then the harvest?
Well, I tell you:
Look around you, look at the fields;
already they are white, ready for harvest!
Already the reaper is being paid his wages,
already he is bringing in the grain for eternal life,
and thus sower and reaper rejoice together.
For here the proverb holds good:
one sows, another reaps;
I sent you to reap
a harvest you had not worked for.
Others worked for it;
and you have come into the rewards of their
    trouble."

Many Samaritans of that town had believed in him on the strength of the woman's testimony when she said, "He told me all I have ever done," so, when the Samaritans came up to him, they begged him to stay with them. He stayed for two days, and when he spoke to them many more came to believe; and they said to the woman, "Now we no longer believe because of what you told us; we have heard him ourselves and we know that he really is the saviour of the world."

This is the Gospel of the Lord.

*Shorter Form, verses 4–5. 15. 19–26. 39–42. Read between *.

3rd SUNDAY OF LENT

Year 2 (Year B)

The readings for Year 1 (Year A) may be used as alternative readings.

First Reading　　　　　　　　　　　　　　　(20:1–17)
A reading from the book of Exodus
The Law was given through Moses.

*God spoke all these words. He said, "I am the Lord your God who brought you out of the land of Egypt, out of the house of slavery.

"You shall have no gods except me.*

"You shall not make yourself a carved image or any likeness of anything in heaven or on earth beneath or in the waters under the earth; you shall not bow down to them or serve them. For I, the Lord your God, am a jealous God and I punish the father's fault in the sons, the grandsons, and the great-grandsons of those who hate me; but I show kindness to thousands of those who love me and keep my commandments.

*"You shall not utter the name of the Lord your God to misuse it, for the Lord will not leave unpunished the man who utters his name to misuse it.

"Remember the sabbath day and keep it holy.* For six days you shall labour and do all your work, but the seventh day is a sabbath for the Lord your God. You shall do no work that day, neither you nor your son nor your daughter nor your servants, men or women, nor your animals nor the stranger who lives with you. For in six days the Lord made the heavens and the earth and the sea and all that these hold, but on the seventh day he rested; that is why the Lord has blessed the sabbath and made it sacred.

*"Honour your father and your mother so that you may have a long life in the land that the Lord your God has given to you.

"You shall not kill.

"You shall not commit adultery.

"You shall not steal.

"You shall not bear false witness against your neighbour.

"You shall not covet your neighbour's house. You shall not covet your neighbour's wife, or his servant, man or woman, or his ox, or his donkey, or anything that is his."

This is the word of the Lord.*

*Shorter Form, verses 1–3. 7–8. 12–17. Read between *.

Responsorial Psalm   (Ps 18:8–11. *R.* Jn 6:69)

Response
You, Lord, have the message of eternal life.

1. The law of the Lord is perfect,
it revives the soul.
The rule of the Lord is to be trusted,
it gives wisdom to the simple. (*R.*)

2. The precepts of the Lord are right,
they gladden the heart.
The command of the Lord is clear,
it gives light to the eyes. (*R.*)

3. The fear of the Lord is holy,
abiding for ever.
The decrees of the Lord are truth
and all of them just. (*R.*)

4. They are more to be desired than gold,
than the purest of gold
and sweeter are they than honey,
than honey from the comb. (*R.*)

Second Reading   (1:22–25)

A reading from the first letter of St Paul to the Corinthians
Here we are preaching a crucified Christ, an obstacle to men,
but to those who are called, the wisdom of God.

And so, while the Jews demand miracles and the Greeks
look for wisdom, here are we preaching a crucified Christ;
to the Jews an obstacle that they cannot get over, to the
pagans madness, but to those who have been called, whether
they are Jews or Greeks, a Christ who is the power and the
wisdom of God. For God's foolishness is wiser than human
wisdom, and God's weakness is stronger than human
strength.

This is the word of the Lord.

Acclamation   (Jn 11:25. 26)

I am the resurrection and the life, says the Lord, whoever
believes in me will never die.

Alternative Acclamations p. 842.

Gospel   (2:13–25)

A reading from the holy Gospel according to John
Destroy this sanctuary, and in three days I will raise it up.

Just before the Jewish Passover Jesus went up to Jerusalem, and in the Temple he found people selling cattle and
sheep and pigeons, and the money changers sitting at their
counters there. Making a whip out of some cord, he drove
them all out of the Temple, cattle and sheep as well, scattered the money changers' coins, knocked their tables over
and said to the pigeon-sellers, "Take all this out of here
and stop turning my Father's house into a market." Then
his disciples remembered the words of scripture: Zeal for
your house will devour me. The Jews intervened and said,
"What sign can you show us to justify what you have
done?" Jesus answered, "Destroy this sanctuary, and in

three days I will raise it up." The Jews replied, "It has taken forty-six years to build this sanctuary: are you going to raise it up in three days?" But he was speaking of the sanctuary that was his body, and when Jesus rose from the dead, his disciples remembered that he had said this, and they believed the scripture and the words he had said.

During his stay in Jerusalem for the Passover many believed in his name when they saw the signs that he gave, but Jesus knew them all and did not trust himself to them; he never needed evidence about any man; he could tell what a man had in him.

This is the Gospel of the Lord.

3rd SUNDAY OF LENT

Year 3 (Year C)

The readings for Year 1 (Year A) may be used as alternative readings.

First Reading   (3:1–8. 13–15)

A reading from the book of Exodus

I Am has sent me to you.

Moses was looking after the flock of Jethro, his father-in-law, priest of Midian. He led his flock to the far side of the wilderness and came to Horeb, the mountain of God. There the angel of the Lord appeared to him in the shape of a flame of fire, coming from the middle of a bush. Moses looked; there was the bush blazing but it was not being burnt up. "I must go and look at this strange sight," Moses said "and see why the bush is not burnt." Now the Lord saw him go forward to look, and God called to him from the middle of the bush. "Moses, Moses!" he said. "Here I am" he answered. "Come no nearer" he said. "Take off your shoes, for the place on which you stand is holy ground. I am the God of your father," he said "the God of Abraham, the God of Isaac and the God of Jacob." At this Moses covered his face, afraid to look at God.

And the Lord said, "I have seen the miserable state of my people in Egypt. I have heard their appeal to be free of their slave-drivers. Yes, I am well aware of their sufferings. I mean to deliver them out of the hands of the Egyptians and bring them up out of that land to a land rich and broad, a land where milk and honey flow."

Then Moses said to God, "I am to go, then, to the sons of Israel and say to them, 'The God of your fathers has sent me to you.' But if they ask me what his name is, what am I to tell them?" And God said to Moses, "I Am who I Am. This" he added "is what you must say to the sons of Israel: 'I Am has sent me to you.'" And God also said to Moses, "You are to say to the sons of Israel: 'The Lord, the God of your fathers, the God of Abraham, the God of Isaac, and the God of Jacob, has sent me to you.' This is my name for all time; by this name I shall be invoked for all generations to come."

This is the word of the Lord.

Responsorial Psalm   (Ps 102:1–4. 6–8. 11. *R*. v. 8)

Response
The Lord is compassion and love.

1. My soul, give thanks to the Lord,
all my being, bless his holy name.
My soul give thanks to the Lord
and never forget all his blessings. (*R*.)

2. It is he who forgives all your guilt,
who heals every one of your ills,
who redeems your life from the grave,
who crowns you with love and compassion. (*R*.)

3. The Lord does deeds of justice,
gives judgement for all who are oppressed.

He made known his ways to Moses
and his deeds to Israel's sons. (*R.*)

4. The Lord is compassion and love,
slow to anger and rich in mercy.
For as the heavens are high above the earth
so strong is his love for those who fear him. (*R.*)

Second Reading   (10:1–6. 10–12)
A reading from the first letter of St Paul to the Corinthians
*The life of the people under Moses in the desert was written
down to be a lesson for us.*

I want to remind you, brothers, how our fathers were all
guided by a cloud above them and how they all passed
through the sea. They were all baptised into Moses in this
cloud and in this sea; all ate the same spiritual food and all
drank the same spiritual drink, since they all drank from
the spiritual rock that followed them as they went, and that
rock was Christ. In spite of this, most of them failed to
please God and their corpses littered the desert.

   These things all happened as warnings for us, not to have
the wicked lusts for forbidden things that they had. You
must never complain: some of them did, and they were
killed by the Destroyer.

   All this happened to them as a warning, and it was written down to be a lesson for us who are living at the end of
the age. The man who thinks he is safe must be careful that
he does not fall.

   This is the word of the Lord.

Acclamation   (Mt 4:17)
Repent, says the Lord, for the kingdom of heaven is close
   at hand.

Alternative Acclamations p. 842.

Gospel (13:1-9)

A reading from the holy Gospel according to Luke

Unless you repent you will all perish as they did.

It was just about this time that some people arrived and told Jesus about the Galileans whose blood Pilate had mingled with that of their sacrifices. At this he said to them, "Do you suppose these Galileans who suffered like that were greater sinners than any other Galileans? They were not, I tell you. No; but unless you repent you will all perish as they did. Or those eighteen on whom the tower at Siloam fell and killed them? Do you suppose that they were more guilty than all the other people living in Jerusalem? They were not, I tell you. No; but unless you repent you will all perish as they did."

He told this parable: "A man had a fig tree planted in his vineyard, and he came looking for fruit on it but found none. He said to the man who looked after the vineyard, 'Look here, for three years now I have been coming to look for fruit on this fig tree and finding none. Cut it down: why should it be taking up the ground?' 'Sir,' the man replied 'leave it one more year and give me time to dig round it and manure it: it may bear fruit next year; if not, then you can cut it down.' "

This is the Gospel of the Lord.

Alternative Readings

The following readings may be used instead of the proper ones any day this week, especially in Years 2 (B) and 3 (C) when the Gospel of the Samaritan woman is not read on the 3rd Sunday.

First Reading (17:1-7)

A reading from the book of Exodus

Water will flow from it for the people to drink.

The whole community of the sons of Israel moved from their camp in the desert of Zin at the Lord's command, to travel the further stages; and they pitched camp at Rephidim where there was no water for the people to drink. So they grumbled against Moses. "Give us water to drink" they said. Moses answered them. "Why do you grumble against me? Why do you put the Lord to the test?" But tormented by thirst, the people complained against Moses. "Why did you bring us out of Egypt?" they said. "Was it so that I should die of thirst, my children too, and my cattle?" Moses appealed to the Lord. "How am I to deal with this people?" he said. "A little more and they will stone me!" The Lord said to Moses, "Take with you some of the elders of Israel and move on to the forefront of the people; take in your hand the staff with which you struck the river, and go. I shall be standing before you there on the rock, at Horeb. You must strike the rock, and water will flow from it for the people to drink." This is what Moses did, in the sight of the elders of Israel. The place was named Massah and Meriba because of the grumbling of the sons of Israel and because they put the Lord to the test by saying, "Is the Lord with us, or not?"

This is the word of the Lord.

RESPONSORIAL PSALM. Ps 94:1–2. 6–9. R. v. 8. See p. 496.
GOSPEL. John 4:5–42, as for Year 1 (Year A), see p. 498.

MONDAY

First Reading (5:1–15)
A reading from the second book of the Kings
There were many lepers in Israel, but none of these was cured, except the Syrian, Naaman.

Naaman, army commander to the king of Aram, was a man who enjoyed his master's respect and favour, since through him the Lord had granted victory to the Aramaeans. But the man was a leper. Now on one of their raids, the Aramaeans had carried off from the land of Israel a little girl who had become a servant of Naaman's wife. She said to

her mistress, "If only my master would approach the prophet of Samaria. He would cure him of his leprosy."
Naaman went and told his master. "This and this" he reported "is what the girl from the land of Israel said." "Go
by all means," said the king of Aram "I will send a letter
to the king of Israel." So Naaman left, taking with him ten
talents of silver, six thousand shekels of gold and ten festal
robes. He presented the letter to the king of Israel. It read:
"With this letter, I am sending my servant Naaman to you
for you to cure him of his leprosy." When the king of Israel
read the letter, he tore his garments. "Am I a god to give
death and life," he said "that he sends a man to me and asks
me to cure him of his leprosy? Listen to this, and take note
of it and see how he intends to pick a quarrel with me."

When Elisha heard that the king of Israel had torn his
garments, he sent word to the king, "Why did you tear your
garments? Let him come to me, and he will find there is a
prophet in Israel." So Naaman came with his team and
chariot and drew up at the door of Elisha's house. And
Elisha sent him a messenger to say, "Go and bathe seven
times in the Jordan, and your flesh will become clean once
more." But Naaman was indignant and went off, saying,
"Here was I thinking he would be sure to come out to me,
and stand there, and call on the name of the Lord his God,
and wave his hand over the spot and cure the leprous part.
Surely Abana and Pharpar, the rivers of Damascus, are
better than any water in Israel? Could I not bathe in them
and become clean?" And he turned round and went off in
a rage. But his servants approached him and said, "My
father, if the prophet had asked you to do something difficult, would you not have done it? All the more reason,
then, when he says to you, 'Bathe and you will become
clean.'" So he went down and immersed himself seven times
in the Jordan, as Elisha had told him to do. And his flesh
became clean once more like the flesh of a little child.

Returning to Elisha with his whole escort, he went in and

stood before him. "Now I know" he said "that there is no
God in all the earth except in Israel."

This is the word of the Lord.

Responsorial Psalm (Pss 41:2–3; 42:3–4. *R.* Ps 41:3)

Response
My soul is thirsting for God,
the God of my life;
when can I enter and see
the face of God?

1. Like the deer that yearns
for running streams,
so my soul is yearning
for you, my God. (*R.*)

2. My soul is thirsting for God,
the God of my life;
when can I enter and see
the face of God? (*R.*)

3. O send forth your light and your truth;
let these be my guide.
Let them bring me to your holy mountain
to the place where you dwell. (*R.*)

4. And I will come to the altar of God,
the God of my joy.
My redeemer, I will thank you on the harp,
O God, my God. (*R.*)

Acclamation (2 Cor 6:2)

Now is the favourable time;
this is the day of salvation.

Alternative Acclamations p. 842.

Gospel   (4:24–30)

A reading from the holy Gospel according to Luke

Like Elijah and Elisha, Jesus is not sent to the Jews only.

Jesus came to Nazara and spoke to the people in the synagogue: "I tell you solemnly, no prophet is ever accepted in his own country.

"There were many widows in Israel, I can assure you, in Elijah's day, when heaven remained shut for three years and six months and a great famine raged throughout the land, but Elijah was not sent to any one of these: he was sent to a widow at Zarephath, a Sidonian town. And in the prophet Elisha's time there were many lepers in Israel, but none of these was cured, except the Syrian, Naaman."

When they heard this everyone in the synagogue was enraged. They sprang to their feet and hustled him out of the town; and they took him up to the brow of the hill their town was built on, intending to throw him down the cliff, but he slipped through the crowd and walked away.

This is the Gospel of the Lord.

TUESDAY

First Reading   (3:25. 34–43)

A reading from the prophet Daniel

May the contrite soul, the humbled spirit be acceptable to you.

Azariah stood in the heart of the fire, and he began to pray:

Oh! Do not abandon us for ever,
for the sake of your name;
do not repudiate your covenant,
do not withdraw your favour from us,
for the sake of Abraham, your friend,
of Isaac your servant,
and of Israel your holy one,

to whom you promised descendants as countless as the
    stars of heaven
and as the grains of sand on the seashore.
Lord, now we are the least of all the nations,
now we are despised throughout the world, today, because
    of our sins.
We have at this time no leader, no prophet, no prince,
no holocaust, no sacrifice, no oblation, no incense,
no place where we can offer you the first-fruits
and win your favour.
But may the contrite soul, the humbled spirit be as accept-
    able to you
as holocausts of rams and bullocks,
as thousands of fattened lambs:
such let our sacrifice be to you today,
and may it be your will that we follow you wholeheartedly,
since those who put their trust in you will not be dis-
    appointed.
And now we put our whole heart into following you,
into fearing you and seeking your face once more.
Do not disappoint us;
treat us gently, as you yourself are gentle
and very merciful.
Grant us deliverance worthy of your wonderful deeds,
let your name win glory, Lord.

    This is the word of the Lord

Responsorial Psalm   (Ps 24:4–9. *R.* v. 6)
Response
Remember your mercy, Lord.

1. Lord, make me know your ways.
Lord, teach me your paths.
Make me walk in your truth, and teach me:
for you are God my saviour. (*R.*)

2. Remember your mercy, Lord,
and the love you have shown from of old.
Do not remember the sins of my youth,
because of your goodness, O Lord. (*R.*)

3. The Lord is good and upright.
He shows the path to those who stray.
He guides the humble in the right path;
he teaches his way to the poor. (*R.*)

Acclamation   (Lk 8:15)

Blessed are those who, with a noble and generous heart,
take the word of God to themselves and yield a harvest
through their perseverance.

Alternative Acclamations p. 842.

Gospel   (18:21–35)

A reading from the holy Gospel according to Matthew

*Your Father will not forgive you unless you each forgive your
brother from your heart.*

Peter went up to Jesus and said, "Lord, how often must I
forgive my brother if he wrongs me? As often as seven
times?" Jesus answered, "Not seven, I tell you, but seventy-
seven times.

"And so the kingdom of heaven may be compared to a
king who decided to settle his accounts with his servants.
When the reckoning began, they brought him a man who
owed ten thousand talents; but he had no means of paying,
so his master gave orders that he should be sold, together
with his wife and children and all his possessions, to meet
the debt. At this, the servant threw himself down at his
master's feet. 'Give me time' he said 'and I will pay the
whole sum.' And the servant's master felt so sorry for him
that he let him go and cancelled the debt. Now as this ser-

vant went out, he happened to meet a fellow servant who owed him one hundred denarii; and he seized him by the throat and began to throttle him. 'Pay what you owe me' he said. His fellow servant fell at his feet and implored him, saying, 'Give me time and I will pay you.' But the other would not agree; on the contrary, he had him thrown into prison till he should pay the debt. His fellow servants were deeply distressed when they saw what had happened, and they went to their master and reported the whole affair to him. Then the master sent for him. 'You wicked servant,' he said. 'I cancelled all that debt of yours when you appealed to me. Were you not bound, then, to have pity on your fellow servant just as I had pity on you?' And in his anger the master handed him over to the torturers till he should pay all his debt. And that is how my heavenly Father will deal with you unless you each forgive your brother from your heart."

This is the Gospel of the Lord.

WEDNESDAY

First Reading   (4:1. 5–9)
A reading from the book of Deuteronomy
Take notice of the laws and observe them.

Moses said to the people: "And now, Israel, take notice of the laws and customs that I teach you today, and observe them, that you may have life and may enter and take possession of the land that the Lord the God of your fathers is giving you. See, as the Lord my God has commanded me, I teach you the laws and customs that you are to observe in the land you are to enter and make your own. Keep them, observe them, and they will demonstrate to the peoples your wisdom and understanding. When they come to know of all these laws they will exclaim, 'No other people is as wise and prudent as this great nation.' And indeed, what great nation is there that has its gods so near as the Lord our God is to us whenever we call to him? And what great nation is there that has laws and customs to match this whole Law that I put before you today?

"But take care what you do and be on your guard. Do not forget the things your eyes have seen, nor let them slip from your heart all the days of your life; rather, tell them to your children and to your children's children."

This is the word of the Lord.

Responsorial Psalm (Ps 147:12–13. 15–16. 19–20. *R*. v. 12)

Response
O praise the Lord, Jerusalem!

1. O praise the Lord, Jerusalem!
Zion, praise your God!
He has strengthened the bars of your gates,
has blessed the children within you. (*R*.)

2. He sends out his word to the earth
and swiftly runs his command.
He showers down snow white as wool,
he scatters hoar-frost like ashes. (*R*.)

3. He makes his word known to Jacob,
to Israel his laws and decrees.
He has not dealt thus with other nations;
he has not taught them his decrees.
Alleluia! (*R*.)

Acclamation   (Jn 8:12)
I am the light of the world, says the Lord, anyone who follows me will have the light of life.

Alternative Acclamations p. 842.

Gospel (5:17–19)

A reading from the holy Gospel according to Matthew

The man who keeps these commandments and teaches them will be considered great in the kingdom of heaven.

Jesus said to his disciples: "Do not imagine that I have come to abolish the Law or the Prophets. I have come not to abolish but to complete them. I tell you solemnly, till heaven and earth disappear, not one dot, not one little stroke, shall disappear from the Law until its purpose is achieved. Therefore, the man who infringes even one of the least of these commandments and teaches others to do the same will be considered the least in the kingdom of heaven; but the man who keeps them and teaches them will be considered great in the kingdom of heaven."

This is the Gospel of the Lord.

THURSDAY

First Reading (7:23–28)

A reading from the prophet Jeremiah

Here is the nation that will not listen to the voice of the Lord its God.

These were my orders: Listen to my voice, then I will be your God and you shall be my people. Follow right to the end the way that I mark out for you, and you will prosper. But they did not listen, they did not pay attention; they followed the dictates of their own evil hearts, refused to face me, and turned their backs on me. From the day your ancestors came out of the land of Egypt until today, day after day I have persistently sent you all my servants the prophets. But they have not listened to me, have not paid attention; they have grown stubborn and behaved worse than their ancestors. You may say all these words to them: they will not listen to you; you may call them: they will not answer. So tell them this, "Here is the nation that will not

listen to the voice of the Lord its God nor take correction.
Sincerity is no more, it has vanished from their mouths."

This is the word of the Lord.

Responsorial Psalm (Ps 94:1–2. 6–9. *R*. v. 8)

Response
O that today you would listen to his voice!
"Harden not your hearts."

1. Come, ring out our joy to the Lord;
hail the rock who saves us.
Let us come before him, giving thanks,
with songs let us hail the Lord. (*R*.)

2. Come in; let us bow and bend low;
let us kneel before the God who made us
for he is our God and we
the people who belong to his pasture,
the flock that is led by his hand. (*R*.)

3. O that today you would listen to his voice!
"Harden not your hearts as at Meribah,
as on that day at Massah in the desert
when your fathers put me to the test;
when they tried me, though they saw my work." (*R*.)

Acclamation (Ez 18:31)
Shake off all your sins – it is the Lord who speaks – and
make yourselves a new heart and a new spirit.

Alternative Acclamations p. 842.

Gospel (11:14–23)
A reading from the holy Gospel according to Luke
He who is not with me is against me.

Jesus was casting out a devil and it was dumb; but when the devil had gone out the dumb man spoke, and the people were amazed. But some of them said, "It is through Beelzebul, the prince of devils, that he casts out devils." Others asked him, as a test, for a sign from heaven; but, knowing what they were thinking, he said to them, "Every kingdom divided against itself is heading for ruin, and a household divided against itself collapses. So too with Satan: if he is divided against himself, how can his kingdom stand – since you assert that it is through Beelzebul that I cast out devils. Now if it is through Beelzebul that I cast out devils, through whom do your own experts cast them out? Let them be your judges, then. But if it is through the finger of God that I cast out devils, then know that the kingdom of God has overtaken you. So long as a strong man fully armed guards his own palace, his goods are undisturbed; but when someone stronger than he is attacks and defeats him, the stronger man takes away all the weapons he relied on and shares out his spoil.

"He who is not with me is against me; and he who does not gather with me scatters."

This is the Gospel of the Lord.

FRIDAY

First Reading   (14:2–10)

A reading from the prophet Hosea
We will not say any more, "*Our God*" *to what our own hands have made.*

The Lord says this:

Israel, come back to the Lord your God;
your iniquity was the cause of your downfall.
Provide yourself with words
and come back to the Lord.

Say to him, "Take all iniquity away
so that we may have happiness again
and offer you our words of praise.
Assyria cannot save us,
we will not ride horses any more,
or say, 'Our God!' to what our own hands have made,
for you are the one in whom orphans find compassion."
– I will heal their disloyalty,
I will love them with all my heart,
for my anger has turned from them.
I will fall like dew on Israel.
He shall bloom like the lily,
and thrust out roots like the poplar,
his shoots will spread far;
he will have the beauty of the olive
and the fragrance of Lebanon.
They will come back to live in my shade;
they will grow corn that flourishes,
they will cultivate vines
as renowned as the wine of Helbon.
What has Ephraim to do with idols any more
when it is I who hear his prayer and care for him?
I am like a cypress ever green,
all your fruitfulness comes from me.
Let the wise man understand these words.
Let the intelligent man grasp their meaning.
For the ways of the Lord are straight,
and virtuous men walk in them,
but sinners stumble.

    This is the word of the Lord.

Responsorial Psalm   (Ps 80:6. 8–11. 14. 17. *R.* vv. 9. 11)

Response
  am the Lord your God.
  Listen, my people, to my warning.

1. A voice I did not know said to me:
"I freed your shoulder from the burden;
your hands were freed from the load.
You called in distress and I saved you. (*R.*)

2. I answered, concealed in the storm cloud,
at the waters of Meribah I tested you.
Listen, my people, to my warning,
O Israel, if only you would heed! (*R.*)

3. Let there be no foreign god among you,
no worship of an alien god.
I am the Lord your God,
who brought you from the land of Egypt. (*R.*)

4. O that my people would heed me,
that Israel would walk in my ways!
But Israel I would feed with finest wheat
and fill them with honey from the rock." (*R.*)

Acclamation

The seed is the word of God, Christ the sower; whoever
finds this seed will remain for ever.

Alternative Acclamations p. 842.

Gospel   (12:28–34)
A reading from the holy Gospel according to Mark
The Lord our God is the one Lord, and you must love him.

One of the scribes came up to Jesus and put a question to
him, "Which is the first of all the commandments?" Jesus
replied, "This is the first: Listen, Israel, the Lord our God
is the one Lord, and you must love the Lord your God with
all your heart, with all your soul, with all your mind, and
with all your strength. The second is this: You must love

your neighbour as yourself. There is no commandment greater than these." The scribe said to him, "Well spoken, Master; what you have said is true: that he is one and there is no other. To love him with all your heart, with all your understanding and strength, and to love your neighbour as yourself, this is far more important than any holocaust or sacrifice." Jesus, seeing how wisely he had spoken, said, "You are not far from the kingdom of God." And after that no one dared to question him any more.

This is the Gospel of the Lord.

SATURDAY

First Reading   (5:15–6:6)
A reading from the prophet Hosea
What I want is love, not sacrifice.

The Lord says this:

They will search for me in their misery:
"Come, let us return to the Lord.
He has torn us to pieces, but he will heal us;
he has struck us down, but he will bandage our wounds;
after a day or two he will bring us back to life,
on the third day he will raise us
and we shall live in his presence.
Let us set ourselves to know the Lord;
that he will come is as certain as the dawn,
he will come to us as showers come,
like spring rains watering the earth."
What am I to do with you, Ephraim?
What am I to do with you, Judah?
This love of yours is like a morning cloud,
like the dew that quickly disappears.

This is why I have torn them to pieces by the prophets,
why I slaughtered them with the words from my mouth,
his judgement will rise like the light,
since what I want is love, not sacrifice;
knowledge of God, not holocausts.

This is the word of the Lord.

Responsorial Psalm (Ps 50:3–4. 18–21. *R.* Hos 6:6)
Response
What I want is love, not sacrifice.

1. Have mercy on me, God, in your kindness.
In your compassion blot out my offence.
O wash me more and more from my guilt
and cleanse me from my sin. (*R.*)

2. For in sacrifice you take no delight,
burnt offering from me you would refuse,
my sacrifice, a contrite spirit.
A humbled, contrite heart you will not spurn. (*R.*)

3. In your goodness, show favour to Zion:
rebuild the walls of Jerusalem.
Then you will be pleased with lawful sacrifice,
burnt offerings wholly consumed. (*R.*)

Acclamation (Ps 94:8)

Harden not your hearts today,
but listen to the voice of the Lord.

Alternative Acclamations p. 842.

Gospel (18:9–14)
A reading from the holy Gospel according to Luke
The tax collector went home again at rights with God; the Pharisee did not.

Jesus spoke the following parable to some people who prided themselves on being virtuous and despised everyone else, "Two men went up to the Temple to pray, one a Pharisee, the other a tax collector. The Pharisee stood there and said this prayer to himself, 'I thank you, God, that I am not grasping, unjust, adulterous like the rest of mankind, and particularly that I am not like this tax collector here. I fast twice a week; I pay tithes on all I get.' The tax collector stood some distance away, not daring even to raise his eyes to heaven; but he beat his breast and said, 'God, be merciful to me, a sinner.' This man, I tell you, went home again at rights with God; the other did not. For everyone who exalts himself will be humbled, but the man who humbles himself will be exalted."

This is the Gospel of the Lord.

4th SUNDAY OF LENT
Year 1 (Year A)

First Reading   (16:1. 6–7. 10–13)
A reading from the first book of Samuel
David is anointed king of Israel.

The Lord said to Samuel, "Fill your horn with oil and go. I am sending you to Jesse of Bethlehem, for I have chosen myself a king among his sons." When Samuel arrived, he caught sight of Eliab and thought, "Surely the Lord's annointed one stands there before him," but the Lord said to Samuel, "Take no notice of his appearance or his height for I have rejected him; God does not see as man sees; man looks at appearances but the Lord looks at the heart." Jesse presented his seven sons to Samuel, but Samuel said to Jesse, "The Lord has not chosen these." He then asked Jesse, "Are these all the sons you have?" He answered, "There is still one left, the youngest; he is out looking after the sheep." Then Samuel said to Jesse, "Send for him; we will not sit down to eat until he comes." Jesse had him sent for, a boy of fresh complexion, with fine eyes and pleasant bearing. The Lord said, "Come, anoint him, for this is the one." At this, Samuel took the horn of oil and anointed him where he stood with his brothers; and the spirit of the Lord seized on David and stayed with him from that day on.

This is the word of the Lord.

Responsorial Psalm   (Ps 22. *R*. v. 1)

Response
The Lord is my shepherd;
there is nothing I shall want.

1. The Lord is my shepherd;
there is nothing I shall want.
Fresh and green are the pastures
where he gives me repose.
Near restful waters he leads me,
to revive my drooping spirit. (*R*.)

2. He guides me along the right path;
he is true to his name.
If I should walk in the valley of darkness
no evil would I fear.
You are there with your crook and your staff;
with these you give me comfort. (*R*.)

3. You have prepared a banquet for me
in the sight of my foes.
My head you have anointed with oil;
my cup is overflowing. (*R*.)

4. Surely goodness and kindness shall follow me
all the days of my life.
In the Lord's own house shall I dwell
for ever and ever. (*R*.)

Second Reading   (5:8–14)

A reading from the letter of St Paul to the Ephesians
Rise from the dead, and Christ will shine on you.

You were darkness once, but now you are light in the Lord;
be like children of light, for the effects of the light are seen
in complete goodness and right living and truth. Try to dis-
cover what the Lord wants of you, having nothing to do
with the futile works of darkness but exposing them by
contrast. The things which are done in secret are things that
people are ashamed even to speak of; but anything exposed
by the light will be illuminated and anything illuminated
turns into light. That is why it is said:

Wake up from your sleep,
rise from the dead,
and Christ will shine on you.

This is the word of the Lord.

Acclamation   (Jn 8:12)

I am the light of the world, says the Lord;
anyone who follows me will have the light of life.

Gospel   (9:1–41)

A reading from the holy Gospel according to John
*He went off and washed himself, and came away with his sight
restored.*

*As Jesus went along, he saw a man who had been blind
from birth.* His disciples asked him, "Rabbi, who sinned,
this man or his parents, for him to have been born blind?"
"Neither he nor his parents sinned," Jesus answered "he
was born blind so that the works of God might be displayed
in him.

"As long as the day lasts
I must carry out the work of the one who sent me;
the night will soon be here when no one can work.
As long as I am in the world
I am the light of the world."

Having said this, *he spat on the ground, made a paste with the spittle, put this over the eyes of the blind man and said to him, "Go and wash in the Pool of Siloam" (a name that means "sent"). So the blind man went off and washed himself, and came away with his sight restored.

His neighbours and people who earlier had seen him begging said, "Isn't this the man who used to sit and beg?" Some said, "Yes, it is the same one." Others said, "No, he only looks like him." The man himself said, "I am the man."* So they said to him, "Then how do your eyes come to be open?" "The man called Jesus" he answered "made a paste, daubed my eyes with it and said to me, 'Go and wash at Siloam'; so I went, and when I washed I could see." They asked, "Where is he?" "I don't know" he answered.

They brought the man who had been blind to the Pharisees. It had been a sabbath day when Jesus made the paste and opened the man's eyes, so when the Pharisees asked him how he had come to see, he said, "He put a paste on my eyes, and I washed, and I can see." Then some of the Pharisees said, "This man cannot be from God: he does not keep the sabbath." Others said, "How could a sinner produce signs like this?" And there was disagreement among them. So they spoke to the blind man again, "What have you to say about him yourself, now that he has opened your eyes?" "He is a prophet" replied the man.

However, the Jews would not believe that the man had been blind and had gained his sight, without first sending for his parents and asking them, "Is this man really your son who you say was born blind? If so, how is it that he is now able to see?" His parents answered, "We know he is our son and we know he was born blind, but we don't know how it is that he can see now, or who opened his eyes. He is old enough: let him speak for himself." His parents spoke like this out of fear of the Jews, who had already agreed to expel from the synagogue anyone who should acknowledge Jesus as the Christ. This was why his parents said, "He is old enough; ask him."

So the Jews again sent for the man and said to him, "Give glory to God! For our part, we know that this man is a sinner." The man answered, "I don't know if he is a sinner; I only know that I was blind and now I can see." They said to him, "What did he do to you? How did he open your eyes?" He replied, "I have told you once and you wouldn't listen. Why do you want to hear it all again? Do you want to become his disciples too?" At this they hurled abuse at him: "You can be his disciple," they said "we are disciples of Moses: we know that God spoke to Moses, but as for this man, we don't know where he comes from." The man replied, "Now here is an astonishing thing! He has opened my eyes, and you don't know where he comes from! We know that God doesn't listen to sinners, but God does listen to men who are devout and do his will. Ever since the world began it is unheard of for anyone to open the eyes of a man who was born blind; if this man were not from God, he couldn't do a thing." *"Are you trying to teach us," they replied "and you a sinner through and through, since you were born!" And they drove him away.

Jesus heard they had driven him away, and when he found him he said to him, "Do you believe in the Son of Man?" "Sir," the man replied "tell me who he is so that I may believe in him." Jesus said, "You are looking at him; he is speaking to you." The man said, "Lord, I believe", and worshipped him.*

Jesus said:

"It is for judgement
that I have come into this world,
so that those without sight may see
and those with sight turn blind."

Hearing this, some Pharisees who were present said to him,
"We are not blind, surely?" Jesus replied:

"Blind? If you were,
you would not be guilty,
but since you say, 'We see',
your guilt remains."
   This is the Gospel of the Lord.

*Shorter Form, verses 1.6–9. 13–17. 34–38. Read between *.

4th SUNDAY OF LENT
Year 2 (Year B)

The readings for Year 1 (Year A) may be used as alternative readings.

First Reading   (36:14–16. 19–23)
A reading from the second book of Chronicles
*The wrath and mercy of God are revealed in the exile and in
the release of his people.*

All the heads of the priesthood, and the people too, added
infidelity to infidelity, copying all the shameful practices
of the nations and defiling the Temple that the Lord had
consecrated for himself in Jerusalem. The Lord, the God
of their ancestors, tirelessly sent them messenger after messenger, since he wished to spare his people and his house.
But they ridiculed the messengers of God, they despised
his words, they laughed at his prophets, until at last the
wrath of the Lord rose so high against his people that there
was no further remedy.

   Their enemies burned down the Temple of God, demol-
ished the walls of Jerusalem, set fire to all its palaces, and

destroyed everything of value in it. The survivors were deported by Nebuchadnezzar to Babylon; they were to serve him and his sons until the kingdom of Persia came to power. This is how the word of the Lord was fulfilled that he spoke through Jeremiah, "Until this land has enjoyed its sabbath rest, until seventy years have gone by, it will keep sabbath throughout the days of its desolation."

And in the first year of Cyrus king of Persia, to fulfill the word of the Lord that was spoken through Jeremiah, the Lord roused the spirit of Cyrus king of Persia to issue a proclamation and to have it publicly displayed throughout his kingdom: "Thus speaks Cyrus king of Persia, 'The Lord, the God of heaven, has given me all the kingdoms of the earth; he has ordered me to build him a Temple in Jerusalem, in Judah. Whoever there is among you of all his people, may his God be with him! Let him go up.' "

This is the word of the Lord.

Responsorial Psalm   (Ps 136. *R*. v. 6)

Response
O let my tongue
cleave to my mouth
if I remember you not!

1. By the rivers of Babylon
there we sat and wept,
remembering Zion;
on the poplars that grew there
we hung up our harps. (*R*.)

2. For it was there that they asked us,
our captors, for songs,
our oppressors, for joy.
"Sing to us," they said,
"one of Zion's songs." (*R*.)

3. O how could we sing
the song of the Lord
on alien soil?
If I forget you, Jerusalem,
let my right hand wither! (*R.*)

4. O let my tongue
cleave to my mouth
if I remember you not,
if I prize not Jerusalem
above all my joys! (*R.*)

Second Reading   (2:4–10)

A reading from the letter of St Paul to the Ephesians
You who were dead through your sins have been saved through grace.

God loved us with so much love that he was generous with his mercy: when we were dead through our sins, he brought us to life with Christ – it is through grace that you have been saved – and raised us up with him and gave us a place with him in heaven, in Christ Jesus.

This was to show for all ages to come, through his goodness towards us in Christ Jesus, how infinitely rich he is in grace. Because it is by grace that you have been saved, through faith; not by anything of your own, but by a gift from God; not by anything that you have done, so that nobody can claim the credit. We are God's work of art, created in Christ Jesus to live the good life as from the beginning he had meant us to live it.

This is the word of the Lord.

Acclamation   (Jn 3:16)

God loved the world so much that he gave his only Son; everyone who believes in him has eternal life.

Gospel   (3:14–21)

A reading from the holy Gospel according to John

God sent his Son so that through him the world might be saved.

Jesus said to Nicodemus:

The Son of Man must be lifted up
as Moses lifted up the serpent in the desert,
so that everyone who believes may have eternal life in him.
Yes, God loved the world so much
that he gave his only Son,
so that everyone who believes in him may not be lost
but may have eternal life.
For God sent his Son into the world
not to condemn the world,
but so that through him the world might be saved.
No one who believes in him will be condemned;
but whoever refuses to believe is condemned already,
because he has refused to believe
in the name of God's only Son.
On these grounds is sentence pronounced:
that though the light has come into the world
men have shown they prefer
darkness to the light
because their deeds were evil.
And indeed, everybody who does wrong
hates the light and avoids it,
for fear his actions should be exposed;
but the man who lives by the truth
comes out into the light,
so that it may be plainly seen that what he does is done in
    God.

    This is the Gospel of the Lord.

4th SUNDAY OF LENT
Year 3 (Year C)

The readings for Year 1 (Year A) may be used as alternative readings.

First Reading   (5:9–12)
A reading from the book of Joshua
The People of God keep the Passover on their entry into the promised land.

The Lord said to Joshua, "Today I have taken the shame of Egypt away from you."

The Israelites pitched their camp at Gilgal and kept the Passover there on the fourteenth day of the month, at evening in the plain of Jericho. On the morrow of the Passover they tasted the produce of that country, unleavened bread and roasted ears of corn, that same day. From that time, from their first eating of the produce of that country, the manna stopped falling. And having manna no longer, the Israelites fed from that year onwards on what the land of Canaan yielded.

This is the word of the Lord.

Responsorial Psalm   (Ps 33:2–7. *R.* v. 9)
Response
Taste and see that the Lord is good.

1. I will bless the Lord at all times,
his praise always on my lips;
in the Lord my soul shall make its boast.
The humble shall hear and be glad. (*R.*)

2. Glorify the Lord with me.
Together let us praise his name.
I sought the Lord and he answered me;
from all my terrors he set me free. (*R.*)

3. Look towards him and be radiant;
let your faces not be abashed.
This poor man called; the Lord heard him
and rescued him from all his distress. (*R.*)

Second Reading   (5:17–21)
A reading from the second letter of St Paul to the
Corinthians
God reconciled us to himself through Christ.

And for anyone who is in Christ, there is a new creation;
the old creation has gone, and now the new one is here. It
is all God's work. It was God who reconciled us to himself
through Christ and gave us the work of handing on this
reconciliation. In other words, God in Christ was reconciling the world to himself, not holding men's faults against
them, and he has entrusted to us the news that they are
reconciled. So we are ambassadors for Christ; it is as
though God were appealing through us, and the appeal that
we make in Christ's name is: be reconciled to God. For our
sake God made the sinless one into sin, so that in him we
might become the goodness of God.

This is the word of the Lord.

Acclamation   (Lk 15:18)
I will leave this place and go to my father and say:
"Father, I have sinned against heaven and against you."

Gospel   (15:1–3. 11–32)
A reading from the holy Gospel according to Luke
Your brother here was dead and has come to life.

The tax collectors and the sinners were all seeking the company of Jesus to hear what he had to say, and the Pharisees
and the scribes complained. "This man" they said "welcomes sinners and eats with them." So he spoke this parable
to them:

"A man had two sons. The younger said to his father, 'Father, let me have the share of the estate that would come to me.' So the father divided the property between them. A few days later, the younger son got together everything he had and left for a distant country where he squandered his money on a life of debauchery.

"When he had spent it all, that country experienced a severe famine, and now he began to feel the pinch, so he hired himself out to one of the local inhabitants who put him on his farm to feed the pigs. And he would willingly have filled his belly with the husks the pigs were eating but no one offered him anything. Then he came to his senses and said, 'How many of my father's paid servants have more food than they want, and here am I dying of hunger! I will leave this place and go to my father and say: Father, I have sinned against heaven and against you; I no longer deserve to be called your son; treat me as one of your paid servants.' So he left the place and went back to his father.

"While he was still a long way off, his father saw him and was moved with pity. He ran to the boy, clasped him in his arms and kissed him tenderly. Then his son said, 'Father, I have sinned against heaven and against you. I no longer deserve to be called your son.' But the father said to his servants, 'Quick! Bring out the best robe and put it on him; put a ring on his finger and sandals on his feet. Bring the calf we have been fattening, and kill it; we are going to have a feast, a celebration, because this son of mine was dead and has come back to life; he was lost and is found.' And they began to celebrate.

"Now the elder son was out in the fields, and on his way back, as he drew near the house, he could hear music and dancing. Calling one of the servants he asked what it was all about. 'Your brother has come' replied the servant 'and your father has killed the calf we had fattened because he has got him back safe and sound.' He was angry then and refused to go in, and his father came out to plead with him;

but he answered his father, 'Look, all these years I have slaved for you and never once disobeyed your orders, yet you never offered me so much as a kid for me to celebrate with my friends. But, for this son of yours, when he comes back after swallowing up your property – he and his women – you kill the calf we had been fattening.'

"The father said, 'My son, you are with me always and all I have is yours. But it is only right we should celebrate and rejoice, because your brother here was dead and has come to life; he was lost and is found.' "

This is the Gospel of the Lord.

Alternative Readings

The following readings may be used instead of the proper ones any day this week, especially in Years 2 (B) and 3 (C) when the Gospel of the man born blind is not read on the 4th Sunday.

First Reading   (7:7–9)

A reading from the prophet Micah
Though I live in darkness, the Lord is my light.

For my part, I look to the Lord,
my hope is in the God who will save me;
my God will hear me.
Do not gloat over me, my enemy:
though I have fallen, I shall rise;
though I live in darkness,
the Lord is my light.
I must suffer the anger of the Lord,
for I have sinned against him,
until he takes up my cause
and rights my wrongs;
he will bring me out into the light
and I shall rejoice to see the rightness of his ways.

This is the word of the Lord.

Responsorial Psalm   (Ps 26:1. 7–9. 13–14. *R*. v. 1)

Response

The Lord is my light and my help.

1. The Lord is my light and my help;
whom shall I fear?
The Lord is the stronghold of my life;
before whom shall I shrink? (*R*.)

2. O Lord, hear my voice when I call;
have mercy and answer.
Of you my heart has spoken:
"Seek his face." (*R*.)

3. It is your face, O Lord, that I seek;
hide not your face.
Dismiss not your servant in anger;
you have been my help. (*R*.)

4. I am sure I shall see the Lord's goodness
in the land of the living.
Hope in him, hold firm and take heart.
Hope in the Lord! (*R*.)

Acclamation   (Jn 8:12)

I am the light of the world, says the Lord, whoever believes
in me will never die.

Alternative Acclamations p. 842.

GOSPEL. John 9:1–41. As for 4th Sunday of Lent, Year 1 (Year A),
p. 525.

MONDAY

First Reading   (65:17–21)

A reading from the prophet Isaiah

*No more will the sound of weeping or the sound of cries be
heard.*

Thus says the Lord: Now I create new heavens and a new
earth, and the past will not be remembered, and will come
no more to men's minds. Be glad and rejoice for ever and

ever for what I am creating, because I now create Jerusalem
"Joy" and her people "Gladness". I shall rejoice over Jerusalem and exult in my people. No more will the sound of
weeping or the sound of cries be heard in her; in her, no
more will be found the infant living a few days only, or the
old man not living to the end of his days. To die at the age
of a hundred will be dying young; not to live to be a hundred
will be the sign of a curse. They will build houses and in-
habit them, plant vineyards and eat their fruit.

    This is the word of the Lord.

Responsorial Psalm   (Ps 29:2. 4–6. 11–13. R. v. 2)
Response
I will praise you, Lord, you have rescued me.

1. I will praise you, Lord, you have rescued me
and have not let my enemies rejoice over me.
O Lord, you have raised my soul from the dead,
restored me to life from those who sink into the grave. (R.)

2. Sing psalms to the Lord, you who love him,
give thanks to his holy name.
His anger lasts but a moment; his favour through life.
At night there are tears, but joy comes with dawn. (R.)

3. The Lord listened and had pity.
The Lord came to my help.
For me you have changed my mourning into dancing;
O Lord my God, I will thank you for ever. (R.)

Acclamation   (Ps 129:5. 7)
My soul is waiting for the Lord,
I count on his word,
because with the Lord there is mercy
and fullness of redemption.

Alternative Acclamations p. 842.

Gospel   (4:43–54)

A reading from the holy Gospel according to John
Go home, your son will live.

Jesus left Samaria for Galilee. He himself had declared that there is no respect for a prophet in his own country, but on his arrival the Galileans received him well, having seen all that he had done at Jerusalem during the festival which they too had attended.

He went again to Cana in Galilee, where he had changed the water into wine. Now there was a court official there whose son was ill at Capernaum and, hearing that Jesus had arrived in Galilee from Judaea, he went and asked him to come and cure his son as he was at the point of death. Jesus said, "So you will not believe unless you see signs and portents!" "Sir," answered the official "come down before my child dies." "Go home," said Jesus "your son will live." The man believed what Jesus had said and started on his way; and while he was still on the journey back his servants met him with the news that his boy was alive. He asked them when the boy had begun to recover. "The fever left him yesterday" they said "at the seventh hour." The father realised that this was exactly the time when Jesus had said, "Your son will live"; and he and all his household believed.

This was the second sign given by Jesus, on his return from Judaea to Galilee.

This is the Gospel of the Lord.

TUESDAY

First Reading   (47:1–9. 12)

A reading from the prophet Ezekiel
I saw a stream of water coming from the Temple, bringing life to all wherever it flowed.

The angel brought me back to the entrance of the Temple, where a stream came out from under the Temple threshold and flowed eastwards, since the Temple faced east. The water flowed from under the right side of the Temple, south of the altar. He took me out by the north gate and led me right round outside as far as the outer east gate where the water flowed out on the right-hand side. The man went to the east holding his measuring line and measured off a thousand cubits; he then made me wade across the stream; the water reached my ankles. He measured off another thousand and made me wade across the stream again; the water reached my knees. He measured off another thousand and made me wade across again; the water reached my waist. He measured off another thousand; it was now a river which I could not cross; the stream had swollen and was now deep water, a river impossible to cross. He then said, "Do you see, son of man?" He took me further, then brought me back to the bank of the river. When I got back, there were many trees on each bank of the river. He said, "This water flows east down to the Arabah and to the sea; and flowing into the sea it makes its waters wholesome. Wherever the river flows, all living creatures teeming in it will live. Fish will be very plentiful, for wherever the water goes it brings health, and life teems wherever the river flows. Along the river, on either bank, will grow every kind of fruit tree with leaves that never wither and fruit that never fails; they will bear new fruit every month, because this water comes from the sanctuary. And their fruit will be good to eat and the leaves medicinal."

This is the word of the Lord.

Responsorial Psalm   (Ps 45:2–3. 5–6. 8–9. *R.* v. 8)
Response
The Lord of hosts is with us:
the God of Jacob is our stronghold.

1. God is for us a refuge and strength,
a helper close at hand, in time of distress:
so we shall not fear though the earth should rock,
though the mountains fall into the depths of the sea. (*R.*)

2. The waters of a river give joy to God's city,
the holy place where the Most High dwells.
God is within, it cannot be shaken;
God will help it at the dawning of the day. (*R.*)

3. The Lord of hosts is with us:
the God of Jacob is our stronghold.
Come, consider the works of the Lord
the redoubtable deeds he has done on the earth. (*R.*)

Acclamation   (Ps 50:12. 14)

A pure heart create for me, O God,
and give me again the joy of your help.

Alternative Acclamations p. 842.

Gospel   (5:1–3. 5–16)
A reading from the holy Gospel according to John
The man was cured at once.

Some time after this there was a Jewish festival, and Jesus
went up to Jerusalem. Now at the Sheep Pool in Jerusalem
there is a building, called Bethzatha in Hebrew, consisting
of five porticos; and under these were crowds of sick people
– blind, lame, paralysed. One man there had an illness
which had lasted thirty-eight years, and when Jesus saw
him lying there and knew he had been in this condition for
a long time, he said, "Do you want to be well again?" "Sir,"
replied the sick man "I have no one to put me into the pool
when the water is disturbed; and while I am still on the way,
someone else gets there before me." Jesus said, "Get up,

pick up your sleeping-mat and walk." The man was cured
at once, and he picked up his mat and walked away.

Now that day happened to be the sabbath, so the Jews
said to the man who had been cured, "It is the sabbath; you
are not allowed to carry your sleeping-mat." He replied,
"But the man who cured me told me, 'Pick up your mat and
walk.' " They asked, "Who is the man who said to you, 'Pick
up your mat and walk'?" The man had no idea who it
was, since Jesus had disappeared into the crowd that filled
the place. After a while Jesus met him in the Temple and
said, "Now you are well again, be sure not to sin any more,
or something worse may happen to you." The man went
back and told the Jews that it was Jesus who had cured him.
It was because he did things like this on the sabbath that
the Jews began to persecute Jesus.

This is the Gospel of the Lord.

WEDNESDAY

First Reading   (49:8–15)

A reading from the prophet Isaiah
*I have appointed you as covenant of the people to restore the
land.*

Thus says the Lord:
At the favourable time I will answer you,
on the day of salvation I will help you.
(I have formed you and have appointed you
as covenant of the people.)
I will restore the land
and assign you the estates that lie waste.
I will say to the prisoners, "Come out",
to those who are in darkness, "Show yourselves".

On every roadway they will graze,
and each bare height shall be their pasture.

They will never hunger or thirst,
scorching wind and sun shall never plague them;
for he who pities them will lead them
and guide them to springs of water.
I will make a highway of all the mountains,
and the high roads shall be banked up.

Some are on their way from afar,
others from the north and the west,
others from the land of Sinim.
Shout for joy, you heavens; exult, you earth!
Your mountains, break into happy cries!
For the Lord consoles his people
and takes pity on those who are afflicted.

For Zion was saying, "The Lord has abandoned me,
the Lord has forgotten me."
Does a woman forget her baby at the breast,
or fail to cherish the son of her womb?
Yet even if these forget,
I will never forget you.

This is the word of the Lord.

Responsorial Psalm (Ps 144:8–9. 13–14. 17–18. *R*. v. 8)
Response
The Lord is kind and full of compassion.

1. The Lord is kind and full of compassion,
slow to anger, abounding in love.
How good is the Lord to all,
compassionate to all his creatures. (*R*.)

2. The Lord is faithful in all his words
and loving in all his deeds.
The Lord supports all who fall
and raises all who are bowed down. (*R*.)

3. The Lord is just in all his ways
and loving in all his deeds.
He is close to all who call him,
who call on him from their hearts. (*R.*)

Acclamation   (Jn 3:16)

God loved the world so much that he gave his only Son;
everyone who believes in him has eternal life.

Alternative Acclamations p. 842.

Gospel   (5:17–30)

A reading from the holy Gospel according to John

*As the Father raises the dead and gives them life, so the Son
gives life to anyone he chooses.*

Jesus answered the Jews: "My Father goes on working,
and so do I." But that only made the Jews even more intent
on killing him, because, not content with breaking the sabbath, he spoke of God as his own Father, and so made himself God's equal.

To this accusation Jesus replied:

"I tell you most solemnly,
the Son can do nothing by himself;
he can do only what he sees the Father doing:
and whatever the Father does the Son does too.
For the Father loves the Son
and shows him everything he does himself,
and he will show him even greater things than these,
works that will astonish you.
Thus, as the Father raises the dead and gives them life,
so the Son gives life to anyone he chooses;
for the Father judges no one;
he has entrusted all judgement to the Son,
so that all may honour the Son
as they honour the Father.

Whoever refuses honour to the Son
refuses honour to the Father who sent him.
I tell you most solemnly,
whoever listens to my words,
and believes in the one who sent me,
has eternal life;
without being brought to judgement
he has passed from death to life.
I tell you most solemnly,
the hour will come – in fact it is here already –
when the dead will hear the voice of the Son of God,
and all who hear it will live.
For the Father, who is the source of life,
has made the Son the source of life;
and, because he is the Son of Man,
has appointed him supreme judge.
Do not be surprised at this,
for the hour is coming
when the dead will leave their graves
at the sound of his voice:
those who did good
will rise again to life;
and those who did evil, to condemnation.
I can do nothing by myself;
I can only judge as I am told to judge,
and my judging is just,
because my aim is to do not my own will,
but the will of him who sent me."

This is the Gospel of the Lord.

THURSDAY

First Reading   (32:7–14)
A reading from the book of Exodus
Do not bring this disaster on your people.

Then the Lord spoke to Moses, "Go down now, because your people whom you brought out of Egypt have apostasised. They have been quick to leave the way I marked out for them; they have made themselves a calf of molten metal and have worshipped it and offered it sacrifice. 'Here is your God, Israel,' they have cried 'who brought you up from the land of Egypt!' " The Lord said to Moses, "I can see how headstrong these people are! Leave me, now, my wrath shall blaze out against them and devour them; of you, however, I will make a great nation."

But Moses pleaded with the Lord his God. "Lord," he said "why should your wrath blaze out against this people of yours whom you brought out of the land of Egypt with arm outstretched and mighty hand? Why let the Egyptians say, 'Ah, it was in treachery that he brought them out, to do them to death in the mountains and wipe them off the face of the earth'? Leave your burning wrath; relent and do not bring this disaster on your people. Remember Abraham, Isaac and Jacob, your servants to whom by your own self you swore and made this promise: I will make your offspring as many as the stars of heaven, and all this land which I promised I will give to your descendants, and it shall be their heritage for ever." So the Lord relented and did not bring on his people the disaster he had threatened.

This is the word of the Lord.

Responsorial Psalm   (Ps 105:19–23. *R*. v. 4)

Response
O Lord, remember me
out of the love you have for your people.

1. They fashioned a calf at Horeb
and worshipped an image of metal,
exchanging the God who was their glory
for the image of a bull that eats grass. (*R*.)

2. They forgot the God who was their saviour,
who had done such great things in Egypt,
such portents in the land of Ham,
such marvels at the Red Sea. (*R.*)

3. For this he said he would destroy them,
but Moses, the man he had chosen,
stood in the breach before him,
to turn back his anger from destruction. (*R.*)

Acclamation   (Jn 6:64. 69)

Your words are spirit, Lord, and they are life; you have the
message of eternal life.

Alternative Acclamations p. 842.

Gospel   (5:31–47)

A reading from the holy Gospel according to John
You place your hope in Moses, and Moses will be your accuser.

Jesus said to the Jews:

"Were I to testify on my own behalf,
my testimony would not be valid;
but there is another witness who can speak on my behalf,
and I know that his testimony is valid.
You sent messengers to John,
and he gave his testimony to the truth:
not that I depend on human testimony;
no, it is for your salvation that I speak of this.
John was a lamp alight and shining
and for a time you were content to enjoy the light that he
    gave.
But my testimony is greater than John's:
the works my Father has given me to carry out,
these same works of mine
testify that the Father has sent me.

Besides, the Father who sent me
bears witness to me himself.
You have never heard his voice,
you have never seen his shape,
and his word finds no home in you
because you do not believe
in the one he has sent.

"You study the scriptures,
believing that in them you have eternal life;
now these same scriptures testify to me,
and yet you refuse to come to me for life!
As for human approval, this means nothing to me.
Besides, I know you too well:
you have no love of God in you.
I have come in the name of my Father
and you refuse to accept me;
if someone else comes in his own name
you will accept him.

"How can you believe,
since you look to one another for approval
and are not concerned
with the approval that comes from the one God?
Do not imagine that I am going to accuse you before the
    Father:
you place your hopes on Moses,
and Moses will be your accuser.
If you really believed him
you would believe me too,
since it was I that he was writing about;
but if you refuse to believe what he wrote,
how can you believe what I say?"

    This is the Gospel of the Lord.

FRIDAY

First Reading   (2:1. 12–22)

A reading from the book of Wisdom
Let us condemn him to a shameful death.

The godless say to themselves, with their misguided
    reasoning:
"Let us lie in wait for the virtuous man, since he annoys us
and opposes our way of life,
reproaches us for our breaches of the law
and accuses us of playing false to our upbringing.
He claims to have knowledge of God,
and calls himself a son of the Lord.
Before us he stands, a reproof to our way of thinking,
the very sight of him weighs our spirits down;
his way of life is not like other men's,
the paths he treads are unfamiliar.
In his opinion we are counterfeit;
he holds aloof from our doings as though from filth;
he proclaims the final end of the virtuous as happy
and boasts of having God for his father.

Let us see if what he says is true,
let us observe what kind of end he himself will have.
If the virtuous man is God's son, God will take his part
and rescue him from the clutches of his enemies.
Let us test him with cruelty and with torture,
and thus explore this gentleness of his
and put his endurance to the proof.
Let us condemn him to a shameful death
since he will be looked after – we have his word for it."
This is the way they reason, but they are misled,
their malice makes them blind.
They do not know the hidden things of God,
they have no hope that holiness will be rewarded,
they can see no reward for blameless souls.

  This is the word of the Lord.

Responsorial Psalm   (Ps 33:16. 18. 19–21. 23. *R.* v. 19)

Response
The Lord is close to the broken-hearted.

1. The Lord turns his face against the wicked
to destroy their remembrance from the earth.
The just call and the Lord hears
and rescues them in all their distress. (*R.*)

2. The Lord is close to the broken-hearted;
those whose spirit is crushed he will save.
Many are the trials of the just man
but from them all the Lord will rescue him. (*R.*)

3. He will keep guard over all his bones,
not one of his bones shall be broken.
The Lord ransoms the souls of his servants.
Those who hide in him shall not be condemned. (*R.*)

Acclamation   (Joel 2:12–13)

Now, now – it is the Lord who speaks –
come back to me with all your heart,
for I am all tenderness and compassion.

Alternative Acclamations p. 842.

Gospel   (7:1–2. 10. 25–30)
A reading from the holy Gospel according to John
They would have arrested him, but his time had not yet come.

After this Jesus stayed in Galilee; he could not stay in
Judaea, because the Jews were out to kill him.
    As the Jewish feast of Tabernacles drew near, after his
brothers had left for the festival, Jesus went up as well,
but quite privately, without drawing attention to himself.

Meanwhile some of the people of Jerusalem were saying, "Isn't this the man they want to kill? And here he is, speaking freely, and they have nothing to say to him! Can it be true the authorities have made up their minds that he is the Christ? Yet we all know where he comes from, but when the Christ appears no one will know where he comes from."

Then, as Jesus taught in the Temple, he cried out:

"Yes, you know me and you know where I came from.
Yet I have not come of myself:
no, there is one who sent me and I really come from him,
and you do not know him,
but I know him
because I have come from him
and it was he who sent me."

They would have arrested him then, but because his time had not yet come no one laid a hand on him.

This is the Gospel of the Lord.

SATURDAY

First Reading   (11:18–20)
A reading from the prophet Jeremiah
I was like a trustful lamb being led to the slaughter-house.

The Lord revealed it to me; I was warned. Lord, that was when you opened my eyes to their scheming. I for my part was like a trustful lamb being led to the slaughter-house, not knowing the schemes they were plotting against me. "Let us destroy the tree in its strength, let us cut him off from the land of the living, so that his name may be quickly forgotten!"
But you, Lord of hosts, who pronounce a just sentence, who probe the loins and heart,

let me see the vengeance you will take on them,
for I have committed my cause to you.

This is the word of the Lord.

Responsorial Psalm (Ps 7:2–3. 9–12. *R.* v. 2)
Response
Lord God, I take refuge in you.

1. Lord God, I take refuge in you.
From my pursuer save me and rescue me,
lest he tear me to pieces like a lion
and drag me off with no one to rescue me. (*R.*)

2. Give judgement for me, Lord; I am just
and innocent of heart.
Put an end to the evil of the wicked!
Make the just stand firm,
you who test mind and heart,
O just God! (*R.*)

3. God is the shield that protects me,
who saves the upright of heart.
God is a just judge
slow to anger;
but he threatens the wicked every day. (*R.*)

Acclamation (Ez 33:11)
I take pleasure, not in the death of a wicked man – it is the
Lord who speaks – but in the turning back of a wicked man
who changes his ways to win life.
Alternative Acclamations p. 842.

Gospel   (7:40–52)

A reading from the holy Gospel according to John
Would the Christ be from Galilee?

Several people who had been listening to Jesus said, "Surely he must be the prophet", and some said, "He is the Christ", but others said, "Would the Christ be from Galilee? Does not scripture say that the Christ must be descended from David and come from the town of Bethlehem?" So the people could not agree about him. Some would have liked to arrest him, but no one actually laid hands on him.

The police went back to the chief priests and Pharisees who said to them, "Why haven't you brought him?" The police replied, "There has never been anybody who has spoken like him." "So" the Pharisees answered "you have been led astray as well? Have any of the authorities believed in him? Any of the Pharisees? This rabble knows nothing about the Law – they are damned." One of them, Nicodemus – the same man who had come to Jesus earlier – said to them, "But surely the Law does not allow us to pass judgement on a man without giving him a hearing and discovering what he is about?" To this they answered, "Are you a Galilean too? Go into the matter, and see for yourself: prophets do not come out of Galilee."

This is the Gospel of the Lord.

5th SUNDAY OF LENT
Year 1 (Year A)

First Reading   (37:12–14)

A reading from the prophet Ezekiel
I shall put my spirit in you, and you will live.

The Lord says this: I am now going to open your graves; I mean to raise you from your graves, my people, and lead you back to the soil of Israel. And you will know that I am the Lord, when I open your graves and raise you from your graves, my people. And I shall put my spirit in you, and you will live, and I shall resettle you on your own soil; and you will know that I, the Lord, have said and done this – it is the Lord who speaks.

This is the word of the Lord.

Responsorial Psalm (Ps 129. *R.* v. 7)

Response
With the Lord there is mercy
and fullness of redemption.

1. Out of the depths I cry to you, O Lord,
Lord, hear my voice!
O let your ears be attentive
to the voice of my pleading. (*R.*)

2. If you, O Lord, should mark our guilt,
Lord, who would survive?
But with you is found forgiveness:
for this we revere you. (*R.*)

3. My soul is waiting for the Lord,
I count on his word.
My soul is longing for the Lord
more than watchman for daybreak
(Let the watchman count on daybreak
and Israel on the Lord.) (*R.*)

4. Because with the Lord there is mercy
and fullness of redemption,
Israel indeed he will redeem
from all its iniquity. (*R.*)

Second Reading   (8:8–11)

A reading from the letter of St Paul to the Romans
The Spirit of him who raised Jesus from the dead is living in you.

People who are interested only in unspiritual things can never be pleasing to God. Your interests, however, are not in the unspiritual, but in the spiritual, since the Spirit of God has made his home in you. In fact, unless you possessed the Spirit of Christ you would not belong to him. Though your body may be dead it is because of sin, but if Christ is in you then your spirit is life itself because you have been justified; and if the Spirit of him who raised Jesus from the dead is living in you, then he who raised Jesus from the dead will give life to your own mortal bodies through his Spirit living in you.

This is the word of the Lord.

Acclamation   (Jn 11:25. 26)

I am the resurrection and the life, says the Lord;
whoever believes in me will never die.

Gospel   (11:1–45)

A reading from the holy Gospel according to John
I am the resurrection and the life.

There was a man named Lazarus who lived in the village of Bethany with the two sisters, Mary and Martha, and he was ill. It was the same Mary, the sister of the sick man Lazarus, who anointed the Lord with ointment and wiped his feet with her hair. *The sisters, Martha and Mary, sent this message to Jesus, "Lord, the man you love is ill." On receiving the message, Jesus said, "This sickness will end not in death but in God's glory, and through it the Son of God will be glorified."

Jesus loved Martha and her sister and Lazarus, yet when he heard that Lazarus was ill he stayed where he was for two more days before saying to the disciples, "Let us go to Judea."*

The disciples said, "Rabbi, it is not long since the Jews wanted to stone you; are you going back again?" Jesus replied:

"Are there not twelve hours in the day?
A man can walk in the daytime without stumbling
because he has the light of this world to see by;
but if he walks at night he stumbles,
because there is no light to guide him".

He said that and then added, "Our friend Lazarus is resting, I am going to wake him." The disciples said to him, "Lord, if he is able to rest he is sure to get better." The phrase Jesus used referred to the death of Lazarus, but they thought that by "rest" he meant "sleep", so Jesus put it plainly, "Lazarus is dead; and for your sake I am glad I was not there because now you will believe. But let us go to him." Then Thomas – known as the Twin – said to the other disciples, "Let us go too, and die with him."

*On arriving, Jesus found that Lazarus had been in the tomb for four days already. Bethany is only about two miles from Jerusalem, and many Jews had come to Martha and Mary to sympathise with them over their brother. When Martha heard that Jesus had come she went to meet him. Mary remained sitting in the house. Martha said to Jesus, "If you had been here, my brother would not have died, but I know that, even now, whatever you ask of God, he will grant you." "Your brother" said Jesus to her "will rise again." Martha said, "I know he will rise again at the resurrection on the last day." Jesus said:

"I am the resurrection.
If anyone believes in me, even though he dies he
    will live,
and whoever lives and believes in me
will never die.
Do you believe this?"

"Yes, Lord," she said "I believe that you are the Christ, the Son of God, the one who was to come into this world."*

When she had said this, she went and called her sister Mary, saying in a low voice, "The Master is here and wants to see you." Hearing this, Mary got up quickly and went to him. Jesus had not yet come into the village; he was still at the place where Martha had met him. When the Jews who were in the house sympathising with Mary saw her get up so quickly and go out, they followed her, thinking that she was going to the tomb to weep there.

Mary went to Jesus, and as soon as she saw him she threw herself at his feet, saying, "Lord, if you had been here, my brother would not have died." At the sight of her tears, and those of the Jews who followed her, *Jesus said in great distress, with a sigh that came straight from the heart, "Where have you put him?" They said, "Lord, come and see." Jesus wept; and the Jews said, "See how much he loved him!" But there were some who remarked, "He opened the eyes of the blind man, could he not have prevented this man's death?" Still sighing, Jesus reached the tomb: it was a cave with a stone to close the opening. Jesus said, "Take the stone away." Martha said to him, "Lord, by now he will smell; this is the fourth day." Jesus replied, "Have I not told you that if you believe you will see the glory of God?" So they took away the stone. Then Jesus lifted his eyes and said:

"Father, I thank you for hearing my prayer.
I know indeed that you always hear me,
but I speak

for the sake of all these who stand round me,
so that they may believe it was you who sent me."

When he had said this, he cried in a loud voice, "Lazarus, here! Come out!" The dead man came out, his feet and hands bound with bands of stuff and a cloth round his face. Jesus said to them, "Unbind him, let him go free."

Many of the Jews who had come to visit Mary and had seen what he did believed in him.

This is the Gospel of the Lord.*

*Shorter Form, verses 3–7. 17. 20. 27. 33–45. Read between *.

5th SUNDAY OF LENT
Year 2 (Year B)

The readings for Year 1 (Year A) may be used as alternative readings.

First Reading   (31:31–34)

A reading from the prophet Jeremiah
I will make a new covenant and never call their sin to mind.

See, the days are coming – it is the Lord who speaks – when I will make a new covenant with the House of Israel (and the House of Judah), but not a covenant like the one I made with their ancestors on the day I took them by the hand to bring them out of the land of Egypt. They broke that covenant of mine, so I had to show them who was master. It is the Lord who speaks. No, this is the covenant I will make with the House of Israel when those days arrive – it is the Lord who speaks. Deep within them I will plant my Law, writing it on their hearts. Then I will be their God and they shall be my people. There will be no further need for neighbour to try to teach neighbour, or brother to say to brother, "Learn to know the Lord!" No, they will all know me, the least no less than the greatest – it is the Lord who speaks – since I will forgive their iniquity and never call their sin to mind.

This is the word of the Lord.

Responsorial Psalm   (Ps 50:3–4. 12–15. *R*. v. 12)

Response
A pure heart create for me, O God.

1. Have mercy on me, God, in your kindness.
In your compassion blot out my offence.
O wash me more and more from my guilt
and cleanse me from my sin. (*R*.)

2. A pure heart create for me, O God,
put a steadfast spirit within me.
Do not cast me away from your presence,
nor deprive me of your holy spirit. (*R*.)

3. Give me again the joy of your help;
with a spirit of fervour sustain me,
that I may teach transgressors your ways
and sinners may return to you. (*R*.)

Second Reading   (5:7–9)
A reading from the letter to the Hebrews
He learnt to obey and became the source of eternal salvation.

During his life on earth, Christ offered up prayer and en-treaty, aloud and in silent tears, to the one who had the power to save him out of death, and he submitted so humbly that his prayer was heard. Although he was Son, he learnt to obey through suffering; but having been made perfect, he became for all who obey him the source of eter-nal salvation.

This is the word of the Lord.

Acclamation   (Jn 12:26)
If a man serves me, says the Lord, he must follow me,
wherever I am, my servant will be there too.

Gospel   (12:20–33)

A reading from the holy Gospel according to John

If a grain of wheat falls on the ground and dies, it yields a rich harvest.

Among those who went up to worship at the festival were some Greeks. These approached Philip, who came from Bethsaida in Galilee, and put this request to him, "Sir, we should like to see Jesus." Philip went to tell Andrew, and Andrew and Philip together went to tell Jesus.

Jesus replied to them:

"Now the hour has come
for the Son of Man to be glorified.
I tell you, most solemnly,
unless a wheat grain falls on the ground and dies,
it remains only a single grain;
but if it dies,
it yields a rich harvest.
Anyone who loves his life loses it;
anyone who hates his life in this world
will keep it for the eternal life.
If a man serves me, he must follow me,
wherever I am, my servant will be there too.
If anyone serves me, my Father will honour him.
Now my soul is troubled.
What shall I say:
Father, save me from this hour?
But it was for this very reason that I have come to this hour.
Father, glorify your name!"

A voice came from heaven, "I have glorified it, and I will glorify it again."

People standing by, who heard this, said it was a clap of thunder; others said, "It was an angel speaking to him." Jesus answered, "It was not for my sake that this voice came, but for yours.

"Now sentence is being passed on this world;
now the prince of this world is to be overthrown.
And when I am lifted up from the earth,
I shall draw all men to myself."
By these words he indicated the kind of death he would die.
  This is the Gospel of the Lord.

5th SUNDAY OF LENT
Year 3 (Year C)

The readings for Year 1 may be used as alternative readings.

First Reading   (43:16–21)
A reading from the prophet Isaiah
See, I am doing a new deed, and I will give my chosen people drink.

Thus says the Lord,
who made a way through the sea,
a path in the great waters;
who put chariots and horse in the field
and a powerful army,
which lay there never to rise again,
snuffed out, put out like a wick:

No need to recall the past,
no need to think about what was done before.
See, I am doing a new deed,
even now it comes to light; can you not see it?
Yes, I am making a road in the wilderness,
paths in the wilds.

The wild beasts will honour me,
jackals and ostriches,
because I am putting water in the wilderness
(rivers in the wild)
to give my chosen people drink.

The people I have formed for myself
will sing my praises.

   This is the word of the Lord.

Responsorial Psalm   (Ps 125. *R.* v. 3)
Response
What marvels the Lord worked for us!
Indeed we were glad.

1. When the Lord delivered Zion from bondage,
It seemed like a dream.
Then was our mouth filled with laughter,
on our lips there were songs. (*R.*)

2. The heathens themselves said: "What marvels
the Lord worked for them!"
What marvels the Lord worked for us!
Indeed we were glad. (*R.*)

3. Deliver us, O Lord, from our bondage
as streams in dry land.
Those who are sowing in tears
will sing when they reap. (*R.*)

4. They go out, they go out, full of tears,
carrying seed for the sowing:
they come back, they come back, full of song,
carrying their sheaves. (*R.*)

Second Reading   (3:8–14)
A reading from the letter of St Paul to the Philippians
*Reproducing the pattern of his death, I have accepted the loss
of everything for Christ.*

I believe nothing can happen that will outweigh the supreme advantage of knowing Christ Jesus my Lord. For him I have accepted the loss of everything, and I look on everything as so much rubbish if only I can have Christ and be given a place in him. I am no longer trying for perfection by my own efforts, the perfection that comes from the Law, but I want only the perfection that comes through faith in Christ, and is from God and based on faith. All I want is to know Christ and the power of his resurrection and to share his sufferings by reproducing the pattern of his death. That is the way I can hope to take my place in the resurrection of the dead. Not that I have become perfect yet: I have not yet won, but I am still running, trying to capture the prize for which Christ Jesus captured me. I can assure you my brothers, I am far from thinking that I have already won. All I can say is that I forget the past and I strain ahead for what is still to come; I am racing for the finish, for the prize to which God calls us upwards to receive in Christ Jesus.

This is the word of the Lord.

Acclamation   (Amos 5:14)

Seek good and not evil so that you may live, and that the Lord God of hosts may really be with you.

Alternative Acclamations p. 242, e.g. nos. 4-6.

Gospel   (8:1–11)

A reading from the holy Gospel according to John

If there is one of you who has not sinned, let him be the first to throw a stone at her.

Jesus went to the Mount of Olives. At daybreak he appeared in the Temple again; and as all the people came to him, he sat down and began to teach them.

The scribes and Pharisees brought a woman along who

had been caught committing adultery; and making her
stand there in full view of everybody, they said to Jesus,
"Master, this woman was caught in the very act of committing adultery, and Moses has ordered us in the Law to
condemn women like this to death by stoning. What have
you to say?" They asked him this as a test, looking for
something to use against him. But Jesus bent down and
started writing on the ground with his finger. As they persisted with their question, he looked up and said, "If there
is one of you who has not sinned, let him be the first to throw
a stone at her." Then he bent down and wrote on the ground
again. When they heard this they went away one by one,
beginning with the eldest, until Jesus was left alone with the
woman, who remained standing there. He looked up and
said, "Woman, where are they? Has no one condemned
you?" "No one, sir," she replied. "Neither do I condemn
you," said Jesus "go away, and don't sin any more."

This is the Gospel of the Lord.

Alternative Readings

The following readings may be used instead of the proper ones any day
this week, especially in Years 2 (B) and 3 (C) when the Gospel of
Lazarus is not read on the 5th Sunday.

First Reading   (4:18–21. 32–37)

A reading from the second book of the Kings

*As Elisha lowered himself on to him, the child's flesh grew
warm.*

One day the son of the Shunammitess went out to his
father who was with the reapers, and exclaimed to his
father, "Oh, my head! My head!" The father told a servant
to carry him to his mother. He lifted him up and took him
to his mother, and the boy sat on her knee until midday,
when he died. She went upstairs, laid him on the bed of
Elisha the man of God, shut the door on him and went out.

Elisha then went to the house, and there on his bed lay

the child, dead. He went in and shut the door on the two of them and prayed to the Lord. Then he climbed on to the bed and stretched himself on top of the child, putting his mouth on his mouth, his eyes to his eyes, and his hands on his hands, and as he lowered himself on to him, the child's flesh grew warm. Then he got up and walked to and fro inside the house, and then climbed on to the bed again and lowered himself on to the child seven times in all; then the child sneezed and opened his eyes. He then summoned Gehazi. "Call our Shunammitess" he said; and he called her. When she came to him, he said, "Take up your son." She went in and, falling at his feet, bowed down to the ground; and taking up her son went out.

This is the word of the Lord.

Responsorial Psalm   (Ps 16:1. 6–8. 15. *R.* v. 15)
Response
I shall be filled, when I awake,
with the sight of your glory.

1. Lord hear a cause that is just,
pay heed to my cry.
Turn your ear to my prayer:
no deceit is on my lips. (*R.*)

2. I am here and I call, you will hear me, O God.
Turn your ear to me; hear my words.
Display your great love, you whose right hand saves
your friends from those who rebel against them. (*R.*)

3. Guard me as the apple of your eye.
Hide me in the shadow of your wings.
As for me, in my justice I shall see your face
and be filled, when I awake, with the sight of your
   glory (*R.*)

Acclamation   (Jn 11:25. 26)

I am the resurrection and the life, says the Lord,
whoever believes in me will never die.

Alternative Acclamations p. 842.
GOSPEL. John 11:1–45. See 5th Sunday of Lent, Year 1 (Year A),
p. 554.

MONDAY

First Reading   (13:1–9. 15–17. 19–30. 33–62)

A reading from the prophet Daniel
Have I to die, innocent as I am?

In Babylon there lived a man named Joakim. He had married Susanna daughter of Hilkiah, a woman of great
beauty; and she was God-fearing, because her parents were
worthy people and had instructed their daughter in the
Law of Moses. Joakim was a very rich man, and had a
garden attached to his house; the Jews would often visit
him since he was held in greater respect than any other
man. Two elderly men had been selected from the people
that year to act as judges. Of such the Lord said, "Wickedness has come to Babylon through the elders and judges
posing as guides to the people." These men were often at
Joakim's house, and all who were engaged in litigation used
to come to them. At midday, when everyone had gone,
Susanna used to take a walk in her husband's garden. The
two elders, who used to watch her every day as she came
in to take her walk, gradually began to desire her. They
threw reason aside, making no effort to turn their eyes to
heaven, and forgetting its demands of virtue. So they waited
for a favourable moment; and one day Susanna came as
usual, accompanied only by two young maidservants. The
day was hot and she wanted to bathe in the garden. There
was no one about except the two elders, spying on her from
their hiding place. She said to the servants, "Bring me some
oil and balsam and shut the garden door while I bathe."
Hardly were the servants gone than the two elders were

there after her. "Look," they said "the garden door is shut, no one can see us. We want to have you, so give in and let us! Refuse, and we will both give evidence that a young man was with you and that was why you sent your maids away." Susanna sighed. "I am trapped," she said "whatever I do. If I agree, that means my death; if I resist, I cannot get away from you. But I prefer to fall innocent into your power than to sin in the eyes of the Lord." Then she cried out as loud as she could. The two elders began shouting too, putting the blame on her, and one of them ran to open the garden door. The household, hearing the shouting in the garden, rushed out by the side entrance to see what was happening; once the elders had told their story the servants were thoroughly taken aback, since nothing of this sort had ever been said of Susanna.

Next day a meeting was held at the house of her husband Joakim. The two elders arrived, in their vindictiveness determined to have her put to death. They addressed the company: "Summon Susanna daughter of Hilkiah and wife of Joakim." She was sent for, and came accompanied by her parents, her children and all her relations.

All her own people were weeping, and so were all the others who saw her. The two elders stood up, with all the people round them, and laid their hands on the woman's head. Tearfully she turned her eyes to heaven, her heart confident in God. The elders then spoke. "While we were walking by ourselves in the garden, this woman arrived with two servants. She shut the garden door and then dismissed the servants. A young man who had been hiding went over to her and they lay down together. From the end of the garden where we were, we saw this crime taking place and hurried towards them. Though we saw them together we were unable to catch the man: he was too strong for us; he opened the door and took to his heels. We did, however, catch this woman and ask her who the young man was. She refused to tell us. That is our evidence."

Since they were elders of the people, and judges, the assembly took their word: *Susanna was condemned to death. She cried out as loud as she could, "Eternal God, you know all secrets and everything before it happens; you know that they have given false evidence against me. And now have I to die, innocent as I am of everything their malice has invented against me?"

The Lord heard her cry and, as she was being led away to die, he roused the holy spirit residing in a young boy named Daniel who began to shout, "I am innocent of this woman's death!" At which all the people turned to him and asked, "What do you mean by these words?" Standing in the middle of the crowd he replied, "Are you so stupid, sons of Israel, as to condemn a daughter of Israel unheard, and without troubling to find out the truth? Go back to the scene of the trial: these men have given false evidence against her."

All the people hurried back, and the elders said to Daniel, "Come and sit with us and tell us what you mean, since God has given you the gifts that elders have." Daniel said, "Keep the men well apart from each other for I want to question them." When the men had been separated, Daniel had one of them brought to him. "You have grown old in wickedness," he said, "and now the sins of your earlier days have overtaken you, you with your unjust judgements, your condemnation of the innocent, your acquittal of guilty men, when the Lord has said, 'You must not put the innocent and the just to death.' Now then, since you saw her so clearly, tell me what tree you saw them lying under?" He replied, "Under a mastic tree." Daniel said, "True enough! Your lie recoils on your own head: the angel of God has already received your sentence from him and will slash you in half." He dismissed the man, ordered the other to be brought and said to him, "Spawn of Canaan, not of Judah, beauty has seduced you, lust has led your heart astray! This is how you have been behaving with the daughters of Israel and they were too frightened to resist; but here is a daughter of Judah who could not stomach your wickedness! Now then, tell me what tree you surprised them under?" He replied, "Under a holm oak." Daniel said, "True enough! Your lie recoils on your own head: the angel of God is waiting, with a sword to drive home and split you, and destroy the pair of you."

Then the whole assembly shouted, blessing God, the saviour of those who trust in him. And they turned on the two elders whom Daniel had convicted of false evidence out of their own mouths. As prescibed in the Law of Moses, they sentenced them to the same punishment as they had intended to inflict on their neighbour. They put them to death; the life of an innocent woman was spared that day.

This is the word of the Lord.*

*Shorter Form, verses 41–62. Read between *.

Responsorial Psalm (Ps 22. *R*. v. 4)

Response
If I should walk in the valley of darkness
no evil would I fear, for you are there.

1. The Lord is my shepherd;
there is nothing I shall want.
Fresh and green are the pastures
where he gives me repose.
Near restful waters he leads me,
to revive my drooping spirit. (*R*.)

2. He guides me along the right path;
he is true to his name.
If I should walk in the valley of darkness
no evil would I fear.
You are there with your crook and your staff;
with these you give me comfort. (*R*.)

3. You have prepared a banquet for me
in the sight of my foes.
My head you have anointed with oil;
my cup is overflowing. (*R.*)

4. Surely goodness and kindness shall follow me
all the days of my life.
In the Lord's own house shall I dwell
for ever and ever. (*R.*)

Acclamation (2 Cor 6:2)

Now is the favourable time;
this is the day of salvation.

Alternative Acclamations p. 842.
GOSPEL. John 8:1–11. As on 5th Sunday of Lent, Year 3 (Year C),
p. 562.

Alternative Gospel

For use in Year 3 (Year C) when John 8:1–11 is read on the preceding
Sunday.

(8:12–20)

A reading from the holy Gospel according to John
I am the light of the world.

When Jesus spoke to the people again, he said:

"I am the light of the world;
anyone who follows me will not be walking in the dark;
he will have the light of life."

At this the Pharisees said to him, "You are testifying
on your own behalf; your testimony is not valid." Jesus
replied:

"It is true that I am testifying on my own behalf,
but my testimony is still valid,
because I know
where I came from and where I am going;

but you do not know
where I come from or where I am going.
You judge by human standards;
I judge no one,
but if I judge,
my judgement will be sound,
because I am not alone:
the one who sent me is with me;
and in your Law it is written
that the testimony of two witnesses is valid.
I may be testifying on my own behalf,
but the Father who sent me is my witness too."

They asked him, "Where is your Father?" Jesus answered:
"You do not know me, nor do you know my Father;
if you did know me, you would know my Father as well."

He spoke these words in the Treasury, while teaching in the Temple. No one arrested him, because his time had not yet come.

This is the Gospel of the Lord.

TUESDAY

First Reading   (21:4–9)

A reading from the book of Numbers
If anyone is bitten and looks at the fiery serpent, he shall live.

The Israelites left Mount Hor by the road to the Sea of Suph, to skirt the land of Edom. On the way the people lost patience. They spoke against God and against Moses, "Why did you bring us out of Egypt to die in this wilderness? For there is neither bread nor water here; we are sick of this unsatisfying food."

At this God sent fiery serpents among the people; their bite brought death to many in Israel. The people came and

said to Moses, "We have sinned by speaking against the
Lord and against you. Intercede for us with the Lord to
save us from these serpents." Moses interceded for the
people, and the Lord answered him, "Make a fiery serpent
and put it on a standard. If anyone is bitten and looks at it,
he shall live." So Moses fashioned a bronze serpent which
he put on a standard, and if anyone was bitten by a serpent, he looked at the bronze serpent and lived.

   This is the word of the Lord.

Responsorial Psalm   (Ps 101:2–3. 16–21. *R.* v. 2)
Response
O Lord, listen to my prayer
and let my cry for help reach you.

1. O Lord, listen to my prayer
and let my cry for help reach you.
Do not hide your face from me
in the day of my distress.
Turn your ear towards me
and answer me quickly when I call. (*R.*)

2. The nations shall fear the name of the Lord
and all the earth's kings your glory,
when the Lord shall build up Zion again
and appear in all his glory.
Then he will turn to the prayers of the helpless;
he will not despise their prayers. (*R.*)

3. Let this be written for ages to come
that a people yet unborn may praise the Lord;
for the Lord leaned down from his sanctuary on high.
He looked down from heaven to the earth
that he might hear the groans of the prisoners
and free those condemned to die. (*R.*)

Acclamation (Jn 8:12)

I am the light of the world, says the Lord, anyone who follows me will have the light of life.

Alternative Acclamations p. 842.

Gospel (8:21–30)

A reading from the holy Gospel according to John
When you have lifted up the Son of Man, then you will know that I am He.

Jesus said to the Pharisees:

"I am going away; you will look for me
and you will die in your sin.
Where I am going, you cannot come."

The Jews said to one another, "Will he kill himself? Is that what he means by saying, 'Where I am going, you cannot come'?" Jesus went on:

"You are from below;
I am from above.
You are of this world;
I am not of this world.
I have told you already: You will die in your sins.
Yes, if you do not believe that I am He,
you will die in your sins."

So they said to him, "Who are you?" Jesus answered:

"What I have told you from the outset.
About you I have much to say
and much to condemn;
but the one who sent me is truthful,
and what I have learnt from him
I declare to the world."

They failed to understand that he was talking to them about the Father. So Jesus said:

"When you have lifted up the Son of Man,
then you will know that I am He
and that I do nothing of myself:
what the Father has taught me
is what I preach;
he who sent me is with me,
and has not left me to myself,
for I always do what pleases him."

As he was saying this, many came to believe in him.
This is the Gospel of the Lord.

WEDNESDAY

First Reading   (3:14–20. 24–25. 28)

A reading from the prophet Daniel
He has sent his angel to rescue his servants.

King Nebuchadnezzar addressed them, "Shadrach, Meshach and Abednego, is it true that you do not serve my gods, and that you refuse to worship the golden statue I have erected? When you hear the sound of horn, pipe, lyre, trigon, harp, bagpipe, or any other instrument, are you prepared to prostrate yourselves and worship the statue I have made? If you refuse to worship it, you must be thrown straight away into the burning fiery furnace; and where is the god who could save you from my power?" Shadrach, Meshach and Abednego replied to King Nebuchadnezzar, "Your question hardly requires an answer: if our God, the one we serve, is able to save us from the burning fiery furnace and from your power, O king, he will save us; and even if he does not, then you must know, O king, that we will not serve your god or worship the statue you have erected." These words infuriated King Nebuchadnezzar; his expression was very different now as he looked at Shadrach, Meshach and Abednego. He gave orders for the furnace to be made seven times hotter than usual, and commanded certain stalwarts from his army to bind Shadrach, Meshach and Abednego and throw them into the burning fiery furnace.

Then King Nebuchadnezzar sprang to his feet in amazement. He said to his advisers, "Did we not have these three men thrown bound into the fire?" They replied, "Certainly, O king." "But," he went on "I can see four men walking about freely in the heart of the fire without coming to any harm. And the fourth looks like a son of the gods."

Nebuchadnezzar exclaimed, "Blessed be the God of Shadrach, Meshach and Abednego: he has sent his angel to rescue his servants who, putting their trust in him, defied the order of the king, and preferred to forfeit their bodies rather than serve or worship any god but their own."

This is the word of the Lord.

Responsorial Psalm   (Dan 3:52–56. R. v. 52)
Response
To you glory and praise for evermore.

1. You are blest, Lord God of our fathers.
To you glory and praise for evermore.
Blest your glorious holy name.
To you glory and praise for evermore. (R.)

2. You are blest in the temple of your glory.
To you glory and praise for evermore. (R.)

3. You are blest on the throne of your kingdom.
To you glory and praise for evermore. (R.)

4. You are blest who gaze into the depths.
To you glory and praise for evermore. (R.)

5. You are blest in the firmament of heaven.
To you glory and praise for evermore. (*R.*)

Acclamation					(Mt 4:4)

Man does not live on bread alone, but on every word that
comes from the mouth of God.

Alternative Acclamations p. 842.

Gospel						(8:31–42)

A reading from the holy Gospel according to John
If the Son of Man makes you free, you will be free indeed.

To the Jews who believed in him Jesus said:

"If you make my word your home
you will indeed be my disciples,
you will learn the truth
and the truth will make you free."

They answered, "We are descended from Abraham and
we have never been the slaves of anyone; what do you mean,
'You will be made free'?"
Jesus replied:

"I tell you most solemnly,
everyone who commits sin is a slave.
Now the slave's place in the house is not assured,
but the son's place is assured.
So if the Son makes you free,
you will be free indeed.
I know that you are descended from Abraham;
but in spite of that you want to kill me
because nothing I say has penetrated into you.
What I, for my part, speak of
is what I have seen with my Father;
but you, you put into action
the lessons learnt from your father."

They repeated, "Our father is Abraham." Jesus said to them:

"If you were Abraham's children,
you would do as Abraham did.
As it is, you want to kill me
when I tell you the truth
as I have learnt it from God;
that is not what Abraham did.
What you are doing is what your father does."

"We were not born of prostitution," they went on "we have one father: God." Jesus answered:

"If God were your father, you would love me,
since I have come here from God; yes, I have come from him;
not that I came because I chose,
no, I was sent, and by him."

This is the Gospel of the Lord.

THURSDAY

First Reading   (17:3–9)

A reading from the book of Genesis
You shall become the father of a multitude of nations.

Abram bowed to the ground and God said this to him, "Here now is my covenant with you: you shall become the father of a multitude of nations. You shall no longer be called Abram; your name shall be Abraham, for I will make you father of a multitude of nations. I will make you most fruitful. I will make you into nations, and your issue shall be kings. I will establish my Covenant between myself and you, and your descendants after you, generation after generation, a Covenant in perpetuity, to be your God and the

God of your descendants after you. I will give to you and to your descendants after you the land you are living in, the whole land of Canaan, to own in perpetuity, and I will be your God."

God said to Abraham, "You on your part shall maintain my Covenant, yourself and your descendants after you, generation after generation."

This is the word of the Lord.

Responsorial Psalm   (Ps 104:4–9. *R*. v. 8)
Response
The Lord remembers his covenant for ever.

1. Consider the Lord and his strength;
constantly seek his face.
Remember the wonders he has done,
his miracles, the judgements he spoke. (*R*.)

2. O children of Abraham, his servant,
O sons of the Jacob he chose.
He, the Lord, is our God:
his judgements prevail in all the earth. (*R*.)

3. He remembers his covenant for ever,
his promise for a thousand generations,
the covenant he made with Abraham,
the oath he swore to Isaac. (*R*.)

Acclamation   (Jn 6:64. 69)

Your words are spirit, Lord, and they are life, you have the message of eternal life.

Alternative Acclamations p. 842.

Gospel   (8:51–59)

A reading from the holy Gospel according to John
Your father Abraham rejoiced to think that he would see my Day.

Jesus said to the Jews:

"I tell you most solemnly,
whoever keeps my word
will never see death."

The Jews said, "Now we know for certain that you are possessed. Abraham is dead, and the prophets are dead, and yet you say, 'Whoever keeps my word will never know the taste of death.' Are you greater than our father Abraham, who is dead? The prophets are dead too. Who are you claiming to be?" Jesus answered:

"If I were to seek my own glory
that would be no glory at all;
my glory is conferred by the Father,
by the one of whom you say, 'He is our God'
although you do not know him.
But I know him,
and if I were to say: I do not know him,
I should be a liar, as you are liars yourselves.
But I do know him, and I faithfully keep his word.
Your father Abraham rejoiced
to think that he would see my Day;
he saw it and was glad."

The Jews then said, "You are not fifty yet, and you have seen Abraham!" Jesus replied:

"I tell you most solemnly,
before Abraham ever was,
I Am."

At this they picked up stones to throw at him; but Jesus hid himself and left the Temple.
This is the Gospel of the Lord.

FRIDAY

First Reading   (20:10–13)

A reading from the prophet Jeremiah
The Lord is at my side, a mighty hero.

I hear so many disparaging me,
" 'Terror from every side!'
Denounce him! Let us denounce him!"
All those who used to be my friends
watched for my downfall,
"Perhaps he will be seduced into error.
Then we will master him
and take our revenge!"
But the Lord is at my side, a mighty hero;
my opponents will stumble, mastered,
confounded by their failure;
everlasting, unforgettable disgrace will be theirs.
But you, Lord of hosts, you who probe with justice,
who scrutinise the loins and heart,
let me see the vengeance you will take on them,
for I have committed my cause to you.
Sing to the Lord,
praise the Lord,
for he has delivered the soul of the needy
from the hands of evil men.

   This is the word of the Lord.

Responsorial Psalm   (Ps 17:2–7. *R*. v. 7)

Response
In my anguish I called to the Lord
and he heard my voice.

1. I love you, Lord, my strength,
my rock, my fortress, my saviour.

My God is the rock where I take refuge;
my shield, my mighty help, my stronghold.
The Lord is worthy of all praise:
when I call I am saved from my foes. (R.)

2. The waves of death rose about me;
the torrents of destruction assailed me;
the snares of the grave entangled me;
the traps of death confronted me. (R.)

3. In my anguish I called to the Lord;
I cried to my God for help.
From his temple he heard my voice;
my cry came to his ears. (R.)

Acclamation (Mt 4:17)

Repent, says the Lord, for the kingdom of heaven is close at hand.

Alternative Acclamations p. 842.

Gospel (10:31–42)

A reading from the holy Gospel according to John
They wanted to arrest Jesus then, but he eluded them.

The Jews fetched stones to stone him, so Jesus said to them, "I have done many good works for you to see, works from my Father; for which of these are you stoning me?" The Jews answered him, "We are not stoning you for doing a good work but for blasphemy: you are only a man and you claim to be god." Jesus answered:

"Is it not written in your Law:
I said, you are gods?
So the Law used the word gods
of those to whom the word of God was addressed,
and scripture cannot be rejected.

Yet you say to someone the Father has consecrated and
    sent into the world,
'You are blaspheming,'
because he says, 'I am the Son of God.'
If I am not doing my Father's work,
there is no need to believe me;
but if I am doing it,
then even if you refuse to believe in me,
at least believe in the work I do;
then you will know for sure
that the Father is in me and I am in the Father."

They wanted to arrest him then, but he eluded them.

He went back again to the far side of the Jordan to stay
in the district where John had once been baptising. Many
people who came to him there said, "John gave no signs,
but all he said about this man was true"; and many of
them believed in him.

This is the Gospel of the Lord.

SATURDAY

First Reading   (37:21–28)

A reading from the prophet Ezekiel
I shall make them into one nation.

The Lord says this: "I am going to take the sons of Israel
from the nations where they have gone. I shall gather them
together from everywhere and bring them home to their
own soil. I shall make them into one nation in my own
land and on the mountains of Israel, and one king is to be
king of them all; they will no longer form two nations, nor
be two separate kingdoms. They will no longer defile themselves with their idols and their filthy practices and all their
sins. I shall rescue them from all the betrayals they have
been guilty of; I shall cleanse them; they shall be my people

and I will be their God. My servant David will reign over them, one shepherd for all; they will follow my observances, respect my laws and practise them. They will live in the land that I gave my servant Jacob, the land in which your ancestors lived. They will live in it, they, their children, their children's children, for ever. David my servant is to be their prince for ever. I shall make a covenant of peace with them, an eternal covenant with them. I shall resettle them and increase them; I shall settle my sanctuary among them for ever. I shall make my home above them; I will be their God, they shall be my people. And the nations will learn that I am the Lord the sanctifier of Israel, when my sanctuary is with them for ever."

This is the word of the Lord.

Responsorial Psalm   (Jer 31:10–13. *R*. v. 10)

Response
The Lord will guard us as a shepherd guards his flock.

1. O nations, hear the word of the Lord,
proclaim it to the far-off coasts.
Say: "He who scattered Israel will gather him
and guard him as a shepherd guards his flock."
For the Lord has ransomed Jacob,
has saved him from an overpowering hand. (*R*.)

2. They will come and shout for joy on Mount Zion,
they will stream to the blessings of the Lord,
to the corn, the new wine and the oil,
to the flocks of sheep and the herds. (*R*.)

3. Then the young girls will rejoice and will dance,
the men, young and old, will be glad.
I will turn their mourning into joy,
I will console them, give gladness for grief. (*R*.)

Acclamation   (Jn 3:16)

God loved the world so much that he gave his only Son;
everyone who believes in him has eternal life.

Alternative Acclamations p. 842.

Gospel   (11:45–57)

A reading from the holy Gospel according to John
To gather together in unity the scattered children of God.

Many of the Jews who had come to visit Mary and had
seen what Jesus did believed in him, but some of them went
to tell the Pharisees what he had done. Then the chief priests
and Pharisees called a meeting. "Here is this man working
all these signs" they said "and what action are we taking?
If we let him go on in this way everybody will believe in
him, and the Romans will come and destroy the Holy Place
and our nation." One of them, Caiaphas, the high priest
that year, said, "You don't seem to have grasped the situation at all; you fail to see that it is better for one man to die
for the people, than for the whole nation to be destroyed."
He did not speak in his own person, it was as high priest
that he made this prophecy that Jesus was to die for the
nation – and not for the nation only, but to gather together
in unity the scattered children of God. From that day they
were determined to kill him. So Jesus no longer went about
openly among the Jews, but left the district for a town
called Ephraim, in the country bordering on the desert, and
stayed there with his disciples.

The Jewish Passover drew near, and many of the country people who had gone up to Jerusalem to purify themselves looked out for Jesus, saying to one another as they
stood about in the Temple, "What do you think? Will he
come to the festival or not?" The chief priests and Pharisees
had by now given their orders: anyone who knew where
he was must inform them so that they could arrest him.

This is the Gospel of the Lord.

HOLY WEEK

PASSION SUNDAY

Palm Sunday

The following Gospels are read at the celebration of our Lord's messianic entry into Jerusalem.

Year 1 (Year A)

Gospel (21:1–11)

A reading from the holy Gospel according to Matthew
Blessings on him who comes in the name of the Lord,

When they were near Jerusalem and had come in sight of Bethphage on the Mount of Olives, Jesus sent two disciples, saying to them, "Go to the village facing you, and you will immediately find a tethered donkey and a colt with her. Untie them and bring them to me. If anyone says anything to you, you are to say, 'The Master needs them and will send them back directly.'" This took place to fulfil the prophecy:

Say to the daughter of Zion:
Look, your king comes to you;
he is humble, he rides on a donkey
and on a colt, the foal of a beast of burden.

So the disciples went out and did as Jesus had told them. They brought the donkey and the colt, then they laid their cloaks on their backs and he sat on them. Great crowds of people spread their cloaks on the road, while others were cutting branches from the trees and spreading them in his path. The crowds who went in front of him and those who followed were all shouting:

"Hosanna to the Son of David!
Blessings on him who comes in the name of the Lord!
Hosanna in the highest heavens!"

And when he entered Jerusalem, the whole city was in turmoil. "Who is this?" people asked, and the crowds answered, "This is the prophet Jesus from Nazareth in Galilee."

This is the Gospel of the Lord.

Year 2 (Year B)

Gospel   (11:1–10)
A reading from the holy Gospel according to Mark
Blessings on him who comes in the name of the Lord.

When they were approaching Jerusalem, in sight of Bethphage and Bethany, close by the Mount of Olives, Jesus sent two of his disciples and said to them, "Go off to the village facing you, and as soon as you enter it you will find a tethered colt that no one has yet ridden. Untie it and bring it here. If anyone says to you, 'What are you doing?' say, 'The Master needs it and will send it back here directly.' " They went off and found a colt tethered near a door in the open street. As they untied it, some men standing there said, "What are you doing, untying that colt?" They gave the answer Jesus had told them, and the men let them go. Then they took the colt to Jesus and threw their cloaks on its back, and he sat on it. Many people spread their cloaks on the road, others greenery which they had cut in the fields. And those who went in front and those who followed were all shouting, "Hosanna! Blessings on him who comes in the name of the Lord! Blessings on the coming kingdom of our father David! Hosanna in the highest heavens!"

This is the Gospel of the Lord.

Alternative Gospel   Year 2 (Year B)
                                                      (12:12–16)

A reading from the holy Gospel according to John
Blessings on him who comes in the name of the Lord.

The next day the crowds who had come up for the festival heard that Jesus was on his way to Jerusalem. They took branches of palm and went out to meet him, shouting, "Hosanna! Blessings on the King of Israel, who comes in the name of the Lord." Jesus found a young donkey and mounted it – as scripture says: Do not be afraid, daughter of Zion; see, your king is coming, mounted on the colt of a donkey. At the time his disciples did not understand this, but later, after Jesus had been glorified, they remembered that this had been written about him and that this was in fact how they had received him.

This is the Gospel of the Lord.

Year 3 (Year C)

Gospel   (19:28–40)

A reading from the holy Gospel according to Luke
Blessings on him who comes in the name of the Lord.

Jesus went on ahead, going up to Jerusalem. Now when he was near Bethphage and Bethany, close by the Mount of Olives as it is called, he sent two of the disciples, telling them, "Go off to the village opposite, and as you enter it you will find a tethered colt that no one has yet ridden. Untie it and bring it here. If anyone asks you, 'Why are you untying it?' you are to say this, 'The Master needs it.'" The messengers went off and found everything just as he had told them. As they were untying the colt, its owner said, "Why are you untying that colt?" and they answered, "The Master needs it."

So they took the colt to Jesus, and throwing their garments over its back they helped Jesus on to it. As he moved off, people spread their cloaks in the road, and now, as he was approaching the downward slope of the Mount of Olives, the whole group of disciples joyfully began to praise God at the top of their voices for all the miracles they had seen. They cried out:

"Blessings on the King who comes,
in the name of the Lord!

Peace in heaven
and glory in the highest heavens!''

Some Pharisees in the crowd said to him, "Master, check
your disciples," but he answered, "I tell you, if these keep
silence the stones will cry out."

This is the Gospel of the Lord.

THE MASS

It is strongly recommended that, unless there is some overriding
pastoral reason against it, all three readings given for this Sunday
be used.
In view of the importance of the reading of the story of the Passion of
the Lord, the priest may, taking into account the particular character
of his congregation, read only one of the readings which precede the
Gospel. Or he may, if necessary, read only the story of the Passion,
even in its shorter form.

Every Year

First Reading (50:4–7)

A reading from the prophet Isaiah
*I did not cover my face against insult – I know I shall not be
shamed.*

The Lord has given me
a disciple's tongue.
So that I may know how to reply to the wearied
he provides me with speech.
Each morning he wakes me to hear,
to listen like a disciple.
The Lord has opened my ear.

For my part, I made no resistance,
neither did I turn away.
I offered my back to those who struck me,
my cheeks to those who tore at my beard;
I did not cover my face
against insult and spittle.

The Lord comes to my help,
so that I am untouched by the insults.

So, too, I set my face like flint;
I know I shall not be shamed.

   This is the word of the Lord.

Responsorial Psalm   (Ps 21:8–9. 17–20. 23–24. *R*. v. 2)

Response
My God, my God, why have you forsaken me?

1. All who see me deride me.
They curl their lips, they toss their heads.
"He trusted in the Lord, let him save him:
let me release him if this is his friend." (*R*.)

2. Many dogs have surrounded me,
a band of the wicked beset me.
They tear holes in my hands and my feet
I can count every one of my bones. (*R*.)

3. They divide my clothing among them.
They cast lots for my robe.
O Lord, do not leave me alone,
my strength, make haste to help me! (*R*.)

4. I will tell of your name to my brethren
and praise you where they are assembled.
"You who fear the Lord give him praise;
all sons of Jacob, give him glory.
Revere him, Israel's sons." (*R*.)

Second Reading   (2:6–11)

A reading from the letter of St Paul to the Philippians
He humbled himself, but God raised him high.

His state was divine,
yet Christ Jesus did not cling

to his equality with God
but emptied himself
to assume the condition of a slave,
and became as men are;
and being as all men are,
he was humbler yet,
even to accepting death,
death on a cross.
But God raised him high
and gave him the name
which is above all other names
so that all beings
in the heavens, on earth and in the underworld,
should bend the knee at the name of Jesus
and that every tongue should acclaim
Jesus Christ as Lord,
to the glory of God the Father.

    This is the word of the Lord.

Acclamation   (Ph 2:8–9)

Christ was humbler yet,
even to accepting death,
death on a cross.
But God raised him high
and gave him the name
which is above all names.

The Passion may be read or sung by three deacons. One reads the narrative and his part is marked C (Chronicler), another the words of Christ, marked ✠, and another the words of other speakers, marked S (the Synagogue).

Year 1 (Year A)

Gospel   (26:14–27:66)

The passion of our Lord Jesus Christ according to Matthew

C. Then one of the Twelve, the man called Judas Iscariot,

went to the chief priests and said, S. "What are you prepared to give me if I hand him over to you?" C. They paid
him thirty silver pieces, and from that moment he looked
for an opportunity to betray him.

Now on the first day of Unleavened Bread the disciples
came to Jesus to say, S. "Where do you want us to make the
preparations for you to eat the passover?" C. He replied ✠
"Go to so-and-so in the city and say to him, 'The Master
says: My time is near. It is at your house that I am keeping
Passover with my disciples.'" C. The disciples did what
Jesus told them and prepared the Passover.

When evening came he was at table with the twelve disciples. And while they were eating he said, ✠ "I tell you
solemnly, one of you is about to betray me." C. They were
greatly distressed and started asking him in turn, S. "Not I,
Lord, surely?" C. He answered, ✠ "Someone who has
dipped his hand into the dish with me, will betray me. The
Son of Man is going to his fate, as the scriptures say he
will, but alas for that man by whom the Son of Man is betrayed! Better for that man if he had never been born!" C.
Judas, who was to betray him, asked in his turn, S. "Not I,
Rabbi, surely?" ✠ "They are your own words" C. Jesus
answered.

Now as they were eating, Jesus took some bread, and
when he had said the blessing he broke it and gave it to the
disciples and said, ✠ "Take it and eat; this is my body."
C. Then he took a cup, and when he had returned thanks he
gave it to them saying, ✠ "Drink all of you from this, for
this is my blood, the blood of the covenant, which is to be
poured out for many for the forgiveness of sins. From now
on, I tell you, I shall not drink wine until the day I drink
the new wine with you in the kingdom of my Father."

C. After psalms had been sung they left for the Mount
of Olives. Then Jesus said to them, ✠ "You will all lose
faith in me this night, for the scripture says: I shall strike
the shepherd and the sheep of the flock will be scattered.

But after my resurrection I shall go before you to Galilee."
C. At this, Peter said, S. "Though all lose faith in you, I
will never lose faith." C. Jesus answered him, ✠ "I tell you
solemnly, this very night, before the cock crows, you will
have disowned me three times." C. Peter said to him,
S. "Even if I have to die with you, I will never disown you."
C. And all the disciples said the same.

Then Jesus came with them to a small estate called Gethsemane; and he said to his disciples, ✠ "Stay here while I
go over there to pray." C. He took Peter and the two sons
of Zebedee with him. And sadness came over him, and
great distress. Then he said to them, ✠ "My soul is sorrowful to the point of death. Wait here and keep awake with
me." C. And going on a little further he fell on his face
and prayed. ✠ "My Father, if it is possible let this cup pass
me by. Nevertheless, let it be as you, not I, would have it."
C. He came back to the disciples and found them sleeping,
and he said to Peter, ✠ "So you had not the strength to
keep awake with me one hour? You should be awake, and
praying not to be put to the test. The spirit is willing, but
the flesh is weak." C. Again, a second time, he went away
and prayed: ✠ "My father, if this cup cannot pass by
without my drinking it, your will be done!" C. And he
came again back and found them sleeping, their eyes were
so heavy. Leaving them there, he went away again and
prayed for the third time, repeating the same words. Then he
came back to the disciples and said to them, ✠ "You can
sleep on now and take your rest. Now the hour has come
when the Son of Man is to be betrayed into the hands of
sinners. Get up! Let us go! My betrayer is already close
at hand."

C. He was still speaking when Judas, one of the Twelve,
appeared, and with him a large number of men armed with
swords and clubs, sent by the chief priests and elders of
the people. Now the traitor had arranged a sign with them.
He had said, S. "The one I kiss, he is the man. Take

him in charge." C. So he went straight up to Jesus and said,
S. "Greetings, Rabbi," C. and kissed him. Jesus said to
him, ✠ "My friend, do what you are here for." C. Then
they came forward, seized Jesus and took him in charge. At
that, one of the followers of Jesus grasped his sword and
drew it; he struck out at the high priest's servant, and cut off
his ear. Jesus then said, ✠ "Put your sword back, for all
who draw the sword will die by the sword. Or do you think
that I cannot appeal to my Father who would promptly
send more than twelve legions of angels to my defence? But
then, how would the scriptures be fulfilled that say this is
the way it must be?" C. It was at this time that Jesus said
to the crowds, ✠ "Am I a brigand, that you had to set out
to capture me with swords and clubs? I sat teaching in the
Temple day after day and you never laid hands on me." C.
Now all this happened to fulfil the prophecies in scripture.
Then all the disciples deserted him and ran away.

The men who had arrested Jesus led him off to Caiaphas
the high priest, where the scribes and the elders were assembled. Peter followed him at a distance, and when he
reached the high priest's palace, he went in and sat down
with the attendants to see what the end would be.

The chief priests and the whole Sanhedrin were looking
for evidence against Jesus, however false, on which they
might pass the death-sentence. But they could not find any,
though several lying witnesses came forward. Eventually
two stepped forward and made a statement, S. "This man
said, 'I have power to destroy the Temple of God and in
three days build it up.'" C. The high priest then stood up
and said to him, S. "Have you no answer to that? What is
this evidence these men are bringing against you?" C. But
Jesus was silent. And the high priest said to him, S. "I put
you on oath by the living God to tell us if you are the Christ,
the Son of God." C. Jesus answered, ✠ "The words are
your own. Moreover, I tell you that from this time on-
ward you will see the Son of Man seated at the right

hand of the Power and coming on the clouds of heaven." C. At this, the high priest tore his clothes and said, S. "He has blasphemed. What need of witnesses have we now? There! You have just heard the blasphemy. What is your opinion?" C. They answered, S. "He deserves to die."

C. Then they spat in his face and hit him with their fists; others said as they struck him, S. "Play the prophet, Christ! Who hit you then?"

C. Meanwhile Peter was sitting outside in the courtyard, and a servant-girl came up to him and said, S. "You too were with Jesus the Galilean." C. But he denied it in front of them all, saying S. "I do not know what you are talking about." When he went out to the gateway another servant-girl saw him and said to the people there, S. "This man was with Jesus the Nazarene." C. And again, with an oath, he denied it, S. "I do not know the man." C. A little later the bystanders came up and said to Peter, S. "You are one of them for sure! Why, your accent gives you away." C. Then he started calling down curses on himself and swearing, S. "I do not know the man." C. At that moment the cock crew, and Peter remembered what Jesus had said, "Before the cock crows you will have disowned me three times." And he went outside and wept bitterly.

When morning came, all the chief priests and the elders of the people met in council to bring about the death of Jesus. They had him bound, and led him away to hand him over to Pilate, the governor.

When he found that Jesus had been condemned, Judas his betrayer was filled with remorse and took the thirty silver pieces back to the chief priests and elders, saying, S. "I have sinned. I have betrayed innocent blood." C. They replied, S. "What is that to us? That is your concern." C. And flinging down the silver pieces in the sanctuary he made off, and went and hanged himself. The chief priests picked up the silver pieces and said, S. "It is against the Law to put this into the treasury; it is blood money."

C. So they discussed the matter and bought the potter's field with it as a graveyard for foreigners, and this is why the field is called the Field of Blood today. The words of the prophet Jeremiah were then fulfilled: And they took the thirty silver pieces, the sum at which the precious One was priced by children of Israel, and they gave them for the potter's field, just as the Lord directed me.

*Jesus, then, was brought before the governor, and the governor put to him this question, S. "Are you the king of the Jews?" C. Jesus replied, ✠ "It is you who say it." C. But when he was accused by the chief priests and the elders he refused to answer at all. Pilate then said to him, S. "Do you not hear how many charges they have brought against you?" C. But to the governor's complete amazement, he offered no reply to any of the charges.

At festival time it was the governor's practice to release a prisoner for the people, anyone they chose. Now there was at that time a notorious prisoner whose name was Barabbas. So when the crowd gathered, Pilate said to them, S. "Which do you want me to release for you: Barabbas, or Jesus who is called Christ?" C. For Pilate knew it was out of jealousy that they had handed him over.

Now as he was seated in the chair of judgement, his wife sent him a message, S. "Have nothing to do with that man; I have been upset all day by a dream I had about him."

C. The chief priests and the elders, however, had persuaded the crowd to demand the release of Barabbas and the execution of Jesus. So when the governor spoke and asked them, S. "Which of the two do you want me to release for you?" C. they said, S. "Barabbas." C. Pilate said to them, what am I to do with Jesus who is called Christ?" C. They all said, S. "Let him be crucified!" "Why? What harm has he done?" C. Pilate asked. But they shouted all the louder, S. "Let him be crucified!" C. Then Pilate saw that he was making no impression, that in fact a riot was imminent. So he took some water, washed his hands in front of the crowd and said, S. "I am innocent of this man's blood. It is your concern." C. And the people, to a man, shouted back, S. "His blood be on us and on our children!" C. Then he released Barabbas for them. He ordered Jesus to be first scourged and then handed over to be crucified.

The governor's soldiers took Jesus with them into the Praetorium and collected the whole cohort round him. Then they stripped him and made him wear a scarlet cloak, and having twisted some thorns into a crown they put this on his head and placed a reed in his right hand. To make fun of him they knelt to him saying, S. "Hail, king of the Jews!" C. And they spat on him and took the reed and struck him on the head with it. And when they had finished making fun of him, they took off the cloak and dressed him in his own clothes and led him away to crucify him.

On their way out, they came across a man from Cyrene, Simon by name, and enlisted him to carry his cross. When they had reached a place called Golgotha, that is, the place of the skull, they gave him wine to drink mixed with gall, which he tasted but refused to drink. When they had finished crucifying him they shared out his clothing by casting lots, and then sat down and stayed there keeping guard over him.

Above his head was placed the charge against him: it read: S. "This is Jesus, the King of the Jews". C. At the same time two robbers were crucified with him, one on the right and one on the left.

The passers-by jeered at him; they shook their heads and said, S. "So you would destroy the Temple and rebuild it in three days! Then save yourself! If you are God's son, come down from the cross!" C. The chief priests, with the scribes and elders mocked him in the same way, saying, S. "He saved others; he cannot save himself. He is the king of Israel; let him come down from the cross now, and we will believe in him. He puts his trust in God; now let God rescue him if he wants him. For he did say, 'I am the son of God.' " C. Even the robbers who were crucified with him taunted him in the same way.

From the sixth hour there was darkness over all the land until the ninth hour. And about the ninth hour, Jesus cried out in a loud voice, ✠ "Eli, Eli, Lama sabachthani?" C. that is, ✠ "My God, my God, why have you deserted me?" C. When some of those who stood there heard this, they said, S. "The man is calling on Elijah," and one of them quickly ran to get a sponge which he dipped in vinegar and, putting it on a reed, gave it him to drink. The rest of them said, S. "Wait! See if Elijah will come to save him." C. But Jesus, again crying out in a loud voice, yielded up his spirit.

At that, the veil of the Temple was torn in two from top to bottom; the earth quaked; the rocks were split; the tombs opened and the bodies of many holy men rose from the dead, and these, after his resurrection, came out of the tombs, entered the Holy City and appeared to a number of people. Meanwhile the centurion, together with the others guarding Jesus, had seen the earthquake and all that was taking place, and they were terrified and said, S. "In truth this was a son of God."

C. And many women were there, watching from a distance, the same women who had followed Jesus from Galilee and looked after him. Among them were Mary of Magdala, Mary the mother of James and Joseph, and the mother of Zebedee's sons.

When it was evening, there came a rich man of Arimathaea, called Joseph, who had himself become a disciple of Jesus. This man went to Pilate and asked for the body of Jesus. Pilate thereupon ordered it to be handed over. So Joseph took the body, wrapped it in a clean shroud and put it in his own new tomb which he had hewn out of the rock. He then rolled a large stone across the entrance of the tomb and went away. Now Mary of Magdala and the other Mary were there, sitting opposite the sepulchre.

Next day, that is, when Preparation Day was over, the chief priests and the Pharisees went in a body to Pilate and said to him, S. "Your Excellency, we recall that this imposter said, while he was still alive, 'After three days I shall rise again.' Therefore give the order to have the sepulchre kept secure until the third day, for fear his disciples come and steal him away and tell the people, 'He has risen from the dead.' This last piece of fraud would be worse than what went before." C. Pilate said to them, "You may have your guards. Go and make all as secure as you know how." C. So they went and made the sepulchre secure, putting seals on the stone and mounting a guard.

This is the Gospel of the Lord.*

*Shorter Form, 27:11–54. Read between *.

Year 2 (Year B)

Gospel   (14:1–15:47)

The passion of our Lord Jesus Christ according to Mark

C. It was two days before the Passover and the feast of Unleavened Bread, and the chief priests and the scribes were looking for a way to arrest Jesus by some trick and have him put to death. For they said, C. "It must not be during the festivities, or there will be a disturbance among the people."

C. Jesus was at Bethany in the house of Simon the leper; he was at dinner when a woman came in with an alabaster jar of very costly ointment, pure nard. She broke the jar and poured the ointment on his head. Some who were there said to one another indignantly, S. "Why this waste of ointment? Ointment like this could have been sold for over three hundred denarii and the money given to the poor"; C. and they were angry with her. But Jesus said, ✠ "Leave her alone. Why are you upsetting her? What she has done for me is one of the good works. You have the poor with you always, and you can be kind to them whenever you wish, but you will not always have me. She has done what was in her power to do: she has anointed my body before-hand for its burial. I tell you solemnly, wherever through-out all the world the Good News is proclaimed, what she has done will be told also, in remembrance of her."

C. Judas Iscariot, one of the Twelve, approached the chief priests with an offer to hand Jesus over to them. They were delighted to hear it, and promised to give him money; and he looked for a way of betraying him when the opportunity should occur.

On the first day of Unleavened Bread, when the Passover lamb was sacrificed, his disciples said to him, S. "Where do you want us to go and make the preparations for you to eat the passover?" C. So he sent two of his disciples, saying to them, ✠ "Go into the city and you will meet a man carrying a pitcher of water. Follow him, and say to the owner of the house which he enters, 'The Master says: Where is my dining room in which I can eat the passover with my disciples?' He will show you a large upper room furnished with couches, all prepared. Make the preparations for us there." C. The disciples set out and went to the city and found everything as he had told them, and prepared the Passover.

When evening came he arrived with the Twelve. And while they were at table eating, Jesus said, ✠ "I tell you solemnly, one of you is about to betray me, one of you eat-ing with me." C. They were distressed and asked him, one after another, S. "Not I, surely?" C. He said to them, ✠ "It is one of the Twelve, one who is dipping into the same dish with me. Yes, the Son of Man is going to his fate, as the scriptures say he will, but alas for that man by whom the Son of Man is betrayed! Better for that man if he had never been born!"

C. And as they were eating he took some bread, and when he had said the blessing he broke it and gave it to them, saying, ✠ "Take it; this is my body." C. Then he took a cup, and when he had returned thanks he gave it to them, and all drank from it, and he said to them, ✠ "This is my blood, the blood of the covenant, which is to be poured out for many. I tell you solemnly, I shall not drink any more wine until the day I drink the new wine in the kingdom of God."

C. After psalms had been sung they left for the Mount of Olives. And Jesus said to them, ✠ "You will all lose faith, for the scripture says: I shall strike the shepherd and the sheep will be scattered. However after my resurrection I shall go before you to Galilee." C. Peter said, S. "Even if all lose faith, I will not." C. And Jesus said to him, ✠ "I tell you solemnly, this day, this very night, before the cock crows twice, you will have disowned me three times." C. But he repeated still more earnestly S. "If I have to die with you, I will never disown you." C. And they all said the same.

They came to a small estate called Gethsemane, and Jesus said to his disciples, ✠ "Stay here while I pray." C. Then he took Peter and James and John with him. And a sudden fear came over him, and great distress. And he said to them, ✠ "My soul is sorrowful to the point of death. Wait here, and keep awake." C. And going on a little further he threw himself on the ground and prayed that, if it were possible, this hour might pass him by. He said ✠ "Abba (Father)! Everything is possible for you. Take this cup away from me. But let it be as you, not I, would have it." C. He came back and found them sleeping, and he said to Peter, ✠ "Simon, are you asleep? Had you not the strength to keep awake one hour? You should be awake, and praying not to be put to the test. The spirit is willing, but the flesh is weak." C. Again he went away and prayed, saying the same words. And once more he came back and found them sleeping, their eyes were so heavy; and they could find no answer for him. He came back a third time and said to them, ✠ "You can sleep on now and take your rest. It is all over. The hour has come. Now the Son of Man is to be betrayed into the hands of sinners. Get up! Let us go! My betrayer is close at hand already."

C. Even while he was still speaking, Judas, one of the Twelve, came up with a number of men armed with swords and clubs, sent by the chief priests and the scribes and the elders. Now the traitor had arranged a signal with them. He had said, S. "The one I kiss, he is the man. Take him in charge, and see he is well guarded when you lead him away." C. So when the traitor came, he went straight up to Jesus and said, S. "Rabbi!" C. and kissed him. The others seized him and took him in charge. Then one of the bystanders drew his sword and struck out at the high priest's servant, and cut off his ear.

Then Jesus spoke, ✠ "Am I a brigand that you had to set out to capture me with swords and clubs? I was among you teaching in the Temple day after day and you never laid hands on me. But this is to fulfil the scriptures." C. And they all deserted him and ran away. A young man who followed him had nothing on but a linen cloth. They caught hold of him, but he left the cloth in their hands and ran away naked.

They led Jesus off to the high priest; and all the chief priests and the elders and the scribes assembled there. Peter had followed him at a distance, right into the high priest's palace, and was sitting with the attendants warming himself at the fire.

The chief priests and the whole Sanhedrin were looking for evidence against Jesus on which they might pass the death-sentence. But they could not find any. Several, indeed, brought false evidence against him, but their evidence was conflicting. Some stood up and submitted this false evidence against him, S. "We heard him say, 'I am going to destroy this Temple made by human hands, and in three days build another, not made by human hands.' " C. But even on this point their evidence was conflicting. The high priest then stood up before the whole assembly and put this question to Jesus, S. "Have you no answer to that? What is this evidence these men are bringing against you?" C. But he was silent and made no answer at all. The high priest put a second question to him, S. "Are you the Christ the Son of the Blessed One?" C. Jesus said, ✠ "I am, and you will see the Son of Man seated at the right hand of the Power and coming with the clouds of heaven." C. The high priest tore his robes, and said, S. "What need of witnesses have we now? You heard the blasphemy. What is your finding?" C. And they all gave their verdict: he deserved to die.

Some of them started spitting at him and, blindfolding him, began hitting him with their fists and shouting, S. "Play the prophet!" C. And the attendants rained blows on him.

While Peter was down below in the courtyard, one of the high priest's servant-girls came up. She saw Peter warming himself there, stared at him and said, S. "You too were with Jesus, the man from Nazareth." C. But he denied it, saying, S. "I do not know, I do not understand, what you are talking about," C. And he went out into the forecourt. The servant-girl saw him and again started telling the bystanders, S. "This fellow is one of them." C. But again he denied it. A little later the bystanders themselves said to Peter, S. "You are one of them for sure! Why, you are a Galilean." C. But he started calling curses on himself and swearing, S. "I do not know the man you speak of." C. At that moment the cock crew for the second time, and Peter recalled how Jesus had said to him, ✠ "Before the cock crows twice, you will have disowned me three times." C. And he burst into tears.

*First thing in the morning, the chief priests together with the elders and scribes, in short the whole Sanhedrin, had their plan ready. They had Jesus bound and took him away and handed him over to Pilate.

Pilate questioned him, S. "Are you the king of the Jews?" He answered, ✠ "It is you who say it," C. And the chief priests brought many accusations against him. Pilate questioned him again, S. "Have you no reply at all? See how many accusations they are bringing against you!" C. But, to Pilate's amazement, Jesus made no further reply.

At festival time Pilate used to release a prisoner for them, anyone they asked for. Now a man called Barabbas was then in prison with the rioters who had committed murder during the uprising. When the crowd went up and began to ask Pilate the customary favour, Pilate answered them, S. "Do you want me to release for you the king of the Jews?" C. For he realised it was out of jealousy that the chief priests had handed Jesus over. The chief priests, however, had incited the crowd to demand that he should release Barabbas for them instead. Then Pilate spoke again. S. "But in that case, what am I to do with the man you call king of the Jews?" C. They shouted back, S. "Crucify him!" C. Pilate asked them, "Why? What harm has he done?" C. But they shouted all the louder, S. "Crucify him!" C. So Pilate, anxious to placate the crowd, released Barabbas for them and, having ordered Jesus to be scourged, handed him over to be crucified.

The soldiers led him away to the inner part of the palace, that is, the Praetorium, and called the whole cohort together. They dressed him up in purple, twisted some thorns into a crown and put it on him. And they began saluting him, S. "Hail, king of the Jews!" C. They struck his head with a reed and spat on him; and they went down on their knees to do him homage. And when they had finished making fun of him, they took off the purple and dressed him in his own clothes.

They led him out to crucify him. They enlisted a passer-by, Simon of Cyrene, father of Alexander and Rufus, who was coming in from the country, to carry his cross. They brought Jesus to the place called Golgotha, which means the place of the skull.

They offered him wine mixed with myrrh, but he refused it. Then they crucified him, and shared out his clothing, casting lots to decide what each should get. It was the third hour when they crucified him. The inscription giving the charge against him read: "The King of the Jews" And they crucified two robbers with him, one on his right and one on his left.

The passers-by jeered at him; they shook their heads and said, S. "Aha! So you would destroy the temple and rebuild it in three days! Then save yourself: come down from the cross!" C. The chief priests and the scribes mocked him among themselves in the same way. They said S. "He saved others, he cannot save himself. Let the Christ, the king of Israel, come down from the cross now, for us to see it and believe." C. Even those who were crucified with him taunted him.

When the sixth hour came there was darkness over the whole land until the ninth hour. And at the ninth hour Jesus cried out in a loud voice, ✠ "Eloi, Eloi, lama sabachthani?" C. This means "My God, my God, why have you deserted me?" When some of those who stood by heard this, they said, S. "Listen, he is calling on Elijah." C. Someone ran and soaked a sponge in vinegar and, putting it on a reed, gave it him to drink saying, S. "Wait and see if Elijah will come to take him down." C. But Jesus gave a loud cry and breathed his last. And the veil of the Temple was torn in two from top to bottom. The centurion, who was standing in front of him, had seen how he had died, and he said, S. "In truth this man was a son of God."

C. There were some women watching from a distance. Among them were Mary of Magdala, Mary who was the mother of James the younger and Joset, and Salome. These used to follow him and look after him when he was in Galilee. And there were many other women there who had come up to Jerusalem with him.

It was now evening, and since it was Preparation Day (that is, the vigil of the sabbath), there came Joseph of Arimathaea, a prominent member of the Council, who himself lived in the hope of seeing the kingdom of God, and he boldly went to Pilate and asked for the body of Jesus. Pilate, astonished that he should have died so soon, summoned the centurion and enquired if he was already dead. Having been assured of this by the centurion, he granted the corpse to Joseph who bought a shroud, took Jesus down from the cross, wrapped him in the shroud and laid him in a tomb which had been hewn out of the rock. He then rolled a stone against the entrance to the tomb. Mary of Magdala and Mary the mother of Joset were watching and took note of where he was laid.

This is the Gospel of the Lord.

*Shorter Form, 15:1–39. Read between *.

Year 3 (Year C)

Gospel   (22:14–23:56)

The passion of our Lord Jesus Christ according to Luke

C. When the hour came Jesus took his place at table, and the apostles with him. And he said to them, ✠ "I have longed to eat this passover with you before I suffer; because, I tell you, I shall not eat it again until it is fulfilled in the kingdom of God."

C. Then, taking a cup, he gave thanks and said, ✠ "Take this and share it among you, because from now on, I tell you, I shall not drink wine until the kingdom of God comes."

C. Then he took some bread, and when he had given thanks, broke it and gave it to them, saying, ✠ "This is my body which will be given for you; do this as a memorial of me." C. He did the same with the cup after supper, and said, ✠ "This cup is the new covenant in my blood which will be poured out for you.

"And yet, here with me on the table is the hand of the man who betrays me. The Son of Man does indeed go to his fate even as it has been decreed, but alas for that man by whom he is betrayed!" C. And they began to ask one another which of them it could be who was to do this thing.

A dispute arose also between them about which should be reckoned the greatest, but he said to them, ✠ "Among pagans it is the kings who lord it over them, and those who have authority over them are given the title Benefactor. This must not happen with you. No; the greatest among you must behave as if he were the youngest, the leader as if he were the one who serves. For who is the greater: the one at table or the one who serves? The one at table, surely? Yet here am I among you as one who serves!

"You are the men who have stood by me faithfully in my trials; and now I confer a kingdom on you, just as my Father conferred one on me: you will eat and drink at my table in my kingdom, and you will sit on thrones to judge the twelve tribes of Israel.

"Simon, Simon! Satan, you must know, has got his wish to sift you all like wheat; but I have prayed for you, Simon, that your faith may not fail, and once you have recovered, you in your turn must strengthen your brothers." He answered, S. "Lord, I would be ready to go to prison with you, and to death." C. Jesus replied, ✠ "I tell you, Peter, by the time the cock crows today you will have denied three times that you know me."

C. He said to them, ✠ "When I sent you out without purse or haversack or sandals, were you short of anything?" S. "No" C. They answered, C. He said to them, ✠ "But now if you have a purse, take it: if you have a haversack, do the same; if you have no sword, sell your cloak and buy one, because I tell you these words of scripture have to be fulfilled in me: He let himself be taken for a criminal. Yes, what scripture says about me is even now reaching its fulfilment." C. They said, "Lord, there are two swords here now." C. He said to them, ✠ "That is enough!"

C. He then left the upper room to make his way as usual to the Mount of Olives, with the disciples following. When they reached the place he said to them, ✠ "Pray not to be put to the test."

C. Then he withdrew from them, about a stone's throw away, and knelt down and prayed, saying ✠ "Father, if you are willing, take this cup away from me. Nevertheless, let your will be done, not mine." C. Then an angel appeared to him, coming from heaven to give him strength. In his anguish he prayed even more earnestly, and his sweat fell to the ground like great drops of blood.

When he rose from prayer he went to the disciples and found them sleeping for sheer grief. He said to them, ✠ "Why are you asleep? Get up and pray not to be put to the test."

C. He was still speaking when a number of men appeared, and at the head of them the man called Judas, one of the Twelve, who went up to Jesus to kiss him. Jesus said, ✠ "Judas, are you betraying the Son of Man with a kiss?" C. His followers, seeing what was happening, said, S. "Lord, shall we use our swords?" C. And one of them struck out at the high priest's servant, and cut off his right ear. But at this Jesus spoke. ✠ "Leave off! That will do!" C. And touching the man's ear he healed him.

Then Jesus spoke to the chief priests and captains of the Temple guard and elders who had come for him. He said, ✠ "Am I a brigand that you had to set out with swords and clubs? When I was among you in the Temple day after day you never moved to lay hands on me. But this is your hour; this is the reign of darkness."

C. They seized him then and led him away, and they

took him to the high priest's house. Peter followed at a distance. They had lit a fire in the middle of the courtyard and Peter sat down among them, and as he was sitting there by the blaze a servant-girl saw him, peered at him, and said, S. "This person was with him too." C. But he denied it, saying S. "Woman, I do not know him." C. Shortly afterwards someone else saw him and said, So. "You are another of them." C. But Peter replied, S. "I am not, my friend." C. About an hour later another man insisted saying. S. "This fellow was certainly with him. Why, he is a Galilean." C. Peter said, S. "My friend, I do not know what you are talking about." C. At that instant, while he was still speaking, the cock crew, and the Lord turned and looked straight at Peter, and Peter remembered what the Lord had said to him, ✠ "Before the cock crows today, you will have disowned me three times." C. And he went outside and wept bitterly.

Meanwhile the men who guarded Jesus were mocking and beating him. They blindfolded him and questioned him, saying S. "Play the prophet. Who hit you then?" C. And they continued heaping insults on him.

When day broke there was a meeting of the elders of the people, attended by the chief priests and scribes. He was brought before their council, and they said to him, S. "If you are the Christ, tell us." C. He replied ✠ "If I tell you, you will not believe me, and if I question you, you will not answer. But from now on, the Son of Man will be seated at the right hand of the Power of God." C. Then they all said, S. "So you are the Son of God then?" C. He answered, ✠ "It is you who say I am." S. "What need of witnesses have we now?" C. they said. S. "We have heard it for ourselves from his own lips." C. *The whole assembly then rose, and they brought him before Pilate.

They began their accusation by saying, S. "We found this man inciting our people to revolt, opposing payment of tribute to Caesar, and claiming to be Christ, a king."

C. Pilate put to him this question, S. "Are you the king of the Jews?" He replied, ✠ "It is you who say it" C. Pilate then said to the chief priests and the crowd, S. "I find no case against this man." C. But they persisted, S. "He is inflaming the people with his teaching all over Judaea; it has come all the way from Galilee, where he started, down to here." C. When Pilate heard this, he asked if the man were a Galilean; and finding that he came under Herod's jurisdiction he passed him over to Herod who was also in Jerusalem at that time.

Herod was delighted to see Jesus; he had heard about him and had been wanting for a long time to set eyes on him; moreover, he was hoping to see some miracle worked by him. So he questioned him at some length; but without getting any reply. Meanwhile the chief priests and the scribes were there, violently pressing their accusations. Then Herod, together with his guards, treated him with contempt and made fun of him; he put a rich cloak on him and sent him back to Pilate. And though Herod and Pilate had been enemies before, they were reconciled that same day.

Pilate then summoned the chief priests and the leading men and the people. He said S. "You brought this man before me as a political agitator. Now I have gone into the matter myself in your presence and found no case against the man in respect of all the charges you bring against him. Nor has Herod either, since he has sent him back to us. As you can see, the man has done nothing that deserves death, so I shall have him flogged and then let him go." C. But as one man they howled, S. "Away with him! Give us Barabbas!" C. (This man had been thrown into prison for causing a riot in the city and for murder.)

Pilate was anxious to set Jesus free and addressed them again, but they shouted back. S. "Crucify him! Crucify him!" C. And for the third time he spoke to them, S. "Why? What harm has this man done? I have found no case against him that deserves death, so I shall have him punished and then let him go." C. But they kept on shouting at the top of their voices, demanding that he should be crucified. And their shouts were growing louder.

Pilate then gave his verdict: their demand was to be granted. He released the man they asked for, who had been imprisoned for rioting and murder, and handed Jesus over to them to deal with as they pleased.

As they were leading him away they seized on a man, Simon from Cyrene, who was coming in from the country, and made him shoulder the cross and carry it behind Jesus. Large numbers of people followed him, and of women too, who mourned and lamented for him. But Jesus turned to them and said, ✠ "Daughters of Jerusalem, do not weep for me; weep rather for yourselves and for your children. For the days will surely come when people will say, 'Happy are those who are barren, the wombs that have never borne, the breasts that have never suckled!' Then they will begin to say to the mountains, 'Fall on us!'; to the hills, 'Cover us!' For if men use the green wood like this, what will happen when it is dry?" C. Now with him they were also leading out two other criminals to be executed.

When they reached the place called The Skull, they crucified him there and the two criminals also, one on the right, the other on the left. Jesus said, ✠ "Father, forgive them; they do not know what they are doing." C. Then they cast lots to share out his clothing.

The people stayed there watching him. As for the leaders, they jeered at him, say S. "He saved others, let him save himself if he is the Christ of God, the Chosen One." C. The soldiers mocked him too, and when they approached to offer him vinegar they said, S. "If you are the king of the Jews, save yourself." C. Above him there was an inscription: "This is the King of the Jews."

One of the criminals hanging there abused him, saying S. "Are you not the Christ? Save yourself and us as well." C. But the other spoke up and rebuked him. S. "Have you no fear of God at all? You got the same sentence as he did, but in our case we deserved it: we are paying for what we did. But this man has done nothing wrong. Jesus, remember me when you come into your kingdom." C. He replied ✠ "Indeed, I promise you, today you will be with me in paradise."

C. It was now about the sixth hour and, with the sun eclipsed, a darkness came over the whole land until the ninth hour. The veil of the Temple was torn right down the middle; and when Jesus had cried out in a loud voice, he said, ✠ "Father, into your hands I commit my spirit." C. With these words he breathed his last.

When the centurion saw what had taken place, he gave praise to God and said, S. "This was a great and good man." C. And when all the people who had gathered for the spectacle saw what had happened, they went home beating their breasts.

All his friends stood at a distance; so also did the women who had accompanied him from Galilee, and they saw all this happen.

Then a member of the council arrived, an upright and virtuous man named Joseph. He had not consented to what the others had planned and carried out. He came from Arimathaea, a Jewish town, and he lived in the hope of seeing the kingdom of God. This man went to Pilate and asked for the body of Jesus. He then took it down, wrapped it in a shroud and put him in a tomb which was hewn in stone in which no one had yet been laid. It was Preparation Day and the sabbath was imminent.

Meanwhile the women who had come from Galilee with Jesus were following behind. They took note of the tomb and of the position of the body.

Then they returned and prepared spices and ointments. And on the sabbath day they rested, as the Law required.

This is the Gospel of the Lord.*

*Shorter Form, 23:1–49. Read between *.

MONDAY

First Reading   (42:1–7)

A reading from the prophet Isaiah
He does not cry out or shout aloud.

Here is my servant whom I uphold,
my chosen one in whom my soul delights.
I have endowed him with my spirit
that he may bring true justice to the nations.

He does not cry out or shout aloud,
or make his voice heard in the streets.
He does not break the crushed reed,
nor quench the wavering flame.

Faithfully he brings true justice;
he will neither waver, nor be crushed
until true justice is established on earth,
for the islands are awaiting his law.

Thus says God, the Lord,
he who created the heavens and spread them out,
who gave shape to the earth and what comes from it,
who gave breath to its people
and life to the creatures that move in it;

I, the Lord, have called you to serve the cause of right;
I have taken you by the hand and formed you;
I have appointed you as covenant of the people and light
   of the nations,

to open the eyes of the blind,
to free captives from prison,
and those who live in darkness from the dungeon.
   This is the word of the Lord.

Responsorial Psalm   (Ps 26:1–3. 13–14. *R*. v. 1)

Response

The Lord is my light and my help.

1. The Lord is my light and my help;
whom shall I fear?
The Lord is the stronghold of my life;
before whom shall I shrink? (*R*.)

2. When evil-doers draw near
to devour my flesh,
it is they, my enemies and foes,
who stumble and fall. (*R*.)

3. Though an army encamp against me
my heart would not fear.
Though war break out against me
even then would I trust. (*R*.)

4. I am sure I shall see the Lord's goodness
in the land of the living.
Hope in him, hold firm and take heart.
Hope in the Lord! (*R*.)

Acclamation

Hail to you, our King!
You alone have had compassion on our sins.

Gospel   (12:1–11)

A reading from the holy Gospel according to John
*Leave her alone; she had to keep this scent for the day of my
burial.*

Six days before the Passover, Jesus went to Bethany, where
Lazarus was, whom he had raised from the dead. They
gave a dinner for him there; Martha waited on them and

Lazarus was among those at table. Mary brought in a pound of very costly ointment, pure nard, and with it anointed the feet of Jesus, wiping them with her hair; the house was full of the scent of the ointment. Then Judas Iscariot – one of his disciples, the man who was to betray him – said. 'Why wasn't this ointment sold for three hundred denarii, and the money given to the poor?" He said this, not because he cared about the poor, but because he was a thief; he was in charge of the common fund and used to help himself to the contributions. So Jesus said, "Leave her alone; she had to keep this scent for the day of my burial. You have the poor with you always, you will not always have me."

Meanwhile a large number of Jews heard that he was there and came not only on account of Jesus but also to see Lazarus whom he had raised from the dead. Then the chief priests decided to kill Lazarus as well, since it was on his account that many of the Jews were leaving them and believing in Jesus.

This is the Gospel of the Lord.

TUESDAY

First Reading   (49:1–6)

A reading from the prophet Isaiah
I will make you the light of the nations so that my salvation may reach to the ends of the earth.

Islands, listen to me,
pay attention, remotest peoples.
The Lord called me before I was born,
from my mother's womb he pronounced my name.

He made my mouth a sharp sword,
and hid me in the shadow of his hand.
He made me into a sharpened arrow,
and concealed me in his quiver.

He said to me, "You are my servant (Israel)
in whom I shall be glorified";
while I was thinking, "I have toiled in vain,
I have exhausted myself for nothing";

and all the while my cause was with the Lord,
my reward with my God.
I was honoured in the eyes of the Lord,
my God was my strength.

And now the Lord has spoken,
he who formed me in the womb to be his servant,
to bring Jacob back to him,
to gather Israel to him:

"It is not enough for you to be my servant,
to restore the tribes of Jacob and bring back the survivors
    of Israel;
I will make you the light of the nations
so that my salvation may reach to the ends of the earth."

This is the word of the Lord.

Responsorial Psalm   (Ps 70:1–6. 15. 17. *R*. v. 15)

Response
My lips will tell of your help.

1. In you, O Lord, I take refuge;
let me never be put to shame.
In your justice rescue me, free me:
pay heed to me and save me. (*R*.)

2. Be a rock where I can take refuge,
a mighty stronghold to save me;
for you are my rock, my stronghold.
Free me from the hand of the wicked. (*R*.)

3. It is you, O Lord, who are my hope,
my trust, O Lord, since my youth.
On you I have leaned from my birth,
from my mother's womb you have been my help. (*R*.)

4. My lips tell of your justice
and day by day of your help
(though I can never tell it all).
O God, you have taught me from my youth
and I proclaim your wonders still. (*R*.)

Acclamation

Hail to you, our King!
Obedient to the Father, you were led to your crucifixion
as a meek lamb is led to the slaughter.

Gospel   (13:21–33. 36–38)

A reading from the holy Gospel according to John
*One of you will betray me . . . Before the cock crows you will
have disowned me three times.*

While at supper with his disciples, Jesus was troubled in
spirit and declared, "I tell you most solemnly, one of you
will betray me." The disciples looked at one another, wondering which he meant. The disciple Jesus loved was re-
clining next to Jesus; Simon Peter signed to him and said,
"Ask who it is he means", so leaning back on Jesus' breast
he said, "Who is it, Lord?" "It is the one" replied Jesus
"to whom I give the piece of bread that I shall dip in the
dish." He dipped the piece of bread and gave it to Judas
son of Simon Iscariot. At that instant, after Judas had taken
the bread, Satan entered him. Jesus then said, "What you
are going to do, do quickly." None of the others at table
understood the reason he said this. Since Judas had charge
of the common fund, some of them thought Jesus was telling him, "Buy what we need for the festival," or telling him

to give something to the poor. As soon as Judas had taken
the piece of bread he went out. Night had fallen.

When he had gone Jesus said:

"Now has the Son of Man been glorified,
and in him God has been glorified.
If God has been glorified in him,
God will in turn glorify him in himself,
and will glorify him very soon.
My little children,
I shall not be with you much longer.
You will look for me,
and, as I told the Jews,
where I am going,
you cannot come."

Simon Peter said, "Lord, where are you going?" Jesus
replied, "Where I am going you cannot follow me now;
you will follow me later." Peter said to him, "Why can't I
follow you now? I will lay down my life for you." "Lay
down your life for me?" answered Jesus. "I tell you most
solemnly, before the cock crows you will have disowned me
three times."

This is the Gospel of the Lord.

WEDNESDAY

First Reading   (50:4–9)

A reading from the prophet Isaiah
I did not cover my face against insult.

The Lord has given me
a disciple's tongue.
So that I may know how to reply to the wearied
he provides me with speech.
Each morning he wakes me to hear,
to listen like a disciple.
The Lord has opened my ear.

For my part, I made no resistance,
neither did I turn away.
I offered my back to those who struck me,
my cheeks to those who tore at my beard;
I did not cover my face
against insult and spittle.

The Lord comes to my help,
so that I am untouched by the insults.
So, too, I set my face like flint;
I know I shall not be shamed.

My vindicator is here at hand. Does anyone start proceed-
    ings against me?
Then let us go to court together.
Who thinks he has a case against me?
Let him approach me.

The Lord is coming to my help,
who dare condemn me?

　　This is the word of the Lord.

Responsorial Psalm (Ps 68:8–10. 21–22. 31. 33–34. R. v. 14)
Response
In your great love, O Lord,
answer my prayer for your favour.

1. It is for you that I suffer taunts,
that shame covers my face,
that I have become a stranger to my brothers,
an alien to my own mother's sons.
I burn with zeal for your house
and taunts against you fall on me. (R.)

2. Taunts have broken my heart;
I have reached the end of my strength.

I looked in vain for compassion,
for consolers; not one could I find.
For food they gave me poison;
in my thirst they gave me vinegar to drink. (R.)

3. I will praise God's name with a song;
I will glorify him with thanksgiving.
The poor when they see it will be glad
and God-seeking hearts will revive;
for the Lord listens to the needy
and does not spurn his servants in their chains. (R.)

Acclamation

Hail to you, our King!
Obedient to the Father, you were led to your crucifixion
as a meek lamb is led to the slaughter.

The Acclamation for Monday may be used as an alternative.

Gospel   (26:14–25)

A reading from the holy Gospel according to Matthew

The Son of Man is going to his fate, as the scriptures say he will, but alas for that man by whom he is betrayed.

Then one of the Twelve, the man called Judas Iscariot, went to the chief priests and said, "What are you prepared to give me if I hand him over to you?" They paid him thirty silver pieces, and from that moment he looked for an opportunity to betray him.

Now on the first day of Unleavened Bread the disciples came to Jesus to say, "Where do you want us to make the preparations for you to eat the passover?" "Go to -so-and-so in the city" he replied "and say to him, 'The master says: My time is near. It is at your house that I am keeping Passover with my disciples.'" The disciples did what Jesus told them and prepared the Passover.

When evening came he was at table with the twelve disciples. And while they were eating he said, "I tell you solemnly, one of you is about to betray me." They were greatly distressed and started asking him in turn, "Not I, Lord, surely?" He answered, "Someone who has dipped his hand into the dish with me, will betray me. The Son of Man is going to his fate, as the scriptures say he will, but alas for that man by whom the Son of Man is betrayed! Better for that man if he had never been born!" Judas, who was to betray him, asked in his turn, "Not I, Rabbi, surely?" "They are your own words" answered Jesus.

This is the Gospel of the Lord.

HOLY THURSDAY

Mass of the Chrism

First Reading   (61:1–3. 6. 8–9)

A reading from the prophet Isaiah
The Lord has anointed me and has sent me to bring good news to the poor and to give them the oil of gladness.

The spirit of the Lord has been given to me,
for the Lord has anointed me.
He has sent me to bring good news to the poor,
to bind up hearts that are broken;
to proclaim liberty to captives,
freedom to those in prison;
to proclaim a year of favour from the Lord,
a day of vengeance for our God.

To comfort all those who mourn and to give them
for ashes a garland;
for mourning robe the oil of gladness,
for despondency, praise.

But you, you will be named "priests of the Lord",
they will call you "ministers of our God".
I reward them faithfully
and make an everlasting covenant with them.

Their race will be famous throughout the nations,
their descendants throughout the peoples.
All who see them will admit
that they are a race whom the Lord has blessed.

This is the word of the Lord.

Responsorial Psalm   (Ps 88:21–22. 25. 27. *R*. v. 2)
Response
I will sing for ever of your love, O Lord.

1. I have found David my servant
and with my holy oil anointed him.
My hand shall always be with him
and my arm shall make him strong. (*R*.)

2. My truth and my love shall be with him;
by my name his might shall be exalted.
He will say to me: "You are my father,
my God, the rock who saves me." (*R*.)

Second Reading   (1:5–8)
A reading from the book of the Apocalypse
He made us a line of kings, priests to serve his God and Father.

Grace and peace to you from Jesus Christ, the faithful witness, the First-born from the dead, the Ruler of the kings of
the earth. He loves us and has washed away our sins with
his blood, and made us a line of kings, priests to serve his
God and Father; to him, then, be glory and power for ever
and ever. Amen. It is he who is coming on the clouds; everyone will see him, even those who pierced him, and all the
races of the earth will mourn over him. This is the truth.
Amen. "I am the Alpha and the Omega" says the Lord
God, who is, who was, and who is to come, the Almighty.
This is the word of the Lord.

Acclamation   (Lk 4:18)

The spirit of the Lord has been given to me;
he has sent me to bring the good news to the poor.

Gospel   (4:16–21)

A reading from the holy Gospel according to Luke
The spirit of the Lord has been given to me, for he has anointed me.

Jesus came to Nazara, where he had been brought up, and went into the synagogue on the sabbath day as he usually did. He stood up to read, and they handed him the scroll of the prophet Isaiah. Unrolling the scroll he found the place where it is written:

The spirit of the Lord has been given to me,
for he has anointed me.
He has sent me to bring the good news to the poor,
to proclaim liberty to captives.
and to the blind new sight,
to set the downtrodden free,
to proclaim the Lord's year of favour.

He then rolled up the scroll, gave it back to the assistant and sat down. And all eyes in the synagogue were fixed on him. Then he began to speak to them. "This text is being fulfilled today even as you listen."
        This is the Gospel of the Lord.

THE EASTER TRIDUUM AND EASTERTIDE

HOLY THURSDAY

Mass of The Lord's Supper

First Reading   (12:1–8. 11–14

A reading from the book of Exodus
Instructions concerning the Passover meal.

The Lord said to Moses and Aaron in the land of Egypt,
"This month is to be the first of all the others for you, the
first month of your year. Speak to the whole community of
Israel and say, 'On the tenth day of this month each man
must take an animal from the flock, one for each family:
one animal for each household. If the household is too
small to eat the animal, a man must join with his neighbour,
the nearest to his house, as the number of persons requires.
You must take into account what each can eat in deciding
the number for the animal. It must be an animal without
blemish, a male one year old; you may take it from either
sheep or goats. You must keep it till the fourteenth day of
the month when the whole assembly of the community of
Israel shall slaughter it between the two evenings. Some of
the blood must then be taken and put on the two doorposts
and the lintel of the houses where it is eaten. That night, the
flesh is to be eaten, roasted over the fire; it must be eaten
with unleavened bread and bitter herbs. You shall eat it
like this: with a girdle round your waist, sandals on your
feet, a staff in your hand. You shall eat it hastily: it is a
passover in honour of the Lord. That night, I will go

through the land of Egypt and strike down all the first-born
in the land of Egypt, man and beast alike, and I shall deal
out punishment to all the gods of Egypt, I am the Lord.
The blood shall serve to mark the houses that you live in.
When I see the blood I will pass over you and you shall
escape the destroying plague when I strike the land of
Egypt. This day is to be a day of remembrance for you, and
you must celebrate it as a feast in the Lord's honour. For all
generations you are to declare it a day of festival, for ever.' "

This is the word of the Lord.

Responsorial Psalm   (Ps 115:12–13. 15–18. *R*. 1 Cor 10:16)
Response
The blessing-cup that we bless
is a communion with the blood of Christ.

1. How can I repay the Lord
for his goodness to me?
The cup of salvation I will raise;
I will call on the Lord's name. (*R*.)

2. O precious in the eyes of the Lord
is the death of his faithful.
Your servant, Lord, your servant am I;
you have loosened my bonds. (*R*.)

3. A thanksgiving sacrifice I make:
I will call on the Lord's name.
My vows to the Lord I will fulfil
before all his people. (*R*.)

Second Reading   (11:23–26)
A reading from the first letter of St Paul to the Corinthians
Every time you eat this bread and drink this cup, you are
proclaiming the death of the Lord.

For this is what I received from the Lord, and in turn passed on to you: that on the same night that he was betrayed, the Lord Jesus took some bread, and thanked God for it and broke it, and he said, "This is my body, which is for you; do this as a memorial of me." In the same way he took the cup after supper, and said, "This cup is the new covenant in my blood. Whenever you drink it, do this as a memorial of me." Until the Lord comes, therefore, every time you eat this bread and drink this cup, you are proclaiming his death.

This is the word of the Lord.

Acclamation (Jn 13:34)

I give you a new commandment:
love one another just as I have loved you,
says the Lord.

Gospel (13:1–15)

A reading from the holy Gospel according to John
Now he showed how perfect his love was.

It was before the festival of the Passover, and Jesus knew that the hour had come for him to pass from this world to the Father. He had always loved those who were his in the world, but now he showed how perfect his love was.

They were at supper, and the devil had already put it into the mind of Judas Iscariot son of Simon, to betray him. Jesus knew that the Father had put everything into his hands, and that he had come from God and was returning to God, and he got up from table, removed his outer garment and, taking a towel, wrapped it round his waist; he then poured water into a basin and began to wash the disciples' feet and to wipe them with the towel he was wearing.

He came to Simon Peter, who said to him, "Lord, are you going to wash my feet?" Jesus answered, "At the moment you do not know what I am doing, but later you will understand." "Never!" said Peter "You shall never wash my feet." Jesus replied, "If I do not wash you, you can have nothing in common with me." "Then, Lord," said Simon Peter "not only my feet, but my hands and my head as well!" Jesus said, "No one who has taken a bath needs washing, he is clean all over. You too are clean, though not all of you are." He knew who was going to betray him, that was why he said, "though not all of you are."

When he had washed their feet and put on his clothes again he went back to the table. "Do you understand" he said "what I have done to you? You call me Master and Lord, and rightly; so I am. If I, then, the Lord and Master, have washed your feet, you should wash each other's feet. I have given you an example so that you may copy what I have done to you."

This is the Gospel of the Lord.

GOOD FRIDAY

First Reading   (52:13–53:12)

A reading from the prophet Isaiah
He was pierced through for our faults.

See, my servant will prosper,
he shall be lifted up, exalted, rise to great heights.

As the crowds were appalled on seeing him
– so disfigured did he look
that he seemed no longer human –
so will the crowds be astonished at him,
and kings stand speechless before him;
for they shall see something never told
and witness something never heard before:
"Who could believe what we have heard,
and to whom has the power of the Lord been revealed?"

Like a sapling he grew up in front of us,
like a root in arid ground.
Without beauty, without majesty (we saw him),
no looks to attract our eyes;
a thing despised and rejected by men,
a man of sorrows and familiar with suffering,
a man to make people screen their faces;
he was despised and we took no account of him.
And yet ours were the sufferings he bore,
ours the sorrows he carried.
But we, we thought of him as someone punished,
struck by God, and brought low.
Yet he was pierced through for our faults,
crushed for our sins.
On him lies a punishment that brings us peace,
and through his wounds we are healed.
We had all gone astray like sheep,
each taking his own way,
and the Lord burdened him
with the sins of all of us.
Harshly dealt with, he bore it humbly,
he never opened his mouth,
like a lamb that is led to the slaughter-house,
like a sheep that is dumb before its shearers
never opening its mouth.

By force and by law he was taken;
would anyone plead his cause?
Yes, he was torn away from the land of the living;
for our faults struck down in death.

They gave him a grave with the wicked,
a tomb with the rich,
though he had done no wrong
and there had been no perjury in his mouth.

The Lord has been pleased to crush him with suffering.
If he offers his life in atonement,
he shall see his heirs, he shall have a long life
and through him what the Lord wishes will be done.

His soul's anguish over
he shall see the light and be content.
By his sufferings shall my servant justify many,
taking their faults on himself.

Hence I will grant whole hordes for his tribute,
he shall divide the spoil with the mighty,
for surrendering himself to death
and letting himself be taken for a sinner,
while he was bearing the faults of many
and praying all the time for sinners.

This is the word of the Lord.

Responsorial Psalm   (Ps 30:2. 6. 12–13. 15–17. 25.
                                              R. Lk 23:46)

Response
Father, into your hands I commend my spirit.

1. In you, O Lord, I take refuge.
Let me never be put to shame.
In your justice, set me free.
Into your hands I commend my spirit.
It is you who will redeem me, Lord. (*R*.)

2. In the face of all my foes
I am a reproach,
an object of scorn to my neighbours
and of fear to my friends. (*R*.)

3. Those who see me in the street
run far away from me.

I am like a dead man, forgotten in men's hearts,
like a thing thrown away. (R.)

4. But as for me, I trust in you, Lord,
I say: "You are my God."
My life is in your hands, deliver me
from the hands of those who hate me. (R.)

5. Let your face shine on your servant.
Save me in your love.
Be strong, let your heart take courage,
all who hope in the Lord. (R.)

Second Reading   (4:14–16;5:7–9)

A reading from the letter to the Hebrews
*He learnt to obey through suffering and became for all who
obey him the source of eternal salvation.*

Since in Jesus, the Son of God, we have the supreme high
priest who has gone through to the highest heaven, we
must never let go of the faith that we have professed. For it
is not as if we had a high priest who was incapable of feeling our weaknesses with us; but we have one who has been
tempted in every way that we are, though he is without sin.
Let us be confident, then, in approaching the throne of
grace, that we shall have mercy from him and find grace
when we are in need of help.

During his life on earth, he offered up prayer and entreaty, aloud and in silent tears, to the one who had the
power to save him out of death, and he submitted so
humbly that his prayer was heard. Although he was a Son,
he learnt to obey through suffering; but having been made
perfect, he became for all who obey him the source of eternal salvation.

This is the word of the Lord.

Acclamation   (Ph 2:8–9)

Christ was humbler yet,
even to accepting death,
death on a cross.
But God raised him high
and gave him the name
which is above all names.

Gospel   (18:1–19:42)

The passion of our Lord Jesus Christ according to John

C. Jesus left with his disciples and crossed the Kedron
valley. There was a garden there, and he went into it with
his disciples. Judas the traitor knew the place well, since
Jesus had often met his disciples there, and he brought the
cohort to this place together with a detachment of guards
sent by the chief priests and the Pharisees, all with lanterns
and torches and weapons. Knowing everything that was
going to happen to him, Jesus then came forward and said,
✠ "Who are you looking for?" C. They answered, S. "Jesus
the Nazarene." C. He said, ✠ "I am he." C. Now Judas the
traitor was standing among them. When Jesus said, "I
am he", they moved back and fell to the ground. He asked
them a second time, ✠ "Who are you looking for?" C. They
said, S. "Jesus the Nazarene." Jesus replied ✠ "I have told
you that I am he. If I am the one you are looking for, let
these others go." C. This was to fulfil the words he had
spoken, "Not one of those you gave me have I lost."

Simon Peter, who carried a sword, drew it and woun-
ded the high priest's servant, cutting off his right ear. The
servant's name was Malchus. Jesus said to Peter, ✠ "Put
your sword back in its scabbard; am I not to drink the cup
that the Father has given me?"

C. The cohort and its captain and the Jewish guards
seized Jesus and bound him. They took him first to Annas,

because Annas was the father-in-law of Caiaphas, who was high priest that year. It was Caiaphas who had suggested to the Jews, "It is better for one man to die for the people."

Simon Peter, with another disciple, followed Jesus. This disciple, who was known to the high priest, went with Jesus into the high priest's palace, but Peter stayed outside the door. So the other disciple, the one known to the high priest, went out, spoke to the woman who was keeping the door and brought Peter in. The maid on duty at the door said to Peter, S. "Aren't you another of that man's disciples?" C. He answered, S. "I am not." C. Now it was cold, and the servants and guards had lit a charcoal fire and were standing there warming themselves; so Peter stood there too, warming himself with the others.

The high priest questioned Jesus about his disciples and his teaching. Jesus answered, ✠ "I have spoken openly for all the world to hear; I have always taught in the synagogue and in the Temple where all the Jews meet together: I have said nothing in secret. But why ask me? Ask my hearers what I taught: they know what I said." C. At these words, one of the guards standing by gave Jesus a slap in the face, saying, S. "Is that the way to answer the high priest?" C. Jesus replied, ✠ "If there is something wrong in what I said, point it out; but if there is no offence in it, why do you strike me?" C. Then Annas sent him, still bound, to Caiaphas the high priest.

As Simon Peter stood there warming himself, someone said to him, S. "Aren't you another of his disciples?" C. He denied it saying, S. "I am not." C. One of the high priest's servants, a relation of the man whose ear Peter had cut off, said, S. "Didn't I see you in the garden with him?" C. Again Peter denied it; and at once a cock crew.

They then led Jesus from the house of Caiaphas to the Praetorium. It was now morning. They did not go into the Praetorium themselves or they would be defiled and unable to eat the passover. So Pilate came outside to them and said, S. "What charge do you bring against this man?" C. They replied, S. "If he were not a criminal, we should not be handing him over to you." C. Pilate said, S. "Take him yourselves, and try him by your own Law." C. The Jews answered, S. "We are not allowed to put a man to death." C. This was to fulfil the words Jesus had spoken indicating the way he was going to die.

So Pilate went back into the Praetorium and called Jesus to him, and asked S. "Are you the king of the Jews?" Jesus replied, ✠ "Do you ask this of your own accord, or have others spoken to you about me?" C. Pilate answered, S. "Am I a Jew? It is your own people and the chief priests who have handed you over to me: what have you done?" C. Jesus replied, ✠ "Mine is not a kingdom of this world; if my kingdom were of this world, my men would have fought to prevent me being surrendered to the Jews. But my kingdom is not of this kind." S. "So you are a king then?" C. said Pilate. Jesus answered ✠ "It is you who say it. Yes, I am a king. I was born for this, I came into the world for this; to bear witness to my truth, and all who are on the side of truth listen to my voice." C. Pilate said S. "Truth? What is that?" and with that he went out again to the Jews and said, S. "I find no case against him. But according to a custom of yours I should release one prisoner at the Passover; would you like me, then, to release the king of the Jews?" C. At this they shouted: S. "Not this man, but Barabbas." C. Barabbas was a brigand.

Pilate then had Jesus taken away and scourged; and after this, the soldiers twisted some thorns into a crown and put it on his head, and dressed him in a purple robe. They kept coming up to him and saying, S. "Hail, king of the Jews!" C. and they slapped him in the face.

Pilate came outside again and said to them, S. "Look, I am going to bring him out to you to let you see that I find no case." C. Jesus then came out wearing the crown of

thorns and the purple robe. Pilate said, S. "Here is the man."
C. When they saw him the chief priests and the guards
shouted, S. "Crucify him! Crucify him!" C. Pilate said,
S. "Take him yourselves and crucify him: I can find no
case against him." C. The Jews replied S. "We have a Law,
and according to the Law he ought to die, because he has
claimed to be the Son of God."

C. When Pilate heard them say this his fears increased.
Re-entering the Praetorium, he said to Jesus S. "Where do
you come from?" C. But Jesus made no answer. Pilate then
said to him, S. "Are you refusing to speak to me? Surely
you know I have power to release you and I have power to
crucify you?" C. Jesus replied ✠ "You would have no
power over me if it had not been given you from above; that
is why the one who handed me over to you has the greater
guilt."

C. From that moment Pilate was anxious to set him free,
but the Jews shouted S. "If you set him free you are no
friend of Caesar's; anyone who makes himself king is de-
fying Caesar." C. Hearing these words, Pilate had Jesus
brought out, and seated himself on the chair of judgement
at a place called the Pavement, in Hebrew Gabbatha. It was
Passover Preparation Day, about the sixth hour. S. "Here
is your king" C. said Pilate to the Jews. They said S. "Take
him away, take him away!" C. they said. S. "Crucify him!"
C. Pilate said, S. "Do you want me to crucify your king?"
C. The chief priests answered, S. "We have no king except
Caesar." C. So in the end Pilate handed him over to them
to be crucified.

They then took charge of Jesus, and carrying his own
cross he went out of the city to the place of the skull or, as
it was called in Hebrew, Golgotha, where they crucified him
with two others, one on either side with Jesus in the middle.
Pilate wrote out a notice and had it fixed to the cross; it
ran: "Jesus the Nazarene, King of the Jews." This notice
was read by many of the Jews, because the place where

Jesus was crucified was not far from the city, and the writing was in Hebrew, Latin and Greek. So the Jewish chief priests said to Pilate, S. "You should not write 'King of the Jews', but 'This man said: I am King of the Jews'." C. Pilate answered, S. "What I have written, I have written."

C. When the soldiers had finished crucifying Jesus they took his clothing and divided it into four shares, one for each soldier. His undergarment was seamless, woven in one piece from neck to hem; so they said to one another, S. "Instead of tearing it, let's throw dice to decide who is to have it." C. In this way the words of scripture were fulfilled:

They shared out my clothing among them.
They cast lots for my clothes.

This is exactly what the soldiers did.

Near the cross of Jesus stood his mother and his mother's sister, Mary the wife of Clopas, and Mary of Magdala. Seeing his mother and the disciple he loved standing near her, Jesus said to his mother, ✠ "Woman, this is your son." C. Then to the disciple he said, ✠ "This is your mother." C. And from that moment the disciple made a place for her in his home.

After this, Jesus knew that everything had now been completed, and to fulfil the scripture perfectly he said:

✠ "I am thirsty."

C. A jar full of vinegar stood there, so putting a sponge soaked in vinegar on a hyssop stick they held it up to his mouth. After Jesus had taken the vinegar he said, ✠ "It is accomplished"; C. and bowing his head he gave up the spirit.

It was Preparation Day, and to prevent the bodies remaining on the cross during the sabbath – since that sabbath was a day of special solemnity – the Jews asked Pilate to have the legs broken and the bodies taken away. Consequently the soldiers came and broke the legs of the first man who had been crucified with him and then of the other. When they came to Jesus, they found he was already dead, and so instead of breaking his legs one of the soldiers pierced his side with a lance; and immediately there came out blood and water. This is the evidence of one who saw it – trustworthy evidence, and he knows he speaks the truth – and he gives it so that you may believe as well. Because all this happened to fulfil the words of scripture:

Not one bone of his will be broken,

and again, in another place scripture says:

They will look on the one whom they have pierced.

After this, Joseph of Arimathaea, who was a disciple of Jesus – though a secret one because he was afraid of the Jews – asked Pilate to let him remove the body of Jesus. Pilate gave permission, so they came and took it away. Nicodemus came as well – the same one who had first come to Jesus at night-time – and he brought a mixture of myrrh and aloes, weighing about a hundred pounds. They took the body of Jesus and wrapped it with the spices in linen cloths, following the Jewish burial custom. At the place where he had been crucified there was a garden, and in this garden a new tomb in which no one had yet been buried. Since it was the Jewish Day of Preparation and the tomb was near at hand, they laid Jesus there.

This is the Gospel of the Lord.

EASTER SUNDAY THE RESURRECTION OF THE LORD

EASTER VIGIL AND MASS

Nine readings, seven from the Old Testament and two from the New, are proposed for the Easter Vigil. The number of readings may be reduced if circumstances demand it for special reasons. But there should be at least three readings from the Old Testament (though these may be reduced to two in special cases) before the Epistle and Gospel. The account of the Crossing of the Red Sea (Third Reading) must always be used.

First Reading   (1:1–2:2)

A reading from the book of Genesis
God saw all he had made, and indeed it was very good.

In the beginning God created the heavens and the earth. Now the earth was a formless void, there was darkness over the deep, and God's spirit hovered over the water.

God said, "Let there be light," and there was light. God saw that light was good, and God divided light from darkness. God called light "day", and darkness he called "night". Evening came and morning came: the first day.

God said, "Let there be a vault in the waters to divide the waters in two." And so it was. God made the vault, and it divided the waters above the vault from the waters under the vault. God called the vault "heaven". Evening came and morning came: the second day.

God said, "Let the waters under heaven come together into a single mass, and let dry land appear." And so it was. God called the dry land "earth" and the mass of water "seas", and God saw that it was good.

God said, "Let the earth produce vegetation: seed-bearing plants, and fruit trees bearing fruit with their seed inside, on the earth." And so it was. The earth produced vegetation: plants bearing seed in their several kinds, and trees bearing fruit with their seed inside in their several kinds. God saw that it was good. Evening came and morning came: the third day.

God said, "Let there be lights in the vault of heaven to divide day from night, and let them indicate festivals, days and years. Let them be lights in the vault of heaven to shine on the earth." And so it was. God made the two great lights: the greater light to govern the day, the smaller light to govern the night, and the stars. God set them in the vault of heaven to shine on the earth, to govern the day and the night and to divide light from darkness. God saw that it was good. Evening came and morning came: the fourth day.

God said, "Let the waters teem with living creatures, and let birds fly above the earth within the vault of heaven." And so it was. God created great sea-serpents and every kind of living creature with which the waters teem, and every kind of winged creature. God saw that it was good. God blessed them, saying "Be fruitful, multiply, and fill the waters of the seas; and let the birds multiply upon the earth." Evening came and morning came: the fifth day.

God said, "Let the earth produce every kind of living creature: cattle, reptiles, and every kind of wild beast." And so it was. God made every kind of wild beast, every kind of cattle, and every kind of land reptile. God saw that it was good.

*God said, "Let us make man in our own image, in the likeness of ourselves, and let them be masters of the fish of the sea, the birds of heaven, the cattle, all the wild beasts and all the reptiles that crawl upon the earth."

God created man in the image of himself,
in the image of God he created him,
male and female he created them.

God blessed them, saying to them, "Be fruitful, multiply, fill the earth and conquer it. Be masters of the fish of the

sea, the birds of heaven and all living animals on the earth."
God said, "See, I give you all the seed-bearing plants that
are upon the whole earth, and all the trees with seed-
bearing fruit; this shall be your food. To all wild beasts,
all birds of heaven and all living reptiles on the earth I give
all the foliage of plants for food." And so it was. God saw
all he had made, and indeed it was very good. Evening came
and morning came: the sixth day.

Thus heaven and earth were completed with all their
array. On the seventh day God completed the work he had
been doing. He rested on the seventh day after all the work
he had been doing.

This is the word of the Lord.*

*Shorter Form, verses 1.26–31. Read between *.

Responsorial Psalm   (Ps 103:1–2. 5–6. 10. 12–14.
                                              24. 35. *R*. v. 30)

Response
Send forth your spirit, O Lord,
and renew the face of the earth.

1. Bless the Lord, my soul!
Lord God, how great you are,
clothed in majesty and glory,
wrapped in light as in a robe! (*R*.)

2. You founded the earth on its base,
to stand firm from age to age.
You wrapped it with the ocean like a cloak:
the waters stood higher than the mountains. (*R*.)

3. You make springs gush forth in the valleys:
they flow in between the hills.
On their banks dwell the birds of heaven;
from the branches they sing their song. (*R*.)

4. From your dwelling you water the hills;
earth drinks its fill of your gift.
You make the grass grow for the cattle
and the plants to serve man's needs. (*R.*)

5. How many are your works, O Lord!
In wisdom you have made them all.
The earth is full of your riches.
Bless the Lord, my soul! (*R.*)

Alternative Psalm   (Ps 32:4–7. 12–13. 20. 22. *R.* v. 5)
Response
The Lord fills the earth with his love.

1. The word of the Lord is faithful
and all his works to be trusted.
The Lord loves justice and right
and fills the earth with his love. (*R.*)

2. By his word the heavens were made,
by the breath of his mouth all the stars.
He collects the waves of the ocean;
he stores up the depths of the sea. (*R.*)

3. They are happy, whose God is the Lord,
the people he has chosen as his own.
From the heavens the Lord looks forth,
he sees all the children of men. (*R.*)

4. Our soul is waiting for the Lord.
The Lord is our help and our shield.
May your love be upon us, O Lord,
as we place all our hope in you. (*R.*)

Second Reading   (22:1-18)

A reading from the book of Genesis
The sacrifice of Abraham, our father in faith.

God put Abraham to the test, "Abraham, Abraham," he called. "Here I am" he replied. "Take your son," God said "your only child Isaac, whom you love, and go to the land of Moriah. There you shall offer him as a burnt offering, on a mountain I will point out to you."

Rising early next morning Abraham saddled his ass and took with him two of his servants and his son Isaac. He chopped wood for the burnt offering and started on his journey to the place God had pointed out to him. On the third day Abraham looked up and saw the place in the distance. Then Abraham said to his servants, "Stay here with the donkey. The boy and I will go over there, we will worship and come back to you."

Abraham took the wood for the burnt offering, loaded it on Isaac, and carried in his own hands the fire and the knife. Then the two of them set out together. Isaac spoke to his father Abraham, "Father" he said. "Yes, my son" he replied. "Look," he said "here are the fire and the wood, but where is the lamb for the burnt offering'?' Abraham answered, "My son, God himself will provide the lamb for the burnt offering." Then the two of them went on together.

*When they arrived at the place God had pointed out to him, Abraham built an altar there, and arranged the wood. Then he bound his son Isaac and put him on the altar on top of the wood. Abraham stretched out his hand and seized the knife to kill his son.

But the angel of the Lord called to him from heaven. "Abraham, Abraham," he said. "I am here" he replied. "Do not harm him, for now I know you fear God. You have not refused me your son, your only son." Then looking up, Abraham saw a ram caught by its horns in a bush.

Abraham took the ram and offered it as a burnt-offering in place of his son.*

Abraham called this place "The Lord provides", and hence the saying today: On the mountain the Lord provides.

*The angel of the Lord called Abraham a second time from heaven. "I swear by my own self – it is the Lord who speaks – because you have done this, because you have not refused me your son, your only son, I will shower blessings on you, I will make your descendants as many as the stars of heaven and the grains of sand on the seashore. Your descendants shall gain possession of the gates of their enemies. All the nations of the earth shall bless themselves by your descendants, as a reward for your obedience."

This is the word of the Lord.*

*Shorter Form, verses 1–2. 9–13. 15–18. Read between *.

Responsorial Psalm   (Ps 15:5. 8–11. *R.* v. 1)

Response
Preserve me, God, I take refuge in you.

1. O Lord, it is you who are my portion and cup;
it is you yourself who are my prize.
I keep the Lord ever in my sight:
since he is at my right hand, I shall stand firm. (*R.*)

2. And so my heart rejoices, my soul is glad;
even my body shall rest in safety.
For you will not leave my soul among the dead,
nor let your beloved know decay. (*R.*)

3. You will show me the path of life,
the fullness of joy in your presence,
at your right hand happiness for ever. (*R.*)

The following reading is obligatory.

Third Reading   (14:15–15:1)

A reading from the book of Exodus
The sons of Israel went on dry ground right into the sea.

The Lord said to Moses, "Why do you cry to me so? Tell the sons of Israel to march on. For yourself, raise your staff and stretch out your hand over the sea and part it for the sons of Israel to walk through the sea on dry ground. I for my part will make the heart of the Egyptians so stubborn that they will follow them. So shall I win myself glory at the expense of Pharaoh, of all his army, his chariots, his horsemen. And when I have won glory for myself, at the expense of Pharaoh and his chariots and his army, the Egyptians will learn that I am the Lord."

Then the angel of the Lord, who marched at the front of the army of Israel, changed station and moved to their rear. The pillar of cloud changed station from the front to the rear of them, and remained there. It came between the camp of the Egyptians and the camp of Israel. The cloud was dark, and the night passed without the armies drawing any closer the whole night long. Moses stretched out his hand over the sea. The Lord drove back the sea with a strong easterly wind all night, and he made dry land of the sea. The waters parted and the sons of Israel went on dry ground right into the sea, walls of water to right and to left of them. The Egyptians gave chase: after them they went, right into the sea, all Pharaoh's horses, his chariots, and his horsemen. In the morning watch, the Lord looked down on the army of the Egyptians from the pillar of fire and of cloud, and threw the army into confusion. He so clogged their chariot wheels that they could scarcely make headway. "Let us flee from the Israelites," the Egyptians cried "the Lord is fighting for them against the Egyptians!" "Stretch out your hand over the sea," the Lord said to Moses "that the waters may flow back on the Egyptians and their chariots and their horsemen." Moses stretched out his hand over the sea and, as day broke, the sea returned to its bed. The fleeing Egyptians marched right into it, and the Lord overthrew the Egyptians in the very middle of the sea. The returning waters overwhelmed the chariots and the horsemen of Pharaoh's whole army, which had followed the Israelites into the sea; not a single one of them was left. But the sons of Israel had marched through the sea on dry ground, walls of water to right and to left of them. That day, the Lord rescued Israel from the Egyptians, and Israel saw the Egyptians lying dead on the shore. Israel witnessed the great act that the Lord had performed against the Egyptians, and the people venerated the Lord; they put their faith in the Lord and in Moses, his servant.

It was then that Moses and the sons of Israel sang this song in honour of the Lord:

The choir takes up the Responsorial Psalm immediately.

Responsorial Psalm   (Ex 15:1–6. 17–18. R. v. 1)

Response
I will sing to the Lord, glorious his triumph!

1. I will sing to the Lord, glorious his triumph!
Horse and rider he has thrown into the sea!
The Lord is my strength, my song, my salvation.
This is my God and I extol him,
my father's God and I gaev him praise. (*R.*)

2. The Lord is a warrior! The Lord is his name.
The chariots of Pharaoh he hurled into the sea,
the flower of his army is drowned in the sea.
The deeps hide them; they sank like a stone. (*R.*)

3. Your right hand, Lord, glorious in its power,
your right hand, Lord, has shattered the enemy.
In the greatness of your glory you crushed the foe. (*R.*)

4. You will lead them and plant them on your mountain,
the place, O Lord, where you have made your home,
the sanctuary, Lord, which your hands have made.
The Lord will reign for ever and ever. (*R*.)

Fourth Reading   (54:5–14)

A reading from the prophet Isaiah
*With everlasting love the Lord your redeemer has taken pity
on you.*

For now your creator will be your husband,
his name, the Lord of hosts;
your redeemer will be the Holy One of Israel,
he is called the God of the whole earth.
Yes, like a forsaken wife, distressed in spirit,
the Lord calls you back.
Does a man cast off the wife of his youth?
says your God.

I did forsake you for a brief moment,
but with great love will I take you back.
In excess of anger, for a moment
I hid my face from you.
But with everlasting love I have taken pity on you,
says the Lord, your redeemer.

I am now as I was in the days of Noah
when I swore that Noah's waters
should never flood the world again.
So now I swear concerning my anger with you
and the threats I made against you;

for the mountains may depart,
the hills be shaken,
but my love for you will never leave you
and my covenant of peace with you will never be shaken,
says the Lord who takes pity on you.

Unhappy creature, storm-tossed, disconsolate,
see, I will set your stones on carbuncles
and your foundations on sapphires.
I will make rubies your battlements,
your gates crystal,
and your entire wall precious stones.
Your sons will all be taught by the Lord.
The prosperity of your sons will be great.
You will be founded on integrity;
remote from oppression, you will have nothing to fear;
remote from terror, it will not approach you.

This is the word of the Lord.

Responsorial Psalm   (Ps 29:2. 4–6. 11–13. R. v. 2)
Response
I will praise you, Lord, you have rescued me.

1. I will praise you, Lord, you have rescued me
and have not let my enemies rejoice over me.
O Lord, you have raised my soul from the dead,
restored me to life from those who sink into the grave. (*R.*)

2. Sing psalms to the Lord, you who love him,
give thanks to his holy name.
His anger lasts but a moment; his favour through life.
At night there are tears, but joy comes with dawn. (*R.*)

3. The Lord listened and had pity.
The Lord came to my help.
For me you have changed my mourning into dancing,
O Lord my God, I will thank you for ever. (*R.*)

Fifth Reading   (55:1–11)
A reading from the prophet Isaiah
*Come to me and your soul will live, and I will make an ever-
lasting covenant with you.*

Thus says the Lord :
Oh, come to the water all you who are thirsty;
though you have no money, come!
Buy corn without money, and eat,
and, at no cost, wine and milk.
Why spend money on what is not bread,
your wages on what fails to satisfy?
Listen, listen to me, and you will have good things to eat
and rich food to enjoy.
Pay attention, come to me;
listen, and your soul will live.

With you I will make an everlasting covenant
out of the favours promised to David.
See, I have made of you a witness to the peoples,
a leader and a master of the nations.
See, you will summon a nation you never knew,
those unknown will come hurrying to you,
for the sake of the Lord your God,
of the Holy One of Israel who will glorify you.

Seek the Lord while he is still to be found,
call to him while he is still near.
Let the wicked man abandon his way,
the evil man his thoughts.
Let him turn back to the Lord who will take pity on him,
to our God who is rich in forgiving;
for my thoughts are not your thoughts,
my ways are not your ways – it is the Lord who speaks.
Yes, the heavens are as high above earth
as my ways are above your ways,
my thoughts above your thoughts.

Yes, as the rain and the snow come down from the heavens
and do not return without watering the earth, making it
yield and giving growth to provide seed for the sower and

bread for the eating, so the word that goes from my mouth does not return to me empty, without carrying out my will and succeeding in what it was sent to do.

This is the word of the Lord.

Responsorial Psalm   (Is 12:2–6. R. v. 3)

Response
With joy you will draw water

1. Truly God is my salvation,
I trust, I shall not fear.
For the Lord is my strength, my song,
he became my saviour.
With joy you will draw water
from the wells of salvation. (*R.*)

2. Give thanks to the Lord, give praise to his name!
make his mighty deeds known to the peoples,
declare the greatness of his name. (*R.*)

3. Sing a psalm to the Lord
for he has done glorious deeds,
make them known to all the earth!
People of Zion, sing and shout for joy
for great in your midst is the Holy One of Israel. (*R.*)

Sixth Reading   (3:9–15. 32–4:4)

A reading from the prophet Baruch
In the radiance of the Lord make your way to light.

Listen, Israel, to commands that bring life;
hear, and learn what knowledge means.
Why, Israel, why are you in the country of your enemies,
growing older and older in an alien land,
sharing defilement with the dead,

reckoned with those who go to Sheol?
Because you have forsaken the fountain of wisdom.
Had you walked in the way of God,
you would have lived in peace for ever.
Learn where knowledge is, where strength,
where understanding, and so learn
where length of days is, where life,
where the light of the eyes and where peace.
But who has found out where she lives,
who has entered her treasure house?

But the One who knows all knows her,
he has grasped her with his own intellect,
he has set the earth firm for ever
and filled it with four-footed beasts,
he sends the light – and it goes,
he recalls it – and trembling it obeys;
the stars shine joyfully at their set times:
when he calls them, they answer, "Here we are";
they gladly shine for their creator.
It is he who is our God,
no other can compare with him.
He has grasped the whole way of knowledge,
and confided it to his servant Jacob,
to Israel his well-beloved;
so causing her to appear on earth
and move among men.

This is the book of the commandments of God,
the Law that stands for ever;
those who keep her live,
those who desert her die.
Turn back, Jacob, seize her,
in her radiance make your way to light:
do not yield your glory to another,
your privilege to a people not your own.

Israel, blessed are we:
what pleases God has been revealed to us.

This is the word of the Lord.

Responsorial Psalm   (Ps 18:8–11. *R.* Jn 6:69)

Response
You have the message of eternal life, O Lord.

1. The law of the Lord is perfect,
it revives the soul.
The rule of the Lord is to be trusted,
it gives wisdom to the simple. (*R.*)

2. The precepts of the Lord are right,
they gladden the heart.
The command of the Lord is clear,
it gives light to the eyes. (*R.*)

3. The fear of the Lord is holy,
abiding for ever.
The decrees of the Lord are truth
and all of them just. (*R.*)

4. They are more to be desired than gold,
than the purest of gold
and sweeter are they than honey,
than honey from the comb. (*R.*)

Seventh Reading   (36:16–17a, 18–28)

A reading from the prophet Ezekiel
I shall pour clean water over you, and I shall give you a new heart.

The word of the Lord was addressed to me as follows:
"Son of man, the members of the House of Israel used to
live in their own land, but they defiled it by their conduct
and actions.

I then discharged my fury at them because of the blood they shed in their land and the idols with which they defiled it. I scattered them among the nations and dispersed them in foreign countries. I sentenced them as their conduct and actions deserved. And now they have profaned my holy name among the nations where they have gone, so that people say of them, 'These are the people of the Lord; they have been exiled from his land.' But I have been concerned about my holy name, which the House of Israel has profaned among the nations where they have gone. And so, say to the House of Israel, 'The Lord says this: I am not doing this for your sake, House of Israel, but for the sake of my holy name, which you have profaned among the nations where you have gone. I mean to display the holiness of my great name, which has been profaned among the nations, which you have profaned among them. And the nations will learn that I am the Lord – it is the Lord who speaks – when I display my holiness for your sake before their eyes. Then I am going to take you from among the nations and gather you together from all the foreign countries, and bring you home to your own land. I shall cleanse you of all your defilement and all your idols. I shall give you a new heart, and put a new spirit in you; I shall remove the heart of stone from your bodies and give you a heart of flesh instead. I shall put my spirit in you, and make you keep my laws and sincerely respect my observances. You will live in the land which I gave your ancestors. You shall be my people and I will be your God.' "

This is the word of the Lord.

Responsorial Psalm   (Pss 41:3. 5;42:3. 4. *R*. 41:2)

Response
Like the deer that yearns
for running streams,
so my soul is yearning
for you, my God.

1. My soul is thirsting for God,
the God of my life;
when can I enter and see
the face of God? (*R*.)

2. These things will I remember
as I pour out my soul :
how I would lead the rejoicing crowd
into the house of God,
amid cries of gladness and thanksgiving,
the throng wild with joy. (*R*.)

3. O send forth your light and your truth;
let these be my guide.
Let them bring me to your holy mountain
to the place where you dwell. (R.)

4. And I will come to the altar of God,
the God of my joy.
My redeemer, I will thank you on the harp,
O God, my God. (*R*.)

If a Baptism takes place, the Responsorial Psalm which follows the
Fifth Reading above, p. 646, is used, or Ps 50 as follows:

Responsorial Psalm   (Ps 50:12–15. 18. 19. *R*. v. 12)

Response
A pure heart create for me, O God.

1. A pure heart create for me, O God,
put a steadfast spirit within me.
Do not cast me away from your presence,
nor deprive me of your holy spirit. (*R*.)

2. Give me again the joy of your help;
with a spirit of fervour sustain me,
that I may teach transgressors your ways
and sinners may return to you. (*R*.)

3. For in sacrifice you take no delight,
burnt offering from me you would refuse,
my sacrifice, a contrite spirit.
A humbled, contrite heart you will not spurn. (*R.*)

THE MASS OF EASTER NIGHT

First Reading   (6:3–11)

A reading from the letter of St Paul to the Romans
Christ, having been raised from the dead, will never die again.

You have been taught that when we were baptised in Christ
Jesus we were baptised in his death; in other words, when
we were baptised we went into the tomb with him and joined
him in death, so that as Christ was raised from the dead by
the Father's glory, we too might live a new life.

If in union with Christ we have imitated his death, we
shall also imitate him in his resurrection. We must realise
that our former selves have been crucified with him to destroy this sinful body and to free us from the slavery of
sin. When a man dies, of course, he has finished with sin.

But we believe that having died with Christ we shall return to life with him: Christ, as we know, having been
raised from the dead will never die again. Death has no
power over him any more. When he died, he died, once for
all, to sin, so his life now is life with God; and in that way,
you too must consider yourselves to be dead to sin but
alive for God in Christ Jesus.

This is the word of the Lord.

Responsorial Psalm   (Ps 117:1–2. 16–17. 22–23)

Response
Alleluia, alleluia, alleluia!

1. Alleluia!
Give thanks to the Lord for he is good,
for his love has no end.
Let the sons of Israel say:
"His love has no end." (*R*.)

2. The Lord's right hand has triumphed:
his right hand raised me up.
I shall not die, I shall live
and recount his deeds. (*R*.)

3. The stone which the builders rejected
has become the corner stone.
This is the work of the Lord,
a marvel in our eyes. (*R*.)

Year 1 (Year A)

Gospel (28:1–10)

A reading from the holy Gospel according to Matthew
He has risen from the dead and now he is going before you into Galilee.

After the sabbath, and towards dawn on the first day of the week, Mary of Magdala and the other Mary went to visit the sepulchre. And all at once there was a violent earthquake, for the angel of the Lord, descended from heaven, came and rolled away the stone and sat on it. His face was like lightning, his robe white as snow. The guards were so shaken, so frightened of him, that they were like dead men. But the angel spoke; and he said to the women, "There is no need for you to be afraid. I know you are looking for Jesus, who was crucified. He is not here, for he has risen, as he said he would. Come and see the place where he lay, then go quickly and tell his disciples, 'He has risen from the dead and now he is going before you to Galilee; it is there you will see him.' Now I have told you." Filled with awe and great joy the women came quickly away from the tomb and ran to tell the disciples.

And there, coming to meet them, was Jesus. "Greetings" he said. And the women came up to him and, falling down before him, clasped his feet. Then Jesus said to them, "Do not be afraid; go and tell my brothers that they must leave for Galilee; they will see me there."

This is the Gospel of the Lord.

Year 2 (Year B)

Gospel   (16:1–8)

A reading from the holy Gospel according to Mark
Jesus of Nazareth, who was crucified, has risen.

When the sabbath was over, Mary of Magdala, Mary the mother of James, and Salome, bought spices with which to go and anoint him. And very early in the morning on the first day of the week they went to the tomb, just as the sun was rising.

They had been saying to one another, "Who will roll away the stone for us from the entrance to the tomb? But when they looked they could see that the stone – which was very big – had already been rolled back. On entering the tomb they saw a young man in a white robe seated on the right-hand side, and they were struck with amazement. But he said to them, "There is no need for alarm. You are look- ing for Jesus of Nazareth, who was crucified: he has risen, he is not here. See, here is the place where they laid him. But you must go and tell his disciples and Peter, 'He is going before you to Galilee; it is there you will see him, just as he told you.' " And the women came out and ran away from the tomb because they were frightened out of their wits; and they said nothing to a soul, for they were afraid.

This is the Gospel of the Lord.

Year 3 (Year C)

Gospel   (24:1–12)

A reading from the holy Gospel according to Luke
Why look among the dead for someone who is alive?

On the first day of the week, at the first sign of dawn, they
went to the tomb with the spices they had prepared. They
found that the stone had been rolled away from the tomb,
but on entering discovered that the body of the Lord Jesus
was not there. As they stood there not knowing what to
think, two men in brilliant clothes suddenly appeared at
their side. Terrified, the women lowered their eyes. But the
two men said to them, "Why look among the dead for someone who is alive? He is not here; he has risen. Remember
what he told you when he was still in Galilee: that the Son
of Man had to be handed over into the power of sinful men
and be crucified, and rise again on the third day?" And they
remembered his words.

When the women returned from the tomb they told all
this to the Eleven and to all the others. The women were
Mary of Magdala, Joanna, and Mary the mother of James.
The other women with them also told the apostles, but this
story of theirs seemed pure nonsense, and they did not believe them.

Peter, however, went running to the tomb. He bent down
and saw the binding cloths, but nothing else; he then went
back home, amazed at what had happened.

This is the Gospel of the Lord.

EASTER SUNDAY
Morning Mass

First Reading   (10:34. 37–43)

A reading from the Acts of the Apostles
We have eaten and drunk with him after his resurrection.

Peter addressed them: "You must have heard about the
recent happenings in Judaea; about Jesus of Nazareth and

how he began in Galilee, after John had been preaching baptism. God had anointed him with the Holy Spirit and with power, and because God was with him, Jesus went about doing good and curing all who had fallen into the power of the devil. Now I, and those with me, can witness to everything he did throughout the countryside of Judaea and in Jerusalem itself: and also to the fact that they killed him by hanging him on a tree, yet three days afterwards God raised him to life and allowed him to be seen, not by the whole people but only by certain witnesses God had chosen beforehand. Now we are those witnesses – we have eaten and drunk with him after his resurrection from the dead – and he has ordered us to proclaim this to his people and to tell them that God has appointed him to judge everyone, alive or dead. It is to him that all the prophets bear this witness: that all who believe in Jesus will have their sins forgiven through his name."

This is the word of the Lord.

Responsorial Psalm   (Ps 117:1–2. 16–17. 22–23. *R*. v. 24)

Response
This day was made by the Lord;
we rejoice and are glad.
Or: Alleluia!

1. Alleluia!
Give thanks to the Lord for he is good,
for his love has no end.
Let the sons of Israel say:
"His love has no end." (*R*.)

2. The Lord's right hand has triumphed;
his right hand raised me up.
I shall not die, I shall live
and recount his deeds. (*R*.)

3. The stone which the builders rejected
has become the corner stone.
This is the work of the Lord,
a marvel in our eyes. (*R.*)

Second Reading (3:1–4)

A reading from the letter of St Paul to the Colossians
*You must look for the things that are in heaven, where Christ
is.*

Since you have been brought back to true life with Christ,
you must look for the things that are in heaven, where
Christ is, sitting at God's right hand. Let your thoughts be
on heavenly things, not on the things that are on the earth,
because you have died, and now the life you have is hidden
with Christ in God. But when Christ is revealed – and he
is your life – you too will be revealed in all your glory with
him.

This is the word of the Lord.

Alternative Reading (5:6–8)

A reading from the first letter of St Paul to the Corinthians
*Get rid of all the old yeast, make yourselves into a com-
pletely new batch of bread.*

The pride that you take in yourselves is hardly to your
credit. You must know how even a small amount of yeast
is enough to leaven all the dough. So get rid of all the old
yeast, and make yourselves into a completely new batch of
bread, unleavened as you are meant to be. Christ, our passover, has been sacrificed; let us celebrate the feast, then, by
getting rid of all the old yeast of evil and wickedness, having
only the unleavened bread of sincerity and truth.

This is the word of the Lord.

Sequence

Christians, to the Paschal Victim offer sacrifice and praise.
The sheep are ransomed by the Lamb;
and Christ, the undefiled,
hath sinners to his Father reconciled.
Death with life contended : combat strangely ended!
Life's own Champion, slain, yet lives to reign.
Tell us, Mary : say what thou didst see upon the way.
The tomb the Living did enclose;
I saw Christ's glory as he rose!
The angels there attesting;
shroud with grave-clothes resting.
Christ, my hope, has risen : he goes before you into Galilee.
That Christ is truly risen from the dead we know.
Victorious king, thy mercy show!
Amen.

Alleluia   (1 Cor 5:7–8)

Alleluia, alleluia!
Christ, our passover, has been sacrificed;
let us celebrate the feast then, in the Lord.
Alleluia!

Gospel   (20:1–9)

A reading from the holy Gospel according to John
He must rise from the dead.

It was very early on the first day of the week and still dark,
when Mary of Magdala came to the tomb. She saw that
the stone had been moved away from the tomb and came
running to Simon Peter and the other disciple, the one Jesus
loved. "They have taken the Lord out of the tomb" she said
"and we don't know where they have put him."

So Peter set out with the other disciple to go to the tomb.
They ran together, but the other disciple, running faster

than Peter, reached the tomb first; he bent down and saw the linen cloths lying on the ground, but did not go in. Simon Peter who was following now came up, went right into the tomb, saw the linen cloths on the ground, and also the cloth that had been over his head; this was not with the linen cloths but rolled up in a place by itself. Then the other disciple who had reached the tomb first also went in; he saw and he believed. Till this moment they had failed to understand the teaching of scripture, that he must rise from the dead.

This is the Gospel of the Lord.

An evening Mass on Easter Sunday the Gospel of Third Sunday of Easter, Year 1, may be read.

EASTER MONDAY

First Reading (2:14. 22–32)

A reading from the Acts of the Apostles
God raised this man Jesus to life, and all of us are witnesses to that.

Then Peter stood up with the Eleven and addressed them in a loud ovice: "Men of Israel, listen to what I am going to say: Jesus the Nazarene was a man commended to you by God by the miracles and portents and signs that God worked through him when he was among you, as you all know. This man, who was put into your power by the deliberate intention and foreknowledge of God, you took and had crucified by men outside the Law. You killed him, but God raised him to life, freeing him from the pangs of Hades; for it was impossible for him to be held in its power since, as David says of him:

I saw the Lord before me always,
for with him at my right hand nothing can shake me.
So my heart was glad
and my tongue cried out with joy;

my body, too, will rest in the hope
that you will not abandon my soul to Hades
nor allow your holy one to experience corruption.
You have made known the way of life to me,
you will fill me with gladness through your presence.

"Brothers, no one can deny that the patriarch David himself is dead and buried: his tomb is still with us. But since he was a prophet, and knew that God had sworn him an oath to make one of his descendants succeed him on the throne, what he foresaw and spoke about was the resurrection of the Christ: he is the one who was not abandoned to Hades, and whose body did not experience corruption. God raised this man Jesus to life, and all of us are witnesses to that."

This is the word of the Lord.

Responsorial Psalm   (Ps 15:1–2. 5. 7–11. *R*. v. 1)

Response
Preserve me, Lord, I take refuge in you.
Or: Alleluia!

1. Preserve me, God, I take refuge in you.
I say to the Lord: "You are my God.
O Lord, it is you who are my portion and cup;
it is you yourself who are my prize." (*R*.)

2. I will bless the Lord who gives me counsel,
who even at night directs my heart.
I keep the Lord ever in my sight:
since he is at my right hand, I shall stand firm. (*R*.)

3. And so my heart rejoices, my soul is glad;
even my body shall rest in safety.
For you will not leave my soul among the dead,
nor let your beloved know decay. (*R*.)

4. You will show me the path of life,
the fullness of joy in your presence,
and your right hand happiness for ever. (*R.*)

Alleluia   (Ps 117:24)

Alleluia, alleluia!
This day was made by the Lord;
we rejoice and are glad.
Alleluia!

Gospel   (28:8–15)

A reading from the holy Gospel according to Matthew
*Tell my brothers that they must leave for Galilee; they will
see me there.*

Filled with awe and great joy the women came quickly away
from the tomb and ran to tell the disciples.

And there, coming to meet them, was Jesus. "Greetings"
he said. And the women came up to him and, falling down
before him, clasped his feet. Then Jesus said to them, "Do
not be afraid; go and tell my brothers that they must leave
for Galilee; they will see me there."

While they were on their way, some of the guard went off
into the city to tell the chief priests all that had happened.
These held a meeting with the elders and, after some discussion, handed a considerable sum of money to the soldiers with these instructions, "This is what you must say,
'His disciples came during the night and stole him away
while we were asleep.' And should the governor come to
hear of this, we undertake to put things right with him ourselves and to see that you do not get into trouble." The
soldiers took the money and carried out their instructions,
and to this day that is the story among the Jews.

This is the Gospel of the Lord.

EASTER TUESDAY

First Reading   (2:36–41)

A reading from the Acts of the Apostles
You must repent and every one of you must be baptised in the name of Jesus.

Peter spoke to the Jews: "The whole House of Israel can be certain that God has made this Jesus whom you crucified both Lord and Christ."

Hearing this, they were cut to the heart and said to Peter and the apostles, "What must we do, brothers?" "You must repent," Peter answered "and every one of you must be baptised in the name of Jesus Christ for the forgiveness of your sins, and you will receive the gift of the Holy Spirit. The promise that was made is for you and your children, and for all those who are far away, for all those whom the Lord our God will call to himself." He spoke to them for a long time using many arguments, and he urged them, "Save yourselves from this perverse generation." They were convinced by his arguments, and they accepted what he said and were baptised. That very day about three thousand were added to their number.

This is the word of the Lord.

Responsorial Psalm   (Ps 32:4–5. 18–20. 22. *R.* v. 5)

Response
The Lord fills the earth with his love.
Or: Alleluia!

1. The word of the Lord is faithful
and all his works to be trusted.
The Lord loves justice and right
and fills the earth with his love. (*R.*)

2. The Lord looks on those who revere him,
on those who hope in his love,

to rescue their souls from death,
to keep them alive in famine. (*R.*)

3. Our soul is waiting for the Lord.
The Lord is our help and our shield.
May your love be upon us, O Lord,
as we place all our hope in you. (*R.*)

Gospel   (20:11–18)

A reading from the holy Gospel according to John
I have seen the Lord and he has spoken to me.

Mary stayed outside near the tomb, weeping. Then, still
weeping, she stooped to look inside, and saw two angels in
white sitting where the body of Jesus had been, one at the
head, the other at the feet. They said, "Woman, why are
you weeping?" "They have taken my Lord away," she replied, "and I don't know where they have put him." As she
said this she turned round and saw Jesus standing there,
though she did not recognise him. Jesus said, "Woman,
why are you weeping? Who are you looking for?" Sup-
posing him to be the gardener, she said, "Sir, if you have
taken him away, tell me where you have put him, and I will
go and remove him." Jesus said, "Mary!" She knew him
then and said to him in Hebrew, "Rabbuni!" – which means
Master. Jesus said to her "Do not cling to me, because I
have not yet ascended to the Father. But go and find the
brothers, and tell them: I am ascending to my Father and
your Father, to my God and your God." So Mary of Magdala went and told the disciples that she had seen the Lord
and that he had said these things to her.

This is the Gospel of the Lord.

EASTER WEDNESDAY

First Reading   (3:1–10)

A reading from the Acts of the Apostles
I will give you what I have: in the name of Jesus stand up and walk!

Once, when Peter and John were going up to the Temple for the prayers at the ninth hour, it happened that there was a man being carried past. He was a cripple from birth; and they used to put him down every day near the Temple entrance called the Beautiful Gate so that he could beg from the people going in. When this man saw Peter and John on their way into the Temple he begged from them. Both Peter and John looked straight at him and said, "Look at us." He turned to them expectantly, hoping to get something from them, but Peter said, "I have neither silver nor gold, but I will give you what I have: in the name of Jesus Christ the Nazarene, walk!" Peter then took him by the hand and helped him to stand up. Instantly his feet and ankles became firm, he jumped up, stood, and began to walk, and he went with them into the Temple, walking and jumping and praising God. Everyone could see him walking and praising God, and they recognised him as the man who used to sit begging at the Beautiful Gate of the Temple. They were all astonished and unable to explain what had happened to him.

This is the word of the Lord.

Responsorial Psalm   (Ps 104:1–4. 6–9. *R*. Ps 32:5)

Response
The Lord fills the earth with his love.
Or: Alleluia!

1. Alleluia!
Give thanks to the Lord, tell his name,
make known his deeds among the peoples.

O sing to him, sing his praise;
tell all his wonderful works! (*R*.)

2. Be proud of his holy name,
let the hearts that seek the Lord rejoice.
Consider the Lord and his strength;
constantly seek his face. (*R*.)

3. O children of Abraham, his servant,
O sons of the Jacob he chose.
He, the Lord, is our God:
his judgements prevail in all the earth. (*R*.)

4. He remembers his covenant for ever,
his promise for a thousand generations,
the covenant he made with Abraham,
the oath he swore to Isaac (*R*.)

ALLELUIA. As for Easter Monday, see p. 660.

Gospel (24:13–35)

A reading from the holy Gospel according to Luke
They recognised Jesus at the breaking of bread.

Two of the disciples were on their way to a village called
Emmaus, seven miles from Jerusalem, and they were talking together about all that had happened. Now as they
talked this over, Jesus himself came up and walked by their
side; but something prevented them from recognising him.
He said to them, "What matters are you discussing as you
walk along?" They stopped short, their faces downcast.
   Then one of them, called Cleopas, answered him, "You
must be the only person staying in Jerusalem who does not
know the things that have been happening there these last
few days." "What things?" he asked. "All about Jesus of
Nazareth" they answered "who proved he was a great
prophet by the things he said and did in the sight of God

and of the whole people; and how our chief priests and our leaders handed him over to be sentenced to death, and had him crucified. Our own hope had been that he would be the one to set Israel free. And this is not all: two whole days have gone by since it all happened; and some women from our group have astounded us: they went to the tomb in the early morning, and when they did not find the body, they came back to tell us they had seen a vision of angels who declared he was alive. Some of our friends went to the tomb and found everything exactly as the women had reported, but of him they saw nothing."

Then he said to them, "You foolish men! So slow to believe the full message of the prophets! Was it not ordained that the Christ should suffer and so enter into his glory?" Then, starting with Moses and going through all the prophets, he explained to them the passages throughout the scriptures that were about himself.

When they drew near to the village to which they were going, he made as if to go on; but they pressed him to stay with them. "It is nearly evening" they said "and the day is almost over." So he went in to stay with them. Now while he was with them at table, he took the bread and said the blessing; then he broke it and handed it to them. And their eyes were opened and they recognised him; but he had vanished from their sight. Then they said to each other, "Did not our hearts burn within us as he talked to us on the road and explained the scriptures to us?"

They set out that instant and returned to Jerusalem. There they found the Eleven assembled together with their companions, who said to them, "Yes it is true. The Lord has risen and has appeared to Simon." Then they told their story of what had happened on the road and how they had recognised him at the breaking of bread.

This is the Gospel of the Lord.

EASTER THURSDAY

First Reading   (3:11–26)

A reading from the Acts of the Apostles

You killed the prince of life. God, however, raised him from the dead.

Everyone came running towards Peter and John in great excitement, to the Portico of Solomon, as it is called, where the man was still clinging to them. When Peter saw the people he addressed them "Why are you so surprised at this? Why are you staring at us as though we had made this man walk by our own power or holiness? You are Israelites, and it is the God of Abraham, Isaac and Jacob, the God of our ancestors, who has glorified his servant Jesus, the same Jesus you handed over and then disowned in the presence of Pilate, after Pilate had decided to release him. It was you who accused the Holy One, the Just One, you who demanded the reprieve of a murderer while you killed the prince of life. God, however, raised him from the dead, and to that fact we are the witnesses; and it is the name of Jesus which, through our faith in it, has brought back the strength of this man whom you see here and who is well known to you. It is faith in that name that has restored this man to health, as you can all see.

"Now I know, brothers, that neither you nor your leaders had any idea what you were really doing; this was the way God carried out what he had foretold, when he said through all his prophets that his Christ would suffer. Now you must repent and turn to God, so that your sins may be wiped out, and so that the Lord may send the time of comfort. Then he will send you the Christ he has predestined, that is Jesus, whom heaven must keep till the universal restoration comes which God proclaimed, speaking through his holy prophets. Moses, for example, said: The Lord God will raise up a prophet like myself for you, from among your own brothers; you must listen to whatever he tells you. The

man who does not listen to that prophet is to be cut off
from the people. In fact, all the prophets that have ever
spoken, from Samuel onwards, have predicted these days.

"You are the heirs of the prophets the heirs of the covenant God made with our ancestors when he told Abraham:
in your offspring all the families of the earth will be blessed.
It was for you in the first place that God raised up his servant and sent him to bless you by turning every one of you
from your wicked ways."

This is the word of the Lord.

Responsorial Psalm   (Ps 8:2.5–9.*R*.v.2)
Response
How great is your name, O Lord our God,
through all the earth!
Or: Alleluia!

1. How great is your name, O Lord our God,
through all the earth!
What is man that you should keep him in mind,
mortal man that you care for him? (*R*.)

2. Yet you have made him little less than a god;
with glory and honour you crowned him,
gave him power over the works of your hand,
put all things under his feet. (*R*.)

3. All of them, sheep and cattle,
yes, even the savage beasts,
birds of the air, and fish
that make their way through the waters. (*R*.)

ALLELUIA. As for Easter Monday, see p. 660.

Gospel   (24:35–48)
A reading from the holy Gospel according to Luke
*It is written that the Christ would suffer and on the third day
rise from the dead.*

The disciples told their story of what had happened on the road and how they had recognised Jesus at the breaking of bread.

They were still talking about all this when Jesus himself stood among them and said to them, "Peace be with you!" In a state of alarm and fright, they thought they were seeing a ghost. But he said, "Why are you so agitated, and why are these doubts rising in your hearts? Look at my hands and feet; yes, it is I indeed. Touch me and see for yourselves; a ghost has no flesh and bones as you can see I have." And as he said this he showed them his hands and feet. Their joy was so great that they still could not believe it, and they stood there dumbfounded; so he said to them, "Have you anything here to eat?" And they offered him a piece of grilled fish, which he took and ate before their eyes.

Then he told them, "This is what I meant when I said, while I was still with you, that everything written about me in the Law of Moses, in the Prophets and in the Psalms, has to be fulfilled." He then opened their minds to understand the scriptures, and he said to them, "So you see how it is written that the Christ would suffer and on the third day rise from the dead, and that, in his name, repentance for the forgiveness of sins would be preached to all the nations, beginning from Jerusalem. You are witnesses to this."

This is the Gospel of the Lord.

EASTER FRIDAY

First Reading   (4:1–12)
A reading from the Acts of the Apostles
This is the only name by which we can be saved.

While Peter and John were talking to the people the priests came up to them, accompanied by the captain of the Temple and the Sadducees. They were extremely annoyed at their teaching the people the doctrine of the resurrection from the dead by proclaiming the resurrection of Jesus. They arrested them, but as it was already late, they held them till the next day. But many of those who had listened to their message became believers, the total number of whom had now risen to something like five thousand.

The next day the rulers, elders and scribes had a meeting in Jerusalem with Annas the high priest, Caiaphas, Jonathan, Alexander and all the members of the high-priestly families. They made the prisoners stand in the middle and began to interrogate them, "By what power, and by whose name have you men done this?" Then Peter, filled with the Holy Spirit, addressed them, "Rulers of the people, and elders! If you are questioning us today about an act of kindness to a cripple, and asking us how he was healed, then I am glad to tell you all, and would indeed be glad to tell the whole people of Israel, that it was by the name of Jesus Christ the Nazarene, the one you crucified, whom God raised from the dead, by this name and by no other that this man is able to stand up perfectly healthy, here in your presence today. This is the stone rejected by you the builders, but which has proved to be the keystone. For of all the names in the world given to men, this is the only one by which we can be saved."

This is the word of the Lord.

Responsorial Psalm   (Ps 117:1–2. 4. 22–27. *R*. v. 22)

Response
The stone which the builder rejected
has become the corner stone.
Or: Alleluia!

1. Alleluia!
Give thanks to the Lord for he is good,
for his love has no end.
Let the sons of Israel say:
"His love has no end."

Let those who fear the Lord say:
"His love has no end." (R.)

2. The stone which the builders rejected
has become the corner stone.
This is the work of the Lord,
a marvel in our eyes.
This day was made by the Lord;
we rejoice and are glad. (R.)

3. O Lord, grant us salvation;
O Lord, grant success.
Blessed in the name of the Lord
is he who comes.
We bless you from the house of the Lord;
the Lord God is our light. (R.)

ALLELUIA As for Easter Monday, see p. 660.

Gospel (21:1–14)

A reading from the holy Gospel according to John
*Jesus stepped forward, took the bread and gave it to them, and
the same with the fish.*

Later on, Jesus showed himself again to the disciples. It
was by the Sea of Tiberias, and it happened like this:
Simon Peter, Thomas called the Twin, Nathanael from
Cana in Galilee, the sons of Zebedee and two more of his
disciples were together. Somon Peter said, "I'm going fishing." They replied, "We'll come with you." They went out
and got into the boat but caught nothing that night.

It was light by now and there stood Jesus on the shore,
though the disciples did not realise that it was Jesus. Jesus
called out, "Have you caught anything friends?" And when
they answered, "No", he said, "Throw the net out to star-
board and you'll find something." So they dropped the net,

and there were so many fish that they could not haul it in. The disciple Jesus loved said to Peter, "It is the Lord." At these words, "It is the Lord", Simon Peter, who had practically nothing on, wrapped his cloak round him and jumped into the water. The other disciples came on in the boat, towing the net and the fish; they were only about a hundred yards from land.

As soon as they came ashore they saw that there was some bread there, and a charcoal fire with fish cooking on it. Jesus said, "Bring some of the fish you have just caught." Simon Peter went aboard and dragged the net to the shore, full of big fish, one hundred and fifty-three of them; and in spite of there being so many the net was not broken. Jesus said to them, "Come and have breakfast." None of the disciples was bold enough to ask, "Who are you?"; they knew quite well it was the Lord. Jesus then stepped forward, took the bread and gave it to them, and the same with the fish. This was the third time that Jesus showed himself to the disciples after rising from the dead.

This is the Gospel of the Lord.

EASTER SATURDAY

First Reading   (4:13–21)

A reading from the Acts of the Apostles
We cannot promise to stop proclaiming what we have seen and heard.

The rulers, elders and scribes were astonished at the assurance shown by Peter and John, considering they were uneducated laymen; and they recognised them as associates of Jesus; but when they saw the man who had been cured standing by their side, they could find no answer. So they ordered them to stand outside while the Sanhedrin had a private discussion. "What are we going to do with these men?" they asked. "It is obvious to everybody in Jerusalem that a miracle has been worked through them in public, and we cannot deny it. But to stop the whole thing spreading any further among the people, let us caution them never to speak to anyone in this name again."

So they called them in and gave them a warning on no account to make statements or to teach in the name of Jesus. But Peter and John retorted, "You must judge whether in God's eyes it is right to listen to you and not to God. We cannot promise to stop proclaiming what we have seen and heard." The court repeated the warnings and then released them; they could not think of any way to punish them, since all the people were giving glory to God for what had happened.

This is the word of the Lord.

Responsorial Psalm   (Ps 117:1. 14–21. *R*. v. 21)

Response
I will thank you, Lord,
for you have given answer.
Or: Alleluia!

1. Alleluia!
Give thanks to the Lord for he is good,
for his love has no end.
The Lord is my strength and my song;
he was my saviour.
There are shouts of joy and victory
in the tents of the just. (*R*.)

2. The Lord's right hand has triumphed;
his right hand raised me up.
The Lord's right hand has triumphed;
I shall not die, I shall live
and recount his deeds.
I was punished, I was punished by the Lord,
but not doomed to die. (*R*.)

3. Open to me the gates of holiness:
I will enter and give thanks.
This is the Lord's own gate
where the just may enter.
I will thank you for you have given answer
and you are my saviour. (*R.*)

Gospel (16:9–15)

A reading from the holy Gospel according to Mark
Go out to the whole world; proclaim the Good News.

Having risen in the morning on the first day of the week.
Jesus appeared first to Mary of Magdala from whom he
had cast out seven devils. She then went to those who had
been his companions, and who were mourning and in tears,
and told them. But they did not believe her when they heard
her say that he was alive and that she had seen him.

After this, he showed himself under another form to two
of them as they were on their way into the country. These
went back and told the others, who did not believe them
either.

Lastly, he showed himself to the Eleven themselves while
they were at table. He reproached them for their incredulity
and obstinacy, because they had refused to believe those
who had seen him after he had risen. And he said to them,
"Go out to the whole world; proclaim the Good News to
all creation."

This is the Gospel of the Lord.

2nd SUNDAY OF EASTER
Year 1 (Year A)

First Reading (2:42–47)

A reading from the Acts of the Apostles
The faithful all lived together and owned everything in common

These (the new converts) remained faithful to the teaching of the apostles, to the brotherhood, to the breaking of bread and to the prayers.

The many miracles and signs worked through the apostles made a deep impression on everyone.

The faithful all lived together, and owned everything in common; they sold their goods and possessions and shared out the proceeds among themselves according to what each one needed.

They went as a body to the Temple every day but met in their houses for the breaking of bread; they shared their food gladly and generously; they praised God and were looked up to by everyone. Day by day the Lord added to their community those destined to be saved.

This is the word of the Lord.

Responsorial Psalm   (Ps 117:2–4. 13–15. 22–24. *R.* v. 1)
Response
Give thanks to the Lord for he is good,
for his love has no end.
Or: Alleluia!

1. Let the sons of Israel say:
"His love has no end."
Let the sons of Aaron say:
"His love has no end."
Let those who fear the Lord say:
"His love has no end." (*R.*)

2. I was thrust, thrust down and falling
but the Lord is my strength and my song;
he was my saviour.
There are shouts of joy and victory
in the tents of the just. (*R.*)

3. The stone which the builders rejected
has become the corner stone.

This is the work of the Lord,
a marvel in our eyes.
This day was made by the Lord;
we rejoice and are glad. (*R*.)

Second Reading (1:3–9)

A reading from the first letter of St Peter
In his great mercy he has given us a new birth as his sons by raising Jesus from the dead.

Blessed be God the Father of our Lord Jesus Christ, who in his great mercy has given us a new birth as his sons, by raising Jesus Christ from the dead, so that we have a sure hope and the promise of an inheritance that can never be spoilt or soiled and never fade away, because it is being kept for you in the heavens. Through your faith God's power will guard you until the salvation which has been prepared is revealed at the end of time. This is a cause of great joy for you, even though you may for a short time have to bear being plagued by all sorts of trials; so that, when Jesus Christ is revealed, your faith will have been tested and proved like gold – only it is more precious than gold, which is corruptible even though it bears testing by fire – and then you will have praise and glory and honour. You did not see him, yet you loved him; and still without seeing him, you are already filled with a joy so glorious, that it cannot be described, because you believe; and you are sure of the end to which your faith looks forward, that is, the salvation of your souls.

This is the word of the Lord.

ALLELUIA and GOSPEL. As for Year 3 (Year C), see p. 680.

2nd SUNDAY OF EASTER
Year 2 (Year B)

First Reading (4:32–35)

A reading from the Acts of the Apostles
United, heart and soul.

The whole group of believers was united, heart and soul; no one claimed for his own use anything that he had, as everything they owned was held in common.

The apostles continued to testify to the resurrection of the Lord Jesus with great power, and they were all given great respect.

None of their members was ever in want, as all those who owned land or houses would sell them, and bring the money from them, to present it to the apostles; it was then distributed to any members who might be in need.

This is the word of the Lord.

Responsorial Psalm (Ps 117:2–4. 15–18. 22–24. *R*. v. 1)

Response
Give thanks to the Lord for he is good,
for his love has no end.
Or: Alleluia!

1. Let the sons of Israel say:
"His love has no end."
Let the sons of Aaron say:
"His love has no end."
Let those who fear the Lord say:
"His love has no end." (*R*.)

2. The Lord's right hand has triumphed;
his right hand raised me up.
I shall not die, I shall live
and recount his deeds.
I was punished, I was punished by the Lord,
but not doomed to die. (*R*.)

3. The stone which the builders rejected
has become the corner stone.
This is the work of the Lord,
a marvel in our eyes.
This day was made by the Lord;
we rejoice and are glad. (*R.*)

Second Reading   (5:1–6)

A reading from the first letter of St John
*Anyone who has been begotten by God has already overcome
the world.*

Whoever believes that Jesus is the Christ
has been begotten by God;
and whoever loves the Father that begot him
loves the child whom he begets.
We can be sure that we love God's children
if we love God himself and do what he has commanded us;
this is what loving God is –
keeping his commandments;
and his commandments are not difficult,
because anyone who has been begotten by God
has already overcome the world;
this is the victory over the world –
our faith.
Who can overcome the world?
Only the man who believes that Jesus is the Son of God;
Jesus Christ who came by water and blood,
not with water only,
but with water and blood;
with the Spirit as another witness –
since the Spirit is the truth.

This is the word of the Lord.

ALLELUIA and GOSPEL. As for Year 3 (Year C), see p. 680.

2nd SUNDAY OF EASTER
Year 3

First Reading   (5:12–16)

A reading from the Acts of the Apostles
The numbers of men and women who came to believe in the
Lord increased steadily.

The faithful all used to meet by common consent in the
Portico of Solomon. No one else ever dared to join them,
but the people were loud in their praise and the numbers
of men and women who came to believe in the Lord increased steadily. So many signs and wonders were worked
among the people at the hands of the apostles that the sick
were even taken out into the streets and laid on beds and
sleeping-mats in the hope that at least the shadow of Peter
might fall across some of them as he went past. People
even came crowding in from the towns round about Jerusalem, bringing with them their sick and those tormented by
unclean spirits, and all of them were cured.

This is the word of the Lord.

Responsorial Psalm   (Ps 11.7:2–4. 22–27. *R*. v. 1)

Response
Give thanks to the Lord for he is good,
for his love has no end.
Or: Alleluia!

1. Let the sons of Israel say:
"His love has no end."
Let the sons of Aaron say:
"His love has no end."
Let those who fear the Lord say:
"His love has no end." (*R*.)

2. The stone which the builders rejected
has become the corner stone.

This is the work of the Lord,
a marvel in our eyes.
This day was made by the Lord;
we rejoice and are glad. (*R.*)

3. O Lord, grant us salvation;
O Lord, grant success.
Blessed in the name of the Lord
is he who comes.
We bless you from the house of the Lord;
the Lord God is our light. (*R.*)

Second Reading   (1:9–13. 17–19)

A reading from the book of the Apocalypse
I was dead and now I am to live for ever and ever.

My name is John, and through our union in Jesus I am
your brother and share your sufferings, your kingdom, and
all you endure. I was on the island of Patmos for having
preached God's word and witnessed for Jesus; it was the
Lord's day and the Spirit possessed me, and I heard a voice
behind me, shouting like a trumpet, "Write down all that
you see in a book." I turned round to see who had spoken
to me, and when I turned I saw seven golden lampstands
and, surrounded by them, a figure like a Son of man,
dressed in a long robe tied at the waist with a golden girdle.

   When I saw him, I fell in a dead faint at his feet, but he
touched me with his right hand and said, "Do not be afraid;
it is I, the First and the Last; I am the Living One. I was
dead and now I am to live for ever and ever, and I hold the
keys of death and of the underworld. Now write down all
that you see of present happenings and things that are still
to come."

   This is the word of the Lord.

Years 1, 2, 3 (Years A, B, C)

Alleluia (Jn 20:29)

Alleluia, alleluia!
Jesus said: "You believe because you can see me.
Happy are those who have not seen and yet believe."
Alleluia!

Gospel (20:19–31)

A reading from the holy Gospel according to John
Eight days later, Jesus came.

In the evening of that same day, the first day of the week, the doors were closed in the room where the disciples were, for fear of the Jews. Jesus came and stood among them. He said to them, "Peace be with you," and showed them his hands and his side. The disciples were filled with joy when they saw the Lord, and he said to them again, "Peace be with you.

"As the Father sent me,
so am I sending you."

After saying this he breathed on them and said:

"Receive the Holy Spirit.
For those whose sins you forgive,
they are forgiven;
for those whose sins you retain,
they are retained."

Thomas, called the Twin, who was one of the Twelve, was not with them when Jesus came. When the disciples said, "We have seen the Lord", he answered, "Unless I see the holes that the nails made in his hands and can put my finger into the holes they made, and unless I can put my hand into his side, I refuse to believe." Eight days later the disciples were in the house again and Thomas was with them. The doors were closed, but Jesus came in and stood among them. "Peace be with you" he said. Then he spoke to Thomas, "Put your finger here; look, here are my hands. Give me your hand; put it into my side. Doubt no longer but believe." Thomas replied, "My Lord and my God!" Jesus said to him:

"You believe because you can see me.
Happy are those who have not seen and yet believe."

There were many other signs that Jesus worked and the disciples saw, but they are not recorded in his book. These are recorded so that you may believe that Jesus is the Christ, the Son of God, and that believing this you may have life through his name.

This is the Gospel of the Lord.

MONDAY

First Reading   (4:23–31)

A reading from the Acts of the Apostles
As they prayed, they were all filled with the Holy Spirit and begin to proclaim the word of God boldly.

As soon as Peter and John were released they went to the community and told them everything the chief priests and elders had said to them. When they heard it they lifted up their voice to God all together. "Master" they prayed "it is you who made heaven and earth and sea, and everything in them; you it is who said through the Holy Spirit and speaking through our ancestor David, your servant:

Why this arrogance among the nations?
these futile plots among the peoples?
Kings on earth setting out to war,
princes making an alliance,
against the Lord and against his Anointed.

"This is what has come true: in this very city Herod and Pontius Pilate made an alliance with the pagan nations and the peoples of Israel, against your holy servant Jesus whom you anointed, but only to bring about the very thing that you in your strength and your wisdom had predetermined should happen. And now, Lord, take note of their threats and help your servants to proclaim your message with all boldness, by stretching out your hand to heal and to work miracles and marvels through the name of your holy servant Jesus." As they prayed, the house where they were assembled rocked; they were all filled with the Holy Spirit and began to proclaim the word of God boldly.

This is the word of the Lord.

Responsorial Psalm   (Ps 2:1–9. *R.* v. 13)

Response
Blessed are they who put their trust in God.
Or: Alleluia!

1. Why this tumult among nations,
among peoples this useless murmuring?
They arise, the kings of the earth,
princes plot against the Lord and his Anointed.
"Come, let us break their fetters,
come, let us cast off their yoke." (*R.*)

2. He who sits in the heavens laughs;
the Lord is laughing them to scorn.
Then he will speak in his anger,
his rage will strike them with terror.
"It is I who have set up my king
on Zion, my holy mountain." (*R.*)

3. I will announce the decree of the Lord:
The Lord said to me: "You are my Son.
It is I who have begotten you this day.

Ask and I shall bequeath you the nations,
put the ends of the earth in your possession.
With a rod of iron you will break them,
shatter them like a potter's jar." (*R.*)

Alleluia   (Col 3:1)

Alleluia, alleluia!
Since you have been brought back to true life with Christ,
you must look for the things that are in heaven where Christ
    is,
sitting at God's right hand.
Alleluia!

Alternative Alleluias, p. 844.

Gospel   (3:1–8)

A reading from the holy Gospel according to John
*Unless a man is born from above, he cannot see the kingdom
of God.*

There was one of the Pharisees called Nicodemus, a leading Jew, who came to Jesus by night and said, "Rabbi, we
know that you are a teacher who comes from God; for no
one could perform the signs that you do unless God were
with him." Jesus answered:

"I tell you most solemnly,
unless a man is born from above,
he cannot see the kingdom of God."

    Nicodemus said, "How can a grown man be born? Can
he go back into his mother's womb and be born again?"
Jesus replied:

"I tell you most solemnly,
unless a man is born through waters of the Spirit,
he cannot enter the kingdom of God:

what is born of the flesh is flesh;
what is born of the Spirit is spirit.
Do not be surprised when I say:
you must be born from above.
The wind blows wherever it pleases;
you hear its sound,
but you cannot tell where it comes from or where it is going.
That is how it is with all who are born of the Spirit.''

This is the Gospel of the Lord.

TUESDAY

First Reading   (4:32–37)

A reading from the Acts of the Apostles
United, heart and soul.

The whole group of believers was united, heart and soul; no one claimed for his own use anything that he had, as everything they owned was held in common.

The apostles continued to testify to the resurrection of the Lord Jesus with great power, and they were all given great respect.

None of their members was ever in want, as all those who owned land or houses would sell them, and bring the money from them, to present it to the apostles; it was then distributed to any members who might be in need.

There was a Levite of Cypriot origin called Joseph whom the apostles surnamed Barnabas (which means "son of encouragement"). He owned a piece of land and he sold it and brought the money, and presented it to the apostles.

This is the word of the Lord.

Responsorial Psalm   (Ps 92:1–2. 5. *R*. v. 1)

Response
The Lord is king, with majesty enrobed.
Or: Alleluia!

1. The Lord is king, with majesty enrobed;
the Lord has robed himself with might,
he has girded himself with power. (*R*.)

2. The world you made firm, not to be moved;
your throne has stood firm from of old.
From all eternity, O Lord, you are. (*R*.)

3. Truly your decrees are to be trusted.
Holiness is fitting to your house,
O Lord, until the end of time. (*R*.)

Alleluia   (Rev 1:5)

Alleluia, alleluia!
You, O Christ, are the faithful witness,
the First-born from the dead;
you have loved us and have washed away our sins
with your blood.
Alleluia!

Alternative Alleluias p. 844.

Gospel   (3:7–15)

A reading from the holy Gospel according to John
*No one has gone up to heaven except the one who came down
from heaven, the Son of Man.*

Jesus said to Nicodemus:

"Do not be surprised when I say:
You must be born from above.
The wind blows wherever it pleases;
you hear its sound,
but you cannot tell where it comes from or where it is
    going.
That is how it is with all who are born in the Spirit."

    "How can that be possible?" asked Nicodemus. "You, a

teacher in Israel, and you do not know these things!" replied Jesus.

"I tell you most solemnly,
we speak only about what we know
and witness only to what we have seen
and yet you people reject our evidence.
If you do not believe me
when I speak about things in this world,
how are you going to believe me
when I speak to you about heavenly things?
No one has gone up to heaven
except the one who came down from heaven,
the Son of Man who is in heaven;
and the Son of Man must be lifted up
as Moses lifted up the serpent in the desert,
so that everyone who believes may have eternal life in him."

This is the Gospel of the Lord.

WEDNESDAY

First Reading (5:17–26)

A reading from the Acts of the Apostles

The men you imprisoned are in the Temple, preaching to the people.

The high priest intervened with all his supporters from the party of the Sadducees. Prompted by jealously, they arrested the apostles and had them put in the common gaol.

But at night the angel of the Lord opened the prison gates and said as he led them out, "Go and stand in the Temple, and tell the people all about this new Life." They did as they were told; they went into the Temple at dawn and began to preach.

When the high priest arrived, he and his supporters convened the Sanhedrin – this was the full Senate of Israel –

and sent to the gaol for them to be brought. But when the officials arrived at the prison they found they were not inside, so they went back and reported, "We found the gaol securely locked and the warders on duty at the gates, but when we unlocked the door we found no one inside." When the captain of the Temple and the chief priests heard this news they wondered what this could mean. Then a man arrived with fresh news. "At this very moment," he said, "the men you imprisoned are in the Temple. They are standing there preaching to the people." The captain went with his men and fetched them. They were afraid to use force in case the people stoned them.

This is the word of the Lord.

Responsorial Psalm   (Ps 33:2–9. *R.* v. 7)

Response
This poor man called
and the Lord heard him.
Or: Alleluia!

1. I will bless the Lord at all times,
his praise always on my lips;
in the Lord my soul shall make its boast.
The humble shall hear and be glad. (*R.*)

2. Glorify the Lord with me.
Together let us praise his name
I sought the Lord and he answered me;
from all my tremors he set me free. (*R.*)

3. Look towards him and be radiant;
let your faces not be abashed.
This poor man called; the Lord heard him
and rescued him from all his distress. (*R.*)

4. The angel of the Lord is encamped
around those who revere him, to rescue them.

Taste and see that the Lord is good.
He is happy who seeks refuge in him. (*R.*)

Alleluia

Alleluia, alleluia!
Christ has risen and shone upon us
whom he redeemed with his blood.
Alleluia!
Alternative Alleluias p. 844.

Gospel   (3:16–21)

A reading from the holy Gospel according to John
God sent his Son into the world so that through him the world
might be saved.

Jesus said to Nicodemus:

"Yes, God loved the world so much
that he gave his only Son,
so that everyone who believes in him may not be lost
but may have eternal life.
For God sent his Son into the world
not to condemn the world,
but so that through him the world might be saved.
No one who believes in him will be condemned;
but whoever refuses to believe is condemned already,
because he has refused to believe
in the name of God's only Son.
On these grounds is sentence pronounced:
that though the light has come into the world
men have shown they prefer
darkness to the light
because their deeds were evil.
And indeed, everybody who does wrong
hates the light and avoids it,
for fear his actions should be exposed;

but the man who lives by the truth
comes out into the light,
so that it may be plainly seen that what he does is done in
    God."

This is the Gospel of the Lord.

THURSDAY

First Reading   (5:27–33)

A reading from the Acts of the Apostles
We are witnesses to all this, we and the Holy Spirit.

When the officials had brought the apostles in to face the Sanhedrin, the high priest demanded an explanation. "We gave you a formal warning" he said "not to preach in his name, and what have you done? You have filled Jerusalem with your teaching, and seem determined to fix the guilt of this man's death on us." In reply Peter and the apostles said, "Obedience to God comes before obedience to men; it was the God of our ancestors who raised up Jesus, but it was you who had him executed by hanging on a tree. By his own right hand God has now raised him up to be leader and saviour, to give repentance and forgiveness of sins through him to Israel. We are witnesses to all this, we and the Holy Spirit whom God has given to those who obey him." This so infuriated them that they wanted to put them to death.

This is the word of the Lord.

Responsorial Psalm   (Ps 33:2. 9. 17–20. *R*. v. 7)

Response
This poor man called
and the Lord heard him.
Or: Alleluia!

1. I will bless the Lord at all times,
his praise always on my lips.

Taste and see that the Lord is good.
He is happy who seeks refuge in him. (*R.*)

2. The Lord turns his eyes to the just
and his ears to their appeal.
They call and the Lord hears
and rescues them in all their distress. (*R.*)

3. The Lord is close to the broken-hearted;
those whose spirit is crushed he will save.
Many are the trials of the just man
but from them all the Lord will rescue him. (*R.*)

Alleluia

Alleluia, alleluia!
Christ has risen: he who created all things,
and has granted his mercy to men.
Alleluia!

Alternative Alleluias p. 844.

Gospel (3:31–36)

A reading from the holy Gospel according to John
The Father loves the Son and has entrusted everything to him.

John the Baptist said to his disciples:

"He who comes from above
is above all others;
he who is born of the earth
is earthly himself and speaks in an earthly way.
He who comes from heaven
bears witness to the things he has seen and heard,
even if his testimony is not accepted;
though all who do accept his testimony
are attesting the truthfulness of God,
since he whom God has sent
speaks God's own words:

God gives him the Spirit without reserve.
The Father loves the Son
and has entrusted everything to him.
Anyone who believes in the Son has eternal life,
but anyone who refuses to believe in the Son will never see
   life:
the anger of God stays on him."

   This is the Gospel of the Lord.

FRIDAY

First Reading   (5:34–42)

A reading from the Acts of the Apostles
*They left, glad to have had the honour of suffering humiliation
for the sake of the name of Jesus.*

One member of the Sanhedrin stood up and asked to have
the apostles taken outside for a time. Then he addressed the
Sanhedrin, "Men of Israel, be careful how you deal with
these people. There was Theudas who became notorious
not so long ago. He claimed to be someone important,
and he even collected about four hundred followers; but
when he was killed, all his followers scattered and that was
the end of them. And then there was Judas the Galilean, at
the time of the census, who attracted crowds of supporters;
but he got killed too, and all his followers dispersed. What
I suggest, therefore, is that you leave these men alone and
let them go. If this enterprise, this movement of theirs, is of
human origin it will break up of its own accord; but if it
does in fact come from God you will not only be unable to
destroy them, but you might find yourselves fighting against
God."
   His advice was accepted; and they had the apostles called
in, gave orders for them to be flogged, warned them not to
speak in the name of Jesus and released them. And so they
left the presence of the Sanhedrin glad to have had the

honour of suffering humiliation for the sake of the name.

They preached every day both in the Temple and in private houses, and their proclamation of the Good News of Christ Jesus was never interrupted.

This is the word of the Lord.

Responsorial Psalm   (Ps 26:1. 4. 13–14. *R*. v. 4)

Response
There is one thing I ask of the Lord,
to live in the house of the Lord.
Or: Alleluia!

1. The Lord is my light and my help;
whom shall I fear?
The Lord is the stronghold of my life;
before whom shall I shrink? (*R*.)

2. There is one thing I ask of the Lord,
for this I long,
to live in the house of the Lord,
all the days of my life,
to savour the sweetness of the Lord,
to behold his temple. (*R*.)

3. I am sure I shall see the Lord's goodness
in the land of the living.
Hope in him, hold firm and take heart.
Hope in the Lord! (*R*.)

Alleluia

Alleluia, alleluia!
We know that Christ is truly risen from the dead;
have mercy on us, triumphant King.
Alleluia!

Alternative Alleluias p. 844.

Gospel   (6:1–15)

A reading from the holy Gospel according to John

To all who were sitting there he gave out as much as they wanted.

Some time after this, Jesus went off to the other side of the Sea of Galilee – or of Tiberias – and a large crowd followed him, impressed by the signs he gave by curing the sick. Jesus climbed the hillside, and sat down there with his disciples. It was shortly before the Jewish feast of Passover.

Looking up, Jesus saw the crowds approaching and said to Philip, "Where can we buy some bread for these people to eat?" He only said this to test Philip; he himself knew exactly what he was going to do. Philip answered, "Two hundred denarii would only buy enough to give them a small piece each." One of his disciples, Andrew, Simon Peter's brother, said, "There is a small boy here with five barley loaves and two fish; but what is that between so many?" Jesus said to them, "Make the people sit down." There was plenty of grass there and as many as five thousand men sat down. Then Jesus took the loaves, gave thanks, and gave them out to all who were sitting ready; he then did the same with the fish, giving out as much as they wanted. When they had eaten enough he said to the disciples, "Pick up the pieces left over so that nothing gets wasted." So they picked them up, and filled twelve hampers with scraps left over from the meal of five barley loaves. The people, seeing this sign that he had given, said, "This really is the prophet who is come into the world." Jesus, who could see they were about to come and take him by force and make him king, escaped back to the hills by himself.

This is the Gospel of the Lord.

SATURDAY

First Reading (6:1–7)

A reading from the Acts of the Apostles
They elected seven men full of the Holy Spirit.

About this time, when the number of disciples was increasing, the Hellenists made a complaint against the Hebrews: in the daily distribution their own widows were being overlooked. So the Twelve called a full meeting of the disciples and addressed them, "It would not be right for us to neglect the word of God so as to give out food; you, brothers, must select from among yourselves seven men of good reputation, filled with the Spirit and with wisdom; we will hand over this duty to them, and continue to devote ourselves to prayer and to the service of the word." The whole assembly approved of this proposal and elected Stephen, a man full of faith and of the Holy Spirit, together with Philip, Prochorus, Nicanor, Timon, Parmenas, and Nicolaus of Antioch, a convert to Judaism. They presented these to the apostles, who prayed and laid their hands on them.

The word of the Lord continued to spread: the number of disciples in Jerusalem was greatly increased, and a large group of priests made their submission to the faith.

This is the word of the Lord.

Responsorial Psalm (Ps 32:1–2. 4–5. 18–19. *R.* v. 22)
Response
May your love be upon us, O Lord,
as we place all our hope in you.
Or: Alleluia!

1. Ring out your joy to the Lord, O you just;
for praise is fitting for loyal hearts.
Give thanks to the Lord upon the harp,
with a ten-stringed lute sing him songs. (*R.*)

2. For the word of the Lord is faithful
and all his works to be trusted.
The Lord loves justice and right
and fills the earth with his love. (R.)

3. The Lord looks on those who revere him,
on those who hope in his love,
to rescue their souls from death,
to keep them alive in famine. (R.)

Alleluia   (Rom 6:9)

Alleluia, alleluia!
Christ, having been raised from the dead,
will never die again.
Death has no power over him any more.
Alleluia!

Alternative Alleluias p. 844.

Gospel   (6:16–12)

A reading from the holy Gospel according to John
They saw Jesus walking on the lake.

In the evening the disciples went down to the shore of the
lake and got into a boat to make for Capernaum on the
other side of the lake. It was getting dark by now and Jesus
had still not rejoined them. The wind was strong, and the
sea was getting rough. They had rowed three or four miles
when they saw Jesus walking on the lake and coming towards the boat. This frightened them, but he said, "It is I.
Do not be afraid." They were for taking him into the boat,
but in no time it reached the shore at the place they were
making for.
     This is the Gospel of the Lord.

3rd SUNDAY OF EASTER
Year 1 (Year A)

First Reading   (2:14. 22–28)

A reading from the Acts of the Apostles
It was impossible for him to be held in the power of Hades.

On the day of Pentecost Peter stood up with the Eleven and addressed the crowd in a loud voice: "Men of Israel, listen to what I am going to say: Jesus the Nazarene was a man commended to you by God by the miracles and portents and signs that God worked through him when he was among you, as you all know. This man, who was put into your power by the deliberate intention and foreknowledge of God, you took and had crucified by men outside the Law. You killed him, but God raised him to life, freeing him from the pangs of Hades; for it was impossible for him to be held in its power since, as David says of him:

I saw the Lord before me always,
for with him at my right hand nothing can shake me.
So my heart was glad
and my tongue cried out with joy;
my body, too, will rest in the hope
that you will not abandon my soul to Hades
nor allow your holy one to experience corruption.
You have made known the way of life to me,
you will fill me with gladness through your presence."

This is the word of the Lord.

Responsorial Psalm   (Ps 15:1–2. 5. 7–11. *R*. v. 11)
Response
Show us, Lord, the path of life.
Or: Alleluia!

1. Preserve me, God, I take refuge in you.
I say to the Lord: "You are my God.

O Lord, it is you who are my portion and cup;
it is you yourself who are my prize." (*R.*)

2. I will bless the Lord who gives me counsel,
who even at night directs my heart.
I keep the Lord ever in my sight:
since he is at my right hand, I shall stand firm. (*R.*)

3. And so my heart rejoices, my soul is glad;
even my body shall rest in safety.
For you will not leave my soul among the dead,
nor let your beloved know decay. (*R.*)

4. You will show me the path of life,
the fullness of joy in your presence,
at your right hand happiness for ever. (*R.*)

Second Reading   (1:17–21)

A reading from the first letter of St Peter
Your ransom was paid in the precious blood of a lamb without
spot or stain, namely, Christ.

If you are acknowledging as your Father one who has no
favourites and judges every one according to what he has
done, you must be scrupulously careful as long as you are
living away from your home. Remember, the ransom that
was paid to free you from the useless way of life your ancestors handed down was not paid in anything corruptible,
neither in silver nor gold, but in the precious blood of a
lamb without spot or stain, namely Christ; who, though
known since before the world was made, has been revealed
only in our time, the end of the ages, for your sake.
Through him you now have faith in God, who raised him
from the dead and gave him glory for that very reason – so
that you would have faith and hope in God.
    This is the word of the Lord.

Alleluia   (Cf. Lk 24:32)

Alleluia, alleluia!
Lord Jesus, explain the scriptures to us.
Make our hearts burn within us
as you talk to us.
Alleluia!

Gospel   (24:13–35)

A reading from the holy Gospel according to Luke
They recognised him at the breaking of bread.

Two of the disciples of Jesus were on their way to a village
called Emmaus, seven miles from Jerusalem, and they were
talking together about all that had happened. Now as they
talked this over, Jesus himself came up and walked by their
side; but something prevented them from recognising him.
He said to them, "What matters are you discussing as you
walk along?" They stopped short, their faces downcast.

Then one of them, called Cleopas, answered him, "You
must be the only person staying in Jerusalem who does not
know the things that have been happening there these last
few days." "What things?" he asked. "All about Jesus of
Nazareth" they answered "who proved he was a great
prophet by the things he said and did in the sight of God
and of the whole people; and how our chief priests and our
leaders handed him over to be sentenced to death, and had
him crucified. Our own hope had been that he would be the
one to set Israel free. And this is not all: two whole days
have gone by since it all happened; and some women from
our group have astounded us: they went to the tomb in the
early morning, and when they did not find the body, they
came back to tell us they had seen a vision of angels who
declared he was alive. Some of our friends went to the tomb
and found everything exactly as the women had reported,
but of him they saw nothing."

Then he said to them, "You foolish men! So slow to believe the full message of the prophets! Was it not ordained that the Christ should suffer and so enter into his glory?" Then, starting with Moses and going through all the prophets, he explained to them the passages throughout the scriptures that were about himself.

When they drew near to the village to which they were going, he made as if to go on; but they pressed him to stay with them. "It is nearly evening" they said "and the day is almost over." So he went in to stay with them. Now while he was with them at table, he took the bread and said the blessing; then he broke it and handed it to them. And their eyes were opened and they recognised him; but he had vanished from their sight. Then they said to each other, "Did not our hearts burn within us as he talked to us on the road and explained the scriptures to us?"

They set out that instant and returned to Jerusalem. There they found the Eleven assembled together with their companions, who said to them, "Yes, it is true. The Lord has risen and has appeared to Simon." Then they told their story of what had happened on the road and how they had recognised him at the breaking of bread.

This is the Gospel of the Lord.

3rd SUNDAY OF EASTER
Year 2 (Year B)

First Reading   (3:13–15. 17–19)

A reading from the Acts of the Apostles
You killed the prince of life. God, however, raised him from the dead.

Peter said to the people: "You are Israelites, and it is the God of Abraham, Isaac and Jacob, the God of our ancestors, who has glorified his servant Jesus, the same Jesus you handed over and then disowned in the presence of Pilate, after Pilate had decided to release him. It was you who accused the Holy One, the Just One, you who demanded the reprieve of a murderer while you killed the prince of life. God, however, raised him from the dead, and to that fact we are the witnesses.

"Now I know, brothers, that neither you nor your leaders had any idea what you were really doing; this was the way God carried out what he had foretold, when he said through all his prophets that his Christ would suffer. Now you must repent and turn to God, so that your sins may be wiped out."

This is the word of the Lord.

Responsorial Psalm (Ps 4:2. 4. 7. 9. *R*. v. 7)

Response
Lift up the light of your face on us, O Lord.
Or: Alleluia!

1. When I call, answer me, O God of justice;
from anguish you released me, have mercy and hear me!
   (*R*.)

2. It is the Lord who grants favours to those whom he loves;
the Lord hears me whenever I call him. (*R*.)

3. "What can bring us happiness?" many say.
Lift up the light of your face on us, O Lord. (*R*.)

4. I will lie down in peace and sleep comes at once,
for you alone, Lord, make me dwell in safety. (*R*.)

Second Reading (2:1–5)

A reading from the first letter of St John
He is the sacrifice that takes our sins away, and not only ours, but the whole world's.

I am writing this, my children,
to stop you sinning;
but if anyone should sin,

we have our advocate with the Father,
Jesus Christ, who is just;
he is the sacrifice that takes our sins away,
and not only ours,
but the whole world's.
We can be sure that we know God
only by keeping his commandments,
Anyone who says, 'I know him',
and does not keep his commandments,
is a liar,
refusing to admit the truth.
But when anyone does obey what he has said,
God's love comes to perfection in him.

This is the word of the Lord.

ALLELUIA. As for year 1 (Year A), see p. 698.

Gospel   (24:35–48)

A reading from the holy Gospel according to Luke

*So you see how it is written that the Christ would suffer and on
the third day rise from the dead.*

The disciples told their story of what had happened on the
road and how they had recognised Jesus at the breaking of
bread.

They were still talking about all this when Jesus himself
stood among them and said to them, "Peace be with you!"
In a state of alarm and fright, they thought they were seeing
a ghost. But he said, "Why are you so agitated, and why
are these doubts rising in your hearts? Look at my hands
and feet; yes, it is I indeed. Touch me and see for yourselves; a ghost has no flesh and bones as you can see I
have." And as he said this he showed them his hands and
feet. Their joy was so great that they could not believe it,
and they stood dumbfounded; so he said to them, "Have
you anything here to eat?" And they offered him a piece of

grilled fish, which he took and ate before their eyes.

Then he told them, "This is what I meant when I said, while I was still with you, that everything written about me in the Law of Moses, in the Prophets and in the Psalms, has to be fulfilled." He then opened their minds to understand the scriptures, and he said to them, "So you see how it is written that the Christ would suffer and on the third day rise from the dead, and that, in his name, repentance for the forgiveness of sins would be preached to all the nations, beginning from Jerusalem. You are witnesses to this."

This is the Gospel of the Lord.

3rd SUNDAY OF EASTER

Year 3 (Year C)

First Reading   (5:27–32. 40–41)

A reading from the Acts of the Apostles
We are witnesses of all this, we and the Holy Spirit.

The high priest demanded an explanation of the apostles. "We gave you a formal warning," he said "not to preach in this name, and what have you done? You have filled Jerusalem with your teaching, and seem determined to fix the guilt of this man's death on us." In reply Peter and the apostles said, "Obedience to God comes before obedience to men; it was the God of our ancestors who raised up Jesus, but it was you who had him executed by hanging on a tree. By his own right hand God has now raised him up to be leader and saviour, to give repentance and forgiveness of sins through him to Israel. We are witnesses to all this, we and the Holy Spirit whom God has given to those who obey him." They warned the apostles not to speak in the name of Jesus and released them. And so they left the presence of the Sanhedrin glad to have had the honour of suffering humiliation for the sake of the name.

This is the word of the Lord.

Responsorial Psalm   (Ps 29:2. 4–6. 11–13. *R.* v. 2)

Response
I will praise you, Lord,
you have rescued me.
Or: Alleluia!

1. I will praise you, Lord, you have rescued me
and have not let my enemies rejoice over me.
O Lord, you have raised my soul from the dead,
restored me to life from those who sink into the grave. (*R.*)

2. Sing psalms to the Lord, you who love him,
give thanks to his holy name.
His anger lasts but a moment; his favour through life.
At night there are tears, but joy comes with dawn. (*R.*)

3. The Lord listened and had pity.
The Lord came to my help.
For me you have changed my mourning into dancing,
O Lord my God, I will thank you for ever. (*R.*)

Second Reading   (5:11–14)

A reading from the book of the Apocalypse
The Lamb that was sacrificed is worthy to be given riches and power.

In my vision, I, John, heard the sound of an immense number of angels gathered round the throne and the animals and the elders; there were ten thousand times ten thousand of them and thousands upon thousands, shouting, "The Lamb that was sacrificed is worthy to be given power, riches, wisdom, strength, honour, glory and blessing." Then I heard all the living things in creation – everything that lives in the air, and on the ground, and under the ground, and in the sea, crying, "To the One who is sitting on the throne and to the Lamb, be all praise, honour, glory and

power, for ever and ever." And the four animals said,
"Amen"; and the elders prostrated themselves to worship.

This is the word of the Lord.

ALLELUIA. As for Year 1 (Year A), see p. 698

Gospel (21:1–19)

A reading from the holy Gospel according to John

*Jesus stepped forward, took the bread and gave it to them, and
the same with the fish.*

*Jesus showed himself again to the disciples. It was by the
Sea of Tiberias, and it happened like this: Simon Peter,
Thomas called the Twin, Nathanael from Cana in Galilee,
the sons of Zebedee and two more of his disciples were
together. Simon Peter said, "I'm going fishing." They replied, "We'll come with you." They went out and got into
the boat but caught nothing that night.

It was light by now and there stood Jesus on the shore,
though the disciples did not realise that it was Jesus. Jesus
called out, "Have you caught anything, friends?" And when
they answered, "No", he said, "Throw the net out to star-
board and you'll find something." So they dropped the net,
and there were so many fish that they could not haul it in.
The disciple Jesus loved said to Peter, "It is the Lord." At
these words "It is the Lord", Simon Peter, who had practically nothing on, wrapped his cloak round him and
jumped into the water. The other disciples came on in the
boat, towing the net and the fish; they were only about a
hundred yards from land.

As soon as they came ashore they saw that there was
some bread there, and a charcoal fire with fish cooking on it.
Jesus said, "Bring some of the fish you have just caught."
Simon Peter went aboard and dragged the net to the shore,
full of big fish, one hundred and fifty-three of them; and in
spite of there being so many the net was not broken. Jesus

said to them, "Come and have breakfast." None of the disciples was bold enough to ask, "Who are you?"; they knew quite well it was the Lord. Jesus then stepped forward, took the bread and gave it to them, and the same with the fish. This was the third time that Jesus showed himself to the disciples after rising from the dead.*

After the meal Jesus said to Simon Peter, "Simon son of John, do you love me more than these others do?" He answered, "Yes Lord, you know I love you." Jesus said to him, "Feed my lambs." A second time he said to him, "Simon son of John, do you love me?" He replied, "Yes, Lord, you know I love you." Jesus said to him, "Look after my sheep." Then he said to him a third time, "Simon son of John, do you love me?" Peter was upset that he asked him the third time, "Do you love me?" and said, "Lord, you know everything; you know I love you." Jesus said to him, "Feed my sheep.

"I tell you most solemnly,
when you were young
you put on your own belt
and walked where you liked;
but when you grow old
you will stretch out your hands,
and somebody else will put a belt round you
and take you where you would rather not go."

In these words he indicated the kind of death by which Peter would give glory to God. After this he said, "Follow me."

This is the Gospel of the Lord.

*Shorter Form, verses 1–14. Read between *.

MONDAY

First Reading   (6:8–15)

A reading from the Acts of the Apostles

They could not get the better of Stephen because of his wisdom, and because it was the Spirit that prompted what he said.

Stephen was filled with grace and power and began to work miracles and great signs among the people. But then certain people came forward to debate with Stephen, some from Cyrene and Alexandria who were members of the synagogue called the Synagogue of Freedmen, and others from Cilicia and Asia. They found they could not get the better of him because of his wisdom, and because it was the Spirit that prompted what he said. So they procured some men to say, "We heard him using blasphemous language against Moses and against God." Having in this way turned the people against him as well as the elders and scribes, they took Stephen by surprise, and arrested him and brought him before the Sanhedrin. There they put up false witnesses to say, "This man is always making speeches against this Holy Place and the Law. We have heard him say that Jesus the Nazarene is going to destroy this Place and alter the traditions that Moses handed down to us." The members of the Sanhedrin all looked intently at Stephen, and his face appeared to them like the face of an angel.

This is the word of the Lord.

Responsorial Psalm (Ps 118:23–24. 26–27. 29–30. *R.* v. 1)

Response

They are happy whose life is blameless.

Or: Alleluia!

1. Though princes sit plotting against me
I ponder on your statutes.
Your will is my delight;
your statutes are my counsellors. (*R.*)

2. I declared my ways and you answered:
teach me your statutes.
Make me grasp the way of your precepts
and I will muse on your wonders. (R.)

3. Keep me from the way of error
and teach me your law.
I have chosen the way of truth
with your decrees before me. (R.)

Alleluia   (Jn 20:29)

Alleluia, alleluia!
You believe, Thomas, because you can see me.
Happy are those who have not seen and yet believe.
Alleluia!

Gospel   (6:22–29)

A reading from the holy Gospel according to John
*Do not work for food that cannot last, but work for food that
endures to eternal life.*

Next day, the crowd that had stayed on the other side saw
that only one boat had been there, and that Jesus had not
got into the boat with his disciples, but that the disciples
had set off by themselves. Other boats, however, had put in
from Tiberias, near the place where the bread had been
eaten. When the people saw that neither Jesus nor his disciples were there, they got into those boats and crossed to
Capernaum to look for Jesus. When they found him on the
other side, they said to him, "Rabbi, when did you come
here?" Jesus answered:

"I tell you most solemnly,
you are not looking for me
because you have seen the signs
but because you had all the bread you wanted to eat.

Do not work for food that cannot last,
but work for food that endures to eternal life,
the kind of food the Son of Man is offering you,
for on him the Father, God himself, has set his seal."

Then they said to him, "What must we do if we are to do the works that God wants?" Jesus gave them this answer, "This is working for God: you must believe in the one he has sent."

This is the Gospel of the Lord.

TUESDAY

First Reading   (7:51–8:1)

A reading from the Acts of the Apostles
Lord Jesus, receive my spirit.

Stephen said to the members of the Sanhedrin: "You stubborn people, with your pagan hearts and pagan ears. You are always resisting the Holy Spirit, just as your ancestors used to do. Can you name a single prophet your ancestors never persecuted? In the past they killed those who foretold the coming of the Just One, and now you have become his betrayers, his murderers. You who had the Law brought to you by angels are the very ones who have not kept it."

They were infuriated when they heard this, and ground their teeth at him.

But Stephen, filled with the Holy Spirit, gazed into heaven and saw the glory of God, and Jesus standing at God's right hand. "I can see heaven thrown open" he said "and the Son of Man standing at the right hand of God." At this all the members of the council shouted out and stopped their ears with their hands; then they all rushed at him, sent him out of the city and stoned him. The witnesses put down their clothes at the feet of a young man called Saul. As they were stoning him, Stephen said in invocation, "Lord Jesus, receive my spirit." Then he knelt down and said aloud,

"Lord, do not hold this sin against them"; and with these
words he fell asleep. Saul entirely approved of the killing.

This is the word of the Lord.

Responsorial Psalm   (Ps 30:3–4. 6–8. 17. 21. *R*. v. 6)
Response
Into your hands, O Lord,
I commend my spirit.
Or: Alleluia!

1. Be a rock of refuge for me,
a mighty stronghold to save me,
for you are my rock, my stronghold.
For your name's sake, lead me and guide me. (*R*.)

2. Into your hands I commend my spirit.
It is you who will redeem me, Lord.
As for me, I trust in the Lord:
let me be glad and rejoice in your love. (*R*.)

3. Let your face shine on your servant.
Save me in your love.
You hide those who trust you in the shelter of your presence
from the plotting of men. (*R*.)

Alleluia   (Jn 10:14)
Alleluia! alleluia!
I am the good shepherd, says the Lord,
I know my sheep and my own know me.
Alleluia!

Alternative Alleluias p. 844.

Gospel   (6:30–35)
A reading from the holy Gospel according to John
*It was not Moses who gave you bread from heaven, it is my
Father who gives you the bread from heaven, the true bread.*

The Jews said to Jesus: "What sign will you give to show us that we should believe in you? What work will you do? Our fathers had manna to eat in the desert; as scripture says: He gave them bread from heaven to eat."

Jesus answered:

"I tell you most solemnly,
it was not Moses who gave you bread from heaven,
it is my Father who gives you the bread from heaven,
the true bread;
for the bread of God
is that which comes down from heaven
and gives life to the world."

"Sir," they said "give us that bread always." Jesus answered:

"I am the bread of life.
He who comes to me will never be hungry;
he who believes in me will never thirst."

This is the Gospel of the Lord.

WEDNESDAY

First Reading (8:1–8)

A reading from the Acts of the Apostles
They went from place to place preaching the Good News.

That day a bitter persecution started against the church in Jerusalem, and everyone except the apostles fled to the country districts of Judea and Samaria.

There were some devout people, however, who buried Stephen and made great mourning for him.

Saul then worked for the total destruction of the Church; he went from house to house arresting both men and women and sending them to prison.

Those who had escaped went from place to place preaching the Good News. One of them was Philip who went to a Samaritan town and proclaimed the Christ to them. The people united in welcoming the message Philip preached, either because they had heard of the miracles he worked or because they saw them for themselves. There were, for example, unclean spirits that came shrieking out of many who were possessed, and several paralytics and cripples were cured. There was great rejoicing in that town as a result.

This is the word of the Lord.

Responsorial Psalm   (Ps 65:1–7. *R*. v. 1)

Response
Cry out with a joy to God all the earth.
Or : Alleluia !

1. Cry out with joy to God all the earth,
O sing to the glory of his name.
O render him glorious praise.
Say to God : "How tremendous your deeds!" (*R*)

2. "Before you all the earth shall bow;
shall sing to you, sing to your name."
Come and see the works of God,
tremendous his deeds among men. (*R*.)

3. He turned the sea into dry land,
they passed through the river dry-shod.
Let our joy then be in him;
he rules for ever by his might. (*R*.)

Alleluia   (Jn 10:27)
Alleluia, alleluia !
The sheep that belong to me listen to my voice,

says the Lord;
I know them and they follow me.
Alleluia!

Alternative Alleluias p. 844.

Gospel   (6:35–40)

A reading from the holy Gospel according to John
*It is my Father's will that whoever sees the Son shall have
eternal life.*

Jesus said to the Jews:

"I am the bread of life.
He who comes to me will never be hungry;
he who believes in me will never thirst.
But, as I have told you,
you can see me and still you do not believe.
All that the Father gives me will come to me,
and whoever comes to me
I shall not turn him away;
because I have come from heaven,
not to do my own will,
but to do the will of the one who sent me.
Now the will of him who sent me
is that I should lose nothing
of all that he has given to me,
and that I should raise it up on the last day.
Yes, it is my Father's will
that whoever sees the Son and believes in him
shall have eternal life,
and that I shall raise him up on the last day."

This is the Gospel of the Lord.

THURSDAY

First Reading   (8:26–40)

A reading from the Acts of the Apostles
If you believe with all your heart, you may be baptised.

The angel of the Lord spoke to Philip saying, "Be ready to
set out at noon along the road that goes from Jerusalem
down to Gaza, the desert road." So he set off on his journey. Now it happened that an Ethiopian had been on pil-
grimage to Jerusalem; he was a eunuch and an officer at the
court of the kandake, or queen, of Ethiopia, and was in fact
her chief treasurer. He was now on his way home; and as
he sat in his chariot he was reading the prophet Isaiah. The
Spirit said to Philip, "Go up and meet that chariot." When
Philip ran up, he heard him reading Isaiah the prophet and
asked, "Do you understand what you are reading?" "How
can I" he replied "unless I have someone to guide me?" So
he invited Philip to get in and sit by his side. Now the passage of scripture he was reading was this:

Like a sheep that is led to the slaughter-house,
like a lamb that is dumb in front of its shearers,
like these he never opens his mouth.
He has been humiliated and has no one to defend him.
Who will ever talk about his descendants,
since his life on earth has been cut short!

The eunuch turned to Philip and said, "Tell me, is the
prophet referring to himself or someone else?" Starting,
therefore, with this text of scripture Philip proceeded to
explain the Good News of Jesus to him.
Further along the road they came to some water, and
the eunuch said, "Look, there is some water here; is there
anything to stop me being baptised?" He ordered the
chariot to stop, then Philip and the eunuch both went down
into the water and Philip baptised him. But after they had

come up out of the water again Philip was taken away by the Spirit of the Lord, and the eunuch never saw him again but went on his way rejoicing. Philip found that he had reached Azotus and continued his journey proclaiming the Good News in every town as far as Caesarea.

This is the word of the Lord.

Responsorial Psalm		(Ps 65:8–9. 16–17. 20. *R*. v. 1)

Response
Cry out with joy to God all the earth.
Or: Alleluia!

1. O peoples, bless our God,
let the voice of his praise resound,
of the God who gave life to our souls
and kept our feet from stumbling. (*R*.)

2. Come and hear, all who fear God.
I will tell what he did for my soul:
to him I cried aloud,
with high praise ready on my tongue. (*R*.)

3. Blessed be God
who did not reject my prayer
nor withhold his love from me. (*R*.)

Alleluia
Alleluia, alleluia!
The Lord, who hung for us upon the tree,
has risen from the tomb.
Alleluia!

Alternative Alleluias p. 844.

Gospel						(6:44–51)
A reading from the holy Gospel according to John
I am the living bread which has come down from heaven.

Jesus said to the Jews:

"No one can come to me
unless he is drawn by the Father who sent me,
and I will raise him up at the last day.
It is written in the prophets:
They will all be taught by God,
and to hear the teaching of the Father,
and learn from it,
is to come to me.
Not that anybody has seen the Father,
except the one who comes from God:
he has seen the Father.
I tell you most solemnly,
everyody who believes has eternal life.
I am the bread of life.
Your fathers ate the manna in the desert
and they are dead;
but this is the bread that comes down from heaven,
so that a man may eat it and not die.
I am the living bread which has come down from heaven.
Anyone who eats this bread will live for ever;
and the bread that I shall give
is my flesh, for the life of the world."

This is the Gospel of the Lord.

FRIDAY

First Reading   (9:1–20)

A reading from the Acts of the Apostles
*This man is my chosen instrument to bring my name before
pagans.*

Meanwhile Saul was still breathing threats to slaughter the
Lord's disciples. He had gone to the high priest and asked
for letters addressed to the synagogues in Damascus, that

would authorise him to arrest and take to Jerusalem any followers of the Way, men or women, that he could find.

Suddenly, while he was travelling to Damascus and just before he reached the city, there came a light from heaven all round him. He fell to the ground, and then he heard a voice saying, "Saul, Saul, why are you persecuting me?" "Who are you, Lord?" he asked, and the voice answered, "I am Jesus, and you are persecuting me. Get up now and go into the city, and you will be told what you have to do." The men travelling with Saul stood there speechless, for though they heard the voice they could see no one. Saul got up from the ground, but even with his eyes wide open he could see nothing at all, and they had to lead him into Damascus by the hand. For three days he was without his sight, and took neither food nor drink.

A disciple called Ananias who lived in Damascus had a vision in which he heard the Lord say to him, "Ananias!" When he replied, "Here I am, Lord," the Lord said, "You must go to Straight Street and ask at the house of Judas for someone called Saul, who comes from Tarsus. At this moment he is praying, having had a vision of a man called Ananias coming in and laying hands on him to give him back his sight."

When he heard that, Ananias said, "Lord, several people have told me about this man and all the harm he has been doing to your saints in Jerusalem. He has only come here because he holds a warrant from the chief priests to arrest everybody who invokes your name." The Lord replied, "You must go all the same, because this man is my chosen instrument to bring my name before pagans and pagan kings and before the people of Israel; I myself will show him how much he himself must suffer for my name." Then Ananias went. He entered the house, and at once laid his hands on Saul and said, "Brother Saul, I have been sent by the Lord Jesus who appeared to you on your way here so that you may recover your sight and be filled with the Holy

Spirit." Immediately it was as though scales fell away from
Saul's eyes and he could see again. So he was baptised there
and then, and after taking some food he regained his
strength.

After he had spent only a few days with the disciples
in Damascus, he began preaching in the synagogues, "Jesus
is the Son of God."

This is the word of the Lord.

Responsorial Psalm   (Ps 116. *R.* Mk 16:15)

Response
Go out to the whole world;
proclaim the Good News.
Or: Alleluia!

1. Alleluia!
O praise the Lord, all you nations,
acclaim him all you peoples! (*R.*)

2. Strong is his love for us;
he is faithful for ever. (*R.*)

Alleluia   (Lk 24:25. 26)

Alleluia, alleluia!
It was ordained that the Christ should suffer
and rise from the dead,
and so enter into his glory.
Alleluia!

Alternative Alleluias p. 844.

Gospel   (6:52–59)

A reading from the holy Gospel according to John
My flesh is real food and my blood is real drink.

The Jews started arguing with one another: "How can this
man give us his flesh to eat?" they said. Jesus replied:

"I tell you most solemnly,
if you do not eat the flesh of the Son of Man
and drink his blood,
you will not have life in you.
Anyone who does eat my flesh and drink my blood
has eternal life,
and I shall raise him up on the last day.
For my flesh is real food
and my blood is real drink.
He who eats my flesh and drinks my blood
lives in me
and I live in him.
As I, who am sent by the living Father,
myself draw life from the Father,
so whoever eats me will draw life from me.
This is the bread come down from heaven;
not like the bread our ancestors ate:
they are dead,
but anyone who eats this bread will live for ever."

He taught this doctrine at Capernaum, in the synagogue.
   This is the Gospel of the Lord.

SATURDAY

First Reading   (9:31–42)

A reading from the Acts of the Apostles
The churches built themselves up and were filled with the
consolation of the Holy Spirit.

The churches throughout Judaea, Galilee and Samaria were
now left in peace, building themselves up, living in the fear
of the Lord, and filled with the consolation of the Holy
Spirit.

   Peter visited one place after another and eventually came
to the saints living down in Lydda. There he found a man
called Aeneas, a paralytic who had been bedridden for eight
years. Peter said to him, "Aeneas, Jesus Christ cures you:

get up and fold up your sleeping mat." Aeneas got up immediately; everybody who lived in Lydda and Sharon saw him, and they were all converted to the Lord.

At Jaffa there was a woman disciple called Tabitha, or Dorcas in Greek, who never tired of doing good or giving in charity. But the time came when she got ill and died, and they washed her and laid her out in a room upstairs. Lydda is not far from Jaffa, so when the disciples heard that Peter was there, they sent two men with an urgent message for him, "Come and visit us as soon as possible."

Peter went back with them straightaway, and on his arrival they took him to the upstairs room, where all the widows stood round him in tears, showing him tunics and other clothes Dorcas had made when she was with them. Peter sent them all out of the room and knelt down and prayed. Then he turned to the dead woman and said, "Tabitha, stand up." She opened her eyes, looked at Peter and sat up. Peter helped her to her feet, then he called in the saints and widows and showed them she was alive. The whole of Jaffa heard about it and many believed in the Lord.

This is the word of the Lord.

Responsorial Psalm   (Ps 115:12–17. *R*. v. 12)

Response
How can I repay the Lord
for his goodness to me?
Or: Alleluia!

1. How can I repay the Lord
for his goodness to me?
The cup of salvation I will raise;
A thanksgiving sacrifice I make:
I will call on the Lord's name. (*R*.)

2. My vows to the Lord I will fulfil
before all his people.

O precious in the eyes of the Lord
is the death of his faithful. (*R.*)

3. Your servant, Lord, your servant am I;
you have loosened my bonds.
A thanksgiving sacrifice I make:
I will call on the Lord's name. (*R.*)

Alleluia

Alleluia, alleluia!
We know that Christ is truly risen from the dead;
have mercy on us, triumphant King.
Alleluia!

Alternative Alleluias p. 844.

Gospel   (6:60–69)

A reading from the holy Gospel according to John
Who shall we go to? You have the message of eternal life.

After hearing his doctrine, many of the followers of Jesus
said, "This is intolerable language. How could anyone accept it?" Jesus was aware that his followers were complain-
ing about it and said, "Does this upset you? What if you
should see the Son of Man ascend to where he was before?

"It is the spirit that gives life,
the flesh has nothing to offer.
The words I have spoken to you are spirit
and they are life.

"But there are some of you who do not believe."

For Jesus knew from the outset those who did not believe,
and who it was that would betray him. He went on, "This is
why I told you that no one could come to me unless the
Father allows him." After this, many of his disciples left
him and stopped going with him.

Then Jesus said to the Twelve. "What about you, do

you want to go away too?" Simon Peter answered, "Lord, who shall we go to? You have the message of eternal life, and we believe; we know that you are the Holy One of God."

This is the Gospel of the Lord.

4th SUNDAY OF EASTER
Year 1 (Year A)

First Reading   (2:14. 36–41)

A reading from the Acts of the Apostles
God has made him both Lord and Christ.

On the day of Pentecost Peter stood up with the Eleven and addressed the crowd with a loud voice: "The whole House of Israel can be certain that God has made this Jesus whom you crucified both Lord and Christ."

Hearing this, they were cut to the heart and said to Peter and the apostles, "What must we do, brothers?" "You must repent," Peter answered "and every one of you must be baptised in the name of Jesus Christ for the forgiveness of your sins, and you will receive the gift of the Holy Spirit. The promise that was made is for you and your children, and for all those who are far away, for all those whom the Lord our God will call to himself." He spoke to them for a long time using many arguments, and he urged them, "Save yourselves from this perverse generation." They were convinced by his arguments, and they accepted what he said and were baptised. That very day about three thousand were added to their number.

This is the word of the Lord.

Responsorial Psalm   (Ps 22:1–6. *R*. v. 1)

Response
The Lord is my Shepherd;
there is nothing I shall want.
Or: Alleluia!

1. The Lord is my shepherd;
there is nothing I shall want.
Fresh and green are the pastures
where he gives me repose.
Near restful waters he leads me,
to revive my drooping spirit. (*R.*)

2. He guides me along the right path;
he is true to his name.
If I should walk in the valley of darkness
no evil would I fear.
You are there with your crook and your staff;
with these you give me comfort. (*R.*)

3. You have prepared a banquet for me
in the sight of my foes.
My head you have anointed with oil;
my cup is overflowing. (*R.*)

4. Surely goodness and kindness shall follow me
all the days of my life.
In the Lord's own house shall I dwell
for ever and ever. (*R.*)

Second Reading   (2:20–25)

A reading from the first letter of St Peter
You have come back to the shepherd of your souls.

The merit, in the sight of God, is in bearing punishment
patiently when you are punished after doing your duty.
   This, in fact, is what you were called to do, because Christ
suffered for you and left an example for you to follow the
way he took. He had not done anything wrong, and there
had been no perjury in his mouth. He was insulted and did
not retaliate with insults; when he was tortured he made
no threats but he put his trust in the righteous judge. He
was bearing our faults in his own body on the cross, so that

we might die to our faults and live for holiness; through
his wounds you have been healed. You had gone astray like
sheep but now you have come back to the shepherd and
guardian of your souls.

This is the word of the Lord.

Alleluia   (Jn 10:14)

Alleluia, alleluia!
I am the good shepherd, says the Lord;
I know my own sheep and my own know me.
Alleluia!

Gospel   (10:1–10)

A reading from the holy Gospel according to John
I am the gate of the sheepfold.

Jesus said to the Jews: "I tell you most solemnly, anyone
who does not enter the sheepfold through the gate, but gets
in some other way is a thief and a brigand. The one who
enters through the gate is the shepherd of the flock; the gate-
keeper lets him in, the sheep hear his voice, one by one he
calls his own sheep and leads them out. When he has
brought out his flock, he goes ahead of them, and the sheep
follow because they know his voice. They never follow a
stranger but run away from him: they do not recognise the
voice of strangers."

Jesus told them this parable but they failed to understand
what he meant by telling it to them.

So Jesus spoke to them again:

"I tell you most solemnly,
I am the gate of the sheepfold.
All others who have come
are thieves and brigands;
but the sheep took no notice of them.
I am the gate.

Anyone who enters through me will be safe:
he will go freely in and out
and be sure of finding pasture.
The thief comes
only to steal and kill and destroy.
I have come
so that they may have life
and have it to the full."

This is the Gospel of the Lord.

4th SUNDAY OF EASTER
Year 2 (Year B)

First Reading   (4:8–12)

A reading from the Acts of the Apostles
This is the only name by which we can be saved.

Peter, filled with the Holy Spirit, addressed them, "Rulers
of the people, and elders! If you are questioning us today
about an act of kindness to a cripple, and asking us how
he was healed, then I am glad to tell you all, and would
indeed be glad to tell the whole people of Israel, that it was
by the name of Jesus Christ the Nazarene, the one you
crucified, whom God raised from the dead, by this name
and by no other that this man is able to stand up perfectly
healthy, here in your presence, today. This is the stone rejected by you the builders, but which has proved to be the
keystone. For of all the names in the world given to men,
this is the only one by which we can be saved."

This is the word of the Lord.

Responsorial Psalm   (Ps 117:1. 8–9. 21–23. 26. 28–29.
                                                   R. v. 22)

Response
The stone which the builders rejected
has become the corner stone.
Or: Alleluia!

1. Alleluia!
Give thanks to the Lord for he is good,
for his love has no end.
It is better to take refuge in the Lord
than to trust in men:
it is better to take refuge in the Lord
than to trust in princes (R.)

2. I will thank you for you have given answer
and you are my saviour.
The stone which the builders rejected
has become the corner stone.
This is the work of the Lord,
a marvel in our eyes. (R.)

3. Blessed in the name of the Lord
is he who comes.
We bless you from the house of the Lord;
I will thank you for you have given answer
and you are my saviour.
Give thanks to the Lord for he is good;
for his love has no end. (R.)

Second Reading   (3:1–2)
A reading from the first letter of St John
We shall see God as he really is.

Think of the love that the Father has lavished on us,
by letting us be called God's children;
and that is what we are.
Because the world refused to acknowledge him,
therefore it does not acknowledge us.
My dear people, we are already the children of God
but what we are to be in the future has not yet been
    revealed;

all we know is, that when it is revealed
we shall be like him
because we shall see him as he really is.

    This is the word of the Lord.

Alleluia   (Jn 10:14)

Alleluia, alleluia!
I am the good shepherd, says the Lord;
I know my own sheep and my own know me.
Alleluia!

Gospel   (10:11–18)

A reading from the holy Gospel according to John
The good shepherd is one who lays down his life for his sheep.

Jesus said:

"I am the good shepherd:
the good shepherd is one who lays down his life for his
    sheep.
The hired man, since he is not the shepherd
and the sheep do not belong to him,
abandons the sheep and runs away
as soon as he sees a wolf coming,
and then the wolf attacks and scatters the sheep;
this is because he is only a hired man
and has no concern for the sheep.
I am the good shepherd;
I know my own
and my own know me,
just as the Father knows me
and I know the Father;
and I lay down my life for my sheep.
And there are other sheep I have
that are not of this fold,
and these I have to lead as well.

They too will listen to my voice,
and there will be only one flock,
and one shepherd.
The Father loves me,
because I lay down my life
in order to take it up again.
No one takes it from me;
I lay it down of my own free will,
and as it is in my power to lay it down,
so it is in my power to take it up again;
and this is the command I have been given by my
    Father."

This is the Gospel of the Lord.

4th SUNDAY OF EASTER
Year 3 (Year C)

First Reading   (13:14. 43–52)

A reading from the Acts of the Apostles
We must turn to the pagans.

Paul and Barnabas carried on from Perga till they reached
Antioch in Pisidia. Here they went to syngagogue on the
sabbath and took their seats.

When the meeting broke up, many Jews and devout converts joined Paul and Barnabas, and in their talks with
them Paul and Barnabas urged them to remain faithful to
the grace God had given them.

The next sabbath almost the whole town assembled to
hear the word of God. When they saw the crowds, the Jews,
prompted by jealousy, used blasphemies and contradicted
everything Paul said. Then Paul and Barnabas spoke out
boldly. "We had to proclaim the word of God to you first,
but since you have rejected it, since you do not think yourselves worthy of eternal life, we must turn to the pagans.
For this is what the Lord commanded us to do when he
said:

I have made you a light for the nations,
so that my salvation may reach the ends of the earth."

It made the pagans very happy to hear this and they thanked the Lord for his message; all who were destined for eternal life became believers. Thus the word of the Lord spread through the whole countryside.

But the Jews worked upon some of the devout women of the upper classes and the leading men of the city and persuaded them to turn against Paul and Barnabas and expel them from their territory. So they shook the dust from their feet in defiance and went off to Iconium; but the disciples were filled with joy and the Holy Spirit.

This is the word of the Lord.

Responsorial Psalm
(Ps 99:1–3. 5. *R*. v. 3)

Response
We are his people, the sheep of his flock.
Or: Alleluia!

1. Cry out with joy to the Lord, all the earth.
Serve the Lord with gladness.
Come before him, singing for joy. (*R*.)

2. Know that he, the Lord, is God.
He made us, we belong to him,
we are his people, the sheep of his flock. (*R*.)

3. Indeed, how good is the Lord,
eternal his merciful love.
He is faithful from age to age. (*R*.)

Second Reading
(7:9. 14–17)

A reading from the book of the Apocalypse
The Lamb will be their shepherd and will lead them to springs of living water.

I, John, saw a huge number, impossible to count, of people from every nation, race, tribe and language; they were standing in front of the throne and in front of the Lamb, dressed in white robes and holding palms in their hands. One of the elders said to me, "These are the people who have been through the great persecution, and because they have washed their robes white again in the blood of the Lamb, they now stand in front of God's throne and serve him day and night in his sanctuary; and the One who sits on the throne will spread his tent over them. They will never hunger or thirst again; neither the sun nor scorching wind will ever plague them, because the Lamb who is at the throne will be their shepherd and will lead them to springs of living water; and God will wipe away all tears from their eyes."

This is the word of the Lord.

Alleluia   (Jn 10:14)

Alleluia, alleluia!
I am the good shepherd, says the Lord;
I know my own sheep and my own know me.
Alleluia!

Gospel   (10:27–30)

A reading from the holy Gospel according to John
I give eternal life to the sheep that belong to me.

Jesus said:

"The sheep that belong to me listen to my voice;
I know them and they follow me.
I give them eternal life;
they will never be lost
and no one will ever steal them from me.
The Father who gave them to me is greater than anyone,

and no one can steal from the Father.
The Father and I are one."

This is the Gospel of the Lord.

MONDAY
First Reading (11:1–18)

A reading from the Acts of the Apostles
God can grant even the pagans the repentance that leads to life.

The apostles and the brothers in Judaea heard that the pagans too had accepted the word of God, and when Peter came up to Jerusalem the Jews criticised him and said, "So you have been visiting the uncircumcised and eating with them, have you?" Peter in reply gave them the details point by point: 'One day, when I was in the town of Jaffa,' he began "I fell into a trance as I was praying and had a vision of something like a big sheet being let down from heaven by its four corners. This sheet reached the ground quite close to me. I watched it intently and saw all sorts of animals and wild beasts – everything possible that could walk, crawl or fly. Then I heard a voice that said to me, 'Now, Peter; kill and eat!' But I answered: Certainly not, Lord; nothing profane or unclean has ever crossed my lips. And a second time the voice spoke from heaven, 'What God has made clean, you have no right to call profane.' This was repeated three times, before the whole of it was drawn up to heaven again.

"Just at that moment, three men stopped outside the house where we were staying; they had been sent from Caesarea to fetch me, and the Spirit told me to have no hesitation about going back with them. The six brothers here came with me as well, and we entered the man's house. He told us he had seen an angel standing in his house who said, 'Send to Jaffa and fetch Simon known as Peter; he has a message for you that will save you and your entire household.'

"I had scarcely begun to speak when the Holy Spirit came down on them in the same way as it came on us at the beginning, and I remembered that the Lord had said, 'John baptised with water, but you will be baptised with the Holy Spirit.' I realised then that God was giving them the identical thing he gave to us when we believed in the Lord Jesus Christ; and who was I to stand in God's way?"

This account satisfied them, and they gave glory to God. "God" they said, "can evidently grant even the pagans the repentance that leads to life."

This is the word of the Lord.

Responsorial Psalm   (Pss 41:2–3; 42:3–4. *R*. Ps 41:3)

Response
My soul is thirsting for God,
the God of my life.
Or: Alleluia!

1. Like the deer that yearns
for running streams,
so my soul is yearning
for you, my God. (*R*.)

2. My soul is thirsting for God,
the God of my life;
when can I enter and see
the face of God? (*R*.)

3. O send forth your light and your truth;
let these be my guide.
Let them bring me to your holy mountain
to the place where you dwell. (*R*.)

4. And I will come to the altar of God,
the God of my joy.
My redeemer, I will thank you on the harp,
O God, my God. (*R*.)

Alleluia (Jn 10:14)

Alleluia, alleluia!
I am the good shepherd, says the Lord,
I know my sheep and my own know me.
Alleluia!

Alternative Alleluias p. 844.

GOSPEL. John 10:1–10. as for 4th Sunday of Easter, Year 1 (Year A).
See p. 723.

The following alternative Gospel is to be used when the above Gospel is read on the 4th Sunday of Easter in Year 1.

Gospel (10:11–18)

A reading from the holy Gospel according to John
The good shepherd is one who lays down his life for his sheep.

Jesus said:

"I am the good shepherd:
the good shepherd is one who lays down his life for his
    sheep.
The hired man, since he is not the shepherd
and the sheep do not belong to him,
abandons the sheep and runs away
as soon as he sees a wolf coming,
and then the wolf attacks and scatters the sheep;
this is because he is only a hired man
and has no concern for the sheep.
I am the good shepherd;
I know my own
and my own know me,
just as the Father knows me
and I know the Father;
and I lay down my life for my sheep.
And there are other sheep I have
that are not of this fold,
and these I have to lead as well.

They too will listen to my voice,
and there will be only one flock,
and one shepherd.
The Father loves me,
because I lay down my life
in order to take it up again.
No one takes it from me;
I lay it down of my own free will,
and as it is in my power to lay it down,
so it is in my power to take it up again;
and this is the command I have been given by my Father."

This is the Gospel of the Lord.

TUESDAY

First Reading   (11:19–26)

A reading from the Acts of the Apostles
*They started preaching to the Greeks, proclaiming the Lord
Jesus.*

Those who had escaped during the persecution that happened because of Stephen travelled as far as Phoenicia and
Cyprus and Antioch, but they usually proclaimed the message only to Jews. Some of them, however, who came from
Cyprus and Cyrene, went to Antioch where they started
preaching to the Greeks, proclaiming the Good News of
the Lord Jesus to them as well. The Lord helped them, and
a great number believed and were converted to the Lord.
    The church in Jerusalem heard about this and they sent
Barnabas to Antioch. There he could see for himself that
God had given grace, and this pleased him, and he urged
them all to remain faithful to the Lord with heartfelt devotion; for he was a good man, filled with the Holy Spirit
and with faith. And a large number of people were won over
to the Lord.

Barnabas then left for Tarsus to look for Saul, and when he found him he brought him to Antioch. As things turned out they were to live together in that church a whole year, instructing a large number of people. It was at Antioch that the disciples were first called "Christians".

This is the word of the Lord.

Responsorial Psalm (Ps 86:1–7. *R.* Ps 116:1)

Response
O praise the Lord, all you nations!
Or: Alleluia!

1. On the holy mountain is his city
cherished by the Lord.
The Lord prefers the gates of Zion
to all Jacob's dwellings.
Of you are told glorious things,
O city of God! (*R.*)

2. "Babylon and Egypt I will count
among those who know me;
Philistia, Tyre, Ethiopia,
these will be her children
and Zion shall be called 'Mother'
for all shall be her children." (*R.*)

3. It is he, the Lord Most High,
who gives each his place.
In his register of peoples he writes:
"These are her children"
and while they dance they will sing:
"In you all find their home." (*R.*)

Alleluia (Jn 10:27)

Alleluia, alleluia!
The sheep that belong to me listen to my voice,
says the Lord;

I know them and they follow me.
Alleluia!

Alternative Alleluias p. 844.

Gospel   (10:22–30)

A reading from the holy Gospel according to John
The Father and I are one.

It was the time when the feast of Dedication was being celebrated in Jerusalem. It was winter, and Jesus was in the Temple walking up and down in the Portico of Solomon. The Jews gathered round him and said, "How much longer are you going to keep us in suspense? If you are the Christ, tell us plainly." Jesus replied:

"I have told you, but you do not believe.
The works I do in my Father's name are my witness;
but you do not believe,
because you are no sheep of mine.
The sheep that belong to me listen to my voice;
I know them and they follow me.
I give them eternal life;
they will never be lost
and no one will ever steal them from me.
The Father who gave them to me is greater than anyone,
and no one can steal from the Father.
The Father and I are one."

This is the Gospel of the Lord.

WEDNESDAY

First Reading   (12:24–13:5)

A reading from the Acts of the Apostles
Set Barnabas and Saul apart.

The word of God continued to spread and to gain followers. Barnabas and Saul completed their task and came back from Jerusalem, bringing John Mark with them.

In the church at Antioch the following were prophets and teachers: Barnabas, Simeon called Niger, and Lucius of Cyrene, Manaen, who had been brought up with Herod the tetrarch, and Saul. One day while they were offering worship to the Lord and keeping a fast, the Holy Spirit said, "I want Barnabas and Saul set apart for the work to which I have called them". So it was that after fasting and prayer they laid their hands on them and sent them off.

So these two, sent on their mission by the Holy Spirit, went down to Seleucia and from there sailed to Cyprus. They landed at Salamis and proclaimed the word of God in the synagogues of the Jews.

This is the word of the Lord.

Responsorial Psalm   (Ps 66:2–3. 5–6. 8. *R.* v. 4)

Response
Let the peoples praise you, O God;
let all the peoples praise you.
Or: Alleluia!

1. O God, be gracious and bless us
and let your face shed its light upon us.
So will your ways be known upon earth
and all nations learn your saving help. (*R.*)

2. Let the nations be glad and exult
for you rule the world with justice.
With fairness you rule the peoples,
you guide the nations on earth. (*R.*)

3. Let the peoples praise you, O God;
let all the peoples praise you.
May God still give us his blessing
till the ends of the earth revere him. (*R.*)

Alleluia   (Jn 20:29)

Alleluia, alleluia!
You believe, Thomas, because you can see me.
Happy are those who have not seen and yet believe.
Alleluia!

Alternative Acclamations p. 844.

Gospel   (12:44–50)

A reading from the holy Gospel according to John
I, the light, have come into the world.

Jesus declared publicly:
"Whoever believes in me
believes not in me
but in the one who sent me,
and whoever sees me,
sees the one who sent me.
I, the light, have come into the world,
so that whoever believes in me
need not stay in the dark any more.
If anyone hears my words and does not keep them
      faithfully,
it is not I who shall condemn him,
since I have come not to condemn the world,
but to save the world:
he who rejects me and refuses my words
has his judge already:
the word itself that I have spoken
will be his judge on the last day.
For what I have spoken does not come from myself;
no, what I was to say, what I had to speak,
was commanded by the Father who sent me,
and I know that his commands mean eternal life.
And therefore what the Father has told me
is what I speak."

    This is the Gospel of the Lord.

THURSDAY

First Reading   (13:13–25)

A reading from the Acts of the Apostles

God has raised up one of David's descendants, Jesus, as Saviour.

Paul and his friends went by sea from Paphos to Perga in Pamphylia where John left them to go back to Jerusalem. The others carried on from Perga till they reached Antioch in Pisidia. Here they went to synagogue on the sabbath and took their seats. After the lessons from the Law and the Prophets had been read, the presidents of the synagogue sent them a message: "Brothers, if you would like to address some words of encouragement to the congregation, please do so." Paul stood up, held up a hand for silence and began to speak:

"Men of Israel, and fearers of God, listen! The God of our nation Israel chose our ancestors, and made our people great when they were living as foreigners in Egypt; then by divine power he led them out, and for about forty years took care of them in the wilderness. When he had destroyed seven nations in Canaan, he put them in possession of their land for about four hundred and fifty years. After this he gave them judges, down from the prophet Samuel. Then they demanded a king, and God gave them Saul son of Kish, a man of the tribe of Benjamin. After forty years, he deposed him and made David their king, of whom he approved in these words, 'I have selected David son of Jesse, a man after my own heart, who will carry out my whole purpose.' To keep his promise, God has raised up for Israel one of David's descendants, Jesus, as Saviour, whose coming was heralded by John when he proclaimed a baptism of repentance for the whole people of Israel. Before John ended his career he said, 'I am not the one you imagine me to be; that one is coming after me and I am not fit to undo his sandal.' "

This is the word of the Lord.

Responsorial Psalm   (Ps 88:2–3. 21–22. 25. 27. *R.* v. 2)
Response
I will sing for ever of your love, O Lord.
Or: Alleluia!

1. I will sing for ever of your love, O Lord;
through all ages my mouth will proclaim your truth.
Of this I am sure, that your love lasts for ever,
that your truth is firmly established as the heavens. (*R.*)

2. I have found David my servant
and with my holy oil anointed him.
My hand shall always be with him
and my arm shall make him strong. (*R.*)

3. My truth and my love shall be with him;
by my name his might shall be exalted.
He will say to me: "You are my father,
my God, the rock who saves me." (*R.*)

Alleluia   (Rev 1:5)

Alleluia, alleluia!
You, O Christ, are the faithful witness,
the First-born from the dead;
you have loved us and have washed away our sins
with your blood.
Alleluia!
Alternative Alleluias p. 844.

Gospel   (13:16–20)

A reading from the holy Gospel according to John
Whoever welcomes the one I send welcomes me.

Jesus said to his disciples:
"I tell you most solemnly,
no servant is greater than his master,
no messenger is greater than the man who sent him.

"Now that you know this, happiness will be yours if you behave accordingly. I am not speaking about all of you: I know the ones I have chosen; but what scripture says must be fulfilled: Someone who shares my table rebels against me.

"I tell you this now, before it happens,
so that when it does happen
you may believe that I am He.
I tell you most solemnly,
whoever welcomes the one I send welcomes me,
and whoever welcomes me welcomes the one who sent me."

This is the Gospel of the lord.

FRIDAY

First Reading (13:26–33)

A reading from the Acts of the Apostles
God has fulfilled his promise by raising Jesus from the dead.

Paul stood up in the synagogue at Antioch in Pisidia, held up a hand for silence and began to speak: "My brothers, sons of Abraham's race, and all you who fear God, this message of salvation is meant for you. What the people of Jerusalem and their rulers did, though they did not realise it, was in fact to fulfil the prophecies read on every sabbath. Though they found nothing to justify his death, they condemned him and asked Pilate to have him executed. When they had carried out everything that scripture foretells about him they took him down from the tree and buried him in a tomb. But God raised him from the dead, and for many days he appeared to those who had accompanied him from Galilee to Jerusalem: and it is these same companions of his who are now his witnesses before our people.

"We have come here to tell you the Good News. It was to our ancestors that God made the promise but it is to us, their children, that he has fulfilled it, by raising Jesus from the dead. As scripture says in the first psalm: You are my son: today I have become your father."

This is the word of the Lord.

Responsorial Psalm (Ps 2:6–11. *R.* v. 7)

Response
You are my Son.
It is I who have begotten you this day.
Or: Alleluia!

1. "It is I who have set up my king
on Zion, my holy mountain."
I will announce the decree of the Lord:
The Lord said to me: "You are my Son.
It is I who have begotten you this day." (*R.*)

2. "Ask and I shall bequeath you the nations,
put the ends of the earth in your possession.
With a rod of iron you will break them,
shatter them like a potter's jar." (*R.*)

3. Now, O kings, understand,
take warning, rulers of the earth;
serve the Lord with awe
and trembling, pay him your homage. (*R.*)

Alleluia (Col 3:1)

Alleluia, alleluia!
Since you have been brought back to true life with Christ,
you must look for the things that are in heaven where Christ
  is,

sitting at God's right hand.
Alleluia!

Alternative Alleluias p. 844.

Gospel   (14:1–6)

A reading from the holy Gospel according to John
I am the Way, the Truth and the Life.

Jesus said to his disciples:
"Do not let your hearts be troubled.
Trust in God still, and trust in me.
There are many rooms in my Father's house;
if there were not, I should have told you.
I am going now to prepare a place for you,
and after I have gone and prepared you a place,
I shall return to take you with me;
so that where I am
you may be too.
You know the way to the place where I am going."

Thomas said, "Lord, we do not know where you are going, so how can we know the way?" Jesus said:

"I am the Way, the Truth and the Life.
No one can come to the Father except through me."

This is the Gospel of the Lord.

SATURDAY

First Reading   (13:44–52)

A reading from the Acts of the Apostles
We must turn to the pagans.

The next sabbath almost the whole town assembled to hear
the word of God. When they saw the crowds, the Jews,
prompted by jealousy, used blasphemies and contradicted

everything Paul said. Then Paul and Barnabas spoke out boldly. "We had to proclaim the word of God to you first, but since you have rejected it, since you do not think yourselves worthy of eternal life, we must turn to the pagans. For this is what the Lord commanded us to do when he said:

I have made you a light for the nations,
so that my salvation may reach the ends of the earth."

It made the pagans very happy to hear this and they thanked the Lord for his message; all who were destined for eternal life became believers. Thus the word of the Lord spread through the whole countryside.

But the Jews worked upon some of the devout women of the upper classes and the leading men of the city and persuaded them to turn against Paul and Barnabas and expel them from their territory. So they shook the dust from their feet in defiance and went off to Iconium; but the disciples were filled with joy and the Holy Spirit.

This is the word of the Lord.

Responsorial Psalm   (Ps 97:1–4. *R.* v. 3)

Response
All the ends of the earth have seen
the salvation of our God.
Or: Alleluia!

1. Sing a new song to the Lord
for he has worked wonders.
His right hand and his holy arm
have brought salvation. (*R.*)

2. The Lord has made known his salvation;
has shown his justice to the nations.
He has remembered his truth and love
for the house of Israel. (*R.*)

3. All the ends of the earth have seen
the salvation of our God.
Shout to the Lord all the earth,
ring out your joy. (*R.*)

Alleluia

Alleluia, alleluia!
Christ, having been raised from the dead
will never died again.
Death has no power over him any more.
Alleluia!

Alternative Alleluias p. 844.

Gospel (14:7–14)

A reading from the holy Gospel according to John
To have seen me is to have seen the Father.

Jesus said to his disciples:

"If you know me, you know my Father too.
From this moment you know him and have seen him."

Philip said, "Lord, let us see the Father and then we
shall be satisfied." "Have I been with you all this time,
Philip," said Jesus to him, "and you still do not know me?"

"To have seen me is to have seen the Father,
So how can you say, 'Let us see the Father'?
Do you not believe
that I am in the Father and the Father is in me?
The words I say to you I do not speak as from
    myself:
it is the Father, living in me, who is doing this work.
You must believe me when I say
that I am in the Father and the Father is in me;

believe it on the evidence of this work, if for no other
    reason.
I tell you most solemnly,
whoever believes in me
will perform the same works as I do myself,
he will perform even greater works,
because I am going to the Father.
Whatever you ask for in my name I will do,
so that the Father may be glorified in the Son.
If you ask for anything in my name,
I will do it."

This is the Gospel of the Lord.

5th SUNDAY OF EASTER
Year 1 (Year A)

First Reading   (6:1-7)

A reading from the Acts of the Apostles
They elected seven men full of the Holy Spirit.

About this time, when the number of disciples was increasing, the Hellenists made a complaint against the Hebrews: in the daily distribution their own widows were being overlooked. So the Twelve called a full meeting of the disciples and addressed them, "It would not be right for us to neglect the word of God so as to give out food; you, brothers, must select from among yourselves seven men of good reputation, filled with the Spirit and with wisdom; we will hand over this duty to them, and continue to devote ourselves to prayer and to the service of the word." The whole assembly approved of this proposal and elected Stephen, a man full of faith and of the Holy Spirit, together with Philip, Prochorus, Nicanor, Timon, Parmenas, and Nicolaus of Antioch, a convert to Judaism. They presented these to the apostles, who prayed and laid their hands on them.

The word of the Lord continued to spread: the number of disciples in Jerusalem was greatly increased, and a large group of priests made their submission to the faith.

This is the word of the Lord.

Responsorial Psalm   (Ps 32:1–2. 4–5. 18–19. *R.* v. 22)

Response
May your love be upon us, O Lord,
as we place all our hope in you.
Or: Alleluia!

1. Ring out your joy to the Lord, O you just;
for praise is fitting for loyal hearts.
Give thanks to the Lord upon the harp,
with a ten-stringed lute sing him songs. (*R.*)

2. For the word of the Lord is faithful
and all his works to be trusted.
The Lord loves justice and right
and fills the earth with his love. (*R.*)

3. The Lord looks on those who revere him,
on those who hope in his love,
to rescue their souls from death,
to keep them alive in famine. (*R.*)

Second Reading   (2:4–9)

A reading from the first letter of St Peter
But you are a chosen race, a royal priesthood.

The Lord is the living stone, rejected by men but chosen by God and precious to him; set yourselves close to him so that you too, the holy priesthood that offers the spiritual sacrifices which Jesus Christ has made acceptable to God, may be living stones making a spiritual house. As scripture says: See how I lay in Zion a precious cornerstone that I have chosen and the man who rests his trust on it will not be disappointed. That means that for you who are believers, it is precious; but for unbelievers, the stone rejected by the builders has proved to be the keystone, a stone to stumble over, a rock to bring men down. They stumble over it because they do not believe in the word; it was the fate in store for them.

But you are a chosen race, a royal priesthood, a consecrated nation, a people set apart to sing the praises of God who called you out of the darkness into his wonderful light.

This is the word of the Lord.

Alleluia   (Jn 14:6)
Alleluia, alleluia!
Jesus said: "I am the Way, the Truth and the Life.
No one can come to the Father except through me."
Alleluia!

Gospel   (14:1–12)
A reading from the holy Gospel according to John
I am the Way, the Truth and the Life.

Jesus said to his disciples:

"Do not let your hearts be troubled.
Trust in God still, and trust in me.
There are many rooms in my Father's house;
if there were not, I should have told you.
I am now going to prepare a place for you,
and after I have gone and prepared you a place,
I shall return to take you with me;
so that where I am
you may be too.
You know the way to the place where I am going."

Thomas said, "Lord, we do not know where you are going, so how can we know the way?" Jesus said:

"I am the Way, the Truth and the Life.
No one can come to the Father except through me.
If you know me, you know my Father too.
From this moment you know him and have seen him."

Philip said, "Lord, let us see the Father and then we shall be satisfied." "Have I been with you all this time, Philip," said Jesus to him "and you still do not know me?

"To have seen me is to have seen the Father,
so how can you say, 'Let us see the Father'?
Do you not believe
that I am in the Father and the Father is in me?
The words I say to you I do not speak as from myself:
it is the Father, living in me, who is doing this work.
You must believe me when I say
that I am in the Father and the Father is in me;
believe it on the evidence of this work, if for no other
    reason.
I tell you most solemnly,
whoever believes in me
will perform the same works as I do myself,
he will perform ever greater works,
because I am going to the Father."

This is the Gospel of the Lord.

5th SUNDAY OF EASTER
Year 2 (Year B)

First Reading   (9:26–31)

A reading from the Acts of the Apostles
Barnabas explained how the Lord had appeared to Saul on his journey.

When Saul got to Jerusalem he tried to join the disciples, but they were all afraid of him: they could not believe he was really a disciple. Barnabas, however, took charge of him, introduced him to the apostles, and explained how the Lord had appeared to Saul and spoken to him on his journey, and how he had preached boldly at Damascus in the name of Jesus. Saul now started to go round with them in Jerusalem, preaching fearlessly in the name of the Lord. But after he had spoken to the Hellenists, and argued with them, they became determined to kill him. When the brothers knew, they took him to Caesarea, and sent him off from there to Tarsus.

The churches throughout Judaea, Galilee and Samaria were now left in peace, building themselves up, living in the fear of the Lord, and filled with the consolation of the Holy Spirit.

This is the word of the Lord.

Responsorial Psalm   (Ps 21:26–28. 30–32. *R*. v. 26)

Response
You, Lord, are my praise in the great assembly.
Or: Alleluia!

1. My vows I will pay before those who fear him.
The poor shall eat and shall have their fill.
They shall praise the Lord, those who seek him.
May their hearts live for ever and ever! (*R*.)

2. All the earth shall remember and return to the Lord,
all families of the nations worship before him.
They shall worship him, all the mighty of the earth;
before him shall bow all who go down to the dust. (*R*.)

3. And my soul shall live for him, my children serve him.
They shall tell of the Lord to generations yet to come,
declare his faithfulness to peoples yet unborn:
"These things the Lord has done." (*R*.)

Second Reading   (3:18–24)

A reading from the first letter of St John
His commandments are these: that we believe in his Son and
that we love one another.

My children,
our love is not to be just words or mere talk,
but something real and active;
only by this can we be certain
that we are the children of the truth
and be able to quieten our conscience in his presence,
whatever accusations it may raise against us,
because God is greater than our conscience and he knows
    everything.
My dear people,
if we cannot be condemned by our own conscience,
we need not be afraid in God's presence,
and whatever we ask him,
we shall receive,
because we keep his commandments
and live the kind of life that he wants.
His commandments are these:
that we believe in the name of his Son Jesus Christ
and that we love one another
as he told us to.
Whoever keeps his commandments
lives in God and God lives in him.
We know that he lives in us
by the Spirit that he has given us.

   This is the word of the Lord.

Alleluia   (Jn 15:4–5)

Alleluia, alleluia!
Make your home in me, as I make mine in you.
Whoever remains in me bears fruit in plenty.
Alleluia!

Gospel　　　　　　　　　　　　　　　　　　(15:1–8)

A reading from the holy Gospel according to John
Whoever remains in me, with me in him, bears fruit in plenty.

Jesus said to his disciples:

"I am the true vine,
and my Father is the vinedresser.
Every branch in me that bears no fruit
he cuts away,
and every branch that does bear fruit he prunes
to make it bear even more.
You are pruned already,
by means of the word that I have spoken to you.
Make your home in me, as I make mine in you.
As a branch cannot bear fruit all by itself,
but must remain part of the vine,
neither can you unless you remain in me.
I am the vine,
you are the branches.
Whoever remains in me, with me in him,
bears fruit in plenty;
for cut off from me you can do nothing.
Anyone who does not remain in me
is like a branch that has been thrown away
– he withers;
these branches are collected and thrown on the fire,
and they are burnt.
If you remain in me
and my words remain in you,
you may ask what you will
and you shall get it.
It is to the glory of my Father that you should bear much
　　fruit,
and then you will be my disciples."

　　This is the Gospel of the Lord.

5th SUNDAY OF EASTER
Year 3 (Year C)

First Reading   (14:21–27)

A reading from the Acts of the Apostles
*They gave an account to the church of all that God had done
with them.*

Paul and Barnabas went back through Lystra and Iconium
to Antioch. They put fresh heart into the disciples, encouraging them to persevere in the faith. "We all have to experience many hardships" they said "before we enter
the kingdom of God." In each of these churches they appointed elders, and with prayer and fasting they commended them to the Lord in whom they had come to believe.

They passed through Pisidia and reached Pamphylia.
Then after proclaiming the word at Perga they went down
to Attalia and from there sailed for Antioch, where they
had originally been commended to the grace of God for the
work they had now completed.

On their arrival they assembled the church and gave an
account of all that God had done with them, and how he
had opened the door of faith to the pagans.

This is the word of the Lord.

Responsorial Psalm   (Ps 144:8–13. *R*. v. 1)

Response
I will bless your name for ever, O God my King.
Or : Alleluia!

1. The Lord is kind and full of compassion,
slow to anger, abounding in love.
How good is the Lord to all,
compassionate to all his creatures. (*R*.)

2. All your creatures shall thank you, O Lord,
and your friends shall repeat their blessing.

They shall speak of the glory of your reign
and declare your might, O God,
to make known to men your mighty deeds
and the glorious splendour of your reign. (*R.*)

3. Yours is an everlasting kingdom;
your rule lasts from age to age. (*R.*)

First Reading   (21:1–5)

A reading from the book of the Apocalypse
God will wipe away all tears from their eyes.

I, John, saw a new heaven and a new earth; the first heaven
and the first earth had disappeared now, and there was no
longer any sea. I saw the holy city, and the new Jerusalem,
coming down from God out of heaven, as beautiful as a
bride all dressed for her husband. Then I heard a loud voice
call from the throne, "You see this city? Here God lives
among men. He will make his home among them; they shall
be his people, and he will be their God; his name is God-
with-them. He will wipe away all tears from their eyes;
there will be no more death, and no more mourning or sadness. The world of the past has gone."

Then the One sitting on the throne spoke: "Now I am
making the whole of creation new" he said.

This is the word of the Lord.

Alleluia   (Jn 13:34)

Alleluia, alleluia!
Jesus said: "I give you a new commandment:
love one another, just as I have loved you."
Alleluia!

Gospel   (13:31–35)

A reading from the holy Gospel according to John
I give you a new commandment: love one another.

When Judas had gone Jesus said:

"Now has the Son of Man been glorified,
and in him God has been glorified.
If God has been glorified in him,
God will in turn glorify him in himself,
and will glorify him very soon.
My little children,
I shall not be with you much longer.
I give you a new commandment:
love one another;
just as I have loved you,
you also must love one another.
By this love you have for one another,
everyone will know that you are my disciples."

This is the Gospel of the Lord.

MONDAY

First Reading   (14:5–18)

A reading from the Acts of the Apostles
*We have come with good news to make you turn from these
empty idols to the living God.*

Eventually with the connivance of the authorities a move
was made by pagans as well as Jews to make attacks on
Paul and Barnabas and to stone them. When the apostles
came to hear of this, they went off for safety to Lycaonia
where, in the towns of Lystra and Derbe and in the surrounding country, they preached the Good News.

A man sat there who had never walked in his life, because his feet were crippled from birth; and as he listened
to Paul preaching, he managed to catch his eye. Seeing that
the man had the faith to be cured, Paul said in a loud voice,
"Get to your feet – stand up," and the cripple jumped up
and began to walk.

When the crowd saw what Paul had done they shouted in the language of Lycaonia, "These people are gods who have come down to us disguised as men." They addressed Barnabas as Zeus, and since Paul was the principal speaker they called him Hermes. The priests of Zeus-outside-the-Gate, proposing that all the people should offer sacrifice with them, brought garlanded oxen to the gates. When the apostles Barnabas and Paul heard what was happening they tore their clothes, and rushed into the crowd, shouting, "Friends, what do you think you are doing? We are only human beings like you. We have come with good news to make you turn from these empty idols to the living God who made heaven and earth and the sea and all that these hold. In the past he allowed each nation to go its own way; but even then he did not leave you without evidence of himself in the good things he does for you: he sends you rain from heaven, he makes your crops grow when they should, he gives you food and makes you happy." Even this speech, however, was scarcely enough to stop the crowd offering them sacrifice.

This is the word of the Lord.

Responsorial Psalm   (Ps 113B:1–4. 15–16. *R*. v. 1)

Response
Not to us, Lord,
but to your name give the glory.
Or: Alleluia!

1. Not to us, Lord, not to us,
but to your name give the glory
for the sake of your love and your truth,
lest the heathen say: "Where is their God?" (*R*.)

2. Our God he is in the heavens;
he does whatever he wills.
Their idols are silver and gold,
the work of human hands. (*R*.)

3. May you be blessed by the Lord,
the maker of heaven and earth.
The heavens belong to the Lord
but the earth he has given to men. (*R.*)

Alleluia
Alleluia, alleluia!
Christ has risen and shone upon us
whom he redeemed with his blood.
Alleluia!

Alternative Alleluias p. 844.

Gospel   (14:21–26)

A reading from the holy Gospel according to John
The Advocate, whom the Father will send in my name, will teach you everything.

Jesus said to his disciples:

"Anybody who receives my commandments and keeps
   them
will be one who loves me;
and anybody who loves me will be loved by my Father,
and I shall love him and show myself to him."

Judas – this was not Judas Iscariot – said to him, "Lord,
what is all this about? Do you intend to show yourself to
us and not to the world?" Jesus replied:

"If anyone loves me he will keep my word,
and my Father will love him,
and we shall come to him
and make our home with him.
Those who do not love me do not keep my words.
And my word is not my own:
it is the word of the one who sent me.

I have said these things to you
while still with you;
but the Advocate, the Holy Spirit,
whom the Father will send in my name,
will teach you everything
and remind you of all I have said to you."

This is the Gospel of the Lord.

TUESDAY

First Reading   (14:19–28)

A reading from the Acts of the Apostles
They gave an account to the church of all that God had done with them.

Some Jews arrived from Antioch and Iconium, and turned the people against the apostles. They stoned Paul and dragged him outside the town, thinking he was dead. The disciples came crowding round him but, as they did so, he stood up and went back to the town. The next day he and Barnabas went off to Derbe.

Having preached the Good News in that town and made a considerable number of disciples, they went back through Lystra and Iconium to Antioch. They put fresh heart into the disciples, encouraging them to persevere in the faith. "We all have to experience many hardships" they said "before we enter the kingdom of God." In each of these churches they appointed elders, and with prayer and fasting they commended them to the Lord in whom they had come to believe.

They passed through Pisidia and reached Pamphylia. Then after proclaiming the word at Perga they went down to Attalia and from there sailed for Antioch, where they had originally been commended to the grace of God for the work they had now completed.

On their arrival they assembled the church and gave an

account of all that God had done with them, and how he had opened the door of faith to the pagans. They stayed there with the disciples for some time.

This is the word of the Lord.

Responsorial Psalm (Ps 144:10–13. 21. *R*. v. 12)

Response
Your friends, O Lord, shall make known
the glorious splendour of your reign.
Or: Alleluia!

1. All your creatures shall thank you, O Lord,
and your friends shall repeat their blessing.
They shall speak of the glory of your reign
and declare your might, O God,
to make known to men your mighty deeds
and the glorious splendour of your reign. (*R*.)

2. Yours is an everlasting kingdom;
your rule lasts from age to age. (*R*.)

3. Let me speak the praise of the Lord,
let all mankind bless his holy name
for ever, for ages unending. (*R*.)

Alleluia

Alleluia, alleluia!
It was ordained that the Christ should suffer
and rise from the dead,
and so enter into his glory.
Alleluia!
Alternative Alleluias p. 844.

Gospel (14:27–31)

A reading from the holy Gospel according to John
My own peace I give you.

Jesus said to his disciples:
"Peace I bequeath to you,
my own peace I give you,
a peace the world cannot give, this is my gift to you.
Do not let your hearts be troubled or afraid.
You heard me say:
I am going away, and shall return.
If you loved me you would have been glad to know
    that I am going to the Father,
For the Father is greater than I.
I have told you this now before it happens,
so that when it does happen you may believe.
I shall not talk with you any longer,
because the prince of this world is on his way.
He has no power over me,
but the world must be brought to know that I love the
    Father
and that I am doing exactly what the Father told me."

This is the Gospel of the Lord.

WEDNESDAY

First Reading   (15:1–6)

A reading from the Acts of the Apostles
*It was arranged that they should go up to Jerusalem and
discuss the problem with the apostles and elders.*

Some men came down from Judaea and taught the brothers,
"Unless you have yourselves circumcised in the tradition of
Moses you cannot be saved." This led to disagreement, and
after Paul and Barnabas had had a long argument with
these men it was arranged that Paul and Barnabas and
others of the church should go up to Jerusalem and discuss
the problem with the apostles and elders.

All the members of the church saw them off, and as they
passed through Phoenicia and Samaria they told how the
pagans had been converted, and this news was received

with the greatest satisfaction by the brothers. When they arrived in Jerusalem they were welcomed by the church and by the apostles and elders, and gave an account of all that God had done with them.

But certain members of the Pharisees' party who had become believers objected, insisting that the pagans should be circumcised and instructed to keep the Law of Moses. The apostles and elders met to look into the matter.

This is the word of the Lord.

Responsorial Psalm   (Ps 121:1–5. R. v. 1)

Response
I rejoiced when I heard them say:
"Let us go to God's house."
Or: Alleluia!

1. I rejoiced when I heard them say:
"Let us go to God's house."
And now our feet are standing
within your gates, O Jerusalem. (*R.*)

2. Jerusalem is built as a city
strongly compact.
It is there that the tribes go up,
the tribes of the Lord. (*R.*)

3. For Israel's law it is,
there to praise the Lord's name.
There were set the thrones of judgement
of the house of David. (*R.*)

Alleluia   (Jn 10:14)

Alleluia, alleluia!
I am the good shepherd, says the Lord,
I know my sheep and my own know me.
Alleluia!

Alternative Alleluias p. 844.

Gospel   (15:1–8)

A reading from the holy Gospel according to John
Whoever remains in me, with me in him, bears fruit in plenty.

Jesus said to his disciples:
"I am the true vine,
and my Father is the vinedresser.
Every branch in me that bears no fruit
he cuts away,
and every branch that does bear fruit he prunes
to make it bear even more.
You are pruned already,
by means of the word that I have spoken to you.
Make your home in me, as I make mine in you.
As a branch cannot bear fruit all by itself,
but must remain part of the vine,
neither can you unless you remain in me.
I am the vine,
you are the branches.
Whoever remains in me, with me in him,
bears fruit in plenty;
for cut off from me you can do nothing.
Anyone who does not remain in me
is like a branch that has been thrown away
– he withers;
these branches are collected and thrown on the fire,
and they are burnt.
If you remain in me
and my words remain in you,
you may ask what you will
and you shall get it.
It is to the glory of my Father that you should bear much
    fruit,
and then you will be my disciples."

This is the Gospel of the Lord.

THURSDAY

First Reading   (15:7–21)

A reading from the Acts of the Apostles
I rule that we do not make things more difficult for pagans who turn to God.

After the discussion had gone on a long time, Peter stood up and addressed the apostles and elders.

"My brothers," he said "you know perfectly well that in the early days God made his choice among you: the pagans were to learn the Good News from me and so become believers. In fact God, who can read everyone's heart, showed his approval of them by giving the Holy Spirit to them just as he had to us. God made no distinction between them and us, since he purified their hearts by faith. It would only provoke God's anger now, surely, if you imposed on the disciples the very burden that neither we nor our ancestors were strong enough to support? Remember, we believe that we are saved in the same way as they are: through the grace of the Lord Jesus."

This silenced the entire assembly, and they listened to Barnabas and Paul describing all the signs and wonders God had worked through them among the pagans.

When they had finished it was James who spoke. "My brothers," he said "listen to me. Simeon has described how God first arranged to enlist a people for his name out of the pagans. This is entirely in harmony with the words of the prophets, since the scriptures say:

After that I shall return
and rebuild the fallen House of David;
I shall rebuild it from its ruins
and restore it.
Then the rest of mankind,
all the pagans who are consecrated to my name,
will look for the Lord,
says the Lord who made this known so long ago.

"I rule, then, that instead of making things more difficult for pagans who turn to God, we send them a letter telling them merely to abstain from anything polluted by idols, from fornication, from the meat of strangled animals and from blood. For Moses has always had his preachers in every town, and is read aloud in the synagogues every sabbath."

This is the word of the Lord.

Responsorial Psalm   (Ps 95:1–3. 10. *R*. v. 3)
Response
Tell the wonders of the Lord
among all the peoples.
Or: Alleluia!

1. O sing a new song to the Lord,
sing to the Lord all the earth.
O sing to the Lord, bless his name. (*R*.)

2. Proclaim his help day by day,
tell among the nations his glory
and his wonders among all the peoples. (*R*.)

3. Proclaim to the nations: "God is king."
The world he made firm in its place;
he will judge the peoples in fairness. (*R*.)

Alleluia

Alleluia, alleluia!
Christ has risen: he who created all things,
and has granted his mercy to men.
Alleluia!
Alternative Alleluias p. 844.

Gospel   (15:9–11)
A reading from the holy Gospel according to John
Remain in my love, and let your joy be complete.

Jesus said to his disciples:
"As the father has loved me,
so I have loved you.
Remain in my love.
If you keep my commandments
you will remain in my love,
just as I have kept my Father's commandments
and remain in his love.
I have told you this
so that my own joy may be in you
and your joy be complete."

This is the Gospel of the Lord.

FRIDAY

First Reading   (15:22–31)

A reading from the Acts of the Apostles
*It has been decided by the Holy Spirit and by ourselves not to
saddle you with any burden beyond essentials.*

The apostles and elders decided to choose delegates to
send to Antioch with Paul and Barnabas; the whole church
concurred with this. They chose Judas known as Barsabbas
and Silas, both leading men in the brotherhood, and gave
them this letter to take with them:

"The apostles and elders, your brothers, send greetings to
the brothers of pagan birth in Antioch, Syria and Cilicia.
We hear that some of our members have disturbed you
with their demands and have unsettled your minds. They
acted without any authority from us, and so we have decided unanimously to elect delegates and to send them to
you with Barnabas and Paul, men we highly respect who
have dedicated their lives to the name of our Lord Jesus
Christ. Accordingly we are sending you Judas and Silas,
who will confirm by word of mouth what we have written
in this letter. It has been decided by the Holy Spirit and by

ourselves not to saddle you with any burden beyond these essentials: you are to abstain from food sacrificed to idols, from blood, from the meat of strangled animals and from fornication. Avoid these, and you will do what is right. Farewell."

The party left and went down to Antioch, where they summoned the whole community and delivered the letter. The community read it and were delighted with the encouragement it gave them.

This is the word of the Lord.

Responsorial Psalm   (Ps 56:8–12. *R*. v. 10)
Response
I will thank you, Lord, among the peoples.
Or: Alleluia!

1. My heart is ready, O God,
my heart is ready.
I will sing, I will sing your praise.
Awake my soul,
awake lyre and harp,
I will awake the dawn. (*R*.)

2. I will thank you Lord among the peoples,
praise you among the nations;
for your love reaches to the heavens
and your truth to the skies.
O God, arise above the heavens;
may your glory shine on earth! (*R*.)

Alleluia   (Jn 10:27)
Alleluia, alleluia!
The sheep that belong to me listen to my voice,
says the Lord;
I know them and they follow me.
Alleluia!

Alternative Alleluias p. 844.

Gospel (15:12–17)

A reading from the holy Gospel according to John
What I command you is to love one another.

Jesus said to his disciples:
"This is my commandment:
love one another,
as I have loved you.
A man can have no greater love
than to lay down his life for his friends.
You are my friends,
if you do what I command you.
I shall not call you servants any more,
because a servant does not know
his master's business;
I call you friends,
because I have made known to you
everything I have learnt from my Father.
You did not choose me,
no, I chose you;
and I commissioned you
to go out and to bear fruit,
fruit that will last;
and then the Father will give you
anything you ask him in my name.
What I command you
is to love one another."

This is the Gospel of the Lord.

SATURDAY

First Reading (16:1–10)

A reading from the Acts of the Apostles
Come across to Macedonia and help us.

From Cilicia Paul went to Derbe, and then on to Lystra.
Here there was a disciple called Timothy, whose mother

was a Jewess who had become a believer; but his father was a Greek. The brothers at Lystra and Iconium spoke well of Timothy, and Paul, who wanted to have him as a travelling companion, had him circumcised. This was on account of the Jews in the locality where everyone knew his father was a Greek.

As they visited one town after another, they passed on the decisions reached by the apostles and elders in Jerusalem, with instructions to respect them.

So the churches grew strong in the faith, as well as growing daily in numbers.

They travelled through Phrygia and the Galatian country, having been told by the Holy Spirit not to preach the word in Asia. When they reached the frontier of Mysia they thought to cross it into Bithynia, but as the Spirit of Jesus would not allow them, they went through Mysia and came down to Troas.

One night Paul had a vision: a Macedonian appeared and appealed to him in these words, "Come across to Macedonia and help us." Once he had seen this vision we lost no time in arranging a passage to Macedonia, convinced that God had called us to bring them the Good News.

This is the word of the Lord.

Responsorial Psalm   (Ps 99:1–3. 5. R. v. 1)

Response
Cry out with joy to the Lord, all the earth.
Or: Alleluia!

1. Cry out with joy to the Lord, all the earth.
Serve the Lord with gladness.
Come before him, singing for joy. (R.)

2. Know that he, the Lord, is God.
He made us, we belong to him,
we are his people, the sheep of his flock. (R.)

3. Indeed, how good is the Lord,
eternal his merciful love.
He is faithful from age to age. (*R.*)

Alleluia

Alleluia, alleluia!
The Lord, who hung for us upon the tree,
has risen from the tomb.
Alleluia!

Alternative Alleluias p. 844.

Gospel   (15:18–21)

A reading from the holy Gospel according to John
*You do not belong to the world because my choice withdrew
you from the world.*

Jesus said to his disciples:
"If the world hates you,
remember that it hated me before you.
If you belonged to the world,
the world would love you as its own;
but because you do not belong to the world,
because my choice withdrew you from the world,
therefore the world hates you.
Remember the words I said to you:
A servant is not greater than his master.
If they persecuted me,
they will persecute you too;
if they kept my word,
they will keep yours as well.
But it will be on my account that they will do all this,
because they do not know the one who sent me."

This is the Gospel of the Lord.

6th SUNDAY OF EASTER
Year 1 (Year A)

First Reading   (8:5–8.14–17)

A reading from the Acts of the Apostles
They laid hands on them, and they received the Holy Spirit.

Philip went to a Samaritan town and proclaimed the Christ
to them. The people united in welcoming the message Philip
preached, either because they had heard of the miracles he
worked or because they saw them for themselves. There
were, for example, unclean spirits that came shrieking out
of many who were possessed, and several paralytics and
cripples were cured. As a result there was great rejoicing in
that town.

When the apostles in Jerusalem heard that Samaria had
accepted the word of God, they sent Peter and John to
them, and they went down there, and prayed for the Samaritans to receive the Holy Spirit, for as yet he had not come
down on any of them: they had only been baptised in the
name of the Lord Jesus. Then they laid hands on them, and
they received the Holy Spirit.

This is the word of the Lord.

Responsorial Psalm   (Ps 65:1–7. 16. 20. *R*. v. 1)

Response
Cry out with joy to God all the earth.
Or: Alleluia!

1. Cry out with joy to God all the earth,
O sing to the glory of his name.
O render him glorious praise.
Say to God: "How tremendous your deeds!" (*R*.)

2. "Before you all the earth shall bow;
shall sing to you, sing to your name!"
Come and see the works of God,
tremendous his deeds among men. (*R*.)

3. He turned the sea into dry land,
they passed through the river dry-shod.
Let our joy then be in him;
he rules for ever by his might. (*R.*)

4. Come and hear, all who fear God.
I will tell what he did for my soul:
Blessed be God who did not reject my prayer
nor withhold his love from me. (*R.*)

Second Reading   (3:15–18)
A reading from the first letter of St Peter
*In the body he was put to death, in the spirit he was raised
to life.*

Reverence the Lord Christ in your hearts, and always have
your answer ready for people who ask you the reason for
the hope that you all have. But give it with courtesy and
respect and with a clear conscience, so that those who slander you when you are living a good life in Christ may be
proved wrong in the accusations that they bring. And if it
is the will of God that you should suffer, it is better to suffer
for doing right than for doing wrong.

Why, Christ himself, innocent though he was, had died
once for sins, died for the guilty, to lead us to God. In the
body he was put to death, in the spirit he was raised to
life.

This is the word of the Lord.

Alleluia   (Jn 14:23)
Alleluia, alleluia!
Jesus said: "If anyone loves me he will keep my word,
and my Father will love him,
and we shall come to him."
Alleluia!

Gospel   (14:15–21)

A reading from the holy Gospel according to John
I shall ask the Father, and he will give you another Advocate.

Jesus said to his disciples:
"If you love me you will keep my commandments.
I shall ask the Father,
and he will give you another Advocate
to be with you for ever,
that Spirit of truth
whom the world can never receive
since it neither sees nor knows him;
but you know him,
because he is with you, he is in you.
I will not leave you orphans;
I will come back to you.
In a short time the world will no longer see me;
but you will see me,
because I live and you will live.
On that day
you will understand that I am in my Father
and you in me and I in you.
Anybody who receives my commandments and keeps them
will be one who loves me;
and anybody who loves me will be loved by my Father,
and I shall love him and show myself to him."

This is the Gospel of the Lord.

6th SUNDAY OF EASTER
Year 2 (Year B)

First Reading   (10:25–26. 34–35. 44–48)

A reading from the Acts of the Apostles
The Holy Spirit has been poured out on the pagans too.

As Peter reached the house Cornelius went out to meet him,
knelt at his feet and prostrated himself. But Peter helped

him up. "Stand up," he said "I am only a man after all!"

Then Peter addressed them: "The truth I have now come to realise" he said "is that God does not have favourites, but that anybody of any nationality who fears God and does what is right is acceptable to him."

While Peter was still speaking the Holy Spirit came down on all the listeners. Jewish believers who had accompanied Peter were all astonished that the gift of the Holy Spirit should be poured out on the pagans too, since they could hear them speaking strange languages and proclaiming the greatness of God. Peter himself then said, "Could anyone refuse the water of Baptism to these people, now they have received the Holy Spirit just as much as we have?" He then gave orders for them to be baptised in the name of Jesus Christ. Afterwards they begged him to stay on for some days.

This is the word of the Lord.

Responsorial Psalm (Ps 97:1–4. *R*. v. 2)

Response
The Lord has shown his salvation to the nations.
Or: Alleluia!

1. Sing a new song to the Lord
for he has worked wonders.
His right hand and his holy arm
have brought salvation. (*R*.)

2. The Lord has made known his salvation;
has shown his justice to the nations.
He has remembered his truth and love
for the house of Israel. (*R*.)

3. All the ends of the earth have seen
the salvation of our God.
Shout to the Lord all the earth,
ring out your joy. (*R*.)

Second Reading   (4:7–10)

A reading from the first letter of St John
God is love.

My dear people,
let us love one another
since love comes from God
and everyone who loves is begotten by God and knows
    God.
Anyone who fails to love can never have known God,
because God is love.
God's love for us was revealed
when God sent into the world his only Son
so that we could have life through him;
this is the love I mean:
not our love for God,
but God's love for us when he sent his Son
to be the sacrifice that takes our sins away.

This is the word of the Lord.

Alleluia   (Jn 14:23)

Alleluia, alleluia!
Jesus said: "If anyone loves me he will keep my word,
and my Father will love him,
and we shall come to him."
Alleluia!

Gospel   (15:9–17)

A reading from the holy Gospel according to John
*A man can have no greater love than to lay down his life for
his friends.*

Jesus said to his disciples:
"As the Father has loved me,

so I have loved you.
Remain in my love.
If you keep my commandments
you will remain in my love,
just as I have kept my Father's commandments
and remain in his love.
I have told you this
so that my own joy may be in you
and your joy be complete.
This is my commandment:
love one another,
as I have loved you.
A man can have no greater love
than to lay down his life for his friends.
You are my friends,
if you do what I command you.
I shall not call you servants any more,
because a servant does not know
his master's business;
I call you friends,
because I have made known to you
everything I have learnt from my Father.
You did not choose me,
no, I chose you;
and I commissioned you
to go out and to bear fruit,
fruit that will last;
and then the Father will give you
anything you ask him in my name.
What I command you
is to love one another."

This is the Gospel of the Lord.

6th SUNDAY OF EASTER
Year 3 (Year C)

First Reading   (15:1–2. 22–29)

A reading from the Acts of the Apostles
*It has been decided by the Holy Spirit and by ourselves not to
saddle you with any burden beyond these essentials.*

Some men came down from Judaea and taught the brothers,
"Unless you have yourselves circumcised in the tradition
of Moses you cannot be saved." This led to disagreement,
and after Paul and Barnabas had had a long argument with
these men it was arranged that Paul and Barnabas and
others of the church should go up to Jerusalem and discuss
the problem with the apostles and elders.

Then the apostles and elders decided to choose delegates
to send to Antioch with Paul and Barnabas; the whole
church concurred with this. They chose Judas known as
Barsabbas and Silas, both leading men in the brotherhood,
and gave them this letter to take with them:

"The apostles and elders, your brothers, send greetings
to the brothers of pagan birth in Antioch, Syria and Cilicia.
We hear that some of our members have disturbed you
with their demands and have unsettled your minds. They
acted without any authority from us, and so we have decided unanimously to elect delegates and to send them to
you with Barnabas and Paul, men we highly respect who
have dedicated their lives to the name of our Lord Jesus
Christ. Accordingly we are sending you Judas and Silas,
who will confirm by word of mouth what we have written
in this letter. It has been decided by the Holy Spirit and by
ourselves not to saddle you with any burden beyond these
essentials: you are to abstain from food sacrificed to idols,
from blood, from the meat of strangled animals and from
fornication. Avoid these, and you will do what is right.
Farewell."

This is the word of the Lord.

Responsorial Psalm   (Ps 66:2–3. 5–6. 8. *R*. v. 4)

Response
Let the peoples praise you, O God;
let all the peoples praise you.
Or: Alleluia!

1. O God, be gracious and bless us
and let your face shed its light upon us.
So will your ways be known upon earth
and all nations learn your saving help. (*R*.)

2. Let the nations be glad and exult
for you rule the world with justice.
With fairness you rule the peoples,
you guide the nations on earth. (*R*.)

3. Let the peoples praise you, O God;
let all the peoples praise you.
May God still give us his blessing
till the ends of the earth revere him. (*R*.)

Second Reading   (21:10–14. 22–23)

A reading from the book of the Apocalypse
He showed me the holy city coming down out of heaven.

In the spirit, the angel took me to the top of an enormous
high mountain and showed me Jerusalem, the holy city,
coming down from God out of heaven. It had all the
radiant glory of God and glittered like some precious jewel
of crystal-clear diamond. The walls of it were of a great
height, and had twelve gates; at each of the twelve gates
there was an angel, and over the gates were written the
names of the twelve tribes of Israel; on the east there were
three gates, on the north three gates, on the south three
gates, and on the west three gates. The city walls stood on

twelve foundation stones, each one of which bore the name of one of the twelve apostles of the Lamb.

I saw that there was no temple in the city since the Lord God Almighty and the Lamb were themselves the temple, and the city did not need the sun or the moon for light, since it was lit by the radiant glory of God and the Lamb was a lighted torch for it.

This is the word of the Lord.

Alleluia   (Jn 14:23)

Alleluia, alleluia!
Jesus said: "If anyone loves me he will keep my word,
and my Father will love him,
and we shall come to him.
Alleluia!

When the Ascension of Our Lord is celebrated on the Seventh Sunday of Easter, the Second Readings and Gospels assigned to the Seventh Sunday may be read on the Sixth Sunday.

Gospel   (14:23–29)

A reading from the holy Gospel according to John
The Holy Spirit will remind you of all I have said to you.

Jesus said to his disciples:
"If anyone loves me he will keep my word,
and my Father will love him,
and we shall come to him
and make our home with him.
Those who do not love me do not keep my words.
And my word is not my own:
it is the word of the one who sent me.
I have said these things to you
while still with you;
but the Advocate, the Holy Spirit,
whom the Father will send in my name,
will teach you everything

and remind you of all I have said to you.
Peace I bequeath to you,
my own peace I give you,
a peace the world cannot give, this is my gift to you.
Do not let your hearts be troubled or afraid.
You heard me say:
I am going away, and shall return.
If you loved me you would have been glad to know that
    I am going to the Father,
for the Father is greater than I.
I have told you this now before it happens,
so that when it does happen you may believe."

This is the Gospel of the Lord.

MONDAY

First Reading   (16:11–15)

A reading from the Acts of the Apostles
The Lord opened her heart to accept what Paul was saying.

Sailing from Troas we made a straight run for Samothrace;
the next day for Neapolis, and from there for Philippi, a
Roman colony and the principal city of that particular district of Macedonia. After a few days in this city we went
along the river outside the gates as it was the sabbath and
this was a customary place for prayer. We sat down and
preached to the women who had come to the meeting. One
of these women was called Lydia, a devout woman from
the town of Thyatira who was in the purple-dye trade. She
listened to us, and the Lord opened her heart to accept
what Paul was saying. After she and her household had
been baptised she sent us an invitation: "If you really think
me a true believer in the Lord," she said "come and stay
with us"; and she would take no refusal.
    This is the word of the Lord.

Responsorial Psalm   (Ps 149:1–6. 9. *R.* v. 4)

Response
The Lord takes delight in his people.
Or: Alleluia!

1. Alleluia!
Sing a new song to the Lord,
his praise in the assembly of the faithful.
Let Israel rejoice in its Maker,
let Zion's sons exult in their king. (*R.*)

2. Let them praise his name with dancing
and make music with timbrel and harp.
For the Lord takes delight in his people.
He crowns the poor with salvation. (*R.*)

3. Let the faithful rejoice in their glory,
shout for joy and take their rest.
Let the praise of God be on their lips:
this honour is for all his faithful. Alleluia! (*R.*)

Alleluia   (Lk 24:25.26)

Alleluia, alleluia!
It was ordained that the Christ should suffer
and rise from the dead,
and so enter into his glory.
Alleluia!

Alternative Alleluias p. 844.

Gospel   (15:26–16:4)
A reading from the holy Gospel according to John
The Spirit of truth will be my witness.

Jesus said to his disciples:
"When the Advocate comes,

whom I shall send to you from the Father,
the Spirit of truth who issues from the Father,
he will be my witness.
And you too will be witnesses,
because you have been with me from the outset.

"I have told you all this
so that your faith may not be shaken.
They will expel you from the synagogues,
and indeed the hour is coming
when anyone who kills you will think he is doing a holy
   duty for God.
They will do these things
because they have never known either the Father or myself.
But I have told you all this,
so that when the time for it comes
you may remember that I told you."

This is the Gospel of the Lord.

TUESDAY

First Reading (16:22–34)

A reading from the Acts of the Apostles
*Become a believer in the Lord Jesus, and you will be saved,
and your household too.*

The crowd joined in and showed its hostility to Paul and
Silas, so the magistrates had them stripped and ordered
them to be flogged. They were given many lashes and then
thrown into prison, and the gaoler was told to keep a close
watch on them. So, following his instructions, he threw
them into the inner prison and fastened their feet in the
stocks.

Late that night Paul and Silas were praying and singing
God's praises, while the other prisoners listened. Suddenly
there was an earthquake that shook the prison to its foun-

dations. All the doors flew open and the chains fell from all the prisoners. When the gaoler woke and saw the doors wide open he drew his sword and was about to commit suicide, presuming that the prisoners had escaped. But Paul shouted at the top of his voice, "Don't do yourself any harm; we are all here."

The gaoler called for lights, then rushed in, threw himself trembling at the feet of Paul and Silas, and escorted them out, saying, "Sirs, what must I do to be saved?" They told him, "Become a believer in the Lord Jesus, and you will be saved, and your household too." Then they preached the word of the Lord to him and to all his family. Late as it was, he took them to wash their wounds, and was baptised then and there with all his household. Afterwards he took them home and gave them a meal, and the whole family celebrated their conversion to belief in God.

This is the word of the Lord.

Responsorial Psalm   (Ps 137:1–3. 7–8. *R*. v. 7)

Response
You stretch out your hand and save me, O Lord.
Or: Alleluia!

1. I thank you, Lord, with all my heart,
you have heard the words of my mouth.
Before the angels I will bless you.
I will adore before your holy temple. (*R*.)

2. I thank you for your faithfulness and love
which excel all we ever knew of you.
On the day I called, you answered;
you increased the strength of my soul. (*R*.)

3. You stretch out your hand and save me,
your hand will do all things for me.
Your love, O Lord, is eternal,
discard not the work of your hands. (*R*.)

Alleluia

Alleluia, alleluia!
Christ has risen and shone upon us
whom he redeemed with his blood.
Alleluia!

Alternative Alleluias p. 844.

Gospel (16:5–11)

A reading from the holy Gospel according to John
Unless I go, the Advocate will not come to you.

Jesus said to his disciples:
"Now I am going to the one who sent me.
Not one of you has asked, 'Where are you going?'
Yet you are sad at heart because I have told you this.
Still, I must tell you the truth:
it is for your own good that I am going
because unless I go,
the Advocate will not come to you;
but if I do go,
I will send him to you.
And when he comes,
he will show the world how wrong it was,
about sin,
and about who was in the right,
and about judgement:
about sin:
proved by their refusal to believe in me;
about who was in the right:
proved by my going to the Father
and your seeing me no more;
about judgement:
proved by the prince of this world being already condemned."

This is the Gospel of the Lord.

WEDNESDAY

First Reading   (17:15.22–18:1)

A reading from the Acts of the Apostles
The God whom I proclaim is in fact the one whom you already worship without knowing it.

Paul's escort took him as far as Athens, and went back with instructions for Silas and Timothy to rejoin Paul as soon as they could.

Paul stood before the whole Council of the Areopagus and made this speech:

"Men of Athens, I have seen for myself how extremely scrupulous you are in all religious matters, because I noticed, as I strolled round admiring your sacred monuments, that you had an altar inscribed: To An Unknown God. Well, the God whom I proclaim is in fact the one whom you already worship without knowing it.

"Since the God who made the world and everything in it is himself Lord of heaven and earth, he does not make his home in shrines made by human hands. Nor is he dependent on anything that human hands can do for him, since he can never be in need of anything; on the contrary, it is he who gives everything – including life and breath – to everyone. From one single stock he not only created the whole human race so that they could occupy the entire earth, but he decreed how long each nation should flourish and what the boundaries of its territory should be. And he did this so that all nations might seek the deity and, by feeling their way towards him, succeed in finding him. Yet in fact he is not far from any of us, since it is in him that we live, and move, and exist, as indeed some of your own writers have said:

'We are all his children.'

"Since we are the children of God, we have no excuse

for thinking that the deity looks like anything in gold, silver or stone that has been carved and designed by a man.

"God overlooked that sort of thing when men were ignorant, but now he is telling everyone everywhere that they must repent, because he has fixed a day when the whole world will be judged, and judged in righteousness, and he has appointed a man to be the judge. And God has publicly proved this by raising this man from the dead."

At this mention of rising from the dead, some of them burst out laughing; others said, "We would like to hear you talk about this again." After that Paul left them, but there were some who attached themselves to him and became believers, among them Dionysius the Areopagite and a woman called Damaris, and others besides. After this Paul left Athens and went to Corinth.

This is the word of the Lord.

Responsorial Psalm (Ps 148:1–2.11–14)

Response
Your glory fills all heaven and earth.
Or: Alleluia!

1. Alleluia!
Praise the Lord from the heavens,
praise him in the heights.
Praise him, all his angels,
praise him, all his host. (*R.*)

2. All earth's kings and peoples,
earth's princes and rulers;
young men and maidens,
old men together with children. (*R.*)

3. Let them praise the name of the Lord
for he alone is exalted.
The splendour of his name
reaches beyond heaven and earth. (*R.*)

4. He exalts the strength of his people.
He is the praise of all his saints,
of the sons of Israel,
of the people to whom he comes close. Alleluia! (*R.*)

Alleluia

Alleluia, alleluia!
Since you have been brought back to true life with Christ,
you must look for the things that are in heaven where Christ
   is,
sitting at God's right hand.
Alleluia!

Alternative Alleluias p. 844.

Gospel   (16:12–15)

A reading from the holy Gospel according to John
The Spirit of truth will lead you to the complete truth.

Jesus said to his disciples:
"I still have many things to say to you
but they would be too much for you now.
But when the Spirit of truth comes
he will lead you to the complete truth,
since he will not be speaking as from himself
but will say only what he has learnt;
and he will tell you of the things to come.
He will glorify me,
since all he tells you
will be taken from what is mine.
Everything the Father has is mine;
that is why I said:
All he tells you
will be taken from what is mine."

   This is the Gospel of the Lord.

THE ASCENSION OF OUR LORD

The first and second readings with the responsorial psalm and alleluia are common to Years 1, 2 and 3 (Years A, B and C).

First Reading   (1:1–11)

A reading from the Acts of the Apostles
He was lifted up while they looked on.

In my earlier work, Theophilus, I dealt with everything Jesus had done and taught from the beginning until the day he gave his instructions to the apostles he had chosen through the Holy Spirit, and was taken up to heaven. He had shown himself alive to them after his Passion by many demonstrations: for forty days he had continued to appear to them and tell them about the kingdom of God. When he had been at table with them, he had told them not to leave Jerusalem, but to wait there for what the Father had promised. "It is" he had said "what you have heard me speak about: John baptised with water but you, not many days from now, will be baptised with the Holy Spirit."

Now having met together, they asked him, "Lord, has the time come? Are you going to restore the kingdom to Israel?" He replied, "It is not for you to know times or dates that the Father has decided by his own authority, but you will receive power when the Holy Spirit comes on you, and then you will be my witnesses not only in Jerusalem but throughout Judaea and Samaria, and indeed to the ends of the earth."

As he said this he was lifted up while they looked on, and a cloud took him from their sight. They were still staring into the sky when suddenly two men in white were standing near them and they said, "Why are you men from Galilee standing here looking into the sky? Jesus who has been taken up from you into heaven, this same Jesus will come back in the same way as you have seen him go there."

This is the word of the Lord.

Responsorial Psalm   (Ps 46:2–3. 6–9. *R.* v. 6)

Response
God goes up with shouts of joy;
the Lord goes up with trumpet blast.
Or: Alleluia!

1. All peoples, clap your hands,
cry to God with shouts of joy!
For the Lord, the Most High, we must fear,
great king over all the earth. (*R.*)

2. God goes up with shouts of joy;
the Lord goes up with trumpet blast.
Sing praise for God, sing praise,
sing praise to our king, sing praise. (*R.*)

3. God is king of all the earth.
Sing praise with all your skill.
God is king over the nations;
God reigns on his holy throne. (*R.*)

Second Reading   (1:17–23)

A reading from the letter of St Paul to the Ephesians
He made him sit at his right hand in heaven.

May the God of our Lord Jesus Christ, the Father of glory,
give you a spirit of wisdom and perception of what is revealed, to bring you to full knowledge of him. May he enlighten the eyes of your mind so that you can see what hope
his call holds for you, what rich glories he has promised the
saints will inherit and how infinitely great is the power that
he has exercised for us believers. This you can tell from the
strength of his power at work in Christ, when he used it to
raise him from the dead and to make him sit at his right
hand, in heaven, far above every Sovereignty, Authority,
Power, or Domination, or any other name that can be

named, not only in this age, but also in the age to come. He
has put all things under his feet, and made him, as the ruler
of everything, the head of the Church; which is his body,
the fullness of him who fills the whole creation.

This is the word of the Lord.

Alleluia   (Mt 28:19–20)

Alleluia, alleluia!
Go, make disciples of all the nations;
I am with you always; yes, to the end of time.
Alleluia!

Year 1 (Year A)

Gospel   (28:16–20)

The end of the holy Gospel according to Matthew
All authority in heaven and on earth has been given to me.

The eleven disciples set out for Galilee, to the mountain
where Jesus had arranged to meet them. When they saw
him they fell down before him, though some hesitated. Jesus
came up and spoke to them. He said, "All authority in
heaven and on earth has been given to me. Go, therefore,
make disciples of all the nations; baptise them in the name
of the Father and of the Son and of the Holy Spirit, and
teach them to observe all the commands I gave you. And
know that I am with you always; yes, to the end of time."

This is the Gospel of the Lord.

Year 2 (Year B)

Gospel   (16:15–20)

The end of the holy Gospel according to Mark
*He was taken up into heaven: there at the right hand of God
he took his place.*

Jesus showed himself to the Eleven, and said to them, "Go
out to the whole world; proclaim the Good News to all

creation. He who believes and is baptised will be saved; he who does not believe will be condemned. These are the signs that will be associated with believers: in my name they will cast out devils; they will have the gift of tongues; they will pick up snakes in their hands, and be unharmed should they drink deadly poison; they will lay their hands on the sick, who will recover."

And so the Lord Jesus, after he had spoken to them, was taken up into heaven: there at the right hand of God he took his place, while they, going out, preached everywhere, the Lord working with them and confirming the word by the signs that accompanied it.

This is the Gospel of the Lord.

Year 3 (Year C)

Gospel   (24:46–53)

The end of the holy Gospel according to Luke
As he blessed them he was carried up to heaven.

Jesus said to his disciples: "You see how it is written that the Christ would suffer and on the third day rise from the dead, and that, in his name, repentance for the forgiveness of sins would be preached to all the nations, beginning from Jerusalem. You are witnesses to this.

"And now I am sending down to you what the Father has promised. Stay in the city then, until you are clothed with the power from on high."

Then he took them out as far as the outskirts of Bethany, and lifting up his hands he blessed them. Now as he blessed them, he withdrew from them and was carried up to heaven. They worshipped him and then went back to Jerusalem full of joy; and they were continually in the Temple praising God.

This is the Gospel of the Lord.

Where the Ascension is celebrated on Sunday, the following readings are used on the Thursday.

THURSDAY

First Reading   (18:1–8)

A reading from the Acts of the Apostles

Paul lodged with them and worked, and he used to hold debates in the synagogues.

Paul left Athens and went to Corinth, where he met a Jew called Aquila whose family came from Pontus. He and his wife Priscilla had recently left Italy because an edict of Claudius had expelled all the Jews from Rome. Paul went to visit them, and when he found they were tentmakers, of the same trade as himself, he lodged with them, and they worked together. Every sabbath he used to hold debates in the synagogues, trying to convert Jews as well as Greeks.

After Silas and Timothy had arrived from Macedonia, Paul devoted all his time to preaching, declaring to the Jews that Jesus was the Christ. When they turned against him and started to insult him, he took his cloak and shook it out in front of them, saying, "Your blood be on your own heads; from now on I can go to the pagans with a clear conscience." Then he left the synagogue and moved to the house next door that belonged to a worshipper of God called Justus. Crispus, president of the synagogue, and his whole household, all became believers in the Lord. A great many Corinthians who had heard him became believers and were baptised.

This is the word of the Lord.

Responsorial Psalm   (Ps 97:1–4. *R.* v. 2)

Response

The Lord has shown his salvation to the nations.

Or: Alleluia!

1. Sing a new song to the Lord
for he has worked wonders.
His right hand and his holy arm
have brought salvation. (*R.*)

2. The Lord has made known his salvation;
has shown his justice to the nations.
He has remembered his truth and love
for the house of Israel. (*R.*)

3. All the ends of the earth have seen
the salvation of our God.
Shout to the Lord all the earth,
ring out your joy. (*R.*)

Alleluia (Col 3:1)

Alleluia, alleluia!
Christ, having been raised from the dead,
will never die again.
Death has no power over him any more.
Alleluia!

Alternative Acclamations p. 844.

Gospel (16:16–20)

A reading from the holy Gospel according to John
You will be sorrowful, but your sorrow will turn to joy.

Jesus said to his disciples:

"In a short time you will no longer see me,
and then a short time later you will see me again."

Then some of his disciples said to one another, "What
does he mean, 'In a short time you will no longer see me,
and then a short time later you will see me again' and, 'I
am going to the Father?' What is this 'short time'? We don't
know what he means." Jesus knew that they wanted to

question him, so he said, "You are asking one another what I meant by saying: In a short time you will no longer see me, and then a short time later you will see me again.

"I tell you most solemnly,
you will be weeping and wailing
while the world will rejoice;
you will be sorrowful,
but your sorrow will turn to joy."

This is the Gospel of the Lord.

FRIDAY

First Reading   (18:9–18)
A reading from the Acts of the Apostles
I have many people on my side in this city.

One night the Lord spoke to Paul in a vision, "Do not be afraid to speak out, nor allow yourself to be silenced: I am with you. I have so many people on my side in this city that no one will even attempt to hurt you." So Paul stayed at Corinth preaching the word of God among them for eighteen months.

But while Gallio was proconsul of Achaia, the Jews made a concerted attack on Paul and brought him before the tribunal. "We accuse this man" they said "of persuading people to worship God in a way that breaks the Law." Before Paul could open his mouth, Gallio said to the Jews, "Listen, you Jews. If this were a misdemeanour or a crime, I would not hesitate to attend to you; but if it is only quibbles about words and names, and about your own Law, then you must deal with it yourselves – I have no intention of making legal decisions about things like that." Then he sent them out of the court, and at once they all turned on Sosthenes, the synagogue president, and beat him in front of the court house. Gallio refused to take any notice at all.

After staying on for some time, Paul took leave of the

brothers and sailed for Syria, accompanied by Priscilla and Aquila. At Cenchreae he had his hair cut off, because of a vow he had made.

 This is the word of the Lord.

Responsorial Psalm   (Ps 46:2–7. *R*. v. 8)

Response
God is king of all the earth.
Or: Alleluia!

1. All peoples, clap your hands,
cry to God with shouts of joy!
For the Lord, the Most High, we must fear,
great king over all the earth. (*R*.)

2. He subdues people under us
and nations under our feet.
Our inheritance, our glory, is from him,
given to Jacob out of love. (*R*.)

3. God goes up with shouts of joy;
the Lord goes up with trumpet blast.
Sing praise for God, sing praise,
sing praise to our king, sing praise. (*R*.)

Alleluia   (Jn 14:26)

When the Ascension is celebrated on the Thursday
Alleluia, alleluia!
The Holy Spirit will teach you everything
and remind you of all I have said to you.
Alleluia!
Alternative Alleluias p. 846.

When the Ascension is celebrated on the 7th Sunday of Easter.
Alleluia, alleluia!
Christ has risen: he who created all things,

and has granted his mercy to men.
Alleluia!

Alternative Alleluias p. 844.

Gospel (16:20–23)

A reading from the holy Gospel according to John
No one shall take your joy from you.

Jesus said to his disciples:
"I tell you most solemnly,
you will be weeping and wailing
while the world will rejoice;
you will be sorrowful,
but your sorrow will turn to joy.
A woman in childbirth suffers,
because her time has come;
but when she has given birth to the child she forgets the
    suffering
in her joy that a man has been born into the world.
So it is with you: you are sad now,
but I shall see you again, and your hearts will be full of joy,
and that joy no one shall take from you.
When that day comes,
you will not ask me any questions."

This is the Gospel of the Lord.

SATURDAY

First Reading (18:23–28)

A reading from the Acts of the Apostles
*Apollos demonstrated from the scriptures that Jesus was the
Christ.*

Paul came down to Antioch where he spent a short time before continuing his journey through the Galatian country
and then through Phrygia, encouraging all the followers.

An Alexandrian Jew named Apollos now arrived in Ephesus. He was an eloquent man, with a sound knowledge of the scriptures, and yet, though he had been given instructions in the Way of the Lord and preached with great spiritual earnestness and was accurate in all the details he taught about Jesus, he had only experienced the baptism of John. When Priscilla and Aquila heard him speak boldly in the synagogue, they took an interest in him and gave him further instruction about the Way.

When Apollos thought of crossing over to Achaia, the brothers encouraged him. When he arrived there he was able by God's grace to help the believers considerably by the energetic way he refuted the Jews in public and demonstrated from the scriptures that Jesus was the Christ.

This is the word of the Lord.

Responsorial Psalm   (Ps 46:2–3. 8–10. R. v. 8)

Response
God is king of all the earth.
Or: Alleluia!

1. All peoples, clap your hands,
cry to God with shouts of joy!
For the Lord, the Most High, we must fear,
great king over all the earth. (R.)

2. God is king of all the earth.
Sing praise with all your skill.
God is king over the nations;
God reigns on his holy throne. (R.)

3. The princes of the peoples are assembled
with the people of Abraham's God.
The rulers of the earth belong to God,
to God who reigns over all. (R.)

Alleluia   (Jn 14:16)

When the Ascension is celebrated on the Thursday.

Alleluia, alleluia!
I shall ask the Father,
and he will give you another Advocate
to be with you for ever.
Alleluia!

Alternative Alleluias p. 846.

When the Ascension is celebrated on the 7th Sunday of Easter.

Alleluia, alleluia!
The Lord, who hung for us upon the tree,
has risen from the tomb.
Alleluia!

Alternative Alleluias p. 844.

Gospel   (16:23–28)

A reading from the holy Gospel according to John
The Father loves you for loving me and believing

Jesus said to his disciples:
"I tell you most solemnly,
anything you ask for from the Father
he will grant in my name.
Until now you have not asked for anything in my name.
Ask and you will receive,
and so your joy will be complete.
I have been telling you all this in metaphors;
the hour is coming
when I shall no longer speak to you in metaphors,
but tell you about the Father in plain words.
When that day comes
you will ask in my name;
and I do not say that I shall pray to the Father for you,
because the Father himself loves you
for loving me
and believing that I came from God.

I came from the Father and have come into the world
and now I leave the world to go to the Father."

   This is the Gospel of the Lord.

7th SUNDAY OF EASTER
Year 1 (Year A)

First Reading   (1:12–14)

A reading from the Acts of the Apostles
All joined in continuous prayer.

From the Mount of Olives, as it is called, the apostles went
back to Jerusalem, a short distance away, no more than a
sabbath walk; and when they reached the city they went
to the upper room where they were staying; there were Peter
and John, James and Andrew, Philip and Thomas, Bartholomew and Matthew, James son of Alphaeus and Simon
the Zealot, and Jude son of James. All these joined in continuous prayer, together with several women, including
Mary the mother of Jesus, and with his brothers.
   This is the word of the Lord.

Responsorial Psalm   (Ps 26:1. 4. 7–8. *R.* v. 13)

Response
I am sure I shall see the Lord's goodness
in the land of the living.
Or: Alleluia!

1. The Lord is my light and my help;
whom shall I fear?
The Lord is the stronghold of my life;
before whom shall I shrink? (*R.*)

2. There is one thing I ask of the Lord,
for this I long,
to live in the house of the Lord,
all the days of my life,

to savour the sweetness of the Lord,
to behold his temple. (R.)

3. O Lord, hear my voice when I call;
have mercy and answer.
Of you my heart has spoken:
"Seek his face." (R.)

Second Reading (4:13–16)

A reading from the first letter of St Peter
It is a blessing for you when they insult you for bearing the name of Christ.

If you can have some share in the sufferings of Christ, be glad, because you will enjoy a much greater gladness when his glory is revealed. It is a blessing for you when they insult you for bearing the name of Christ, because it means that you have the Spirit of glory, the Spirit of God resting on you. None of you should ever deserve to suffer for being a murderer, a thief, a criminal or an informer; but if anyone of you should suffer for being a Christian, then he is not to be ashamed of it; he should thank God that he has been called one.

This is the word of the Lord.

Alleluia (Jn 14:18)

Alleluia, alleluia!
I will not leave you orphans, says the Lord;
I will come back to you,
and your hearts will be full of joy.
Alleluia!

Gospel (17:1–11)

A reading from the holy Gospel according to John
Father, glorify your Son.

Jesus raised his eyes to heaven and said:
"Father, the hour has come:
glorify your Son
so that your Son may glorify you;
and, through the power over all mankind that you have
    given him,
let him give eternal life to all those you have entrusted to
    him.
And eternal life is this:
to know you,
the only true God,
and Jesus Christ whom you have sent.
I have glorified you on earth
and finished the work
that you gave me to do.
Now, Father, it is time for you to glorify me
with that glory I had with you
before ever the world was.
I have made your name known
to the men you took from the world to give me.
They were yours and you gave them to me,
and they have kept your word.
Now at last they know
that all you have given me comes indeed from you;
for I have given them
the teaching you gave to me,
and they have truly accepted this, that I came from you,
and have believed that it was you who sent me.
I pray for them;
I am not praying for the world
but for those you have given me,
because they belong to you:
all I have is yours
and all you have is mine,
and in them I am glorified.
I am not in the world any longer,

but they are in the world,
and I am coming to you."

This is the Gospel of the Lord.

7th SUNDAY OF EASTER
Year 2 (Year B)

First Reading   (1:15–17. 20–26)

A reading from the Acts of the Apostles
We must choose one of these to be a witness to his resurrection with us.

One day Peter stood up to speak to the brothers – there were about a hundred and twenty persons in the congregation: "Brothers, the passage of scripture had to be fulfilled in which the Holy Spirit, speaking through David, foretells the fate of Judas, who offered himself as a guide to the men who arrested Jesus – after having been one of our number and actually sharing this ministry of ours.

In the Book of Psalms it says:

Let someone else take his office.

"We must therefore choose someone who has been with us the whole time that the Lord Jesus was travelling round with us, someone who was with us right from the time when John was baptising until the day when he was taken up from us – and he can act with us as a witness to his resurrection."

Having nominated two candidates, Joseph known as Barsabbas, whose surname was Justus, and Matthias, they prayed, "Lord, you can read everyone's heart; show us therefore which of these two you have chosen to take over this ministry and apostolate, which Judas abandoned to go to his proper place." They then drew lots for them, and as the lot fell to Matthias, he was listed as one of the twelve apostles.

This is the word of the Lord.

Responsorial Psalm (Ps 102:1–2. 11–12. 19–20. *R*. v. 19)

Response
The Lord has set his sway in heaven.
Or: Alleluia!

1. My soul, give thanks to the Lord,
all my being, bless his holy name.
My soul, give thanks to the Lord
and never forget all his blessings. (*R*.)

2. For as the heavens are high above the earth
so strong is his love for those who fear him.
As far as the east is from the west
so far does he remove our sins. (*R*.)

3. The Lord had set his sway in heaven
and his kingdom is ruling over all.
Give thanks to the Lord, all his angels,
mighty in power, fulfilling his word. (*R*.)

Second Reading (4:11–16)

A reading from the first letter of St John
Anyone who lives in love lives in God, and God lives in him.

My dear people,
since God has loved us so much,
we too should love one another.
No one has ever seen God;
but as long as we love one another
God will live in us
and his love will be complete in us.
We can know that we are living in him
and he is living in us
because he lets us share his Spirit.
We ourselves saw and we testify
that the Father sent his Son
as saviour of the world.

If anyone acknowledges that Jesus is the Son of God,
God lives in him, and he in God.
We ourselves have known and put our faith in
God's love towards ourselves.
God is love
and anyone who lives in love lives in God,
and God lives in him.

This is the word of the Lord.

Alleluia (Jn 14:18)

Alleluia, alleluia!
I will not leave you orphans, says the Lord;
I will come back to you,
and your hearts will be full of joy.
Alleluia!

Gospel (17:11–19)

A reading from the holy Gospel according to John
That they may be one like us!

Jesus raised his eyes to heaven and said:

"Holy Father,
keep those you have given me true to your name,
so that they may be one like us.
While I was with them,
I kept those you had given me true to your name.
I have watched over them and not one is lost
except the one who chose to be lost,
and this was to fulfil the scriptures.
But now I am coming to you
and while still in the world I say these things
to share my joy with them to the full.
I passed your word on to them,
and the world hated them,
because they belong to the world
no more than I belong to the world.

I am not asking you to remove them from the world,
but to protect them from the evil one.
They do not belong to the world
any more than I belong to the world.
Consecrate them in the truth;
your word is truth.
As you sent me into the world,
I have sent them into the world,
and for their sake I consecrate myself
so that they too may be consecrated in truth."

This is the Gospel of the Lord.

7th SUNDAY OF EASTER
Year 3 (Year C)

First Reading   (7:55–60)

A reading from the Acts of the Apostles
I can see the Son of Man standing at the right hand of God.

Stephen, filled with the Holy Spirit, gazed into heaven and
saw the glory of God, and Jesus standing at God's right
hand. "I can see heaven thrown open" he said "and the
Son of Man standing at the right hand of God." At this all
the members of the council shouted out and stopped their
ears with their hands; then they all rushed at him, sent him
out of the city and stoned him. The witnesses put down their
clothes at the feet of a young man called Saul. As they were
stoning him, Stephen said in invocation, "Lord Jesus, receive my spirit." Then he knelt down and said aloud,
"Lord, do not hold this sin against them"; and with these
words he fell asleep.
     This is the word of the Lord.

Responsorial Psalm   (Ps 96:1–2. 6–7. 9. *R*. vv. 1.9)

Response
The Lord is king, most high above all the earth.
Or: Alleluia!

1. The Lord is king, let earth rejoice,
the many coastlands be glad.
His throne is justice and right. (*R.*)

2. The skies proclaim his justice;
all peoples see his glory.
All you spirits, worship him. (*R.*)

3. For you indeed are the Lord
most high above all the earth
exalted far above all spirits. (*R.*)

Second Reading (22:12–14. 16–17. 20)

A reading from the book of the Apocalypse
Come, Lord Jesus!

I, John, heard a voice speaking to me: "Very soon now, I shall be with you again, bringing the reward to be given to every man according to what he deserves. I am the Alpha and the Omega, the First and the Last, the Beginning and the End. Happy are those who will have washed their robes clean, so that they will have the right to feed on the tree of life and can come through the gates into the city."

I, Jesus, have sent my angel to make these revelations to you for the sake of the churches. I am of David's line, the root of David and the bright star of the morning.

The Spirit and the Bride say, "Come." Let everyone who listens answer, "Come." Then let all who are thirsty come; all who want it may have the water of life, and have it free.

The one who guarantees these revelations repeats his promise: I shall indeed be with you. Amen; come, Lord Jesus.

This is the word of the Lord.

Alleluia (Jn 14:18)

Alleluia, alleluia!
I will not leave you orphans, says the Lord;

I will come back to you,
and your hearts will be full of joy.
Alleluia!

Gospel   (17:20–26)

A reading from the holy Gospel according to John
May they be completely one.

Jesus raised his eyes to heaven and said:
"Holy Father,
I pray not only for these,
but for those also
who through their words will believe in me.
May they all be one.
Father, may they be one in us,
as you are in me and I am in you,
so that the world may believe it was you who sent me.
I have given them the glory you gave to me,
that they may be one as we are one.
With me in them and you in me,
may they be so completely one
that the world will realise that it was you who sent me
and that I have loved them as much as you loved me.
Father,
I want those you have given me
to be with me where I am,
so that they may always see the glory
you have given me
because you loved me
before the foundation of the world.
Father, Righteous One,
the world has not known you,
but I have known you,
and these have known
that you have sent me.
I have made your name known to them

and will continue to make it known,
so that the love with which you loved me may be in them,
and so that I may be in them."

This is the Gospel of the Lord.

MONDAY

First Reading (19:1–8)

A reading from the Acts of the Apostles
Did you receive the Holy Spirit when you became believers?

While Apollos was in Corinth, Paul made his way over-
land as far as Ephesus, where he found a number of disciples. When he asked, "Did you receive the Holy Spirit
when you became believers?" they answered, "No, we were
never even told there was such a thing as a Holy Spirit."
"Then how were you baptised?" he asked. "With John's
baptism" they replied. "John's baptism" said Paul "was a
baptism of repentance; but he insisted that the people
should believe in the one who was to come after him – in
other words Jesus." When they heard this, they were baptised in the name of the Lord Jesus, and the moment Paul
had laid hands on them the Holy Spirit came down on
them, and they began to speak with tongues and to prophesy. There were about twelve of these men.

He began by going to the synagogue, where he spoke out
boldly and argued persuasively about the kingdom of
God. He did this for three months.

This is the word of the Lord.

Responsorial Psalm (Ps 67:2–7. *R*. v. 33)

Response
Kingdoms of the earth, sing to God.
Or: Alleluia!

1. Let God arise, let his foes be scattered.
Let those who hate him flee before him.
As smoke is blown away so will they be blown away;
like wax that melts before the fire,
so the wicked shall perish at the presence of God. (*R.*)

2. But the just shall rejoice at the presence of God,
they shall exult and dance for joy.
O sing to the Lord, make music to his name;
rejoice in the Lord, exult at his presence. (*R.*)

3. Father of the orphan, defender of the widow,
such is God in his holy place.
God gives the lonely a home to live in;
he leads the prisoners forth into freedom. (*R.*)

Alleluia   (Jn 16:28)

Alleluia, alleluia!
I came from the Father
and have come into the world,
and now I leave the world
to go to the Father.
Alleluia!

Alternative Alleluias p. 846.

Gospel   (16:29–33)

A reading from the holy Gospel according to John
Be brave: I have conquered the world.

His disciples said to Jesus, "Now you are speaking plainly
and not using metaphors! Now we see that you know everything, and do not have to wait for questions to be put into
words; because of this we believe that you came from
God." Jesus answered them:

"Do you believe at last?
Listen; the time will come – in fact it has come already –

when you will be scattered, each going his own way
and leaving me alone.
And yet I am not alone,
because the Father is with me.
I have told you all this
so that you may find peace in me.
In the world you will have trouble,
but be brave:
I have conquered the world."

This is the Gospel of the Lord.

TUESDAY

First Reading   (20:17–27)

A reading from the Acts of the Apostles
*I am finishing my race and carrying out the mission the Lord
Jesus gave me.*

From Miletus Paul sent for the elders of the church of
Ephesus. When they arrived he addressed these words to
them:

"You know what my way of life has been ever since the
first day I set foot among you in Asia, how I have served
the Lord in all humility, with all the sorrows and trials that
came to me through the plots of the Jews. I have not hesitated to do anything that would be helpful to you; I have
preached to you, and instructed you both in public and in
your homes, urging both Jews and Greeks to turn to God
and to believe in our Lord Jesus.

"And now you see me a prisoner already in spirit; I am
on my way to Jerusalem, but have no idea what will happen to me there, except that the Holy Spirit, in town after
town, has made it clear enough that imprisonment and persecution await me. But life to me is not a thing to waste
words on, provided that when I finish my race I have car-

ried out the mission the Lord Jesus gave me – and that was to bear witness to the Good News of God's grace.

"I now feel sure that none of you among whom I have gone about proclaiming the kingdom will ever see my face again. And so here and now I swear that my conscience is clear as far as all of you are concerned, for I have without faltering put before you the whole of God's purpose."

This is the word of the Lord.

Responsorial Psalm   (Ps 67:10–11. 20–21. R. v. 33)

Response
Kingdoms of the earth, sing to God.
Or: Alleluia!

1. You poured down, O God, a generous rain:
when your people were starved you gave them new life.
It was there that your people found a home,
prepared in your goodness, O God, for the poor. (*R.*)

2. May the Lord be blessed day after day.
He bears our burdens, God our saviour.
This God of ours is a God who saves.
The Lord our God holds the keys of death. (*R.*)

Alleluia   (Jn 14:18)

Alleluia, alleluia!
I will not leave you orphans, says the Lord;
I go, but I will come back to you,
and your hearts will be full of joy.
Alleluia!

Alternative Alleluias p. 846.

Gospel   (17:1–11)
A reading from the holy Gospel according to John
Father, glorify your Son.

Jesus raised his eyes to heaven and said:
"Father, the hour has come:
glorify your Son
so that your Son may glorify you;
and, through the power over all mankind that you have
   given him,
let him give eternal life to all those you have entrusted to
   him.
And eternal life is this:
to know you,
the only true God,
and Jesus Christ whom you have sent.
I have glorified you on earth
and finished the work
that you gave me to do.
Now, Father, it is time for you to glorify me
with that glory I had with you
before ever the world was.
I have made your name known
to the men you took from the world to give me.
They were yours and you gave them to me,
and they have kept your word.
Now at last they know
that all you have given me comes indeed from you;
for I have given them
the teaching you gave to me,
and they have truly accepted this, that I came from you,
and have believed that it was you who sent me.
I pray for them;
I am not praying for the world
but for those you have given me,
because they belong to you:
all I have is yours
and all you have is mine,
and in them I am glorified.
I am not in the world any longer,

but they are in the world,
and I am coming to you."

This is the Gospel of the Lord.

WEDNESDAY

First Reading   (20:28–38)

A reading from the Acts of the Apostles
I commend you to God, who has power to build you up and to give you your inheritance.

Paul addressed these words to the elders of the church of Ephesus: "Be on your guard for yourselves and for all the flock of which the Holy Spirit has made you the overseers, to feed the Church of God which he bought with his own blood. I know quite well that when I have gone fierce wolves will invade you and will have no mercy on the flock. Even from your own ranks there will be men coming forward with a travesty of the truth on their lips to induce the disciples to follow them. So be on your guard, remembering how night and day for three years I never failed to keep you right, shedding tears over each one of you. And now I commend you to God, and to the word of his grace that has power to build you up and to give you your inheritance among all the sanctified.

"I have never asked anyone for money or clothes; you know for yourselves that the work I did earned enough to meet my needs and those of my companions. I did this to show you that this is how we must exert ourselves to support the weak, remembering the words of the Lord Jesus, who himself said, 'There is more happiness in giving than in receiving.' "

When he had finished speaking he knelt down with them all and prayed. By now they were all in tears; they put their arms round Paul's neck and kissed him; what saddened

them most was his saying they would never see his face
again. Then they escorted him to the ship.

This is the word of the Lord.

Responsorial Psalm   (Ps 67:29–30. 33–36. *R*. v. 33)
Response
Kingdoms of the earth, sing to God.
Or: Alleluia!

1. Show forth, O God, show forth your might,
your might, O God, which you have shown for us.
For the sake of your temple high in Jerusalem
may kings come to you bringing their tribute. (*R*.)

2. Kingdoms of the earth, sing to God, praise the Lord
who rides on the heavens, the ancient heavens.
He thunders his voice, his mighty voice.
Come, acknowledge the power of God. (*R*.)

3. His glory is over Israel; his might is in the skies.
God is to be feared in his holy place.
He is the Lord, Israel's God.
He gives strength and power to his people.
Blessed be God! (*R*.)

Alleluia   (Mt 28:19. 20)
Alleluia, alleluia!
Go, make disciples of all the nations:
I am with you always; yes, to the end of time.
Alleluia!

Alternative Acclamations p. 846.

Gospel   (17:11–19)
A reading from the holy Gospel according to John
May they be one like us.

Jesus raised his eyes to heaven and said:
"Holy Father,
keep those you have given me true to your name,
so that they may be one like us.
While I was with them,
I kept those you had given me true to your name.
I have watched over them and not one is lost
except the one who chose to be lost,
and this was to fulfil the scriptures.
But now I am coming to you
and while still in the world I say these things
to share my joy with them to the full.
I passed your word on to them,
and the world hated them,
because they belong to the world
no more than I belong to the world.
I am not asking you to remove them from the world,
but to protect them from the evil one.
They do not belong to the world
any more than I belong to the world.
Consecrate them in the truth;
your word is truth.
As you sent me into the world,
I have sent them into the world,
and for their sake I consecrate myself
so that they too may be consecrated in truth."

This is the Gospel of the Lord.

THURSDAY

First Reading   (22:30; 23:6–11)

A reading from the Acts of the Apostles
Now you must bear witness in Rome.

Since the tribune wanted to know what precise charge the
Jews were bringing against Paul, he freed him and gave

orders for a meeting of the chief priests and the entire San-hedrin; then he brought Paul down and stood him in front of them.

Now Paul was well aware that one section was made up of Sadducees and the other of Pharisees, so he called out in the Sanhedrin, "Brothers, I am a Pharisee and the son of Pharisees. It is for our hope in the resurrection of the dead that I am on trial." As soon as he said this a dispute broke out between the Pharisees and Sadducees, and the assembly was split between the two parties. For the Sadducees say there is neither resurrection, nor angel, nor spirit, while the Pharisees accept all three. The shouting grew louder, and some of the scribes from the Pharisees' party stood up and protested strongly, "We find nothing wrong with this man. Suppose a spirit has spoken to him, or an angel?" Feeling was running high, and the tribune, afraid that they would tear Paul to pieces, ordered his troops to go down and haul him out and bring him into the fortress.

Next night, the Lord appeared to him and said, "Courage! You have borne witness for me in Jerusalem, now you must do the same in Rome."

This is the word of the Lord.

Responsorial Psalm (Ps 15:1–2. 5. 7–11. R. v. 1)

Response
Preserve me, God, I take refuge in you.
Or : Alleluia!

1. Preserve me, God, I take refuge in you.
I say to the Lord : "You are my God."
O Lord, it is you who are my portion and cup;
it is you yourself who are my prize. (*R.*)

2. I will bless the Lord who gives me counsel,
who even at night directs my heart.
I keep the Lord ever in my sight :
since he is at my right hand, I shall stand firm. (*R.*)

3. And so my heart rejoices, my soul is glad;
even my body shall rest in safety.
For you will not leave my soul among the dead,
nor let your beloved know decay. (*R.*)

4. You will show me the path of life,
the fullness of joy in your presence,
at your right hand happiness for ever. (*R.*)

Gospel   (17:20–26)

A reading from the holy Gospel according to John
May they be completely one.

Jesus raised his eyes to heaven and said:

"Holy Father,
I pray not only for these,
but for those also
who through their words will believe in me.
May they all be one.
Father, may they be one in us,
as you are in me and I am in you,
so that the world may believe it was you who sent me.
I have given them the glory you gave to me,
that they may be one as we are one.
With me in them and you in me,
may they be so completely one
that the world will realise that it was you who sent me
and that I have loved them as much as you loved me.
Father,
I want those you have given me
to be with me where I am,
so that they may always see the glory
you have given me
because you loved me
before the foundation of the world.

Father, Righteous One,
the world has not known you,
but I have known you,
and these have known
that you have sent me.
I have made your name known to them
and will continue to make it known,
so that the love with which you loved me may be in them,
and so that I may be in them."

This is the Gospel of the Lord.

FRIDAY

First Reading (25:13–21)

A reading from the Acts of the Apostles
A dead man called Jesus whom Paul alleged to be alive.

King Agrippa and Bernice arrived in Caesarea and paid their respects to Festus. Their visit lasted several days, and Festus put Paul's case before the king, "There is a man here" he said "whom Felix left behind in custody, and while I was in Jerusalem the chief priests and elders of the Jews laid information against him, demanding his condemnation. But I told them that Romans are not in the habit of surrendering any man, until the accused confronts his accusers and is given an opportunity to defend himself against the charge. So they came here with me, and I wasted no time but took my seat on the tribunal the very next day and had the man brought in. When confronted with him, his accusers did not charge him with any of the crimes I had expected; but they had some argument or other with him about their own religion and about a dead man called Jesus whom Paul alleged to be alive. Not feeling qualified to deal with questions of this sort, I asked him if he would be willing to go to Jerusalem to be tried there on this issue. But Paul put in an appeal for his case to be reserved for the judgement of the august emperor, so I ordered him to be remanded until I could send him to Caesar."

This is the word of the Lord.

Responsorial Psalm   (Ps 102:1–2. 11–12. 19–20. *R*. v. 19)
Response
The Lord has set his sway in heaven.
Or: Alleluia!

1. My soul, give thanks to the Lord,
all my being, bless his holy name.
My soul, give thanks to the Lord
and never forget all his blessings. (*R*.)

2. For as the heavens are high above the earth
so strong is his love for those who fear him.
As far as the east is from the west
so far does he remove our sins. (*R*.)

3. The Lord has set his sway in heaven
and his kingdom is ruling over all.
Give thanks to the Lord, all his angels,
mighty in power, fulfilling his word. (*R*.)

Alleluia   (Jn 14:26)
Alleluia, alleluia!
The Holy Spirit will teach you everything
and remind you of all I have said to you.
Alleluia!
Alternative Alleluias p. 846.

Gospel   (21:15–19)
A reading from the holy Gospel according to John
Feed my lambs, feed my sheep.

After the meal Jesus said to Simon Peter, "Simon son of John, do you love me more than these others do?" He answered, "Yes Lord, you know I love you." Jesus said to him, "Feed my lambs." A second time he said to him, "Simon son of John, do you love me?" He replied, "Yes, Lord, you know I love you." Jesus said to him, "Look after my sheep." Then he said to him a third time, "Simon son of John, do you love me?" Peter was upset that he asked him the third time, "Do you love me?" and said, "Lord, you know everything; you know I love you." Jesus said to him, "Feed my sheep."

"I tell you most solemnly,
when you were young
you put on your own belt
and walked where you liked;
but when you grow old
you will stretch out your hands,
and somebody else will put a belt round you
and take you where you would rather not go."

In these words he indicated the kind of death by which Peter would give glory to God. After this he said, "Follow me."

This is the Gospel of the Lord.

VIGIL OF PENTECOST
Years 1, 2, 3 (Years A, B, C)
Morning Mass

First Reading   (28:16–20. 30–31)

A reading from the Acts of the Apostles
Paul stayed in Rome, proclaiming the kingdom of God.

On our arrival in Rome Paul was allowed to stay in lodgings of his own with the soldier who guarded him.

After three days he called together the leading Jews. When they had assembled, he said to them, "Brothers, although I have done nothing against our people or the customs of our ancestors, I was arrested in Jerusalem and handed over to the Romans. They examined me and would have set me free, since they found me guilty of nothing involving the death penalty; but the Jews lodged an objection, and I was forced to appeal to Caesar, not that I had any accusation to make against my own nation. That is why I have asked to see you and talk to you, for it is on account of the hope of Israel that I wear this chain."

Paul spent the whole of the two years in his own rented lodging. He welcomed all who came to visit him, proclaiming the kingdom of God and teaching the truth about the Lord Jesus Christ with complete freedom and without hindrance from anyone.

This is the word of the Lord.

Responsorial Psalm   (Ps 10:4–5. 7. *R.* v. 7)

Response
The upright shall see your face, O Lord.
Or: Alleluia!

1. The Lord is in his holy temple,
the Lord, whose throne is in heaven.
His eyes look down on the world;
his gaze tests mortal men. (*R.*)

2. The Lord tests the just and the wicked:
the lover of violence he hates. (*R.*)

3. The Lord is just and loves justice:
the upright shall see his face. (*R.*)

Alleluia   (Col 3:1)

Alleluia, alleluia!
Since you have been brought back to true life with Christ,

you must look for the things that are in heaven where Christ
is,
sitting at God's right hand.
Alleluia!

Alternative Alleluias p. 846.

Gospel (21:20–25)

The end of the holy Gospel according to John
*This disciple is the one who has written these things down, and
we know that his testimony is true.*

Peter turned and saw the disciple Jesus loved following
them – the one who had leaned on his breast at the supper
and had said to him, "Lord, who is it that will betray you?"
Seeing him, Peter said to Jesus, "What about him, Lord?"
Jesus answered, "If I want him to stay behind till I come,
what does it matter to you? You are to follow me." The
rumour then went out among the brothers that this disciple
would not die. Yet Jesus had not said to Peter, "He will not
die," but, "If I want him to stay behind till I come."

This disciple is the one who vouches for these things and
has written them down, and we know that his testimony is
true.

There were many other things that Jesus did; if all were
written down, the world itself, I suppose, would not hold
all the books that would have to be written.

This is the Gospel of the Lord.

Evening Mass

Any of the following readings from the old Testament may be chosen
for Evening Mass on the Vigil of Pentecost.

First Reading (11:1–9)

A reading from the book of Genesis
*It was named Babel because there the language of the whole
earth was confused.*

Throughout the earth men spoke the same language, with the same vocabulary. Now as they moved eastwards they found a plain in the land of Shinar where they settled. They said to one another, "Come, let us make bricks and bake them in the fire." – For stone they used bricks, and for mortar they used bitumen. – "Come," they said "let us build ourselves a town and a tower with its top reaching heaven. Let us make a name for ourselves, so that we may not be scattered about the whole earth."

Now the Lord came down to see the town and the tower that the sons of man had built. "So they are all a single people with a single language!" said the Lord. "This is but the start of their undertakings! There will be nothing too hard for them to do. Come, let us go down and confuse their language on the spot so that they can no longer understand one another." The Lord scattered them thence over the whole face of the earth, and they stopped building the town. It was named Babel therefore, because there the Lord confused the language of the whole earth. It was from there that the Lord scattered them over the whole face of the earth.

This is the word of the Lord.

Alternative First Reading   (19:3–8. 16–20)
A reading from the book of Exodus
The Lord came down on the mountain of Sinai before all the people.

Moses went up to God, and the Lord called to him from the mountain, saying, "Say this to the House of Jacob, declare this to the sons of Israel, 'You yourselves have seen what I did with the Egyptians, how I carried you on eagle's wings and brought you to myself. From this you know that now, if you obey my voice and hold fast to my covenant, you of all the nations shall be my very own for all the earth is mine. I will count you a kingdom of priests, a consecrated nation.' Those are the words you are to speak to the sons of Israel." So Moses went and summoned the elders of the people, putting before them all that the Lord had bidden him. Then all the people answered as one, "All that the Lord has said, we will do."

Now at daybreak on the third day there were peals of thunder on the mountain and lightning flashes, a dense cloud, and a loud trumpet blast, and inside the camp all the people trembled. Then Moses led the people out of the camp to meet God; and they stood at the bottom of the mountain. The mountain of Sinai was entirely wrapped in smoke, because the Lord had descended on it in the form of fire. Like smoke from a furnace the smoke went up, and the whole mountain shook violently. Louder and louder grew the sound of the trumpet. Moses spoke, and God answered him with peals of thunder. The Lord came down on the mountain of Sinai, on the mountain top, and the Lord called Moses to the top of the mountain.

This is the word of the Lord.

Alternative First Reading (37:1–14)

A reading from the prophet Ezekiel
Dry bones, I am going to make the breath enter you, and you will live.

The hand of the Lord was laid on me, and he carried me away by the spirit of the Lord and set me down in the middle of a valley, a valley full of bones. He made me walk up and down among them. There were vast quantities of these bones on the ground the whole length of the valley; and they were quite dried up. He said to me, "Son of man, can these bones live?" I said, "You know, Lord." He said, "Prophesy over these bones. Say, 'Dry bones, hear the word of the Lord. The Lord says this to these bones: I am now going to make the breath enter you, and you will live. I shall put sinews on you, I shall make flesh grow on you, I shall cover you with skin and give you breath, and you will live; and you will learn that I am the Lord.' " I prophesied as I had been ordered. While I was prophesying, there was a noise, a sound of clattering; and the bones joined together. I looked, and saw that they were covered with sinews; flesh was growing on them and skin was covering them, but there was no breath in them. He said to me, "Prophesy to the breath; prophesy, son of man. Say to the breath, 'The Lord says this: Come from the four winds, breath; breathe on these dead; let them live!' " I prophesied as he had ordered me, and the breath entered them; they came to life again and stood up on their feet, a great, an immense army.

Then he said, "Son of man, these bones are the whole House of Israel. They keep saying, 'Our bones are dried up, our hope has gone; we are as good as dead.' So prophesy. Say to them, 'The Lord says this: I am now going to open your graves; I mean to raise you from your graves, my people, and lead you back to the soil of Israel. And you will know that I am the Lord, when I open your graves and raise you from your graves, my people. And I shall put my spirit in you, and you will live, and I shall resettle you on your own soil; and you will know that I, the Lord, have said and done this – it is the Lord who speaks.' "

This is the word of the Lord.

Alternative First Reading   (3:1–5)

A reading from the prophet Joel
Even on the slaves, men and women, will I pour out my Spirit.

Thus says the Lord:

"I will pour out my spirit on all mankind.
Your sons and daughters shall prophesy,
your old men shall dream dreams,
and your young men see visions.

Even on the slaves, men and women,
will I pour out my spirit in those days.
I will display portents in heaven and on earth.
blood and fire and columns of smoke."

The sun will be turned into darkness,
and the moon into blood,
before the day of the Lord dawns,
that great and terrible day.
All who call on the name of the Lord will be saved,
for on Mount Zion there will be some who have escaped,
as the Lord has said,
and in Jerusalem some survivors whom the Lord will call.

This is the word of the Lord.

Responsorial Psalm   (Ps 103:1–2. 24. 27–30. 35. R. v. 30)
Response
Send forth your Spirit, O Lord,
and renew the face of the earth.
Or: Alleluia!

1. Bless the Lord, my soul!
Lord God, how great you are,
clothed in majesty and glory,
wrapped in light as in a robe! (R.)

2. How many are your works, O Lord!
In wisdom you have made them all.
The earth is full of your riches.
Bless the Lord, my soul. (R.)

3. All of these look to you
to give them their food in due season.
You give it, they gather it up:
you open your hand, they have their fill. (R.)

4. You take back your spirit, they die,
returning to the dust from which they came.
You send forth your spirit, they are created;
and you renew the face of the earth. (*R.*)

Second Reading   (8:22–27)

A reading from the letter of St Paul to the Romans
*The Spirit himself expresses our plea in a way that could never
be put into words.*

From the beginning till now the entire creation, as we know,
has been groaning in one great act of giving birth; and not
only creation, but all of us who possess the first-fruits of
the Spirit, we too groan inwardly as we wait for our bodies
to be set free. For we must be content to hope that we shall
be saved – our salvation is not in sight, we should not have
to be hoping for it if it were – but, as I say, we must hope to
be saved since we are not saved yet – it is something we
must wait for with patience.

The Spirit too comes to help us in our weakness. For
when we cannot choose words in order to pray properly, the
Spirit himself expresses our plea in a way that could never
be put into words, and God who knows everything in our
hearts knows perfectly well what he means, and that the
pleas of the saints expressed by the Spirit are according to
the mind of God.

This is the word of the Lord.

Alleluia

Alleluia, alleluia!
Come, Holy Spirit, fill the hearts of your faithful,
and kindle in them the fire of your love.
Alleluia!

Gospel   (7:37–39)

A reading from the holy Gospel according to John
From his breast shall flow fountains of living water.

On the last day and greatest day of the festival, Jesus stood there and cried out:
"If any man is thirsty, let him come to me!
Let the man come and drink who believes in me!"
As scripture says: From his breast shall flow fountains of living water.

He was speaking of the Spirit which those who believed in him were to receive; for there was no Spirit as yet because Jesus had not yet been glorified.

This is the Gospel of the Lord.

PENTECOST SUNDAY
(Whitsunday)

First Reading   (2:1–11)

A reading from the Acts of the Apostles
They were all filled with the Holy Spirit and began to speak.

When Pentecost day came round, the apostles had all met in one room, when suddenly they heard what sounded like a powerful wind from heaven, the noise of which filled the entire house in which they were sitting; and something appeared to them that seemed like tongues of fire; these separated and came to rest on the head of each of them. They were all filled with the Holy Spirit, and began to speak foreign languages as the Spirit gave them the gift of speech.

Now there were devout men living in Jerusalem from every nation under heaven, and at this sound they all assembled, each one bewildered to hear these men speaking his own language. They were amazed and astonished. "Surely" they said "all these men speaking are Galileans? How does it happen that each of us hears them in his own native language? Parthians, Medes and Elamites; people

from Mesopotamia, Judaea and Cappadocia, Pontus and
Asia, Phrygia and Pamphylia, Egypt and the parts of Libya
round Cyrene; as well as visitors from Rome – Jews and
proselytes alike – Cretans and Arabs; we hear them preaching in our own language about the marvels of God."

This is the word of the Lord.

Responsorial Psalm   (Ps 103:1. 24. 29–31. 34. *R.* v. 30)

Response
Send forth your Spirit, O Lord,
and renew the face of the earth.
Or: Alleluia!

1. Bless the Lord, my soul!
Lord God, how great you are,
How many are your works, O Lord!
The earth is full of your riches. (*R.*)

2. You take back your spirit, they die,
returning to the dust from which they came.
You send forth your spirit, they are created;
and you renew the face of the earth. (*R.*)

3. May the glory of the Lord last for ever!
May the Lord rejoice in his works!
May my thoughts be pleasing to him.
I find my joy in the Lord. (*R.*)

Second Reading   (12:3–7. 12–13)

A reading from the first letter of St Paul to the Corinthians
In the one Spirit we were all baptised.

No one can say, "Jesus is Lord" unless he is under the
influence of the Holy Spirit.

There is a variety of gifts but always the same Spirit; there
are all sorts of service to be done, but always to the same

Lord; working in all sorts of different ways in different people, it is the same God who is working in all of them. The particular way in which the Spirit is given to each person is for a good purpose.

Just as a human body, though it is made up of many parts, is a single unit because all these parts, though many, make one body, so it is with Christ. In the one Spirit we were all baptised, Jews as well as Greeks, slaves as well as citizens, and one Spirit was given to us all to drink.

This is the word of the Lord.

SEQUENCE Holy Spirit, Lord of Light.

Alleluia

Alleluia, alleluia!
Come, Holy Spirit, fill the hearts of your faithful,
and kindle in them the fire of your love.
Alleluia!

Gospel   (20:19–23)

A reading from the holy Gospel according to John
As the Father sent me, so am I sending you: receive the Holy Spirit.

In the evening of that same day, the first day of the week, the doors were closed in the room where the disciples were, for fear of the Jews. Jesus came and stood among them. He said to them, "Peace be with you," and showed them his hands and his side. The disciples were filled with joy when they saw the Lord, and he said to them again. "Peace be with you.

"As the Father sent me,
so am I sending you."

After saying this he breathed on them and said:

"Receive the Holy Spirit.
For those whose sins you forgive,
they are forgiven;
for those whose sins you retain,
they are retained."

This is the Gospel of the Lord.

Where Monday or Tuesday after Pentecost is a day on which it is
obligatory or customary for the faithful to attend Mass, the
Mass of Pentecost Sunday may be used, or alternatively the Mass of
the Holy Spirit.

PROPER OF THE SAINTS*

February 2
THE PRESENTATION OF THE LORD
Years 1, 2, 3 (Years A, B, C)

First Reading (3:1–4)

A reading from the prophet Malachi
The Lord you are seeking will suddenly enter his Temple.

The Lord God says this: Look, I am going to send my
messenger to prepare a way before me. And the Lord you
are seeking will suddenly enter his Temple; and the angel
of the covenant whom you are longing for, yes, he is coming, says the Lord of hosts. Who will be able to resist the
day of his coming? Who will remain standing when he appears? For he is like the refiner's fire and the fullers' alkali.
He will take his seat as refiner and purifier; he will purify
the sons of Levi and refine them like gold and silver, and
then they will make the offering to the Lord as it should be
made. The offering of Judah and Jerusalem will then be
welcomed by the Lord as in former days, as in the years of
old.

This is the word of the Lord.

Responsorial Psalm (Ps 23:7–10. R. v. 8)

Response
Who is the king of glory?
It is the Lord.

1. O gates, lift up your heads;
grow higher, ancient doors.
Let him enter, the king of glory! (R.)

*Only Solemnities, which may take the place of the Sunday Mass, for
the time from Advent – Pentecost, are given here.

2. Who is the king of glory?
The Lord, the mighty, the valiant,
the Lord, the valiant in war. (*R.*)

3. O gates, lift high your heads;
grow higher, ancient doors.
Let him enter, the king of glory! (*R.*)

4. Who is he, the king of glory?
He, the Lord of armies,
he is the king of glory. (*R.*)

Second Reading   (2:14–18)

A reading from the letter to the Hebrews
It was essential that he should in this way become completely
like his brothers.

Since all the children share the same blood and flesh, he
too shared equally in it, so that by his death he could take
away all the power of the devil, who had power over
death, and set free all those who had been held in slavery all
their lives by the fear of death. For it was not the angels
that he took to himself; he took to himself descent from
Abraham. It was essential that he should in this way become completely like his brothers so that he could be a
compassionate and trustworthy high priest of God's religion, able to atone for human sins. That is, because he has
himself been through temptation he is able to help others
who are tempted.

This is the word of the Lord.

Alleluia   (Lk 2:32)

Alleluia, alleluia!
The light to enlighten the Gentiles
and give glory to Israel, your people.
Alleluia!

Gospel   (2:22–40)

A reading from the holy Gospel according to Luke

My eyes have seen your salvation.

*When the day came for them to be purified as laid down by the Law of Moses, the parents of Jesus took him up to Jerusalem to present him to the Lord – observing what stands written in the Law of the Lord: Every first-born male must be consecrated to the Lord – and also to offer in sacrifice, in accordance with what is said in the Law of the Lord, a pair of turtle-doves or two young pigeons. Now in Jerusalem there was a man named Simeon. He was an upright and devout man; he looked forward to Israel's comforting and the Holy Spirit rested on him. It had been revealed to him by the Holy Spirit that he would not see death until he had set eyes on the Christ of the Lord. Prompted by the Spirit he came to the Temple; and when the parents brought in the child Jesus to do for him what the Law required, he took him into his arms and blessed God; and he said:

"Now, Master, you can let your servant go in peace,
just as you promised;
because my eyes have seen the salvation
which you have prepared for all the nations to see,
a light to enlighten the pagans
and the glory of your people Israel."*

As the child's father and mother stood there wondering at the things that were being said about him, Simeon blessed them and said to Mary his mother, "You see this child: he is destined for the fall and for the rising of many in Israel, destined to be a sign that is rejected – and a sword will pierce your own soul too – so that the secret thoughts of many may be laid bare."

There was a prophetess also, Anna the daughter of

Shorter Form, verses 2:22–23. Read between.

Phanuel, of the tribe of Asher. She was well on in years. Her days of girlhood over, she had been married for seven years before becoming a widow. She was now eighty-four years old and never left the Temple, serving God night and day with fasting and prayer. She came by just at that moment and began to praise God; and she spoke of the child to all who looked forward to the deliverance of Jerusalem.

When they had done everything the Law of the Lord required, they went back to Galilee, to their own town of Nazareth. Meanwhile the child grew to maturity, and he was filled with wisdom; and God's favour was with him.

This is the Gospel of the Lord.

December 8
SOLEMNITY OF THE IMMACULATE CONCEPTION OF THE BLESSED VIRGIN MARY
Years 1, 2, 3 (Years A, B, C)

First Reading   (3:9–15.20)

A reading from the book of Genesis
I will make you enemies of each other: your offspring and her offspring.

After Adam had eaten of the tree, the Lord God called to him. "Where are you?" he asked. "I heard the sound of you in the garden," he replied. "I was afraid because I was naked, so I hid." "Who told you that you were naked?" he asked. "Have you been eating of the tree I forbade you to eat?" The man replied, "It was the woman you put with me; she gave me the fruit, and I ate it." Then the Lord God asked the woman, "What is this you have done?" The woman replied, "The serpent tempted me and I ate."

Then the Lord God said to the serpent, "Because you have done this,

"Be accursed beyond all cattle,
all wild beasts.
You shall crawl on your belly and eat dust
every day of your life.

I will make you enemies of each other:
you and the woman,
your offspring and her offspring.
It will crush your head
and you will strike its heel."

The man named his wife "Eve" because she was the mother of all those who live.

This is the word of the Lord.

Responsorial Psalm (Ps 97:1–4. *R.* v. 1)

Response
Sing a new song to the Lord
for he has worked wonders.

1. Sing a new song to the Lord
for he has worked wonders.
His right hand and his holy arm
have brought salvation. (*R.*)

2. The Lord has made known his salvation;
has shown his justice to the nations.
He has remembered his truth and love
for the house of Israel. (*R.*)

3. All the ends of the earth have seen
the salvation of our God.
Shout to the Lord all the earth,
ring out your joy. (*R.*)

Second Reading (1:3–6. 11–12)

A reading from the letter of St Paul to the Ephesians
Before the world was made, God chose us in Christ.

Blessed be God the Father of our Lord Jesus Christ,
who has blessed us with all the spiritual blessings of heaven
  in Christ.

Before the world was made, he chose us, chose us in Christ,
to be holy and spotless, and to live through love in his
    presence,
determining that we should become his adopted sons,
    through Jesus Christ
for his own kind purposes,
to make us praise the glory of his grace,
his free gift to us in the Beloved.
And it is in him that we were claimed as God's own,
chosen from the beginning,
under the predetermined plan of the one who guides all
    things
as he decides by his own will;
chosen to be,
for his greater glory,
the people who would put their hopes in Christ before he
    came.

This is the word of the Lord.

Alleluia   (Lk 1:28)
Alleluia, alleluia!
Hail, Mary, full of grace; the Lord is with thee!
Blessed art though among women.
Alleluia!

Gospel   (1:26–38)
A reading from the holy Gospel according to Luke
Rejoice, so highly favoured! The Lord is with you.

The angel Gabriel was sent by God to a town in Galilee
called Nazareth, to a virgin betrothed to a man named
Joseph, of the House of David; and the virgin's name was
Mary. He went in and said to her, "Rejoice, so highly fav-

oured! The Lord is with you." She was deeply disturbed by these words and asked herself what this greeting could mean, but the angel said to her, "Mary, do not be afraid; you have won God's favour. Listen! You are to conceive and bear a son, and you must name him Jesus. He will be great and will be called Son of the Most High. The Lord God will give him the throne of his ancestor David; he will rule over the House of Jacob for ever and his reign will have no end." Mary said to the angel, "But how can this come about, since I am a virgin?" "The Holy Spirit will come upon you" the angel answered "and the power of the Most High will cover you with its shadow. And so the child will be holy and will be called Son of God. Know this too: your kinswoman Elizabeth has, in her old age, herself conceived a son, and she whom people called barren is now in her sixth month, for nothing is impossible to God." "I am the handmaid of the Lord," said Mary "let what you have said be done to me." And the angel left her.

This is the Gospel of the Lord.

ALLELUIA AND ACCLAMATIONS

The following Alleluia and Acclamation verses may be used *ad libitum* for the periods noted.

FOR WEEKDAYS OF ADVENT UNTIL 16 DECEMBER

(Ps 79 : 4)

1. Alleluia, alleluia!
God of hosts, bring us back;
let your face shine on us and we shall be saved.
Alleluia!

(Ps 84 : 8)

2. Alleluia, alleluia!
Let us see, O Lord, your mercy
and give us your saving help.
Alleluia!

(Is 33 : 22)

3. Alleluia, alleluia!
The Lord is our judge, the Lord our lawgiver,
the Lord our king and our saviour.
Alleluia!

(Is 40 : 9–10)

4. Alleluia, alleluia!
Shout with a loud voice, joyful messenger to Jerusalem.
Here is the Lord God coming with power.
Alleluia!

(Is 45 : 8)

5. Alleluia, Alleluia!
Send victory like a dew, you heavens,
and let the clouds rain it down.

Let the earth open
and bring forth the saviour.
Alleluia!

(Is 55 : 6)

6. Alleluia, alleluia!
Seek the Lord while he is still to be found,
call to him while he is still near.
Alleluia!

(Lk 3 : 4. 6)

7. Alleluia, alleluia!
Prepare a way for the Lord,
make his paths straight.
And all mankind shall see the salvation of God.
Alleluia!

8. Alleluia, alleluia!
Come Lord! Do not delay.
Forgive the sins of your people.
Alleluia!

9. Alleluia, alleluia!
Behold, our Lord will come with power
and will enlighten the eyes of his servants.
Alleluia!

10. Alleluia, alleluia!
Come to us, Lord, with your peace
that we may rejoice in your presence with sincerity of heart.
Alleluia!

11. Alleluia, alleluia!
See, the king, the Lord of the world, will come.
He will free us from the yoke of our bondage.
Alleluia!

12. Alleluia, alleluia!
The day of the Lord is near;
Look, he comes to save us.
Alleluia!

13. Alleluia, alleluia!
The Lord will come, go out to meet him.
Great is his beginning and his reign will have no end.
Alleluia!

14. Alleluia, alleluia!
Look, the Lord will come to save his people.
Blessed those who are ready to meet him.
Alleluia!

17–24 DECEMBER*

1. Alleluia, alleluia!
Wisdom of the Most High, ordering all things with strength and gentleness, come and teach us the way of truth.
Alleluia!

2. Alleluia, alleluia!
Ruler of the House of Israel, who gave the law to Moses on Sinai, come and save us with outstretched arm.
Alleluia!

3. Alleluia, alleluia!
Root of Jesse, set up as a sign to the peoples, come to save us and delay no more.
Alleluia!

4. Alleluia, alleluia!
Key of David, who open the gates of the eternal kingdom, come to liberate from prison the captive who lives in darkness.
Alleluia!

*Except on 4th Sunday of Advent and at Evening Mass, 24 December.

5. Alleluia, alleluia!

Morning star, radiance of eternal light, sun of justice, come and enlighten those who live in darkness and in the shadow of death. Alleluia!

6. Alleluia, alleluia!

King of the peoples and corner-stone of the Church, come and save man whom you made from the dust of the earth. Alleluia!

7. Alleluia, alleluia!

Emmanuel, our king and lawgiver, come and save us, Lord our God. Alleluia!

BETWEEN CHRISTMAS AND EPIPHANY

(Jn 1:14. 12)

1. Alleluia, alleluia!
The Word became flesh, and dwelt among us.
To all who received him he gave power to become children
    of God.
Alleluia!

2. Alleluia, alleluia!
At various times in the past
and in various different ways,
God spoke to our ancestors through the prophets;
but in our own time, the last days,
he has spoken to us through his Son.
Alleluia!

3. Alleluia, alleluia!
A hallowed day has dawned upon us.
Come, you nations, worship the Lord,
for today a great light has shone down upon the earth.
Alleluia!

ON THE WEEKDAYS [IF ANY] BETWEEN THE EPIPHANY AND THE 1st SUNDAY AFTER THE EPIPHANY

(Mt 4:16)

1. Alleluia, alleluia!
The people that lived in darkness
has seen a great light;
on those who dwell in the land and shadow of death
a light has dawned.
Alleluia!

(Mt 4:23)

2. Alleluia, alleluia!
Jesus proclaimed the Good News of the kingdom
and cured all kinds of diseases among the people.
Alleluia!

(Lk 4:18–19)

3. Alleluia, alleluia!
The Lord has sent me to bring the Good News to the poor,
to proclaim liberty to the captives.
Alleluia!

(Lk 7:16)

4. Alleluia, alleluia!
A great prophet has appeared among us;
God has visited his people.
Alleluia!

(1 Tim 3:16)

5. Alleluia, alleluia!
Glory be to you, O Christ,
proclaimed to the pagans;
glory be to you, O Christ,
believed in by the world.
Alleluia!

FOR THE DAYS OF LENT

During Lent, both before and after the Acclamation, one or other of the following phrases may be used:

Praise to you, O Christ, king of eternal glory;
Praise and honour to you, Lord Jesus;
Glory and praise to you, O Christ;
Glory to you, O Christ, you are the Word of God.

Other similar phrases may be used.

(Ps 50:12. 14)

1. A pure heart create for me, O God,
and give me again the joy of your help.

(Ps 94:8)

2. Harden not your hearts today,
but listen to the voice of the Lord.

(Ps 129:5. 7)

3. My soul is waiting for the Lord,
I count on his word,
because with the Lord there is mercy
and fullness of redemption.

(Ez 18:31)

4. Shake off all your sins – it is the Lord who speaks – and make yourselves a new heart and a new spirit.

(Ez 33:11)

5. I take pleasure, not in the death of a wicked man – it is the Lord who speaks – but in the turning back of a wicked man who changes his ways to win life.

6. Now, now – it is the Lord who speaks –
come back to me with all your heart,
for I am all tenderness and compassion.

(Amos 5 : 14)

7. Seek good and not evil so that you may live, and that the Lord God of hosts may really be with you.

(Mt 4 : 4)

8. Man does not live on bread alone, but on every word that comes from the mouth of God.

(Mt 4 : 17)

9. Repent, says the Lord, for the kingdom of heaven is close at hand.

(Lk 8 : 15)

10. Blessed are those who, with a noble and generous heart, take the word of God to themselves and yield a harvest through their perseverance.

(Lk 15 : 18)

11. I will leave this place and go to my father and say: "Father, I have sinned against heaven and against you."

(Jn 3 : 16)

12. God loved the world so much that he gave his only Son; everyone who believes in him has eternal life.

(Jn 6 :64. 69)

13. Your words are spirit, Lord, and they are life; you have the message of eternal life.

(Jn 8 : 12)

14. I am the light of the world, says the Lord, anyone who follows me will have the light of life.

(Jn 11:25. 26)

15. I am the resurrection and the life, says the Lord, whoever believes in me will never die.

(2 Cor 6:2)

16. Now is the favourable time;
this is the day of salvation.

17. The seed is the word of God, Christ the sower; whoever finds this seed will remain for ever.

FOR WEEKDAYS OF PASCHAL TIME BEFORE THE ASCENSION

(Lk 24:25. 26)

1. Alleluia, alleluia!
It was ordained that the Christ should suffer
and rise from the dead,
and so enter into his glory.
Alleluia!

(Jn 10:14)

2. Alleluia, alleluia!
I am the good shepherd, says the Lord,
I know my sheep and my own know me.
Alleluia!

(Jn 10:27)

3. Alleluia, alleluia!
The sheep that belong to me listen to my voice,
says the Lord;
I know them and they follow me.
Alleluia!

(Jn 20:29)

4. Alleluia, alleluia!
You believe, Thomas, because you can see me.
Happy are those who have not seen and yet believe.
Alleluia!

(Rom 6:9)

5. Alleluia, alleluia!
Christ, having been raised from the dead,
will never die again.
Death has no power over him any more.
Alleluia!

(Col 3:1)

6. Alleluia, alleluia!
Since you have been brought back to true life with Christ,
you must look for the things that are in heaven where Christ
    is,
sitting at God's right hand.
Alleluia!

(Rev 1:5)

7. Alleluia, alleluia!
You ,O Christ, are the faithful witness,
the First-born from the dead;
you have loved us and have washed away our sins
with your blood.
Alleluia!

8. Alleluia, alleluia!
Christ has risen and shone upon us
whom he redeemed with his blood.
Alleluia!

9. Alleluia, alleluia!
The Lord, who hung for us upon the tree,
has risen from the tomb.
Alleluia!

10. Alleluia, alleluia!
Christ has risen : he who created all things.
and has granted his mercy to men.
Alleluia!

11. Alleluia, alleluia!
We know that Christ is truly risen from the dead;
have mercy on us, triumphant King.
Alleluia!

FOR WEEKDAYS OF PASCHAL TIME AFTER THE ASCENSION

(Mt 28 : 19.20)

1. Alleluia, alleluia!
Go, make disciples of all the nations:
I am with you always; yes, to the end of time.
Alleluia!

(Jn 14 : 16)

2. Alleluia, alleluia!
I shall ask the Father,
and he will give you another Advocate
to be with you for ever.
Alleluia!

(Jn 14 : 18)

3. Alleluia, alleluia!
I will not leave you orphans, says the Lord;
I go, but I will come back to you,
and your hearts will be full of joy.
Alleluia!

(Jn 14 : 26)

4. Alleluia, alleluia!
The Holy Spirit will teach you everything
and remind you of all I have said to you.
Alleluia!

(Jn 16:7. 13)

5. Alleluia, alleluia!
I will send you the Spirit of truth, says the Lord;
he will lead you to the complete truth.
Alleluia!

(Jn 16 : 28)

6. Alleluia, alleluia!
I came from the Father
and have come into the world,
and now I leave the world
to go to the Father.
Alleluia!

(Col 3 : 1)

7. Alleluia, alleluia!
Since you have been brought back to true life with Christ,
you must look for the things that are in heaven where Christ
    is,
sitting at God's right hand.
Alleluia!

FOR THE WEEKDAYS OF THE TIME
THROUGHOUT THE YEAR

(1 Sam 3 : 9; Jn 6 : 68)

1. Alleluia, alleluia!
Speak, Lord, your servant is listening:
you have the message of eternal life.
Alleluia!

(Ps 18 : 9)

2. Alleluia, alleluia!
Your words gladden the heart, O Lord,
they give light to the eyes.
Alleluia!

(Ps 24 : 4. 5)

3. Alleluia, alleluia!
Teach me your paths, my God,
make me walk in your truth.
Alleluia!

(Ps 26 : 11)

4. Alleluia, alleluia!
Instruct me, Lord, in your way;
on an even path lead me.
Alleluia!

(Ps 94 : 8)

5. Alleluia, alleluia!
Harden not your hearts today,
but listen to the voice of the Lord.
Alleluia!

(Ps 110 :7. 8)

6. Alleluia, alleluia!
Your precepts, O Lord, are all of them sure;
they stand firm for ever and ever,
Alleluia!

(Ps 118 : 18)

7. Alleluia, alleluia!
Open my eyes, O Lord, that I may consider
the wonders of your law.
Alleluia!

(Ps 118 : 27)

8. Alleluia, alleluia!
Make me grasp the way of your precepts,
and I will muse on your wonders.
Alleluia!

(Ps 118 : 34)

9. Alleluia, alleluia!
Train me, Lord, to observe your law,
to keep it with my heart.
Alleluia!

(Ps 118 : 29.35)

10. Alleluia, alleluia!
Bend my heart to your will, O Lord,

and teach me your law.
Alleluia!

(Ps 118 : 88)

11. Alleluia, alleluia!
Because of your love give me life,
and I will do your will.
Alleluia!

(Ps 118 : 105)

12. Alleluia, alleluia!
Your word is a lamp for my steps
and a light for my path.
Alleluia!

(Ps 118 : 135)

13. Alleluia! alleluia!
Let your face shine on your servant,
and teach me your decrees.
Alleluia!

(Ps 129 : 5)

14. Alleluia, alleluia!
My soul is waiting for the Lord,
I count on his word.
Alleluia!

(Ps 144 : 13)

15. Alleluia, alleluia!
The Lord is faithful in all his words
and loving in all his deeds.
Alleluia!

(Ps 147 : 12.15)

16. Alleluia, alleluia!
O praise the Lord, Jerusalem!
He sends out his word to the earth.
Alleluia!

(Mt 4:4)

17. Alleluia, alleluia!
Man does not live on bread alone,
but on every word that comes from the mouth of God.
Alleluia!

(Mt 11:25)

18. Alleluia, alleluia!
Blessed are you, Father,
Lord of Heaven and earth,
for revealing the mysteries of the kingdom
to mere children.
Alleluia!

(Lk 8:15)

19. Alleluia, alleluia!
Blessed are those who,
with a noble and generous heart,
take the word of God to themselves
and yield a harvest through their perseverance.
Alleluia!

(Jn 6:63.68)

20. Alleluia, alleluia!
Your words are spirit, Lord,
and they are life:
you have the message of eternal life.
Alleluia!

(Jn 8:12)

21. Alleluia, alleluia!
I am the light of the world, says the Lord,
anyone who follows me
will have the light of life.
Alleluia!

(Jn 10:27)

22. Alleluia, alleluia!
The sheep that belong to me listen to my voice,
says the Lord,
I know them and they follow me.
Alleluia!

(Jn 14:5)

23. Alleluia, alleluia!
I am the Way, the Truth and the Life, says the Lord;
no one can come to the Father except through me.
Alleluia!

(Jn 14:23)

24. Alleluia, alleluia!
If anyone loves me he will keep my word,
and my Father will love him,
and we shall come to him.
Alleluia!

(Jn 15:15)

25. Alleluia, alleluia!
I call you friends, says the Lord,
because I have made known to you
everything I have learnt from my Father.
Alleluia!

(Jn 17:17)

26. Alleluia, alleluia!
Your word is truth, O Lord,
consecrate us in the truth.
Alleluia!

(Acts 16:14)

27. Alleluia, alleluia!
Open our heart, O Lord,
to accept the words of your Son.
Alleluia!

(2 Cor 5 : 19)

28. Alleluia, alleluia!
God in Christ was reconciling the world to himself,
and he has entrusted to us the news that they are reconciled.
Alleluia!

(Eph 1 : 17.18)

29. Alleluia, alleluia!
May the Father of our Lord Jesus Christ
enlighten the eyes of our mind,
so that we can see what hope his call holds for us.
Alleluia!

(Phil 2 : 15–16)

30. Alleluia, alleluia!
You will shine in the world like bright stars
because you are offering it the word of life.
Alleluia!

(Col 3:16. 17)

31. Alleluia, alleluia!
Let the message of Christ, in all its richness,
find a home with you;
through him give thanks to God the Father.
Alleluia!

(I Thess 2 : 13)

32. Alleluia, alleluia!
Accept God's message for what it really is:
God's message, and not some human thinking.
Alleluia!

(2 Thess 2 : 14)

33. Alleluia, alleluia!
Through the Good News God called us
to share the glory of our Lord Jesus Christ.
Alleluia!

(2 Tim 1 : 10)

34. Alleluia, alleluia!
Our Saviour Christ Jesus abolished death,
and he has proclaimed life through the Good News.
Alleluia!

(Heb 4 : 12)

35. Alleluia, alleluia!
The word of God is something alive and active;
it can judge secret emotions and thoughts.
Alleluia!

(James 1 : 18)

36. Alleluia, alleluia!
By his own choice the Father made us his children
by the message of the truth,
so that we should be a sort of first-fruits
of all that he created.
Alleluia!

(James 1 : 21)

37. Alleluia, alleluia!
Accept and submit to the word
which has been planted in you
and can save your souls.
Alleluia!

(1 Peter 1 : 25)

38. Alleluia, alleluia!
The word of the Lord remains for ever:
What is this word?
It is the Good News that has been brought to you.
Alleluia!

(1 Jn 2 : 5)

39. Alleluia, alleluia!
When anyone obeys what Christ has said,
God's love comes to perfection in him.
Alleluia!

FOR THE SUNDAYS OF THE YEAR

(1 Sam 3:9; Jn 6:68)

1. Alleluia, alleluia!
Speak, Lord, your servant is listening:
you have the message of eternal life. Alleluia!

(Mt 11:25)

2. Alleluia, alleluia!
Blessed are you, Father,
Lord of heaven and earth,
for revealing the mysteries of the kingdom
to mere children. Alleluia!

(Lk 19:38)

3. Alleluia, alleluia!
Blessings on the King who comes,
in the name of the Lord!
Peace in heaven
and glory in the highest heavens! Alleluia!

(Jn 1:12.14)

4. Alleluia, alleluia!
The Word was made flesh and lived among us;
to all who did accept him
he gave power to become children of God.
Alleluia!

(Jn 6:63. 68)

5. Alleluia, alleluia!
Your words are spirit, Lord,
and they are life:
you have the message of eternal life. Alleluia!

(Jn 8:12)

6. Alleluia, alleluia!
I am the light of the world, says the Lord,
anyone who follows me
will have the light of life. Alleluia!

(Jn 10:27)

7. Alleluia, alleluia!
The sheep that belong to me listen to my voice,
says the Lord,
I know them and they follow me. Alleluia!

(Jn 14:5)

8. Alleluia, alleluia!
I am the Way, the Truth and the Life, says the Lord;
no one can come to the Father except through me. Alleluia!

(Jn 14:23)

9. Alleluia, alleluia!
If anyone loves me he will keep my word,
and my Father will love him,
and we shall come to him. Alleluia!

(Jn 15:15)

10. Alleluia, alleluia!
I call you friends, says the Lord,
because I have made known to you
everything I have learnt from my Father. Alleluia!

(Jn 17:17)

11. Alleluia, alleluia!
Your word is truth, O Lord,
consecrate us in the truth. Alleluia!

(Acts 16:14)

12. Alleluia, alleluia!
Open our heart, O Lord,
to accept the words of your Son. Alleluia!

(Eph 1:17. 18)

13. Alleluia, alleluia!
May the Father of our Lord Jesus Christ
enlighten the eyes of our mind,
so that we can see what hope his call holds for us.
Alleluia!

THE ORDER OF MASS

The Introductory Rites

The priest and the ministers go to the altar and the entrance song is sung. When the entrance song is ended the priest and the faithful cross themselves.

Celebrant. In the name of the Father, and of the Son, and of the Holy Spirit.
People. **Amen.**
C. The Lord be with you.
P. **And also with you.**

Other forms of greeting
2. *C.* The grace of our Lord Jesus Christ and the love of God and the fellowship of the Holy Spirit be with you all.

   P. **And also with you.**
or
3. *C.* The grace and peace of God our Father and the Lord Jesus Christ be with you.

   P. **Blessed be God, the Father of our Lord Jesus Christ.**
or
   P. **And also with you.**

The Penitential Rite
C. My brothers and sisters,* to prepare ourselves to celebrate the sacred mysteries, let us call to mind our sins.
After a brief silence all say:
All. **I confess to almighty God,**
   and to you, my brothers and sisters,
   that I have sinned through my own fault
   (*All strike their breast*)

---

*Other words, such as "my dear people, friends, dearly beloved, brethren", may be used here and in similar places in the liturgy.

      in my thoughts and in my words,
      in what I have done,
      and in what I have failed to do;
      and I ask blessed Mary, ever virgin,
      all the angels and saints,
      and you, my brothers and sisters,
      to pray for me to the Lord our God.

The priest says the absolution

Other forms of the Penitential Rite

2. *C.* My brothers and sisters, to prepare ourselves to celebrate the sacred mysteries, let us call to mind our sins.

After a brief silence, the celebrant says:

C. Lord, we have sinned against you:
     Lord, have mercy.

P. **Lord, have mercy.**

C. Lord, show us your mercy and love.

P. **And grant us your salvation.**

The priest says the absolution.

or

3. *C.* My brothers and sisters, to prepare ourselves to celebrate the sacred mysteries, let us call to mind our sins.

After a brief silence, the celebrant says:

C. You were sent to heal the contrite:
     Lord, have mercy.

P. **Lord, have mercy.**

C. You came to call sinners:
     Christ, have mercy.

P. **Christ, have mercy.**

C. You plead for us at the right hand of the Father:
     Lord, have mercy.

P. **Lord, have mercy.**

The priest says the absolution.

The absolution

C. May almighty God have mercy on us,
         forgive us our sins,
         and bring us to everlasting life.

P. **Amen.**

The following is not said if it has already been incorporated in the penitential rite

C. Lord, have mercy.

P. **Lord, have mercy.**

C. Christ, have mercy.

P. **Christ, have mercy.**

C. Lord, have mercy.

P. **Lord, have mercy.**

The Gloria

(When it is prescribed. This may be said or sung.)

C. Glory be to God on high,

All. **And on earth peace to men who are God's friends.**
           We praise thee.
           We bless thee.
           We adore thee.
           We glorify thee.
           We give thee thanks for thy great glory.
           Lord God, heavenly King, God the almighty Father.
           Lord Jesus Christ, only-begotten Son.
           Lord God, Lamb of God, Son of the Father.
           Thou who takest away the sins of the world,
           have mercy on us.
           Thou who takest away the sins of the world,
           receive our prayer.
           Thou who art seated at the right hand of the Father,
           have mercy on us.
           For thou alone art the Holy One.
           Thou alone art the Lord.
           Thou alone art the Most High, Jesus Christ.

With the Holy Spirit; in the glory of God the Father.
    Amen.

C. Let us pray.

All pray silently with the priest for a while. Then the priest says the opening prayer (collect), to which the people respond:

P. **Amen.**

THE LITURGY OF THE WORD

First Reading

At the end of the first reading:

Reader. This is the Word of the Lord.

All.   **Thanks be to God.**

Responsorial Psalm

The Cantor sings or recites the psalm, and the people make the response (see Proper of the Mass for the Day).

Second Reading

At the end of the Second Reading:

Reader. This is the Word of the Lord.

All.   **Thanks be to God.**

Alleluia or Acclamation

The Alleluia or another chant follows (see Proper of the Mass or the Day). The people sing or say this chant.

The Gospel

C. The Lord be with you.

P. **And also with you.**

C. A reading from the holy gospel according to N.

P. **Glory to you, Lord.**

At the end of the Gospel:

C. This is the gospel of the Lord.

P. **Praise to you, Lord Jesus Christ.**

Homily

Creed

C. I believe in one God,

All. The almighty Father, maker of heaven and earth,
Maker of all things, visible and invisible.
I believe in one Lord, Jesus Christ,
The only-begotten Son of God,
Born of the Father before time began,
God from God, Light from Light, true God from true God;
Begotten, not made, one in substance with the Father;
And through him all things were made.
For us men and for our salvation he came down from heaven,

(All bow up to the words 'made man'.)

Was incarnate of the virgin Mary by the power of the Holy Spirit,
and was made man.
For our sake, too, under Pontius Pilate, he was crucified, suffered death, and was buried.
The third day he rose from the dead, as the scriptures had foretold.
He ascended to heaven, where he is seated at the right hand of the Father.
He will come again in glory to judge the living and the dead, and his kingdom will have no end.
I believe in the Holy Spirit, the Lord, the giver of life, who proceeds from the Father and the Son.
Together with the Father and the Son he is adored and glorified;
He it was who spoke through the prophets.
I believe in one, holy, catholic, and apostolic church.
I profess one baptism for the remission of sins.
And I look forward to the resurrection of the dead, and the life of the world to come. Amen.

Then follows
The prayer of the faithful
(*The prayer begins with an invitation, followed by a series of petitions to which the people answer* **Lord, graciously hear us,** *and concludes with a prayer by the celebrant to which the people answer* **Amen.**)

THE LITURGY OF THE EUCHARIST

The offering
During the offertory, the people may sing an offertory song, while the priest says the following quietly. If no song is sung then the people may make the responses given here to the prayer of offering.

C. Blessed are you, Lord, God of all creation.
     Through your goodness we have this bread to offer,
     which earth has given and human hands have made.
     It will become for us the bread of life.

P. **Blessed be God for ever.**

C. By the mystery of this water and wine
     may we come to share in the divinity of Christ,
     who humbled himself to share in our humanity.

     Blessed are you, Lord, God of all creation.
     Through your goodness we have this wine to offer,
     fruit of the vine and work of human hands.
     It will become our spiritual drink.

P. **Blessed be God for ever.**

C. Lord God, we ask you to receive us
     and be pleased with the sacrifice we offer you
     with humble and contrite hearts.

The priest washes his hands, saying quietly:

C. Lord, wash away my iniquity;
     cleanse me from my sin.

Pray, brethren, that our sacrifice
may be acceptable to God, the almighty Father.
P. **May the Lord accept the sacrifice at your hands**
for the praise and glory of his name,
for our good, and the good of all his Church.
The priest says or sings the prayer over the gifts.
P. **Amen.**

The Eucharistic Prayer
C. The Lord be with you.
P. **And also with you.**
C. Let us lift up our hearts.
P. **We have raised them up to the Lord.**
C. Let us give thanks to the Lord our God.
P. **It is right and fitting.**

The Preface
The celebrant continues alone. At the end of the Preface:
All. **Holy, holy, holy, Lord God of Hosts.**
Thy glory fills all heaven and earth.
Hosanna in the highest.
Blessed is he who comes in the name of the Lord.
Hosanna in the highest.

Eucharistic Prayer I

(*The passages within the brackets may be omitted if the celebrant wishes.*)

The celebrant continues:
We come to you, Father,
with praise and thanksgiving,
through Jesus Christ your Son.
Through him we ask you to accept and bless
these gifts we offer you in sacrifice.

We offer them for your holy catholic Church,

watch over it, Lord, and guide it;
grant it peace and unity throughout the world.
We offer them for N. our Pope,
for N. our bishop,
and for all who hold and teach the catholic faith
that comes to us from the apostles.

Remember, Lord, your people,
especially those for whom we now pray, N. and N.
Remember all of us gathered here before you.
You know how firmly we believe in you
and dedicate ourselves to you.
We offer you this sacrifice of praise
for ourselves and those who are dear to us.
We pray to you, our living and true God,
for our well-being and redemption.

In union with the whole Church
we honour Mary,
the ever-virgin mother of Jesus Christ our Lord and God.
We honour Joseph, her husband,
the apostles and martyrs
Peter and Paul, Andrew,
(James, John, Thomas,
James, Philip,
Bartholomew, Matthew, Simon and Jude;
we honour Linus, Cletus, Clement, Sixtus,
Cornelius, Cyprian, Lawrence, Chrysogonus,
John and Paul, Cosmas and Damian)
and all the saints.
May their merits and prayers
gain us your constant help and protection.
(Through Christ our Lord. Amen.)

Father, accept this offering
from your whole family.

Grant us your peace in this life,
save us from final damnation,
and count us among those you have chosen.
(Through Christ our Lord. Amen.)

Bless and approve our offering;
make it acceptable to you,
an offering in spirit and in truth.
Let it become for us
the body and blood of Jesus Christ,
your only Son, our Lord.

The day before he suffered
he took bread in his sacred hands
and looking up to heaven,
to you, his almighty Father,
he gave you thanks and praise.
He broke the bread,
gave it to his disciples, and said:

Take this, all of you, and eat it:
this is my body which will be given up for you.

When supper was ended,
he took the cup.
Again he gave you thanks and praise,
gave the cup to his disciples, and said:

Take this, all of you, and drink from it:
this is the cup of my blood,
the blood of the new and everlasting covenant.
It will be shed for you and for all men
so that sins may be forgiven.
Do this in memory of me.

C. Let us proclaim the mystery of faith:

Memorial acclamation of the people
P. **1. Christ has died,**
      Christ is risen,
      Christ will come again.

Alternative acclamations
P. **2. Dying you destroyed our death,**
      rising you restored our life.
      Lord Jesus, come in glory.

    3. When we eat this bread and drink this cup,
      we proclaim your death, Lord Jesus,
      until you come in glory.

    4. Lord, by your cross and resurrection
      you have set us free.
      You are the Saviour of the world.

Father, we celebrate the memory of Christ, your Son.
We, your people and your ministers,
recall his passion,
his resurrection from the dead,
and his ascension into glory;
and from the many gifts you have given us
we offer to you, God of glory and majesty,
this holy and perfect sacrifice:
the bread of life
and the cup of eternal salvation.

Look with favour on these offerings
and accept them as once you accepted
the gifts of your servant Abel,
the sacrifice of Abraham, our father in faith,

and the bread and wine offered by your priest Melchisedech.
Almighty God,
we pray that your angel may take this sacrifice
to your altar in heaven.
Then, as we receive from this altar
the sacred body and blood of your Son,
let us be filled with every grace and blessing.
(Through Christ our Lord. Amen.)

Remember, Lord, those who have died
and have gone before us marked with the sign of faith,
especially those for whom we now pray, N. and N.
May these, and all who sleep in Christ,
find in your presence
light, happiness, and peace.
(Through Christ our Lord. Amen.)

For ourselves, too, we ask
some share in the fellowship of your apostles and
    martyrs,
with John the Baptist, Stephen, Matthias, Barnabas,
(Ignatius, Alexander, Marcellinus, Peter,
Felicity, Perpetua, Agatha, Lucy,
Agnes, Cecilia, Anastasia)
and all the saints.
Though we are sinners,
we trust in your mercy and love.
Do not consider what we truly deserve,
but grant us your forgiveness.

Through Christ our Lord
you give us all these gifts.
You fill them with life and goodness,
you bless them and make them holy.

Through him,
with him,
in him,
in the unity of the Holy Spirit,
all glory and honour is yours,
almighty Father,
for ever and ever.

P. **Amen.**

Continue on p. 878

Eucharistic Prayer II

C. Father, it is our duty and our salvation,
      always and everywhere
      to give you thanks
      through your beloved Son, Jesus Christ.
      He is the Word through whom you made the universe,
      the Saviour you sent to redeem us.
      By the power of the Holy Spirit
      he took flesh and was born of the Virgin Mary.
      For our sake he opened his arms on the cross;
      he put an end to death
      and revealed the resurrection.
      In this he fulfilled your will
      and won for you a holy people.
      And so we join the angels and the saints
      in proclaiming your glory
      as we sing (say):

First acclamation of the people
All. **Holy, holy, holy . . .**

C. Lord, you are holy indeed,
      the fountain of all holiness.

Let your Spirit come upon these gifts to make them
   holy,
so that they may become for us
the body and blood of our Lord, Jesus Christ.

Before he was given up to death,
a death he freely accepted,
he took bread and gave you thanks.
He broke the bread,
gave it to his disciples, and said:
Take this, all of you, and eat it:
this is my body which will be given up for you.

When supper was ended, he took the cup.
Again he gave you thanks and praise,
gave the cup to his disciples, and said:

Take this, all of you, and drink from it:
this is the cup of my blood,
the blood of the new and everlasting covenant.
It will be shed for you and for all men
so that sins may be forgiven.
Do this in memory of me.

C. Let us proclaim the mystery of faith:

Memorial acclamation of the people
P. **1. Christ has died,**
      Christ is risen,
      Christ will come again.

Alternative acclamations
P. **2. Dying you destroyed our death,**
      rising you restored our life.
      Lord Jesus, come in glory.

3. **When we eat this bread and drink this cup,**
   we proclaim your death, Lord Jesus,
   until you come in glory.

4. **Lord, by your cross and resurrection**
   you have set us free.
   You are the Saviour of the world.

C. In memory of his death and resurrection,
   we offer you, Father, this life-giving bread,
   this saving cup.
   We thank you for counting us worthy
   to stand in your presence and serve you.

   May all of us who share in the body and blood of Christ
   be brought together in unity by the Holy Spirit.

   Lord, remember your Church throughout the world;
   make us grow in love,
   together with N. our Pope,
   N. our bishop, and all the clergy.

(*In Masses for the Dead the following may be added:*
   Remember N., whom you have called from this life.
   In baptism he [she] died with Christ:
   may he [she] also share his resurrection.)

   Remember our brothers and sisters
   who have gone to their rest
   in the hope of rising again;

bring them and all the departed
into the light of your presence.

Have mercy on us all;
make us worthy to share eternal life
with Mary, the virgin mother of God,
with the apostles,
and with all the saints who have done your will throughout the ages.
May we praise you in union with them,
and give you glory
through your Son, Jesus Christ.

Through him,
with him,
in him,
in the unity of the Holy Spirit,
all glory and honour is yours,
almighty Father,
for ever and ever.

P. **Amen.**

Continued on p. 878.

Eucharistic Prayer III

C. Father, you are holy indeed,
and all creation rightly gives you praise.
All life, all holiness comes from you
through your Son, Jesus Christ our Lord,
by the working of the Holy Spirit.
From age to age you gather a people to yourself,
so that from east to west
a perfect offering may be made
to the glory of your name.

And so, Father, we bring you these gifts.
We ask you to make them holy by the power of your
    Spirit,
that they may become the body and blood
of your Son, our Lord Jesus Christ,
at whose command we celebrate this eucharist.

On the night he was betrayed,
he took bread and gave you thanks and praise.
He broke the bread, gave it to his disciples, and said:

Take this, all of you, and eat it:
this is my body which will be given up for you.

When supper was ended, he took the cup.
Again he gave you thanks and praise,
gave the cup to his disciples, and said:

Take this, all of you, and drink from it:
this is the cup of my blood,
the blood of the new and everlasting covenant.
It will be shed for you and for all men
so that sins may be forgiven.
Do this in memory of me.

C. Let us proclaim the mystery of faith:

Memorial acclamation of the people
P. **1. Christ has died,**
        Christ is risen,
        Christ will come again.

Alternative acclamations
P. **2. Dying you destroyed our death,**
        rising you restored our life.
        Lord Jesus, come in glory.

3. **When we eat this bread and drink this cup,**
   we proclaim your death, Lord Jesus,
   until you come in glory.

4. **Lord by your cross and resurrection**
   you have set us free.
   You are the Saviour of the world.

C. Father, calling to mind the death your Son endured
  for our salvation,
 his glorious resurrection and ascension into heaven,
 and ready to greet him when he comes again,
 we offer you in thanksgiving this holy and living
  sacrifice.

 Look with favour on your Church's offering,
 and see the Victim whose death has reconciled us to
  yourself.

 Grant that we, who are nourished by his body and
  blood,
 may be filled with his Holy Spirit,
 and become one body, one spirit in Christ.

 May he make us an everlasting gift to you
 and enable us to share in the inheritance of your saints,
 with Mary, the virgin Mother of God;
 with the apostles, the martyrs,
 (Saint N.—the patron saint or saint of the day) and all
  your saints,
 on whose constant intercession we rely for help.

 Lord, may this sacrifice, which has made our peace with
  you,

advance the peace and salvation of all the world.

Strengthen in faith and love your pilgrim Church on
  earth;

your servant, Pope N., our bishop N., and all the
  bishops,

with the clergy and the entire people your Son has
  gained for you.

Father, hear the prayers of the family you have gathered
  here before you.

In mercy and love unite all your children
wherever they may be.

[In Masses for the Dead the following is said:
Remember N.
In baptism he [she] died with Christ:
may he [she] also share his resurrection,
when Christ will raise our mortal bodies
and make them like his own in glory.]

Welcome into your kingdom our departed brothers
  and sisters,

and all who have left this world in your friendship.

We hope to enjoy for ever the vision of your glory,

through Christ our Lord, from whom all good things
  come.

Through him,
with him,
in him,
in the unity of the Holy Spirit,
all glory and honour is yours,
almighty Father,
for ever and ever.

P. **Amen.**
Continue on p. 878.

Eucharistic Prayer IV

Preface

C.   Father in heaven, it is right that we should give you
        thanks and glory:
        you alone are God, living and true.
        Through all eternity you live in unapproachable light.
        Source of life and goodness, you have created all
        things, to fill your creatures with every blessing
        and lead all men to the joyful vision of your light.
        Countless hosts of angels stand before you to do your
        will;
        they look upon your splendour
        and praise you, night and day.
        United with them, and in the name of every creature
        under heaven,
        we too praise your glory as we sing (say):

First acclamation of the people

P.   **Holy, holy, holy . . .**

C.   Father, we acknowledge your greatness:
        all your actions show your wisdom and love.
        You formed man in your own likeness
        and set him over the whole world
        to serve you, his creator,
        and to rule over all creatures.
        Even when he disobeyed you and lost your friendship
        you did not abandon him to the power of death,
        but helped all men to seek and find you.
        Again and again you offered a covenant to man,
        and through the prophets taught him to hope for
        salvation.
        Father, you so loved the world

that in the fullness of time you sent your only Son to be
our Saviour.
He was conceived through the power of the Holy
Spirit, and born of the Virgin Mary,
a man like us in all things but sin.
To the poor he proclaimed the good news of salvation,
to prisoners, freedom,
and to those in sorrow, joy.
In fulfilment of your will
he gave himself up to death;
but by rising from the dead,
he destroyed death and restored life.
And that we might live no longer for ourselves but
for him,
he sent the Holy Spirit from you, Father,
as his first gift to those who believe,
to complete his work on earth
and bring us the fullness of grace.

Father, may this Holy Spirit sanctify these offerings.
Let them become the body and blood of Jesus Christ
our Lord
as we celebrate the great mystery
which he left us as an everlasting covenant.

He always loved those who were his own in the world.
When the time came for him to be glorified by you,
his heavenly Father,
he showed the depth of his love.
While they were at supper,
he took bread, said the blessing, broke the bread
and gave it to his disciples, saying:

Take this, all of you, and eat it:
this is my body which will be given up for you.

In the same way, he took the cup, filled with wine.
He gave you thanks, and giving the cup to his disciples,
said:

Take this all of you, and drink from it:
this is the cup of my blood,
the blood of the new and everlasting covenant.
It will be shed for you and for all men
so that sins may be forgiven.
Do this in memory of me.

Let us proclaim the mystery of faith:

Memorial acclamation of the people
P. **1. Christ has died,**
Christ is risen,
Christ will come again.

Alternative acclamations
P. **2. Dying you destroyed our death,**
rising you restored our life.
Lord Jesus, come in glory.

3. When we eat this bread and drink this cup,
we proclaim your death, Lord Jesus,
until you come in glory.

4. Lord, by your cross and resurrection
you have set us free.
You are the Saviour of the world.

C. Father, we now celebrate this memorial of our redemption.
We recall Christ's death, his descent among the dead,

his resurrection, and his ascension to your right hand;
and, looking forward to his coming in glory, we offer
  you his body and blood,
the acceptable sacrifice which brings salvation to the
  whole world.

Lord, look upon this sacrifice which you have given to
  your Church;
and by your Holy Spirit, gather all who share this
  bread and wine
into the one body of Christ, a living sacrifice of praise.

Lord, remember those for whom we offer this sacrifice,
especially N. our Pope,
N. our bishop, and bishops and clergy everywhere.
Remember those who take part in this offering,
those here present and all your people,
and all who seek you with a sincere heart.

Remember those who have died in the peace of Christ
and all the dead whose faith is known to you alone.

Father, in your mercy grant also to us, your children,
to enter into our heavenly inheritance
in the company of the Virgin Mary, the Mother of
  God,
and your apostles and saints.
Then, in your kingdom, freed from the corruption of
  sin and death,
we shall sing your glory with every creature through
  Christ our Lord,
through whom you give us everything that is good.

Through him,
with him,
in him,

in the unity of the Holy Spirit,
all glory and honour is yours,
almighty Father,
for ever and ever.

P. **Amen.**

Rite of Communion

C. Let us pray with confidence to the Father
in the words our Saviour gave us:

All. **Our Father, who art in heaven,
hallowed be thy name;
Thy kingdom come;
Thy will be done on earth as it is in heaven.
Give us this day our daily bread;
and forgive us our trespasses
as we forgive those who trespass against us;
and lead us not into temptation,
but deliver us from evil.**

C. Deliver us, Lord, from every evil,
and grant us peace in our day.
In your mercy keep us free from sin
and protect us from all anxiety
as we wait in joyful hope
for the coming of our Saviour, Jesus Christ.

All. **For the kingdom, the power, and the glory are yours,
now and for ever.**

C. Lord Jesus Christ, you said to your apostles:
I leave you peace, my peace I give you.
Look not on our sins, but on the faith of your Church,
and grant us the peace and unity of your kingdom
where you live for ever and ever.

P. **Amen.**

C.   The peace of the Lord be with you always.

P.   **And also with you.**

[*Then the deacon, or the priest, may add:*

C.   Let us offer each other the sign of peace.

All make a sign of peace according to local custom.]

C.   May this mingling of the body and blood of our Lord
     Jesus Christ
    bring eternal life to us who receive it.

Meanwhile the following is sung or said:

All.   **Lamb of God, you take away the sins of the world:**
     have mercy on us.
    Lamb of God, you take away the sins of the world:
     have mercy on us.
    Lamb of God, you take away the sins of the world:
     grant us peace.

C.   Lord Jesus Christ, Son of the living God,
    by the will of the Father and the work of the Holy
     Spirit
    your death brought life to the world.
    By your holy body and blood
    free me from all my sins and from every evil.
    Keep me faithful to your teaching,
    and never let me be parted from you.

or

    Lord Jesus Christ,
    with faith in your love and mercy
    I eat your body and drink your blood.
    Let it not bring me condemnation,
    but health in mind and body.

C.   This is the Lamb of God
    who takes away the sins of the world.
    Happy are those who are called to his supper.

All.   **Lord, I am not worthy to receive you,**
    but only say the word and I shall be healed.

The priest's communion
While the priest is receiving the body of Christ, the communion song is begun.
The people's communion
C. The body of Christ.
P. **Amen.**
After the communion of the people, a period of silence may be observed, or a psalm or song of praise may be sung. Then:
C. Let us pray.
Priest and people pray in silence for a while, unless the silence has already been observed. Then the priest sings or says the prayer after communion. The people respond:
P. **Amen.**

Concluding rite

If there are any short announcements, they are made at this time. Then:
C. The Lord be with you.
P. **And also with you.**
C. May almighty God bless you, the Father, and the Son, and the Holy Spirit.
P. **Amen.**
C. The Mass is ended, go in peace.
P. **Thanks be to God.**

Alternative dismissals
C. Go in the peace of Christ.
or
C. Go in peace to love and serve the Lord.
P. **Thanks be to God.**